CO-ASP-591

YALE HISTORICAL PUBLICATIONS

THE IDEA OF

Progress

IN EIGHTEENTH-

CENTURY BRITAIN

DAVID SPADAFORA

YALE UNIVERSITY PRESS

NEW HAVEN & LONDON

Published under the direction of the Department of
History of Yale University with assistance from the
income of the Frederick John Kingsbury Memorial
Fund and with assistance from the Frederick W. Hilles
Publication Fund of Yale University.

Designed by Robert Kirkpatrick and set in Trump
Roman types by The Composing Room of Michigan,
Inc. Printed in the United States of America by
BookCrafters, Inc., Chelsea, Michigan.

Library of Congress Cataloging-in-Publication Data

Spadafora, David, 1951–
    The idea of progress in eighteenth-century Britain/
David Spadafora.
        p.   cm. — (Yale historical publications)
    Includes bibliographical references.
    ISBN 0–300–04671–5
    1. Great Britain—Social conditions—18th
century. 2. Progress. 3. Great Britain—
Intellectual   life—18th century.
    I. Title. II. Series.
HN385.S73   1990
306′.0941′09033—dc20   89–29303
                                        CIP

The paper in this book meets the guidelines for
permanence and durability of the Committee on
Production Guidelines for Book Longevity of the
Council on Library Resources.

10 9 8   7 6 5 4 3 2 1

TO MY MOTHER AND FATHER

Contents

Illustrations

Preface

This book has three closely related purposes of approximately equal weight. First, as a contribution to the historical study of a particular idea, it seeks to remedy some of the substantial deficiencies, in both focus and method, of existing scholarship on the history of the idea of progress. Second, as an essay in modern European intellectual history and in British history, it attempts to demonstrate that, during the age of the Enlightenment, the idea of progress *was* a characteristic and important part of the world-view of the educated, literate citizens of at least one country; and to identify the intellectual and social factors which led to the development and prevalence of that idea in that nation. Finally, as an experiment in the historiography of thought, it offers a response, mainly at the practical level, to recent criticisms of the goals and methods traditionally adopted by intellectual historians and historians of ideas.

Inseparable from these purposes is a fundamental assumption: although the idea of progress requires generalized definition in order to be studied historically, as a product of human thinking it can be given many forms and is not monolithic. What were the most prominent of these forms in eighteenth-century British thought, and especially during the period between 1730 and 1789? How did they arise, develop, and become widespread? Answering these questions has demanded an examination of the opinions of a substantial range of contemporaries, from the obscure to the famous, who wrote for publication on a broad spectrum of subjects, from eschatology to philology. Only in this context is it possible to determine the degree to which the belief in progress—a term used here and in the text interchangeably with "the idea of progress," for the sake of convenience— pervaded historical thinking at the time. Because the actual nature and forms of that belief emerge most clearly in the idiom of the age, copious quotation is employed throughout the book.

This entire enterprise, it has all along seemed to me, involves some not inconsiderable risks. The idea of progress and the Enlightenment itself are generally out of fashion in the later twentieth century, both philosophically and politically. To write about that idea's development in that period will therefore almost inevitably seem old-fashioned to some. It may appear contradictory to others, because the scholarship of the past generation has portrayed the French philosophes—the presumed leaders of eighteenth-century thought— as rather modern in having exhibited considerable skepticism about at least some kinds of historical optimism. Still others may wonder whether, in an era of *mentalité* and popular-culture studies, we should really be examining the views of the educated elite on a topic that J. B. Bury covered with so much apparent thoroughness seventy years ago. Or, it may be asked, is it legitimate to study the history of an idea at all, in the wake of the Wittgensteinian-inspired methodological revolution associated with Quentin Skinner? The impression of being out of bounds, or at least out of date, in method may appear to have confirmation from the fact that the "civic humanist tradition" is a concept that receives little attention here.

The risks of encountering these kinds of reactions are well worth taking, I believe. It is time for traditional intellectual history to reassert its legitimacy and proper place. The field has profited and should continue to profit from contemporary language philosophy, hermeneutics, the history of political discourse, and other disciplines associated with methodology. But it should not become disabled over concern with how to recover the "intention" of "speech acts" in "texts," should not obscure the thought of the past with the latest post-structuralist jargon, should not look for political "weapons" on every page or in every book, should not spend so much of its energy on tracking down the meaning of special "languages" or "idioms" that they receive more attention than the ideas couched in them. Likewise, the field should continue to make room, indeed plenty of room, to study the thought of those who stood below the lofty intellectual peaks of their age, and it should also continue to learn from social history and the social sciences about the best ways to link thought and social context. But we should remember that the fundamental interest of intellectual history lies in the written word, not rituals, and that until we know with precision what the elite were thinking we would do well not to ignore them out of a politically generated fear of writing history "from the top down." In an era of great turmoil and creativity among the disciplines, with ever-greater narrowness of focus and ever-more stimulus to cross-disciplinary endeavor, intellectual history—whose purview is the entire range of disciplines—has a significant part to play in the world of scholarship.

As for the idea of progress and the thought of the eighteenth century, it is also time to recognize again that they were inextricable, if in ways more complicated than Bury imagined. French thought was crucial in the age of the Enlightenment, to be sure, but we must now imagine that the version of the Enlightenment found among the philosophes of Paris and Geneva was not the only one—and thus that in their reservations about historical optimism and their high degree of secularity the philosophes were not necessarily reflective of the rest of Western European thinkers. Nor were they invariably the pathbreakers down every intellectual trail of the century. Among the English and the Scots, although the civic humanist tradition had a far from negligible influence at the time, there were other important intellectual traditions, too, and these were quite regularly associated in some substantial way with Newton and, yes, Locke. In Britain the idea of progress, in particular, was so crucial a concept and was so closely interwoven with so many major intellectual trends of the time that we cannot understand eighteenth-century thought without understanding it. Indeed, we would do well to keep the era's doctrines of progress in mind when we explore the impact of British thought on the Continent, the meaning of Victorian optimism, or the sources of the Industrial Revolution.

This book could not have been completed without my having had access to the outstanding collection of eighteenth-century British materials in the Yale University Library system, and at the Yale Center for British Art. To the staff of each, I extend my appreciation for the assistance they have given me. I want particularly to thank Joan Hall Sussler of the Lewis Walpole Library, Ferenc A. Gyorgyey and Susan Alon of the Yale Medical History Library, and Laura Guadagnoli of the Center for British Art for their kind aid in locating and obtaining images for some of the illustrations.

Yale University Press has been a most supportive publisher. I am especially grateful to Charles Grench for his welcoming encouragement and overall cooperativeness, and to Judith Calvert for the great care, patience, and friendly humor with which she has overseen the manuscript's final preparations.

What now seems like a good many years ago, Dudley W. R. Bahlman stimulated my interest in British and intellectual history, and encouraged my first attempts at understanding the history of the idea of progress. At about the same time, Francis C. Oakley introduced me to the history of ideas as a discipline, and he later read and made useful comments on the earliest versions of two chapters. Peter Gay and John Brewer also read and offered valuable suggestions on several chapters at an early stage. Jaroslav Pelikan read the entire text in its dissertation form, and I have profited much from his observations on it—as well as from his having heartened me in my efforts to keep my scholarship alive while performing decanal duties, and having suggested that I consider Yale University Press as a publisher. W. Warren Wagar has now spent more time with this book than he may care to remember, but greatly to my advantage; would that every author received the kind of painstaking, insightful assessment and recommendations that he has offered me. I consider myself fortunate indeed to have had such helpful criticism, and moral support, from all of these scholars. For the book's remaining errors, of course, I alone am responsible.

Frank M. Turner has given me much encouragement in this project at almost every step, and I owe much to him for what I have learned in the many conversations we have had about intellectual history. My debt is all the greater for his having persistently but politely urged me to turn a Yale Ph.D. dissertation into a book.

For opening so many windows on European intellectual history, and for allowing me to pursue my historical interests in my own way while giving me direction every time I needed it, I shall always be grateful to Franklin L. Baumer. His patience and sagacious counsel, his understanding and support, his insistence that I ask the difficult questions and recognize the wider context, made him the best of graduate advisers. I am thankful, too, for his gracious friendship.

I am under an even greater obligation to my wife, Carolyn. In recent months she has given her careful, professional eye to the text of this book, as it has been readied for publication. But across the years she has journeyed along with me through the ups and downs of research, writing, and career, offering her common sense, humor, and love while postponing some of her dreams so that I could pursue some of mine. For these things no words of thanks could ever be sufficient.

A Note on Usage and References

Quotations from eighteenth-century texts almost always preserve the vagaries of contemporary British spelling, capitalization, and punctuation; occasional emendations appear in brackets. Unless specifically noted to the contrary, emphasis is universally in the original.

The initial reference to a work gives its full title (except where unusually long) and, if a later edition has been cited, the date of the first edition. In some instances, especially when a book was published posthumously, the year of composition is given. Once a work has been cited, the first reference to it in any subsequent chapter gives only one date, that of the edition used, and the title may be shortened somewhat.

In any footnote containing references to more than one writer, the order in which the writers are cited corresponds to the order in which the relevant paragraph of text first mentions each of them or their opinions. The same principle applies to the order in which multiple works by one author are cited in a footnote, and, wherever possible, to the order of pages as cited from any single work.

For all too many eighteenth-century works, standard editions do not exist. The best and most widely available edition is ordinarily used in such cases, and if the book has organizational divisions citations are made to structural part (e.g., chapter, section, or lecture) as well as to page number.

1 Introduction

The recognition of temporal movement in life unquestionably lies near the center of human consciousness. In the eighteenth-century phrase of the Scottish moral philosopher Adam Ferguson, man is always and everywhere "employed in the exercise of recollection and foresight," and this universal activity constitutes one of his fundamental characteristics. The human being necessarily experiences the immediate flow of time, he remembers, he prognosticates. His "knowledge of *the Future*," perceived Ferguson's English contemporary James Harris, "comes from knowledge of *the Past*; as does knowledge of *the Past* from knowledge of *the Present*, so that their *Order to us* is that of PRESENT, PAST, and FUTURE." Because of this temporal experience, as a twentieth-century student of political and social thought has argued, man

> cannot help but see himself a traveller, and can change his mind only about the road he is taking. He cannot be aware of himself as a person, cannot know that he is alive, without looking back to a past and forward to a future. Whoever can put to himself the question, What am I? will also be tempted to ask, And where am I going? Again, man knows himself as one among others of his kind, as a member of society, as an heir and an ancestor; and so passes easily from seeing himself to seeing his kind as a traveller.[1]

1. Adam Ferguson, *An Essay on the History of Civil Society* (1767), ed. Duncan Forbes (Edinburgh, 1966), 3; James Harris, *Hermes: or a Philosophical Inquiry, concerning Universal Grammar* (1751), in *The Works of James Harris, Esq.*, 2 vols. (London, 1801), 1:277; John Plamenatz, *Man and Society: A Critical Examination of Some Important Social and Political Theories from Machiavelli to Marx*, 2 vols. (London, 1963), 2:409. Elsewhere (*Institutes of Moral Philosophy. For the use of Students in the College of Edinburgh* [1768], 2d ed., rev. and corr. [Edinburgh, 1773], 59, 65), Ferguson defined his terms: "Memory is the recollection of subjects past"; "Foresight is the faculty of conjecturing what is to follow from the past or present."

The fact of movement or of a journey in time, then, has perpetually and unavoidably confronted self-conscious man, forcing him to grapple with it and make it comprehensible.

In the modern world, the single most influential result of these continuing efforts to fashion a historical understanding is the idea of progress. This idea, according to a recent writer on its history, "has inspired most of the great political and intellectual movements of the last two hundred years. It is perhaps the most characteristic and pervasive theme in modern Western thought." Although some historians might consider these claims excessive, nearly all commentators on the idea agree that it has played a truly significant role among intellectuals and in society at large, both as a historiographical or sociological hypothesis and, frequently, as an almost religious credo canonizing change. During the first three-quarters of the nineteenth century, in particular, the belief in progress was widespread and sometimes seemed virtually unchallenged. Since the 1870s and 1880s, and certainly since the cataclysm of the Great War, the idea has been placed on trial and, increasingly, found unpersuasive and out of date. Still, the gospel of progress has hardly wanted for prophets in the present century. And important traces of the old faith remain apparent, in the hopes of intellectuals as well as the assumptions of the general public, in the rhetoric of politicians as well as the salesmanship of commercial advertisers. The idea continues to hold sway especially with regard to the common expectation of future beneficial developments in science and technology (though even here doubts have crept in, as a result of growing fears of nuclear catastrophe and environmental degradation).[2]

For more than a century, awareness of the centrality of the idea of progress to modern thought has led to a continuing interest in its history. A voluminous literature has grown up in this field since Auguste Javary published his groundbreaking *De l'idée de progrès* in 1851.[3] Several general historical accounts have been written, one as

2. W. Warren Wagar, *The Idea of Progress Since the Renaissance* (New York, 1969), 192; idem, *Good Tidings: The Belief in Progress from Darwin to Marcuse* (Bloomington, Ind., 1972), 8. Revealing examples of the contemporary view of progress were presented in an American television program prepared and narrated by Frank McGee: "But Is This Progress?," NBC Reports (broadcast July 31, 1973). Among them was the statement of a young woman that "I want to stop progress . . . before it goes too far," which succinctly expresses late twentieth-century confusion about progress.

3. For secondary works dealing with the idea of progress and its history, see below, Bibliographical Essay.

recently as 1980; specialized studies have found the roots of the idea among Renaissance artisans, the early Church Fathers, and even the classical Greeks and Romans; many monographs have focused on eighteenth- and early nineteenth-century France, and on individual members of the French Enlightenment; and one volume has examined the fate of the idea since the time of Darwin. As this fragmentary list suggests, the history of the idea has been explored from numerous perspectives, so that much raw information about it is now available.

In spite of its vastness, however, this body of scholarship is actually a badly flawed torso. First, most of it deals with France, to the relative neglect of its neighbor across the Channel. J. B. Bury's deservedly famous book *The Idea of Progress* (1920) illustrates this fact: for the century before the 1790s, it devotes seven chapters to the French, one to the English and Scots. Furthermore, Bury argues that in Britain at the time the idea of progress was merely an import from France and never attained the kind of popularity it enjoyed among its exporters.[4] Such an opinion by a highly influential authority on the subject undoubtedly helps to explain why only two major works about British versions of the idea have been published since 1934— and the later of these appeared in 1949. Yet it was Britain that possessed a constitution widely hailed at home and abroad as unparalleled, that gave birth to the technological marvels of the Industrial Revolution, and that eventually became redolent with "Victorian optimism." On the basis of these considerations alone, might we not reasonably expect the idea of progress to have flourished vigorously in the Georgian mental climate? Would the country that built the foundations of Enlightenment thought have merely borrowed this idea, rather than have played an important, independent role in its development? Surely the history of the idea in eighteenth-century Britain deserves more careful attention than it has so far received.

Second, although—in the words of Karl Mannheim—"Constructive abstraction is a prerequisite for empirical investigation," few historians of the idea have defined it with precision. The result has been terminological confusion of the worst sort. For instance, to say

4. J. B. Bury, *The Idea of Progress: An Inquiry into Its Origin and Growth* (London, 1920), 217–18. The other large-scale history of the idea—Jules Delvaille, *Essai sur l'histoire de l'idée de progrès jusqu'à la fin du XVIIIe siècle* (Paris, 1910)—allots three times as many pages to the French as to the British.

The enormous influence exerted by Bury on the historiography of the idea is discussed in W. Warren Wagar, "Modern Views of the Origins of the Idea of Progress," *Journal of the History of Ideas* 28 (Jan.–March 1967): 61.

without further clarification that both Jean-Jacques Rousseau and the Marquis de Condorcet believed in progress actually means very little and could well lead to a misunderstanding of their thought. Among those historians who have explicitly stated a definition, the dictum advanced by Bury seventy years ago has generally remained the standard:

> This idea means that civilisation has moved, is moving, and will move in a desirable direction.
>
> . . . .
>
> It is based on an interpretation of history which regards men as slowly advancing—*pedetemtim progredientes*—in a definite and desirable direction, and infers that this progress will continue indefinitely. And it implies that, as "The issue of the earth's great business," a condition of general happiness will ultimately be enjoyed, which will justify the whole process of civilisation; for otherwise the direction would not be desirable. There is also a further implication. The process must be the necessary outcome of the psychical and social nature of man; it must not be at the mercy of any external will; otherwise there would be no guarantee of its continuance and its issue, and the idea of Progress would lapse into the idea of Providence.

Broad as it may seem, Bury's definition nonetheless does not range widely enough to encompass men who, like Thomas Babington Macaulay, did not consider progress from the point of view of world "civilization" or did not believe that improvement could continue gradually and indefinitely. Yet does it make any sense to exclude from the ranks of believers in progress those who held, as Macaulay did, that in certain areas of human or national life advances had occurred in the past and would continue for at least some time in the future? And what of Lord Acton, who late in life "thought that Providence was progress and progress was the *raison d'être* of history," or of Herbert Butterfield, who contended that "progress . . . is itself the work of Providence"? These and related questions demand that the definition of the idea be reconsidered, and made more general.[5]

5. Karl Mannheim, *Ideology and Utopia: An Introduction to the Sociology of Knowledge*, trans. Louis Wirth and Edward Shils (New York, 1936), 202; Bury, *Idea of Progress*, 2, 5. Butterfield's *Christianity and History* (New York, 1950), 95–97, contains the quotation on Acton as well as his own remarks on providence and progress.

Third, the traditional view that acceptance of the idea became widespread among European intellectuals during the eighteenth century has lately been called into doubt. Henry Vyverberg and Peter Gay contend that the belief in progress in the age of the Enlightenment (and particularly in France) was neither so customary nor so unalloyed and comprehensive as previously assumed. Gay censures the indiscriminate efforts of some historians at "seeking out, and finding, clues to a theory of progress everywhere" in this period. These criticisms have much merit and must be observed in all future work on the history of the idea among the French philosophes and their contemporaries. Such men often had high hopes, but they also *did* occasionally become gloomy, and it was rare for them to treat the past uncritically as a record of ceaseless linear improvement. Not surprisingly, therefore, very few of them foreshadowed the nineteenth-century creation by men like Auguste Comte and Henry Thomas Buckle of what Gay refers to as a "theory of progress," that "metaphysical claim that progress is an inevitable process immanent in history."[6] Yet although it would be unhistorical to display their optimism while ignoring their pessimism, it would also be useful finally to ascertain the precise balance between those two moods.

Finally, there are problems of methodology in the historical literature on the idea of progress. The argument that it is either absurdly ambitious or conceptually illegitimate to attempt the reconstruction of the history of an idea may be rejected without denying that such an enterprise can easily stumble into methodological pitfalls.[7] As pointed out in recent criticisms, the historiography of thought has all too

---

For definitions similar to—though usually not as detailed as—that of Bury, see Frederick J. Teggart, ed., *The Idea of Progress: A Collection of Readings*, rev. ed. (Berkeley, 1949), 3–4; John Baillie, *The Belief in Progress* (New York, 1951), 2; Morris Ginsberg, *The Idea of Progress: A Revaluation* (London, 1953), 3; Plamenatz, *Man and Society*, 2:410.

The desirability of a broad definition of the idea of progress was noted by C. F. (probably Charles Frankel), reviewing Ernest Lee Tuveson's *Millennium and Utopia*, in *Journal of Philosophy* 48 (March 1, 1951): 169. Wagar makes the same point but still defines the idea in a relatively narrow way: Wagar, "Modern Views," 69–70, 55; idem, *Good Tidings*, 3–7.

6. Peter Gay, *The Enlightenment: An Interpretation*, 2 vols. (New York, 1966–69), 2:606; idem, *The Party of Humanity: Essays in the French Enlightenment* (New York, 1964), 271; Henry Vyverberg, *Historical Pessimism in the French Enlightenment* (Cambridge, Mass., 1958), 1–6 and passim.

7. For a discussion of the argument mentioned here and of methodological issues in general, see below, Appendix.

often unconsciously reified ideas, ignored their social context, and concentrated solely on the intellectual elite. Scholarship on the history of the idea of progress is generally subject to these same limitations, and to others of an even more serious nature. Most of it proceeds descriptively rather than analytically, tending merely to relate who believed in progress during a given period and to record the words into which those individuals put their belief. With few exceptions (including work by R. S. Crane, Ernest Lee Tuveson, Charles Frankel, and W. Warren Wagar), it rarely explores in more than cursory fashion the process by which this idea developed, and therefore it offers few insights into what intellectual—let alone social—conditions contributed to the rise and spread of the idea. In addition, the descriptive technique itself operates at a rudimentary level. There has been no effort, for example, to determine whether at any time there were identifiable social groups or intellectual contexts in which the belief in progress customarily appeared. Quite simply, then, the methods employed in the historical study of the idea of progress are inadequate.

Because of these four basic deficiencies, this book adopts a new approach to the history of the idea, while focusing on Britain during the eighteenth century, and especially during the years between about 1730 and 1789.

In order to permit systematic discussion of this subject, a new definition of the idea is required, one that avoids the weaknesses of Bury's. Consequently, the idea of progress will here be taken to mean the belief in the movement over time of some aspect or aspects of human existence, within a social setting, toward a better condition. This definition is necessarily provisional, designed to assist historical reconstruction. But it escapes the difficulties of excessive narrowness and, by virtue of its generality, considerably limits the dangers of reifying ideas. For present purposes, it has the added justification of corresponding fairly closely to later eighteenth-century usage. In English dictionaries published between 1720 and 1791, the primary meaning of the term "progress" and its derivatives was stated to be "a going forward or proceeding in any undertaking" or a "course, procession, passage." This neutral conception permitted negative connotations, as in William Hogarth's famous engravings *A Harlot's Progress* (1732) and *A Rake's Progress* (1735). From the 1750s, however, a secondary meaning with a clearly meliorative outlook was added: "motion forward," in the sense of "advancement" or "improvement."[8]

When defined in so broad a way, the idea of progress can obviously take on many shapes in human use. The individual forms into which it is cast will vary in relation to how the components of the definition are conceived. Progressive temporal movement may be found in the past, the present, the future, or some combination thereof; it may be considered linear or spiral, continuous or interrupted, gradual or rapid, limited or indefinitely extended. The aspect of human affairs that appears to advance may have very narrow boundaries, like the art of painting, or immensely wide ones, like happiness. Since people do not have the same preferences, their notions of what is "better" will differ dramatically. In looking to the future, for example, some will envision the coming of needed reform,[9] and others positive innovation; but in both cases the expectation is for improvement over the present. Overall, then, the way in which a given exponent of the idea of progress conceives of movement, betterment, and the facet of existence undergoing beneficial change will determine the precise form he or she gives to that idea.

This means that although there is only one *idea* of progress, there is a multitude of possible *expressions* of the idea (referred to in this book as "doctrines" of progress). Of these expressions, two types

8. On the usefulness of generality in the definition of historical ideas, see below, Appendix. The eighteenth-century definitions referred to are contained in the following dictionaries, s.v. "Progress," "Progression," "Progressional," and "Progressive": Edward Phillips, *The New World of Words: Or, Universal English Dictionary*, 7th ed. (London, 1720); N. Bailey, *Dictionarium Britannicum*, 1st ed. (London, 1730) and 2d ed. (London, 1736); Samuel Johnson, *A Dictionary of the English Language* (1755), 2d ed., 2 vols. (London, 1755–56), vol. 2; James Buchanan, *Linguae Britannica Vera Pronunciatio: Or, A New English Dictionary* (London, 1757); William Rider, *A New English Dictionary* (London, 1759); *A New Universal Etymological English Dictionary* [a revised and expanded version of Bailey's] (London, 1764); Thomas Sheridan, *A General Dictionary of the English Language*, 2 vols. (London, 1780), vol. 2; John Walker, *A Critical Pronouncing Dictionary and Expositor of the English Language* (London, 1791).

The philosophical problem of defining historical ideas is thoroughly discussed in Gerhart B. Ladner, *The Idea of Reform: Its Impact on Christian Thought and Action in the Age of the Fathers*, enl. ed. (New York, 1967), 425–32. Mannheim argues that although such definitions are created by the historian only for working purposes, they have special merit when they "are not just arbitrary and wilful constructions, but have their roots in historical reality": *Ideology and Utopia*, 201–02.

9. According to its historian, "the idea of reform is an idea of progress": Ladner, *Idea of Reform*, 31.

achieved considerable currency before the eighteenth century: doctrines of religious progress, usually found among Christian eschatologists and prophets of the millennium; and doctrines of progress in learning or knowledge, enunciated especially by Baconians
and other partisans of modernity in their famous *querelle* with the
supporters of the ancients. But if some Europeans expressed a belief in
progress before 1700, many more did so during the next hundred
years. The idea of progress unquestionably became far more widespread in the age of the Enlightenment than in previous centuries,
even though historical pessimism of various kinds coexisted with it.
And in spite of the relative scarcity in the eighteenth century of a true
"theory" of progress, it was just at that time that broadly gauged
doctrines of secular progress first began to appear. Instead of the Baconian concept of the advancement of learning, Continental thinkers
like Anne-Robert-Jacques Turgot, Condorcet, and Immanuel Kant
talked about the improvement of civilization; instead of the Christian dream of a divine millennium, others looked for the self-perfecti-
bility of man in this world.

In eighteenth-century Britain, too, the idea of progress burst forth
with new vigor and in new forms, particularly from the 1730s
through the 1780s. These years, the high eighteenth century,[10] com-
prise a period of British history that can properly be treated as a
whole. To be sure, in politics and the economy there is a recognizable
break that centers on 1760. The ascension of Sir Robert Walpole
ushered in an age of political stability and government by oligarchy
that lasted from the mid-1720s until George III came to the throne, an
age largely free from the earlier agitation produced by parties and
issues. All of this changed under the third Hanoverian king. In the
1760s and again after 1776, issues and party organization re-emerged
and new forms of political activity appeared, bringing with them
renewed agitation. Economically, a similar change occurred. The relatively stagnant pre-industrial economy of the early eighteenth century, with its poverty and agricultural orientation, began to give way
by 1750—and increasingly by the 1760s—to substantial technological innovation, significantly increased enclosure of farm land, greater
consumer demand, and the first phases of the Industrial Revolution.

From other perspectives, however, the high eighteenth century

10. This term is taken from J. G. A. Pocock, who uses it without attaching an exact
chronology to it: *The Ancient Constitution and the Feudal Law: A Study of English
Historical Thought in the Seventeenth Century*, 2d ed. (New York, 1967), 244.

appears far more unified. In society and politics, it represents a *relatively* placid interlude between two great historical storms. Before it came the tumultuous "Century of Revolution," whose turbulence spilled over into the more than three decades of political instability that succeeded 1689. Following the 1780s came the unsettling influences of the French Revolution and its aftermath, which provoked domestic radicalism and reaction; and of the height of the Industrial Revolution, which, together with the impact of the French wars, altered British society forever and made constitutional change imperative. In contrast to both of these epochs, the high eighteenth century can be characterized as comparatively tranquil. Politically, it was far more stable than either the years between 1675 and 1725 or the period from 1789 to 1832. If the pattern of politics changed between Walpole and the younger Pitt, dramatic modification of the constitution did not occur. The tremors of the 1760s and the years of the American Revolution may have jostled and even cracked but did not overturn the edifice of oligarchic control. Socially, it was an age of dynamic equilibrium. The grip of the elite on the reins of power was strong enough to prevent changes in the structure of society, yet sufficiently loose to permit assimilation of the successful from below and to keep discontent and riot from burgeoning into full-scale revolt. This equilibrium began to give way only in the 1780s, after which class consciousness, social antagonism, and the class system began to emerge in their modern forms.

Intellectually, too, the high eighteenth century in England and Scotland constitutes a unified period. By 1727, when Sir Isaac Newton died, the great seventeenth-century revolution in thought had ended, as for the most part had the Augustan fear of science. But if the age of Newton and Locke was over, the age of Newtonianism and Lockeanism had just begun. For the next six decades, the influence of these two giants dominated British thought. Their method—the use of critical reason and empiricism—was widely considered to be the only one through which the various disciplines could achieve the desirable status of sciences, on the model of Newton's natural philosophy. Not until the true emergence of Romanticism at the very end of the century, among men like Blake and Coleridge, were these intellectual heroes and this outlook seriously challenged. This was also true on the Continent and especially in France, the headquarters of the Enlightenment during precisely these years after the 1720s. The philosophes who formed this movement had an ambitious pro-

gram of "secularism, humanity, cosmopolitanism, and freedom," a
program characterized by its appeal to pagan antiquity, attack upon
Christianity, and pursuit of modernity through reform and science.[11]
Its avowed technique was criticism and the use of Newtonian and
Lockean critical reason. In France, the movement was organized, if
somewhat loosely and with substantial differences of opinion about
strategy and tactics, by the philosophes' deeply held belief in the need
for reform in church and state, and among other things by their contribution to the *Encyclopédie* of Diderot and d'Alembert. In England,
however, there was no real organization because there was relatively
little social and political discontent among the educated, and no institutional focus for reformist intellectual activity like the encyclopedic project. Moreover, very few English thinkers of the high
eighteenth century waged war against the Christian religion. During
the early 1730s, William Law, George Berkeley, and Joseph Butler
essentially put an end to more than three decades of theological polemics by replying effectively to the deist critique of revealed religion. Traditional Christianity was thereafter not nearly so much
under attack, and it is even appropriate to speak of a revival of belief
inaugurated by the Wesley brothers and George Whitefield before
1740. In spite of the charges of "enthusiasm" lodged against these
evangelicals at the time, the post-deist era was quiescent in matters
of religion. For the fact of toleration prevented turmoil over faith, as
Voltaire understood so well. Whether High Anglican, Latitudinarian,
Methodist, or Nonconformist, virtually all the English were at least
formally Christian. And until the 1790s they countenanced wide
variety in theology and worship, except for Catholicism and, occasionally, Judaism.

Clearly, then, there was no English Enlightenment comparable to
that in France. This does not mean that there were *no* philosophes of
the French type in England; among better known figures, the sometime-
Englishman Thomas Paine and the young Jeremy Bentham probably
qualify as such, and so to some degree does Edward Gibbon. Nor
should it be imagined that neither the empirical spirit of the French
Enlightenment nor portions of its program failed to find a home between the Channel and the Tweed. The legacy of Newton, Locke, and
critically vigorous Augustan humanism made that impossible. Yet to
the extent that the French Enlightenment had anything like a British

11. Gay, *The Enlightenment*, 1:3, 8.

counterpart, it was located not in England but in Scotland. There, in the new political world of the post-Union period and amid a changing economy, the universities, the legal profession, the "improving" clubs and societies of the time, and even the Church helped to provide an institutional foundation for the growth of the Enlightenment vision. Beginning with Francis Hutcheson in the later 1720s, Scottish scholars—primarily though not exclusively academics and jurists—constructed a science of man and society along lines consonant with the views of the French. Indeed, a few men like David Hume and Adam Smith were thoroughly sympathetic to much of the basic philosophe program. Nevertheless, the heights of the Scottish intellectual milieu were broad enough to encompass Lord Monboddo's Aristotelianism, Thomas Reid's common-sense philosophy, and William Robertson's moderate Presbyterianism, all of which were in fundamental ways alien to the Enlightenment of France. Distinguishing the Scottish Enlightenment even more from the French scene was the fact that most of its leaders were prominent members of the country's elite, holding positions of importance in key institutions and often wielding some political power. Further, in spite of the critical, scientific ethos so widespread in Scotland, that country experienced an evangelical revival contemporaneous with and similar to that in England. So although the intellectual trends of Paris were eminently visible in Edinburgh, Glasgow, and even Aberdeen, they did not completely dominate the climate of opinion there.

In Britain as a whole, therefore, although many features of the enlightened outlook were present, the Enlightenment in its typically French form *generally* was not.[12] What nearly all strands of high eighteenth-century British thought had in common, however, was the tendency to use, interpret, consolidate, and even criticize the intellectual heritage of the previous period, especially that of Locke and Newton. But criticism did not yet amount to rejection, as it came to do with Burke and the Romantics from the 1790s on. In thought as in literature, the era between the 1730s and 1789 stands distinct from its Augustan forerunner and its Romantic successor, even though it grew out of the former and stimulated the latter.

It was during the eighteenth century, and especially these six decades, that the idea of progress first became a prominent element in

12. Nor should the French philosophes necessarily be taken as the prototypes for other national forms of the Enlightenment. See, for example, Roy Porter and Mikuláš Teich, eds., *The Enlightenment in National Context* (Cambridge, 1981), vii.

British thought, receiving expression in a variety of ways. Of these, the most widespread and significant are described and analyzed in this book.[13] Two of them—doctrines of progress in the arts and sciences and in religion and the conditions of spiritual life—had notable predecessors, and for that reason they constitute the ultimate foundations of the idea as it existed in Britain during the eighteenth century. But if the old "Battle of Ancients and Moderns" and the still-older traditional Christian vision of history served as the intellectual inheritance from which the idea grew, that legacy was substantially modified after 1730. A dramatic change occurred in the character of the controversy over ancient and modern achievements, and with it came victory for the proponents of modernity, even (to a considerable degree) in the field of the fine arts. Likewise, the scholarly eschatology of the time became at once less scientific and more believable than that of the preceding period at the end of the seventeenth century, and doctrines of progress in religion had greater popularity and a stronger future orientation than ever before.

Contemporaries also gave expression to several new kinds of doctrines of progress in the eighteenth century. One of these derived from Locke and concerned the mental and emotional pliability of man. It found favor with writers on education and the psychology of association, who depicted man as a creature shaped far more by his surroundings and experience than by any innate endowment, and therefore as capable of progress through environmental control. Another new variety of belief in progress emerged in discussions of language. Speech and writing were considered to have improved dur-

13. Compared to the forms of the idea mentioned in this and the next paragraph and discussed at length in chaps. 2 through 5, doctrines of economic and political progress, considered on their own, were not nearly as common. (For some evidence relating to them, if almost always in contexts other than the history of the idea of progress, see especially Caroline Robbins, *The Eighteenth-Century Commonwealthman: Studies in the Transmission, Development and Circumstance of English Liberal Thought from the Restoration of Charles II until the War with the Thirteen Colonies*, Atheneum ed. [New York, 1968], 177–377 passim; Isaac Kramnick, *Bolingbroke and His Circle: The Politics of Nostalgia in the Age of Walpole* [Cambridge, Mass., 1968], 127–36; J. G. A. Pocock, "Machiavelli, Harrington and English Political Ideologies in the Eighteenth Century," *Politics, Language and Time: Essays on Political Thought and History* [New York, 1971], 140–42; John Brewer, *Party Ideology and Popular Politics at the Accession of George III* [Cambridge, 1976], 253–64; Richard C. Wiles, "Mercantilism and the Idea of Progress," *Eighteenth-Century Studies* 8 [Fall 1974]: 56–74.) But the belief in progress in the political and social realms was necessarily an integral part of the notions of general progress discussed in chaps. 6 through 8 and receives consideration there.

ing the past, and conscious attempts were made to foster further linguistic advance in the future. The progress of language seemed to have special significance because of its intimate relation to positive intellectual and social change.

Surpassing in breadth all these forms of the idea were doctrines of general progress, of which one version appeared in England and one in Scotland, especially after about 1760. On the whole, the Scots in question envisioned the "progress of human culture" as a somewhat less comprehensive and temporally indefinite historical process than did the English. But both groups believed that improvement had already occurred or eventually would take place across virtually all fronts of human life. What is more, this belief normally included and combined elements of each of the other, narrower doctrines of progress that were popular at the time.

The men whose published writings enunciated the idea of progress in all these various shapes constitute a virtual cross-section of the educated and literate strata of British society. Most of them were natives of England and Scotland, although some were Welsh and Irish by birth. A vast majority belonged to the middle ranks of society and practiced one of the by then traditional non-military professions. Thus, they included clergymen at all levels, lawyers and judges, professors and schoolmasters, and physicians. Others were engaged in what we would today call the sciences, the fine arts and literature, or commerce and manufacturing, and a few were members of the leisured gentry. They had diverse political affiliations, ranging (in only somewhat anachronistic terms) from conservative to liberal to radical. Religiously, most—whether moderates or high churchmen—were members of the established churches of England and Scotland, but a good many were Dissenters or evangelicals; only a handful took a deist or skeptical position on matters of faith, and these were usually Scots. In brief, they may be considered representative of the entire contemporary republic of letters and its readership, a fact indicating that acceptance of the idea was pervasive and cut through multiple climates of opinion at the time.

This does not mean that the upper one-quarter of British society, to say nothing of everyone else, believed in progress with a uniform level of conviction, or even at all. Some men set out to prove that there had been or would be progress in certain facets of life, while others, both consciously and unconsciously, simply *assumed* that this was the case. And as in France during the same period, still others

held completely different views of the pattern of historical movement. We can in fact find three related forms of historical pessimism
in contemporary British thought, each of which combined a well-
known intellectual tradition with specific features of the eighteenth-
century scene.

In spite of successful attacks since the 1620s against the doctrine
of the continuous degeneration of man and nature, the old idea
of historical decline or decay lingered on in new (though less all-
encompassing) forms. It appeared, for example, in the context of the
cultural primitivism of proto-Romanticism, which emphasized the
aesthetic superiority of the "natural" to the "refined," and the physical and moral advantages of the emotional "noble savage" over the
reasoning European. Related to this partial condemnation of modern
civilization was the widespread outcry, among the British as well as
the French, against the purportedly deleterious effects of commercial
society, especially luxury. The private vices of Bernard Mandeville's
mercantile world had their supporters, but they also had many critics, who feared the results of the excessive accumulation and enjoyment of wealth. This economic notion of decay occasionally emerged
in the context of the decline of Rome, a subject that excited both
historical scholarship and polemical comparisons between the actual
collapse of an ancient state and the potential demise of Britain.[14]

Frequently blending with such conceptions of decay and decline
was the idea of the historical cycle, the chief eighteenth-century
theoretician of which was Henry St. John, Viscount Bolingbroke.
Following Machiavelli, earlier Renaissance commentators, and
classical writers like Livy and Polybius, he believed that "physical
and moral systems are carried round in one perpetual revolution,
from generation to corruption, and from corruption to generation;
from ignorance to knowledge, and from knowledge to ignorance;
from barbarity to civility, and from civility to barbarity." Of course,

14. On the various doctrines of decline, see Peter Burke, "Tradition and Experi-
ence: The Idea of Decline from Bruni to Gibbon," in G. W. Bowersock, John Clive, and
Stephen R. Graubard, eds., *Edward Gibbon and the Decline and Fall of the Roman
Empire* (Cambridge, Mass., 1977), 87–102; Lois Whitney, *Primitivism and the Idea of
Progress in English Popular Literature of the Eighteenth Century* (Baltimore, 1934),
42–136; Simeon M. Wade, Jr., "The Idea of Luxury in Eighteenth-Century England,"
Ph.D. diss. (Harvard Univ., May 1968), 1–172; Brewer, *Party Ideology and Popular
Politics*, 258–59; H. R. Trevor-Roper, "The Idea of the Decline and Fall of the Roman
Empire," in W. H. Barber et al., eds., *The Age of Enlightenment: Studies Presented to
Theodore Besterman* (Edinburgh, 1967), 413–30.

Bolingbroke was only the best known of a substantial number of "neo-Harringtonians," reformers, and members of the political opposition who at least occasionally espoused the cyclical view. They tended to apply it, as he himself did in *The Idea of a Patriot King* (written 1738–39), to the history of government and especially to the British state, which, they worried, might be caught in the same cycle of corruption that had long before destroyed Rome. Conyers Middleton's biography of Cicero illustrates how they feared a repetition of the pattern in which the rise of the Roman state to a condition of plenty, liberty, and refinement was succeeded by a declension

> from virtuous industry to wealth; from wealth, to luxury; from luxury to an impatience of discipline and corruption of morals; till by a total degeneracy and loss of virtue, being grown ripe for destruction, it falls a prey at last to some hardy oppressor, and, with the loss of liberty, losing every thing else, that is valuable, sinks gradually again into it's [*sic*] original barbarism.[15]

The third tradition of historical pessimism that survived in the eighteenth century was social lamentation, in the form of jeremiads on the failures of and evils present in Britain. Naturally, the launching of litanies of woe had always been common practice in Western culture, and they had found many targets. Under the first three Georges, the customary focuses for attack were irreligion, faction, political corruption, and, above all, luxury. Anti-luxury polemical literature tended to appear in bursts coinciding with times of military conflict or severe economic dislocation: the War of the Spanish Succession, the South Sea Bubble, the War of the Austrian Succession, the Forty-Five, the Seven Years' War, the American Revolution, and the wars of the French Revolution. These periodic "choruses of Catonism" had in common a "consumptive" theory of history, in both senses of the term. They judged general changes in society and morality on the basis of shifts in the pattern of economic consumption; and they declared that when the economy permitted this pat-

---

15. Henry St. John, Viscount Bolingbroke, "Essay the Third," *Essays addressed to Mr. Pope* (published 1754), in *The Works of the Late Right Honorable Henry St. John, Lord Viscount Bolingbroke,* ed. David Mallet, 5 vols. (London, 1754), 4:235–36; idem, *The Idea of a Patriot King,* in *Works,* 3:76; Conyers Middleton, *The History of the Life of Marcus Tullius Cicero,* 2 vols. (London, 1741), 1:495. For general remarks on the Augustan polemical use of the cyclical theory of history, see Robbins, *Eighteenth-Century Commonwealthman,* 293; J. G. A. Pocock, *The Machiavellian Moment: Florentine Political Thought and the Atlantic Republican Tradition* (Princeton, 1975), 477.

tern to become excessive and overly refined, a nation would lose its political equilibrium and spirit of patriotism and collapse internally, as if suffering from the disease consumption. Paradoxically, prosperity was thus the forerunner and cause of decay. This negative assessment of luxury took place within the larger context of a cyclical rise and retrogression, but most of its emphasis clearly fell on the decline that seemed inevitable when a society became prosperous. Appearing to have reached just such an economic situation, Britain was considered by the opponents of luxury to be headed for its mortal illness.[16]

These varieties of pessimism undoubtedly constituted a more than negligible portion of the historical outlook of the eighteenth century. But their force was limited in important ways throughout the period. A number of primitivists, for instance, held their critical views of modern civilization in an uneasy tension with a belief in progress. The "gloom of the Tory satirists" was sometimes brightened, as in the case of Swift, by an ultimate dream of divine intervention that would alter the course of history in a positive direction. And, in more secular terms, Bolingbroke looked forward to the breaking of the historical cycle in Britain by a patriot king, under whose auspices "concord will appear, brooding peace and prosperity on the happy land; joy sitting in every face, content in every heart; a people unoppressed, undisturbed, unalarmed; busy to improve their private property and the public stock." Even the authors of the jeremiads often held out hopes for social improvement through individual self-regeneration.[17] Undeniably, then, much of the pessimism of the eighteenth century was tempered with optimism, many of its fears with hopes.

Moreover, the extent of historical pessimism (except for its primitivist version) began to wane with the end of the Augustan age in the

16. Wade, "Idea of Luxury," 80–113, 7, 277–78. For a somewhat different assessment of the eighteenth-century attack on luxury, see John Sekora, *Luxury: The Concept in Western Thought, Eden to Smollett* (Baltimore, 1977), 63–131.

17. Whitney, *Primitivism and the Idea of Progress*, esp. 137, 277–97, and passim; James William Johnson, "Swift's Historical Outlook," *Journal of British Studies*, 4, no. 2 (May 1965): 57–58, 76–77; Bolingbroke, *Idea of a Patriot King*, in *Works*, 3:125; Wade, "Idea of Luxury," 91. For an example of the jeremiads that culminated in hopefulness, see George Berkeley, *A Discourse addressed to Magistrates and Men in Authority, Occasioned by the enormous Licence and Irreligion of the Times* (1736), in *The Works of George Berkeley, Bishop of Cloyne*, ed. A. A. Luce and T. E. Jessop, 9 vols. (London, 1948–57), 6:201, 221–22.

1730s and diminished substantially after about 1760.[18] Just the opposite was true of the idea of progress. Already widely expressed before the 1750s, from that decade on it became an increasingly common feature of British thought and was given its most general forms. Indeed, it was the dominant element in the historical outlook of the high eighteenth century, far more popular than pessimism.

That it flourished so vigorously was due in part to the temperateness of the surrounding social climate, which might best be described as confidence without complacency. Fundamentally, confidence was bred of pride in the institutions of politics and society, which normally seemed at the time—and relative to the rest of the world—to provide stability and liberty, power and prosperity. These blessings had been won only with difficulty, but their very winning made the present appear secure and boded well for the future. The sense of confidence also derived, after mid-century, from the heightened visibility of scientific and technological advance, especially those improvements in machinery and transportation associated with the onset of the Industrial Revolution. And, in a more particular way, it received added impetus from the sudden burst of national optimism that accompanied the favorable turn taken by the Seven Years' War during 1759 and 1760. But the mood of confidence rarely amounted to unrealistic smugness. Political critics of all types found the constitution to be good but hardly perfect, and others lamented the state of religion and education. Military defeats fostered occasional moments of gloom, as happened in the three years before 1759. If optimism tempered pessimism, optimism was itself kept in bounds by self-criticism, worries, and even the literature of pessimism. With few exceptions, to educated Britons of the eighteenth century whatever was, was not necessarily or entirely right. Lacking complacency, they possessed sufficient confidence to point out problems and propose solutions.

Although the idea of progress blossomed in this social atmosphere, it could not have done so without the fertile soil of intellectual tradition. By the late seventeenth century, it was already customary to think about religion and learning as progressive. These and

18. On the shift away from pessimism, see Louis I. Bredvold, "The Gloom of the Tory Satirists," in James L. Clifford and Louis A. Landa, eds., *Pope and His Contemporaries: Essays Presented to George Sherburn* (Oxford, 1949), 15–18. Evidence of historical pessimism is much harder to find for the first three decades of the reign of George III than for the previous thirty years.

the other narrower forms of the idea gradually became well-established habits of mind that could feed on themselves. And on each other: through conceptual "displacement," the idea was transferred or extended from one sphere of application to another. This process goes far to explain how doctrines of general progress arose, and why they appeared latest in time.

For all these social and intellectual reasons, the idea of progress was the normal vision of history in high eighteenth-century Britain, and it became increasingly dominant as the period proceeded. Probably more than at any other time in British history, including the Victorian era, when educated men of this age looked back to the past or forward to the future, when they engaged in recollection or foresight or both, what they usually saw, in various shapes, was progress.

*P*art One
The Modified Inheritance

The emergence of the idea of progress in Britain, as in Europe generally, has often been associated with two intellectual traditions. One of these, the Judeo-Christian conception of history, ranks among the oldest and most influential of all the major streams of Western thought. The other, a belief in the advancement of knowledge, has less ancient roots. It did not appear until the Renaissance, and only in the early seventeenth century did it become prominent, primarily in England. Then, in the years between the accession of Charles I and the Restoration, a substantial number of English Puritans joined the two traditions, in a millennial context. During the eighteenth century this link did not survive completely intact.[1] But together the traditions continued in that period to play a crucial role: simultaneously drawn upon and transformed, they served as the intellectual inheritance out of which the idea of progress developed in Britain.

---

1. See below, chap. 3. For the joining of the traditions, see Charles Webster, *The Great Instauration: Science, Medicine and Reform 1626–1660* (London, 1975), 1–2, 506–07.

2 Ancients and Moderns, Arts and Sciences

The belief that knowledge about man and the external world could and did advance followed, as is well known, in the wake of the scientific, technological, and geographical discoveries that rapidly multiplied after the late fifteenth century. These achievements led a number of sixteenth-century Continental writers, from Albrecht Dürer to Jean Bodin and Louis LeRoy, to conclude that learning developed *cumulatively*, and that it could never reach completeness. At the same time, the great thinkers of ancient Greece and Rome began to lose some of the prestige accorded them by earlier generations of humanists. In the light shed by the journeys of discovery and the new physics, it became clear that the ancients neither possessed all possible knowledge nor were entirely free from error. A new attitude to authority was in the making. Merely to recover and adopt the wisdom of classical antiquity (and early Christianity) no longer sufficed to understand the workings of the world; instead, men were slowly coming to see the value of observation.

By the start of the seventeenth century, a scientist like William Gilbert could express his impatience with those who simply copied old books instead of examining the book of nature. In his treatise *De Magnete* (1600), he emphasized empirical observation and largely avoided the use of Greek words and the arguments of Greek authors, which to him did not seem helpful in demonstrating the truth about nature. Moreover, he went so far as actually to attack the authority of the ancients. This new attitude was epitomized and popularized by Francis Bacon, who during the reign of James I presented his contemporaries with a comprehensive doctrine of progress in knowledge. Most of his intellectual labors were inspired by a desire to extend the frontiers of learning. For Bacon, this goal was to be attained primarily

21

through the rallying of all men to empirical activities in a common effort to investigate nature.[1]

His fleshing out of this prescription, in *The Advancement of Learning* (1605) and *Novum Organum* (1620), made it apparent that he looked upon useful, scientific knowledge or learning as progressive. According to his famous paradox of the ancients, "the old age of the world is to be accounted the true antiquity; and this is the attribute of our own times, not of that earlier age of the world in which the ancients lived; and which, though in respect of us it was the elder, yet in respect of the world it was the younger." And just as one can expect "greater knowledge of human things" in the old man than the young because of his experience, so more can rightly be expected of modernity than antiquity because "it is a more advanced age of the world, and stored and stocked with infinite experiments and observations."[2] This paradox made the same point as the giant-and-dwarf metaphor so popular in the seventeenth century: because knowledge is cumulative and progressive, because it is naturally subject to advancement, those who live later will inevitably have more of it than their predecessors, even if the predecessors stood taller.

Bacon was not only arguing in favor of the notion that knowledge advances; he was also conducting a polemic on behalf of the moderns and the new scientific method against the ancients and adherence to authority. Not that he outwardly wished to demean the men of the classical world: he claimed that he left the "honor of the ancients untouched." But in fact he often did disparage their intellectual achievements and, especially, their method. The "wisdom which we have derived principally from the Greeks," he wrote, "is but like the boyhood of knowledge, and has the characteristic property of boys: it can talk, but it cannot generate; for it is fruitful of controversies but barren of works."[3] With this valuation of the ancients as with the belief in the advancement of knowledge, Bacon sounded themes that the English echoed and elaborated down to the time of Macaulay.

From the 1620s through the 1690s these themes played important

1. On Bacon and Gilbert, see Richard Foster Jones, *Ancients and Moderns: A Study of the Rise of the Scientific Movement in Seventeenth-Century England*, 2d ed. (Berkeley, 1965), 16–21, 41–61.

2. Francis Bacon, *Novum Organum*, in *The Works of Francis Bacon*, ed. James Spedding, R. L. Ellis, and D. D. Heath, new ed., 7 vols. (London, 1870–72), 4:82 (Bk. I, Aph. lxxxiv).

3. Ibid., 4:62 (Bk. I, Aph. lxi); idem, *The Great Instauration*, in *Works*, 4:14 ("Preface").

roles in what has come to be called the "Battle"—or, among the French, the *querelle*—of Ancients and Moderns. The English title is really a misnomer, for if anything the controversy in question was a war, a kind of intellectual Hundred Years' War. Like that medieval conflict, it proceeded intermittently in a number of stages and continued for more than a century. Having begun in late Renaissance Italy, it eventually spread to France, where in the 1680s and 1690s the likes of Perrault, Fontenelle, and Boileau fought its most renowned engagements. Meanwhile, the English theater of the conflict became equally active. There the first phase of the war, in the decade after Bacon's death in 1626, centered on the popular theory of the decay of nature, with George Hakewill championing the cause of the moderns. Unlike the arch-pessimist Godfrey Goodman, Hakewill insisted that there was no inherent tendency for either nature or man to degenerate over the centuries, and part of his proof for this contention consisted of a detailed comparison of ancient with modern times. He found the two periods to be equal in life span and physical stature and strength; although the same was largely true with regard to learning, he considered the moderns actually to have excelled in such areas as painting, philology, medicine, religion and morals, science, and inventions. Consequently he condemned excessive veneration of antiquity and concluded that the moderns were not inferior—and in some respects were superior—to the ancients.[4]

Hakewill laid a firm foundation for the succeeding controversy by establishing a basis for comparison of achievements in the various fields of endeavor. During the period of the English Revolution, many other writers followed him in upholding the moderns against the ancients, and Bacon in accepting the theory of the advancement of learning. After 1660 a new stage of the controversy developed, this

4. Hakewill developed his argument in *An Apologie of the Power and Providence of God in the Government of the World* (3 eds., 1627–35), which is thoroughly analyzed in Victor Harris, *All Coherence Gone* (Chicago, 1949), 47–85; and Jones, *Ancients and Moderns*, 22–40. On the history of the Ancients-and-Moderns controversy from Hakewill to Swift, explored in the next several paragraphs, see Jones, *Ancients and Moderns*, 183–267; idem, "The Background of *The Battle of the Books*," in *The Seventeenth Century: Studies in the History of English Thought and Literature from Bacon to Pope* (Stanford, 1951), 10–40; Hippolyte Rigault, *Histoire de la querelle des anciens et des moderns* (1856), in *Oeuvres complètes de H. Rigault*, 4 vols. (Paris, 1859), 1:295–374 ("Deuxième partie"). The concept of a *war* between ancients and moderns was present in the eighteenth century: see, for example, [John Gordon], *Occasional Thoughts on the Study and Character of Classical Authors, on the Course of Literature, and the present Plan of a Learned Education* (London, 1762), 3–5.

time focusing on the value of the Royal Society. One of the chief proponents of the moderns in this engagement was Thomas Sprat, author of the first history of the society, who rested his case for the superiority of the moderns solely on their experimental method and its anticipated future results. Another significant modernist was Joseph Glanvill. In his *Plus Ultra* (1668) and polemical writings aimed at Henry Stubbe, an opponent of the society, Glanvill made the same argument as Sprat. But he also utilized the technique of Hakewill, to whom he referred, and outlined the superior accomplishments of the moderns field by field. According to this analysis, the moderns exceeded the ancients in three broad areas: useful knowledge, in chemistry, anatomy, mathematics, astronomy, optics, geography, and the study of living things; scientific instruments, particularly the microscope, telescope, thermometer, barometer, and air pump; and the means of spreading knowledge and communicating (printing, the compass, and the Royal Society itself).[5]

This was a strong case for the moderns. Ultimately, such an argument would necessarily bring triumph to them, for it was difficult to deny the compelling evidence of their concrete and demonstrable achievements in science and technology. Still, victory did not come in 1668, as was made apparent by the attacks launched against Glanvill's book in the next few years by Stubbe and Meric Casaubon. And although the war entered a period of quiescence in England from the early 1670s through the 1680s, it boiled over again in 1690.

That year saw the appearance of Sir William Temple's *Essay upon the Ancient and Modern Learning*, which opened and served as a center for the final phase of the controversy during the seventeenth century. Without clearly reasserting the doctrine of degeneration, Temple nonetheless still gave the palm to the ancients in genius, using the giant-and-dwarf metaphor to prove his point. Yet he refused to grant the modern dwarfs the comfort implied by that metaphor. The moderns, he claimed, did not see farther than—indeed, they did not see as far as—the ancients on whose shoulders they tried to stand. For they were inferior in virtually every department of learning and knowledge. This Temple believed to be true not only of philosophy and science (including astronomy and medicine, recent "discoveries" which he doubted to be either new or accurate) but also of lan-

---

5. Joseph Glanvill, *Plus Ultra: Or, the Progress and Advancement of Knowledge Since the Days of Aristotle* (London, 1668), 7–92.

guage, prose literature, and the arts of music, architecture, painting, and sculpture. Evidence of this kind led him to conclude that learning, like an organism, was subject to decay and could not continue to advance indefinitely.[6]

Temple's essay and the warm response with which the reading public greeted it indicate that the Glanvillian position had not yet achieved complete supremacy. Further, they suggest that for the first time the French *querelle* was making itself felt across the Channel. Previously, in England the war had been fought almost entirely over science and philosophy, whereas in France the combatants had accepted the superiority of the moderns in these areas and had limited their polemics to literature and the arts. Now Temple, as a result of his reading of the modernist Fontenelle, helped to make the latter two fields new territory over which the war could rage in his own country. The defenders of the moderns, however, were largely not yet prepared to contest this ground, as demonstrated by the response that Temple's essay evoked from them. Sir Thomas Pope Blount, for instance, replied in two essays of 1692 by using the categories and restating the arguments of Hakewill and Glanvill. He recurred both to Bacon's paradox of the ancients and to the giant-and-dwarf metaphor, but he made no attempt to claim superiority in literature and the arts for the moderns.

The same was true of William Wotton, who in 1694 published his *Reflections upon Ancient and Modern Learning*, the most comprehensive and fair-minded contribution to the war that appeared in either France or England during the seventeenth century. Wotton cited Fontenelle and Perrault in his book and like them he refused to accept the theory of degeneration. In addition, like Fontenelle (and, to some extent, Perrault) he believed that it was necessary to divide the corpus of thought and culture into two parts. He argued that there were some areas—especially philosophy, the sciences, and those fields closely related to or dependent on them—in which achievements could be judged by definite criteria. In this context, Wotton illustrated at length how learning had slowly advanced and he argued that the moderns exceeded the ancients. On the other hand, he conceded that achievements in the arts (poetry, oratory, architecture, painting, and sculpture) were a matter of opinion only. And here

6. Sir William Temple, *An Essay upon the Ancient and Modern Learning*, in *The Works of Sir William Temple, Bart.*, 1st ed., 2 vols. (London, 1720), 1:151–69.

Wotton was prepared to follow the opinion of what he called the majority of learned men in giving up the cause to the ancients, or at least admitting that the moderns had not gone beyond their predecessors. In a posthumously published essay, Temple made much of this admission. But he did not and could not provide evidence to attack Wotton's position on the advancement of knowledge outside the arts: the case for the moderns was simply too concrete and too strong. It led Wotton to conclude that "the World has gone on, from Age to Age, Improving; and consequently . . . it is at present much more Knowing than it ever was since the earliest Times to which History can carry us."[7]

Nevertheless, in spite of Wotton's declared intention of mediating between the respective proponents of the ancients and moderns and of setting forth the true facts of the matter in final form, he was not successful in bringing the war to an end. Indeed, he managed to provoke further polemical writings. Most of these, concerning the authenticity of the letters of Phalaris (praised so highly by Temple), were tangential to the central issues of the war. Jonathan Swift, however, in both *Tale of a Tub* and *Battle of the Books*, came to the defense of his patron Temple and presented a satirical bird's-eye view of the course of the war. Swift brought forth no new arguments on behalf of either the ancients or the moderns. But he did express an important truth about the whole controversy when he wrote that "we cannot learn to which side the Victory fell."[8] For the ultimate outcome of the war had not been definitively decided by 1704, when he published the two satires, although the ancients appeared to have gained the upper hand in the arts and the moderns in knowledge and the sciences. It was the task of the eighteenth century to continue the search for final answers.

THE BOUNDARIES AND TERMS OF DISCOURSE

After a hiatus of about a quarter-century during which comparatively few works relevant to the war appeared, serious dis-

7. William Wotton, *Reflections upon Ancient and Modern Learning*, 3d ed., corr. (London, 1705), v. Temple's reply to Wotton, "Some Thoughts Upon Reviewing the Essay of Ancient and Modern Learning," was first published by Swift in 1701 and appears in *Works of Temple*, 1:290–304.

8. Jonathan Swift, *A Full and True Account of the Battel Fought last Friday, Between the Ancient and the Modern Books in St. James's Library* (written 1697), in

cussion of the merits of the ancients and moderns resumed in England and Scotland in the 1730s and 1740s. And it continued, among more people and with fewer interruptions than ever before, from the 1750s to the time of the French Revolution. The war itself, however, had become a relatively peaceable affair by 1730. With the exception of the related yet substantially different controversy surrounding John Brown's *Estimate of the Manners and Principles of the Times* during the years after 1757,[9] the heated debates marking each stage of the seventeenth-century war gave way to largely non-polemical consideration of an important intellectual question. This discussion did not proceed in phases but formed a whole in which the same issues were consistently addressed.

These characteristics indicate that by the fourth decade of the eighteenth century an intellectual tradition relating to the question of ancients and moderns had already emerged. When Swift published his satires, the basic approaches to this question were largely determined, and the men of the eighteenth century who concerned themselves with the ancients and moderns thought and wrote within that established framework. This is not to suggest that they had nothing new to say: on the contrary, their discussion of the question was very productive of conceptions about progress in knowledge, practical skills, and—especially—the fine arts. But their ideas were strongly conditioned by the tradition of the seventeenth-century war. They recognized, as was pointed out by Hugh Blair (1718–1800), Professor of Rhetoric at the University of Edinburgh and a key member of the Scottish Enlightenment, that the issue of the "comparative merit of the Antients and the Moderns" had produced "no small controversy in the Republic of Letters." They were familiar with both the English and the French participants in the war, and they even continued to use the metaphor of the giant and dwarf and the paradox of the ancients.[10]

The Prose Works of Jonathan Swift, ed. Herbert Davis, 14 vols. (Oxford, 1951–68), 1:141 ("The Bookseller to the Reader").

9. On the Brown controversy, see below, chap. 6. Among the most important early eighteenth-century defenders of the moderns were the poets and critics Sir Richard Blackmore (ca. 1650–1729), in his "Essay upon Epic Poetry" (1716); John Dennis (1657–1734), especially in *The Advancement and Reformation of Modern Poetry* (1701); and Charles Gildon (1665–1724), throughout his critical writings.

10. Hugh Blair, *Lectures on Rhetoric and Belles Lettres* (1783), ed. Harold F. Harding, 2 vols. (Carbondale, Ill., 1965), 2:247. In his amusing and imaginatively written *On the Shoulders of Giants: A Shandean Postscript* (New York, 1965), Robert K. Merton

Still, there were basic differences between them and their predecessors. They not only avoided the polemical orientation of the past but also tended to explore the issues at hand in a more profound and analytical way. And as a group they exhibited a much stronger, more widely accepted conviction that the "moderns" were superior to the "ancients" in the "arts" and "sciences." If we are to understand precisely what this conviction meant we must first discover how they used these terms.

For the first of these pairs of words, "ancients" and "moderns," they rarely offered anything approaching exact definition. Invariably, the writers of eighteenth-century English dictionaries followed the Renaissance distinction between *antiqua* and *nova* and merely denominated as moderns "those who have lived lately, opposed to the ancients." What it meant to have "lived lately" was generally not specified, although one dictionary did suggest that some people considered as moderns "all those Authors who have written since *Boet*[h]*ius.*"[11] On the whole, the context in which most of those who directly treated the question of ancients and moderns were writing makes it clear that they considered the fall of the Roman Empire in the West as a chronological dividing line. Before that time the ancients lived. But immediately afterward came a kind of historical no-man's land whose inhabitants, neither ancient nor modern, were not made parties to the question at all because of their lack of learning. Here appears in another guise the common tendency of historians in the age of the Enlightenment (except for a few, like William Robertson) to dismiss the Middle Ages and concentrate instead on what they considered the great ages of "civilization." Therefore, unlike the dictionary writer who mentioned Boethius, eighteenth-century British students of the question of the ancients and moderns treated the latter as if they had first appeared with the Renaissance.

---

cites no instances of the use of the giant-dwarf metaphor between 1705 and 1812. But there were many: see, for example, J.[ames] B.[urgh], *The Dignity of Human Nature. Or, A brief Account of the certain and established Means for attaining the true End of our Existence*, 1st ed. (London, 1754), 143; Oliver Goldsmith, *An Enquiry into the Present State of Polite Learning in Europe* (1759), in *Collected Works of Oliver Goldsmith*, ed. Arthur Friedman, 5 vols. (Oxford, 1966), 1:264; J.[ohn] Aikin, "On Attachment to the Ancients," *Letters from a Father to His Son, on Various Topics, relative to Literature and the Conduct of Life* (London, 1793), 18. Burgh and Aikin, among others, also mentioned the paradox of the ancients.

11. William Rider, *A New Universal English Dictionary* (London, 1759), s.v. "Moderns"; N. Bailey, *Dictionarium Britannicum*, 1st ed. (London, 1730), s.v. "Moderns."

Blair, intimate of the chief Scottish *literati*, explicitly stated this view in his comments on the four periods in history that he found distinguished above all others for learning. In chronological order these were the "Grecian Age" from the Peloponnesian Wars to Alexander the Great, the "Roman Age" of Julius Caesar and Augustus, the "restoration of Learning" in the era of the Renaissance, and the "Age of Louis XIV. and Queen Anne." When speaking comparatively of the ancients and the moderns, he wrote,

> we generally mean by the Ancients, such as lived in the two first of these periods, including also one or two who lived more early, as Homer in particular; and by the Moderns, those who flourished in the two last of these ages, including also the eminent Writers down to our own times.[12]

The second pair of words, "arts" and "sciences," is even more problematic than the first. For the thinkers of eighteenth-century Britain and, in fact, Europe as a whole had not yet decided in a definitive way how to categorize the various disciplines and branches of knowledge. That they were aware of this situation appears from two dictionaries published in the 1750s. The compiler of one of these conceded that the terms art and science were "used promiscuously by authors, for want of affixing certain ideas to their words." In the other, the author agreed that "it must be confessed, that our ideas are, in this case, not sufficiently precise." Definitions in still other dictionaries, like that of Samuel Johnson, frequently equated science with "Any art or species of knowledge" and "Art attained by precepts or built on principles," thereby providing evidence of a state of terminological confusion.[13]

Such confusion resulted from the presence of two conflicting tendencies in contemporary thought on the subject of the arts and sciences. To begin with, there was a desire, epitomized by the *Encyclopédie*, to consider all fields of knowledge as a unified and interconnected whole. This desire, flowing from Bacon, Descartes,

12. Blair, *Lectures on Rhetoric*, 2:248–49.
13. Rider, *New Universal English Dictionary*, s.v. "Art"; [John Barrow], *A Supplement to the New and Universal Dictionary of Arts and Sciences* (London, 1754), 6 ("Preface"); Samuel Johnson, *A Dictionary of the English Language* (1755), 2d ed., 2 vols. (London, 1755–56), vol. 2, s.v. "Science." Johnson's definition of "science" reappeared verbatim in Thomas Sheridan, *A General Dictionary of the English Language*, 2 vols. (London, 1780), vol. 2, s.v. "Science"; and John Walker, *A Critical Pronouncing Dictionary and Expositor of the English Language* (London, 1791), s.v. "Science."

and Leibniz, gained added strength from the achievement of the *Principia Mathematica*, as theoreticians in the various fields sought to become the Newtons of their own disciplines by grounding them in fundamental laws. As Goldsmith declared, the writers of France had lately "fallen into a method of considering every part of art and science, as arising from simple principles." The search for basic laws led, in part, to the first truly systematic examinations of the philosophy of the fine arts and to the application of the term "aesthetics" to studies of this kind. It also was intimately connected to what has been called the "neoclassical revolution," that late eighteenth-century attempt to create a changeless and harmonious art (in the modern sense of the word) based upon unalterable principles.[14]

In essence, then, during this period "art" aspired to become "science" or, at least, to follow other disciplines in adopting the scientific approach. British definitions of "art" often reflected this aspiration. According to one dictionary, art was "any branch of knowledge, capable of being reduced to determinate invariable rules, independent of caprice or opinion." Elsewhere it was called "a Collection of Rules, Inventions and Experiments" and a "collection of certain rules from observation and experience."[15] The linkage with Newtonian science is apparent.

But if eighteenth-century thinkers wished to treat all disciplines as a unit, they also tended to recognize within that whole a crucial distinction between theory, contemplation, or speculation, and practice, action, or application. This difference was discussed by Diderot in his famous article "Art" (1751), prepared for the *Encyclopédie*. He gave the name "art" to any set of rules whose formal object was a form of *action*, and "science" to a technically organized set of observations about an object merely *contemplated* in its various facets. Diderot was not the first to draw such a distinction. It had appeared more than twenty years before in the statement of Nathan (or

14. Goldsmith, *Enquiry*, in *Collected Works*, 1:304; Ernst Cassirer, *The Philosophy of the Enlightenment*, trans. Fritz C. A. Koelln and James Pettegrove (Princeton, 1951), 278–82; Paul Oskar Kristeller, "The Modern System of the Arts," *Renaissance Thought II: Papers on Humanism and the Arts* (New York, 1965), 163–65; Peter Gay, *The Enlightenment: An Interpretation*, 2 vols. (New York, 1966–69), 2:219; Hugh Honour, *Neo-classicism* (Harmondsworth, Eng., 1968), 13.

15. Barrow, *Supplement*, 6 ("Preface"); Bailey, *Dictionarium Britannicum*, s.v. "Art"; Rider, *New Universal Dictionary*, s.v. "Art." In each case, "art" was intended to include what was frequently called "the liberal arts," among which poetry and painting were usually ranked.

Nathaniel) Bailey (d. 1742), an English lexicographer, that "Science, as opposed to Art, is a formed System of any Branch of Knowledge, comprehending the Doctrine, Reason or Theory of a Thing, without any immediate Application of it to any Uses or Offices of Life." And throughout the second half of the century British writers continued to assert, with the *Encyclopaedia Britannica*, that "Art is principally used for a system of rules serving to facilitate the performance of certain actions; in which sense it stands opposed to science, or a system of speculative principles."[16]

Here is what appears to be a clear-cut definition of art and science. And yet many eighteenth-century thinkers were not satisfied with it. As John Barrow (fl. 1735–56), the author of a dictionary of arts and sciences, admitted, "We are often at a loss in naming such branches of knowledge where speculation is joined with practice," and he used for an example the fact that "it is frequently disputed in the schools, whether logic be an Art or a Science." The solution he adopted was simple and ingenious: "the question might easily be solved," he wrote, "by saying it is both the one and the other," adding that "in this sense, several Sciences, considered in their practical use, may be termed Arts." The same point was made from a slightly different perspective by George Campbell (1719–96), Professor of Divinity and Principal of Marischal College at Aberdeen. For him, "All art is founded in science, and the science is of little value which does not serve as a foundation to some beneficial art." This consideration led him to remark that valuable knowledge always produces and arrives at perfection in some practical skill, and that such skills lack complete beauty and utility when they do not originate in knowledge. Therefore, he concluded, a natural relationship exists "between the sciences and the arts, like that which subsists between the parent and the offspring." Sir Joshua Reynolds, in remarks addressed to the students of the Royal Academy in 1776, took a similar approach to the specific subject of painting. "As our art is not a divine *gift*," he declared, "so neither is it a mechanical *trade*. Its foundations are laid in

16. Denis Diderot, "Art," *Encyclopédie ou Dictionnaire raisonné des sciences, des arts et des métiers,* 17 vols. (Paris, 1751–57, and Neuchâtel, 1765), 1:714:1; Bailey, *Dictionarium Britannicum,* s.v. "Science"; *Encyclopaedia Britannica: Or, A Dictionary of Arts, Sciences, &c.,* 2d ed., enl., 10 vols. (Edinburgh, 1778–83), 1:708:2 (s.v. "Art"). For other examples of this distinction, see Barrow, *Supplement,* 6 ("Preface"); Rider, *New Universal Dictionary,* s.v. "Art" and "Science." An exception is Johnson, who listed "Speculation" as his sixth definition for "art": Johnson, *Dictionary,* vol. 1, s.v. "Art."

solid science: and practice, though essential to perfection, can never attain that to which it aims, unless it works under the direction of principle." Likewise, in the same year the young Jeremy Bentham—future inventor of the master "art-and-science" of eudaemonics—wrote that "the same object which is called *an art*, viewed in another light is called *a science.*"[17]

In these views the opposition between the two conflicting tendencies of eighteenth-century thought on the nature of science and art achieved resolution. Science and art were seen to exist in an intimate relationship, like the sides of a single coin, even though they differed with respect to speculation and application. Yet this outlook, while logical and understandable when spelled out in detail, could easily make for confusion. Its existence explains why some writers of the period defined art as "a science, as the liberal arts"; why others referred to certain disciplines sometimes as "liberal arts" and sometimes as "liberal sciences"; why Samuel Johnson listed what he called the "seven liberal arts" under the heading "SCIENCE." It also illuminates the fact that what in the nineteenth century came to be known as "science" was previously called "natural philosophy," merely one science among many, some of which later lost that appellation.[18]

Thus, although in eighteenth-century Britain there was an attempt to distinguish between science and art, it had neither clear-cut nor invariably applied results. If anything like such a comprehensive,

---

17. Barrow, *Supplement*, 6 ("Preface"); George Campbell, *The Philosophy of Rhetoric* (1776), 2d ed., 2 vols. (London, 1801), 1:i–ii ("Introduction"); Sir Joshua Reynolds, *Discourses on Art*, ed. Robert R. Wark, Yale ed. (New Haven, 1975), 117 (Discourse VII, delivered Dec. 10, 1776). Bentham's statement comes from unpublished papers cited in Mary P. Mack, *Jeremy Bentham: An Odyssey of Ideas, 1748–1792* (London, 1962), 136.

Similar ideas appeared in France at this time. D'Alembert claimed that several sciences could be considered arts when seen from their practical side, and Diderot believed that each art had both speculative and practical features: Jean Le Rond d'Alembert, *Preliminary Discourse to the Encyclopedia of Diderot* (1751), trans. Richard N. Schwab (Indianapolis, 1963), 40; Diderot, "Art," *Encyclopédie*, 1:714:1. Barrow clearly took his solution directly from d'Alembert.

18. Sheridan, *General Dictionary*, vol. 1, s.v. "Art"; Walker, *Critical Pronouncing Dictionary*, s.v. "Art"; Bailey, *Dictionarium Britannicum*, 2d ed. (1736), s.v. "Art" (subsection entitled "The Liberal Arts"); Johnson, *Dictionary*, vol. 2, s.v. "Science." Natural philosophy was called a single, distinct science in, for example, Bailey, *Dictionarium Britannicum*, 1st ed., s.v. "Natural Philosophy"; [John Barrow], *A New and Universal Dictionary of Arts and Sciences* (London, 1751), s.v. "Natural Philosophy"; James Buchanan, *Linguae Britannicae Vera Pronunciatio: Or, A New English Dictionary* (London, 1757), s.v. "Natural Philosophy."

widely acknowledged distinction did exist, it was within the arts themselves. Here most writers differentiated between the mechanical and the liberal or polite arts. To the former, which encompassed trades like weaving, baking, brewing, and carpentry, they attributed the characteristics of requiring physical more than mental exertion, and of aiming at the provision of the necessities of life or even profit. The liberal or polite arts, however, depended on the mind rather than the body and did not have economic or financial ends. They were nearly always considered to include the seven members of the medieval Trivium and Quadrivium, grammar, rhetoric, logic, arithmetic, geometry, astronomy, and music; occasionally navigation, poetry, and painting were added to the list.[19]

This bifurcation seems straightforward enough, but it was complicated by the question of the nature of the "polite" or "fine" arts. These terms appeared in the *Encyclopaedia Britannica* as synonyms for the liberal arts, and in juxtaposition to the mechanical or "useful" arts. Among British writers, the polite arts were considered to have pleasure for their goal and, universally, to include painting, sculpture, music, and poetry (sometimes joined by architecture, eloquence, dancing, and engraving). So the polite arts overlapped with but were not identical to the liberal arts. Moreover, an influential theoretician on the arts, Campbell, muddied the waters of definition even further. He argued that eloquence and architecture were at once "polite" *and* "useful" arts, that some "liberal" arts—such as navigation—were also "useful," and that the "polite" arts of painting and sculpture were "mechanical" with regard to their execution. Compounding the problem still more was the existence of yet another category, "belles lettres" or polite literature. Two dictionaries stated that the French term meant "Literature, the Knowledges of Languages and Science also." Another lexicographer expanded on this imprecise formulation when he commented that "Languages, classical learning, both Greek and Latin, geography, rhetoric, chronology, and history may be accounted the chief parts of learning contained under this term."[20]

19. The mechanical arts are discussed under the heading "Art" in Bailey, *Dictionarium Britannicum*, 1st and 2d eds.; Barrow, *New and Universal Dictionary*; Rider, *New Universal English Dictionary*; Anon., *A New Universal Etymological English Dictionary* (London, 1764). Under the same heading in these sources also appear comments on the liberal arts, which are discussed, in addition, under "Science" in Johnson, *Dictionary*, vol. 2; Buchanan, *Linguae Britannicae*.

20. *Encyclopaedia Britannica*, 1:708:2, 710:2, 715:2–716:1; Campbell, *Philosophy*

All these considerations together indicate that during the high eighteenth century in Britain, and probably throughout Europe, consistent, comprehensive definition of science and art had not yet been achieved. This fact presents a formidable though not insurmountable obstacle to the examination of the question of ancients and moderns in this period. With one exception, it makes impossible the use of contemporary categories to analyze contemporary thought, because those categories were fluctuating and confused. The exception, the concept denoted by the phrase "arts and sciences" or its singular form, was nearly universally used in an inclusive sense. It referred both to knowledge in general and to the performance of what in the strict sense could be called useful and ornamental activities. Otherwise, the precise meaning of many relevant statements containing terms like "art" and "science" emerges only from the particular context in which those statements appear. Conclusions about them must necessarily be drawn in terms of externally imposed (but not completely anachronistic) categories: learning, encompassing the method and all fields of knowledge; practical skills and techniques, including what eighteenth-century Britons typically called trades and mechanical or useful arts; and what later became regularly known as the fine arts, particularly poetry, painting, sculpture, music, and architecture.

GENERAL VIEWS

Some of the high eighteenth-century writers who discussed the question of ancient and modern achievements admitted that answers were difficult or even impossible to reach. Hugh Blair,

---

of Rhetoric, v–vii [misnumbered as vi] ("Introduction"). For the "polite" or "fine" arts, see also [John Hippisley], *The Polite Arts, or, a Dissertation on Poetry, Painting, Musick, Architecture, and Eloquence* (London, 1749), 5–6; Cosmetti [pseud.], *The Polite Arts. Dedicated to the Ladies* (London, 1767), 1; Thomas Robertson, *An Inquiry into the Fine Arts* (London, 1784), 14–17; Sir William Jones, "On the Arts Commonly Called Imitative" (1772), in Scott Elledge, ed., *Eighteenth-Century Critical Essays,* 2 vols. (Ithaca, N.Y., 1961), 2:872–73. On "belles lettres" and polite literature, see the following under the heading "Belles Lettres": Bailey, *Dictionarium Britannicum,* 2d ed.; *Etymological English Dictionary;* Rider, *New Universal English Dictionary;* Johnson, *Dictionary,* vol. 1. Blair considered "belles lettres" to form a part of the liberal arts: *Lectures on Rhetoric,* 1:4. Goldsmith wrote a whole book about "polite learning" without defining the term. But he clearly meant it to include literature and what has come to be known as the fine arts, but not natural science or philosophy: see, for example, *Enquiry,* in *Collected Works,* 1:269.

for instance, argued that "Any comparison between these two classes of Writers, cannot be other than vague and loose."[21] But others disagreed with this assessment and did not hesitate to deal with the question at both general and specific levels. Among those who arrived at the broadest kinds of conclusions about the issue, we find considerable difference of opinion.

To begin with, there was the conviction that many contemporaries had an unbounded admiration for the ancients, preferring them, as the political commentator and reformer James Burgh (1714–75) put it, "universally and in the gross, to the moderns." According to a writer in a magazine of the 1780s, these men—"who are perpetually dinning our ears with the praises of time past, who are fond of drawing comparisons between the ancients and moderns, much to the disparagement of the latter"—believed that the arts and sciences had declined from the heights formerly attained. The same writer argued that such an outlook was held in conjunction with the notion of decay or degeneration. The supporters of the ancients, he stated, "take a misanthropical delight in representing mankind as degenerating from age to age, both in mental and corporeal endowments. . . . Even the human figure is dwindling away in stature, and diminishing in strength; the climates are altered, the seasons become yearly more inclement; the earth is losing its fertility, and the sun its heat."[22]

In fact, however, those who adopted this opinion must have been very few in number. Virtually no direct evidence exists to support claims about the popularity of the doctrine of progressive degeneration. When contemporaries spoke of decay, as they sometimes did, they meant a decline vis-à-vis the recent past (as in the Brown contro-

21. Blair, *Lectures on Rhetoric*, 2:249.
22. Burgh, *Dignity of Human Nature*, 145; Paul Pasquin [pseud. for Alexander Fraser Tytler?], "Comparison of ancient with modern times, much to the advantage of the latter," *The Lounger*, no. 19 (June 11, 1785), 2d ed., 3 vols. (Edinburgh, 1787), 1:172–73. For other comments on the popularity of these views, see [Peter Shaw], *The Reflector: Representing Human Affairs, As they are; and may be improved* (London, 1750), 131; [Philip Stanhope, Lord Chesterfield], "On the Notion of Decay," *The World*, no. 197 (Oct. 7, 1756), new ed. (London, 1767), 254; Sir John Hawkins, *A General History of the Science and Practice of Music* (1776), repr. of 1853 ed. (New York, 1963), xxviii:1 ("Preliminary Discourse").
A limited understanding of the history of the idea of degeneration could also be found at this time. See Samuel Johnson, "Milton," *Lives of the Poets*, ed. George Birkbeck Hill, 3 vols. (Oxford, 1905), 1:137; John Hookham Frere, contribution to *The Microcosm* (May 7, 1787), in *The Works of John Hookham Frere in Verse and Prose*, ed. W. E. Frere and Sir Bartle Frere, 1st ed., 2 vols. (London, 1872), 1:21.

versy on luxury) or a relative difference between primitive and civilized man, not a continuous, eternal process. The notion of an ever-worsening deterioration of man and nature was dead by this period.[23]

But for some men, like Lord Chesterfield, the belief in the general superiority of the ancients remained. He admitted to his conviction as a youth that

> there had been no common sense nor common honesty in the world for these last fifteen hundred years; but that they were totally extinguished with the ancient Greek and Roman governments. Homer and Virgil could have no faults, because they were ancients; Milton and Tasso could have no merit because they were modern.

The same view was put forth by Louis Dutens (1730–1812), a French Huguenot who migrated to England and performed many diplomatic missions for the British government, and was seconded by his popularizer, John Wesley. Dutens claimed superiority for the ancients not only in the fine arts but also, to a certain extent, in inventions and the sciences, "insomuch that there is no part of knowledge in which they have not either preceeded [sic] us, directed us, or surpassed us." Without holding such extreme opinions, many other Britons expressed their admiration for antiquity by imitating it and appealing to its authority. During the first decades after 1700, this was true of those caught up in the Palladian craze, from architects like Colen Campbell to the men who patronized and worked with them, such as the earl of Burlington. In building churches and country houses, they derived a large part of their inspiration from the Romans, as Alexander Pope made clear in his line addressed to Burlington, "be whate'er Vitruvius was before." Similarly, neoclassicists in literature and, later, architecture consciously learned from the ancients, even though Pope's dictum that "to copy *Nature* is to copy *Them*" was by no means universally accepted.[24]

23. One historian of ideas has suggested that the idea of progressive degeneration "remained one of the popular favorites in the eighteenth century": Lois Whitney, *Primitivism and the Idea of Progress in English Popular Literature of the Eighteenth Century* (Baltimore, 1934), 43. She produces no convincing evidence to support this contention, although she does make clear the existence of primitivism and concerns about the ill effects of luxury.

24. Lord Chesterfield to Philip Stanhope, Feb. 7, 1749 (O.S.), in *The Letters of Philip Dormer Stanhope, 4th Earl of Chesterfield*, ed. Bonamy Dobrée, 6 vols. (London, 1932), 4:1305; [Louis] Dutens, *An Inquiry into the Origin of the Discoveries attributed to the*

However expressed, the veneration often directed toward classical culture in eighteenth-century Britain should hardly be surprising. It clearly derived in part from the traditional evaluation of the ancients epitomized by Temple's *Essay*. But it was also fostered by the education that the ruling classes typically received. The curriculum of the endowed grammar schools of England still focused primarily on the classics (although the speaking of Latin in the schools became much less common), and the same was largely true at Oxford (whereas Cambridge was going its own way by emphasizing mathematics). Visits to Italy and sometimes to Greece, as part of the Grand Tour, brought young gentlemen into direct contact with the monuments of a past about which they had previously only read, and often into actual possession of its treasures. To be sure, there were critics of this whole system of education, and the Dissenting academies and Scottish universities offered a broader range of instruction (which included such subjects as modern languages and all fields of natural philosophy, as well as ancient literature). But no one would have disagreed with Blair's assertion that only a considerable acquaintance with the classics permitted a man to write and speak well and be "reckoned a polite scholar."[25]

Gibbon understood full well the effect of such an education: "those impressions, engraved in our minds, before we reflect, grow up with us afterwards, and . . . when we look abroad, into the Moral and natural world, which these companions, often prevent us from doing, we see it only with the eyes of the ancients." Seeing through the classical lens was the "certain spirit" that the young Gibbon elsewhere praised, and that so often led even educational reformers, Scots, and Nonconformists to cite ancient texts in their writings, much like the English politicians whose speeches were studded with

---

Moderns: Wherein it is demonstrated, That our most celebrated Philosophers have, for the most part, taken what they advance from the Works of the ancients. . . . Translated from the French. . . . With considerable Additions communicated by the Author (London, 1769), 453–55; Alexander Pope, *Epistles to Several Persons* (1731–35), in *The Twickenham Edition of the Poems of Alexander Pope*, ed. John Butt, 1st ed., 11 vols. (London, 1951–69), 3:ii (*Epistles to Several Persons [Moral Essays]*, ed. F. W. Bateson [1951]), 150 ("Epistle IV," l. 194); idem, *An Essay on Criticism* (1711), in *Twickenham Edition*, vol. 1 (*Pastoral Poetry and An Essay on Criticism*, ed. E. Audra and Aubrey Williams [1961]), 255 (l. 140). See also James Beattie, "Remarks on the Utility of Classical Learning" (written 1769), *Essays* (Edinburgh, 1776), 752–53.

25. Blair, *Lectures on Rhetoric*, 2:258. On criticism of traditional education, see below, chap. 4. For a defense of an education in the classics, see Beattie, "Classical Learning," *Essays*, esp. 712, 728, 735.

quotations from the Greeks and Romans.[26] The kind of education that permitted such references to be made and understood also allowed classical scholarship to continue to flourish, if at a less erudite level than during the preceding period. Although there was a long interval from Richard Bentley to Richard Porson, in between Conyers Middleton's *Life of Cicero*, Hume's essay on ancient population, Adam Ferguson's volumes on the history of republican Rome, and, of course, Gibbon's *Decline and Fall* itself all testify that some of the best minds of the age were still attracted to and skillful at the scholarly use of antique sources.

Not everyone attributed the love of antiquity merely to the "classical prejudices" instilled by traditional education. Psychological explanations were also put forward. For instance, the writer and royal physician Peter Shaw (1694–1763) traced the tendency to praise the past and blame the present to the disappointment of old men. Vicesimus Knox (1752–1821), a schoolmaster and Anglican cleric, agreed with this assessment and added that the exaltation of past genius derived as well from "a secret desire to degrade living merit by introducing an invidious comparison." Chesterfield explained how this could be when he suggested that some men of letters, through anger and despair, devalued the achievements of their own times, "which, till brought very low indeed, they are conscious they cannot equal." Such "consolatory expedients," to use Samuel Johnson's term, could easily be manufactured not just by writers but by mankind in general. According to a magazine article published in 1787 by John Hookham Frere (1769–1846), a young writer and poet who later helped to found the *Quarterly Review*, the constant failure of men to achieve the happiness they seek led to the "invention of lenitives." By considering themselves constitutionally incapable of reaching the heights attained by the past, men gained substantial "protection from the feelings of conscious humiliation, and the agonies of conviction and remorse."[27]

26. Edward Gibbon, "Hurd on Horace," in *The English Essays of Edward Gibbon*, ed. Patricia B. Craddock (Oxford, 1972), 47; idem, "Essai sur l'étude de la littérature" (1759), in *The Miscellaneous Works of Edward Gibbon, Esq.*, ed. John, Lord Sheffield, 2d ed., 5 vols. (London, 1814), 4:27.

27. Shaw, *The Reflector*, 135; Vicesimus Knox, "The Complaints Against Modern Literature Probably Ill-Founded" and "On Some Inconveniences which Unavoidably Attend Living Writers," *Essays, Moral and Literary* (1778), nos. CVII and CXI, in *The Works of Vicesimus Knox, D.D.*, 7 vols. (London, 1824), 1:525, 540; Chesterfield, "On the Notion of Decay," *The World*, 257; Samuel Johnson, "Preface to Shakespeare"

In a different way, James Boswell also located the cause of the veneration of antiquity in human nature. He quoted as the epigraph to an essay of 1782 the observation of Velleius Paterculus that men were more inclined to praise things of which they had only heard than things which they themselves saw, adding that distance in both time and place affected the imagination with "mysterious feelings of preference." To this fact Boswell attributed the tendency of every age to lament its degeneracy in comparison to former times.[28]

With their overtones of cultural self-examination, these various attempts to account for the long-standing adulation of antiquity rightly serve as indicators of a changing mental world. Contemporaries were seeking to understand that traditional attitude precisely because it now faced notable, ever-increasing challenges. So great were these that, if from the political perspective it is inappropriate to call the eighteenth century "Augustan," it is equally wrong to use the labels "classical" or "neoclassical" to describe the mainstream of British thought or English literature after about 1730.[29] In fact, just as we can find relatively few high eighteenth-century minds that were convinced of the general superiority of the ancient to the modern world, so there was at the time a tendency to look away from the past and toward the future. To be sure, notwithstanding Gibbon's claim in 1759 that his century found it easier to ignore and scorn the ancients than to study and admire them, they were rarely rejected outright. Some contemporaries believed with Goldsmith that the general contest between ancient and modern achievements "can be decided in favour of neither." As the mature Chesterfield concluded, rejecting his youthful outlook, "the ancients had their excellencies and their defects, their virtues and their vices, just like the moderns." Or, in

---

(1765), in *The Yale Edition of the Works of Samuel Johnson*, ed. John E. Middendorf, 13 vols. to date (New Haven, 1958–), vol. 7 (*Johnson on Shakespeare*, ed. Arthur Sherbo [1968]), 59; John Hookham Frere, *The Microcosm* (May 7, 1787), in *Works*, 1:23–24. On the role of education in the classics, see Blair, *Lectures on Rhetoric*, 2:251; Hawkins, *History of the Science and Practice of Music*, 1:xxviii:1; Aikin, "On Attachment to the Ancients," *Letters from a Father*, 33.

28. James Boswell, "On Past & Present," *The Hypochondriack*, ed. Margery Bailey, 2 vols. (Stanford, 1928), 2:141 (no. 52, Jan. 1782).

29. See, for example, James William Johnson, *The Formation of English Neo-Classical Thought* (Princeton, 1967), especially xi, 3–30, in which neoclassicism as "reverence for classical civilization" becomes the leitmotiv of the entire era from Dryden to Gibbon. On the problems associated with the term "Augustan," see Howard D. Weinbrot, *Augustus Caesar in "Augustan" England: The Decline of a Classical Norm* (Princeton, 1978).

the words of Shaw, "If the Cause should be brought to the Bar, the Judge might have some Doubt in passing Sentence. Were I an Arbitrator; I should award both Parties to pay their own Costs."[30]

But others found decisively for the moderns. Sir John Hawkins (1719–89), a magistrate and eminent historian of music, claimed that "when appearances every where around us favor the opinion of our improvement [over the ancients] not only in literature, but in the sciences and all the manual arts, it is wonderful that the contrary notion should ever have got footing among mankind." At an early age Jeremy Bentham wrote that there are even more reasons "for the times that are called modern having it over times that are called ancient" than for the old man to have an advantage over the young. Johnson not only spoke "favourably of his own age" but also "maintained its superiority [to the ancients] in every respect, except in its reverence for government." In fact, he was reported by Boswell to have said that "'I am always angry when I hear ancient times praised at the expence of modern times.'" Boswell himself took the same view, stating that "I do sincerely think that this age is better than ancient times."[31]

This kind of broad appraisal rested at least in part on the popular eighteenth-century theory of uniformitarianism, as did the conviction that antiquity and modernity were essentially equal. The outlook of Hakewill and Wotton had triumphed: man and nature in the modern world were no longer considered inherently inferior to their classical predecessors. For example, John Aikin (1747–1822), a London physician, asserted simply that "nature herself does not alter" and advised his son "not [to] think that the powers of men have declined." The importance of this general point for the specific question of ancient and modern achievements was elaborated by William Benwell (1765–96), a student at Trinity College, Oxford, who set forth his conviction that

30. Gibbon, "Essai sur l'étude de la littérature," Miscellaneous Works, 4:17; Goldsmith, Enquiry, in Collected Works, 2:273; Letters of Chesterfield, 4:1306; Shaw, The Reflector, 143.

31. Hawkins, History of the Science and Practice of Music, 1:xxix:1; Jeremy Bentham, "Préjugés in favour of Antiquity" (memorandum of 1773–74), in The Works of Jeremy Bentham, ed. John Bowring, 11 vols. (Edinburgh, 1843), 10:69:1; Boswell's Life of Johnson, ed. George Birkbeck Hill, rev. and enl. L. F. Powell, 6 vols. (Oxford, 1934–50), 3:3, and 4:217; Boswell, "On Past & Present," The Hypochondriack, 2:143. On Johnson as a modern, see also the views of Richard B. Schwartz, Samuel Johnson and the New Science (Madison, Wis., 1971), 26, 106–07.

the powers of genius and intellect still exist in their original and native energy: that arts and sciences, however easily and skil[l]fully managed by the ancients, were not, like the spear of Achilles, too mighty to be handled by posterity; and that a mental superiority is no more to be attributed to the early ages of mankind, than the fabulous pretences of gigantic stature.[32]

Of course, uniformity of natural *powers* did not necessarily imply equality of *accomplishments*, although for Chesterfield it certainly did. His decision not to prefer either the attainments of the ancients or those of the moderns followed directly from his belief "that nature was the same three thousand years ago as it is at present; that men were but men then as well as now; that modes and customs vary often, but that human nature is always the same." Yet such other believers in uniformitarianism as Hawkins and Johnson advocated modern superiority. In doing so they implicitly accepted a principle enunciated, although not applied, by Chesterfield when he paradoxically argued that man "has always been invariably the same, tho' always varying"; that is, constant in "substance" (passions, affections, and appetites) while changing in the "forms and modes" of life (due to the operation of climate, education, and accident). Barrow made this principle explicit in his comments on the "dark ages." "Those unhappy times," he wrote, "were not less fruitful than others in extraordinary genius. Nature continues always the same: But what could geniuses do . . . ?"[33]

Nor, as Barrow's remarks suggest, did the combination of uniformitarianism with the principle of variability in circumstances lead ineluctably to a doctrine of *continuous* progress in the arts and sciences. In fact, it was quite possible for such a firm believer in the constancy of man and nature as Lord Bolingbroke to apply the cyclical theory of history to the whole field of science and art. "Arts and sciences," he declared, "grow up, flourish, decay, die, and return again under the same, or other forms, after periods which appear long to us." The Welsh educator, writer, and Anglican cleric Peter Williams (1756?–1837) held a similar perspective. He considered the

32. Aikin, "On Attachment to the Ancients," *Letters from a Father*, 20, 38; William Benwell, "In What Arts Have the Moderns Excelled the Ancients?" (June 1787), in *The Oxford English Prize Essays*, 4 vols. (Oxford, 1830), 1:105–06.

33. *Letters of Chesterfield*, 4:1305; Chesterfield, "On the Notion of Decay," *The World*, 256; Barrow, *New and Universal Dictionary*, 20 ("Preface").

chief operation performed in the study of history in general to be "tracing, with care and judgment, thè *Rise,* the *Progress,* the *Decline,* and again the *Revival* of the Sciences, and of the liberal and necessary Arts." Barrow prefaced his lengthy examination of the history of the arts and sciences with the comment that they

> have had their happy ages, in which they have appeared with greater splendor, and cast a stronger light: But this splendor, this light, was soon obscured, and these times of perfection [were] of no long continuance. . . . The misfortune is, that this perfection itself, when arrived at its supreme degree, is the forerunner of the decline of Arts and Sciences.

He then proceeded to examine four such happy ages of perfection: in the Near East between the Deluge and the time of the Greeks' travels into Egypt and Babylon, in Greece from Perikles to the death of Alexander's immediate successors, in the Roman Empire until its devastation by the Goths, and in Europe since the Renaissance.[34]

The cyclical theory was also occasionally linked to a version of the old idea of the *translatio imperii.* This connection emerged in James Thomson's long poem *The Castle of Indolence* (1748), in which art and science were depicted as having moved westward over the centuries, rising and falling successively in Egypt, Greece, and Rome before reaching western Europe. Carrying this conception to its logical conclusion, Bishop Berkeley at the end of his life looked forward to the flight of culture from the Old World to America, where "shall be sung another golden Age, / The rise of empire and of Arts." The poet and civil servant Leonard Welsted (1688–1747) did not think that such a migration was imminent, but he projected that the "Arts and Sciences, with their Train of Blessings, shall visit, in their Turn, all Parts of the Globe, and . . . every Part, in its Turn, shall lie sunk in Desolation and Barbarism."[35]

34. Lord Bolingbroke, "Essay the Third," *Essays addressed to Mr. Pope,* in *The Works of the Late Right Honorable Henry St. John, Lord Viscount Bolingbroke,* ed. David Mallet, 5 vols. (London, 1754), 4:236; Peter Williams, *Letters concerning Education: Addressed to a Gentleman Entering at the University* (London, 1785), 182–83; Barrow, *New and Universal Dictionary,* 1, 6, 20–21 ("Preface").

35. James Thomson, *The Castle of Indolence,* in *Liberty, The Castle of Indolence and Other Poems,* ed. James Sambrook (Oxford, 1986), 203–04 (II, xvi–xx); Bishop Berkeley, "Verses . . . on the prospect of Planting Arts and Learning in America" (published 1752), in *The Works of George Berkeley, Bishop of Cloyne,* ed. A. A. Luce and T. E. Jessop, 9 vols. (London, 1948–1957), 7:373; Leonard Welsted, *A Dissertation*

In these various ways the history of art and science, considered as a unit, was frequently stamped with a cyclical pattern. Almost never was it claimed to be *continually* progressive, primarily because the recognition of early medieval cultural desolation naturally militated against the acceptance of any notion of uninterrupted advance. Nevertheless, the arts and sciences did appear to at least some men to exhibit progress on the whole, without threat of decline. As an anonymous Irish writer on the fine arts declared, "Knowledge is gradual in its progress; we should therefore no more expect it can come to perfection all at once, than that a man can be born at his full growth: It has its infancy, nonage and maturity." To this Baconian principle he added that "What is said of the Sciences, holds equally true of the Arts. There is, in this respect, an exact analogy between them." Others argued that continuing advance in these fields could actually be discovered in history. For instance, James Wadham Whitchurch (1749?–76), a young Anglican priest, found it disgraceful that education alone had remained static when the "useful and ornamental Arts, with some few Exceptions, have been for many Centuries, in a State of Progression; when the Sciences have received continual Improvements." For precisely how many centuries? Whitchurch did not say, but ordinarily it was the Renaissance that seemed to have inaugurated the advance. This was certainly what Thomas Barnes (1747–1810), Arian minister of the Cross Street Presbyterian Congregation in Manchester, had in mind when he proclaimed it the honor of modernity to have "extended the Empire of SCIENCE, and of the Arts, so far beyond its antient boundary." In one of the first futuristic novels, *Memoirs of the Twentieth Century* (1733), Samuel Madden (1686–1765) adopted a similar *terminus a quo*. In the postscript to his massive work, this Anglican priest, poet, and playwright from Ireland, who helped to found the Dublin Society of Arts, pointed out

> how few years are past, since we improv'd Astronomy by a true system, verified by demonstration, and founded Philosophy on actual experiments, not on imaginary notions and opinions; since the compass and the needle trac'd out the mariner's unerring road on the ocean, and war join'd fire to the sword, or muskets banish'd bows and arrows; since the invention of

Concerning the Perfection of the English Language, the State of Poetry, &c. (1724), in Willard Higby Durham, ed., *Critical Essays of the Eighteenth Century* (New Haven, 1915), 360–61.

printing gave new lights and aids to the arts; since musick and painting had a new birth in the world; . . . since Physicians found out either new drugs or specificks, or even the secrets of Anatomy, or the circulation of the blood; . . . or that even one half of the earth had found out the other.[36]

The eighteenth century itself appeared to contemporaries to be playing an important role in this progress. Writing of his own time, the poet Edward Young declared in 1759 that "all arts and sciences are making considerable advance." And since improvements in this general sphere seemed to have taken place throughout the modern era and were currently continuing, it was natural to expect that more of the same would come later. Projecting the progress of the past into the future, the anonymous Irish writer declared that "If the moderns have improved on those who went before them, those who come after will improve upon us." Likewise, one of the main points of Madden's novel was to foretell the "vast discoveries and improvements" that would take place during the next 250 years, which he argued should "not appear surprizing, and much less absurd," in light of the advances of recent centuries. Madden specifically underscored the progress that would occur in Great Britain, as did George Turnbull (1698–1748), an Aberdeen professor-turned-Anglican cleric. He looked forward to a Britain in which wealth is "employed in the Encouragement of every kind of Ingenuity and Invention, [and] Philosophy moral and natural, Mathematicks, Poetry, Architecture, Painting, Statuary, Sculpture, and all the Arts, are daily making new Improvements and Advances."[37]

Alongside the relatively small number of men who expressed such unambiguous opinions, there were those who obviously wanted to agree but hesitated to do so. Their reluctance derived from the

36. Anon., *An Essay on Perfecting the Fine Arts in Great Britain and in Ireland* (Dublin, 1767), 5; James Wadham Whitchurch, *An Essay upon Education* (London, 1772), 7; Thomas Barnes, "A Plan for the Improvement and Extension of Liberal Education in Manchester" (read April 9, 1783), *Memoirs of the Literary and Philosophical Society of Manchester* (1785), 2d ed. (London, 1789), 2:16; Samuel Madden, *Memoirs of the Twentieth Century. Being Original Letters of State under George the Sixth*, repr. ed. (New York, 1972), 512.

37. Edward Young, *Conjectures on Original Composition* (1759), ed. Edith A. Morley (Manchester, 1918), 33; Anon., *Essay on Perfecting the Fine Arts*, 4; Madden, *Memoirs of the Twentieth Century*, 505, 513–14; George Turnbull, *A Treatise on Ancient Painting, containing Observations on the Rise, Progress, and Decline of that Art amongst the Greeks and Romans* (London, 1740), 124.

theory (put forth in the late seventeenth century, especially by Fontenelle and Wotton) that with respect to the question of progress there was a division running through the whole body of the arts and sciences. As Benwell observed,

> works of imagination and taste [the fine arts] . . . appear to resemble the great source that produces them: active and vigorous in their progress, and soon arriving at a degree of perfection beyond which no advances can be made. The very reverse may be observed with regard to science [philosophy and knowledge in general], which, as it proceeds with cautiousness and deliberation, and has for its object the unlimited series of causes and effects, is slow and regular in its course, and seems ever capable of increasing excellence, as the experience of the ages is united in its behalf.

In spite of this theory, however, he could not imagine that so many ages had elapsed since antiquity "without suggesting some improvement" in creative literature, pre-eminently a field of imagination and taste. Blair had equal difficulty in reaching a firm conclusion on this issue. He argued that although the world may be expected to know more as time passes, "nothing of this kind holds as to matters of Taste; which depend not on the progress of knowledge and science, but upon sentiment and feeling." Yet he also stated that in "some studies too, that relate to taste and fine writing . . . the progress of Society must, in equity, be admitted to have given us some advantages" over the ancients. Aikin similarly hesitated to draw a clear-cut distinction between knowledge and the fine arts. He suggested that in many arts, especially painting and sculpture, the "excellence of a particular artist cannot be transmitted to a successor; hence a later age does not stand on the shoulders of an earlier one with respect to them." Just a few pages later, however, he declared that "any kind of intellectual product" must partake of the general improvement of the mind. Therefore, he failed to see why not only the moralist and philosopher but "the historian, the critic, the orator, and the poet, too, should not be benefited by the progress" of knowledge.[38]

These equivocating pronouncements reinforce the impression that contemporary thinking about the history of the totality of the

38. Benwell, "Moderns Excelled," in *Oxford Prize Essays*, 1:76–77; Blair, *Lectures on Rhetoric*, 2:250–51, 253; Aikin, "On Attachment to the Ancients," *Letters from a Father*, 18–19, 27–28.

arts and sciences lacked clarity and unanimity. Were the achievements of the moderns in this broad area inferior, equal, or superior to
those of the ancients? What did the principle of uniformitarianism
imply about this problem? Did the arts and sciences follow a cyclical
pattern or develop progressively, and, if the latter, was progress a
natural characteristic of *all* of them? The eighteenth century answered none of these questions definitively and with one voice. That
its outlook on the subject of progress in the whole realm of art and
science displayed considerable diversity is hardly surprising, however, if we remember that the hold exercised by the ancients over the
British mind had loosened but by no means entirely relaxed. It was
virtually impossible for an educated person not to feel at least some
prejudice in favor of classical antiquity, not to find some form of
unchallengeable superiority among the Greeks and Romans. And yet
ever since the *querelle* it had also become increasingly difficult to
accept the ancients unhesitatingly as guides and arbiters. The result
was an intellectual and cultural tension, a tension deriving from a
fundamental realignment of thought. It manifested itself in the varying views of individuals who wrote on art and science, and it goes far
to explain what Paul Fussell has insightfully identified as "the opposition between humanist and 'modern' in the eighteenth century."[39]

But if we look further, to examine not just general views of art and
science, where some praise for the ancients was virtually inevitable,
but also the specific constituent elements of that complex whole, we
will uncover less reluctance to stand up for the moderns. We will
find, in fact, a broad consensus: the men of the high eighteenth century believed in the supremacy of the moderns—and the existence or
possibility of progress—in learning, practical skills and techniques,
and, to a significant degree, the fine arts.

The evidence for this consensus is to be found in the published
writings of the clergy, both Anglican and Dissenting; civil servants
and lawyers; schoolmasters, professors, and university students;
writers of all types, from political commentators to poets, and including several outstanding men of letters; and practitioners of the arts of
painting and music. It is confirmed by the programs of "improving"

39. Paul Fussell, *The Rhetorical World of Augustan Humanism: Ethics and Imagery from Swift to Burke* (Oxford, 1965), 23.

societies whose members included not only the professional classes but also landowners and businessmen. Thus, the group under examination may be considered a microcosm of the most literate classes of eighteenth-century Britain. Equally important, its members far outnumbered those who held opposite views on the subject of progress in the various arts and sciences.

LEARNING

In Britain during this period there was essentially no doubt that the moderns excelled their predecessors in learning. Dutens was almost alone in claiming that the ancients had preceded or surpassed the moderns in knowledge. But even he never attempted actually to prove the superiority of the ancients, resting his case instead on the contention that they had foreshadowed recent "discoveries" in philosophy, mathematics, and natural philosophy. And he was compelled to surrender "to the partizans of the moderns every advantage" in all fields that "require long experience and practice to bring them to perfection."[40] Clearly, he was conducting a kind of rearguard action aimed at salvaging as much respect as he could for his beloved classical antiquity.

Dutens's arguments did not, however, represent a reaction to derisive treatment of the ancients by proponents of the moderns, because intemperate abuse of the Greeks and Romans had very largely disappeared with polemics like Glanvill's *Plus Ultra*. From the time of Wotton on, the ancients received due measure of recognition for their achievements in knowledge. If Shaw, for instance, held that the "Sciences, and Learning in general, flourish more at present, than anciently," he also acknowledged that it was "easy to improve upon Things already begun." And the significance of ancient learning in such areas as moral philosophy was reported by all hands. The point of the advocates of the moderns was not to belittle their forerunners but to distinguish, in Blair's words, "a just and high regard for the prime writers of antiquity . . . from that contempt of every thing

40. Dutens, *Discoveries attributed to the Moderns*, 446, 56, xi–xiii. Wesley agreed with Dutens that "little new has been discovered" by the moderns, concluding triumphantly "How plain is it, that in Philosophy, as well as the course of human affairs, *there is nothing new under the sun!*": [John Wesley], *A Survey of the Wisdom of God in the Creation: or, A Compendium of Natural Philosophy* (1763), 3d ed., further expanded, 5 vols. (London, 1777), 5:169.

which is Modern, and that blind veneration for all that has been written in Greek and Latin, which belongs only to pedants."[41]

Even so, respect for the past did not inhibit praise for modern learning. Again and again, contemporaries echoed Burgh's assertion that the moderns

> have acquired incomparably the superiority over [the ancients] in almost all parts of real knowledge drawn from actual observation, in method and closeness of reasoning; in depth of enquiry; in more various ways, as well as more compendious methods, of coming at truth; and in general, in whatever is useful for improving the understanding.

Or as Aikin expressed it, "modern times, in extent and accuracy of knowledge, have far surpassed those periods which ought rather to be regarded as the *infancy* than the *antiquity* of the world." These claims were often supported by references to specific fields of intellectual endeavor, such as natural history (including geology), chemistry, mathematics, astronomy, geography, and history. Modern supremacy in the content and method of philosophy and "natural philosophy" was particularly insisted upon. "The Antients were indeed but very poor Philosophers," commented the schoolmaster John Clarke (1687–1734), "prodigiously short of the Moderns. With regard to the Knowledge of Nature, the Thing is too notorious to admit of any Dispute at all." It was so obvious especially because of Newton, whose endeavors by themselves seemed to amount to "a hundred times more than what all the antient Philosophers knew put together."[42]

41. Shaw, *The Reflector*, 141–42; Blair, *Lectures on Rhetoric*, 2:258. On the outstanding accomplishments of antiquity in moral philosophy, see George Turnbull, *The Principles of Moral Philosophy* (London, 1740), 431, 433; Knox, "On the Superficial Nature and Pernicious Tendency of Modern Ethics," *Essays*, in *Works*, 1:119 (no. XXII). Similarly, a Fellow of the Royal Society, citing Dutens, felt both that the moderns were superior in natural philosophy and that in this field "the ignorance of the ancients has been overrated": William Falconer, "Remarks on the Knowledge of the Ancients" (read Oct. 16, 1782), *Memoirs of the Literary and Philosophical Society of Manchester*, 2d ed., 1:261.

42. Burgh, *Dignity of Human Nature*, 145; Aikin, "On Attachment to the Ancients," *Letters from a Father*, 27; John Clarke, *An Essay upon Study* (1731), 2d ed. (London, 1737), 45. For some other examples of comments on modern superiority in learning, see Knox, "Tendency of Modern Ethics," *Essays*, in *Works*, 1:118–19; Blair, *Lectures on Rhetoric*, 2:253–57; Benwell, "Moderns Excelled," in *Oxford Prize Essays*, 1:84–95, 98–101. On philosophy and natural philosophy in particular, see Turnbull, *Principles of Moral Philosophy*, 432; David Hartley, *Observations on Man, His Frame,*

Like the tendency (inherited from Hakewill and Glanvill) to list one recent achievement in knowledge after another, down to the latest discoveries about electricity, Clarke's statement illustrates how the eighteenth-century mind was influenced by what might best be called the "visibility of progress." Looking around them, the men of the period could not help but see an accumulation of accomplishments in learning. The "advancement of valuable science," thought Knox, "has been disproportionably rapid within the space of the last two or three centuries." Clarke agreed, referring to the "prodigious Progress of the finest and most useful Parts of Learning amongst us" since the Reformation. He pointed especially to the later seventeenth century, when

> those Parts of Learning, which at any Time before, had only crept in the World, begun [sic] to advance apace; and presently run forwards, with such an amazing Rapidity, that the Modern Improvements therein, have infinitely outdone all the Attainments of the Sons of Men in that Kind before them put together. And this Mighty Progress of the Sciences (with Joy I speak it, for the Sake of my Country's Honour) was Principally owing to the Immortal Genius of the Great NEWTON.

Here as in other areas of thought during the age of the Enlightenment, the influence of the *Principia Mathematica* and its author was immense. Newton's achievement allowed or even forced men to see in the relatively recent past a tremendous leap forward in knowledge. Colin Maclaurin (1698–1746), Professor of Mathematics at the University of Edinburgh and one of the leading Scottish Newtonians, underscored this point with his careful account of developments in natural philosophy from the time of Copernicus onward, culminating in Newton. The great Sir Isaac, he proclaimed, had "opened matter for the enquiries of future ages, which may confirm and enlarge his doctrines, but can never refute them," and Maclaurin added that "by following the excellent models which he has given us, we may be able to make farther advances."[43]

His Duty, and His Expectations, 2 vols. (London, 1749), 2:444; Burgh, *Dignity of Human Nature*, 144–45; James Beattie, "An Essay on Laughter and Ludicrous Composition" (written 1764), *Essays*, 688.

43. Knox, "On the Reasonableness of the Antiquarian Taste," *Essays*, in *Works*, 1:357 (no. LXIII); Clarke, *Essay upon Study*, 16, 122; Colin Maclaurin, *An Account of Sir Isaac Newton's Philosophical Discoveries*, 2d ed. (London, 1750), 10, 14 (Newton's precursors are described on pp. 43–66).

Such improvements appeared already to be taking place in the eighteenth century, an age full of what Tobias Smollett called the "advances which mankind are daily making in useful knowledge." In Maclaurin's view, the "valuable discoveries . . . which learned men are still in pursuit of" no less than the achievements of recent centuries gave good reason to believe that it would be long before the "happy revolution" in learning inaugurated by the Renaissance came to an end. Even the sober young Jeremy Bentham could not help but celebrate the intellectual accomplishments of his time:

> The age we live in is a busy age; an age in which knowledge is rapidly advancing towards perfection. In the natural world, in particular, every thing teems with discovery and with improvement. The most distant and recondite regions of the earth traversed and explored—the all-vivifying and subtle element of the air so recently analyzed and made known to us [by Lavoisier and Priestley, presumably],—are striking evidences, were all others wanting, of this pleasing truth.

These statements eloquently testify to the impact of the piling up of new knowledge, a central feature of the contemporary intellectual environment, and one that led men almost inexorably to favor the moderns.[44]

A number of specific factors were cited to explain modern superiority and the progress of knowledge since the Renaissance. The migration of Byzantine scholars and the invention of printing and the compass were seen as having helped to initiate the advances, which later received added impetus from scientific societies and (in the eighteenth century) relative freedom from war and religious strife. Throughout the entire period that began with the fifteenth century, it was said, learning gained much from the patronage of the wealthy and powerful, the stimulating and diffusing effect of such intellectual tools as dictionaries, and the liberal spirit pervading European thought. This spirit appeared to have engendered a disinterested pursuit of knowledge, a questioning of received opinions, and a positive attitude toward innovation in ideas.[45]

44. Tobias Smollett, *The Present State of All Nations* (1768–1769), 2d ed., 8 vols. (London, 1768–69), 1:v; Maclaurin, *Account of Newton's Discoveries*, 43–44; Jeremy Bentham, *A Fragment on Government* (1776), in *Works*, 1:227:1 ("Preface to the First Edition").

45. Barrow, *New and Universal Dictionary*, "Dedication" (unpaginated), 21, 32

Although eighteenth-century British writers called attention to these social and cultural factors, they did so almost offhandedly, focusing instead on two other, more general and abstract explanations. First, they pointed to dramatic changes for the better in intellectual method. D'Alembert himself, in his *Discours préliminaire*, offered no more effective a presentation of the subject of methodology than did Maclaurin in his book on the Newtonian achievement. There the "systems of ancient philosophers" were once again depicted as the work of boys: "generally speaking," Maclaurin wrote, the ancients "indulged themselves too much in abstruse fruitless disquisitions concerning the hidden essences of things, and sought after a knowledge that was not suited to the grounds they had to build on." With Bacon, however, came a "thorough reformation in the way of treating natural knowledge," an understanding that "all theory was to be laid aside that was not founded on experiment." His "exhortations and example had a good effect," and by the time of Boyle and then Newton "We are . . . arrived at the happy Æra of experimental philosophy; when men, having got into the right path, prosecuted useful knowledge."[46]

Second, there was a related emphasis on the actual process by which knowledge piled up. In Burgh's opinion, for example, the advance of learning was simply a question of succeeding to the labors of predecessors, of making use of the inquiries and observations of past ages. Or as the Scottish common-sense philosopher James Beattie (1735–1803) remarked, modern pre-eminence is the "consequence of our being posterior in time, and enjoying the benefit of [ancient] discoveries and examples, as well as the fruits of our own industry." David Hartley employed a mathematical analogy to describe how knowledge advanced by "every preceding Discovery being made the Foundation for a subsequent one, and the Equation resolving itself, as it were, gradually." "Now this is indeed the Way," he wrote, "in which all Advances in Science are carried on; and scientific Persons are in general aware, that it is and must be so." Typically, Johnson's *Rambler* essay on useful knowledge put the matter most forcefully: "all that is great was at first little, and rose to its present bulk by gradual accessions, and accumulated labours." In such views, the

---

("Preface"); Knox, "Antiquarian Taste," *Essays*, in *Works*, 1:357; Frere, *The Microcosm* (May 7, 1787), in *Works*, 1:23; Benwell, "Moderns Excelled," in *Oxford Prize Essays*, 1:106–07; Maclaurin, *Account of Newton's Discoveries*, 44.

46. Maclaurin, *Account of Newton's Discoveries*, 40, 59, 62, 65.

traditional Baconian concept of cumulatively improving learning became a law of nature, what Blair called "the natural progress of knowledge."[47]

Thus, it was generally believed that for several reasons the moderns were pre-eminent in knowledge and that, since the Renaissance, progress had become an inherent characteristic of learning. But would the advances continue in the future? Most writers of the period agreed with Benwell that "there are many parts of science which are yet comparatively in their infancy" and in which the achievements of the present may "be considered by posterity as very confined." Nature, thought Maclaurin, had "discoveries in store for future times also," and provided that men did not engage in rash system-building he saw good reason to expect that "every age will add to the common stock of knowledge," that the "mysteries that still lie concealed in nature may be gradually opened," and that mankind will "approach more towards a perfect knowledge of nature." Even Dutens, the admirer of antiquity, conceded that whatever efforts had been made to date to bring knowledge toward perfection, "there will remain something still to be done in that respect, by us and our posterity." Hartley put his finger on the reason for these expectations. The present state of relative ignorance made it difficult, in his opinion, to comprehend or accept as a fact the "great Increase of Knowlege [sic], which may come in future Ages." Nevertheless, "the great, and to former Times inconceivable, Advancement of Knowlege, which has been made in the two last Centuries, may help a little to qualify our Prejudices." Unquestionably, it was a projection of the relatively recent past into the future that illuminated the continuing character of the progress of learning.[48]

47. Burgh, *Dignity of Human Nature*, 143, 145; Beattie, "Laughter and Ludicrous Composition," *Essays*, 688; Hartley, *Observations*, 1:349; Samuel Johnson, *The Rambler*, no. 83 (Jan. 1, 1751), in *Yale Edition*, vol. 4 (*The Rambler*, ed. W. J. Bate and Albrecht B. Strauss [1969]), 72; Blair, *Lectures on Rhetoric*, 2:252. See also Bentham, "Préjugés in favour of Antiquity," *Works*, 10:69:1. Maclaurin described this cumulative piling-up process but argued that although it applied to mathematics it did not suit the case of natural philosophy, where there had been so many fits and starts. He preferred to ascribe progress in that realm to the motivation of a psychological mechanism by which "every step in true knowledge gives a glimpse or faint view of what lies next beyond it," so that "the mind is kept in a pleasing expectation of making a further progress": *Account of Newton's Discoveries*, 98–99, 47, 3.

48. Benwell, "Moderns Excelled," in *Oxford Prize Essays*, 1:106; Maclaurin, *Account of Newton's Discoveries*, 95–96; Dutens, *Discoveries attributed to the Moderns*, 456–57; Hartley, *Observations*, 1:316. For an interesting satirical view of the progress of learning, see Laurence Sterne, *The Life and Opinions of Tristram Shandy, Gentle-*

PRACTICAL SKILLS AND TECHNIQUES

If the moderns had achieved superiority in learning, and if there had been progress in knowledge, the same was true in the realm of practical skills and techniques. Inventions provided a crucial case in point. Printing, the compass, the microscope, engraving, the telescope, the air pump: all had come from the hands of the moderns, and all were perceived as setting recent times apart from and above antiquity. Indeed, the age was fascinated with new instruments of all types, as appears from such paintings by Joseph Wright of Derby (1734–97) as *A Philosopher Giving a Lecture on the Orrery*. Dutens tried to minimize the importance of modern inventions, calling them the result of mere chance, not of surpassing genius. But he could not deny that these instruments and techniques belonged to the moderns alone. Nor could he refuse to admit that, with the assistance of the compass, the moderns had "certainly perfected the art of navigation," a fact that the painter James Barry (1741–1806) used his *Navigation, or the Triumph of the Thames* to illustrate. In this work of about 1778, the personified nations, called by Mercury (the god of commerce), pour their products into the lap of Father Thames. He is carried along by the great British navigators (Drake, Raleigh, Cabot, and Cook), portrayed as Tritons, and he steers his vessel by means of a marine compass. Because of this device, noted Barry, "modern navigation has arrived at a certainty, importance, and magnitude, superior to anything known in the ancient world." Of course, navigation did not stand alone in this respect. Modern superiority seemed manifest in all of what Benwell called "those arts which contribute to the support of civil life," and which others referred to as the manual, mechanical, practical, or necessary arts.[49]

man (1759–67), ed. James Aiken Work (New York, 1940), 64. Sterne argued that knowledge had been increasing enormously during the previous two hundred years and would soon reach an acme of perfection. He projected that there would follow—as war begets poverty and poverty peace—"an end to all kinds of knowledge,——and then—— we shall have to begin over again; or, in other words, be exactly where we started."

49. Dutens, *Discoveries attributed to the Moderns*, x–xiii; James Barry, *An Account of a Series of Pictures in the Great Room of the Society of Arts. . . at the Adelphi* (1783), in *The Works of James Barry, Esq.*, 2 vols. (London, 1809), 2:323, 332–33; David Allen, "The Progress of Human Culture and Knowledge," *The Connoisseur*, 186, no. 748 (June 1974): 107:2, 109:1; Benwell, "Moderns Excelled," in *Oxford Prize Essays*, 1:105. See also Campbell, *Philosophy of Rhetoric*, 1:ix ("Introduction"). On modern supremacy in inventions and useful arts, see, for example, Burgh, *Dignity of Human Nature*, 145; Knox, "Antiquarian Taste," *Essays*, in *Works*, 1:357; Benwell, "Moderns Excelled," in *Oxford Prize Essays*, 1:84, 95–96, 102–03.

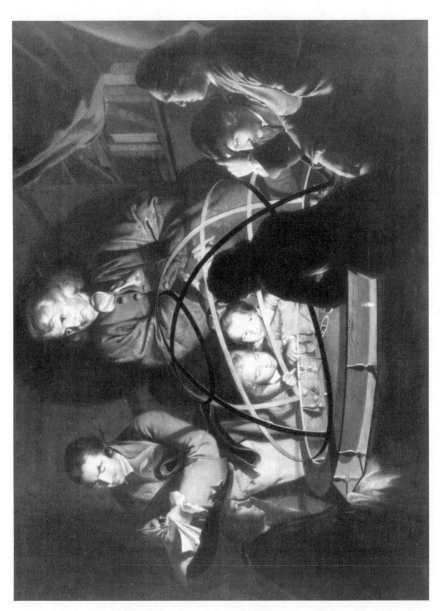

Joseph Wright of Derby. *A Philosopher Giving a Lecture on the Orrery.*

After James Barry. *The Thames, or the Triumph of Navigation.*

Moreover, as with learning, these arts were considered to have made substantial progress in recent times. The useful arts, wrote Whitchurch, "have been, for many Centuries, in a State of Progression." Benwell agreed, noting that the "same active spirit of improvement [found in navigation] has communicated itself to every other art of public concern, on which the wealth and prosperity of nations more immediately depend," including agriculture and the mechanical skills of manufacturing. And the poet Young declared that the "arts Mechanic are in perpetual progress, and increase." This comment and the accompanying metaphorical description of the useful arts as an ever-widening river suggest that he believed in their future progress. So did many others like Campbell, who, with regard to these arts, found it impossible to say

> what is the perfection of the art, since we are incapable of perceiving how far the united discernment and industry of men, properly applied, may yet carry them. For some centuries backwards, the men of every age have made great and unexpected improvements on the labours of their predecessors. And it is very probable that the subsequent age will produce discoveries and acquisitions, which we of this age are as little capable of foreseeing, as those who preceded us in the last century were capable of conjecturing the progress that would be made in the present.

Once again, projection led to an expectation of indefinite advance.[50]

Showing the same kind of interest in the useful arts that, under Diderot's guidance, had characterized its French forerunner, the *Encyclopaedia Britannica* pointed to a number of factors that brought about the progress of these arts on a national level. Included were contact with other peoples, sudden prosperity, engagement in a struggle of doubtful outcome (such as fighting for liberty or resisting invasion), and, when not carried to extremes, specialization of activity and the division of labor. But the ultimate explanation of advances in the practical arts, as in learning, appeared to lie in what Campbell

50. Whitchurch, *Essay upon Education*, 7; Benwell, "Moderns Excelled," in *Oxford Prize Essays*, 1:101–02; Young, *Conjectures*, 19; Campbell, *Philosophy of Rhetoric*, 1:viii ("Introduction"). This sort of projection is very clearly at work in Madden's novel, as exemplified by his comments on twentieth-century telescopes that could be used to glimpse hills, rivers, forests, and towns on the moon: *Memoirs of the Twentieth Century*, 135, 310.

called improvement on the labor of forerunners. Practitioners of the mechanical arts, wrote Young, were "ever endeavouring to go beyond their predecessors," and they could do so because of the accumulation of skill. In the manual arts it was the "natural course and order of things," said Hawkins, "that those who begin to learn them, in their noviciate often attain to that degree of perfection at which their teachers stopped."[51] In fact, the classicism of Josiah Wedgwood, as expressed in such designs as the reproduction of the Portland Vase and the portraits of modern heroes, like Newton, after the manner of ancient cameos, can appropriately be considered the attempt of that enterprising industrialist "to excel the noblest works produced at any place or in any period."[52]

That the high eighteenth century looked upon the useful arts as progressive followed in part from a well-established tradition of citing new inventions to prove the inferiority of the ancients. But it also resulted from the evidence on all sides of substantial technological advance. This was, after all, the age that saw the developments associated with the early Industrial Revolution. In agriculture, for instance, many large farmers and a few great landlords introduced new systems of crop cultivation and rotation, new methods of drainage and livestock breeding, and the use of a few new farm implements (including threshing machines and improved ploughs). These slow but steady changes found in Arthur Young only one, if the best known, of a number of celebrators and popularizers. Even more dramatic and widespread were developments in transportation. Better vehicle design made for greater speed over the ground, as did the multiplication of turnpikes, many with engineering improvements: the time for the journey from London to Birmingham was cut by more than half between the 1740s and the 1780s. In addition, the third duke of Bridgewater and others built several hundred miles of canals by the 1770s, thereby significantly easing the flow of goods and almost overnight becoming national heroes. As Arthur Young himself proclaimed, Bridgewater's undertakings "must command our admiration," because they "tend so greatly to advance the agriculture,

51. *Encyclopaedia Britannica*, 1:708:2–710:2; Young, *Conjectures*, 19; Hawkins, *History of the Science and Practice of Music*, 2:918:2. The comments of the *Encyclopaedia Britannica* on this subject are drawn largely from the work of Henry Home, Lord Kames: see below, chap. 7.

52. Francis D. Klingender, *Art and the Industrial Revolution*, ed. and rev. Arthur Elton (New York, 1968), 46, 48.

manufactures, and commerce, of an extensive neighbourhood" and "improve and adorn his country." Indeed, Young called the planned crossing of the River Mersey at Runcorn Gap the "greatest undertaking (if executed) that ever yet was thought of, . . . [which] will exceed the noblest works of the *Romans*, when masters of the world; or the legendary tales even of *Semiramis* herself." A print of 1766 shows the duke pointing to a similar, already realized achievement at Barton in Lancashire and contrasting the new technology of summit-level canals with the old, far slower methods of river navigation. "Vessels o'er vessels, water under water, /" went a contemporary poem, "Bridgewater triumphs—art has conquered nature." Henry Homer (1719–91), a Warwickshire rector, echoed these sentiments in 1767. He claimed that there had never been a "more astonishing Revolution accomplished in the internal System of any Country, than has been within the Compass of a few Years in that of *England*," with regard to transportation. Because of the "valuable Project of increasing inland Navigation" and the "Improvements, which have been made in our publick Roads," carriages now "travel with almost winged Expedition" and "Every Thing wears the Face of Dispatch."[53]

Along with changes in transit and farming went innovations in manufacturing. Beginning in the 1760s, a rapid transformation occurred in the cotton industry, with Richard Arkwright's water-frame, James Hargreave's spinning-jenny, Samuel Crompton's "mule," and Edmund Cartwright's power-loom. Advances in the iron and steel industry continued apace, especially at Sheffield and Coalbrookdale, from the discovery of Huntsman's process in 1740 to the invention of puddling and rolling in the 1780s. Meanwhile, Wedgwood pioneered many new techniques in the manufacture of pottery at his Etruria works. And these and other industries came to benefit after 1775 from a new source of power, the steam engine produced by James Watt and Matthew Boulton.

The invention and, where feasible, application of labor-saving devices was so clearly the order of the day that Johnson, in one of his

53. [Arthur Young], *A Six Months Tour through the North of England*, 4 vols. (London, 1768–70), 3:290, 288; Henry Homer, *An Enquiry into the Means of Preserving and Improving the Publick Roads of this Kingdom* (Oxford, 1767), 8, 6, 3. On the public's perception of the canal builders, and for the poem cited, see Hugh Malet, *Bridgewater: The Canal Duke, 1736–1803* (Manchester, 1977), 66–68. Interestingly, in his futuristic novel of 1733, Madden referred to "the great canals cut by *George III.* and *Frederick II.* from *Bristol* to the *Thames*, from *Southampton* to *Winchester*, and from sea to sea from *Carlisle* to the *Humber*": *Memoirs of the Twentieth Century*, 371.

The Most Noble Francis Egerton, Duke of Bridgewater and Marquis of Brackley.

conservative moods, could sarcastically declare in 1783 that "'The age is running mad after innovation; and all the business of the world is to be done in a new way; men are to be hanged in a new way; Tyburn itself is not free from the fury of innovation.'" The statistics support his observation. Only 56 patents were granted in the 1730s, 82 in the 1740s, and 92 in the 1750s; but in the next three decades there were 205, then 294, and finally 477, respectively. Others looked upon this multitude of inventions and changes in technique with a far less jaundiced eye than Johnson in his remarks about Tyburn Prison—and even Johnson himself, who was very interested in mechanical contrivances, usually approved of technological advance. The magazines and newspapers devoted considerable attention to industrial developments, describing them with adjectives like "great and extraordinary," "almost miraculous," "unparalleled," "incredible," and "amazing." In this period it was the benefits of innovation, not the dangers, to which commentators pointed. As a surveyor of trade for the government reported to the Colonial Secretary in 1775, while in the Midlands he had seen "great improvements in Machinery, by which the expense of labour is much diminished and the perfection of the work increased."[54]

The future looked even rosier. Erasmus Darwin (1731–1802), poet-physician and grandfather of the great evolutionist, discussed Watt's steam engine and its industrial uses at length and predicted that

> it may in time be applied to the rowing of barges, and the moving of carriages along the road. As the specific levity of air is too great for the support of great burthens by balloons, there seems no probable method of flying conveniently but by the power of steam, or some other explosive material, which another half-century may probably discover.

Although Darwin held little hope for the future of balloon flight, many others were more optimistic. The excitement generated by the

54. *Boswell's Life of Johnson*, 4:188. The patent figures are drawn from B. R. Mitchell with Phyllis Deane, *Abstract of British Historical Statistics* (Cambridge, 1962), 268. On the terms used to describe industrial technology, see Dorothy Marshall, *England in Transition: Life and Work in the Eighteenth Century*, Penguin ed. (Harmondsworth, Eng., 1953), 107; Asa Briggs, *The Age of Improvement, 1783–1867*, corr. ed. (London, 1960), 18. Marshall's book (p. 110) is also the source of the ms. letter from the trade surveyor. For Johnson as proponent of technological advance, see Schwartz, *Johnson and the New Science*, 41.

Francis Jukes (after Brewer). *The First Balloon Ascent in England, September 1784, from the Artillery Ground, Moorfields.*

first ascents by balloon and flights across the Channel in the 1780s led, among a large segment of the educated public, to great expectations regarding rapid travel through the air. As one of the first British balloonists wrote in 1784, "By this invention the schemes of transporting people through the atmosphere, formerly thought chimerical, are realized; and it is impossible to say how far the art of navigation may be improved, or with what advantages it may be attended."[55]

Steam and balloons, power and speed: these were the quintessential symbols of contemporary technological advance. They and the other inventions and new processes—the tools of the Industrial Revolution—encouraged men to proclaim the superiority of modernity and the existence of progress in practical skills and techniques. As with learning, it was the visibility of innovation in this sphere that made possible the belief in progress, past and future.

THE FINE ARTS

Opinion on the fine arts presents a somewhat different picture. It has been argued that the prevailing tendency in eighteenth-century British speculation about the history of these arts was to deny that they had improved and would continue to do so, and to assert instead that they had necessarily declined after attaining perfection at an earlier stage of civilization.[56] To date this thesis has not been contradicted, and, indeed, there is a considerable amount of evidence to support it.

For example, a substantial number of writers contended that the ancients excelled the moderns in achievements in the fine arts. Dutens, although on the defensive with respect to learning and the mechanical arts, felt it needless to prove the pre-eminence of antiquity

55. [Erasmus Darwin], *The Botanic Garden, A Poem. In Two Parts* (1789–91), 4th ed., 2 vols. (London, 1799), 1:31n. On the impact of balloon flights, see Maurice J. Quinlan, "Balloons and the Awareness of a New Age," *Studies in Burke and His Time* 14 (Spring 1973): 222–31; I. F. Clarke, *The Pattern of Expectation, 1644–2001* (New York, 1979), 29–34 (quotation on p. 30).

56. John D. Scheffer, "The Idea of Decline in Literature and the Fine Arts in Eighteenth-Century England," *Modern Philology* 34 (Nov. 1936): 155–78; Murray Krieger, "The Arts and the Idea of Progress," in Gabriel A. Almond, Marvin Chodorow, and Roy Harvey Pearce, eds., *Progress and Its Discontents* (Berkeley, 1982), 450–58. See also Henry Vyverberg, *Historical Pessimism in the French Enlightenment* (Cambridge, Mass., 1958), 86–95.

in the fine arts, asserting that the "moderns themselves will not contest" this fact. The Anglican cleric, Winchester headmaster, and literary critic Joseph Warton (1722–1800) agreed with Addison that "'we fall short at present of the ancients in poetry, painting, oratory, history, architecture, and all the noble arts and sciences which depend more upon genius than experience.'" Many others made similar claims about specific arts. Benwell found for the ancients in the arts of design generally. Barrow granted them supremacy in painting, and Thomas Kirshaw (fl. 1783) and Robert Cullen (d. 1810) in sculpture; Warton was particularly emphatic about the surpassing greatness of their architecture, and Blair joined him in conferring superiority on ancient eloquence and oratory. A few writers, including Dutens, preferred the music of antiquity. Nor did ancient literature lack for supporters. Blair and Benwell conceded the advantage to the Greeks and Romans in "elegant Composition" and the "higher species" of verse and prose. Ancient poetry, especially, in all its forms from panegyric to epic to drama, received high praise. The statement by Robert Wood (1717?–71), an influential writer on Homer, that among the early Greeks "Poetry had acquired a greater degree of perfection than it has ever since obtained," spoke for more than a few men of his era, including Gibbon.[57]

In addition, the cyclical theory of the history of art and science found application in the realm of the fine arts more than anywhere else. Archibald Alison (1757–1839), the Scottish literary critic, epitomized this outlook when he wrote that "the Arts of Taste, in every country, after a certain period of perfection, [have] degenerated into

57. Dutens, *Discoveries attributed to the Moderns*, 364–65, 372–87; Joseph Warton, "In What Arts the Ancients excel the Moderns," *The Adventurer*, no. 127 (Jan. 22, 1754), in Alexander Chalmers, ed., *The British Essayists*, 45 vols. (London, 1802–03), 25:225, 230, 228; Benwell, "Moderns Excelled," in *Oxford Prize Essays*, 1:80–82, 77; Barrow, *New and Universal Dictionary*, 15 ("Preface"); Thomas Kirshaw, "On the comparative Merit of the Ancients and Moderns, with respect to the imitative Arts" (read Feb. 19, 1783), *Memoirs of the Literary and Philosophical Society of Manchester*, 2d ed., 1:407; [Robert Cullen], article in *The Lounger*, no. 73 (June 24, 1786), 2d ed., 3:36–37; Blair, *Lectures on Rhetoric*, 2:256–57; Robert Wood, *An Essay on the Original Genius and Writings of Homer* (1769), 2d ed. (London, 1775), 245, 171; Gibbon, "Essai sur l'étude de la littérature," *Miscellaneous Works*, 4:24–25. On the belief in the superiority of ancient music, see Herbert M. Schueller, "The Quarrel of the Ancients and the Moderns," *Music and Letters* 41 (Oct. 1960): 313–30. Other examples of proponents of ancient poetry include Peter Williams, *Letters concerning Education*, 284, 297; George Richards, "On the Characteristic Differences between Ancient and Modern Poetry, and the several Causes from which they result" (June 26, 1789), in *Oxford Prize Essays*, 1:115–16, 124, 126–27, 130.

the mere Expressions of the Skill and Execution of the Artist, and gradually sunk into a state of barbarity, almost as great as that from which they at first arose." Similarly, the *Encyclopaedia Britannica* considered these arts far more precarious and subject to decline than their "useful" cousins. Hildebrand Jacobs (1693–1739), a playwright and writer on aesthetics, focused more narrowly on poetry, which he argued "has had its Nourishment with *Learning*, and with *Learning* too it has constantly decay'd and dwindled into *Barbarism*."[58]

Several general explanations were advanced to account for the cyclical rise and decline of the fine arts and for ancient superiority in this field of culture. To begin with, earlier ages appeared to have had certain unique characteristics beneficial to art. Great poetry, as one Oxford student wrote, seemed peculiarly the "natural offspring of an illiterate age"—in part because, according to Wood, "in a rude and unlettered state of society the memory [of the poet] is loaded with nothing that is either useless or unintelligible." He added that without an advanced division of labor, "the business and pleasures of life were rude, simple, and confined," and therefore "they lay more open to the Poet's observation." Indeed, he agreed with many of his contemporaries that in the Homeric age culture as a whole was "addressed more to the passions than [to] the understanding." But passion and imagination were thought to have diminished with the gradual advance of civilization and reason, causing poetry to lose in simplicity and force while it gained in sophistication. As Johnson's character Imlac suggested in *Rasselas* (1759), the "early writers are in possession of nature, and their followers of art: . . . the first excel in strength and invention, and the latter in elegance and refinement." A balance of nature and art, of imagination and reason, of simplicity and elegance was not in itself considered bad. "But refinement," as was noted by George Richards, another Oxford student essayist, "is ever verging towards degeneracy . . . and poetry, when to chaste and simple delineations of nature it has united ornament and splendour, will soon transgress the limits of a judicious and decent embellishment."[59]

58. Archibald Alison, *Essays on the Nature and Principles of Taste* (Edinburgh, 1790), 337; *Encyclopaedia Britannica*, 1:715:2; Hildebrand Jacob, *Of the Sister Arts: an Essay* (London, 1734), 7.

59. A. Robertson, "On Original Composition" (1782), in *Oxford Prize Essays*, 1:50; Wood, *Essay on Homer*, 260, 247, 269; Samuel Johnson, *The History of Rasselas, Prince of Abyssinia*, in *The Yale Edition of the Works of Samuel Johnson*, vol. 16 (*Rasselas and Other Tales*, ed. Gwin J. Kolb [1990]), Ch. X; Richards, "Ancient

Modern artists were thought to be subject to other disadvantages, as well. Unlike their predecessors, they labored under the heavy burden of learning and information, argued Richards and Joseph Warton (much as did d'Alembert), which led them toward the creation of pedantic rather than beautiful works. According to such writers as Warton, criticism had the same depressing effect. But the most serious problem of all for the art of modernity seemed to lie in past artistic achievements themselves. Benwell looked at this difficulty from one perspective when he announced that the fine arts "have certain boundaries, which human nature does not suffer us to pass," and which the ancients had already reached. From another viewpoint, the problem appeared to be the psychologically restricting effect of ancient success. Thus, in Cullen's opinion, when any art had attained a high degree of perfection, the spirit of emulation was thereafter destroyed in that field. "Conscious of being unable to surpass the great models which he sees, the artist is discouraged from making attempts." On the other hand, some writers found the culprit in emulation itself. Aikin spoke of the "shackles of imitation," created by the early appearance of extraordinary works of poetry that "became models in their respective kinds, and restricted all subsequent efforts of genius to mere imitation." The *Encyclopaedia Britannica* commented that while emulation benefited any maturing art, "after arriving at maturity, its downfal[l] is not less promoted by it." For artists, ambitious to outstrip their predecessors, could not submit to being mere imitators, "but must strike out something new, which, in an art advanced to ripeness, seldom fails to be a degeneracy." In this context the pursuit of novelty was frequently condemned.[60]

and Modern Poetry," in *Oxford Prize Essays*, 1:130–31. On this whole subject, see also the discussion of the literary views of Bishop Richard Hurd and Thomas Warton in René Wellek, *A History of Modern Criticism*, 6 vols. to date (New Haven, 1955–), 1:130–32, and the opinions of the leading proponent of Macpherson's Ossian and its "Poetry of the Heart," Hugh Blair, in his *A Critical Dissertation on the Poems of Ossian, the Son of Fingal*, 2d ed. (London, 1765), 1–4, 37. For what he called the "gradual desertion of the End of the Art, for the display of the Art itself," see also Alison, *Essays on Taste*, 335–38.

60. Richards, "Ancient and Modern Poetry," in *Oxford Prize Essays*, 1:132–33; Joseph Warton, "Ancients excel Moderns," *The Adventurer*, in *British Essayists*, 1:231; Benwell, "Moderns Excelled," in *Oxford Prize Essays*, 1:105; Cullen, *The Lounger* (June 24, 1786), 2d ed., 3:40; Aikin, "On Attachment to the Ancients," *Letters from a Father*, 23; *Encyclopaedia Britannica*, 1:713:2. On the disrepute of novelty in the fine arts, see Scheffer, "Idea of Decline," *Modern Philology* 34 (Nov. 1936): 162, 164. Cullen's comments follow, without acknowledgment, the argument and even the words of David Hume: see below, chap. 7.

Modern art, and specifically that of the eighteenth century, appeared to suffer from one final disadvantage, a decline of patronage. Jacob stated that the fine arts had received more encouragement from great men in antiquity than they did at present. The poet Thomson wrote that in earlier ages "great patrons" had called these arts "Up to the Sun-shine of uncumber'd Ease, / Where no rude Care the mounting Thought may thrall, / And where they nothing have to do but please." "But now," he lamented, "alas! we live too late in Time: / Our Patrons now even grudge that little Claim." And the *Encyclopaedia Britannica* warned that the fine arts would "never flourish in any country, unless patronized by the sovereign, or by men of power and opulence." These comments point to a contemporary development that helps to explain pessimistic thinking about the history of the fine arts: the shrinkage of patronage—far more in literature than in architecture, painting, or landscape gardening—by court and nobility, and the parallel transformation, centering on the middle class, of culture into an industry.[61] If some men, like Johnson in his famous letter to Chesterfield, proclaimed their willingness to exchange the security and dependence offered by patronage for autonomy and reliance on the public, others, like Thomson, had no desire to do so. The latter group regretted both the diminution of patronage and the new appeal to a wider and less sophisticated audience, the effects of which were thought to include the production of popular but artistically destructive "novelties." Of course, the preference granted to the ancients and the perception of artistic decline must also have been matters of education and mere taste. Still, the new cultural scene undoubtedly played a part in the tendency to depict modern art in somber hues.

But this was, in fact, only *one* tendency in thinking about the history of the fine arts. Many eighteenth-century Britons reached rather different conclusions concerning the comparison of ancient and modern accomplishments in the arts. In painting, for instance, Turnbull found a "very like degree of Beauty and Excellence" in the works of the Renaissance and antiquity, an assessment with which

61. Jacob, *Sister Arts*, 35; Thomson, *Castle of Indolence*, in *Liberty, The Castle of Indolence and Other Poems*, 205 (II, xxii–xxiii); *Encyclopaedia Britannica*, 1:715:2. On patronage and the new shape of culture, see Ian Watt, *The Rise of the Novel: Studies in Defoe, Richardson and Fielding* (Berkeley, 1960), 35–59; J. H. Plumb, "The Public, Literature, and the Arts in the Eighteenth Century," in Michael R. Marrus, ed., *The Emergence of Leisure* (New York, 1974), 11–37.

Joseph Wharton agreed. The anonymous author of a poem on painting argued for the equality not only of the Renaissance with the ancients, but also of the seventeenth and eighteenth centuries with the Renaissance. Speaking about Raphael and Michelangelo, Reynolds went even further and stated that these two "carried some of the higher excellencies of the art to a greater degree of perfection than probably they ever arrived at before." Kirshaw extended this judgment, noting that works of "ancient Painting are much inferior to modern productions," especially in landscape. The case of Cullen illustrates how a belief in the superiority of the ancients in one area did not preclude the opposite view of other arts. For although he granted supremacy to classical sculpture, he contended that in "Painting, . . . whatever we may be told of the high admiration in which a Zeuxis and an Apelles were held by their countrymen, yet there is very good reason to believe that the moderns have far exceeded the ancients."[62]

As for eloquence, Clarke was virtually alone in awarding superiority to modernity in even some aspects of that art. He also argued that the moderns "have carried almost all the most valuable Parts of Literature to a Height, vastly beyond what the Antients arrived at." Others were not quite so sanguine. The Welsh educator and writer David Williams (1738–1816) believed that "we have some authors who compose with the truest elegance, and who might dispute the palm of fine writing with the best of their predecessors." Cullen considered ancient and modern poetry essentially equal, and Blair commented that "Milton and Shakespeare are inferior to no Poets in any age." He also conceded the moderns some advantages in the "more complex kinds of Poetry" and in drama. While Wharton advanced the claims of antiquity in the higher and more serious forms of literature, he and Beattie admitted modern superiority in the genres of humor and ridicule (comedy, satire, and burlesque). Richards agreed and added that parallel to the "advancement of modern literature in comedy, is its improvement likewise in tragedy." Mark Akenside (1721–70), author of the renowned *Pleasures of Imagination*, offered a general comparison of poetic achievements in his curious

62. Turnbull, *Treatise on Ancient Painting*, 47; Joseph Warton, "Ancients excel Moderns," *The Adventurer*, in *British Essayists*, 25:227–28; Anon., "The Progress of Painting," *Gentleman's Magazine*, 12 (Feb.–March 1743): 100:2, 153:2–154:1; Reynolds, *Discourses on Art*, 84 (Discourse V, delivered Dec. 10, 1772); Kirshaw, "Merit of the Ancients and Moderns," *Memoirs of the Literary and Philosophical Society of Manchester*, 2d ed., 1:408, 411; Cullen, *The Lounger* (June 24, 1786), 2d ed., 3:36.

"Ballance of Poets," a kind of eighteenth-century analogue to late twentieth-century "performance ratings." Akenside awarded modern poets of all sorts 167 points to 105 for the ancients.[63]

In music, too, the moderns had many proponents, including both of the great eighteenth-century English historians of music, Hawkins and Charles Burney (1726–1814). The former asserted against Sir William Temple that in comparing "the modern with the ancient music it must evidently appear that that of the present day has the advantage, whether we consider it in theory or practice." He found the same to be true with regard to musical instruments. At one point Burney refused to make a comparison because of the impossibility of hearing the music of antiquity performed. Nevertheless, he elsewhere concluded that it was not

> superiour to the modern in any other respects than its simplicity, and strict adherence to metrical feet, when applied to poetry. For, *as music*, considered abstractedly, it appears to have been much inferiour to the modern, in the two great and essential parts of the art, *melody* and *harmony*.

Lesser lights took the same position. "The *Moderns*," wrote Jacob, "seem to have surpass'd the *Ancients* in *Music* to so great a Degree, that they may be said, in some Measure, to be the *Inventers* [*sic*] of it." Granting some excellence to the ancients in rhythm, Richard Brockelsby (1722–97), a physician interested in the medical uses of music, nonetheless contended that a perfect judge of the music of both ages "would prefer that of the moderns, just as much as ours exceeds the antients['] in uniformity amidst variety." And in Benwell's view, the key to modern superiority lay in its instruments and discovery of counterpoint.[64]

63. Clarke, *Essay upon Study*, 176, 43; David Williams, *A Treatise on Education* (London, 1774), 152; Cullen, *The Lounger* (June 24, 1786), 2d ed., 3:36; Blair, *Lectures on Rhetoric*, 2:253–54; Joseph Warton, "In what Arts the Moderns excel the Ancients," *The Adventurer*, no. 133 (Feb. 12, 1754), in *British Essayists*, 25:260, 265; Beattie, "Laughter and Ludicrous Composition," *Essays*, 683, 687; Richards, "Ancient and Modern Poetry," in *Oxford Prize Essays*, 1:119–23; Musiphron [Mark Akenside], "The Ballance of Poets," *The Museum* [*Dodsley's Museum*] 2 (Dec. 6, 1746): 169.

64. Hawkins, *History of the Science and Practice of Music*, 2:917:1, 918:1, and 1:xxx:2; Charles Burney, *A General History of Music, From the Earliest Ages to the Present Period* (1776–89), ed. Frank Mercer, 2 vols. (London, 1935), 1:149; Jacob, *Sister Arts*, 14; Richard Brockelsby, *Reflections on Antient and Modern Musick, with the Application to the Cure of Diseases* (London, 1749), 80–81; Benwell, "Moderns Ex-

Along with the advocacy of the moderns, there was also considerable discussion, in three basic ways, of progress in the fine arts. First, the natural course of development of these arts was widely considered to be gradual and progressive. Turnbull called it an indisputable principle that "no Art is invented and perfected at once, and that according to the nature of things Painting, like other Arts, must have advanced gradually, and from very small Beginnings to any very considerable Pitch of Excellence." Reynolds accepted this "common observation" and speculated on how the process worked. The first man who, from empirical study of an art, arrived at a general principle could not pursue it very far. "He himself worked on it, and improved it; others worked more, and improved further; until the secret was discovered, and the practice made as general, as refined practice can be made." Or as Barrow succinctly put it, "Most Arts, indeed, are discovered by degrees; and ages have been employed in bringing some of them to perfection." The parallel between the fine arts and learning was made clear by Barry when he wrote that "it is the property and particular nature of these arts, that, from a low beginning, they advance by little and little, by which they finally arrive at the top of perfection; . . . it is the same thing in other faculties, there being amongst all the liberal arts a certain relation." The accumulative effect operated here no less than in the sciences since, in the words of the anonymous Irish writer on the arts, the "improvements of all arts are gradual; the scholar adds to the progress of the master."[65]

This general concept of a process of gradual development was applied to individual arts as well. Aikin disputed the notion that poetry emerged suddenly and full-blown at a very early stage of history, noting that it tended to "keep pace with other choice products of the mind in their progress towards perfection." (He admitted, however, that his theory of the "progressive improvement of poetry" did not always work in practice, because of the inhibiting effect of imitation.) Reynolds made the same point about painting when he commented that the "progress of an individual Student"—which, using

celled," in *Oxford Prize Essays*, 1:83. See also Cullen, *The Lounger* (June 24, 1786), 2d ed., 3:36.

65. Turnbull, *Treatise on Ancient Painting*, 39–41; Reynolds, *Discourses on Art*, 95, 97 (Discourse VI, delivered Dec. 10, 1774); Barrow, *Supplement*, 6 ("Preface"); James Barry, *An Inquiry into the Real and Imaginary Obstructions to the Acquisition of the Arts in England* (1775), in *Works*, 2:186; Anon., *Essay on Perfecting the Fine Arts*, 31.

the example of his friend and competitor Gainsborough, he called "gradual advancement" and the "slow progress of advancement"— "bears a great resemblance to the progress and advancement of the Art itself." In addition, he spoke of painting as an art developing in stages from its infancy. Hawkins drew a direct parallel between music and natural philosophy. As the inherent movement of sciences like physics and mathematics "is ever towards perfection," he wrote, so

> of music it may be said, that the discoveries of one age have served but as a foundation for improvements in the next; the consequence whereof is, that the fund of harmony is ever increasing. . . . Now, the greater the fund of knowledge above spoken of is, the greater is the source from whence the invention of the artist or composer is supplied; and the benefits thereof are seen in new combinations and phrases, capable of variety and permutation without end.[66]

Clearly, the process of cumulative progress was often held to apply to the fine arts, just as to learning and practical skills.

Second, progress in this area was found actually to have occurred in the past. Examining the history of the fine arts in England, Welsted noted that they began to advance after the Restoration, became vigorous under William III, and since that time had "kept on in a progressive State." The *Encyclopaedia Britannica* indicated that in England the fine arts "are in a progress . . . toward maturity," although at a slow pace. Looking around him, Reynolds saw "a greater number of excellent Artists than were ever known before at one period" and the "Arts in a state to which they never before arrived in this nation." In his final address to the students of the Royal Academy, he singled out his own achievement in the theory of painting for special recognition: building on the discoveries of others, he wrote, "I have succeeded in establishing the rules and principles of our Art on a more firm and lasting foundation than that on which they had formerly been placed." Advances were also thought to have occurred in music, over the long term. Much of the music criticism of the eighteenth century contained an implicit belief in progress. Burney, for instance,

66. Aikin, "On Attachment to the Ancients," *Letters from a Father*, 22; Reynolds, *Discourses on Art*, 152, 249 (Discourses VIII and XIV, delivered Dec. 10, 1778 and Dec. 10, 1788, respectively); Hawkins, *History of the Science and Practice of Music*, 1:xxx:2–xxxi:1.

began to write his history intending "to trace the genealogy of Music in a *right line*," without, however, violating the appropriate reverence for antiquity. And he unquestionably plotted the ascent of that line on the basis of the advances made by the composers of the past toward the harmonic perfection of the present. Hawkins's *History of Music* similarly depicted a slow, steady progress of music from the eleventh century through the Renaissance to the "state of perfection in which we hold it at this day."[67]

The same outlook penetrated thinking about the history of English poetry. Johnson believed that the poetry of his country had marched continuously toward the establishment of a timeless norm with Dryden and Pope, from which there could be no relapse into its former savagery. "From the time of Gower and Chaucer," he stated, "the English writers have studied elegance, and advanced their language, by successive improvements, to as much harmony as it can easily receive, and as much copiousness as human knowledge has hitherto required." The general scheme of Thomas Warton's *History of English Poetry* (1774–81) was to "pursue the progress of our national poetry, from a rude origin and obscure beginnings, to its perfection in a polished age." He claimed that his book exhibited "without transposition the gradual improvements of our poetry." This view was quite common among high eighteenth-century commentators on the history of poetry.[68]

Third, even more was expected or hoped of the fine arts in the future. Horace Walpole wrote a series of *Anecdotes of Painting in England* (1762–80) similar in many ways to Vasari's *Lives of the Artists*. But whereas Vasari's aim was to preserve the memory of an

67. Welsted, *Dissertation*, in Durham, *Critical Essays*, 357–58; *Encyclopaedia Britannica*, 1:715:1; Reynolds, *Discourses on Art*, 14, 169, 269 (Discourses I, IX, and XV, delivered Jan. 2, 1769, Oct. 16, 1780, and Dec. 10, 1790, respectively); Burney, *General History of Music*, 1:20; Hawkins, *History of the Science and Practice of Music*, 1:xxxiv:1–xxxvi:2. On the belief in progress held by Burney, Hawkins, and other music critics, see Lawrence Lipking, *The Ordering of the Arts in Eighteenth-Century England* (Princeton, 1970), 259, 276, 303, 386; Schueller, "Quarrel of Ancients and Moderns," *Music and Letters* 41 (Oct. 1960): 328.

68. Johnson, "Dryden," *Lives of the Poets*, 1:421; idem, *The Idler*, no. 63 (June 30, 1759), in *Yale Edition*, vol. 2 ("*The Idler*" and "*The Adventurer*," ed. W. J. Bate et al. [1963]), 198; Thomas Warton, *The History of English Poetry, from the Close of the Eleventh to the Commencement of the Eighteenth Century*, 3 vols. (London, 1774–81), 1:ii, v; René Wellek, *The Rise of English Literary History* (Chapel Hill, N.C., 1941), 136, 139–40, 158, 180–82; idem, *History of Modern Criticism*, 1:104, 131; Frances Schouler Miller, "The Historic Sense of Thomas Warton, Junior," *ELH* 5 (March 1938): 82; Lipking, *Ordering of Arts*, 384–86.

age that he felt had achieved perfection, Walpole chronicled the past with the desire of stimulating the painters of the future to achieve greater things. Welsted believed it reasonable to hope that the coming age would move the arts beyond the already high levels attained since the Restoration, "to that *Standard* or Perfection, which denominates a Classical Age." The anonymous Irish writer thought that "*London* may yet rival *Rome* in the Fine Arts; and *England* may, in future times, be as celebrated for Painting, Sculpture and Architecture, as she is at present for Poetry, Philosophy, or the Mathematicks." From the imagined vantage point of the twentieth century, Madden could contend that "we have made *Great Britain*, the Seat of these lovely Arts, and have drawn hither, the first Masters of the World," so that "we have better new Pictures and Statues in *Great Britain*, than in all *Europe* besides; and perhaps Italy her self, will not, in a little Time, be able to excel the Palaces we have built here." Three decades later the architect and decorator Robert Adam (1728–92) similarly suggested that in the "Arts of Elegance" the reign of George III "promises an Age of Perfection, that will . . . fix an Æra no less remarkable than that of PERICLES, AUGUSTUS, or the MEDICIS."[69]

In addressing this comment to the young king himself, Adam may perhaps have exaggerated in order to ingratiate. Yet others who had no sycophantish motives held equally high hopes, as the case of Edward Young exemplifies. He lamented the present "great inferiority" of the moderns in poetry and found that their "performance in general is deplorably short" of the level set by antiquity. He even believed that the liberal arts, in contrast with the mechanical, "are in retrogradation, and decay." Nevertheless, he asked, who could dare affirm that poets as great as or even greater than the ancients would not arise in the future or the present? Was it presumptuous to hope to surpass antiquity, or was "it not, rather, contrary to nature to fail in it?" For all knowledge and the conveniences of life were increasing, "and these are new food to the genius of a polite writer; these are as the root, and composition, as the flower; and as the root spreads, and

69. Welsted, *Dissertation*, in Durham, *Critical Essays*, 358; Anon., *Essay on Perfecting the Fine Arts*, 9; Madden, *Memoirs of the Twentieth Century*, 138–39; R[obert] Adam, *Ruins of the Palace of the Emperor Diocletian at Spalatro in Dalmatia* ([London], 1764), iv. On Walpole, see Lipking, *Ordering of Arts*, 155. Even Alison saw some good reasons to hope that the cycle of progress and decay that he described could be broken "in the modern state of Europe": *Essays on Taste*, 339.

thrives, shall the flower fail?" In Young's view, the key to a future brilliant blossoming lay in loosening the shackles of imitation:

> if antients and moderns were no longer considered as masters and pupils, but as hard-matched rivals for renown; then moderns, by the longevity of their labours, might, one day, become antients themselves: And old time, that best weigher of merits, to keep his balance even, might have the golden weight of an *Augustan* age in both his scales: Or rather our scale might descend; and that of antiquity (as a modern match for it [i.e., Milton] strongly speaks) might *kick the beam.*

The day might come when moderns would proudly look back on the comparative darkness of antiquity and consider Homer and Demosthenes mere infants in their arts. "It is prudence to read, genius to relish, glory to surpass, antient authors."[70]

Johnson thought that Young's ideas were rather commonplace, and the evidence of the counsel offered by Reynolds to the students in the Royal Academy suggests that this was so. Reynolds hoped that the fine arts would flower again as they did in the Renaissance, and that the present era might become the rival of the age of Pope Leo X. For this to occur, artists must first study the ancients diligently and treat them as masters. "But an artist should not be contented with this only; he should enter into a competition with his original, and endeavour to improve what he is appropriating to his own work." The technique of studying and borrowing from the ancients "will enable him to make new combinations, perhaps, superior to what had ever before been in the possession of the art," and to "approach nearer to perfection than any one of his masters." Reynolds was really arguing that art, like learning, could advance cumulatively. Artists must turn to the great men of the past not simply to imitate or copy, but "to shorten our labour." For without making use of the "advantages which our predecessors afford us, the art would be always to begin, and consequently remain always in its infant state." Thus, in Reynolds's opinion, the "true and liberal ground of imitation is an open field; where, though he who precedes has the advantage of starting before you, you may always propose to overtake him; you need not

---

70. Young, *Conjectures*, 10, 21, 19, 12, 31–33. Beattie was not so disturbed about imitation, if it was ingenious: "Classical Learning," *Essays*, 744–45.

tread in his footsteps; and you certainly have a right to outstrip him if you can."[71] As these comments by one of its chief exponents quite clearly reveal, neoclassical theory assumed the need for imitation, but only because of the potential that models contained for the future progress of art.

In his discussion of the proper form of imitation, Reynolds pointed out a widely recognized cause of artistic progress. Young described it in his own terminology: "Imitation is inferiority confessed; emulation is superiority contested, or denied; imitation is servile, emulation generous; that fetters, this fires." By all means imitate, he advised poets, but imitate appropriately. For those who do more than merely copy, who instead strive to compete with their models by achieving originality, "extend the republic of letters, and add a new province to its dominion." Johnson took the same line. He knew that the world of letters must always remain in a rude condition if no use were made of the labors of past ages. But he also proclaimed that the writer who "wishes to be counted among the benefactors of posterity, must add by his own toil to the acquisitions of his ancestors, and secure his memory from neglect by some valuable improvement."[72] The accumulative effect was thus often seen to be the process of progress in the fine arts, as well as in learning and practical skills.

Other explanations of artistic progress were also put forth. In Reynolds's view, the establishment of rules for art permitted it to advance, as did the invention of engraving. Barry believed that the mutual interaction of the fine arts was important to their improvement. According to Burney, projects such as his *History of Music* served as repositories for all past achievements and thereby encouraged future progress. Goldsmith considered a temperate climate to be a prerequisite for the attainment of literary excellence. While some contemporaries looked askance at the effects of learning and criticism on art, many held an opposite opinion. Turnbull, for example, discovered in history a conjunction of great periods in painting with times of high learning. This had been more than coincidental, since in these ages the "Learned willingly gave all the assistance they were

71. *Boswell's Journal of A Tour to the Hebrides with Samuel Johnson, LL.D*, ed. Frederick A. Pottle and Charles H. Bennett (New York, 1936), 234 (entry for Sept. 30, 1773); Reynolds, *Discourses on Art*, 21, 106–07, 103, 101, 95 (Discourses I and VI).

72. Young, *Conjectures*, 29, 11, 6–7; Samuel Johnson, *The Rambler*, no. 154 (Sept. 7, 1751), in *Yale Edition*, vol. 5 (*The Rambler*), 55, 57–58. Many neoclassical artists and theorists, including Winckelmann, observed the distinction between what Young called "imitation" and "emulation": Honour, *Neo-Classicism*, 107, 111–13, 61.

able to the Artists, of whom many were themselves very learned."
Likewise, he asserted, "Painting and all Arts have been, and only can
be polished and improved by free Criticism." Or as Campbell wrote,
"observations derived from the productions of an art" provided the
means by which "every art, liberal or mechanical, elegant or useful,
except those founded in pure mathematics, advances toward perfection."[73]

Taking a wider view, some writers attempted to account for progress in all the arts and sciences, including the fine arts. In doing so
they sometimes focused on economic factors. Turnbull and Reynolds, for instance, thought that trade and the riches flowing from it
were the instruments for the acquisition of intellectual and artistic
excellence. More often, political factors seemed crucial, especially
liberty, which Thomson called the *"Eternal Patron"* and Turnbull
the *"Parent and Patron"* of the arts and sciences. Goldsmith agreed
and added that the permanence of the state was essential for the
endeavors of the mind and hand.[74]

Finally, it was argued that the fine arts prospered when society
made direct efforts to encourage them. Turnbull suggested that the
advances achieved during the great eras of painting in the past flowed
in large part from the "Encouragement given to every Kind and Degree of Merit in it, by the Rewards and Honours that were chearfully
conferred on all who excelled in any part of the Profession." A similar
comment addressed by Welsted to the duke of Newcastle was followed by a plea for aristocratic patronage:

> all would conspire to make this Nation the Rival of the most
> renown'd among the Ancients for Works of Wit and Genius;
> could we but once see that amiable Temper of Humanity, and
> the Love of Learning, which distinguish your GRACE, more
> generally prevail among Persons of your Rank: Give us our
> *Holles's*, and we shall not be long without our Poets.[75]

73. Reynolds, *Discourses on Art*, 97, 107 (Discourse VI); Barry, *Inquiry*, in *Works*,
2:246, 280; Burney, *General History of Music*, 1:11; Goldsmith, *Enquiry*, in *Collected
Works*, 1:263; Turnbull, *Treatise on Ancient Painting*, 47–48, xxx; Campbell, *Philosophy of Rhetoric*, 1:xx ("Introduction").

74. Turnbull, *Treatise on Ancient Painting*, 124, 99; Reynolds, *Discourses on Art*,
169 (Discourse IX); Thomson, *Castle of Indolence*, in *Liberty, The Castle of Indolence
and Other Poems*, 205 (II, xxiii); Goldsmith, *Enquiry*, in *Collected Works*, 1:262–63.

75. Turnbull, *Treatise on Ancient Painting*, 42–43; Welsted, *Dissertation*, in Durham, *Critical Essays*, 363.

This and other explanations were advanced to account for that progress in the fine arts which was seen in the past or envisioned for the future. Of course, not everyone believed in the existence or possibility of progress, or championed the cause of the moderns, in this field. Yet many—probably most—members of the intellectual and cultural elite did, just as nearly all of them conceived of learning and practical skills as progressive.

In some respects, the belief in progress in these three fields was essentially abstract, often based upon assessments of ages remote in time or space, and frequently concerned with impersonal facts in confused, shifting disciplinary categories. But this gulf between opinion about the operation of the real world and reality itself was bridged at a number of points, particularly by the visible, palpable signs of progressive change confronting educated men and women at the time: Newton, the steam engine, and balloons symbolized while reifying progress. And certain important institutions that grew up during the high eighteenth century had the same kind of effect, in an even more personal way.

INSTITUTIONS AND PROGRESS

Bacon's program for the enlargement of the human empire contained a vision, set forth in the *New Atlantis* (1626) and elsewhere, of the possibilities of cooperative endeavor in science, all the arts, manufacturing, and inventions. During the seventeenth century, his vision began to become reality with the establishment throughout Europe of a number of organizations like the Royal Society of London, primarily (though not exclusively) dedicated to and concerned with the advancement of the new natural philosophy. It was the enterprise in which these societies were engaged that some proponents of the moderns, like Glanvill and Sprat, found so exciting and sought to defend. In the eighteenth century, such group-oriented activity continued, but with two significant changes. The number of societies aiming at improvement or advancement multiplied enormously. And the focus of their efforts expanded to encompass not just knowledge of the natural world but the arts and sciences as a whole, in the contemporary inclusive sense of that term.

The need for encouragement of the arts and sciences by society was, of course, widely recognized, and not only because some poets and prose writers feared the ill effects of a decline in aristocratic patronage. For as Turnbull wrote, the

Progress of the Arts and Sciences, as well as innumerable other Blessings of Life, depend greatly on the Care of Society to encourage, assist, and promote them. . . . Nor can it be otherwise with regard to Beings made for Society, and fitted to acquire Knowledge, and to refine and polish Life gradually, by united Study and Industry. This is the Law of Nature, with respect to our Improvement in Sciences, and all useful or ornamental Arts: "That Knowledge shall be advanced and improved in proportion to our Application to cultivate and promote it in a social confederate way, by joining and combining our natural Stocks and Forces for that end."

Understanding this to be the case, the men of the eighteenth century undertook projects like the *Encyclopédie* and *Encyclopaedia Britannica*. More importantly, they also established a whole range of "improving" institutions, generally modeled on the existing scientific societies. Academies of the fine arts sprang up, and in provincial towns as well as in capital cities new "philosophical" societies developed. Meanwhile, beginning in the 1720s more than fifty groups concerned with the practical arts came into existence throughout Europe and America.[76] Complementing all of these were museums (or *cabinets*) and botanical gardens. Since governments usually lacked the will and resources to do more than offer their imprimatur and limited assistance, most of these organizations grew out of the efforts of private individuals.

Nowhere did such institutions flourish more vigorously than in eighteenth-century Britain. In London, to begin with there was the exhibition craze, as a cultural climate that encouraged the pursuit of knowledge also stimulated the formation and public, for-profit display of innumerable private collections of various sorts. These ranged from curios and other artifacts to specimens of fauna and flora to ingenious mechanical contrivances, such as the automatons in Cox's Museum (1772–75). Beyond the realm of popular culture, to the Royal Society were added in 1753 the British Museum, a year later the Society for the Promotion of Arts, Manufactures, and Commerce (usually called the London Society of Arts and later chartered as the

76. Turnbull, *Treatise on Ancient Painting*, 109. On the new learned organizations formed during the eighteenth century, see Roger Hahn, "The Application of Science to Society: The Societies of Arts," *Studies on Voltaire and the Eighteenth Century* 25 (1963): 829–36; James E. McClellan III, *Science Reorganized: Scientific Societies in the Eighteenth Century* (New York, 1985), esp. 145–51.

Royal Society of Arts), and in 1768 the Royal Academy. Virtually every major English provincial town also came to have at least one "improving" society during the period. Outside England, Edinburgh had several organizations of this sort, led by the principal figures of the Scottish Enlightenment, and Aberdeen, Glasgow, and Dublin had one each. Overall, the men who participated in these groups unquestionably numbered in the thousands and included both Anglicans and Nonconformists, landed gentlemen and merchants, members of the traditional professions and manufacturers, artists and amateur scientists, and, at least in the case of the Edinburgh and London organizations, many of the most powerful and influential figures on both the local and national scenes.[77]

All of these various British institutions, like their Continental counterparts, were permeated in one way or another by a spirit of progress. The private museums have appropriately been called a "faithful . . . manifestation of the spirit of the age," in the sense that they reflected the prevailing faith in the expansion of knowledge and the development of technology. Johnson recognized that this was so, and he argued that collecting

> the productions of art, and examples of mechanical science or manual ability, is unquestionably useful . . . because it is always advantageous to know how far the human powers have proceeded, and how much experience has [been] found to be within the reach of diligence. Idleness and timidity often despair without being overcome, and forbear attempts for fear of being defeated; and we may promote the invigoration of faint endeavours, by shewing what has been already performed. It may sometimes happen that the great efforts of ingenuity may

77. On the exhibitions and private museums, see Richard D. Altick, *The Shows of London* (Cambridge, Mass., 1978), 20–33, 64–76. For work on the membership of the societies, see Davis D. McElroy, *Scotland's Age of Improvement: A Survey of Eighteenth-Century Literary Clubs and Societies* ([Pullman, Wash.], 1969); Roger L. Emerson, "The Social Composition of Enlightened Scotland: The Select Society of Edinburgh, 1754–1764," *Studies on Voltaire and the Eighteenth Century* 114 (1973): 291–329; Robert E. Schofield, *The Lunar Society of Birmingham: A Social History of Provincial Science and Industry in Eighteenth-Century England* (Oxford, 1963); D. G. C. Allan, "The Society of Arts and Government, 1754–1800: Public Encouragement of Arts, Manufactures, and Commerce in Eighteenth-Century England," *Eighteenth-Century Studies* 7 (Summer 1974): 443–45.

Among the English towns that had such societies were Bath, Birmingham, Bristol, Derby, Exeter, Leeds, Leicester, Liverpool, Maidstone, Manchester, Newcastle, Northampton, Norwich, Peterborough, Plymouth, Spalding, and York.

have been exerted in trifles, yet the same principles and expedients may be applied to more valuable purposes, and the movements which put into action machines of no use but to raise the wonder of ignorance, may be employed to drain fens, or manufacture metals, to assist the architect, or preserve the sailor.

It was even possible for the raffle liquidating Cox's Museum to be advertised in doggerel that not only made use of the conflict between ancients and moderns ("See here more than Athens or Rome ever knew") but also connected the expansion of national commerce with the advancement of knowledge: "Thus Britain's white sails shall be kept unfurl'd, / And our commerce extend, as our thunders are hurl'd, / Till the Empress of Science is Queen of the World, / If we haste to buy into the Lott'ry."[78]

The other institutions may rightly be characterized as "improving" because their very goal was to bring about progress. The British Museum, according to the act founding it, was intended to yield "*advancement and improvement*" in natural philosophy and other branches of knowledge. Reynolds stated that the purpose of the Royal Academy was to "contribute to advance our knowledge of the Arts, and bring us nearer to that ideal excellence, which it is the lot of genius always to contemplate and never to attain." The Scottish societies sought to promote improvement in every part of national life, from agriculture and industry to science to culture and literature. In proposing the establishment of the London Society of Arts in 1753, William Shipley (1715–1803), who is known as its founder, expressed his hope that it would "prove an effectual means to embolden enterprise, to enlarge Science, to refine Art, to improve our Manufactures, and extend our Commerce; in a word, to render Great Britain the school of instruction, as it is already the centre of traffic to the greatest part of the known world." Thirty-three years later, after the Society of Arts had become thoroughly successful, he was once again promoting a new institution, this time the expansion of the Maidstone Society into a society for promoting useful knowledge in all of Kent. This latter proposal contended that his envisioned organization would not only stimulate agricultural improvement and enhanced landowner profits but also introduce new employments for the poor,

78. Altick, *Shows of London*, 22:1–23:1, 71:2–72:1; Samuel Johnson, *The Rambler*, no. 83, in *Yale Edition*, 4:73.

thereby reducing poor rates and making the previously unemployed "much better members of the community than they are at present."[79]

In order to achieve their ends, many societies utilized the technique of offering rewards for notable accomplishments. The members of the Edinburgh Society for the Encouragement of Arts, Sciences, Manufactures, and Agriculture (founded 1755) believed that the useful "arts and manufactures can never be effectually promoted, unless a spirit of emulation be excited in the various artists and manufacturers," and a "proper distribution of premiums" seemed to them to be the most reasonable method of exciting this spirit." Cash prizes were to be awarded for achievements in the useful arts, and gold and silver medals for those in the fine arts. The Dublin Society had earlier adopted a similar plan, on the urgings of Samuel Madden himself, and the London Society of Arts disbursed more than £30,000 by 1766, while pursuing Shipley's plan of awarding premiums in such areas as education, naval affairs, husbandry, new manufactures, and "those Arts and Sciences which are at low ebb amongst us; as Poetry, Painting, Tapestry, Architecture, &c."[80]

The notion that these institutions held great potential for progress was widespread. As Shipley put it, "Encouragement is much the same to Arts and Sciences as culture is to Vegetables: they always advance and flourish in proportion to the rewards they acquire, and the honours they obtain." A member of the Northampton Philosophical Society (founded 1743) noted with great pleasure in 1747 that "societies for inquiring into the productions of nature, and the im-

79. "An act for the purchase of the Museum, or collection of Sir Hans Sloane, and of the Harleian collection of manuscripts; and for providing one general repository for the better reception and more convenient use of the said collections. . . ," in Danby Pickering, ed., *The Statutes at Large*, 46 vols. (Cambridge, 1762–1807), 21:68 (26 Geo. II, cap. 22); Reynolds, *Discourses on Art*, 14 (Discourse I); McElroy, *Scotland's Age of Improvement*, 9, 49–50, 54; William Shipley, "Proposals for raising by subscription a fund to be distributed in Premiums for the promoting of improvements in the Liberal Arts and Sciences, Manufactures, &c." (June 8, 1753), and "A Proposal to Establish a Society for Promoting Useful Knowledge in the County of Kent. Addressed to the Inhabitants of the Said County" (1786), printed in D. G. C. Allan, *William Shipley, Founder of the Royal Society of Arts: A Biography with Documents*, corr. ed. (London, 1979), 43–44, 203.

80. *Rules and Orders of the Edinburgh Society for the Encouragement of Arts, Sciences, and Manufactures* ([Edinburgh, 1758]), 3–4; Robert Dossie, *Memoirs of Agriculture, and other Œconomical Arts*, 3 vols. (London, 1768–82), 1:27; William Shipley, "A Scheme for putting the Proposals in Execution" (Dec. 7, 1753), printed in Allan, *Shipley*, 46.

provement of art, are forming in different parts of the King's dominions. . . . When ingenious people meet to communicate their several observations, with a sincere desire to discover truth, great advances may be made in knowledge." The *Memoirs* of the Manchester Literary and Philosophical Society (founded 1781) explained why this was so, pointing to the cumulatively progressive effect of cooperative enterprise. When learned men

> have frequent opportunities of meeting and conversing together, thought begets thought, and every hint is turned to advantage. A spirit of inquiry glows in every breast. Every new discovery relative to the natural, intellectual or moral world, leads to a farther investigation; and each man is zealous to distinguish himself in the interesting pursuit.

The fine arts also appeared to most men of the age to benefit from the institutional setting. Writing in 1740, Turnbull called academies and schools of the arts one of the chief "necessary Means for improving, or even calling forth [artistic] Genius," and he expressed his unhappiness that they had not yet appeared in Britain. With the same unhappiness and regret, the anonymous essayist on the fine arts called for the establishment of painting academies and public art museums. "For had the same steps been taken here as in France" under Louis XIV, he argued, "our Arts would have made the same approaches to perfection."[81]

The advancement of the practical and mechanical arts seemed almost to *require* the cooperative efforts of societies. One competitor for an essay prize offered by the Select Society of Edinburgh (founded 1754) contended that nothing did more than such groups to promote the progress of the useful arts and manufacturing. The reason for this fact, in the view of the London Society of Arts, lay in the need for a close relationship between science and industry (as they became known in the next century): "unless Labour be assisted by Art, unless the Knowledge of the Learned be communicated to direct the Hand of the Industrious, the Labourer may waste his Time and Strength in

81. Shipley, "Proposals," in Allan, *Shipley*, 42; Henry Baker to Philip Doddridge, Nov. 24, 1747, quoted in A. E. Musson and Eric Robinson, *Science and Technology in the Industrial Revolution* (Manchester, 1969), 380; *Memoirs of the Literary and Philosophical Society of Manchester*, 2d ed., 1:vi–vii; Turnbull, *Treatise on Ancient Painting*, 110; Anon., *Essay on Perfecting the Fine Arts*, 32, 35, 38–39, 26–28. Goldsmith, however, had some doubts about the potential usefulness of societies as they were then constituted: *Enquiry*, in *Collected Works*, 1:279–81.

vain, and Study degenerate into Amusement." It was such a linkage between pure science and industry that the London Society set out to provide. On the related issue of mechanical contrivances, Thomas Barnes asked his fellow members of the Manchester Literary and Philosophical Society what the genius of the solitary inventor could "have achieved, if fostered by science, by liberality, and by honour! . . . What, if to genius and application had been added, a larger field of observation, a more general acquaintance with the mechanical powers . . . ! How much further might he have advanced!"[82] Unquestionably, the London Society of Arts and its provincial brethren were seeking to unite science or theory with art or practice, to create eighteenth-century versions of twentieth-century research and development programs.

These organizations seemed uniquely able to bring about progress in all the arts and sciences. Indeed, according to their members they had already been doing so. As the *Memoirs* of the Manchester society declared, the

> numerous Societies, for the promotion of Literature and Philosophy, which have been formed in different parts of Europe, in the course of the last and present centuries, have been not only the means of diffusing knowledge more extensively, but have contributed to produce a greater number of important discoveries, than have been effected in any other equal space of time.
>
> The progress that has been made in Physics and the Belles Lettres, owes its rapidity, if not its origin, to the encouragement which these Societies have given to such pursuits, and to the emulation which has been excited between different academical bodies, as well as among the individual Members of each institution.

Naturally, individual societies pointed with pride to their own accomplishments. For example, one important member of the London Society of Arts, Robert Dossie (d. 1777), particularly discussed its contribution to agricultural improvement and its advancement of "almost every branch of [the fine] arts, to such an approach toward

82. McElroy, *Scotland's Age of Improvement*, 66; *Rules and Orders of the Society, Established at London, for the Encouragement of Arts, Manufactures, and Commerce* (London, 1758), 4; Thomas Barnes, "On the Affinity subsisting between the Arts, with a Plan for promoting and extending Manufactures, by encouraging those Arts, on which Manufactures principally depend" (read Jan. 9, 1782), *Memoirs of the Literary and Philosophical Society of Manchester*, 2d ed., 1:84. See also Allan, *Shipley*, 7.

perfection as was scarcely to be expected." Shipley was even more emphatic as he looked back on the work of the London Society of Arts. From its efforts, he contended, "more solid benefits have been derived to our country, within the short space of thirty years, than from all the improvements that have been made throughout this kingdom in half a century before that time." And in his final presidential remarks, Reynolds claimed that the Royal Academy had achieved at least as much as "has been effected by other societies formed in this nation for the advancement of useful and ornamental knowledge."[83]

The members of the various societies also looked optimistically toward the future. Barnes felt sure that all of his fellows in the Manchester institution would agree that "human ingenuity is not exhausted; that machines are not yet carried to their highest improvement." Addressing the Derby Philosophical Society, which he had founded, Dr. Darwin prophesied that the "common heap of knowledge . . . will never cease to accumulate so long as the human footstep is seen upon the earth." Not surprisingly, it was expected that the societies themselves would play a key part in future progress. As Barrow asked rhetorically, "What Progress in Literature! What sublime Discoveries may we not expect from so learned a Body" as the Royal Society, especially in light of the contribution it had already made to science and inventions. The implication of Barrow's comment appeared in explicit form in the statement by Dossie that the members of the Society of Arts

> have inspired an ardent spirit of general pursuit of improvements, as well as a keen attention to the discovery, or rendering perfect, [of] many particulars which have already been brought into agitation. The future benefits of their unremitted efforts, will, nevertheless, in all probability, exceed those already reaped.[84]

83. *Memoirs of the Literary and Philosophical Society of Manchester*, 2d ed., 1: sig. A3r; Dossie, *Memoirs of Agriculture*, 1:33, 37, 319; Shipley, "A Proposal to Establish a Society in Kent," in Allan, *Shipley*, 201; Reynolds, *Discourses on Art*, 266 (Discourse XV). See also *Transactions of the Royal Society of Edinburgh* 1 (1788): vi–viii.

84. Barnes, "Affinity subsisting between the Arts," *Memoirs of the Literary and Philosophical Society of Manchester*, 2d ed., 1:84; Erasmus Darwin, Inaugural Address to the Derby Philosophical Society (July 18, 1784), quoted in Eric Robinson, "The Derby Philosophical Society," *Annals of Science* 9 (Dec. 15, 1953): 361; Barrow, *New and Universal Dictionary*, "Dedication"; Dossie, *Memoirs of Agriculture*, 1:321.

As for so many others in the eighteenth century, for the members of these societies visible progress in the present gave a promise of still greater things to come.

Thus, a spirit of progress pervaded all of these institutions. In a personal and intimate way, their originators and members engaged in an attempt to bring about advancement of the arts and sciences, thereby treating the societies as tools of progress. Because that attempt was believed to be succeeding, the institutions also served as concrete evidence of improvement, making progress appear as a fact of life. The mood of the societies and their members is captured in a description of Shipley by a younger friend: "When he contemplated the plan of that society which he afterwards formed and matured, I have known him [to] sit for hours . . . and with a loquacity unusual to him, discuss the rise and the progress of, and the improvements that had been, and might be, made in a variety of arts and manufactures."[85]

The hundreds or even thousands of educated men associated with the improving societies typify eighteenth-century attitudes toward the history of the arts and sciences. Looking back, they and their contemporaries saw progress in learning, practical skills and techniques, and (to a significant degree) the fine arts; projecting this image into the future, they envisioned more of the same. Proponents of the ancients and the cyclical theory of history did not completely disappear, especially with regard to the polite arts, and Paul Fussell is right to consider the confrontation between what he calls the "humanist" and "modern" traditions in literature as "a continuation clear through the century of the old Renaissance battle of the Ancients and the Moderns."[86] Increasingly, however, this confrontation was a one-sided affair, as we have seen: for the most part, the adherents of the moderns were triumphant and their belief in progress in the arts and sciences prevailed. With their victory came crucial change, and not just in literature and art as the more imitative brand of classicism decayed. Relying on the visible evidence of the Newtonian and commercial revolutions, the moderns were helping to make the full-blown Industrial Revolution possible by shaping its mental climate.

85. Joseph Moser, "Vestiges, Collected and Recollected," *European Magazine* 44 (July–Dec. 1803): 176:1–2. See also Allan, *Shipley*, 128.

86. Fussell, *Rhetorical World of Augustan Humanism*, 25.

3 The Christian Vision of History

In Britain during the eighteenth century, those who advanced doctrines of progress in the arts and sciences inherited and transformed certain by-then traditional modes of thought, which concerned secular subjects centering on the "Battle of Ancients and Moderns." Some of the same men, along with a substantial number of their contemporaries, also believed that there had been or would be improvement in religion and spiritual life. And here, too, the resulting pattern of recollection and foresight represents the modification of an intellectual heritage—in this case, the Christian vision of history.

The problem of determining the logical and historical connection between this vision and the modern European belief in progress has received much attention since the late nineteenth century. But the most influential explanation remains that of J. B. Bury, writing in 1920. He contended that the idea of progress—which, according to his view of it, implies that human improvement occurs gradually and springs from the nature of man—is fundamentally incompatible with those key elements of the Christian faith, providentialism and the doctrine of original sin. At the same time, however, he argued that Christianity did make a contribution to the development of the idea: medieval theology depicted the past as leading to the definite and desirable goal of salvation, thereby shattering the ancient cyclical theory of history and forcing modern men to seek a new, linear replacement for it.[1]

Although these two points have been widely accepted, they are not entirely satisfactory. The first rests on what we have already seen to be an unwarrantedly narrow definition of the idea. When defined (as it should be) in broader terms, this idea *does* encompass among its

1. J. B. Bury, *The Idea of Progress: An Inquiry into Its Origin and Growth* (London, 1920), 4–5, 20–29.

various forms certain Christian historical conceptions.[2] Two such forms arose in late antiquity and, along with several others of more recent origin, became popular in Britain after about 1700. Bury's second point embodies an important truth. The simplistic form in which he presented it, however, does not offer the kind of precision and factual underpinnings necessary for historical demonstration. Later scholars have tried to remedy this deficiency, but their conclusions do not fit the case of British eschatologists of the high eighteenth century. These commentators on "the last things," along with their contemporaries who believed that there was progress in religion, offer strong evidence that the role of Christian conceptions in the historical development of the idea of progress was more intimate and complex than Bury allowed, and considerably different from what his followers have suggested.

PROGRESS IN RELIGION

During the first centuries of Christianity, a significant number of prominent religious thinkers put forth several kinds of doctrines of progress. Theodor Mommsen uncovered one of these, which he called the "Christian idea of progress," in the writings of such Church Fathers and apologists as Melito of Sardis, Tertullian, Origen, Arnobius, Lactantius, Eusebius, Ambrose, Jerome, Cyril of Alexandria, and Prudentius. They believed that under the auspices of the new religion "the world had made concrete progress in historical time and that further progress could be expected." Claiming that earthly and material progress was impossible, Augustine decisively rejected this belief (along with millennialism), and it became untenable after the early fifth century because of his enormous influence and the fall of the western Roman Empire.[3]

Yet Augustine helped to establish another sort of doctrine of progress. He thought that real *spiritual* improvement had taken place in the past, that there had been "a gradual revelation of the divine truth communicated by God to man, especially through the prophecies" that predicted the coming of the Messiah. Other Christian writers—including some whose "Christian idea of progress" he opposed—

2. On the weaknesses of Bury's definition and the need for one that is far more comprehensive, see above, chap. 1.

3. Theodor E. Mommsen, "St. Augustine and the Christian Idea of Progress: The Background of the City of God," *Journal of the History of Ideas* 12 (June 1951): 357–74.

joined him in detecting this process at work in history up to the promulgation of the gospel. Unlike Gotthold Lessing centuries later, they did not foresee any future advances in the revelatory "education of the human race" (to use Augustine's own phrase). But Vincent of Lerins, writing at the same time as Augustine, did suggest in his *Commonitorium* that although the true faith must never be altered, doctrine should nonetheless be clarified and consolidated over time, and "the knowledge, the wisdom . . . of the whole Church, ought, in the course of ages and centuries, to increase and make much and vigorous progress." Here was a notion of the possibility of doctrinal development, a belief in the potential progress of religious knowledge independent of further revelation.[4]

This second kind of Christian doctrine of progress did not die out with late antiquity. By the twelfth and thirteenth centuries it was appearing among medieval theologians like Hugh of St. Victor and Thomas Aquinas alongside the version of belief in religious progress that had been commonly found among the Fathers. That belief also came to have numerous proponents in the later sixteenth and seventeenth centuries, including Grotius, Jurieu, and Spinoza on the Continent, and Hooker, Milton, and Henry More in England. R. S. Crane long ago argued that the whole conception of progressive religious understanding was vigorously reasserted and extended between 1699 and 1745 primarily by three Anglican clerics, John Edwards, William Worthington, and Edmund Law. Drawing upon the relatively new belief in the ongoing advance of secular knowledge, as well as upon the Augustine-Vincent tradition, they concluded that religious knowledge had increased in the past and would unquestionably continue to do so. For God, they assumed, reveals His truth in stages appropriate to the intellectual conditions of particular times and places. According to Crane, this assumption illuminated the fundamentally polemical motivation of these clergymen: they were attempting to defend the orthodox faith against deist attacks, particularly with regard to the troublesome issue of local revelation. That is, their concept of "religious progressivism" allowed them to explain

4. Ibid., 372–73; Saint Augustine, *The City of God*, trans. Marcus Dods et al. (New York, 1950), 319; R. S. Crane, "Anglican Apologetics and the Idea of Progress, 1699–1745," *Modern Philology* 31 (Feb. and May 1934), reprinted with corrections in idem, *The Idea of the Humanities and Other Essays Historical and Critical*, 2 vols. (Chicago, 1967), 1:216–18. Vincent is also discussed in this context by Gerhart B. Ladner, *The Idea of Reform: Its Impact on Christian Thought and Action in the Age of the Fathers*, enl. ed. (New York, 1967), 411–12.

why the true religion had not been vouchsafed all at once and to all nations.[5]

Although Crane largely focused on three individuals, during the eighteenth century there were in fact a substantial number of Anglicans—ranging theologically from conservatives to liberals, and including some quite prominent churchmen—who believed in the past and future improvement of religious understanding.

Occasionally, such advance was considered to be entirely the work of God. Thomas Hartley (1709–84), a Northamptonshire rector and budding mystic, wrote in 1764 that although complete knowledge of the meaning of the scriptures had not yet been attained, eventually "they shall be understood in perfection . . . since to that end they were given." He had no doubt that this further progress would come "not in the way of human learning and criticism, but by larger communications of the Spirit of wisdom from the Father of lights." The spiritually educative process that Hartley had in mind was essentially what Benjamin West (1738–1820), the famous Anglo-American painter, proposed to illustrate pictorially. Around 1779, he suggested to George III that a new chapel the king wanted to build could be decorated with a series of thirty-five pictures on the history of revealed religion. With the advice of a half-dozen bishops, the king, a supporter of the High Church party, approved the project and became its patron. West never entirely completed this *Progress of Revelation*, as it was called, but he made its intended theme clear in a meeting with the king and bishops. He explained that he wanted to depict the course of divine revelation over four successive "Dispensations": the Antediluvian and Patriarchal, the Mosaic, the Gospel, and the Revelation (of "John"). The subjects of his pictures were to begin with the expulsion from Eden and conclude with the Last Judgment and New Jerusalem. Among the works in this series that he did finish were five from the Gospel Dispensation, which he sketched as they were to be displayed on a side wall of the proposed royal chapel.[6]

Adopting an Augustinian perspective, Hartley and West focused exclusively on the role of God in what John Gill (1697–1771), a well-

5. Crane, "Anglican Apologetics," 215–26, 229, 233–36, 246–48, 268–72. Worthington and Law are discussed below in chap. 6, and their views on religious progress are examined in chap. 8.

6. Thomas Hartley, *Paradise Restored: Or A Testimony to the Doctrine of the Blessed Millennium* (London, 1764), 174–75; Robert C. Alberts, *Benjamin West: A Biography* (Boston, 1978), 158–59; Joseph Burke, *English Art, 1714–1800* (Oxford, 1976), 248.

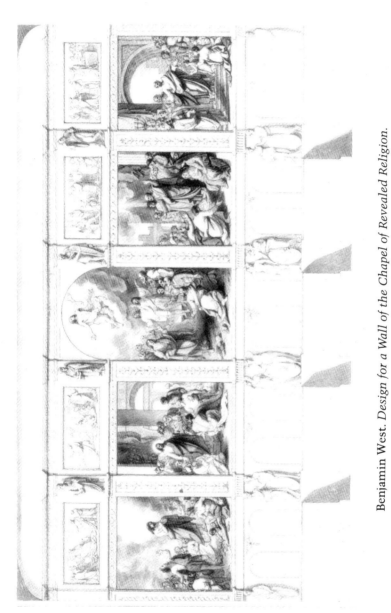

Benjamin West. *Design for a Wall of the Chapel of Revealed Religion.*

known Baptist minister from London, called the "gradual progress of light, thro' the various dispensations of the church." Even though all of these men unquestionably conceived of divine revelation as dynamic, none of them expected a new, more sophisticated future revelation along the lines of Lessing's vision of 1780. There is at least some evidence, however, that a tendency toward this radical opinion may have appeared in Scotland about 1770.[7]

In any case, it was more common during the high eighteenth century to ascribe the improvement of religious knowledge at least partially to human actions than entirely to divine revelation. Thus, John Ross (1719–92), the moderate bishop of Exeter, declared that even though a full understanding of the prophecies would probably not be attained "till the great designs of Providence are accomplished, and *the mystery of God is finished*," still much of the obscurity of prophetic texts could be removed by the "frequent and gradual attempts" of their interpreters. In fact, Ross claimed, substantial advances along these lines had recently occurred. Another bishop, the contentious William Warburton (1698–1779), likewise believed that the increase of religious wisdom could flow from the efforts of man as well as from the unvarying divine "method of the GRADUAL COMMUNICATION of Truth." He expected that future "advances in the knowledge of God's WILL should haply prove as considerable as those in the discovery of his WORKS," quoting with approval Bacon's remark that men should endeavor to make progress in both fields of study.[8]

This last comment implied that there was a similarity between the progress of secular and religious knowledge. The parallel became

7. John Gill, *The Watchman's Answer to the Question, What of the Night? A Sermon Preached . . . December 27, 1750* (London, 1751), 18–19. Thomas Gillespie (1708–74), a member of the Popular party within the Scottish Church and a focus of debate during the Inverkeithing Affair of 1752–53, was at pains to brand as heretical the view that God *might* make additions to scripture beyond the Book of Revelation. He seemed to be suggesting that some of his Scottish contemporaries (the Moderates?) held this view, although he mentioned no names. See his *An Essay on The continuance of immediate revelations of facts and future events in the Christian church* (Edinburgh, 1771), 2, 16.

8. John [Ross], *A Sermon Preached before the Incorporated Society for the Propagation of the Gospel in Foreign Parts . . . February 18, 1785* (London, 1785), 3–4; William Warburton, *The Divine Legation of Moses Demonstrated* (1737–41), Bk. IX, in *The Works of the Right Reverend William Warburton*, new ed., 12 vols. (London, 1811), 6:228, 232. The first quotation from Warburton is cited in Gerald R. Cragg, *Reason and Authority in the Eighteenth Century* (Cambridge, 1964), 42. For similar views, see also William Berriman, *The Gradual Revelation of the Gospel; from the Time of Man's Apostacy* (1733), quoted in Crane, "Anglican Apologetics," 238–39.

explicit in the *Analogy of Religion* written by Joseph Butler (1692–1752), ultimately bishop of Durham and perhaps the most influential opponent of the deists. Butler assumed, like Warburton, that the divine scheme of things was "not a fixed but a progressive one," and that God "accomplishes his natural ends by slow successive steps." Consequently, he did not find it at all surprising that the Bible contained truths not yet discovered, which could only be apprehended

> in the same way as natural knowledge is come at: by the continuance and progress of learning and liberty; and by particular persons attending to, comparing and pursuing, intimations scattered up and down [the scriptures], which are overlooked and disregarded by the generality of the world. For this is the way, in which all improvements are made.

The same basic view was reiterated half a century later by John Napleton (1738–1817), a theological conservative who was chaplain to the bishop of Hereford. He contended that religious knowledge advanced like the arts and sciences, which to him meant cumulatively and collectively.[9]

The physician, psychologist, and liberal Anglican layman David Hartley extended the parallel between religious and secular knowledge by arguing that God intended the two to proceed hand in hand. The scriptural dispensations, he wrote, had always been "perfectly suited" to the state of the world—including its intellectual conditions—at the respective times of their reception. Hence, gospel precepts appeared as if "under a Veil" in the patriarchal era but "were gradually opened more and more under the later Prophets." More recently, just as (and partly because) the whole realm of learning had continued to progress, so scholarship had produced great "Improvement of the historical Evidences" of Christianity and refinement in the interpretation of prophecy. These beneficial changes had permitted the "Knowlege [*sic*] of true, pure, and perfect Religion" to become "advanced and diffused more and more every Day," and this was precisely as it should have been. For it was more agreeable to the divine plan and the nature of man that "the Bulk of Mankind should have such a Knowledge of God, as suits their intellectual Faculties,

---

9. Joseph Butler, *The Analogy of Religion* (1736), in *The Works of Joseph Butler*, ed. W. E. Gladstone, 2 vols. (Oxford, 1896), 1:176, 234–35, 251; John Napleton, *A Sermon Preached in the Cathedral Church of Hereford . . . September IX, MDCCLXXXIX* (Oxford, 1789), 9–11.

and other Circumstances, . . . than that all should stand still or go backwards, or make less Improvements in Religion, than tallies with their Improvements in other Things."[10]

Underlying these views of Hartley was a version of the common eighteenth-century attempt to accommodate revealed religion to human reason, and it became pronounced in a long poem of 1751 by James Fortescue (1716–77), another Northamptonshire cleric. He traced the rise of "Sacred Science" from fable (the "dawning of Science") through the gospel (the "completion of Science") to the use of reason in examining the "credentials of religion." The overall tendency of this development, he thought, was to eliminate superstition and ignorance, and ultimately to inculcate through intellectual conviction a submission to the authority of revelation.[11]

In all these various forms, therefore, belief in the past and future improvement of religious knowledge was quite common among Anglicans of the high eighteenth century.[12] The same was probably true of the Moderates in the Church of Scotland, who in the 1770s and 1780s argued that all creeds and confessions were incomplete. In spite of the work of the Reformation, wrote one Moderate,

> Something is still left to reform; . . . we have the same *right*, nay we have the same calls from duty and conscience, to review received opinions, even though they should be found in our standards, as our fathers had, and to reject them if they are discovered to be erroneous. . . . This age is superior to the age

10. David Hartley, *Observations on Man, His Frame, His Duty, and His Expectations*, 2 vols. (London, 1749), 2:187, 172, 376, 150, 379, 176, 137–38.

11. [James Fortescue], *Science; A Poem. (In a Religious View) On It's* [sic] *Decline and Revival. With a particular regard to the Mission of Moses, And the Coming of the Messiah* (Oxford, 1751), iii, 1–7.

12. Going much further than Crane, Owen Chadwick asserts that this belief was "assumed by the main stream of English thought in the eighteenth century": *From Bossuet to Newman: The Idea of Doctrinal Development* (Cambridge, 1957), 77. The evidence presented in the preceding five paragraphs gives such a generalization considerable support, even though Chadwick himself cites only Joseph Butler and the clergymen whom Crane examined. In any event, Sir Leslie Stephen was clearly wrong when he declared that in the eighteenth century there was "a curious inability" to accept the view that "man in the infancy of the race was fitted for an order of [religious] ideas entirely different from that which would be appropriate at a later epoch." He went on to comment that "nothing can more distinctly indicate how modern is that conception of progress which is now so familiar to us all": *History of English Thought in the Eighteenth Century* (3d ed., 1902), repr., 2 vols. (New York, 1962), 1:119–20.

of the Reformation; our sentiments may be presumed juster, and more correct than theirs.[13]

The old view of Vincent and Augustine, of Hugh of St. Victor and Aquinas, had its eighteenth-century versions north of the Tweed as well as south.

But whether expressed by the English or the Scots, this concept of the advance of religious understanding was only one sort of Christian doctrine of progress put forth at the time. Breaking new ground, a group of notable Anglicans also believed in the progressive spread of Christianity. For instance, Brownlow North (1741–1820), bishop of Worcester and brother of Lord North, considered the discovery of the western hemisphere to have marked "a material and important step in the purpose of God, to bring all nations of the earth to bless him." Exactly why this should have been so was made clear by Richard Osbaldeston (1690–1764), bishop of Carlisle. Like North, he adopted an interesting version of the old theory of *translatio imperii* and claimed that the "Progress of true Religion has been similar to the Course of the Sun from East to West." Continuing westward from Europe, it will eventually "illuminate and refresh all Places and Regions of the Earth." As the conservative bishop of Oxford, John Butler (1717–1802), put it in 1784, "Christianity is evidently in a progressive state; and the great design of Infinite Wisdom and Goodness, to bring all men into the Faith of Christ, will be finally accomplished, however slow the progress."[14]

North, Osbaldeston, and Butler made their comments in sermons delivered to annual meetings of the Society for the Propagation of the Gospel in Foreign Parts, chartered in 1701. The S.P.G. had been found-

13. Christianus [pseud. for J. Mackenzie], *The Religious Establishment of Scotland Examined* (London, 1771), 73, quoted in Ian D. L. Clark, "From Protest to Reaction: The Moderate Regime in the Church of Scotland, 1752–1805," in N. T. Phillipson and Rosalind Mitchison, eds., *Scotland in the Age of Improvement: Essays in Scottish History in the Eighteenth Century* (Edinburgh, 1970), 205.

14. Brownlow [North], *A Sermon Preached before the Incorporated Society for the Propagation of the Gospel in Foreign Parts . . . February 20, 1778* (London, 1778), 5; Richard [Osbaldeston], *A Sermon Preached before the Incorporated Society for the Propagation of the Gospel in Foreign Parts . . . February 21, 1752* (London, 1752), 8–9; John [Butler], *A Sermon Preached before the Incorporated Society for the Propagation of the Gospel in Foreign Parts . . . February 20, 1784* (London, 1784), 17. Chadwick does not mention the presence of such views in eighteenth-century Britain, although he points out that they had earlier been accepted by Bossuet: *From Bossuet to Newman,* 17.

ed to help effect just such ends as the bishops envisioned, and the same was true of the Society for Promoting Christian Knowledge (established 1699) and its Scottish namesake (1708). From the 1730s, when these missionary organizations were becoming increasingly active, many of the clergymen who belonged to them undoubtedly subscribed to the bishops' optimism about the expansion of Christianity. That such sentiments were more than mere institutional propaganda is apparent from the case of Richard Watson (1737–1816), the extremely liberal bishop of Llandaff. Though a long-time member of the s.p.g., he never participated in its enterprises and did "not, indeed, expect much success in propagating Christianity by missionaries." Nevertheless, he thought it likely that the faith, "a rational religion," would continue to spread—but by means of the civilizing extension of commerce and, especially, "science":

> the Romans, the Athenians, the Corinthians and others, were highly civilized, far advanced in the rational use of their intellectual faculties, and they all, at length, exchanged Paganism for Christianity; the same change will take place in other countries, as they become enlightened by the progress of European literature, and become capable of justly estimating the weight of historical evidence, on which the truth of Christianity must, as to them, depend.[15]

So in spite of his misgivings about the value of the s.p.g., Watson believed as firmly as its other members in the inevitable expansion of the true religion.

In fact, some who had no connection whatever to the missionary societies held similar views. David Hartley, for example, pointed to the rapid early spread of Christianity, "the Progress it has since made, and the Reception which it meets with at present," as evidence of its divine origin. He thought that the number of faithful "increases every Day" and, looking to the future, expected that the Christian religion ultimately "will be preached to, and received by, all Nations." In this great work, several "natural Causes" would play their part, including the advance of knowledge and enlargement of international com-

---

15. Richard Watson, *Anecdotes of the Life of Richard Watson, Bishop of Llandaff*, ed. Richard Watson, Jr. (London, 1817), 196, 198 (remarks on a proposal of 1788 to send missionaries to India). On the s.p.g. and related societies, see J. A. De Jong, *As the Waters Cover the Sea: Millennial Expectations in the Rise of Anglo-American Missions, 1640–1810* (Kampen, 1970), 85, 115–58.

merce and communication cited by Watson. Even the challenges of unbelievers would lead the faithful to purify their religion and develop new evidence for its truths, "by which means its Progress amongst the yet Heathen Nations will be much forwarded." Hartley clearly agreed with what a leader of the so-called Popular party in the Church of Scotland, Dr. Alexander Webster (1707–84), wrote in 1741: the "'Sun of Righteousness' has gone on *gradually* enlightening those 'dark Places of the Earth'; and . . . 'the Fulness of Time' is fast approaching" when all peoples would be united in the true church. Or as Fortescue put it, the rule of Christ is "Ever progressive," and "From age to age his kingdom shall increase."[16]

John Wesley took an almost identical position and added some personal observations. In two sermons of the 1780s, he suggested that the beginnings of his own movement at Oxford half a century before had initiated an enormous spreading of religion throughout the English-speaking world. He believed that the gospel had never been more widely preached than in the recent past, and that "myriads" of sinners had been converted. These successes were not diminishing in the present and would continue into the future. The kingdom of God would "silently increase . . . and spread from heart to heart, from house to house, from town to town, from one kingdom to another"— even among the heathen nations—until the whole world would be "leavened."[17] No less than orthodox Anglican bishops or Scottish "High Flyers" like Webster, the leader of English evangelicalism was optimistic about the spread of Christianity.

Related to this outlook was an innovative belief in the overall improvement of religion. Bishop John Green (1706?–79), a liberal from Lincoln, felt convinced that "circumstances are at present favourable to the farther progress of the Gospel; that it may be published to people among whom it is now unknown; and have more influence on those by whom it has been received." Eventually, wrote Charles Moss (1711–1802), moderate bishop of St. David's, Christianity not only would be established across the earth but also would flourish as never before and "bring forth its genuine fruits." At that

16. David Hartley, *Observations*, 2:189–90, 376–80, 186; Alexander Webster, *Supernatural Revelation the Only Sure Hope of Sinners* (Edinburgh, 1741), 29, 49, quoted in De Jong, *As the Waters Cover the Sea*, 149; Fortescue, *Science; A Poem*, 11, 19.

17. John Wesley, "The General Spread of the Gospel" (delivered 1783) and "The Signs of the Times" (delivered 1787), in *The Works of the Rev. John Wesley, A.M.*, 14 vols. (London, 1872), 6:281–86, 307–08, 310.

point, Gill thought, the church would "enjoy purity of doctrine, discipline and ordinances, as well as have honour and authority." Bishop Ross likewise expected an ultimately "glorious and flourishing state of religion and virtue, in which the Gospel will not only be taught and professed throughout the world, but taught and professed in the purity and simplicity in which it began, and have a suitable influence over the lives and manners of men."[18]

An explanation of why this general religious progress was to occur came from John Taylor (1694–1761), an English Presbyterian minister with Socinian tendencies who taught divinity at the Dissenting academy in Warrington. He asserted that the design of God was "to carry religion, both in its personal influences, and general prevalence, to the highest perfection our present condition will admit." To that end, he believed, the scriptural dispensations had each been "adapted to the then capacities and improvements, the moral state and circumstances of mankind," so that, for instance, the Adamic dispensation "was very different from that which we are under." Taylor could easily have borrowed this line of reasoning from David Hartley's discussion of advances in religious knowledge, and he certainly did borrow and recast for his own purposes two traditional Baconian arguments. "The several ages of the world," he continued,

> may be compared to the several stages of human life, infancy, youth, manhood, and old-age. Now, as a man under due culture gradually improves in knowledge and wisdom, from infancy to old-age, so we may conceive of the world, from the beginning to the end, as gradually improving in mental and religious attainments under the several divine dispensations. . . .
>
> COROLLARY. *A preceding dispensation is intended and adapted to introduce and prepare for that which comes after it.* . . . It is therefore agreeable to the nature of things, that . . . what we already have experienced should be a step to further advances. . . . Thus mankind, reflecting upon preceding dispensations, will be admonished and directed to reform old errors and corruptions; and thus, even the monstrous apostasy of

18. John [Green], *A Sermon Preached before the Incorporated Society for the Propagation of the Gospel in Foreign Parts . . . February 19, 1768* (London, 1768), 22; Charles [Moss], *A Sermon Preached before the Incorporated Society for the Propagation of the Gospel in Foreign Parts . . . February 21, 1772* (London, 1772), xv; Gill, *Watchman's Answer*, 20; Ross, *Sermon before the S.P.G. 1785*, 18.

the church of *Rome* may serve to introduce and establish that most perfect state of Christianity, which we expect will succeed the dispensation we are now under.

The old paradox of the ancients and the notion of cumulative intellectual progress were here given new applications, in order to provide a foundation for Taylor's conception of what he referred to as *"the progress of religion."*[19]

In eighteenth-century Britain, then, there were Christian doctrines of progress that depicted religious knowledge as advancing, the true faith as spreading, and, in more general terms, Christianity as improving.[20] Taken together, these doctrines amounted to a belief that there had been or would be progress in religion. The writers who expressed such a view were largely Anglican clerics (of most theological persuasions), along with some notable Dissenters and evangelical leaders. As a group, they do not constitute a microcosm of British Christianity,[21] in light of the underrepresentation not only of laity but also of ordinary parish clergy. Nonetheless, these were respectable and often influential men, and they undoubtedly reflected a very substantial body of religious opinion.

Why was it that doctrines of progress in religion became so widespread at the time? Part of the answer to this question must be sought in the realm of intellectual tradition and influence. Two of the clerics

19. John Taylor, *A Scheme of Scripture-Divinity, formed upon the Plan of the Divine Dispensations. With a Vindication of the Sacred Writings* (London, 1762), in Richard Watson, ed., *A Collection of Theological Tracts* (1785), 2d ed., 6 vols. (London, 1791), 1:15–16. Taylor concluded his remarks on this subject by displaying a Bentham-like calculating instinct. He suggested that it was possible to compute the progress of religion under any dispensation. This could be done simply by measuring *"the quantity of knowledge and religion"* (or, more precisely, *"the advances of knowledge and religion"*) among individual members—"how few soever"—of *"the righteous"*!

20. The three types of doctrines can be found together in Edmund [Keene], *A Sermon Preached before the Incorporated Society for the Propagation of the Gospel in Foreign Parts . . . February 18, 1757* (London, 1757), 7, 14, 19–20; John Willison, *The Balm of Gilead, for Healing a Diseased Land* (1742), in *The Works of the Reverend and Learned Mr. John Willison*, new ed., 3 vols. (Edinburgh, 1818), 2:94–98; James Brown, *The Extensive Influence of Religious Knowledge* (Edinburgh, 1769), 3–4, 42, quoted in De Jong, *As the Waters Cover the Sea,* 150–51.

21. In one respect they come close to doing so, however, since the bulk of them were Anglican: in the eighteenth century, Dissenters comprised only perhaps 6 percent of the population of England and Wales, and Scotland had between 15 and 17 percent of the people of Great Britain as a whole (calculations based on figures in Michael R. Watts, *The Dissenters: From the Reformation to the French Revolution* [Oxford, 1978], Appendix, and M. W. Flinn, *British Population Growth, 1700–1850* [London, 1970], 17, 21).

analyzed by Crane—namely, Edwards and Law—cited passages from Vincent's *Commonitorium* to buttress their argument that religious knowledge had been increasing. Whether others also drew directly upon the Augustine-Vincent tradition cannot be known, for they left no similar record of their indebtedness. There clearly was at least an indirect link to the Fathers, however: the layman David Hartley read and referred in print to Law on the advancement of religious understanding, as did several of the clergymen.[22] Where Warburton and Joseph Butler derived their views on this subject is uncertain. But those views had an excellent opportunity to reach a large readership, because they appeared in contemporary bestsellers.

Influence of this sort, coupled with the continuation of a centuries-old tradition, certainly helped to give currency to doctrines of religious progress. Nonetheless, their popularity owed even more to the fact that they were useful and appealing in several ways. To begin with, they sometimes served a strategic function in the battle of orthodoxy against deism. No less than for Crane's three clerics, the notion of improvement in religious understanding made it possible for David Hartley to assert that "a gradual and partial Promulgation is not inconsistent with the Supposition of a true Revelation." This argument also provided Joseph Butler and Warburton with a weapon in their antideist arsenal, although such was no longer the case among ecclesiastics writing after mid-century, when the deist controversy had virtually spent itself.[23]

Even then, however, the belief in religious progress retained psychological appeal. Emotion had largely been drained from religion during the late seventeenth and early eighteenth century, in reaction to what were perceived to be the excesses of Puritanism. But "enthusiasm" could not be constantly and indefinitely repressed, and it took more than one shape when it reappeared from the 1730s on: mysticism and Swedenborgianism, Hutchinsonianism, and, of course, Methodism in England and evangelicalism in Scotland. Contemporaneously with these movements, enthusiasm also appeared in the somewhat more subtle forms of interest in eschatology and belief in

22. Crane, "Anglican Apologetics," 227, 234n, 264n–65n, 274–75, 277, 282; David Hartley, *Observations*, 2:186. See also Conyers Middleton, *An Inquiry into the Miraculous Powers, Which are supposed to have subsisted in the Christian Church* (London, 1749), 57n.

23. David Hartley, *Observations*, 2:186–87; Chadwick, *From Bossuet to Newman*, 85–86.

religious progress. The vision of an advancing Christianity provided, in effect, an acceptable vent for religious emotion in otherwise sober ecclesiastics, such as the bishops who annually addressed the s.p.g. Contemplating the future spread of true religion, Richard Terrick (1710–77), the conservative bishop of London, declared to his s.p.g. colleagues in 1764, "what a happy glorious Scene may this open to our view!" How "would the heart of the good Christian overflow with joy," he asked rhetorically, "to see the approach of those happy days foretold by the Prophets, when the earth shall be filled with the knowledge of the Lord." The expression of such sentiment obviously had much less in common with John Tillotson, that exemplar of the staid, temperate preaching style, than with Wesley and George Whitefield. It partook of a recognizable shift in the emphasis of British religion as a whole from the head toward the heart, from a strictly intellectual orientation toward greater devotional feeling.[24]

The expectation of future religious progress was psychologically appealing for another reason, too. In the eighteenth century, just when the use of critical reason produced a serious challenge to orthodoxy, anticlericalism reached more massive proportions in Britain than at any time since the Lollards. Ecclesiastics were fully aware of this situation. "Christianity is now ridiculed and railed at, with very little Reserve: and the Teachers of it, without any at all," said Thomas Secker (1693–1768) in 1738. The future archbishop of Canterbury added that "an open and professed Disregard to Religion is become, through a Variety of unhappy Causes, the distinguishing Character of the present Age." Such negativism about the contemporary state of religion was quite common throughout the century. Joseph Butler expressed it in the "Advertisement" to his *Analogy* and again a few years later in a charge to the diocesan clergy of Durham, where he lamented the "general decay of religion." Yet pessimism of this type, no less than others at the time, was almost never unalloyed:

24. Richard [Terrick], *A Sermon Preached before the Incorporated Society for the Propagation of the Gospel in Foreign Parts . . . February 17, 1764* (London, 1764), 30–31. On the outlets that developed for previously stifled religious enthusiasm, and on the related increase from the 1730s in spiritual vitality, religious feeling, and vigorous belief, see John H. Overton and Frederic Relton, *The English Church from the Accession of George I. to the End of the Eighteenth Century (1714–1800)* (London, 1906), 203, 4; Stephen, *English Thought in the Eighteenth Century*, 2:324; Gerald R. Cragg, *The Church and the Age of Reason, 1648–1789* (Harmondsworth, Eng., 1970), 139. R. A. Knox argues that enthusiasm and keen interest in the last things have historically gone hand in hand: *Enthusiasm: A Chapter in the History of Religion; With Special Reference to the XVII and XVIII Centuries* (Oxford, 1950), 157, 545–46.

it usually led not to gloom but to optimism about the future of religion. Butler himself counseled against despair on the grounds that scripture predicted the "great defection from . . . religion which should be in the latter days," that is, just before the glorious millennium. As "miserable as the condition of [religion] is at present," wrote Warburton in 1771, "I am confident it will revive again."[25]

Hopefulness grew out of negativism in a kind of wish-fulfillment. John Warren (1730–1800), bishop of Bangor, told the s.p.g. in 1787 that the present dissolute state of the Christian world hindered the progress of the gospel. Nonetheless, he fully expected Christianity to spread and improve. Though all efforts to propagate the word of God "have not hitherto proved very effectual," he said, "yet great and glorious changes, even a *New Earth, wherein dwelleth Righteousness,* may be produced by ways and means, of which we are now ignorant." Speaking to the same group eighteen years earlier, Thomas Newton (1704–82), a fairly conservative theologian who held the see of Bristol, contended that in "these degenerate times" Christianity has been "retarded in its progress" by heresy, schism, and debauchery. He declared, however, that present conditions actually served the "wise ends and purposes of providence," since they permitted God to "bring good out of evil, light out of darkness, and turn even the infidelity of some into arguments to beget and nourish faith in others." He urged men to participate in realizing the divine aim of making Christianity universal, as did Edmund Keene (1714–81), bishop of Chester. Keene knew of people who were "disheartened at the gloomy and melancholy State of Christianity." But instead of sinking into despondency, he asserted, "we ought rather to be stimulated on that Account, to a more vigorous Exertion of our own Endeavours to enlarge the Kingdom of Christ." Furthermore, the Christian who is grieved at the "State to which Christianity is reduced . . . will com-

25. [Thomas Secker], *The Charge of Thomas Lord Bishop of Oxford to the Clergy of his Diocese, In his Primary Visitation 1738,* 2d ed. (London, 1739), sig. A2r[3]-4; Butler, *Analogy* and "A Charge delivered to the Clergy at the Primary Visitation of the Diocese of Durham, in the year MDCCLI," in *Works,* 1:1–2, and 2:397–98; Warburton to Richard Hurd, Sept. 23, 1771, in *Letters from a Late Eminent Prelate, to One of His Friends* (Kidderminster, [1809]), 347. For views strikingly similar to those of Butler, see George Berkeley, "Primary Visitation Charge" (delivered to the clergy of the diocese of Cloyne, mid-1730s), in *The Works of George Berkeley, Bishop of Cloyne,* ed. A. A. Luce and T. E. Jessop, 9 vols. (London, 1948–57), 7:161. Anticlericalism and the perception (among Dissenters as well as Anglicans) of religious decay are discussed in Overton and Relton, *The English Church 1714–1800,* 63, 164; Cragg, *Reason and Authority,* 25; idem, *The Church and the Age of Reason,* 134.

fort himself" with the "pleasing Hope" that true religion "is likely to make its Progress into those Places where it shineth not at present," and with the promise of Christ "that he will, in his own good Time, render it triumphant in every Part of the World."[26]

This pattern of thought—the sense of living in times of religious trouble, accompanied by the dream of a far better future brought about by redoubled human effort working in concert with the divine plan—has been called the "afflictive model of progress." It is at least as old as the prophets of the eighth century B.C. and has often appeared in Christianity when the faith has come under attack or the faithful have encountered hard times.[27] In this historical context, it should not be surprising that the expectation of improvement in religion provided psychological comfort to eighteenth-century clerics. Confronted with deism, anticlericalism, and what they thought to be increasing irreligion, they found solace in hopes of a new world to come.

Doctrines of progress in religion had intellectual as well as psychological appeal, because of their kinship with other, quite common conceptions. One of these was the idea of the pilgrim's progress. From St. Peter and Augustine to Langland and Bunyan, the image of an individual's advance toward salvation through an ever-closer approach to the way of Christ lay near the center of Christian thought, and it remained familiar in the eighteenth century. The Yorkshire vicar Wilson Bewicke (fl. 1747–88) reasserted it in a sermon of 1759, drawing an analogy between the growth of a seed "by a regular Progress to produce the full Corn in the Ear" and the germination of the "good Seed of the Gospel . . . in the Heart, until it grows up by gradual Advances, and brings forth the Fruits of Righteousness to Perfection" in a Christian. Bewicke focused on the individual man, but it was only a short step from the idea of a single pilgrim's progress to the notion of the collective pilgrims' progress of all Christianity or even

26. John [Warren], A Sermon Preached before the Incorporated Society for the Propagation of the Gospel in Foreign Parts . . . February 17, 1787 (London, 1787), xiii–xiv, xxxvi; Thomas Newton, On the imperfect Reception of the Gospel. A Sermon Preached before the Incorporated Society for the Propagation of the Gospel in Foreign Parts . . . February 17, 1769 (London, 1769), 11, 14–15, 17–18; Keene, Sermon before the S.P.G. 1757, 5–6, 19–21. See also George Berkeley, A Sermon Preached before the Incorporated Society for the Propagation of the Gospel in Foreign Parts . . . February 18, 1732, in Works, 7:124–28.

27. On the "afflictive model of progress" and the eighteenth-century New England eschatologists who used it, see James West Davidson, The Logic of Millennial Thought: Eighteenth-Century New England (New Haven, 1977), 129–41.

all humankind. Thus, David Hartley could discuss both the "gradual Progress in the spiritual Life" of one soul and the "Progress that Christ's Religion made" in ancient and more recent times.[28]

In high eighteenth-century Britain, such conceptual transference or "displacement" was facilitated by the emergence of a more social view of religion and by the growth of domestic and foreign missionary activity. A new emphasis (except among some evangelicals) on moral rather than personal religious concerns and the rise of movements like the s.p.g. and s.p.c.k. testify to the increasingly social outlook of British Christianity. The same is true of the heightened sensitivity of the clergy to contemporary social problems, ranging from "Gin Lane" to slavery to the penal system anathematized by the Vicar of Wakefield. It was no accident that men like Wesley—who declared that the "gospel of Christ knows no religion, but social; no holiness but social holiness"—and the bishops who spoke before the s.p.g. conceived of religious progress in collective terms.[29]

Perhaps even more important to the popularity of doctrines of progress in religion was their close affinity to the belief that the arts and sciences had advanced and would continue to do so. Warburton, Joseph Butler, Napleton, David Hartley, and Taylor all justified their opinion that religion was progressive by pointing to positive changes in worldly learning. As Terrick remarked, Christianity must slowly improve, just like science. In addition, Hartley and Watson agreed with Green that religion benefited from the "gradual improvement in arts and knowledge." Living in an enlightened age "in which knowledge is still increasing," wrote Robert Lowth (1710–87), bishop of London, "may we not hope that these improvements will have their proper and natural effect . . . in introducing a reformation of another nature . . . ?"[30] Quite clearly, then, those who found the idea

28. Wilson Bewicke, *The State of Grace illustrated from Nature: Or, Its Growth shewn to be gradual, its Operation imperceptible, but by its Fruits; and its Fruits a proper Ground of Assurance* (London, 1760), vi, 3; David Hartley, *Observations*, 2:132, 189–90. For an extended contemporary treatment of the pilgrim's progress, see the well-known work of the Nonconformist educator Philip Doddridge, *The Rise and Progress of Religion in the Soul* (1745), in *The Miscellaneous Works of Philip Doddridge, D.D.* (London, 1839), 7–114.

29. John Wesley and Charles Wesley, *Hymns and Sacred Poems* (1739), in *Works of John Wesley*, 14:321. On the degree to which religion had a developing social orientation, see G. R. Cragg, "The Churchman," in James L. Clifford, ed., *Man versus Society in Eighteenth-Century Britain: Six Points of View* (Cambridge, 1968), 63–69. Conceptual displacement is discussed below, chap. 8.

30. Terrick, *Sermon before the S.P.G. 1764*, 8; Green, *Sermon before the S.P.G.*

of progress to fit the case of the sciences and arts could easily apply it to the subject of religion, and this extension of the idea occurred with considerable frequency.

Tradition and influence, strategic, psychological, and intellectual appeal: each of these helped to make the belief in religious progress widespread. But regardless of its sources and popularity, was R. S. Crane right to claim that this belief grew into a "comprehensive progressivist philosophy," "a distinctive theory of the general progress of man"? In fact, such displacement frequently *did* occur from about 1770 on. Bishop Moss, for example, after predicting the universal establishment and full flowering of Christianity, went on to describe the consequences of that development. Human nature would change, he said, and with the subduing of passions and cessation of violence would come an "uninterrupted scene of peace, harmony, and joy." Furthermore, the earth would yield up its fruits in "constant and uniform abundance," copiously rewarding the diligence of its tillers. During that "golden aera," mankind would enjoy "a state of plenty, ease and splendor; and partake of every blessing that can exalt the mind or gratify the heart." In short, men would find themselves once again in "an earthly paradise."[31]

Moss's expectations were unique in their degree of utopianism. But other clergymen who did not foresee the coming of a second paradise, and who reflected on the past as well as the future, also traced broad, secular progress to a divine plan for propagating and perfecting religion. Brownlow North declared that the

> history of man, considered as to the various circumstances of his condition, during the course of God's dispensations towards him, affords ample proof that all moral and literary improvement, the unfolding and spreading of science, throughout different ages, and in different countries, are all conducted by the hand of Providence; and made instrumental in this one great design.

Likewise, Lowth discovered the "hand of Providence" in many important events that had distinguished recent times, including the revival and increase of the arts and sciences, the invention of print-

1768, 22; *Sermons, and Other Remains, of Robert Lowth, D.D.*, ed. Peter Hall (London, 1834), 91 (sermon delivered July 27, 1758).

31. Crane, "Anglican Apologetics," 225–26, 286–87; Moss, *Sermon before the S.P.G. 1772*, xv–xvi.

ing, the Reformation, geographical discoveries, the improvement of navigation, and the extension of commerce. These developments, he thought, mutually promoted each other. Together they were evidence of "a general effort, under a superior direction," toward a single goal: the "union and comprehension of the affairs of mankind in one great system," namely, the "spiritual Kingdom of Christ." Claiming that "civilization and knowledge are in a progressive state," John Moore (1729–1802), bishop of Bangor, took great comfort in the developments cited by Lowth. For he regarded them as "circumstances favourable to the dissemination of true Christianity," and as "so many signs . . . that the great plan of Providence, with respect to its future prevalence and completion, is gradually unfolding itself."[32]

As their comments indicate, these clergymen held a view of history very similar to the old "Christian idea of progress" described by Mommsen. Unlike Augustine, they thought that improvement in secular affairs played a role in God's program for mankind. As with him and the other Fathers, however, so with them it was the divine scheme that really mattered, that gave context and focus to their historical thinking. Their belief in secular progress formed part of a Christian, not a secularized vision of history. Except on the basis of Bury's opinion, it is no paradox that for them progress and providence were conjoined rather than divorced. And this is equally true of the others who, in eighteenth-century Britain, enunciated doctrines of progress in religion.

ESCHATOLOGY

Following in Bury's footsteps, a number of mid-twentieth-century scholars from various disciplines accepted his definition of the idea of progress while expanding upon his general theory that Christianity contributed to the development of the idea. Christopher Dawson, Carl Becker, John Baillie, and Rudolph Bultmann, for instance, all claimed that the modern belief in progress—which they saw as an exclusively modern belief—actually derived from Christian conceptions. In their opinion, teleology and providentialism,

32. North, Sermon before the S.P.G. 1778, 5; Robert [Lowth], A Sermon Preached before the Incorporated Society for the Propagation of the Gospel in Foreign Parts . . . February 15, 1771 (London, 1771), 26–27; John [Moore], A Sermon Preached before the Incorporated Society for the Propagation of the Gospel in Foreign Parts . . . February 15, 1782 (London, 1782), 14–15.

eschatology[33] and redemptionism sank so deeply into the European mind as to be ineradicable, even when Christianity itself had serious challenges to confront. But what could not be extirpated, these scholars argued, could be and eventually was secularized, largely by the philosophes. Through one general agency or another, ranging from social discontents to anti-Christian polemics to general opposition to supernaturalism, the men of the Enlightenment shifted the perceived goal of history from otherworldly salvation to continual betterment of temporal life in posterity, and they located the supposed source of positive change in reasoning, perfectible man rather than in divine providence or the returned Christ. Yet the resulting idea of progress, in the nineteenth century as well as the eighteenth, retained a strong if usually hidden dependence on the old faith of Christianity in a future goal. The modern idea of progress is therefore what Karl Löwith has called a "secular religion of progress," simply "substituting an indefinite and immanent *eschaton* for a definite and transcendent one."[34]

This thesis has considerable merit. It properly points out that the Christian expectation of the coming kingdom of God and the belief in the historical improvement of worldly affairs have much in common, especially when seen in contrast to the nonhistorical or cyclical thought of oriental and classical cultures. It also correctly indicates

33. In what follows, the term "eschatology" is used to refer to the analysis of "the last things" as a whole. "Apocalypticism" and "chiliasm" denote a variety of eschatology that concentrates on the destruction and revolutionary changes to be brought about by the Second Coming of Christ. "Millennialism" (referred to by some scholars as "millenarianism")—a brand of eschatology that particularly focuses on the millennium and its arrival—is of two types: "premillennialism" places the thousand-year period after the Parousia, while "postmillennialism" places it before that event.

34. Christopher Dawson, *Progress and Religion: An Historical Enquiry* (New York, 1929), 190–91; Carl Becker, *The Heavenly City of the Eighteenth-Century Philosophers* (New Haven, 1932), 122–30, 139–51; idem, "Progress," in *Encyclopedia of the Social Sciences*, 15 vols. (New York, 1930–35), 12:495:2–497:2; John Baillie, *The Belief in Progress* (New York, 1951), 94–95, 106, 113–14, 187; Rudolf Bultmann, *History and Eschatology: The Presence of Eternity* (New York, 1957), 65–73; Karl Löwith, *Meaning in History* (Chicago, 1949), 83–84, 113–14, 61–62, 91–112. For similar views, see Helmut Richard Niebuhr, *The Kingdom of God in America* (Chicago, 1937), 182–83, 189–90; Charles Frankel, *The Faith of Reason: The Idea of Progress in the French Enlightenment* (New York, 1948), 126, 154; Frank E. Manuel, *The Prophets of Paris: Turgot, Condorcet, Saint-Simon, Fourier, and Comte* (Cambridge, Mass., 1962), 46–48; Charles Webster, *The Great Instauration: Science, Medicine and Reform 1626–1660* (London, 1975), 506–07. Much of the literature on this issue is reviewed in W. Warren Wagar, "Modern Views of the Origins of the Idea of Progress," *Journal of the History of Ideas* 28 (Jan.–March 1967): 62–66.

that modern advocates of progress, unlike medieval Christians, have frequently envisioned ever-continuing, man-made improvements in history. Nevertheless, the theory of *secularization* erected by Dawson, Becker, and the others rests on rather unstable ground. For one thing, many of the philosophes actually had serious reservations about the possibility of ongoing human advancement and hence hardly turned Christian conceptions, or anything else, into a secular religion of progress. Equally important, very little concrete evidence (and none at all from British sources) has been offered to demonstrate with exactness—rather than merely to suggest—how this transformation occurred. Vague references to the naturalistic predisposition, social discontentment, and antireligious polemics of the Enlightenment can perhaps establish the tone of a secularizing process but not the method by which it took place.

In an attempt to bridge the gap between theory and proof, Ernest Lee Tuveson considered this process in a different context, that of seventeenth- and eighteenth-century English Christian thought. He, too, made the assumption that the idea of progress was distinctively modern, but his thesis about its emergence offers greater precision and sophistication. The idea developed, he contended, through the combination of a revived millennialism with the "New Philosophy." In this partnership, the older element played the larger conceptual role, while the new science and its method served as secularizing agents: they transformed the Christian millennium into an earthly utopia and transferred the action of providence in history to natural laws.[35]

To substantiate his argument, Tuveson analyzed in detail the late seventeenth-century eschatological writings of the Cambridge Platonist Henry More, the scientist Robert Boyle, the conservative religious controversialist John Edwards, and, especially, the Anglican physico-theologian Thomas Burnet. These scholars, he asserted, displayed a decidedly naturalistic outlook in their discussion of the future events prophesied in the Bible, especially by attempting to account for any coming changes in the earthly environment without recourse to immediate divine intervention. In addition, they foresaw the advance of scientific knowledge as an integral feature of the mil-

35. Ernest Lee Tuveson, *Millennium and Utopia: A Study in the Background of the Idea of Progress*, Harper Torchbook ed. (New York, 1964), vi, viii–xi, 3–7, 201. This edition contains an interesting additional preface not appearing in the first edition (Berkeley, 1949).

lennium, which all of them except Edwards believed would *follow* the conflagration and transformation of the earth mentioned in the Book of Revelation. During this thousand-year period, there would be great improvement in the moral nature of man and in the conditions of human existence. Life would become happy, just, and (in the opinion of Burnet and Edwards, at least) convenient and easy, with increased soil fertility, lengthened life spans, and a common language for all mankind. In short, these eschatologists looked upon the millennium as a paradisiacal, utopian era. According to Tuveson, this general position was reasserted and elaborated by a "group of influential eighteenth-century millennialists." He represented them as continuing to substitute the laws of nature for providence in the working out of historical improvement, and as producing an increasingly secularized notion of progress.[36]

This analysis would seem to provide a solid basis of support for the broad claim of Löwith and the others that Christian historical conceptions were transformed into the modern idea of progress, and that the change had been essentially completed by the time of the Enlightenment. And in fact Tuveson's line of argument is unquestionably correct in one important respect. For seventeenth-century English eschatology *did* mark the emergence of some important new trends in the interpretation of prophecies relating to "the last things"— trends of great significance for the eighteenth century.

Although the ultimate source of Christian eschatological thought lies in ancient Judaic culture, not until the late first-century Book of Revelation was a definite program for the last things mapped out. The writer of Revelation combined Jewish apocalyptic imagery (including the Beast of the Book of Daniel) with Christian ideas to foretell a great struggle, in a number of divinely ordained stages, between the powers of good and evil, culminating in the defeat of the latter. The precise chronological arrangement of these stages is not entirely clear, which goes far to explain the existence over the centuries of many conflicting interpretations of Revelation. In any case, the author of this account predicted the eventual defeat of Antichrist and the binding of his master Satan, a thousand-year period of peace and bliss followed by a brief time of renewed struggle against Gog and Magog, the resurrection of the saints, the general judgment conducted under the auspices of a returned Christ, the destruction of the present heavens and

---

36. Ibid., 71–183 passim (and esp. 93, 120, 123–24, 131–33, 137, 139–51).

earth, and the creation of a new sublunary environment—though not necessarily in that order.[37]

Through the mid-fourth century, Revelation and similar early Christian prophecies enjoyed a considerable theological vogue. Thereafter eschatology began to lose its fascination for Christian intellectuals, and for the next thousand years Augustine's de-historicized brand of eschatology, usually called "amillennialism," held sway (except, of course, in popular apocalypticism). Until the Reformation, virtually all theologians believed that there would never be any millennium other than the one in which all people had been living since the time of Christ. But the emergence of Protestantism was accompanied by a reinvigoration of interest in eschatology, beginning on the Continent and spreading quickly to the British Isles. By the Elizabethan era English and Scottish theologians had become familiar with the ideas that the popes were the embodiment of Antichrist and that Revelation and Daniel could serve as forecasting tools. Shortly after 1600 came a fundamental change in interpretation, when several Continental Reformed theologians like Johann Heinrich Alsted and Johann Piscator reached the conclusion that the millennium lay not in the past or present but in the future. Joseph Mede (1586–1638), a Cambridge theologian and professor of Greek, popularized this new view in England, arguing that the millennium might occur as soon as the early 1700s, with the reappearance of Christ. In this form, belief in a future millennium became quite common among English divines in the era of the Civil Wars and Interregnum. Meanwhile, the pope was often replaced by the Anglican episcopacy, Parliament, the Protectorate, or even the universities as the incarnation of Antichrist. These years also saw the emergence among Puritans and Separatists of a scholarly premillennialism fathered by Mede, and among sectarians like the Fifth Monarchists a more militant apocalypticism of the sort that had appeared so frequently in medieval and Renaissance Europe.[38]

37. For an excellent short account of the eschatology in the Book of Revelation, see Davidson, *Logic of Millennial Thought*, 3–12.

38. For the eschatology of late antiquity, the Middle Ages, and the Continental Reformation, I draw here especially on Norman Cohn, *The Pursuit of the Millennium: Revolutionary Messianism in Medieval and Reformation Europe and Its Bearing on Modern Totalitarian Movements*, 2d ed. (New York, 1961), 8–123, 251–306; Peter Toon, "Introduction," in idem, ed., *Puritans, the Millennium and the Future of Israel: Puritan Eschatology 1600–1660* (Cambridge, 1970), 9–19; Mommsen, "Christian Idea of Progress," 349–50, 355–57, 370–73; Tuveson, *Millennium and Utopia*, 14–18, 24–

What these two brands of eschatology had in common was the expectation of an imminent millennium, which enabled them to provide a useful ideological framework for the religious, political, and sometimes social reforms their proponents desired. Not surprisingly, the more conservative Anglicans and Scottish Presbyterians tended to oppose and even directly to attack eschatology of both varieties. Meanwhile, premillennialism was establishing a close relationship to the new science, especially because the study of the last things could provide natural philosophy with a new context and new goals. According to Daniel 12:4, in the latter ages "many shall run to and fro and knowledge shall be increased." This passage had been central to the *instauratio magna* of Bacon and the *pansophia* of Comenius, and it served as a rallying cry for Puritan scientists and eschatologists. They believed with Hakewill that knowledge had been increasing in recent centuries and that in many respects the moderns were superior to the ancients. As a result, they thought that Daniel's prophecy was being fulfilled and looked forward to its completion in an imminent era of great intellectual achievement: the advancement of human learning, guided by the programs of Bacon and Comenius, was to be an integral part of the millennium. Furthermore, when applied to practical pursuits this advance in learning would restore the lost human dominion over nature and thereby improve society.

In short, many Puritan reformers envisioned the millennium as a scientifically created utopia—"a dramatic leap forward which would achieve not only totally successful religious concord, but also social amelioration and intellectual renewal." Here was a doctrine of general progress surpassing in vision even the old "Christian idea of progress." But it, too, was ultimately "religious in motivation," not secu-

---

34, 36–43; John W. O'Malley, "Historical Thought and the Reform Crisis of the Early Sixteenth Century," *Theological Studies* 28 (Sept. 1967): 534–35, 544–46; Katharine R. Firth, *The Apocalyptic Tradition in Reformation Britain 1530–1645* (Oxford, 1979), 9–13, 32–37. The interpretation of English and Scottish eschatology here and in the next paragraph represents an attempt to reconcile the following sources: Bernard Capp, "*Godly Rule* and English Millenarianism," *Past and Present*, no. 52 (Aug. 1971): 106–17; idem, "The Millennium and Eschatology in England," *Past and Present*, no. 57 (Nov. 1972): 156–62; Firth, *Apocalyptic Tradition*; Christopher Hill, *Antichrist in Seventeenth-Century England* (London, 1971); William M. Lamont, "Puritanism as History and Historiography: Some Farther Thoughts," *Past and Present*, no. 44 (Aug. 1969): 133–46; idem, "Richard Baxter, the Apocalypse and the Mad Major," *Past and Present*, no. 55 (May 1972): 68–90; Toon, *Puritans, Millennium and Israel*, 23–114; Tuveson, *Millennium and Utopia*, 34–36, 43–54, 75–92; Webster, *Great Instauration*, 1–31.

lar. For it was God who "would allow science to become the means to bring about a new paradise on earth," and Puritan science was dominated by eschatological aims and pursued rather "for its value in confirming the power of providence" than as an end in itself.[39]

With the Restoration, Puritan hopes for an imminent millennium quite naturally receded from the center of English thought, and militant apocalypticism largely disappeared. But concern with the last things was by then too deeply traditional a current of British Protestantism to dry up altogether. From the 1660s through the 1690s it flowed on very largely in the form of scholarly interpretations of Biblical prophecies. The clerics who undertook this exegetical labor included Anglicans like Drue Cressener and Scottish Presbyterians like Robert Fleming and his son of the same name, as well as Dissenters such as Hanserd Knollys, William Sherwin, and Thomas Beverley. They uniformly placed the millennium in the future, coincident with or after the Second Coming, and (though this is not entirely true of Richard Baxter during the 1680s) they reverted to the old tendency to identify Antichrist exclusively with the papacy. In spite of the occasional calculation of dates for key eschatological events, the fervent sense of enormous impending changes and the expectation of a utopian millennium, so common during the Civil Wars and Interregnum, became exceptional after 1660.[40] Likewise, in the late seventeenth century the Puritan linkage of science to eschatology seems to have survived only among the handful of men whom Tuveson analyzed, More, Boyle, Burnet, Whiston, and Edwards. But they did add a new strand to this linkage: a *somewhat* more naturalistic outlook on the last things, reflected principally in their frequent ascription of the physical changes associated with the conflagration and arrival of the millennium to the operation of uniform natural laws.

39. Webster, *Great Instauration*, 7, 506–07, xvi, 27, 30.
40. Christopher Hill, *Puritanism and Revolution: Studies in Interpretation of the English Revolution of the 17th Century*, new ed. (New York, 1964), 328–36; Le Roy Edwin Froom, *The Prophetic Faith of Our Fathers: The Historical Development of Prophetic Interpretation*, 4 vols. (Washington, D.C., 1946–54), 2:576–96, 642–49; De Jong, *As the Waters Cover the Sea*, 81–82; Capp, "*Godly Rule* and English Millenarianism," 117; idem, "The Millennium and Eschatology in England," 160–61; Lamont, "Richard Baxter, the Apocalypse and the Mad Major," 68, 80, 83, 87; Davidson, *Logic of Millennial Thought*, 57–59, 161–63. It is certainly not the case that during the period from the 1680s through the reign of Anne "It was . . . left to Baptists and other sectarians, and perhaps more significantly to the astrologers, to bring millenarianism before the wider public": Bernard Capp, *English Almanacs, 1500–1800: Astrology and the Popular Press* (Ithaca, 1979), 251.

Here obviously we find a new departure in eschatology, one that can be traced to the "new philosophy" of the *virtuosi.* Nonetheless, too much can be attributed to what these millennialists were saying. Tuveson referred to the "naturalistic bias" and "insistence on the operation of regular [physical] laws" in More's account of the last things. He claimed that according to Burnet the Deluge "came about through no divine intervention, but only the natural and inescapable sequence of physical events," just as eventually, "again by the operation of physical forces, the earth will be set on fire, something like the Stoic rebirth of nature will take place, and a renovated earth will rise like a phoenix." This conception was treated by Tuveson as part of "a theory of progress" in which the history of the earth and the history of man were reconciled "as parallel developments, caused by the workings of natural law." Similarly, he contended that Whiston—whom he called one of "the scientific, progressive millennialists"—sought to demonstrate that the transformation of the earth and the inauguration of the millennium "could be accounted for without recourse to the immediate intervention of Providence." And Edwards, according to Tuveson, carried this "secularizing tendency" even further. In other words, late seventeenth-century English eschatology "tended more and more to become a dogma of this worldly progress implemented by secondary causes."[41]

But this line of argument does not entirely stand up under careful scrutiny. Like their Puritan predecessors, Burnet and the others *did* contend that the millennium would see a great advance in human knowledge, and they *did* believe in broadly gauged future progress. This belief, however, continued to remain within a decidedly eschatological context, and the preoccupation with an earth-destroying great conflagration, resurrected saints, and the return of Christ can hardly be considered secular. Moreover, any description of these commentators on the last things as displaying a naturalistic bias requires substantial qualification.

It is true that Burnet, for instance, did not want to "flie to miracles, where Man and Nature are sufficient" for the explanation of particular physical events, since this "breaks the chains of Natural Providence, when it is done without necessity, that is, when things are otherwise intelligible from second Causes." But he also insisted that the "other extream is worse than this, for to deny all Miracles, is

41. Tuveson, *Millennium and Utopia,* 93, 117, 131–33; idem, "Swift and the World-Makers," *Journal of the History of Ideas* 11 (Jan. 1950): 55–58.

in effect to deny all reveal'd Religion." And so he asserted that along with

> the ordinary Providence of God in the ordinary course of Nature, there is doubtless an extraordinary Providence that doth attend the greater Scenes and the greater revolutions of Nature. This, methinks, besides all other proof from the Effects, is very rational and necessary in it self; for it would be a limitation of the Divine Power and Will so to be bound up to second causes, as never to use, upon occasion, an extraordinary influence or direction: And 'tis manifest, taking any Systeme of Natural causes, if the best possible, that there may be more and greater things done, if to this, upon certain occasions you joyn an extraordinary conduct.

Such occasions were just the ones with which Burnet was most concerned, and he found "an extraordinary Providence" or "miraculous hand" at work in the formation of the earth and in the Deluge. He expected similar departures from the operation of secondary causes in the conflagration, when angels would manage the consuming fires, and in the Second Coming of Christ, which would be "wholly out of the way of Natural Causes." The heavenly bodies would then be "confus'd and irregular, both in their light and motions; as if the whole frame of the Heavens was out of order, all the laws of Nature were broken or expir'd."[42]

Likewise, Whiston contended in *A New Theory of the Earth* (1696) that God had originally formed the natural world along the lines of a great machine, so that secondary causes alone (specifically, comets) could account for the Flood and the conflagration. This opinion continued to appear in the last edition of the book that he personally prepared for the press before the end of his long life in 1752, as did the general comment that God governs the world without disturbances to "the settled Course of Nature, or a miraculous Interposition on every Occasion." But if Whiston thought that "*Miracles are not ordinarily to be expected,*" he did not deny that they *could* occur. In fact, he wrote in 1749 that "I verily believe Providence is, in an extraordinary Degree, now interposing in the Affairs of the World,

---

42. Thomas Burnet, *The Sacred Theory of the Earth* (1684–90; 2d ed., 1691), repr. ed. (Carbondale, Ill., 1965), 220–21, 280–83, 88–89, 299–301 (Bk. II, Chap. xi; Bk. III, Chaps. viii, xii; Bk. I, Chap. viii).

and beginning to set up the *Millennium,* or the Kingdom of our Lord *Christ.*"[43]

The next year two earthquakes shook London, and Whiston publicly described them as fulfilling some of the prophecies about the last things. Many of "our *minute Philosophers,*" he said in a lecture, "(and very *minute Philosophers* they must be who reason thus) pretend, that all this is done by the *Air,* or *Water,* or *Earth,* or *Fire;* that all this is no more than the necessary Effects of natural Causes." But he knew better. In his view, "an higher Agent or Agents are concern'd in these aerial Explosions" (as he believed the earthquakes to be), so that

> Our Business therefore, is not here with aerial Vapours, with Sulphur, or Nitre, which are the inanimate Instruments on these occasions, &c. but with the rational Instruments themselves employ'd by God . . . no other than the *Angels of Peace,* or *good Angels,* acting according to the Direction of God himself; or else the *evil Angels,* or *wicked Daemons,* acting according to their own evil Inclinations, by God's Permission.[44]

There was clearly room in Whiston's causal analysis of eschatological events for divine interpositions and supernatural beings as well as for the operation of natural laws.

In the same vein, More had serious reservations about the new scientific world-view, which led him to formulate the Platonist notion of a supernatural "Spirit of Nature" and to compile a list of examples demonstrating divine intervention in nature. And as for Boyle himself, although he must be considered an influential popularizer of mechanical philosophy, he always preserved a place in his conception of the operation of the universe for miracles and other suspensions of natural laws by the deity. Such views were quite normal at the time: the belief in and recording of "special" or "extraordinary" providences remained widespread in England, just as in Massachusetts. Even Sir Isaac Newton, as is well known, suggested that the

43. William Whiston, *A New Theory of the Earth, From its Original to the Consummation of All Things. Wherein The Creation of the World in Six Days, The Universal Deluge, And the General Conflagration, As Laid down in the Holy Scriptures, Are shewn to be perfectly agreeable to Reason and Philosophy,* 6th ed. (London, 1755), 431–37, 439, 445 (cf. 1st ed. [London, 1696], 357–63, 367, 371); idem, *Memoirs of the Life and Writings of Mr. William Whiston,* 1st ed. (London, 1749), 626.

44. Idem, *Memoirs,* 2d ed., 2 vols. (London, 1753), 2:58–69, 190, 195, 192–93.

solar system might occasionally require a renewal by its divine artificer. Defending Newton against Leibniz on this and other issues, Samuel Clarke as late as 1715 argued against the analogy of the universe to "a great machine, going on without the interposition of God, as a clock continues to go without the assistance of a clock maker." For this notion "tends, (under the pretence of making God a *supramundane intelligence,*) to exclude providence and God's government in reality out of the world," even in the act of creation, whereas actually "nothing is done without his continual government and inspection." Thus, Tuveson was right for the wrong reasons when he wrote that contemporary scientists "accepted generally [Burnet's] basic assumptions as to the place of natural law in carrying out the will of Providence." In England, at least, if the physico-theologians and others were engaged in "transferring the burden of Providence to 'nature,'" they had not carried the process very far with regard either to cosmology or to eschatology.[45]

Tuveson argued that the secularizing trends he found in late seventeenth-century eschatology became even more pronounced after 1700. But the "group of influential eighteenth-century millennialists" upon whom he based this conclusion actually includes only three men, Bishop Thomas Sherlock, Law, and Worthington. Sherlock and Law cannot really be considered "millennialists" at all, since their writings virtually never mention the millennium or the last things in general. And while it is true that Worthington wrote much more extensively on this topic than did either of the others, his opinions do not completely support Tuveson's theory of seculariza-

---

45. Samuel Clarke, "First Reply" (Nov. 26, 1715), in H. G. Alexander, ed., *The Leibniz-Clarke Correspondence* (Manchester, 1956), 14; Tuveson, "Swift and the World-Makers," 55–56; idem, *Millennium and Utopia*, 119. On More, Boyle, and Newton (who certainly was of two minds on this whole question), see Webster, *Great Instauration*, 149–50; Richard S. Westfall, *Science and Religion in Seventeenth-Century England* (New Haven, 1958) 73–92, 200–06. Examples of the continued belief—throughout the seventeenth century—in divine intervention through the exercise of "special" providences are contained in Perry Miller, *The New England Mind: The Seventeenth Century* (Boston, 1961), 224–31; Keith Thomas, *Religion and the Decline of Magic* (New York, 1971), 89–96, 109.

Burnet and Whiston were criticized by contemporaries (including, significantly, Edwards) for going even so far as they did in a naturalistic direction: J.[ohn] Keill, *An Examination of Dr. Burnet's Theory of the Earth: with some Remarks on Mr. Whiston's New Theory of the Earth* (1698), 2d ed., corr. (Oxford, 1734), 16–28; Davidson, *Logic of Millennial Thought*, 89–90.

tion.[46] In fact, almost no evidence for that theory can be adduced from eighteenth-century British eschatology.

Nonetheless, there *was* a widespread and enduring British interest in the last things from the reign of Anne through the era of the French Revolution, and it took two basic forms. One of these was that ever-recurring feature of the history of Christianity, popular apocalypticism, which erupted quite visibly on several occasions. Early in the century, for example, the exiled French Camisards and their English converts prophesied the return of Christ, the burning of London, and the end of the world. They despised learning, encouraged a withdrawal from earthly affairs, and often claimed to possess special gifts and miraculous powers. These characteristics and the accompanying adventist outlook make it clear that the Camisards did not secularize eschatology or possess anything like a naturalistic bias. Much the same is true of the many clerics and laymen who associated the earthquakes at London and Lisbon (and elsewhere) during the 1750s with the working out of the last things. There were some attempts at the time to explain these phenomena in a wholly naturalistic way, but not among the eschatologically minded—who, like Whiston, pointed instead to God's will as the ultimate or even immediate cause of the upheavals. The Anglican Thomas Wilson (1703–84) and many other clergymen preached on this subject to "very attentive and serious" congregations. At the time of the London temblors, he was typical in praying that "God fit us for whatever His Providence shall think fit." According to one "A. B—e," writing in the *Gentleman's Magazine*, the Lisbon catastrophe heralded the "glorious kingdom of the millennium" and was "seemingly supernatural, as if it came to pass under the direction of a *particular* providence." The same mixture of apocalyptic despair and millennial optimism in evidence during the earthquake frenzy also permeated the numerous chiliastic movements of the 1790s, which sprang up among radicals and the common people. At that time Richard Brothers and many

46. On Worthington's eschatology, see below, chap. 8. The book by Law in which Tuveson found "millennialist" ideas dealt very briefly with eschatological subjects in only two places, where Law indicated that men should study the signs of the times and that the latter days "cannot be far off": *Considerations on the Theory of Religion* (1745), ed. George Henry Law, new ed. (London, 1820), 202n, 221–22. Law's other works do not show even this much interest in eschatology. Sherlock was concerned with Old Testament prophecies about the coming of the Messiah rather than with Revelation and the last things.

others predicted both the coming great destruction and the arrival of an egalitarian paradise. But their dreams of a better society, unlike those of nineteenth-century Owenism, were not yet grounded in the scientific spirit or a faith in the possibilities of science.[47]

During the eighteenth century, the other basic form of concern with the last things was study and elucidation of the prophecies of Daniel and the New Testament. Such work was undertaken by British Protestant ecclesiastics of virtually all persuasions, and it enjoyed great popularity and respectability throughout the period, especially from the 1730s on.[48]

47. *The Diaries of Thomas Wilson, D.D., 1731–1737 and 1750*, ed. C. L. S. Linnell (London, 1964), 231–32; A. B—e, contribution to *The Gentleman's Magazine* 26 (Feb. 1756): 69:1–2. On the three outbursts of eschatological fervor mentioned, see W. H. G. Armytage, *Heavens Below: Utopian Experiments in England, 1560–1960* (Toronto, 1961), 39–43; Hillel Schwartz, "The French Prophets in England," Ph.D. diss., Yale Univ. (Dec. 1974), and its published version, *The French Prophets: The History of a Millenarian Group in Eighteenth-Century England* (Berkeley, 1980); G. S. Rousseau, "The London Earthquakes of 1750," *Cahiers d'histoire mondiale* 11 (1968): 436–51; T. D. Kendrick, *The Lisbon Earthquake* (Philadelphia, [1957]), 11–44, 219–43; E. P. Thompson, *The Making of the English Working Class* (New York, 1963), 48–50, 116–19, 382; Clarke Garrett, *Respectable Folly: Millenarians and the French Revolution* (Baltimore, 1975). British almanacs continued their long tradition of concern with eschatology throughout the eighteenth century, and it is appropriate to contend that "the attempt to fit contemporary events into a millennial pattern was popular with the vast readership": Capp, *English Almanacs*, 252–53, 265, 286.

For a later movement—Owenism—whose interest in the last things more nearly fits Tuveson's secularization thesis, see J. F. C. Harrison, *Quest for the New Moral World: Robert Owen and the Owenites in Britain and America* (New York, 1969), 92–139, and below, chap. 9. Harrison distinguishes between popular apocalypticism and scholarly eschatology (see also his *The Second Coming: Popular Millenarianism, 1780–1850* [New Brunswick, N.J., 1979], 5–7, 231n5), as, in a slightly different way, does Schwartz ("French Prophets," 55–56).

48. In spite of the lack of historical scholarship on this subject for the years 1700–89, Garrett asserts—in his monograph on the 1790s—that there was a "Millenarian Tradition in English Dissent" and that "in the eighteenth century, millenarianism still enjoyed a currency and respectability, even in intellectual circles": *Respectable Folly*, 121–22 (see also Harrison, *Second Coming*, 5, 13–14, and *Quest for the New Moral World*, 95). As we will see, this contention is undoubtedly correct, and it applies to the Anglican and Scottish churches as well as to Nonconformity. Indeed, it is also true of the New England clergy in this period: Davidson, *Logic of Millennial Thought*, 12–13 and passim.

In the following discussion, I focus especially on the years between about 1730 and the outbreak of the French Revolution, in part because of the chronological emphasis of this book, but also because there were relatively fewer eschatological writers during the preceding three decades. The most notable of these were Whiston, Daniel Whitby, Matthew Henry, William Lowth, and Richard Roach, along with Sir Isaac Newton (whose exposition of Daniel and Revelation was not published until 1733) and the

In large measure, the currency of eschatological study was a simple matter of the continuation of an old tradition. Constantly citing the work of their predecessors, the "scholarly eschatologists" of the eighteenth century were merely the latest in a long line of prophecy expositors. But they had special incentives to carry on the labors of the past. Like the belief in religious progress, eschatology provided an acceptable vent for repressed enthusiasm. Thus, Adam Gib (1714–88), a minister of the Church of Scotland, could summarize the sentiments that the prospect of the latter days evoked in him by quoting Vergil's lines:

> O let my soul incessantly presage
> The blissful glories of the coming age!
> May yet my life till then protracted be
> With strength and spirit still enough in me;
> To see and praise that end of present crimes,
> The hopeful dawning of those happy times!

That Gib felt this way in spite of being aware of "the manifold and horrible darkness of the present" is illustrative of another incentive to eschatology: it was—again, like the belief in religious progress—a source of psychological comfort. The Book of Revelation, stated Robert Clayton (1695–1758), an Arian and bishop of Clogher, was written "to enliven our Hopes; to comfort and keep up our Spirits in the Warfare of this Life, with the general Expectation of better Things to come." For him and other clergymen, this warfare had much to do with what John Willison (1680–1750) referred to as the "melancholy" state of the church, "her groans and grievances, defections and backslidings, and the power and success of [her] enemies." In the face of these troubles, Willison, an evangelical from Dundee, believed that good eschatological tidings "may be of *consolation* to all the friends of Christ."[49]

Huguenot exile Charles Daubuz. Some of them are occasionally cited below, since their opinions generally conform to those of their successors.

49. Adam Gib, *A Memorial and Remonstrance, Read before the Associate Synod, at Edinburgh; May 2, 1782* (Edinburgh, 1784), 60; Robert [Clayton], *A Dissertation on Prophecy, Wherein the Coherence and Connexion of the Prophecies in both the Old and New Testament are fully considered; Together with an Explanation of the Revelation of St. John* (London, 1749), 150; Willison, *Balm of Gilead*, in *Works*, 2:108. See also John Milner, *Signs of the Times. In Two Discourses Delivered at Peckham in Surrey: On the General Fast, February 11, 1757. Wherein some Grand Events of Scripture Prophecy are considered and improved* (London, 1757), 33–44. Garrett is right to claim that English scholarly eschatology was a continuing tradition which fed on itself,

Indeed, the challenge of the later deists provided yet one more incentive for studying scriptural texts relating to the last things. In the mid-1720s, Anthony Collins launched a vigorous attack on the belief that Biblical prophecy as a whole had been fulfilled. Thereafter, orthodoxy and its opponents alike treated prophecy as one of the twin pieces of evidence (miracles being the other) on which the case of Christianity would stand or fall. This outlook remained long after the deist controversy had subsided. As late as 1768, Warburton founded an annual lectureship designed to establish the truth of prophecy and, therefore, of the Christian faith. In such a theological climate, it was natural that there should have been a proportionately larger number of scholarly eschatologists after the 1720s than before. The Baptist Gill reflected their conscious motivation when he noted that by proving prophecies about the last things to have been fulfilled, "we may be assured the scripture is divinely inspired."[50]

For all these reasons, scholarly eschatology flourished in eighteenth-century Britain. And in several respects its practitioners did not significantly modify the conclusions of their late seventeenth-century predecessors. For example, they accepted the conviction of the Continental Reformers and their English successors that, as Gill wrote, "whereas great part of prophecy, particularly in the book of Revelations, has been already fulfilled, there is great reason to believe the rest will be." Adopting the historical approach to the study of the last things, they argued "from the actual accomplishment of some things relating to the kingdom of Christ, to the certain completion of others; . . . as sure as the one is fulfilled, so sure shall the other [be]." Consequently, they ransacked the works of historians and antiquarians to find evidence of the realization of sacred predictions in profane history.[51]

although the tradition was broader and deeper than he indicates: Respectable Folly, 15, 125–26, 145, 152–53.

50. John Gill, The sure Performance of Prophecy. A Sermon Preached . . . in Great Eastcheap, Jan. 1st, 1755, 6th ed. (London, 1812), 36. See also David Hartley, Observations, 2:150; Samuel Hallifax, Twelve Sermons on the Prophecies Concerning the Christian Church; and in particular, Concerning the Church of Papal Rome: Preached . . . at the Lecture of The Right Reverend William Warburton (London, 1776), 1, 7. The importance of prophecy and of deist attacks on it is discussed in Roland M. Stromberg, Religious Liberalism in Eighteenth-Century England (Oxford 1954), 71–72; Cragg, Reason and Authority, 54–56, 84–85.

51. Gill, The sure Performance of Prophecy, 3–4. See also Moses Lowman, A Paraphrase on the Revelation of St. John (1737), in A Critical Commentary and Paraphrase on the Old and New Testament and the Apocrypha. By Patrick, Lowth, Arnald, Whit-

They also accepted the by-then traditional view of Mede that the millennium lay in the future, not the past. In fact, most of them simply assumed that this was the case. The others, like the well-preferred liberal Anglican prebendary Thomas Broughton (1704–74), made the assumption explicit by pointedly attempting to expose the "Mistake of supposing [the millennium] to be *already past.*"[52] Since about 1660, this "error" had been committed only by some Continental expositors of prophecy.

In addition, high eighteenth-century eschatologists continued to devote much attention to the figure of Antichrist. Contrary to recent claims, the theory that Antichrist existed was perfectly respectable at this time.[53] Almost no treatment of the prophecies failed to mention him, and many contained elaborate discussions of his past and future role in the last things. Furthermore, as had previously been customary (except for the period from the 1630s to 1660), Antichrist was almost always equated with the Roman Catholic Church in general or the papacy in particular. Broughton saw no need to "spend any Time in proving what has been so often and clearly made out by

by, and Lowman, new ed., 4 vols. (Philadelphia, 1846–48), 4:1011:1, 1014:2, 1018:1–2, 1020:1–2; [John Erskine], *The Signs of the Times Consider'd* (Edinburgh, 1742), iii–iv, 9–13, 15–33; Robert [Clayton], *An Enquiry into the Time of the Coming of the Messiah, and the Restoration of the Jews* (London, 1751), 34–35; John Milner, *Signs of the Times*, 24; Samuel Chandler, *The Signs of the Times* (London, [1759]), 26–27; Thomas Broughton, *A Prospect of Futurity, in Four Dissertations on the Nature and Circumstances of the Life to Come* (London, 1768), 252n; Richard Hurd, *An Introduction to the Study of the Prophecies Concerning the Christian Church; and, in particular, Concerning the Church of Papal Rome* (1772), 4th ed., 2 vols. (London, 1776), 2:201–02; Henry Taylor, *Thoughts on the Nature of the Grand Apostacy* (London, 1781), 169.

52. Broughton, *Prospect of Futurity*, 288–90. For other explicit statements that the millennium was reserved for the future, see Robert Hort, *A Sermon on the Glorious Kingdom of Christ upon Earth, or the Millennium* (Dublin, 1748), 21–22; Thomas Hartley, *Paradise Restored*, 152–68; John Wesley, "The New Creation" (1785), in *Works of John Wesley*, 6:289.

53. Christopher Hill has argued that concern with Antichrist died out about the time of the Restoration and was not revived until the late eighteenth century: *Antichrist in Seventeenth-Century England*, 164, 167. But even in the period 1700–30 the Beast was far from neglected in respected commentaries: see Daniel Whitby, *A Treatise on the True Millennium* (1703), in *Critical Commentary*, 4:1123:2–1125:2; William Whiston, *An Essay on the Revelation of Saint John, So far as concerns the Past and Present Times* (Cambridge, 1706), 85, 88–92, 106–07, 110–16, 191, 252; Matthew Henry, *An Exposition of the Old and New Testament* (1710), 1st American ed., 6 vols. (Philadelphia, 1828), 6:904:1, 911:2, 921:1–922:2; William Lowth, *A Commentary Upon the Larger and Lesser Prophets* (1714–25), in Froom, *Prophetic Faith*, 2:670–71; Isaac Newton, *Observations upon the Prophecies of Daniel, and the Apocalypse of St. John* (London, 1733), 75. In early eighteenth-century almanacs the pope was widely portrayed as Antichrist: Capp, *English Almanacs*, 252.

learned Protestants, that the *Pope* (or *Succession* of *Popes*) or the
Papal Power, is the true ANTICHRIST." (Even so, he devoted ten pages
to correlating prophecies about the Beast with the history of the
papacy.) Other, more conservative Anglicans took the same position.
One of the "learned Protestants" cited by Broughton, Thomas Newton, wrote in great detail on the prophecies fulfilled by various actions of the Antichristian popes. Richard Hurd (1720–1808), archdeacon of Gloucester and an intimate of Warburton, felt that few men
could any longer doubt "this great Protestant principle, *That the Pope
is Antichrist.*" These views also appeared among Scottish Presbyterians like Willison and English Nonconformists such as Gill. Clearly,
d'Alembert was wrong when in 1757 he wrote that in his enlightened
century the pope "is no longer Antichrist for anyone."[54]

When contemporary eschatologists discussed the Beast, they
were not merely repeating accepted platitudes about him. He—and
therefore the papacy—inspired them with real, deep-seated fears and
hopes associated with the supernatural. The fears were similar to the
age-old sense of insidious subversion awakened in Christians by the
contemplation of the devil. Ecclesiastics responded to this sentiment
by urging their fellow men to remain on guard against Antichrist.
John Milner (1687?–1757), a Dissenting minister in Surrey, told his
congregation in 1757 that he found it necessary to discuss this malignant being in order "to awaken your jealousy and zeal against this
power, which we are yet in danger from." Even those few eschatologists who had doubts about the specific identity of the Beast still felt a
dread of permitting him to infiltrate their souls. As Thomas Hartley
declared to his readers in 1764, "look around thee, spectator, and thou
shalt see Anti christ and his retinue also behind thee and on each
hand of thee; and beware lest he be not also within thee." As for the
supernatural hopes connected with Antichrist, they sprang from the

54. Broughton, *Prospect of Futurity*, 260–70; Thomas Newton, *Dissertations on
the Prophecies* (1754), 11th ed., 3 vols. (Perth, 1794), 3:133–60, 322–28; Hurd, *Introduction to the Study of the Prophecies*, 2:53, 217; Willison, *Balm of Gilead*, in *Works*,
2:98–100; Gill, *Watchman's Answer*, 27; idem, *The sure Performance of Prophecy*, 13;
Jean le Rond d'Alembert, "Genève," *Encyclopédie ou Dictionnaire raisonné des sciences, des arts et des métiers*, 17 vols. (Paris, 1751–57, and Neuchâtel, 1765), 7:575:2.
See also David Hartley, *Observations*, 2:370, 450; Henry Taylor, *The Apology of Benjamin Ben Mordecai to His Friends for Embracing Christianity* (1771–77), 2d ed., 2
vols. (London, 1784), 2:903–07, 907n; Hallifax, *Twelve Sermons*, 29; Gib, *Memorial
and Remonstrance*, 7, 10–14. In Scotland, attitudes toward Roman Catholics and the
pope were much more hostile among members of the Popular party than among the
Moderates.

belief that his ultimate defeat and the subsequent millennium would be caused by providential intervention in earthly affairs. "The *Destruction* of the *Papacy*," wrote Broughton, "will be the Work of successive *Judgments* from Heaven."[55]

These fears and hopes illustrate yet another way in which eighteenth-century eschatologists remained within the traditions established by their predecessors: they continued to emphasize the role of the supernatural in the proximate causation of eschatological events. Samuel Chandler (1693–1766), a well-known English Presbyterian and fellow of the Royal Society, was unique in adopting an entirely naturalistic perspective on the last things. He argued in a sermon of 1759 that God, in bringing prosperity or affliction to humankind, never arbitrarily interposed himself so as to "interrupt and pervert his own original constitution." Instead, divine providence acted in concurrence with the laws of nature in order—according to Chandler's curious reasoning—"finally to secure their effect . . . to make the natural connection of things more respectible [sic], and to declare his purpose not to contravene or destroy it." Chandler clearly intended this general thesis to apply to the particular case of the latter days, thereby exceeding even Burnet's degree of naturalism in eschatology. Broughton seemed to do the same when he wrote in 1768 that "the Providence of God, in his greatest and most important Dispensations, acts by the instrumentality of *Natural Causes*." But while Broughton also sought a naturalistic explanation for the conflagration, he admitted, much like Burnet, that the earth could be destroyed by any means that God wished, no matter how unlikely it might seem to human reason. Further, he found it "highly probable, that God will interpose, by a *Special Providence*," to bring about beneficial conditions of life in the millennium.[56]

The other eschatologists who discussed the question of causation insisted even more emphatically on divine interpositions. Robert Hort (b. 1709), chaplain to an Anglican archbishop in Ireland, focused on Providence as the immediate director of eschatological changes in the sublunary world. He asserted that the restoration of the earth to "its primitive Perfection" would come about "through the Merit and

55. Milner, *Signs of the Times*, 22; Thomas Hartley, *Paradise Restored*, 274–75; Broughton, *Prospect of Futurity*, 263.

56. Chandler, *The Signs of the Times*, 24–25; Broughton, *Prospect of Futurity*, 502–13, 294–95. David Hartley, too, seemed to desire to account for the conflagration in a naturalistic way: *Observations*, 2:400.

Power of *Christ*," citing with approval the antique "heathen" belief
that the renovation of the earth would be brought about "by some
Divine Hero." Not confining the operation of the divine plan for the
last things to the laws of nature, he emphasized that God could do
with this world as He pleased. Soon after Hort expressed these views
in 1747, the influential Dissenter and educator Philip Doddridge
(1702–51) took a similar position on the matter of the conflagration.
He believed that "no natural cause could be assigned" to explain the
burning of the earth; he looked instead to "the miraculous power of
Christ, or agency of his angels."[57]

Analyzing causation with regard to prophecies in general, Bishop
Clayton wrote that Biblical predictions did not depend on any visible
"chain of necessary Causes," for only God could fulfill them. In the
historical realization of prophecies, therefore, "the Operation of natural and necessary Causes is excluded." The Nonconformist Milner
agreed with this broad assessment, and he noted specific contemporary signs of the coming of the latter days in which he thought he had
"seen providence step out of its usual course." These signs manifested themselves in the natural as well as the moral world, and they
included unusually strong earthquakes and tidal waves. Were such
events, he inquired, only "the accidental and irregular efforts of natural causes?" Since he did not believe that this view could be reconciled with the "consummate wisdom and goodness, which preside
over the world," he argued that the agitations arose instead from a
divinely ordained alteration of nature. "Don't these shocks," he
asked rhetorically, "seem to be the struggles and pangs of nature,
preceding some change in its constitution? Or rather, is not this the
voice of heaven; the thunder of the Almighty . . . ?"[58]

In a sermon of 1785, John Wesley foresaw a similar dramatic
change in the laws of nature. At the time of the renovation of nature,
there would be no more comets, and "All the elements (taking the

57. Hort, *Sermon on the Glorious Kingdom*, 7, 12, 20, 33, 35; Philip Doddridge, *A Course of Lectures on the Principal Subjects in Pneumatology, Ethics, and Divinity* (written ca. 1749–51; 1st ed. 1763), in *Miscellaneous Works*, 524:1. See also David Imrie, *A Letter From the Reverend Mr. David Imrie. . . . To a Gentleman in the City of Edinburgh. Predicting The speedy Accomplishment of the great, awful and glorious events which the Scriptures say are to be brought to pass in the Latter Times* (Edin-burgh, 1755), 16. Doddridge discussed the London earthquakes in somewhat more naturalistic terms: "The Guilt and Doom of Capernaum" (1750), in *Miscellaneous Works*, 806–07.

58. Clayton, *Dissertation on Prophecy*, 29, 31; Milner, *Signs of the Times*, 30–32.

word in the common sense, for the principles of which all natural beings are compounded) will be new indeed." For example, while fire would retain its "vivifying power," it would lose its ability to destroy. With Wesley, as with Milner, eternal and immutable laws of nature did not exist: God could—and in the last things would—bring about a new order.[59]

The views of Thomas Hartley aptly summarize the eschatologists' attitude toward natural laws and providence in the working out of the last things. He frowned upon "that irreligious kind of philosophy, which teaches men now-a-days to explain away God's warnings and judgments into unmeaning effects from natural causes." Men, he thought, should not "give laws to God," since the deity "is not bound by human prescription, but is pleased at times to vary his proceedings from the ordinary course of things." With this assumption in mind, Hartley went on to discuss the eschatological renovation of nature. When that transformation occurred, he wrote, the present laws of nature would be changed and a new set of "heavenly-physical powers" would replace them. Therefore, he concluded,

> to set up our mechanical philosophy as the test of what is possible or impossible in nature restored, is just as wise, and to as good effect, as to put on spectacles to see what is transacting on the moon.[60]

With only slight dissent, then, contemporary eschatologists retained God as the proximate cause of the events prophesied in the Bible, and they minimized the importance of constant laws of nature. This was not a new tendency in the study of the last things. Nor does it support the theory that an empirical, naturalistic outlook on the world grew up among the members of the British social and political elite between 1680 and 1720 only to be largely rejected by them in the reign of George III, meanwhile finding a new home among the lower orders, Dissenters, and others outside the establishment. In fact, the shift in the "search for causation" from the "providential world" of

59. Wesley, "New Creation," in *Works of John Wesley*, 6:290–91.
60. Thomas Hartley, *Paradise Restored*, 311, 328, 251–52. Belief in the continuing possibility of miracles or special providences was not confined to eschatology and appeared throughout the century, among laymen with scientific interests as well as among clerics. For only a few examples, see David Hartley, *Observations*, 2:138, 143–45, 149; Henry Taylor, *Apology of Ben Mordecai*, 2:938–41; Abraham Tucker, *The Light of Nature Pursued* (1768–78), 3d ed., 2 vols. (London, 1834), 1:527–30 and 2:167; Napleton, *Sermon Preached in the Cathedral Church*, 6–7.

the earlier seventeenth century to the "observable world" associated with the Enlightenment[61] had only barely begun in the age of Newton, as the case of Burnet makes clear. And to the limited degree that there was a naturalistic perspective on the last things in the high eighteenth century, the Anglican Broughton reflects it as much as the Nonconformist Chandler. In the interpretation of prophecy, providentialism did not disappear and then recur; it simply remained the norm, a tradition not yet replaced by the scientific spirit. Tuveson to the contrary notwithstanding, the union of eschatology with the "new philosophy" was still very far from complete during the eighteenth century.

Further evidence of this fact can be found in commentaries on Daniel's prophecy that "knowledge shall be increased." Of all high eighteenth-century eschatologists, only the aged Whiston pointed to a connection between the latter days and scientific progress, writing in his *Memoirs* about the "wonderful *Newtonian* philosophy . . . as an eminent prelude and preparation to those happy times of the restitution of all things." Everyone else focused on the progress of religious—not scientific—knowledge. John Erskine (1721?–1813), a principal leader of the Popular party in the Church of Scotland and a long-time opponent of William Robertson, was typical in this regard. He contended that the religious revivals of his own era provided evidence that the fulfillment of Daniel's prophecy had begun. In the future, he claimed, mankind could expect an even greater "Advance in Divine Knowledge," because of the "Progress that has of late been made in the Study of several Sciences subservient to Divinity, and the clear Views of certain Truths of Religion which the Opposition of Enemies has occasioned." Or as Thomas Hartley put it, "the *knowledge* that shall be *increased*, according to the prophet Daniel, means nothing less than a fruitful, influencing knowledge, a knowledge of things pertaining to God and true godliness."[62] Although it had been

61. The theory and the terms quoted are those of J. H. Plumb, in his "Reason and Unreason in the Eighteenth Century: The English Experience," in idem, *In the Light of History* (New York, 1972), 324.

62. Whiston, *Memoirs*, 2d ed., 1:34 and 2:133–34 (and see also idem, *Essay on Revelation*, 238–39; idem, *The Literal Accomplishment of Scripture Prophecies* [London, 1724], 76–77, 85–86); Erskine, *Signs of the Times Consider'd*, 12–14, 26; Thomas Hartley, *Paradise Restored*, 324–25. Similar statements on this matter are contained in Clayton, *Dissertation on Prophecy*, 142–43; Gill, *Watchman's Answer*, 39; Chandler, *The Signs of the Times*, 44; Wesley, "General Spread of the Gospel," in *Works of John Wesley*, 6:277, 279.

reasserted by a handful of men after the Restoration, the short-lived Puritan dream of the latter days as a time of immense scientific progress did not revive in the next century.

Nonetheless, just as the Puritans, Burnet, and Edwards had turned the millennium into a utopian or paradisiacal state, so did some of their successors. While Hort, for instance, provided few details, he certainly envisioned the millennium as a return to something approximating Eden. The earth, he believed, would regain "its primitive Perfection," and the New Jerusalem would "be, if . . . not the *original* Paradise, analogous to it, and equal to it in Happiness." With righteousness and spiritual enlightenment abounding, mankind would live free from infirmities, pain, sorrow, and even death. Richard Clarke (b. 1723), an Anglican preacher originally from Winchester, similarly looked forward to a *"paradisiacal* world," in which the curses introduced by the Fall would "go away gradually, as the progressive restitution of all things comes on, and is ripening through this *Millennial* reign." Thomas Hartley added flesh to the bare bones of this conception of the millennium. He expected a physical paradise, replete with the sources of happiness: the heavenly bodies would shine forth as never before, the Babel of languages cease, the beasts grow tame, and the earth improve in climate and fertility. Such a view was accepted with only a few modifications by Wesley. He added more material conveniences to Hartley's list and agreed with Hort that "there will be no more death." For him, the millennium would represent not a return to but an actual advance upon Eden: "an unmixed state of holiness and happiness, far superior to that which Adam enjoyed in Paradise," "a more beautiful Paradise than Adam ever saw."[63]

Clayton and Gill went only part way toward the utopian vision. The former emphasized that the millennium would "in general be a Period of great Bliss and Righteousness, over the Face of the whole Earth," but he also mentioned that this "Life of Righteousness" would be set "in the midst of Peace and Plenty." Gill placed spiritual and material factors in balance. After the defeat of Antichrist, he claimed, would come "a time of great prosperity, both temporal and

63. Hort, *Sermon on the Glorious Kingdom*, 8–10, 34; Richard Clarke, *A Series of Letters, Essays, Dissertations, and Discourses on Various Subjects* (London, n.d. [1790?]), 258; Thomas Hartley, *Paradise Restored*, 1, 17, 26–27, 35–36, 81–82, 86–87, 102–03, 135–36, 219, 341–42, 348; Wesley, "New Creation," in *Works of John Wesley*, 6:290–96.

spiritual: . . . the *righteous* will *flourish*, both in things outward and inward." Other eschatologists depicted the millennium in completely spiritual terms, as an epoch in which true religion would flower as never before. Referring to Burnet and Thomas Hartley, Broughton rejected the supposition of "*Millenary* Writers" that the "Earth will be restored to its original *Paradisal* [sic] State." He preferred to interpret prophecy about the millennium as denoting "*figuratively* some or other of those *Spiritual Benefits* and Advantages to Mankind, which are the grand Objects of the *Christian Dispensation.*" Although Doddridge expected a few earthly pleasures during this period, he, too, repudiated the theory that paradise would be restored and evil and death ended. He asserted to the contrary that the "reasonings by which these conjectures are supported are . . . too superficial to need to be confuted." Likewise, the Dissenter Milner and the Scottish evangelical Erskine both treated the millennium as a "*final glorious period of peace, righteousness, and perfection,*" when true religion would permeate every social action and Christian brotherhood would spread. Henry Taylor (1711–85), a Hampshire rector and an Arian, agreed with these assessments. He spoke for many of his contemporaries in arguing that the future new Jerusalem would not be a city of material bliss but "*a political and religiou[s] society,* a people living by certain rules founded on the doctrines of the prophets and apostles," "a state of many years Rest and happiness to [Christ's] Church."[64]

All of the eschatologists, then, anticipated a great increase in righteousness, brotherly love, and religious purity during the millennium. Perhaps half of them went further and predicted the coming of something like the material paradise envisioned by Burnet. But of those who did so not one adopted a naturalistic perspective on the causes of the last things. To the degree that the millennium became a utopia in eschatology, that transformation had nothing to do with the scientific spirit. Certainly, the utopians' view of the future does bear

---

64. Clayton, *Dissertation on Prophecy*, 141, 145; Gill, *Watchman's Answer*, 40; idem, *The Glory of the Church in the Latter Day* (preached 1752), 5th ed. (London, 1793), 33–34 and passim; Broughton, *Prospect of Futurity*, 286n (also 270–73, 286–88, 294–99, 312–13); Doddridge, *Lectures on Pneumatology*, in *Miscellaneous Works*, 527:2–528:1; Milner, *Signs of the Times*, 12, 17; Erskine, *Signs of the Times Consider'd*, 14; Taylor, *Thoughts on the Grand Apostacy*, 199, 190. See also Imrie, *A Letter Predicting glorious Events*, 9. Technically, Gill was referring to conditions in the "spiritual reign of Christ," which would follow the defeat of Antichrist but precede the millennium.

a slight resemblance to the hopes of later European advocates of broadly gauged secular progress. As in past centuries, however, the overriding concern of eschatology remained the divinely ordained program for mankind's religious advancement. The expositors of prophecy uniformly believed deeply that the spiritual relationship between God and man was destined to improve dramatically in the latter days. Like several of the s.p.g. bishops and others, they put forth a doctrine of general religious progress, according to which religion and the church would eventually flourish far more vigorously than ever before. And it was this spiritual progress rather than any change in the secular side of life that really mattered to them. Therefore, they do not provide evidence to support Tuveson's theory that eschatology was secularized by science into the "modern" idea of progress.

Yet if they were not secularizing eschatology in the way Tuveson imagined, they did give the coming of the last things a large and, in some respects, new measure of verisimilitude. Embedded within the interpretive intricacies of their scholarly studies are certain details that indicate a tendency to make the fulfillment of optimistic scriptural predictions as believable as possible, to bring prophecy down to earth and into the realm of the here and now.

This was so in part because they often broke with their predecessors on the crucial question of the order of eschatological events. For instance, many of them rejected premillennialism and placed the Parousia *after* the millennium. "Postmillennialism," as it later came to be known, was popularized by Daniel Whitby's *Treatise of the True Millennium*, an appendix to his *Paraphrase and Commentary on the New Testament* (1703). As a result of an unusual textual reading of Romans 11, Whitby (1638–1726), a Latitudinarian rector and friend of Nonconformity, repositioned the thousand-year period between the fall of Antichrist on the one hand and the Second Advent and resurrection of the saints on the other. The *Treatise* was reprinted seven times by 1760, and Whitby's new theory consequently achieved great popularity. Scottish evangelicals adopted it almost to a man, and so did influential English Nonconformists like Moses Lowman (1680–1752), the well-known Presbyterian. Citing Whitby, he looked for the millennium to take place before the Parousia and general resurrection, and he noted that it could be called the "Kingdom of God, and of his Christ" only in a figurative sense. Doddridge agreed, referring respectfully to both Whitby and Lowman. Postmillennialism was also accepted by such liberal Anglicans as Clayton.

He claimed that while Christ would probably appear to men at some point so as to encourage righteousness, he would reign solely "in the Hearts of Men" and not remain on earth as a temporal ruler.[65]

By keeping Christ and the resurrected saints out of the millennium, these eschatologists made that period seem more commensurable to the present state of affairs than it would otherwise have been. The transition from contemporary to millennial life was made to appear less abrupt and drastic as a result. Arguing that "Christ will reign . . . though not in person" during the thousand years, Broughton declared that the "Government of the *Millennial Kingdom* will not be altogether different from That of the Ante-millennial or present *Kingdom of Christ*."[66] Thus, the coming of the millennium became a more readily conceivable phenomenon, more conformable to human experience.

A similar tendency can be found in the contemporary treatment of the conflagration and creation of the new heavens and earth. More and Burnet accepted the traditional Protestant view that these events would precede the millennium. At the turn of the century, however, Edwards and Whitby rejected such catastrophism on the grounds that a careful reading of scripture did not substantiate it. By the 1730s, their belief that the conflagration could only follow the millennium had become the customary interpretation. Some eschatologists still felt compelled to attack the earlier theory of Burnet in detail. Lowman, for example, argued that it was "attended with a very great, and, as I think, an unanswerable difficulty": if there was to be a universal destruction and purification by fire before the thousand years, how

65. Whitby, *Treatise on the Millennium*, in *Critical Commentary*, 4:1123:2, 1131:1, and passim; Lowman, *Paraphrase on Revelation*, in *Critical Commentary*, 4:1014:1, 1105:2, 1021:2, 1106:2; Doddridge, *Lectures on Pneumatology*, in *Miscellaneous Works*, 527:1–2, 530:2–532:1; Clayton, *Dissertation on Prophecy*, 141, 144, 147; idem, *Enquiry into the Time of the Coming*, 4. See also John Wesley, *Explanatory Notes upon The New Testament* (London, 1755), 748:1–2. On "Whitbyanism" and its influence, see Froom, *Prophetic Faith*, 2:649–55; De Jong, *As the Waters Cover the Sea*, 38–39, 82–83, 120–21, 153–54. As De Jong makes clear, traces of postmillennial sentiment can be found in the half-century before Whitby wrote.

Although it no longer dominated eschatology, premillennialism did continue after 1730, among both Anglicans and Nonconformists. See Hort, *Sermon on the Glorious Kingdom*, 4, 16–17, 29, 35; Gill, *Watchman's Answer*, 41; idem, *The sure Performance of Prophecy*, 33; Sayer Rudd, *An Essay Towards a New Explication of the Doctrines of the Resurrection, Millennium, and Judgment* (London, 1734), 196–97, 273, as quoted in Froom, *Prophetic Faith*, 2:682. But as Hort admitted, this was no longer the "generally received" theory.

66. Broughton, *Prospect of Futurity*, 297.

could the evil Gog and Magog later arise? Broughton was more caustic in his criticism, arguing that Burnet's ideas about the timing of the cosmological revolution were "strange Absurdities" and "a Fable much fitter for Ovid's *Metamorphoses,* than [for] a *Sacred Theory of the Earth.*" Nearly all of the other students of the last things—from the Dissenter Doddridge to liberal Anglicans like Clayton and David Hartley to conservative members of the religious establishment such as Hallifax—merely took for granted that the conflagration and re-creation could only *follow* the millennium. Even the premillennialist Hort adopted this position. Henry Taylor went further and denied that prophecies about the conflagration should be taken literally, writing that "none of these threats could relate to the dissolution of the natural, but merely of the political world."[67] This view was extreme, but it clearly was of a piece with the new tendency to keep the millennium free of the wholly unfamiliar and catastrophic.

High eighteenth-century eschatologists made the fulfillment of optimistic Biblical prophecies more conceivable in still another way: they placed the happy events of the latter days well within the range of their historical vision. Frequently this process occurred by means of correlating past historical events (especially those concerning the papacy and the Reformation) with scriptural predictions. Lowman's *Paraphrase on Revelation* (1737) and Thomas Newton's *Dissertations on the Prophecies* (1754), which became standard works soon after their publication, were largely based on the attempt to establish this correlation as fully as possible. Such efforts led to the acceptance of an eschatology in which—as recollection became foresight—the gradual accomplishment of one prophecy after another created a sense of inevitable movement toward a final goal. "And now," wrote Henry Taylor, "we begin to see many plain appearances that the prophecies are approaching to a completion."[68]

Among these appearances were present as well as past occur-

67. Whitby, *Treatise on the Millennium,* in *Critical Commentary,* 4:1130:2, 1133:1–2; Lowman, *Paraphrase on Revelation,* in *Critical Commentary,* 4:1107:1; Broughton, *Prospect of Futurity,* 290–94, 305; Doddridge, *Lectures on Pneumatology,* in *Miscellaneous Works,* 526:2; Clayton, *Dissertation on Prophecy,* 148–52; David Hartley, *Observations,* 2:380, 381, 400; Hallifax, *Twelve Sermons,* 249–50; Hort, *Sermon on the Glorious Kingdom,* 36–37; Taylor, *Thoughts on the Grand Apostacy,* 188–90. Gill was unique in expecting the destruction and re-creation to precede the millennium: *Glory of the Church in the Latter Day,* 40–41.

68. Taylor, *Thoughts on the Grand Apostacy,* 169. The sense of inevitability is perhaps most strikingly conveyed by a table of prophecies with dates of completion in Lowman, *Paraphrase on Revelation,* in *Critical Commentary,* 4:1020–21.

rences. The "signs of the times" held a powerful fascination for the eschatologists: Erskine, Clayton, Milner, Thomas Hartley, and Wesley all included the phrase in the titles of their books or sermons. What they had in mind was contemporary events which, in their interpretation of the prophecies, they took to be indications of even greater spiritual developments soon to come. Religious awakenings and the purported decline of papal power, for example, seemed to bode well for the future and provided encouragement to the hopes of the faithful. But the afflictions of the age, whether meteorological and seismological disturbances or the excessive desire for pleasure and luxury, were also perceived as eschatological landmarks, since it was assumed that "God mingled light and darkness to bring history to its consummation." Whatever the sign, therefore, the intention in citing it remained the same: to portray a foreshadowing of a season of great change which, as Chandler wrote, "surely cannot be far" since "events seem to be ripening towards the full accomplishing of it."[69]

Complementing the examination of the signs of the times were frequent attempts to determine when the key events of the last things would occur. Of those eschatologists who did not predict exact dates, most believed with Hurd and John Gillies (1712–96), minister of the college church at Glasgow and another member of the Popular party, that the "glory of the latter days is . . . necessarily approaching" and that the "happy period cannot be far off." Others were far more precise, generally arguing that their own age lay about halfway between the glorious Reformation and the even more brilliant millennium. The fall of Antichrist (immediately preceding the millennium) would occur, said Gib, in 2016 or even considerably earlier. Gill preferred the date 1902 or sooner, and Doddridge could not decide between 1998 and 1848. Willison fixed on 1866, while Broughton and Wesley selected 1836. David Imrie (fl. 1754), a Scottish minister from Annandale, chose the year 1794. Lowman expected the commencement of the millennium after 2016, and both Milner and Clayton thought it might occur a few years earlier than that. Chandler went so far as to express the hope, in 1759 at the age of sixty-six, that he might live to see the inauguration of that period, as did Whiston in 1751 at the age

69. Davidson, *Logic of Millennial Thought*, 140; Chandler, *The Signs of the Times*, 51, 33–48. See also Whiston, *Memoirs*, 2d ed., 2:1–45; Milner, *Signs of the Times*, 30–44; Erskine, *Signs of the Times Consider'd*, 19; Wesley, "The Signs of the Times," in *Works of John Wesley*, 6:304–11; Hallifax, *Twelve Sermons*, 97, 320–21, 379; Hurd, *Introduction to the Study of the Prophecies*, 72; Clarke, *Series of Letters*, 289–91.

of eighty-four. In short, the destruction of Antichrist and the start of the thousand-year era of spiritual triumph were usually placed in the not-too-distant future, and occasionally they were envisioned as near at hand indeed. As Gillies declared, this relatively imminent prospect "is no small encouragement."[70]

Correlation of past events with scriptural predictions, discussion of the signs of the times, determination of the proximity of the last things: in these various ways the eschatologists of high eighteenth-century Britain gave the Biblical prophetic program a concrete chronological order and made it amenable to their historical understanding. By linking the future with the past in a historical chain, by binding recollection to foresight, they added credibility to their eschatological hopes, just as they did by removing Christ from the millennial scene and positioning the conflagration after the millennium. As a result, they could look confidently toward the vista of a better life to come, an earthly life neither so distant in time as to be eons away nor so different in quality as to take place in a radically changed environment ruled by a divine figure in person. Here was hopefulness born of an eschatology "secularized" only in terms of the new verisimilitude it possessed, not in terms of any rapprochement with science. And this optimism about the future did not transform the concern with the last things into what Löwith called the "secular religion of progress." It simply strengthened by making more conceivable the old Christian belief—flowing from the interpretation of prophecy—in man's advance toward an improved relationship with God.

The writers who expressed this eschatological doctrine of progress were representative of nearly the entire range of the British ecclesiastical community. They included bishops like the politically important Thomas Newton and obscure rural clergymen like Milner.

70. John Gillies, *Historical Collections Relating to Remarkable Periods of the Success of the Gospel* (1754), ed. Horatius Bonar (Kelso, 1845), viii:2 ("Author's Preface"); Hurd, *Introduction to the Study of the Prophecies*, 228; Gib, *Memorial and Remonstrance*, 7–8, 15–18; Gill, *The Practical Improvement of the Watchman's Answer. A Sermon Preached . . . January 1, 1752*, 5th ed. (London, 1793), 13; Doddridge, *Lectures on Pneumatology*, in *Miscellaneous Works*, 530:1–2; Willison, *Balm of Gilead*, in *Works*, 2:105; Broughton, *Prospect of Futurity*, 267–68, 300–01, 307, 356; John Wesley, *Explanatory Notes*, 739:1; Imrie, *A Letter Predicting glorious Events*, 6, 11; Lowman, *Paraphrase on Revelation*, in *Critical Commentary*, 4:1020:2, 1021:2, 1082:1, 1083:2; Milner, *Signs of the Times*, 28n; Clayton, *Dissertation on Prophecy*, 80–81; Chandler, *The Signs of the Times*, 27; Whiston, *Memoirs*, 1st ed., 398, 608, 636, and 2d ed., 2:2, 80, 88.

There were High Churchmen like Hallifax and Arians like Henry Taylor, liberal Anglicans like Broughton and evangelicals like Wesley and the Scotsman Willison, Dissenters like Doddridge and ministers aligned with the Popular party of the Scottish church like Erskine. There was even a mystic, Thomas Hartley. Inasmuch as this diverse group of expositors of prophecy published books and delivered sermons on the last things throughout the century, the optimism they expressed was widespread and enduring and must have reached and persuaded a large audience of laymen.

In eighteenth-century Britain, at least, it is the existence of this pervasive, long-lasting optimism that most closely links Christian historical conceptions to the development of the idea of progress. For when contemporary Protestants looked closely at history, they saw progress. To their eyes such progress had a specific form: the overarching divine program for spiritual improvement discerned by eschatologists as well as by those who believed in the improvement of religious knowledge, the spread of the true faith, and the general advancement of religion. As their occasional utopian dreams illustrate, this program did not completely exclude or deny the secular side of life, but rather subordinated it to or absorbed it within the religious.

By about 1760, however, the Christian vision of history had helped to create a climate in which it was possible for some Englishmen, such as Joseph Priestley, to conceive of spiritual and general secular progress *together*, as mutually important parts of the same historical process. That climate was in fact also the product of the prevalent belief in the advance of the arts and sciences. And it became complete only with the acceptance of new views of the nature of human beings and their linguistic capacities.

*P*art Two
New Expressions

  Doctrines of progress in learning and the arts, in religion, religious knowledge, and the fulfillment of eschatological prophecies: these eighteenth-century British expressions of the idea of progress derived from and modified earlier patterns of recollection and foresight. Their proponents pointed to the fact of past advancement, envisioned future improvement, or both. But in these doctrines man himself frequently did not occupy the center of the stage. To be sure, his roles were not insignificant: he was the bearer, accumulator, and user of knowledge and the arts, the Christian soldier marching onward under the leadership of a divine commander. Still, the unfolding of a higher drama concerning abstractions—the arts and sciences, religion, God—tended to overshadow the acting out of these parts.

  Some contemporary doctrines of progress, however, were almost entirely new, and they directed the spotlight at man himself. In one of them, he appeared as a patient requiring and able to profit from "medical" treatment. In another, his power of communication in society became the center of attention. That eighteenth-century conceptions about the human mind and education and about language should have been so substantially penetrated by the idea of progress provides important evidence of how prominent a role the idea was coming to play in British thought.

4 *Medicine of the Mind*

Where "shall one with hopes of success begin the cure?" asked John Locke about what he called "a disease of the mind as hard to be cured as any," the association of ideas. This question, with its emphasis on disease and cure, clearly suggests a medical approach to psychology.[1] And it thereby foreshadows much eighteenth-century British thinking about the operation and regulation of the human mind. For the attitude to this subject found in many contemporary British writers on psychology and education, especially from the 1730s through the 1780s, makes it possible to characterize them as practitioners of a kind of medicine of the mind, in the two primary senses of the term.

First of all, they sought to construct a science of the mind just as Sydenham, Boerhaave, and others had created a science of the body. Their great hero was Newton, and they endeavored to find as satisfying an explanation for the functioning of the mind as Newton's principle of gravitation was for the operation of the physical universe. Thus, they had in common with most other contemporary students of the mind the aim of elaborating what Hume called "the science of MAN," whose "only solid foundation . . . must be laid on experience and observation."[2] At the same time, though, the contents of this science led them to believe that they could treat the ills to which man's mind made him subject in much the same way as physicians could treat gout or the stone. That is, they intended to use their descriptive science of the mind prescriptively, to dispense

---

1. John Locke, *Of the Conduct of the Understanding* (1706), ed. Francis W. Garforth (New York, 1966), 114–15 (sect. 41). As will appear below, the term "psychology" was just coming into use in its modern sense during the eighteenth century.

2. David Hume, *A Treatise of Human Nature* (1739–40), ed. L. A. Selby-Bigge, 2d ed., rev. Peter H. Nidditch (Oxford, 1978), xv–xvi.

medicine—if not a panacea—that would improve the condition of humankind and create progress.

The parallelism in eighteenth-century British thought between medical science and the study of the mind was natural, for several reasons. In England throughout the century, the two works that probably had most influence on the continuing analysis of the mind's operations were written by physicians, Locke and David Hartley. In addition, the fact that the mind and body were intimately related was never forgotten, from at least the time of Newton's *Opticks*. Further, as Peter Gay has noted, the philosophes considered medicine a model, test, and guarantee of their new philosophy;[3] and this philosophy, after all, concerned the science of man in a central way.

Of course, the evidence for the rapport with medicine comes largely from French philosophes, most of whom seem to have been quite conscious of and explicit about the ties of medicine to philosophy or psychology. In contrast, only some of the contemporary British writers on the mind and education established the connection in direct fashion. But those who did made the link very apparent. On the simplest level, there was widespread recognition, as an anonymous writer put it in 1745, that "our Minds are subject to many Diseases, as well as our Bodies." Three years later one James Forrester (who was probably a teacher), with somewhat more sophistication, considered the discovery of the "Diseases of the Mind" a principal goal of education. He drew a parallel between the physician's treatment of disease and the handling of the passions of children by the educator (or "moral Physician"). Likewise, George Chapman, a Scottish grammar-school master, wrote metaphorically in 1773 that "where medicine may be necessary for the mind, it should be adapted, with a skilful hand, to the temper of the child, and the mental diseases to which it is most liable."[4]

Two Scotsmen associated with the colleges at Aberdeen carried the parallel of medicine and psychology considerably farther. George Turnbull (1698–1748), who had taught Thomas Reid and others at

3. Peter Gay, "The Enlightenment as Medicine and as Cure," in W. H. Barber et al., eds., *The Age of Enlightenment: Studies Presented to Theodore Besterman* (Edinburgh, 1967), 375. See also Gay, *The Enlightenment: An Interpretation*, 2 vols. (New York, 1966–69), 2:12–13.

4. Anon., *A Letter from a Man to his Fellow-Creatures, relating to Several Important Points of Religion and Morality* (London, 1745), 37; James Forrester, *Dialogues on the Passions, Habits, and Affections Peculiar to Children* (London, 1748), 12, 14–15; George Chapman, *A Treatise on Education* (Edinburgh, 1773), 39.

Marischal College before becoming an Anglican curate and chaplain to the Prince of Wales, wrote in 1740 that he had long before decided to apply himself "to the study of the human mind in the same way as to that of the human body." No doubt it was as a result of this approach that he discussed the "anatomy, so to speak, of the human mind" and described the "science" concerning the relationship of mind and body as the "medicine of the mind." David Fordyce (1711–51), professor of moral philosophy at Marischal, used similar terminology, writing of "Systems of spiritual Medicines," "moralizing Medicine," "Moral or Spiritual Medicine," and the "MEDICINE of the Mind." He went so far as to outline a pathology "on which to erect the whole Superstructure of our *moral* Medicine," which would serve as an integral part of education. These contemporary academics were engaged in the kind of intellectual project championed by a later, anonymous writer in a popular magazine who called himself "The Physician of the Heart":

> We must know the nature of man, and how he is affected by pleasure and pain, by moral and physical good and evil; and where they mingle, and to what degree, before we can pretend to regulate the intellectual machine, or tune the chords of the heart. The soul and body are intimately connected, and have a necessary influence on each other. Every philosopher should, perhaps, be a physician, and every physician a philosopher.

This approach was of "importance to society," because its ultimate goal was "to heal those complaints [of the heart] for which physic has no remedy, and surgery no salve."[5]

If others who considered this whole subject did not explicitly establish a correlation between medicine and psychology, still they had the same fundamental intentions as Turnbull, Fordyce, and the magazine writer. They all aimed at determining how the human mind functioned and developed, and at applying that knowledge to cure the troubles of humankind. These intentions appeared in two kinds of discourses for which, once again, Locke provided the archetypes: the analysis of psychology (found in the *Essay Concerning*

5. George Turnbull, *The Principles of Moral Philosophy* (London, 1740), iii ("Preface"), 79; idem, *Observations upon Liberal Education* (London, 1742), 233; David Fordyce, *Dialogues Concerning Education*, 2 vols. (London, 1745–48), 2:97–98, 353, 362, 368, 417, 438; Anon., "The Physician of the Heart," *Sentimental Magazine* 1 (Nov. 1773): 409:2–410:1.

Human Understanding) and the treatise on educational theory and practice (*Some Thoughts Concerning Education*). Although usually distinct and separable, these discourses sometimes overlapped in the same writer or work. Moreover, the educational writings almost always relied quite heavily for their assumptions on the psychological treatises. In both cases, however, the conclusion, whether stated or implied, was that the nature of human beings made them the fit object for progress—through appropriate nurture.

PSYCHOLOGY

During the 1730s and 1740s a new subject loomed ever larger on the horizon of the British intellectual world, the association of ideas. The subject had made its first appearance under this title in a chapter added to Book II of the fourth edition of Locke's *Essay* (1700), called "Of the Association of Ideas." There Locke distinguished ideas that had "a natural Correspondence and Connexion one with another" from the "Connexion of *Ideas* wholly owing to Chance or Custom." To the latter he attributed most of the extravagances, antipathies, and unreasonableness of men and women. Although such errors in "Tenets and Conduct" might seem to be innate, Locke wrote, "a great part of those which are counted Natural, would have been known to be from unheeded, though, perhaps, early Impressions . . . if they had been warily observed." They arose from the uniting in the mind of ideas not naturally correspondent, so that one idea no sooner entered the understanding than its associates appeared with it. They followed one another "in an habitual train, when once they are put into that tract." These "undue Connexions of *Ideas*" were so common and "of so great force to set us awry in our Actions, as well Moral as Natural, Passions, Reasonings, and Notions themselves, that, perhaps, there is not any one thing that deserves more to be looked after," especially by parents and educators.[6]

Locke clearly viewed associations of ideas as essentially objectionable phenomena. For him they were the immensely powerful springs of error, playing a harmful if important role in intellectual and moral life, in the course of reasoning and the formation of the passions. Yet with proper care, he intimated, they could be overcome.

6. John Locke, *An Essay Concerning Human Understanding* (1690), ed. Peter H. Nidditch (Oxford, 1975), 394–97 (Bk. II, Ch. xxxiii, Sects. 1–9).

For they were not natural but rather developed out of subtle impressions left by the environment; that is, by education in the broadest sense. This assessment and the principle giving it coherence—the central thesis of the existence of an associating process—provided a framework for discussion within which the development of the psychology of association took place in eighteenth-century Britain.

Francis Hutcheson, the philosophic mentor of so many leading Scottish thinkers of the century, added to this development in two ways. The less important part of his contribution was his treatment of association itself. As with Locke, he took a dim view of the value of connections of ideas, referring, for example, to "some *foolish Associations of Ideas.*" Arising not naturally but accidentally or casually, these "*Conjunctions of Ideas* may give a Disgust, where there is nothing disagreeable," so that they constituted "one great Cause of the apparent Diversity of Fancys [*sic*] in the *Sense of Beauty.*" Also like Locke, Hutcheson believed that these prejudices arising from association, "without any natural Connection," could be rooted out. Separate contemplation of wrongly associated objects could "at last disjoin the unreasonable Association, especially if we can join new agreeable ideas to them."[7]

These comments of 1725 represented no substantial enlargement on Locke's views of a quarter-century before. But Hutcheson did contribute to the growth of the concept of association in a more significant manner. He brought it into contact with the equally important concept of what he called the "internal Sense," which was popularized by Lord Shaftesbury and pursued by British writers throughout the century. Hutcheson divided this internal sense into a sense of beauty and a moral sense. In relation largely to the former, but with obvious implications for the latter as well, he wrote that "by *Education* there are some strong Associations of Ideas . . . which it is very hard for us ever after [their formation] to break asunder." Yet in all these instances, education never caused the mind to apprehend any qualities of objects that the internal senses could not have perceived.

> Thus *Education* and *Custom* may influence our *internal Senses*, where they are antecedently, by enlarging the Capacity of our Minds to retain and compare the Parts of complex

7. Francis Hutcheson, *An Inquiry into the Original of our Ideas of Beauty and Virtue, In Two Treatises*, 1st ed. (London, 1725), 67–68, 76, 85.

Compositions. . . . But all this presupposes our *Sense* of *Beauty* to be *natural*.[8]

In Hutcheson's view, then, the shaping of aesthetic and moral judgments proceeded primarily from the internal sense and only in a subsidiary way from education and association of ideas.

This position proved widely influential in Scottish intellectual circles for the rest of the century, but many English thinkers criticized it strongly. Nevertheless, even English moral philosophers continued to pursue the question of the relation of the associative process to the formation of moral judgments. Indeed, this very issue became the primary concern of one of Hutcheson's earliest critics, John Gay.

Gay (1699–1745) held a fellowship at Sidney Sussex College, Cambridge, from 1724 to 1732, after which he served as a vicar in Bedfordshire. A year before the end of his Cambridge career he contributed anonymously a *Preliminary Dissertation Concerning the Fundamental Principle of Virtue or Morality* to the translation by Edmund Law of Archbishop William King's Latin treatise on the origin of evil.[9] It was Gay's principal object in this essay to attack Hutcheson directly by denying that the moral sense and benevolence were "innate or implanted in us." Instead, he claimed, they were "acquired either from our own observation or the imitation of others." The process of acquisition went forward by means of "reason pointing out private happiness," the pursuit of happiness itself being innate. Whenever this ultimate utilitarian end was not perceived by the individual, his "approbation of morality, and all affections whatsoever . . . are to be accounted for from the association of ideas, and may properly enough be called habits." That is, an individual frequently did not by reason reach the ultimate end of his or her actions (happiness), because he or she stopped upon arriving at "resting places" or principles that, through experience, had already become associated with happiness. For proof of this theory Gay cited the

8. Ibid., 82–84.

9. This essay has always been ascribed to Gay, and there is no reason to doubt the general accuracy of the attribution. It should be noted, however, that in the preface to the fourth edition of his translation Law stated that the "*Dissertation was composed chiefly by the Late Reverend Mr. Gay*": William King, *An Essay on the Origin of Evil*, trans. and ed. Edmund Law, 4th ed., corr. (Cambridge, 1758), xx. No hint is given as to who the collaborator might have been, although it would be natural to look to Law himself, in light of his role in the production of the translation and his interest in moral philosophy and psychology (see below, chap. 8).

example of how association could transform the knowledge of advantages arising from the possession of money into the love of money for its own sake.[10]

Such, according to Gay, were the mechanics of association. As for its powers, they were far stronger in his view than Hutcheson had admitted, and not purely destructive as they had seemed to Locke. In Gay's opinion association constituted one of the most fundamental principles of the mind, for good as well as ill. Further, he asserted that it was closely bound up with education in the broadest sense. Writing in response to hypothetical objections from Hutcheson, he observed that "we do not always (and perhaps not for the most part) make this association ourselves, but learn it from others: . . . Hence national virtues and vices, dispositions and opinions: And from hence we may observe how easy it is to account for what is generally call'd the prejudice of education."[11] Association played both an individual and a social role.

The *Preliminary Dissertation* clearly marked the emergence of the principle of association from its position as a kind of afterthought in British psychology and moral philosophy. After Gay it rapidly became a central feature of these subjects. There is perhaps no better evidence of this change than the young David Hume's views on association. They probably owed something to Gay, for Hume undoubtedly read Gay's essay before he wrote the *Treatise of Human Nature*. When the first two books of this work appeared in 1739, they contained a section entitled "Of the connexion or association of ideas." There Hume discussed what he thought to be the three modes of association: resemblance, contiguity in time or place, and cause and effect. Association itself he called "a gentle force, which commonly prevails"; commonly, but not always, because it was not in his view the infallible or sole cause of the union of ideas. Nonetheless, he certainly thought it played a crucial role in mental operations, for he drew a parallel between it and Newton's principle of gravitation. "Here is a kind of ATTRACTION," he wrote, "which in the mental world will be found to have as extraordinary effects as in the natural,

<hr />

10. John Gay, *Preliminary Dissertation Concerning the Fundamental Principle of Virtue or Morality* (1731), in L. A. Selby-Bigge, *British Moralists: Being Selections from Writers Principally of the Eighteenth Century*, 2 vols. (Oxford, 1897), 2:285, 270, 278, 282–83. Selby-Bigge reprints the version appearing in the fifth edition of Law's translation of King's *Origin of Evil* (1781).

11. Ibid., in Selby-Bigge, *British Moralists*, 2:285.

and to shew itself in as many and as various forms." The three modes of association together had "vast consequence . . . in the science of human nature," because "they are really *to us* the cement of the universe, and all the operations of the mind must, in a great measure, depend on them." In fact, association struck Hume as so important that he declared in the *Abstract of a Treatise of Human Nature* (1740) that "if any thing can intitle [*sic*] the author [of the *Treatise*] to so glorious a name as that of an *inventor*, 'tis the use he makes of the principle of the association of ideas, which enters into most of his philosophy."[12]

Of course, the principle of association did not provide the entire foundation for Hume's philosophy. On the contrary, he considered human beings as innately possessing common moral sentiments and, therefore, stood somewhat closer to the position of Hutcheson than to that of Gay in their controversy. Yet the fact remains that Hume, one of Britain's most creative and independent thinkers, found the association of ideas to be fascinating and highly significant for any discussion of human nature. Nor, from the late 1730s on, was such an attitude any longer unusual in British thought.

In 1741 and 1747 there appeared two anonymous treatises entitled, respectively, *An Introduction towards an essay on the origin of the Passions, in which is endeavoured to be shown how they are all acquired and that they are no other than Associations of Ideas of our own making, or what we learn of others,* and *An Enquiry into the Origin of the Human Appetites and Affections, Shewing how each arises from Association.* These works were certainly written by the same person, and the titles by themselves suggest that Gay might well have been their author.[13] Whatever the identity of the writer, he

12. Hume, *Treatise*, 10–13, 92; idem, *Abstract of A Treatise of Human Nature*, in *Treatise*, 661–62. Hume's familiarity with Gay's *Preliminary Discourse* was brought to light in Ernest Campbell Mossner, *The Life of David Hume*, 1st ed. (Austin, Tex., 1954), 80.

13. It is undoubtedly the case that the same person wrote both treatises. The first treatise ends with the statement that it is a prospectus of a "work which probably some time hence will make its appearance in the world": Anon., *An Introduction towards an Essay on the origin of the Passions* (London, 1741), reprinted in Maria Heider, *Studien über David Hartley. (1705–1757)* (Bergische Gladbach, 1913), 42. More important, the treatises are similar in structure and style, containing numerous parallel or identical passages, such as those defining association and discussing the approval or disapproval of virtue or vice: see, for example, *Introduction towards an Essay*, in Heider, *Studien*, 34–36; Anon., *An Enquiry into the Origin of the Human Appetites and Affections* (Lincoln, 1747), 35, 18, as reprinted in Paul McReynolds, ed., *Four Early*

made the same general case as Gay did in his dissertation of 1731, but with greater elaboration at certain crucial points. He began by rejecting Hutcheson's notion of a moral sense, and by considering as innate only the desire for self-preservation, happiness, and pleasure. He then proceeded to attribute the development of all the passions to the power of association. Those actions, he wrote, "which we stile [sic] moral or immoral, virtuous or vicious, are approved and disapproved, not by nature and constitution, but by habit and association." In fact, the "human soul is made up of nothing but associations." This claim led him, as a "Newton of the mind" like Hume, to a still grander one: "association is the law of the soul in a sense analogous to that in which gravitation is said to be a law of matter."[14]

Hume had suggested that there might be a physiological cause for association; the anonymous author believed that, in fact, there was such a cause, and he attempted to elucidate it. He wrote, initially, of the "intimate relation betwixt soul and body," a relation in which

---

Works on Motivation (Gainesville, Fla., 1969), 281–476. In his "Two Early Works by David Hartley," Journal of the History of Philosophy 19 (April 1981): 174–75, Stephen Ferg now also argues that both works came from the hands of one author.

Ferg attempts to demonstrate that the author was David Hartley, just as (apparently unknown to Ferg) Heider had earlier argued that Hartley wrote the Introduction towards an Essay. Neither case is persuasive, for at least two reasons. To begin with, the man who wrote both treatises was not a physician, as Hartley was: Enquiry into the Origin of Human Appetites and Affections, 61. In addition, a second edition of this Enquiry was published in 1753, and it is highly unlikely that this would have occurred if Hartley had been the author. Having already published Observations on Man (1749), a book whose insights into association and related subjects were far more sophisticated than those of the Enquiry, Hartley would have had no incentive to bring out another edition of a superseded, shorter work that contained no reference to his masterpiece.

The British Museum Catalogue ascribes the Enquiry to one James Long of Lincoln, but this attribution cannot be confirmed because nothing is known of him (unless he was the James Long from Wells who matriculated at Lincoln College, Oxford in March 1721 at the age of sixteen, graduating B.A. in 1724). There is some reason, however, for considering John Gay as the author of the two treatises. For example, his Preliminary Dissertation (in Selby-Bigge, British Moralists, 2:269) and the Introduction towards an Essay (in Heider, Studien, 39) and Enquiry, 87, use the phrase "the ingenious Author of the Enquiry into the Original of our Idea of Virtue" to refer to Hutcheson. In addition, unlike any other eighteenth-century moral philosopher of whom I am aware, both Gay and whoever wrote the two treatises in question distinguished between the passions and the affections in precisely the same way: Gay, Preliminary Dissertation, in Selby-Bigge, British Moralists, 2:276; Introduction towards an Essay, in Heider, Studien, 27; Enquiry into the Origin of Human Appetites and Affections, 68. Of course, this is hardly definitive evidence.

14. Introduction towards an Essay, in Heider, Studien, 27–28, 30, 34, 39, 42. See also Enquiry into the Origin of Human Appetites and Passions, 6–8, 18, 87–88, 93–94, 106–08.

"whatever passes in the one, affects the other: . . . certain motions of the nerves raise certain perceptions in the soul! and vice versa." Therefore, he argued, it was probable that

> Association may be the Result of, and owing to, that Relation.
> . . . And since by Ideas are understood certain Motions of the Nerves *as* felt and perceiv'd by the Soul; then probably, the Reason of Ideas when once united keeping ever after in Company together is owing to a Succession of Motions in the Body, or, rather, to those Motions of the Nerves always producing one another.

In brief, the author was indicating that "Associations are subject to the Laws of Matter and Motion" of the physical world. As such they—or at least most of them—"grow out of the Circumstances we are placed in." The environment conditioned their formation and subjected them to alteration and obliteration. "For Motions are ever and anon overcome by contrary ones, and in resisting Mediums they decay."[15]

This position provided a basis in psychology for arguing that, since the environment determined associations and their changes, proper control of the environment could be made to produce *positive* changes. The anonymous author did not develop this argument in its entirety. But he did believe wholeheartedly in the ability of human beings to alter associations of ideas for the better. Admitting that many associations "arise mechanically as it were from our Circumstances, and the Relation we stand in to things around us," he nevertheless declared that "we have it very much in our Power, either to strengthen and confirm, or to impair and eradicate, them." Good habits could be formed and bad ones broken, he thought, because the soul was able to strengthen or weaken its desires and form new associations or end old ones, as it found necessary. The author attempted to prove his case solely on the evidence of introspection. Necessitarians might consider man wholly passive, like a machine. "But I would appeal to those Gentlemen, whether they do not feel within

---

15. Hume, *Treatise*, 60–61; *Introduction towards an Essay*, in Heider, *Studien*, 35–36; *Enquiry into the Origin of Human Appetites and Affections*, 21–22, 35–36, 40, 63. The anonymous author of the two essays did not believe that all associations came directly from the surroundings in which one found oneself. Some were "voluntary and from ourselves": *Enquiry into the Origin of Human Appetites and Affections*, 63; *Introduction towards an Essay*, in Heider, *Studien*, 37.

themselves a Power both of determining and acting independently on the Objects which solicit their Choice! They must allow it to be so." It was the will, then, that provided control of association—the will tempered by judgment, that "Power of taking a Survey of those Effects which . . . Associations, if indulg'd, will probably produce." Man possessed "Free-agency," which permitted him to direct the operation of his mind in a beneficial direction.[16]

Thus, although the author cannot be classed as one of the rigorous environmentalists such as Helvétius, he accepted essentially the same notion of the malleability or, in his words, "Pliableness" of the human mind as they did. And like them he advocated using this mental characteristic to promote progress. "Associations must be made in Favour of Virtue," he declared, in order to convert the selfish passions into benevolent ones. For, humankind "being created mutually dependent," each person could best secure happiness by promoting that of his or her fellows. This practice, "agreeably to the Doctrine of Association above, will in time produce benevolent Appetites, public Dispositions, Love of a System, &c. whence the Source of moral Pleasures." Social change for the better, therefore, rested upon individual advancement through proper associations, and the perfectibility of the individual seemed to the writer a certainty. "'Tis without Dispute," he stated flatly, "a remarkable Property of our Nature (if but rightly turn'd at first and improved afterwards) to be ever advancing itself towards Perfection." To him, social progress seemed assured, assuming only a proper "Foundation being once laid in Childhood for raising Associations upon" and the control by the will of connections of ideas in later life.[17]

In relating the theory of association to progress, the anonymous author prescribed a role for the new psychology not even hinted at by Locke, Hutcheson, Gay, or Hume. Yet neither in this nor in his general belief in the pliableness of man was he unusual or truly original by

16. *Enquiry into the Origin of Human Appetites and Affections*, 43–44, 47, 8. See also *Introduction towards an Essay*, in Heider, *Studien*, 30, 36.

17. *Enquiry into the Origin of Human Appetites and Affections*, 16, 131, 124–25, 135, 153–54. See also *Introduction towards an Essay*, in Heider, *Studien*, 33, 41–42.

I prefer the term "pliability" (or "pliableness") to "malleability" (see John Passmore, "The Malleability of Man in Eighteenth-Century Thought," in Earl R. Wasserman, *Aspects of the Eighteenth Century* [Baltimore, 1965], 21–46), because it was used in the eighteenth century. In addition, the adjective "malleable" describes a characteristic associated with inorganic materials, while "pliable" is ordinarily used to describe yielding and adaptable organic substances.

the time he wrote. Most of his ideas had, in fact, already appeared in print the year before the first of his anonymous essays were published. In 1740, George Turnbull, presumably as a result of having fulfilled his intention to "anatomize" the mind, published an account of the elements of moral philosophy. As befitted his Scottish background, he accepted in this work Hutcheson's theory of a moral sense, and to this extent he differed from the anonymous author. With regard to the association of ideas, however, the two held essentially the same views. Turnbull considered association a signally important mental operation, affecting all or nearly all the ideas that "excite our warmest and keenest affections." Along with that parallel and related phenomenon, the formation of habits, he placed the association of ideas under the heading of a general principle of human nature that he called the "law of custom."[18]

Turnbull regarded association as integrally related to the external physical world. For the human being, he thought, was "a compound of moral and sensitive powers and affections," and the body and mind existed in a state of reciprocal dependence. Taken together the moral and material worlds comprised "one strictly, connected system." Having laid this groundwork, he proceeded to make the environmentalist argument that the anonymous author did not. The dependence of the mind on the physical universe led him to suggest as a "good consequence" that

> whereas the tempers, characters, abilities, and dispositions of our minds, would be utterly unalterable by us, if they were not dependent in that manner upon us; being so dependent, they may in a great measure be changed by our own proper care; or to do so only requires, that we should give due attention to the natural connexions [that is, associations] on which they depend; and conformably to them take proper measures to make fit changes.

Association, he believed, provided the key to the strengthening of pleasures and the diminution of pains, to "our happiness, as far as it depends on ourselves."[19]

But how far did Turnbull think this dependence actually extended (since, after all, he believed in an innate moral sense)? Quite far, for

18. Turnbull, *Principles*, x, 39, 111, 137–39, 86, 81–83.
19. Ibid., 77–80, 95, 433, 92, 437.

although human nurture could not create the moral sense or affections of humankind, it could surely work "change to the better or worse upon what nature hath implanted in our breasts." Like an innate ear for music, the moral sense was "greatly improveable by instruction and exercise . . . to a great pitch of perfection," and "it is in our power to change any temper we may have contracted, and to form ourselves to any desireable one." Individuals possessed such power because of their capacity to form correct habits and associations, through the *"deliberative temper or habit"* of judging before acting and of discovering the component parts of an associated idea and the process by which they became united. For these reasons, Turnbull rejected necessitarianism (which he called the "doctrine of inactivity") and pronounced that "we are capable of liberty, or are free agents."[20]

Thus, a proponent of the moral-sense theory could agree with an opponent of Hutcheson on a central proposition. Together with the anonymous author of 1741 and 1747, Turnbull felt sure that "changing and reforming" the minds of human beings depended very largely on men and women themselves, on their judgment and will. And, as with the anonymous writer, in Turnbull this certainty excited a grand dream. It encouraged him to hope that men would make greater use of the fact of the interdependence of mind and body than they had in the past. He thought it possible to develop a "rule and standard for associating and dissociating" experiences, through the careful use of which the "medicinal art would extend further than to the body." By means of this hitherto neglected science, which he called the "medicine of the mind," individuals could discipline the sensitive side of their beings to form and preserve virtuous habits. In the context of the hope of tending to the moral and mental health of humankind, Turnbull wrote that the law of habit and association might justly claim the title of the *"law of improvement to perfection,"* and that human beings were "made for progress in virtue." So his dream was really a vision of progress, the progress of the individual *and* of society. For the happiness of each person, he insisted, lay in the "exercise of the same virtuous temper, which fits for and points to the proper manner of uniting [society] in order to promote general happiness or perfection." As the development of virtue could take place only by correct associations and habits, Turnbull's medicine of the mind was in

20. Ibid., 104–05, 139–40, 97, 437–38, 16–18, 106.

effect both a private and a public nostrum, since nature intended men and women "to arrive at perfection in a social way; or by united endeavours."[21]

Views very similar to these of Turnbull appeared in an anonymous *Letter from a Man to His Fellow-Creatures* of 1745. Beginning with the assumption that the human condition had always been and remained unhappy, the author located the source of this sad situation in the misapplication of the faculties, specifically in the "fixing on improper Objects, and neglecting those that are proper." According to him, the objects to which an individual directed his or her attention had such great importance because ideas arose entirely from sensory experience and, in turn, all human actions followed from them. At birth a person had no innate ideas or any moral predisposition. Indeed, this writer called the doctrine of original sin a "vile and ungodly, . . . inhuman and most odious Notion" and presented what he considered convincing evidence against it. In his view, the only innate attribute of humankind was self-love or a general desire for happiness.[22]

The author believed that this set of facts not only explained the cause of human misery but also pointed to a cure: men and women had to direct their attention to appropriate objects. Since actions depended on ideas and ideas on objects, a "Liberty of Application of Faculties to Objects is a sufficient Foundation whereon to build . . . either true and substantial Happiness, or all the Unhappiness, Calamity and Affliction of a miserable and disordered World." Necessity ruled humankind to the extent that sensation forced all their ideas on them. But this process operated only through the appearance of things, and appearance varied with the use of the general power of "Application and Examination" (judgment) regarding sensory objects. Hence, with judgment affecting appearances there existed the "plain Possibility of introducing different Ideas into the Mind; and consequently, if different Ideas, different Volitions, and different Actions." To this extent man possessed liberty, consisting "solely in the Power he has of directing his Faculties among Objects, and ordering his Ideas."[23]

The author proposed to harness this power to produce progress. In

21. Ibid., 97, 79–80, vi, 84, 90, 223, 272, 202, 411, 37.
22. Anon., *Letter from a Man to his Fellow-Creatures*, 1–2, 4–5, 8, 21–23, 31.
23. Ibid., 6, 8, 18–19.

order to do so, he believed, it would be necessary to place the knowledge of human nature on a scientific basis. He did not describe the nature of this knowledge in detail and never specifically discussed the principle of association. Like Turnbull and the other anonymous writer, however, he clearly thought it necessary for his projected science to deal with the general issue of the mind's mechanism for ordering and connecting ideas, "what we act or think being progressive or in train." At any rate, he had great hopes for this science. If properly studied, it

> would soon make us happier than our Species has ever been. This is that Science which shall make the first Nation or People that shall study and understand it, the wisest, happiest, richest, and greatest People that ever were upon this Globe. In fine, this is that Science, by studying which we might soon become happy; and without which Man shall never be so.

Thus, he expected the knowledge of human nature and the mind to yield immense benefits not only to the individual but also to humankind in general. Ignorance of mental operations and, thereby, failure to exercise the ability to control sensory experience in the proper way was "sufficient not only to ruin one particular Man, or any one Nation, but all Nations upon Earth." But by recognizing and utilizing their pliableness, the human race could advance toward happiness.[24]

Positive change for individuals and society through a scientific understanding of the pliant human mind: such was the hope of these British writers on psychology between 1740 and 1747. The cases of Turnbull and the two anonymous writers demonstrate the close relation of this hope to the acceptance and psychology of association. In the first half of the eighteenth century, however, such a connection had not yet become a common feature of British thought. It was left to David Hartley to bring about the popularization of associationism and to weld this psychology firmly to the belief in progress through the pliability of man.

Hartley (1705–57) received his education at Jesus College, Cambridge, graduating B.A. in 1726 and holding a fellowship from 1727 to 1730. Since John Gay was a resident fellow at Sidney Sussex for eight years after 1724, it is likely that the two men were acquainted. But whereas Gay left Cambridge to become an Anglican vicar, Hartley's

24. Ibid., 16–17, 21–22, 8–9.

David Hartley

scruples concerning the Thirty-Nine Articles prevented him from taking orders (although he always remained a practicing member of the Church of England). With the path to an ecclesiastical career blocked, he decided to pursue the medical profession. After studying medicine at Norwich, he practiced at Bury St. Edmunds and then, from about 1735 to 1742, in London, before moving permanently to Bath. While in London he became a fellow of the Royal Society, and his friends in the metropolis included Joseph Butler, Edmund Law, William Warburton, William Whiston, and Edward Young.

Throughout the 1730s and 1740s Hartley explored the operation of the mind. His initial motivation for this work came from Gay's theory of deriving all ideas and moral convictions from association. He had been informed of Gay's opinions before the publication of the *Preliminary Dissertation*. As early as 1735 he composed, but did not publish, two essays that he entitled "The Progress to Happiness deduced from Reason—and from Scripture," the first of which sought to show that "all our intellectual pleasures and pains are formed either immediately or mediately from sensible ones by association." In 1746 he published anonymously a short Latin treatise, *Conjecturae quaedem de Sensu, Motu et Idearum*, summarizing the results of fifteen years of study and preparing the way for his massive *Observations on Man, His Frame, His Duty, and His Expectations* (1749). This latter book, which remained for more than half a century the standard discussion of psychology in England, maintained and elaborated the views Hartley had held since he moved to London—and it constituted his final word on moral philosophy and the mind.[25]

One of the two most prominent intentions underlying Hartley's *Observations* was a desire to set the study and knowledge of the mind on a solid scientific foundation. Not surprisingly, therefore, he refused to apply to himself the appellation of "System-maker" and emphasized his adherence, with most of his contemporaries, to the "Method of Analysis and Synthesis recommended and followed by Sir *Isaac Newton*." By pursuing this method he sought to establish a science of the human mind as a part of natural philosophy, alongside

25. David Hartley to Rev. John Lister, Dec. 2, 1736, in W. B. Trigg, "The Correspondence of Dr. David Hartley and Rev. John Lister," *Transactions of the Halifax Antiquarian Society* (Oct. 4, 1938), 236. The fact, all too frequently overlooked, that Hartley knew of Gay's work before it appeared in print was made plain by Hartley: *Observations on Man, His Frame, His Duties, and His Expectations*, 2 vols. (London, 1749), 1:v ("Preface"). Unless otherwise noted, all references to the *Observations* are to this first edition.

mechanics, astronomy, and chemistry. He hoped that this science—which he may well have been the first English writer to call "psychology"—would be able "to analyse all that vast Variety of complex Ideas, . . . into their simple compounding Parts, *i.e.* into the simple Ideas of Sensation, of which they consist," and to determine "a few simple Principles" governing the relationship of external stimuli to the generation of sensations. He expected that psychologists, like all practitioners of natural philosophy, ultimately would be able to place the contents of their science in the purity and simplicity of a mathematical form. Psychology, Hartley thought, was especially closely related to one branch of natural philosophy: medicine. "Physic" and psychology, he argued, had much to contribute to each other. Indeed, the realization of his whole program for the science of the mind, like that of the subsidiary task of enlarging the boundaries of logic and ethics, would require the "allied efforts of physicians and philosophers who follow in the footsteps of Locke and Newton."[26] Hartley—physician, philosopher, and disciple of Locke and Newton—obviously considered himself well equipped to analyze the human mental constitution.

His analysis led him, like Gay, Turnbull, and the others, to view the principle of association as the cornerstone of psychology. This principle he defined by exemplification as follows:

> *Any sensations* A, B, C, *&c. by being associated with one another a sufficient Number of Times, get such a Power over the corresponding Ideas* a, b, c, *&c. that any one of the Sensations* A, *when impressed alone, shall be able to excite in the Mind* b, c, *&c. the Ideas of the rest.*
>
> Sensations may be said to be associated together, when their Impressions are either made precisely at the same Instant of Time, or in the contiguous successive Instants.

Unlike Hume, then, Hartley recognized only one mode of associa-

---

26. Hartley, *Observations*, 1:vi ("Preface"), 6, 354, 76, 30, 351, 264–67; idem, *Conjectures on the Perception, Motion, and Generation of Ideas (1746)*, trans. Robert E. A. Palmer (Los Angeles, 1959), 57. On the use of the terms "psychology and "psychologist," see G. S. Rousseau, "Psychology," in Rousseau and Roy Porter, *The Ferment of Knowledge: Studies in the Historiography of Eighteenth-Century Science* (Cambridge, 1980), 146. Although N. Bailey's *Dictionarium Britannicum* (London, 1730) contains definitions of these words (respectively, "a Discourse of the Soul" and "one who treats concerning the soul"), neither Johnson's *Dictionary* nor other high eighteenth-century dictionaries include similar listings.

tion, contiguity in time. But how powerful he thought that one mode to be! For simple ideas of sensation—and Hartley considered sensation the sole source of ideas, thereby dissenting from Locke's emphasis on the independent importance of reflection—merged by association into clusters and combinations and finally into complex ideas. The ideas of men belonging "to the Heads of Beauty, Honour, moral Qualities, &c. are, in Fact, thus composed of Parts, which, by degrees, coalesce into one complex Idea."[27] Clearly, Hartley believed that association lay at the base of the entire range of mental operations.

Another key feature of the mind, he agreed with Turnbull and the anonymous author of 1741 and 1747, was its intimate connection with the body and the external physical world. In this context, his thinking proceeded from the assumption that since the body was composed of the same matter as the rest of the universe (Newton's hypothetical particles), the same physical laws prevailed within it as elsewhere. Following Newton's lead in the *Opticks*, Hartley suggested that sensation occurred through the transfer of external particle motion to the nervous system of the body. This system, the immediate instrument of sensation and motion, included the white medullary substance of the brain, the spinal marrow, and the nerves leading from them to the sensory organs. The whole system was constructed of infinitesimal medullary particles. Exterior objects impressed themselves upon the sensory organs by particle motion, stimulating in the nerves and finally, by transference of movement, in the brain the corresponding vibrations of the medullary particles. Sensations derived from these corporeal vibrations. But since the medullary substance of the brain was also the immediate instrument by which ideas presented themselves to the mind, "*whatever Changes are made in this Substance* [by vibrations], *corresponding Changes are made in our Ideas.*" Hartley related the corporeal changes to the mental ones in a fairly simple way. The sensations occasioned by vibrations impressed by an external object remained for a brief time even after the object was removed. Frequent repetition of these vibrations and sensations magnified this tendency, engendering in the medullary substance of the brain a disposition to produce weaker vibrations ("Vibratiuncles"), similar to the original vibrations. These vestiges Hartley called "Simple Ideas of Sensation."[28] Thus, vibra-

27. *Observations*, 1:65, 74–75, 360.
28. Ibid., 1:62, 12, 11, 8, 9, 56, 58.

tory motions imposed from without and recreated within explained for him the basis of the relationship between matter and mind.

This famous theory of vibrations was the first detailed modern treatment of physiological psychology, and it won Hartley considerable renown both in the eighteenth century and after. He himself, like some of those influenced by him after 1750, sometimes derogated from the importance of the vibration theory to his science of the mind as a whole. He certainly did believe it impossible to determine with precision how corporeal phenomena passed into mental ones, and he refused to claim that inorganic matter could be imbued with sensation. But in spite of occasional statements weakening his materialist position, he still proclaimed himself satisfied that "there is a certain Connexion, of one Kind or other, between the Sensations of the Soul, and the Motions excited in the medullary Substance of the Brain." And usually he argued that his vibration theory constituted the most convincing explanation of this connection of which he knew. "Sensation, Thought, and Motion," he wrote, "must all be performed by Vibrations."[29]

Hartley believed that his theories of association and vibration complemented each other. Vibrations could not leave any vestiges of themselves and thereby produce ideas, he argued, unless their many parts cohered together "through joint Impression; i.e. Association." Further, the principle of association applied to vibrations just as much as to sensations and ideas: any group of vibrations, by being associated together through repetition, gained such power over the corresponding vibratiuncles that the occurrence of any single vibration from the group occasioned all of the vibratiuncles. On the other hand, the association of ideas required vibrations, since ideas "must first be generated . . . before they can be associated." Consequently, as the body and the mind existed in an intimate relation, that was necessarily the case also with vibrations and associations. "Vibrations should infer Association as their Effect, and Association point to Vibrations as its Cause."[30]

In devising this psychology, Hartley certainly needed to draw on his medical knowledge. But Observations on Man was the book of an eighteenth-century moral philosopher as well as of a physician. Its author attempted to explain all mental and moral phenomena on the basis of his combination of association and vibration. In this regard he

29. Ibid., 1:416, 33–34, 72, 512, 88.
30. Ibid., 1:70–71, 67, 6.

discussed the five senses, sexual desire, memory, revery, and language. Like John Gay, the anonymous author of the *Letter from a Man to his Fellow-Creatures*, and the anonymous author of 1741 and 1747, he rejected the notion of the moral sense as a distinct faculty. He also denied, however, that self-interest and the desire for pleasure and aversion to pain were innate. Instead, he derived all the passions and moral ideas from the association of simple ideas and sensation. By means of vibrations, he suggested, sensations (or at least the stronger of them) caused pleasure or pain, the latter differing from the former only in degree and not in kind. These pleasures and pains were themselves sensations or ideas, and the passions were "States of considerable Pleasure or Pain." As a result, the passions or affections could only be combinations of simple ideas of sensation united by association, "Aggregates of the Ideas, or Traces of the sensible Pleasures and Pains." Therefore, "all Love and Hatred, all Desire and Aversion, are factitious, and generated by Association."[31] Unlike Gay, Hartley was certainly no utilitarian.

With this foundation in place, Hartley proceeded to explain the six classes of what he called "intellectual Affections": imagination, ambition, self-interest, sympathy, theopathy, and the moral sense. To do so he explored how the "intellectual Pleasures and Pains" attaching to each of the species of affection derived ultimately from sensible pleasures and pains. In the course of this analysis he dealt with a number of important issues in eighteenth-century moral philosophy. His discussion of ambition, for instance, centered on a problem also investigated by Hume, Smith, and other contemporaries, the social reactions of approbation or honor and disapprobation or shame. He concluded that association caused men to seek the pleasures of the former reaction and avoid the pains of the latter, since the opinions of others constituted the principal source of human happiness or misery.[32]

Hartley treated the six classes of pleasures and pains as an interdependent hierarchy, based ultimately on sensation and association. Thus, sensation generated imagination by means of association; sensation and imagination together yielded ambition; sensation, imagination, and ambition produced self-interest; and so on. In addition, each affection reacted upon all those lower than it on the scale of

31. Ibid., 1:ii ("Introduction"), 34–35, 368–71. Even the desire for happiness was only the result of association: ibid., 1:465; 2:21, 197–98.
32. Ibid., 1:416–17, 443–57.

pleasures and pains, so that the passions actually comprised an immensely complex whole. But regardless of the complexity of the passions or affections, Hartley saw clearly and placed great emphasis on two points. First, association provided the key to the entire system, the instrument by which the movement from one level to another in the hierarchy was effected. With Newton's principle of gravitation obviously in mind, Hartley declared that "Association itself [is] the general Law, according to which the intellectual World is framed and conducted."[33]

Second, the end products of the system were theopathy and the famous moral sense, so much debated in the eighteenth century. All the pleasures and pains of sensation, imagination, ambition, self-interest, sympathy, and theopathy

> beget in us a Moral Sense, and lead us to the Love and Approbation of Virtue, and to the Fear, Hatred, and Abhorrence of Vice. This Moral Sense therefore carries its own Authority with it, inasmuch as it is the Sum total of all the rest, and the ultimate Result from them. . . .
>
> It appears also, that the Moral Sense [reacting back on theopathy] carries us perpetually to the pure Love of God, as our highest and ultimate Perfection, End, Centre, and only Resting-place, to which yet we can never attain.

Hartley concluded that through association the moral sense would at last make the performance of duty to God a pleasure and the commission of sin a pain, "without any express Recollection of the Hopes and Fears of another World, just as in other Cases of Association." Similarly, when the moral sense "is advanced to considerable Perfection, a Person may be made to love and hate, merely because he ought."[34]

That Hartley should have used the words "made to" in this context is not at all surprising, for he also wrote that the moral sense was "generated necessarily and mechanically." Such statements accord precisely with his view of mental phenomena in general. From his analysis of vibrations to his treatment of the hierarchy of intellectual pleasures and pains, he clearly depicted the mind as a mechanism. The external world impressed itself on the mind, triggering natural mechanical responses; pleasures and pains arose mechanically from

33. Ibid., 1: 368–69; 2:21.
34. Ibid., 1:497–98.

sensation, and they in turn manufactured one affection after another. Hartley made no effort to disguise this picture of the mind. Indeed, he brought the first volume of his *Observations* to a close with "Some Remarks on the Mechanism of the Human Mind." And in his correspondence he discoursed on the "mechanism" of man's nature and wrote, "I am mechanical."[35] Although profoundly different in many other ways, on this particular subject the views of Hartley and those of his fellow physician La Mettrie, the French materialist and author of *L'Homme machine* (1748), were strikingly similar.

The analogy of man and the mind to a machine logically led Hartley to disapprove of the notion of "Free-will in the philosophical Sense." He understood free will of this sort to mean a power of spontaneously initiating action, of performing any act or its contrary while previous circumstances remained unchanged. Such liberty, he argued, could not exist, since every action arose necessarily out of the prior conditions occurring in the mind (as a result of impressed vibrations and their concomitant associated sensations and ideas). Yet human beings did possess "Free-will in the popular and practical Sense." This he defined as the power "of doing what a Person desires or wills to do, of deliberating, suspending, choosing, *&c.* or of resisting the Motives of Sensuality, Ambition, Resentment, *&c.*" Turnbull and the anonymous author of 1745 had taken a similar position. But Hartley attempted to justify his attitude in greater detail than they. As he defined it the will was that state of mind or set of compound vibratiuncles existing immediately previous to and causing all acts of memory, imagination, or bodily motion. Whenever an action proceeded directly from such a state of mind, without the mind perceiving the intervention of any other sensation, idea, or motion, that action was voluntary. Therefore, all voluntary actions depended on ideas and consequently on associations. The voluntary powers included the ability to attend to an idea for a brief time; to recall a name, fact, or idea; to stimulate or restrain affections; to perform or refrain from actions; and to excite moral motives by reading or reflection. As Hartley himself argued, the existence of such powers obviously did not contradict but actually flowed from the mechanism of human nature. Clearly, much more than the other writers on association in

35. Ibid., 1:504, 500; Hartley to Lister, May 13, 1739, and Aug. 7, 1739, in Trigg, "Correspondence of Hartley and Lister," 254–55, 257.

the 1740s, Hartley was—and admitted to being—a proponent of the doctrine of philosophical necessity.[36]

The analysis of free will and mechanism completed Hartley's psychological system. With this system he believed that he had fulfilled his intention of erecting a theory of the human mind on a scientific basis. But since he thought of psychology and natural philosophy in general as preparatory to religion, ethics, and politics, he aimed at more than merely a science of the mind. In his opinion, an understanding of the "Frame and Constitution" of man would contribute much to the "Determination of Man's Duty and Expectations." So he wished, like Turnbull and the anonymous writers, to apply his knowledge of mental operations to the problems of human life. And he felt that these problems could be solved, just as machines could be repaired or illnesses cured. Adopting the perspective of the engineer and the physician, he wrote that the mechanical nature of the body and mind provided "Encouragements to study them faithfully and diligently, since what is mechanical *may* be both understood and remedied."[37]

Hartley was, at bottom, an essentially religious man, in spite of the materialist tendencies of his psychology. He proclaimed the goal of life to be "Happiness in being united to God," an end attainable through the transformation of sensuality into spirituality ("perfect Self-annihilation, and the pure Love of God"). Because of the Fall, however, men inhabited a "ruined World" and lived in a "degenerate and corrupt State." How, then, were they to make the transition to spirituality and true happiness? Hartley argued that the answer lay in association.[38]

To begin with, he thought that association had a *natural* tendency to promote pleasure and happiness at the expense of pain and misery. This conclusion followed in part from his observation that pains arose from stronger vibrations than did pleasures. Frequent repetition of the relatively violent vibrations of pain occasioned changes in the

36. *Observations*, 1:500–01, vi–viii ("Preface"), iii–iv ("Introduction"), 82, 112. On the mechanical nature of the will, see also ibid., 1:371.

37. Ibid., 1:354, 366; 2:iii ("Introduction").

38. Ibid., 2:183, 282, 236, 203, 214; 1:240. For Hartley's religiosity, see a prayer composed by him in 1734 in which he declared that "all worldly joys are nothing but vanity and vexation of spirit; . . . they are all but loss in comparison of the excellency of the knowledge of JESUS CHRIST my lord": Hartley, *Prayers and Religious Meditations*, in *Observations*, 5th ed., 2 vols. (London, 1810), 2:486. Hartley's views on some of the effects of the Fall appear in *Observations*, 1st ed., 2:257.

brain that made it disposed to receive only weaker—and therefore more pleasurable—vibrations. In addition, he also assumed that there was somewhat more pleasure than pain in the world. As a result, on the whole associated combinations of pleasures and pains would contain more pleasurable elements and appear to be simple pleasures, "equal in Quantity to the Excess of Pleasure above Pain, in each Combination." Thus, concluded Hartley, "Association would convert a State, in which Pleasure and Pain were both perceived by Turns, into one in which pure Pleasure alone would be perceived." Such a natural power of obtaining pleasure and removing pain increased with every day of a person's life, and through association it converted a state in which there was a mixture of happiness and misery "into one of pure Happiness, into a paradisiacal one."[39]

This process occurred on its own, without the need for any human intervention. The same was true of the generation of intellectual pleasures and pains from sensible ones, and of the rise of the higher intellectual affections, such as theopathy and the moral sense (including benevolence), from the lower ones. But Hartley was not satisfied with this natural operation of association. As with Turnbull and both anonymous authors, he wanted humankind to enhance the effect of association by making controlled use of it. It was this desire that lay behind such statements as the one previously cited in which he wrote of people being made to love and hate. For in his view the principal use of the doctrine of association was its contribution to the "amendment of ethics and morals." Association gave human beings, in essence, the ability to produce progress in their moral and religious lives:

> It is of the utmost Consequence to Morality and Religion, that the Affections and Passions should be analysed into their simple compounding Parts, by reversing the Steps of the Associations which concur to form them. For thus we may learn how to cherish and improve good ones, check and root out such as are mischievous and immoral, and how to suit our Manner of Life, in some tolerable Measure, to our Religious Wants.

Similarly, since association also explained how the voluntary powers of man developed and functioned, it also "teaches us how to regulate

39. *Observations*, 1:38–40, 82–83, and 2:15, 359–62, 16–17, 26–27; *Various Conjectures*, 50. With his reference to the excess of pleasure over pain, Hartley anticipated in a general way Bentham's felicific calculus.

and improve these Powers." In sum, by using association "we have a Power of suiting our Frame of Mind to our Circumstances, of correcting what is amiss, and improving what is right."[40]

As a practical moralist, Hartley devoted a long chapter of the *Observations* (entitled "Of the Rule of Life") to specific suggestions about how people might make these corrections and improvements. His theme was that the precepts of benevolence (sympathy), piety (theopathy), and the moral sense ought to regulate the pleasures of sensation and convert them into the higher intellectual pleasures. Because the moral sense coincided with benevolence and piety, it should become the immediate guide of all actions. Its mechanical generation through associations occasioned by the impressions of external objects made it a particularly useful and improvable governor of life. Study of the scriptures and the writings and deeds of good men, for example, enlarged the moral sense and permitted it, in turn, to transform the sympathetic and theopathic affections into the pure love of God. In this process education in the broad sense obviously worked hand in hand with association. Hartley made this linkage clear when he wrote that the power of custom, example, education, and learning had association for "its Foundation, and may be considered as the Detail of it, in various Circumstances."[41]

Thus, association, acting through the moral sense, created moral and religious progress by turning sensuality into spirituality and self-annihilation. But was this conception of Hartley's really a belief in progress at all? Was it not merely a theory of the advance of the individual man to a kind of mystical union with the deity, rather than a notion of the movement of men toward an improved state of temporal affairs by means of exercising control over the pliable nature of the mind?[42]

In fact, it was both. Hartley undeniably considered the question of the spiritual improvement of the individual at great length. His for-

40. *Observations*, 1:81–84, and 2:213; *Various Conjectures*, 54.
41. *Observations*, 2:337–40; 1:65.
42. So one student of the *Observations* has argued. She contends that Hartley's reputation as "a progressivist . . . is entirely mistaken," because "his references to progress, like Bunyan's, refer to the spiritual progress of the individual. In the ordinary sense of the term, he was not a believer in progress at all. . . . For when Hartley talked about progress, as he frequently did, he meant the progress of the individual mind from carnality to spirituality." See Margaret Leslie, "Mysticism Misunderstood: David Hartley and the Idea of Progress," *Journal of the History of Ideas* 33 (Oct.–Dec. 1972): 627, 631.

mal conclusion in this regard stated that the "Progress of every Individual in his Passage through an eternal Life is from imperfect to perfect, particular to general, less to greater, finite to infinite, and from the Creature to the Creator." He believed that for many men and women the transition to spiritual perfection would require a long period of suffering after death.[43] But this treatment of the eternal spiritual development of the individual represents only one side of his thought. The other side concerns things temporal and social. Having established to his satisfaction the method by which ideas and the affections develop in the individual, he proceeded to suggest some social implications for earthly life.

At the simplest level, he claimed that what was true for one person was also true for the group. Since benevolence, piety, and the moral sense provided the true foundations of private happiness, "that the public Happiness arises from them, cannot be doubted by anyone." And because these three classes of affections produced progressively greater felicity in the individual by association, they would achieve the same effect in society. Hartley defined the social group as a system of beings who could cause each other happiness or misery, and he assumed that everyone had the same kind of mental processes and the same desire (from association) to achieve private happiness. Given these premises it followed that

the Scale will turn more and more perpetually in favour of the Production of Happiness: For the Happiness which A receives from B, will lead him by Association to love B, and to wish and endeavour B's Happiness, in return: B will therefore have a Motive, arising from his Desire of his own Happiness, to continue his good Offices to A: Whereas the Misery that A receives from B will lead him to hate B, and to deter him from farther Injuries.[44]

To this extent, the progress of public happiness occurred naturally. But Hartley argued that humankind could accelerate it through their own efforts, especially with the proper use of language. If they would only simplify and refine their language, individuals in society

43. *Observations*, 2:439, 419–37.
44. Ibid., 2:263–64, 20–21. It clearly is not true, as Sir Leslie Stephen claimed, that Hartley failed to consider the "reciprocal action upon each other of different members of the race": *History of English Thought in the Eighteenth Century* (3d ed., 1902), repr. ed., 2 vols. (New York, 1962), 2:59.

might become new senses and powers of perception to each other and thereby give happiness to each other indefinitely. Then, through association, they would find that the mixture of pleasures and pains they currently experienced would "gradually tend to a Collection of pure Pleasures only." In making this prognostication, Hartley was acting on the decidedly anti-Mandevillian principle that "public Happiness, which arises from the Cultivation of private Virtues, includes private Happiness within itself." But he was also relying heavily upon the efficacy of the power of association simultaneously to improve both the individual *and* society. Writing as a physician of the body and of the mind, he declared that association could "illuminate the ways by which the good motivations of the spirit may be fostered, the bad restrained, and how each one of us can both take *the beam out of one's own eye and the mote from the eye of one's neighbor.*"[45]

Hartley was convinced that this medicine for the public mind and morals would have its most important uses among the young. He considered it quite apparent from common experience and especially from his doctrine of association that "Children may be formed and moulded as we please." Given their pliability, whoever took pains with their education might be "the Instrument of Salvation, temporal and eternal, to Multitudes."[46] Clearly, Hartley's conception of the uses of association and the pliable nature of man extended farther than a theory of the spiritual ascent of the individual. Like Turnbull and the two anonymous writers earlier in the 1740s, he dreamed also of earthly progress toward a happier social existence.

Hartley's views on association, pliability, and progress were not substantially different from those of other writers on psychology in the decade before midcentury. But he sought to provide his case in far greater detail than they, and in constructing his elaborate system he made the principle of association the key to both pliability and progress. This system, as expressed in *Observations on Man*, did not become highly influential until after Joseph Priestley published abbreviated versions of that book in 1775 and 1790. Thereafter, Hartley's popularity soared and his ideas on psychology found their way into the writings of such a diverse group of famous thinkers as Bentham, James Mill, Godwin, Erasmus Darwin, Burke, Coleridge, and Wordsworth. According to John Stuart Mill's *Autobiography*,

45. *Observations*, 1:315–21, and 2:210; *Various Conjectures*, 55. For a more detailed analysis of Hartley's views on language and progress, see below, chap. 5.
46. *Observations*, 2:453–54. See also *Various Conjectures*, 55.

Hartley had numerous readers as late as 1830.[47] But although it required more than forty years for the *Observations* to reach a wide audience, the British intellectual world did not suddenly forget about associationism and the doctrine of pliable man after 1749. For example, by creating a controversy over Hartley's position on these subjects, Scottish philosophers such as James Beattie and Thomas Reid helped to keep his ideas before the eyes of an important segment of the reading public. Meanwhile, English writers on psychology and moral philosophy continued to take the Hartleyan line.

Between 1749 and his death in 1751, the Nonconformist Philip Doddridge was at work on a set of lectures concerning "pneumatology" (the science relating to such "spirits" as the human mind) and ethics, for delivery to the students at his Dissenting academy. In these lectures he considered such issues as the relation of the mind to the body and associations or trains of ideas. He also emphasized the great extent to which human beings were shaped by education in the broad sense, and the consequent need for control of the habit-forming process. When Doddridge wrote these lectures he had already studied the *Observations*, so at least some of his views may have been derivative. In any event he clearly agreed with Hartley that man was pliable, and both of them believed what another moralist, Peter Shaw, wrote so succinctly in 1750: "Men's Minds are improveable."[48]

The most voluminous commentary on these points came from Abraham Tucker (1705–74), a retiring Surrey squire who had attended Oxford and received legal training at the Inner Temple. In about 1756 he began to write a treatise on psychology, moral philoso-

47. On Hartley's later influence, see below, chap. 9, and John Stuart Mill, *Autobiography*, in *Collected Works of John Stuart Mill*, 29 vols. to date (Toronto, 1963–), vol. 1 (*Autobiography and Literary Essays*, ed. John M. Robson and Jack Stillinger [1981]), 125–27; G. S. Bower, *David Hartley and James Mill* (New York, 1881), 226–27; Martin Kallich, *The Association of Ideas and Critical Theory in Eighteenth-Century England: A History of a Psychological Method in English Criticism* (The Hague, 1970), 129–31.

In his editions of the *Observations*, Priestley omitted most of the second volume (on religion and morals) and the majority of what Hartley had written about vibrations. For Priestley's reasoning in doing so, and for a discussion of what he quietly *added* to the book, see Ronald B. Hatch, "Joseph Priestley: An Addition to Hartley's *Observations*," *Journal of the History of Ideas* 36 (July–Sept. 1975): 548–50; and see below, chap. 8.

48. Philip Doddridge, *A Course of Lectures on the Principal Subjects in Pneumatology, Ethics, and Divinity* (published 1763), in *The Miscellaneous Works of Philip Doddridge, D.D.* (London, 1839), 220:1–238:2, 522:2; Peter Shaw, *The Reflector, Representing Human Affairs, As they are, and may be improved* (London, 1750), 5.

phy, and religion, and this task required the remainder of his life to complete. The result of his labors, *The Light of Nature Pursued*, appeared between 1768 and 1778 in seven prolix volumes. Tucker called himself a follower of Locke, and this work certainly substantiates that claim. But his reading of Hartley served to modify the psychological theory he had inherited from Locke, so that his chapters on the mental and moral operations of man took the same general perspective as had the writers on psychology of the 1740s.

In his attempt to explore scientifically the wilderness of the human mind, Tucker made use of a few well-established guideposts: the existence of an intellectual and moral tabula rasa at birth, the interdependence of mind and body, and the omnipresence of the power of association. From these bases, and from the utilitarian assumption that each person's pleasure and happiness was "the true original spring and proper first mover of all his actions," he arrived at essentially the same psychology as that of his immediate predecessors. He argued that sensations produced ideas, which in turn became linked together through juxtaposition to form associations or trains; trains grew habitual with repetition. A similar process occurred in the realm of motivation. Association or "translation" could make what a person first considered only a means to happiness (such as money or benevolent actions) into an end in itself. Such transformations became habitual with time and gave rise to tastes, inclinations, sentiments, the moral sense, the regard paid to reputation, and virtues and vices. Therefore, Tucker believed, although man had freedom of the will and his actions followed directly from his volitions, he derived "from prior sources the springs of action determining what he shall please to do." Man and the will operated mechanically, and virtue was a "habit."[49]

With this psychology in mind, Tucker characterized the material composition of the brain and nervous system as "extremely soft and pliable," and the mind itself as having a "soft and pliable temper." Because the mind could be gradually and easily diverted from one habitual track to another, he believed that it was possible to produce progress by controlling mental and moral habits or behavior patterns. An inclination or motivation could "like a tender twig . . . be brought to grow in any shape by continual bending." Consequently, since habits of one sort or another were unavoidable, men should seek to

49. Abraham Tucker, *The Light of Nature Pursued*, 3d ed., 2 vols. (London, 1834), 1:87–104, 128, 150–53, 157–59, 215; 2:569, 609, 619, 669–70, 678.

cultivate good ones and uproot evil ones, quickening their "progress in virtue" by instruction, exhortation, example, and their own industry. The ultimate aim of this moral advancement in each person ought to be the achievement of bliss in heaven. But the individual's spiritual progress had a direct relationship with social progress on earth. For to reach the final spiritual goal, each person had to pursue the "temporal happiness" of his or her fellow creatures. And the promotion of the general good redounded to the benefit of the individual: every act of benevolence "tends something towards the general good, wherein a prudent man will see his own contained."[50] In Tucker's opinion, then, the pliability of the individual permitted the spiritual advancement of each through the temporal progress of all. He believed with Hartley and the others that the key to progress lay in that medicine of the mind, the formation of proper associations and habits.

The Light of Nature Pursued was the longest and most detailed expression of the belief in progress through association and the pliability of man to appear in Britain between 1749 and the French Revolution, but it was not the last during the period. The well-known Anglican theologian and theological utilitarian William Paley (1743–1805) considered the same issues in his *Principles of Moral and Political Philosophy* (1785) and later works. As a disciple of Tucker, however, he merely presented in shortened form ideas derived from his master, without making an original contribution to the study of mental operations.

The works of Tucker and Paley mark the end of a half-century-long series of discourses on the mind in which the principle of association played a prominent role. The writers of these treatises all wanted to set psychology and moral philosophy on a solid foundation, and beginning with John Gay they found in associationism a satisfying explanation of the functioning of the mental and moral world; from 1740 they tied the psychology of association tightly to the related concepts of pliability and progress. Unquestionably, the single most important figure in this group was Hartley, and in many respects he was representative of them all. Like him they were English (though Turnbull had been born and educated in Scotland), liberal Anglican in religion (except for the Dissenter Doddridge), and tended to have strong Cambridge ties (especially Gay, the anony-

50. Ibid., 1:149, 104, 100, 254, 218, 156–57, 255–56, 259; 2:569–70, 680.

mous author of 1741 and 1747, and Paley, as well as Hartley). In addition, like Hartley they all acknowledged themselves followers of Locke and Newton and did their thinking about human nature within the confines of British empirical philosophy.

This last characteristic provides the most significant context for their thought. Their ideas about the mind developed as an essentially self-contained, self-influencing intellectual tradition that worked out many of the implications of Lockean sensationalist psychology. In exploring these implications, the members of this group do not appear to have been influenced by contemporary French ideas on psychology. Nor did they receive the impulse for their work from any specific social condition, such as probably occurred in the somewhat earlier case of the impact of the new commercial culture on Bernard de Mandeville's moral philosophy—although it is undoubtedly true that the development of the whole field of psychology and the rise of the concept of the self owed much to the advance of a secular outlook in eighteenth-century Europe.[51] The very fact that the work of the writers under examination here spanned fifty years militates against the existence of a particular social influence common to most or all of them. To be sure, they were certainly not cut off from the social world. Their experience in a society that was poised on the brink of a period of great changes and stresses must have contributed in a general way to their assessment that the human condition was not entirely healthy. Likewise, their observation of at least a few early examples of the dogged entrepreneurial personality later celebrated by Samuel Smiles undoubtedly helped to foster their belief in the power of individuals to make (or remake) themselves. But as with eighteenth-century eschatology, the psychological theories and accompanying belief in progress of these men from Turnbull to Paley fundamentally represented much more a response to intellectual than social factors.

EDUCATION

Hartley and his predecessors and successors were not alone in preparing medicine for the mind in eighteenth-century Brit-

51. Their writings do not contain—and before 1748 could not have contained—any evidence of familiarity with La Mettrie, Condillac, or Helvétius. On the social context of Mandeville's thought, see Isaac Kramnick, *Bolingbroke and His Circle: The Politics of Nostalgia in the Age of Walpole* (Cambridge, Mass., 1968), 201–04. On secularization and psychology and "the self," see G. S. Rousseau, "Psychology," in

ain. Another and larger group, whose concern was education in the narrower sense, undertook the same task of curing the ills of humankind by administering mental remedies. Side by side with and frequently influenced by the associationist psychologists, these educational thinkers from the 1740s to 1790 produced a series of writings on the theme that education could promote progress because of the pliability of man.

The development of this motif in educational thought was foreshadowed and stimulated by John Locke. In *Some Thoughts Concerning Education*, he commented that each child was unique and born with certain natural tendencies in temper, constitution, and abilities, so that the human mind, like the body, "may perhaps be a little mended; but can hardly be totally alter'd, and transform'd into the contrary." Notwithstanding these suggestions on the importance of the innate element in human temperament, Locke placed stronger emphasis on the predominance of nurture over nature. As he declared in what have become some of his most famous words, "of all the Men we meet with, Nine Parts of Ten are what they are, Good or Evil, useful or not, by their Education." Children he considered "only as white Paper, or Wax, to be moulded and fashioned as one pleases;" their minds were "pliant to Reason . . . most easy to be bowed." Consequently, it was the business of the educator to inculcate proper habits in the child and to promote virtue—the goal of education— "by Custom, made easy and familiar by an *early* Practice." In Locke's opinion the education of the young in virtue had important ramifications for society as well as for the character of the individual. He wished that those

> who complain of the great Decay of Christian Piety and Vertue every where, and of Learning and acquired Improvements in the Gentry of this Generation, would consider how to retrieve them in the next. This I am sure, That if the Foundation of it be not laid in the Education and Principling of Youth, . . .'twill be ridiculous to expect, that those who are to succeed next on the Stage, should abound in that Vertue, Ability, and Learning, which has hitherto made *England* considerable in the World.[52]

Rousseau and Porter, *Ferment of Knowledge*, 147; John O. Lyons, *The Invention of the Self: The Hinge of Consciousness in the Eighteenth Century* (Carbondale, Ill., 1978).

52. John Locke, *Some Thoughts Concerning Education* (1693), in *The Educational Writings of John Locke: A Critical Edition with Introduction and Notes*, ed. James L. Axtell (Cambridge, 1968), 244, 159, 114, 325, 138, 237, 169–70.

Locke's *Some Thoughts* reached a wide audience in eighteenth-century Britain (going through twenty-five printings in England and Scotland before 1780), and the book set the tone and marked the chief point of reference for most thinking about education at the time. Not surprisingly, therefore, his ideas on the supremacy of nurture over nature and on the general significance of education for the improvement of the individual and society became highly influential in pedagogical treatises. Thus, as in the case of the psychology of association, Locke once again initiated and provided the groundwork for a line of thought. Of course, his emphasis on nurture and pliability harmonized nicely with that psychology as developed by Hartley and others. As we have seen, Hartley himself called the principle of association the foundation of education, and this notion was not lost upon those among his readers who were especially interested in pedagogy. As Hartley's popularizer Priestley argued, the "most important application of Dr. Hartley's doctrine of the association of ideas is to *the conduct of human life,* and especially the business of *education.*" Taking this view to heart, the American Benjamin Rush in the 1780s made Hartleyan psychology the basis of his whole program for learning and perfectibility in the new republic.[53] Perhaps no one in Britain had quite the exuberance of Rush, but like him many British educational thinkers proceeded from the arguments of Locke's *Some Thoughts* and from the psychology of association to claim that education was the means of progress.

The educationalists who took this position in published works during the high eighteenth century comprised a diverse group from considerably different backgrounds, and they therefore represent a large body of contemporary opinion. Among them may be numbered the authors of some of the best-known educational treatises of the age, such as Vicesimus Knox and David Williams, as well as obscure pedagogical writers. In politics the group included proponents of extensive parliamentary reform as well as a follower of Lord Bute; in religion an Anglican cleric, a Unitarian minister, and a deist. Coming from all four geographical subdivisions of the British Isles, they pursued a wide variety of careers. About half were directly involved in

53. Joseph Priestley, *An Examination of Dr. Reid's Inquiry into the Human Mind* (1774), in *The Theological and Miscellaneous Works of Joseph Priestley,* ed. John Towill Rutt, 25 vols. in 26 [London, 1817–32], 3:6. On Rush, see Donald J. D'Elia, "Benjamin Rush, David Hartley, and the Revolutionary Uses of Psychology," *Proceedings of the American Philosophical Society* 114 (April 13, 1970): 109:1–118:2.

teaching or the operation of schools, but some were best known as controversialists, "miscellaneous writers," or even actors. What they had in common besides their general interest in education was the same sense of decay in virtue that Locke had mentioned as a lament of *his* age, decay that they attributed to the failure of education.

Such an outlook was expressed succinctly in 1756 by Thomas Sheridan (1719–88), Dublin actor and theater manager, writer on language and education, and father of Richard Brinsley Sheridan. He proclaimed that in his age "irreligion, immorality, and corruption are visibly increased, and daily gather new strength," and he traced the source of all these troubles to "a defective education, which, not taking care to settle the notions of men upon the basis of right reason, leaves their unfurnished minds open to receive any opinion that chance may throw in their way." But with a proper education, as the Aberdeen professor David Fordyce wrote in 1745, a "sober, manly, virtuous Youth" would grow up to replace the present "lazy, effeminate, dissolute Race, who do such dishonour to their Country, and bear too evident Marks of an idle enervated Education."[54]

At base, then, these commentators on education desired reform of the pedagogical system that they saw around them. In this respect they typified the widespread tendency in eighteenth-century England to view traditional educational institutions—grammar schools, public schools, and the universities—with dissatisfaction.[55] Throughout

54. Thomas Sheridan, *British Education: Or, The Source of the Disorders of Great Britain* (Dublin, 1758), 1, 7–8; Fordyce, *Dialogues Concerning Education*, 1:344. For some similar disparaging remarks on contemporary virtue and the situation of education, see Forrester, *Dialogues on Children*, 59; James Wadham Whitchurch, *An Essay upon Education* (London, 1772), 7; Vicesimus Knox, *Liberal Education: Or, A Practical Treatise on the Methods of Acquiring Useful and Polite Learning* (London, 1781), 253; Richard Shepherd, *An Essay on Education* (Holborn, 1782), 15; Catharine Macaulay Graham, *Letters on Education. With Observations on Religious and Metaphysical Subjects* (Dublin, 1790), 9. Exceptions to the general attack on contemporary education may be seen in such Scots as Adam Smith, whose experience with the parish schools of the Lowlands had been favorable, and in those English Nonconformists who had attended Dissenting academies. See, for example, the talk by Warrington Academy graduate Thomas Barnes, "A Plan for the Improvement and Extension of Liberal Education in Manchester" (read April 9, 1783), in *Memoirs of the Literary and Philosophical Society of Manchester*, 2d ed., 2 (1789): 16.
55. On the declining reputation of the English grammar and public schools during the eighteenth century, see Frank Musgrove, "Middle Class Families and Schools, 1780–1880: Interaction and Exchange of Function between Institutions," *Sociological Review*, n. s., 7 (Dec. 1959): 171. Although its exaggerations are now recognized, the most famous account of the universities remains Gibbon's indictment: Edward Gibbon, *Memoirs of My Life*, ed. Georges A. Bonnard (New York, 1969), 47–55.

the century, concern over the failures of these institutions was at least partly responsible for such innovations as the spread of domestic instruction, the new learning techniques encouraged by the Lunar Society of Birmingham and the Literary and Philosophical Society of Manchester, and the Charity and Sunday School movements. Some of the educationalists under consideration here had in mind specific improvements of their own. But whatever changes they proposed, they agreed on fundamental principles very similar to those laid down by Locke and the associationist psychologists.

The most significant assumption that they held in common was the doctrine of the pliability of man. Fordyce, who had spent some time at Doddridge's academy in Northampton, posed a question that concerned them all: did the prejudices, errors, and follies of life come from the innate passions and nature of human beings, or were "they bent and fashioned by Culture, Example, and the Variety of Accidents with which Life is chequered . . . ?" In their answer, they took the position of Locke that although innate endowments could not be entirely ignored, nurture played a larger role than nature in the formation of men and women. While rejecting the view that education in the broad sense was "all in all" in life, since it could not give a person "new Capacities or Springs of Action," Fordyce argued that it could "direct and cultivate" these capacities in the "waxen Mind of Youth." Similar views were held by David Williams, the Welsh deist and writer on religion and moral philosophy, who founded a school in London and encouraged parliamentary reform and full religious toleration. He responded to his reading of Helvétius and Rousseau by claiming that everyone was born with a certain "texture" to his or her nervous system and a disposition and capabilities that no education (in the narrow sense) could entirely change, and that individuals did not all have the same potential for intellectual and moral improvement. Nevertheless, education could "considerably correct and improve" men, since habits, which had such great importance, were changeable and not "original inclinations of nature." Catharine Macaulay Graham (1731–91), the famous historian and radical, also in-

---

Scottish educational institutions generally performed better and thus received less criticism, except for burgh schools. But see the criticism of higher education and proposals for change described in Peter Jones, "The Scottish Professoriate and the Polite Academy, 1720–46," in Istvan Hont and Michael Ignatieff, eds., *Wealth and Virtue: The Shaping of Political Economy in the Scottish Enlightenment* (Cambridge, 1983), 89–117.

sisted on the influence of nurture or "art" in forming the character of the species. "Nature," she wrote, "indeed supplies the raw materials, and the capacity of the workman; but the effect is the mere production of art. . . . No; there is not a virtue or vice that belongs to humanity, which we do not make ourselves."[56]

In asserting the claims of nurture, these educationalists recurred frequently to the analogy of the mind to a garden or plant. Turnbull, who published a book on education two years after his treatise on moral philosophy, suggested that just as the soil requires proper preparation for seeding, "so the mind must by apposite care be moulded into a fit temperament or disposition for embracing and cherishing the seeds of good doctrine." The main difference between the mind and crops was that the "culture of our minds is much more dependent upon us than that of our gardens and fields." Fordyce similarly declared that "as the Minds of Children resemble the uncultivated Garden of Nature, their Improvement will be according to the Nature of the Soil, and the Care and Skill of the Gardeners they meet with. A bad Soil may be greatly rectified and improved by kindly Culture."[57]

Like Locke himself, then, these eighteenth-century writers on education adopted a modified environmentalist position. They attributed more to nature, to the initially existing soil of the mind, than did Locke's French followers such as Helvétius. But they considered art or nurture—the cultivation of the mind—to be superior to innate endowment in the development of the person. Thomas Barnes, the Arian minister who helped to found the Manchester Literary and Philosophical Society and became theological tutor at Manchester Academy, spoke for all of them when he stated in 1783 that although the "original differences stamped upon human minds" were significant, "yet education [in the broad sense] marks far greater and stronger lines of distinction, between one mind and another." Having made

56. Fordyce, *Dialogues Concerning Education*, 1:177–78, 180, and 2:98, 57; David Williams, *A Treatise on Education* (London, 1774), 65–67, 215, 41–42; Macaulay Graham, *Letters on Education*, 53, 7. For similar comments on nurture versus nature, see also Turnbull, *Observations upon Liberal Education*, 155, 178, 196, 206; Forrester, *Dialogues on Children*, 11–12, 19; Juliana-Susannah Seymour [pseud. for John Hill], *On the Management and Education of Children* (London, 1754), 21–22, 29–30, 139–40, 145; Whitchurch, *Essay upon Education*, 12–14, 17–18, 22–23, 27, 101, 119.

57. Turnbull, *Observations upon Liberal Education*, 216, 198; Fordyce, *Dialogues Concerning Education*, 1:191–92. Some of the many other examples of this metaphor appear in Forrester, *Dialogues on Children*, 9–10, 57; Hill, *Management and Education of Children*, 194–95; Whitchurch, *Essay upon Education*, 97, 160–61; Knox, *Liberal Education*, 285.

this assumption about the pliability of man, Barnes and the others naturally concluded that there were "few questions more important, when considered in every point of view, than those which relate to EDUCATION."[58]

Chief among these questions was how the general power of the environment to shape pliable man could be beneficially harnessed in the specific context of the rearing and instruction of children. The educationalists responded to this large problem with a complex solution. To begin with, they contended that education required a worthy goal if deleterious effects from its immense power were to be avoided. For, as Macaulay Graham wrote, it could lead a person to adopt absurd doctrines as easily as reasonable ones. Consequently, these writers agreed with Locke that education ought to have for its object the cultivation of virtue. Richard Shepherd (1732?–1809), an Anglican cleric from Lincolnshire, claimed in 1782 that "virtue is the main object of education. Without it all the learning of the world will render us neither of use or ornament." Of course, it was not necessary to be an ecclesiastic to adopt such an attitude. James Forrester, for example, agreed with Shepherd's assessment. Writing in 1748, he asserted that the "Culture of the Heart" was the most important part of education, far greater in significance than mere learning. Thomas Sheridan echoed the same sentiments by stating that the primary aim of the education of youth ought to be "to make them good men, good members of the universal society of mankind."[59]

In addition, the educationalists argued that the practice of good pedagogy required a correct understanding of mental operations. As the Scottish schoolmaster and writer George Chapman (1723–1806)

58. Barnes, "A brief Comparison of some of the principal Arguments in Favour of Public and Private Education" (read May 7, 1783), in *Memoirs of the Literary and Philosophical Society of Manchester*, 2d ed., 2 (1789): 1. It has been suggested by Frank Musgrove that there was a debate in eighteenth-century educational thought over the question of nature versus nurture: "Two Educational Controversies in Eighteenth Century England. Nature and Nurture: Private and Public Education," *Paedagogica Historica*, 2 (1962): 81–94. But he cites only Hannah More (writing in 1799) as an eighteenth-century defender of the nature position, and the only evidence I have found of other support for this viewpoint is the unclear attitude of Knox on the subject (see *Liberal Education*, 220n–21n).

59. Macaulay Graham, *Letters on Education*, 80; Shepherd, *Essay on Education*, 17; Forrester, *Dialogues on Children*, 7–8; Sheridan, *British Education*, 10. Other varieties of the emphasis on virtue in eighteenth-century writings on education are in John Clarke, *An Essay upon Study* (1731), 2d ed. (London, 1737), 5; Turnbull, *Observations upon Liberal Education*, 179; James Burgh, *Thoughts on Education* (London, 1747), 3; Knox, *Liberal Education*, 13.

put it, "those who have the charge of youth, ought in a particular manner to study the nature of the human mind." Others desired even more: like the associationist psychologists, they sought the development and spread of a science of the mind. This desire naturally appeared in the educational treatise of Turnbull, who wanted both teachers and students to explore the mind. It also manifested itself in Macaulay Graham. She stressed the need for education to be based on a "just insight into the mechanism of the human mind, and the proper exertion of its various faculties." Williams viewed Hartley's *Observations* as the first step toward a "simple, compleat, and intelligible idea of a human mind," without which teachers would "have no rules to go by in education." Although he believed that contemporary psychology required great refinement, he looked forward to the eventual perfection of a "compleat system of education." Fordyce thought that to create a scientific system of education "it would be necessary to give a *Theory* of *Imagination*; to deduce the *Laws* and *Powers* of *Association*; and to trace those Causes, whether *External* or *Internal*, more *Immediate* or more *Remote*, which influence our Views and Passions, and form our Manners."[60]

As the references by Fordyce to association and by Williams to Hartley suggest, the educationalists considered the role of association and habit to be at the core of their science of the mind. Although they specifically mentioned the psychologists of association only on occasion, their picture of mental operations was essentially the same as that painted by Hartley and the others. Fordyce, for example, wrote of the importance of associations of ideas to the foundation of habits, tempers, and manners in men. In Chapman's opinion, the passions derived largely from associated ideas. Williams traced the notions of justice, truth, and beneficence to simple associations, and he indicated that a man's character depended "on the impressions first made on his senses, on the method in which he is led to associate those impressions, and to prepare them as the materials of habits and affections." Although she preferred Tucker to Hartley, Macaulay Graham argued that it was possible on the basis of the system of either one to discover the "cause and course of our ideas, their propensity to run into clusters . . . , and the vast power and strength of such

60. Chapman, *Treatise on Education*, 2–3; Turnbull, *Observations upon Liberal Education*, 157, 349; Macaulay Graham, *Letters on Education*, 265, 283; Williams, *Treatise on Education*, 43–44, 99–100; Fordyce, *Dialogues Concerning Education*, 2:405–06.

associations"—and thereby to account for the "various turns of character we find in our species, by the early impressions made on the infant mind."[61]

This associationist science of the mind constituted the means by which the educational writers thought progress could be made toward their goal of virtue. For like medicine, theirs was to be an *applied* science of preventing and remedying the ills of men. In fact, the analogy of education to medicine was specifically made by Fordyce, Chapman, and others. Fordyce extended the metaphor farther than anyone else. He divided education into two parts, the first of which was preventive. It concerned the formation of wise and good people by exposing them to positive environmental influences and shielding them from deleterious ones. The second part ("SANATORY, or RESTORATIVE") aimed at counteracting wrong principles and manners—such as sudden impulses of passion or desire, envy, avarice, and vanity, all of which Fordyce called mental "Diseases" or "Distempers"—by eliminating from the mind harmful ideas and habits, in order "*to restore it to its sound and healthful State.*"[62]

With or without the trappings of the medical analogy, this was the program of all the educationalists. Williams's phrase, "the art of educating children, by directing the formation of habits," could well have served as their motto. They considered supervision of the establishment of habits and associations to be central to education. For instance, Knox, the Anglican cleric who was headmaster of Tunbridge School, wrote about the need for the teacher to encourage in the child associations connecting virtue with pleasures, honors, and rewards. He also noted that after the formation of wrong associations, it became "a great part of the care of the preceptor to remedy in future what it could not prevent." Chapman thought it paramount that parents and teachers endeavor "to prevent those false associations of ideas which are so destructive of human happiness" and so easily formed during impressionable childhood. In Macaulay Graham's opinion, the wise teacher, knowing the power of association and habit, would accustom his or her pupils to "the practice of habits

---

61. Fordyce, *Dialogues Concerning Education*, 1:269, and 2:393–94; Chapman, *Treatise on Education*, 33; Williams, *Treatise on Education*, 3, 221–22; Macaulay Graham, *Letters on Education*, 85, 44. See also Forrester, *Dialogues on Children*, 34–37.

62. Fordyce, *Dialogues Concerning Education*, 2:97–98, 377. For other references to the medicine metaphor, see the beginning of this chapter.

which tend to confirm those qualities . . . and those affections which are favourable to wise and virtuous volitions." Summing up all these comments, Fordyce pointed to associations as the spring of happiness and misery in life and declared that

> It must, therefore, be an Affair of the utmost Importance in Education, to set the just *Associations* in the Minds of Youth, and to break and disunite wrong ones. The doing this aright, I take to be the grand Art or Engine of *moral Culture*.[63]

Seen from this perspective, education constituted a remedy for the actual and potential ills of the mind, a means of improving the individual in virtue. But the educationalists considered it to have important implications for society as a whole. Indeed, some of them believed that education and an advanced state of civilization went hand in hand. According to Chapman, history "exhibits to our view the fortune of mankind ever varying in proportion to their care or negligence in the training of youth." Although Macaulay Graham attempted to describe this correlation in more detail, Sheridan was satisfied to claim that by education alone the northern and western regions of Europe, "once rude and savage, have risen to their present splendour."[64]

Others described the social role of education in more general terms. Referring particularly to the cultivation of good habits and morals, Williams claimed that the "prosperity and happiness of a people, are produced by causes, which begin their operations on individuals." Likewise, Knox felt certain that the valuable qualities of virtue and learning inculcated by education "operate in augmenting the general sum of human happiness, while they advance the dignity, and increase the satisfactions, of the individual." Turnbull wrote his book on education "to shew, 'How greatly private and publick happiness depends upon the right education of youth.'" Forrester, too, insisted on the importance of education in the principles of morals both "for the Happiness of Society in general, and consequently that

63. Williams, *Treatise on Education*, 42; Knox, *Liberal Education*, 198–99; Chapman, *Treatise on Education*, 5–6; Macaulay Graham, *Letters on Education*, 300–03; Fordyce, *Dialogues Concerning Education*, 1:270. For other comments on the place of habit and association formation in education, see Turnbull, *Observations upon Liberal Education*, 204, 235; Hill, *Management and Education of Children*, 30; Whitchurch, *Essay upon Education*, 27.

64. Chapman, *Treatise on Education*, 10; Macaulay Graham, *Letters on Education*, 149–50; Sheridan, *British Education*, 4–5.

of every Individual."[65] Clearly, these writers thought that the interests of society were closely bound to the education of its members.

The existence of this connection meant, to them, that education offered a way to produce social progress. As Sheridan wrote, the "well-being of a state depends upon the education of their youth," which, if correctly regulated, would "make them most useful to that society." With this principle in mind, he and others argued that the improvement of conditions in Britain—specifically the overcoming of that decay in virtue that so concerned them—could "be effected only by a right system of education." More broadly, Williams argued that because no government could make a nation happy whose members were not virtuous, and because virtue came from education, "whatever effectual steps are taken towards a public reformation, must be taken in the education of our youth." He concluded that "the people may be reformed," but only if "that reformation . . . be the effect of education." Macaulay Graham envisioned a larger role for government in the creation of virtuous society than Williams did. But she agreed with him and all the other educationalists that, in the words of Chapman, the mind by its constitution was "highly susceptible of improvement," and that this improvement was "closely connected with the perfection and happiness of mankind."[66]

The writers on education therefore looked upon education as an instrument not only for the advancement of the individual in virtue but also for the progress of society. From their perspective, it appeared to be a remedy—indeed, the chief remedy—for the afflictions of the minds of men and women. And its efficacy as a cure seemed to them assured, as long as its power over pliable human beings was understood and properly regulated.

In essence, the writers on psychology and education shared the same outlook on the nature of man. They adhered to the doctrine of

65. Williams, *Treatise on Education*, 20; Knox, *Liberal Education*, 12–13; Turnbull, *Observations on Liberal Education*, 2; Forrester, *Dialogues on Children*, x. See also Thomas Barnes, "Proposals for Establishing in Manchester a Plan of Liberal Education" (dated July 9, 1783), in *Memoirs of the Literary and Philosophical Society of Manchester*, 2d ed., 2 (1789): 30.

66. Sheridan, *British Education*, 6, 10, 3–4; Williams, *Treatise on Education*, 22–24, 27–28; Macaulay Graham, *Letters on Education*, 171; Chapman, *Treatise on Education*, 2. For some other comments on the role of education in the improvement of Britain, see Burgh, *Thoughts on Education*, 3; Fordyce, *Dialogues Concerning Education*, 1:296–97, 329, 344.

pliability and explained mental operations on the basis of the principle of association. This outlook led them to suggest that the mind could be comprehended scientifically, and could be controlled by adjusting environmental influences. Hence, perceiving the need for such regulation, they proposed that it offered great potential for progress, not just in the individual but in society generally. In their common view, the medicine of the mind, whether psychology or education in the narrower sense, could administer remedies to the ills of humankind. By producing healthy minds, it would naturally produce progress.

To be sure, not every eighteenth-century believer in progress followed men like Hartley and Williams in describing the human being as a fundamentally pliable creature. And among some Scottish common-sense philosophers, such as Reid and Beattie, there was outright opposition both to this general notion of human nature and to the psychology of association. But in spite of these exceptions, the belief in progress through pliability was obviously widespread at the time, and most educationalists and a large number of important moral philosophers and students of psychology gave expression to it.

Moreover, in many respects it represented in latent form much later British social thought, as the following observation suggests:

> where we have power to direct the course of [sense] impressions, we have power to command the state of the passions; and as laws, example, precept, and custom, are the prime sources of all our impressions, it must be greatly in the power of government to effect, by a proper use of these sources, that improvement on which true civilization depends.

Although this statement was actually made by Macaulay Graham, it could as easily have been written by Jeremy Bentham. In fact, Bentham had much in common with the advocates of the doctrine of progress through pliability. As is well known, he admired Hartley's *Observations*, and the principle of association occupied a central position in his "art-and-science" of legislation. In addition, he wrote on education (the *Chrestomathia*) and claimed that government "may be termed the art of *education*."[67] Of course, the complexity of his thought set him apart from the educationalists and psychologists

67. Macaulay Graham, *Letters on Education*, 172; Jeremy Bentham, *An Introduction to the Principles of Morals and Legislation*, Hafner ed. (New York, 1948), 311–12. For a reference to Hartley, see *Principles*, 124n.

who preceded him. As in the case of Macaulay Graham's statement on government, they threw out hints; but he built a system. They wrote in a general way about education, while he planned "Chresto-mathic" schools. They talked about encouraging good associations, he about the associations of crimes with punishments. He harvested many of the implications of their ideas in fields that they did not themselves cultivate.

Yet he and they shared some basic concerns. Desiring that refor-mation in the moral world keep pace with the progress of scientific knowledge, he proposed to establish a comprehensive system of legis-lation analogous to medicine. Writing in the 1770s, he declared that the "art of legislation is but the art of healing practised upon a large scale. It is the common endeavour of both to relieve men from the miseries of life. But the physician relieves them one by one: the legislator by millions at a time."[68] In various forms, this medical analogy reappeared countless times throughout Bentham's writings, and his use of it suggests that his fundamental intentions were the same as those of Hartley, Fordyce, and the others. Like them he aspired to remedy and prevent social ills, to administer what he called "medicine of the soul." And like them he considered these remedies and, therefore, social progress possible because of the pliable nature of the patient, man.

68. Quotation from unpublished papers cited in Mary P. Mack, *Jeremy Bentham: An Odyssey of Ideas, 1748–1792* (London, 1962), 264. I am largely indebted to Mack for my interpretation of Bentham. She cites many examples of his use of the medical analogy. For two of the earlier ones, see *Principles*, xxv, xxxi.

5 Language and Progress

"The Consideration . . . of *Ideas* and *Words*, as the great Instruments of Knowledge," wrote John Locke in concluding his *Essay Concerning Human Understanding*, "makes no despicable part of their Contemplation, who would take a view of humane Knowledge in the whole Extent of it."[1] Adopting this modestly stated suggestion, many members of the eighteenth-century European republic of letters undertook an examination in depth of the nature and formation of ideas. One important result of their work, particularly but not exclusively in Britain, was the emphasis they came to place on the pliability of the human mind, an emphasis full of consequence for the emerging idea of progress. Nor did they neglect the other side of the Lockean program, words. For the study of language took many forms and occupied many of the best minds of the period, from Vico to Turgot to Herder and the young Bentham. And here, too, the implications for the belief in progress were significant.

To be sure, language was hardly a virgin field of intellectual endeavor by the eighteenth century. Beginning with Bacon and his animadversion on the Idols of the Marketplace, some philosophers of the previous century had discussed the role of existing languages in human communication, and their inadequacies. Appearing in 1660, the Port-Royal Grammar of Claude Lancelot and Antoine Arnauld broke new ground by outlining a universal grammar—those parts of speech and grammatical categories believed to be common to all languages. A number of *virtuosi* and their friends in England, along with Descartes and Leibniz on the Continent, developed schemes for reforming language or promulgating a world-wide linguistic currency.

---

1. John Locke, *An Essay Concerning Human Understanding*, ed. Peter H. Nidditch (Oxford, 1975), 721 (Bk. IV, Ch. xxi, Sect. 4).

Locke himself introduced the problem of the connection between thought and language, ideas and verbal signs.

All of this work strongly influenced the philosophes and their contemporaries. What was new about the eighteenth-century study of language was not that it lacked precursors or prior intellectual foundations but rather, first of all, that it was a highly popular activity conducted with new-found intensity. In France, virtually every major philosophe (and many minor ones, as well) wrote about language, some at considerable length. For example, a number of important articles on language by various writers appeared in the *Encyclopédie*, and language lay at the center of the thought of Condillac, chief philosopher to the philosophes. As their debates on the whole subject demonstrate, the members of the French Enlightenment may have disagreed about various aspects of language, but they were eager to study it.

The same was true elsewhere. The Prussian Royal Academy sponsored several essay contests dealing with language and received many entries from all over Europe. One of these, Herder's famous "On the Origin of Language," emerged triumphant in the competition of 1771. The focus of this essay on the natural growth of language illustrates the second way in which eighteenth-century language study was new: it was frequently concerned with the history of language. The question of the origin of speech fascinated the thinkers of the age, whether they accepted the traditional "divine gift" theory or adopted the heterodox "human invention" interpretation (and some, like Herder over the course of his life, did both). Conceiving of language as a developing and not a static entity, they also attempted to specify how it had changed since its beginning, whatever that might have been, and in what manner these changes related to the history of society. Not surprisingly, therefore, the "relation of language to progress was one of their central themes."[2]

These tendencies manifested themselves in Britain no less than across the Channel. Among English-speakers the study of language was undertaken by a substantial and wide-ranging group of men from the educated and literate social orders. Most of this group came from some of the traditional professions: Anglican clerics (including bishops as well as one poverty-ridden man who could not gain ecclesiasti-

2. Pierre Juliard, *Philosophies of Language in Eighteenth-Century France* (The Hague, 1970), 15.

cal preferment), lawyers, and university professors. Joining them in language scholarship were such men as physicians, a mathematician and scientific popularizer, a gentleman member of Parliament, a government employee, two poets, an Irish actor-turned-elocutionist, and a great man of letters. In all, this group comprised a fairly representative cross-section of well-educated society. With some notable exceptions like Lord Monboddo and Joseph Priestley, these British students of language tended to take a somewhat less sophisticated and advanced approach to the subject than did their French counterparts, from whom they nevertheless derived many of their ideas.[3] Still, as suggested by the large number of works they wrote and by the debates emerging in those works, issues relating to language fascinated them. Three such major issues were preeminent at the time. What had been the origin and history of language? How were language, thought, and society developmentally related? And in what ways and with what consequences could language be improved? As it deals with these questions, the literature of British language study indicates the existence in eighteenth-century thought of a close connection between opinions on language and the idea of progress.

THE HISTORY OF LANGUAGE

Throughout the eighteenth century, British writers on language felt a necessity, as Hugh Blair put it, "to enquire in what manner, and by what steps, Language advanced to the state in which we now find it."[4] Like the other Europeans who took up this inquiry, they were particularly intrigued by the first such steps, the origin and early history of language.

Human speech, they thought, must have had an origin because it

---

3. About the ideas on language of Monboddo, Priestley, and other believers in general progress, see below, chap. 8. With regard to the influence of Continental on British language study, Hugh Blair provides a fairly typical example. In listing sources for his lecture on the "Rise and Progress of Language," he noted twice as many French as British titles: *Lectures on Rhetoric and Belles Lettres* (1783), ed. Harold F. Harding, 2 vols. (Carbondale, Ill., 1965), 1:97n–98n. Several important French works on language, such as Jean Frain du Tremblay's *Traité des Langues* (1709) and Condillac's *Essai sur l'origine des connaissances humaines* (1746), were translated into English, the former in 1725 and the latter in 1756. This is not to suggest that the British merely borrowed and did little original work on language, but rather that here, more than in any other area relating to the idea of progress, the French influence was significant.

4. Blair, *Lectures on Rhetoric*, 1:101.

was not natural (in the sense of being instinctive, like the cries of animals). Bernard Mandeville's *Fable of the Bees. Part II* (1729) made this assumption explicit early in the century, and the *Encyclopaedia Britannica* later provided evidence to support it: for instance, solitary "wild men"—those notorious Enlightenment test cases of the nature of man—had never been observed to use articulate speech, although they possessed all the faculties and vocal organs common to other men. Since language could not be considered natural, either it "must have been originally revealed from heaven, or it must be the fruit of human industry." The *Encyclopaedia Britannica* discussed both viewpoints and their merits, concluding safely that although "We pretend not to decide for our readers in a question of this nature . . . our own judgment leans to the side of revelation."[5]

In Britain (though not in France) this position was the norm. To be sure, there were a few advocates of a purely human origin. Mandeville cautiously advanced such a theory, and Samuel Johnson stated bluntly that "speech was not formed by an analogy sent from heaven." Similarly, Richard Wynne (1719–99), a Hertfordshire rector who wrote grammar manuals and edited the New Testament, suggested that it was unnecessary to conclude that the first human beings "derived their language from heaven by immediate inspiration." For the most part, however, the more traditional opinion prevailed, as expressed by William Warburton's belief that "*language* . . . had, for its sole original, divine instruction," and by Thomas Sheridan's claim that "Speech is the universal gift of God to all mankind." The orthodox theory held its ground not only because of contemporary faith in the Book of Genesis, but also because no other account of the origin seemed logically satisfactory. As Blair reasoned, the origin of all language had to be referred to divine inspiration because "either how Society could form itself, previously to Language; or how words could

---

5. Bernard Mandeville, *The Fable of the Bees. Part II* (1729), in *The Fable of the Bees: or, Private Vices, Publick Benefits*, ed. F. B. Kaye, 2 vols. (Oxford, 1924), 2:286; *Encyclopaedia Britannica; Or, A Dictionary of the Arts, Sciences, &c.*, 3d ed., 15 vols. (Edinburgh, 1787–97), 9:529:2–534:1 (s.v. "Language"). Certain elements of language, however, were considered to be natural, in the sense of being universal to all tongues or in accord with natural reason: see, for example, Thomas Stackhouse, *Reflections on the Nature and Property of Languages in General, And on the Advantages, Defects, and Manner of Improving the English Tongue in Particular* (London, 1731), 25; L. D. Nelme, *An Essay towards an Investigation of the Origin and Elements of Language and Letters* (London, 1772), 16, 20, 132.

rise into a Language, previously to Society formed, seem to be points attended with equal difficulty."[6]

If there was general agreement that God had bestowed language on man, there was less unanimity about the dimensions of that gift. At one extreme, the language of Adam could be considered complete and perfect. It possessed "all the Force, all the Richness, and, in a word, all the Excellence whereof a *Tongue* is capable," wrote Thomas Stackhouse (1677–1752), a religious writer and impoverished Anglican cleric. But it was also, and more frequently, held to have been merely an inchoate scheme, consisting of the faculty of speech and perhaps the basic elements of grammar. In David Hartley's phrase, the "Language, which *Adam* and *Eve* were possessed of in Paradise, was very narrow" and probably "monosyllabic in great measure." Yet this rude foundation was said to have had sufficient strength to support the largest linguistic superstructure that men might later have occasion to raise.[7]

Two approaches were taken to describe and explain the process by which this edifice was erected during the first ages of man. One relied primarily on Genesis 9–11, with some admixture of speculative history. Adam was thought to have transmitted to his descendants his divinely inspired form of speech. According to those writers, like James Beattie, who claimed perfection for the first language, this inheritance underwent no change from the Fall to the time of Babel.

6. Mandeville, *Fable*, 2:288–89; Samuel Johnson, *The Plan of an English Dictionary* (1747), in *The Works of Samuel Johnson, LL.D.*, 11 vols. (Oxford, 1825), 5:11; R.[ichard] Wynne, *Essays on Education. . . . To which are added Observations on the ancient and modern Languages* (London, 1761), 199; William Warburton, *The Divine Legation of Moses Demonstrated* (1737–41), Bk. IV, Sect. iv, note, in *The Works of the Right Reverend William Warburton*, new ed., 12 vols. (London, 1811), 4:391; Thomas Sheridan, *A Discourse . . . Introductory to . . . Lectures on Elocution and the English Language* (London, 1759), 15; Blair, *Lectures on Rhetoric*, 1:100. Near the end of his life, Johnson was recorded as saying that the origin of speech could have lain only in divine inspiration: *Boswell's Life of Johnson*, ed. George Birkbeck Hill, rev. and enl. L. F. Powell, 6 vols. (Oxford, 1934–50), 4:207.

For another assessment of problems attendant on a nondivine theory of origins, see James Beattie, *Dissertations Moral and Critical* (London, 1783), 452–53 (dissertation entitled "The Theory of Language").

7. Stackhouse, *Reflections*, 35; David Hartley, *Observations on Man, His Frame, His Duties, and His Expectations*, 2 vols. (London, 1749), 1:298; *Encyclopaedia Britannica*, 9:533:1. For other comments on the extent of the first language, see Locke, *Essay*, 402 (IV, i, 1); Rowland Jones, *The Origin of Language and Nations* (London, 1764), sig. Bᵛ ("Preface"); Beattie, *Dissertations*, 304; Blair, *Lectures on Rhetoric*, 1:101.

Hartley, however, supposed that during this period modifications and additions occurred both in Adam's speech and in the form of writing imparted to him by God. But regardless of what happened before Babel, there was no question that the divine response to the building of the tower at Babylon had enormous linguistic ramifications. Reacting to the pride and new-found power of humankind, God confounded the single tongue that all people had previously spoken, scattering them across the earth, and forced upon them a multiplication and diversification of language. This miraculous interposition alone, it was widely believed, could account for the existence of the number of primitive tongues necessary to give rise to the present variety of languages in the world. Bringing diversity, Babel at the same time created confusion and therefore what Rowland Jones (1722–74), a Welsh philologist and solicitor living in London, called "great disorder, disputes, and disunion." Yet Babel also appeared to Hartley to be a "beneficial Gift and Blessing to Mankind," for the "new Languages far exceeded the old common one in the Number and Variety of Words."[8]

Having analyzed the immediate effects of Babel, some proponents of the biblically oriented history of language went on to describe the further spread of language. Above all, this expansion meant continued diversification. As Stackhouse argued, tongues having once multiplied by means of a miracle "went on, as it were naturally to multiply into so many, that we can now neither know nor count the Number of them." But other students of language thought that within this shell of diversity lay an inner core of unity, a root from which had grown the classical and modern European languages. For Jones, the father tongue was Celtic; for James Parsons (1705–70), a London physician and fellow of the Royal Society who wrote on medical as well as philological subjects, it was "Japhetan" or "Pelasgian" (after a branch of the descendants of Noah who supposedly came to inhabit the region of Asia Minor and Greece).[9] Whatever the name selected,

8. Beattie, *Dissertations*, 304–05; Hartley, *Observations*, 1:298–305; Jones, *Origin of Language*, sigs. B2ʳ, A2ʳ ("Preface"). On Babel and its effects, see also Stackhouse, *Reflections*, 24, 39; Wynne, *Essays*, 199–200; James Parsons, *Remains of Japhet: Being Historical Enquiries into the Affinity and Origin of the European Languages* (London, 1767), 25.

9. Stackhouse, *Reflections*, 40; Jones, *Origin of Language*, sigs. B2ʳ, B4ʳ ("Preface"); idem, *The Philosophy of Words, in Two Dialogues* (London, 1769), 8; Parsons, *Remains*, xi–xii, 25, 367. For a substantially similar theory of a root language, see Nelme, *Origin and Elements*, 4, 7–8, 14, 87–89.

this root tongue was considered to have branched out over many centuries, and the various bifurcations were etymologically traced to reveal the common lost ancestor of the known languages. The nineteenth- and twentieth-century search for Indo-European, initiated by the English orientalist Sir William Jones shortly before 1800, is clearly foreshadowed in these earlier speculations. The major difference in method between modern comparative philology and that of the eighteenth century in Britain is the fact that Rowland Jones and Parsons began with a biblical presupposition: they believed that the language of Japhet's family did not suffer confusion at Babel, which enabled them to treat it as the link between Adamic and modern languages.

The biblical orientation of writers like Parsons also distinguished them from those who took the other approach to the early history of language. This latter group attempted to construct a "natural" or theoretical history of speech and writing, without reference to Genesis, along the lines of that put forth by the philosophes in France and by Monboddo and Adam Smith in Scotland. This approach, with its emphasis on human invention rather than divine intervention, was adopted even by some of those who believed that God had originated language. For as Warburton declared, "God taught man, language: yet we cannot reasonably suppose it to be any other than what served his present use: after this, he was able of himself to improve and enlarge it, as his future occasions should require."[10]

In brief, according to this nonbiblical approach, the process of enlargement began with the inarticulate cries of passion that broke forth from the earliest human beings. Eventually, these cries, together with gestures and facial expressions, were used by people to communicate basic wants and desires to one another. Continued exercise of the vocal organs ultimately led to the production of articulated sounds (that is, words), some of which gradually became associated with particular passions and with the ideas of individual, familiar tasks and objects. In the case of an object making a sound in some manner, the associated articulated sound imitated that object (this view marks the beginning of the "bow-wow" theory of language acquisition). At this point, the process of generalization of objects into classes had not yet occurred, nor had an even partial separation of articulation and gesture been achieved. Nevertheless, the use of

10. Warburton, *Divine Legation*, IV, iv, note, in *Works*, 4:393.

words as the signs of ideas was passed on from one generation to another and thereby continued to increase. Finally, with the constant multiplication of words, the need for order in speech gave rise to the invention of lexical rules, and recognizable language was born. The first syntax was inverted (for example, "fruit me give") in order to direct attention to the desired object, but over time a syntax more in harmony with the order of the understanding came into existence ("give me fruit").[11]

It was also possible by means of the nonbiblical approach to account for the spread of language across the earth. An increase in the population of the first human beings was supposed to have dispersed them into different nations or to have vastly expanded the geographical extent of one nation. In either case, groups of people began to come into contact with new objects and environments, which occasioned the invention of new words for previously unfamiliar things and tasks. At the same time these people lost contact with certain elements of their former locale, as a result of which old words became disused and in the end were forgotten. By such means the natural creation of separate nations or subgroups of one nation brought about the deviation of the first language into dialects, and ultimately into discrete languages.[12]

Whether they relied fundamentally on Genesis or referred solely to human activity, many students of language in eighteenth-century Britain sought to describe the early history of language. Even with their significant differences, the two approaches had in common an emphasis on linguistic change. That this was so followed from the fact that change was recognized to be an inherent characteristic of language. Benjamin Martin (1704–82), a mathematician and instrument-maker who championed Newtonianism in his voluminous writings on science and technology, stated that no language "can ever be permanently the same, but will always be in a mutable and fluctuating state." He thought that change could, in fact, be observed in no facet of human life more than in speech and writing, which seemed to be "in a state of mutation from age to age." This outlook was typical. Certainly, Jonathan Swift had found evidence of

11. The account in this paragraph is a summary drawn from the following: Mandeville, *Fable*, 2:287–89; *Encyclopaedia Britannica*, 9:530:2–531:2; Blair, *Lectures on Rhetoric*, 1:99–125; Thomas Astle, *The Origin and Progress of Writing* (1st ed., 1784; London, 1876), 2–3.

12. *Encyclopaedia Britannica*, 9:533:1–2.

stability in Chinese, classical Greek, and, to some extent, modern German, Spanish, and Italian, and Beattie insightfully pointed out that languages "become in some degree stationary from the moment they begin to be visible in writing." But the overwhelming weight of opinion agreed with the *Encyclopaedia Britannica* that language, whatever its origin, "must be subject to perpetual changes from its very nature, as well as from the variety of incidents which affect all sublunary things." Even Johnson, "being able to produce no example of a nation that has preserved their words and phrases from mutability," conceded that neither his nor any other "dictionary of a living tongue ever can be perfect," since language was caught up in a continuing process of change.[13]

Johnson asserted that a living tongue varied "by the caprice of everyone that speaks it," so that "words are hourly shifting their relations." Taking the vantage of a longer perspective, however, he also wrote of "the gradual changes" of language. And it was this kind of slow modification to which eighteenth-century writers on language were usually referring when they discussed linguistic history. Mandeville claimed that language came into the world among savages by "slow degrees, as all other Arts and Sciences have done, and length of time." Later commentators likewise tended to emphasize gradualness in their depiction of the initial period of the history of language. Wynne, for instance, believed that "our first parents probably formed a Language by degrees," and in concluding its description of the speculative "human invention" theory of the origin of speech the *Encyclopaedia Britannica* also adopted the gradualist perspective. Even according to those who relied on Genesis, gradualness seemed to characterize the early history of language (except for the cataclysm at Babel). Warburton noted that simple, primitive modes of speaking and writing "did not always straight grow into disuse on the invention of a more improved manner." The probable source of this kind of outlook was the model of scientific advance portrayed most concretely by Bacon and all later champions of the moderns against the ancients. Stackhouse made this connection patent. Echoing Mandeville's analogy, he observed that just "as Sciences did not

13. B.[enjamin] Martin, *Institutions of Language* (London, 1748), 111, 6; Jonathan Swift, *A Proposal for Correcting, Improving and Ascertaining the English Tongue* (1712), in *The Prose Works of Jonathan Swift*, ed. Herbert Davis, 14 vols. (Oxford, 1951–68), 4:9; Beattie, *Dissertations*, 377; *Encyclopaedia Britannica*, 9:534:1–2; Samuel Johnson, "Preface to the English Dictionary" (1755), in *Works* (1825 ed.), 5:46, 50.

arise to the highest degree of their Perfection all on a Sudden, so Languages crept on but slowly."[14]

What was true of the early period of language in particular was also true of its history in general: it changed gradually. Hartley likened its growth to the slow increase of an amount of money at compound interest. Stackhouse declared that its "Progress . . . is by a long Series of Years, and, as it were, insensibly brought about," and Parsons stated flatly that every language "was gradually formed." With these views Beattie agreed, and he adduced as evidence the contention that classical Greek and Latin developed even more slowly than had the Romance languages and English, which themselves "were formed gradually, and without plan or method." Such a gradualist outlook was also central to those few accounts of the history of writing that appeared in eighteenth-century Britain. It undergirded all that Hartley had to say on that subject and also emerged clearly in discussions by Blair and Thomas Astle (1735–1803, Parliament's editor for ancient documents and keeper of records in the Tower) of the slow transition from picture-writing to hieroglyphics to the use of alphabets. As Astle noted with regard to the shift from pictures to arbitrary written signs, "these signs were introduced slowly, and by degrees . . . until generally known and adopted."[15]

But if both speech and writing had changed, and if they had done so gradually, what had been the direction of that change? Many of the comments made about linguistic history by contemporaries have already suggested the existence of a widespread belief in the progress of language. And in fact such a belief was popular and even dominant in the eighteenth century. Still, it did not have the intellectual field entirely to itself at the time. Just as with the case of the ancients and moderns and arts and sciences,[16] so with the case of language not everyone considered the historical changes in question to have been progressive.

For example, Thomas Wilson (1663–1755), the long-time bishop of Sodor and Man, suggested that on the whole language might have

14. Johnson, "Preface" and *Plan*, in *Works* (1825 ed.), 5:35, 20; Mandeville, *Fable*, 2:287; Wynne, *Essays*, 199; *Encyclopaedia Britannica*, 9:531:2; Warburton, *Divine Legation*, IV, iv, in *Works*, 4:140; Stackhouse, *Reflections*, 47.

15. Hartley, *Observations*, 1:298–302; Stackhouse, *Reflections*, 47; Parsons, *Remains*, 256; Beattie, *Dissertations*, 273, 376, 378; Blair, *Lectures on Rhetoric*, 1:125–35; Astle, *Origin and Progress of Writing*, 4–61 (quotation on p. 5).

16. See above, chap. 2.

declined (and certainly had not improved) since the invention of writing. More specifically, Parsons pointed to the "mutilation and degeneracy of languages" that occurred when words, in the process of use, deviated from their normal meaning, syllabification, or pronunciation. He also argued that it was the fate of all languages over a long period of time to split into many dialects. Parson's message was Johnson's, too: tongues, said the great lexicographer, "have a natural tendency to degeneration." Early in the century Swift had taken the same perspective with regard to English itself. He wondered whether since 1642 the "Corruptions in our Language have not, at least, equalled the Refinements of it." This note was sounded later by Beattie, who considered the nearly exclusive use of the indicative mood to be "gradually corrupting the purity of our tongue." And Thomas Sheridan delivered a virtual jeremiad on the subject in 1756. He found no difficulty in proving that the structure of English was worse in his day than at the time of Chaucer, and that in all other respects the language "has been declining since the reign of Charles the first."[17]

But the notion of language decline was a minority opinion in eighteenth-century Britain, as was the concept that the history of language followed a cyclical pattern. Leonard Welsted succinctly stated the theory of a cycle when he wrote that "it is with Languages, as it is with Animals, Vegetables, and all other Things; they have their Rise, their Progress, their Maturity, and their Decay." He illustrated this point by claiming that Greek and Latin, having reached a state of perfection, had then declined from it. Stackhouse used the same example to make a similar claim, adding to Welsted's cycle a final phase of "entire *Extinction*" when languages "cease to live and give way to others to take place in the Commerce of Life." Johnson, too, argued that "every language has a time of rudeness antecedent to perfection, as well as of false refinement and declension." Sheridan at

17. Anon. [Thomas Wilson, probable author], *The Many Advantages of a Good Language to any Nation: With An Examination of the present State of our own* (London, 1724), 17; Parsons, *Remains*, 245–46, 57; Johnson, "Preface," in *Works* (1825 ed.), 5:49; Swift, *A Proposal*, in *Prose Works*, 4:9–10; Beattie, *Dissertations*, 421; Thomas Sheridan, *British Education: Or, the Source of the Disorders of Great Britain* (Dublin, 1756), 188. On the decline of English, see also Johnson, *Plan* and "Preface," in *Works* (1825 ed.), 5:18, 23–24, 39; and Crito, "Remarks upon the Character of some of the most celebrated Languages, ancient and modern," *Sentimental Magazine* 1 (July 1773): 225 [misnumbered as 115], in which the influence of French was charged with responsibility for what appeared to be the current decline of English. Sheridan's use of such constructions as "have wrote" and of "it's" as a possessive pronoun could have provided documentation for his claim.

one point placed his worries about the state of English in a cyclical context, observing that "our language, instead of a progressive motion towards perfection, . . . has really been describing a circular one, and constantly, tho' imperceptibly, bending towards the point of it's [sic] original barbarity."[18]

But the case of Sheridan himself provides evidence that students of language did not always hold notions of decay and circularity unalloyed. For although he bewailed the present "desolate" state of English and perceived its cyclical relapse, he could also contend that it had received as many improvements as corruptions since the Elizabethan period. More significantly, he even stated bluntly that

> the language itself has been so much enlarged and improved since those days [the age of the Reformation], that it is rendered capable of answering every end, whether of profit or pleasure, to us at least, better than all others [especially Latin and Greek] put together, and consequently is become more worthy to be studied.

This kind of ambivalent or dual outlook also permeated the groundbreaking *Diversions of Purley* (1786) written by John Horne Tooke (1736–1812), the famous English philologist and political radical. Tooke clearly agreed with Condillac's contention that considerably more philosophical perfection and, therefore, clarity of expression was to be found in the early state of language than later. Yet if from this perspective there had been corruption and decline in the shift from savage languages to "languages of art," from another there had been improvement, inasmuch as Tooke believed that the use of abbreviated signs in modern speech permitted greater brevity and dispatch. Remarks by Bishop Wilson on a different topic contained a similar dualism. He claimed that speakers of English "must be contented to be like over-grown School-boys" compared to the Greeks and Romans. In opposition to this assertion of decline from antique heights, however, he also argued that the lack of inflection in English constituted an improvement and advantage.[19]

18. Leonard Welsted, *A Dissertation Concerning the Perfection of the English Language, the State of Poetry, &c.* (1724), in Willard Higby Durham, ed., *Critical Essays of the Eighteenth Century* (New Haven, 1915), 359–60; Stackhouse, *Reflections*, 4, 47–49, 53; Johnson, "Preface," in *Works* (1825 ed.), 5:40; Sheridan, *British Education*, 220–21.

19. Sheridan, *British Education*, 162, 158, 164; Wilson, *Many Advantages*, 29, 20. For Tooke, see Hans Aarsleff, *The Study of Language in England, 1780–1860* (Prince-

Many other eighteenth-century students of language followed Wilson in weighing the respective merits of the languages of classical and more recent times. By doing so they were actually opening up a new theater in the peaceful contemporary war of ancients and moderns. Stackhouse recognized this fact when he wrote that "those who take part with the *Dead* against the *Living* Tongues, do likewise take part with the *Ancients* against the *Moderns*, and . . . these Sentiments mutually produce each other." Further evidence of this linkage was provided by James Harris (1709–80), a classicist and aesthetician who represented the Wiltshire gentry in the House of Commons from 1761 to his death. He was exceptional in granting relatively complete preference to the ancient languages (and especially to Greek). This outlook, presented in *Hermes* (1751), undoubtedly followed from his announced intention "to revive the decaying taste of [*sic*] antient Literature; to lessen the bigotted contempt of every thing not modern." Stackhouse found the existing prejudice to be just the opposite. He believed that his age had an excessive esteem for Latin and Greek, which he traced primarily to educational convention and to a veneration of "Every thing that is ancient, even to old Trees and old Houses." As a conclusive objection to such veneration, he produced the familiar "paradox of the ancients" and, giving it a new twist, applied it not only to knowledge but also to language. "Mankind at this time are older than they ever were," he argued, "and should therefore be suppos'd to speak and think better than they ever did." Consequently, "'tis in this latter Age . . . that we must expect to find the Perfection of Languages"—as well as the perfection of science.[20]

The bulk of opinion on this topic lay between the extremes represented by Harris and Stackhouse. Sheridan, for example, strongly believed that the use of inflection gave an advantage to the ancient languages. But he also stated that English was as capable as Greek or Latin of conveying knowledge, and that the use of printing provided the moderns with "an amazing advantage over the ancients" regard-

---

ton, 1967), 68–69. On Condillac, see Isabel F. Knight, *The Geometric Spirit: The Abbé de Condillac and the French Enlightenment* (New Haven, 1968), 170–71.

20. Stackhouse, *Reflections*, 153, 147–49; James Harris, *Hermes: or a Philosophical Inquiry, concerning Universal Grammar*, in *The Works of James Harris, Esq.*, 2 vols. (London, 1801), 1:317, 441, 214. On several occasions Stackhouse proclaimed that all languages were equal: *Reflections*, 66, 68, 107. But this was merely a rhetorical attempt "to cut short the Controversy" (*Reflections*, 149), and his real opinion was the one presented in this paragraph.

ing the stabilization of word meanings. The *Encyclopaedia Britannica*, George Campbell, and Blair were agreed that inflection made the ancient languages superior in elegance. Yet they also held that modern speech possessed greater simplicity and perspicuity (because of the use of auxiliaries) and a broader range of expression (which Campbell specifically attributed to the progress of knowledge). From all these considerations, Blair was able to conclude that "Language is become, in modern times, more correct, indeed, and accurate; but, however, less striking and animated."[21] Overall, then, in this skirmish the moderns managed to achieve at least a draw, though not a decisive victory. In some but not all respects, modern language was believed to have advanced beyond that of antiquity.

That eighteenth-century British writers could go even this far is evidence of the strength of their belief in the progress of language. After all, the bias in favor of Latin and Greek, arising from the traditional educational emphasis on those languages even at the expense of the vernacular, must have been harder to escape than any other prejudice or argument conferring veneration on antiquity. But the tendency to view language as progressive also emerged in other, more directly stated ways. In particular, in spite of the views of Swift and (sometimes) Sheridan, English was more frequently considered to have made significant advances than to have declined. Wynne wrote that the language had eventually "attained to a tolerable degree of perfection" by the time of Tillotson, Locke, and Addison. The advance necessary to reach such a state was pointed out by George Harris (1722–96), a wealthy civil lawyer and commentator on the Institutes of Justinian, when he referred to the "great Improvement of our Language, during the last Century." Likewise, Wilson asserted that English was at present "better than it was two Hundred Years ago." Although conceding some loss since the age of Chaucer "with regard to the pleasingness of sound alone," the *Encyclopaedia Britannica* traced the general process of advance back even farther, noting the "great improvements which have been made in our language since the revival of letters in Europe." Taking a total view, Welsted stated that the "most beautiful Polish is at length given to our

---

21. Sheridan, *British Education*, 206, 174, 185; *Encyclopaedia Britannica*, 9:535:1–549:2; George Campbell, *The Philosophy of Rhetoric* (1775), 2d ed., 2 vols. (London, 1801), 2:353–61; Blair, *Lectures on Rhetoric*, 1:122–24. See also Beattie, *Dissertations*, 376, 468; Crito, "Remarks upon celebrated Languages," *Sentimental Magazine* 1 (July 1773): 225:2 [misnumbered as 115:2].

Tongue, and its *Teutonic* Rust quite worn away." For him the "present Perfection of the *English* Language" demonstrated just as much as progress in the arts and sciences how far "are we advanced towards what I have call'd a *Classical* Age." More than forty years later Parsons made essentially the same claim. He wrote that in considering

> the state of the *English* Language at this time, and its condition before, and at the time of, *Chaucer*, surely we must own it to be now in its perfection, and that it required a long time to bring it to its present improvement. . . . Many would be apt to say, the language of *Chaucer* was very barbarous; and, perhaps, he might have thought that of his ancient predecessors was so too, compared with his own.[22]

If, as Parsons thought, English had achieved a high degree of perfection, to have done so it "required no less time to ripen . . . than every one of the *European* tongues has taken up for its cultivation." This comment illustrates how slow, progressive growth was perceived not only in English but in language generally. Warburton contended that man had gradually been able to "improve and enlarge" speech from its early "extremely rude, narrow, and equivocal" state to a condition "more cultivated . . . smoothed and polished." According to Gregory Sharpe (1713–71), Kentish vicar and scholar of Hebrew, it was in principle possible to trace the "several steps or outlines of language, from the natural notes of man in his infant state, through its progress to perfection." This type of improvement from early rudeness had actually occurred, Beattie wrote, "in many, and perhaps in all nations." Blair had no doubts about the broad contours of the process of linguistic advance, and, speaking for most contem-

---

22. Wynne, *Essays*, 234–35; Anon. [George Harris], *Observations upon the English Language* (London, [1752]), sig. B2ʳ; Wilson, *Many Advantages*, 25; *Encyclopaedia Britannica*, 9:548:2–549:1; Welsted, *Dissertation Concerning the Perfection of English*, in Durham, *Critical Essays*, 358, 361; Parsons, *Remains*, 376. In the only work of modern scholarship to examine a large number of eighteenth-century British studies on language, a thesis entirely contrary to the one put forth here is expressly stated. The "conviction that the Golden Age was irrevocably past and the [English] language [was] suffering constant degradation, was the most common and positive idea in the eighteenth century"; the "view almost without exception expressed by the grammarians, was that the language had passed its golden age and was far gone in decadence": Sterling Andrus Leonard, *The Doctrine of Correctness in English Usage 1700–1800* (Madison, Wis., 1929), 128, 135. But Leonard offers *no* solid evidence to support his claim and, in fact, very little exists. The views of Swift and, occasionally, of Sheridan are far outweighed by the opposite opinion.

porary students of language, he marveled at it. "This artificial meth-od of communicating thought," he declared, "we now behold carried to the highest perfection."

> But carry your thoughts back to the first dawn of Language among men. Reflect upon the feeble beginnings from which it must have arisen, and upon the many and great obstacles which it must have encountered in its progress; and you will find reason for the highest astonishment, on viewing the height which it has now attained. We admire several of the inventions of art; we plume ourselves on some discoveries which have been made in latter ages, serving to advance knowledge, and to render life comfortable; we speak of them as the boast of human reason. But certainly no invention is en-titled to any such degree of admiration as that of Language.[23]

Thus, language—whatever its origin—was recognized to have un-dergone many changes over time. And most writers on language in the high eighteenth century agreed with Blair that these modifica-tions had been for the better. Here is the first connection between the idea of progress and the study of language in this period: the history of language itself was considered progressive.

LANGUAGE, THOUGHT, AND SOCIETY

But what exactly caused progress or, more generally, change in language? During the eighteenth century, this question was part of a far broader issue, the relationship of language to thought and society. It was precisely this problematic interconnection that so many of the best-known language students of the period sought to explain. Condillac and Monboddo explored it in depth, and the Royal Academy in Berlin elicited analyses of it by proposing as the subject of its essay contest for 1759 the "Influence of Opinions on Language and of Language on Opinions."[24] In Britain, the issue received sub-

23. Parsons, *Remains*, 376; Warburton, *Divine Legation*, IV, iv and note in *Works*, 4:393, 133, 137; Gregory Sharpe, *Two Dissertations. I. Upon the Origin, Construction, Division and Relation of Languages* . . . (London, 1751), 17; Beattie, *Dissertations*, 372; Blair, *Lectures on Rhetoric*, 1:98–99.

24. The component parts of this issue—the relationship of language and thought and that of language and society—have rightly been called the "two great themes" around which late eighteenth-century European writings on the nature and function of

stantial discussion throughout the century, from which a broad consensus emerged. Language, on the one hand, and thought and society, on the other, were considered to be reciprocally influential and productive of progressive change.

At bottom this outlook rested upon two universally held assumptions. To begin with, language and thought were recognized to be inextricably bound together. Locke had earlier argued that the connection between ideas and words was so close that it was impossible to analyze human knowledge without also considering the "Nature, Use, and Signification of Language." For in order to "communicate our Thoughts to one another, as well as record them for our own use, Signs of our *Ideas*"—words—were no less necessary than the ideas themselves. The reference to communication in this statement points to the other assumption, that language and society were also intimately related. As Locke had also made clear, language was the "great Instrument, and common Tye of Society," the "Comfort, and Advantage of Society, not being [able] to be had without Communication of Thoughts." The two assumptions appear together in standard eighteenth-century definitions of language. "Articulate sounds," wrote Wynne, "form an Artificial [that is, non-instinctual] Language, which serves to convey the ideas of the speaker to the hearer." Or as Blair put it, "Language, in general, signifies the expression of our ideas by certain articulate sounds, which are used as the signs of those ideas," and a national language was a "set of articulate sounds" chosen by a people "for communicating their ideas." Writers on language further revealed their understanding of its social context when they treated it as a usage established by "compact" or "tacit consent," akin to Locke's social compact.[25]

These assumptions underlay contemporary views of the developmental interconnection of society, thought, and language. In France, the philosophes raised the question of whether the progress of language was the offspring or the handmaiden of social and intellectual advance, but they did not offer a common answer. They were agreed

---

language clustered: Lia Formigari, "Language and Society in the Late Eighteenth Century," *Journal of the History of Ideas* 35 (April–June 1974): 275.

The winning entry in the Prussian Academy's contest, by Johann David Michaelis, was translated into English in 1769.

25. Locke, *Essay*, 401, 721, 402, 405 (II, xxxiii, 19; IV, xxi, 4; III, i, 1; III, ii, 1); Wynne, *Essays*, 199, 231–33; Blair, *Lectures on Rhetoric*, 1:98. For references to the linguistic compact (also discussed by Locke, Wynne, and Blair), see James Harris, *Hermes*, in *Works*, 1:385, 393; Astle, *Origin and Progress of Writing*, 2.

only that the state of a people's language mirrored or provided a means for measuring the level of thought in that nation. This concept of a linguistic index also appeared across the Channel, beginning with Locke. As Wilson argued, an uncouth, ambiguous, and imperfect language "is a sure Sign of a slothful or low Genius in the People," while a copious and clear form of verbal communication "shews a good Understanding and Capacity." Likewise, the *Encyclopaedia Britannica* declared that generally the "language of any people is a very exact index of the state of their minds," and Jeremy Bentham wrote that the "state of language marks the progress of ideas."[26] But for British writers language was far more than just a gauge of intellectual conditions. They depicted it as simultaneously playing two parts in its relationship with thought and society: it was the improver no less than the improved.

Considered in its role as the improved, language was ordinarily believed to change through the action of social and intellectual influences. Other factors, lying at least partially outside the intellectual and social matrix in which a given language normally operated, were sometimes cited as reasons for the alteration of speech and writing. These included contact between peoples, especially in commerce and cases of military conquest; contact between languages, as by translation; and even exposure by migration to different climates. Normally, however, linguistic change was explained by reference to what Johnson called "internal causes": those coming from within a society and its thought. This was true of negative changes. Swift and Sheridan, for example, attributed the decline of Latin to the loss of liberty and rise of tyranny among the Romans (which destroyed the art of oratory), and to the corruption of manners brought about by luxury. According to Stackhouse, when the manners of the Hebrews became barbarous and they neglected the arts and sciences, their language also decayed.[27]

Linguistic *progress* was accounted for in a similar way. First of all,

26. Locke, *Essays*, 403 (III, i, 5); Wilson, *Many Advantages*, 4; *Encyclopaedia Britannica*, 9:534:2; Jeremy Bentham, *An Introduction to the Principles of Morals and Legislation*, Hafner ed. (New York, 1948), 215n2. On the views of the philosophes, see Juliard, *Philosophies of Language*, 60–68.

27. Johnson, "Preface," in *Works* (1825 ed.), 5:47; Swift, *A Proposal*, in *Prose Works*, 4:8; Sheridan, *British Education*, 189, 194; Stackhouse, *Reflections*, 29. For references to causes of linguistic change that were neither intellectual nor social, see Stackhouse, *Reflections*, 40–41; Hartley, *Observations*, 1:305–06; Johnson, "Preface," in *Works* (1825 ed.), 5:48; Parsons, *Remains*, 246, 260.

it was believed that intellectual advance brought with it the enlargement and improvement of language. "In proportion to their progress in knowlege [sic]," stated Sheridan, men "will find adequate powers in the organs of speech, to communicate that knowlege." Stackhouse was convinced that the more a people "advance their Knowledge, the more their *Language* will become enrich'd." And Hartley contended that writing, even more directly than speech, would "grow with the Growth of Knowlege." The reason for this kind of natural correlation between thought and language was highlighted by Johnson's remark that a language was amplified through the cultivation of the various sciences. Stackhouse agreed that the sciences and knowledge of the arts "embellish'd" languages, explaining that "discoveries of new Matters and new Truths, must in proportion multiply Terms necessary to express them. For the greatness and excellence of Things is necessarily follow'd by that of Language, without much Application or Labour." The existence of such an inevitable connection appeared to be supported by the evidence of history. At the general level, Beattie argued that the shift from uncultivated to refined language grew out of the parallel change from disconnected to more methodical and rational modes of thought. More specifically, Campbell held that English was richer and fitter for philosophy and criticism than Latin, because the "materials which constitute the riches of a language"— clearly enlarged since antiquity by intellectual progress—"always bear a proportion to the acquisitions in knowledge made by the people."[28]

Second, the advance of society itself appeared to provide a fundamental impulse to linguistic progress. This was so because the state of society conditioned the state of the intellect, which in turn influenced language. Stackhouse understood this relationship. The progress of language required the improvement of knowledge. But knowledge, he thought, flourished best "in settl'd and establish'd Governments, whose People live in a regular Society," secure from violence, with "wholesome Laws," and "provided with all the Necessaries of Life." Under such social conditions, language, through the mediation of intellectual advance, would "be Embellish'd and Enrich'd." Johnson, too, ultimately traced the enlargement of language

28. Sheridan, *A Discourse*, 16; Stackhouse, *Reflections*, 192, 44–45; Hartley, *Observations*, 1:300; Johnson, "Preface," in *Works* (1825 ed.), 5:47; Beattie, *Dissertations*, 478, 482; Campbell, *Philosophy of Rhetoric*, 2:360.

back to an enabling social situation. He believed that the speech of a barbarous people, "totally employed in procuring the conveniencies of life," would remain relatively static. In a more polished nation, however, where a division of labor had created social stratification, those who had sufficient leisure to think would "always be enlarging the stock of ideas; and every increase of knowledge . . . will produce new words, or combinations of words." Astle made the same argument with regard to writing. The rude state of society, he contended, did not provide men with enough leisure, inclination, or inducement to cultivate the powers of their minds to the degree required for the formation of an alphabet. But when a people reached a state of civilization that necessitated the representation of abstract conceptions, then they would be compelled to abandon picture-writing for the use of an alphabet. This would occur "whenever a nation began to improve in arts, manufactures, and commerce; and the more genius such a nation had, the more improvements would be made in the notation of their language." Meanwhile, those peoples who had made "less progress in civilization and science" would have a less perfect system of writing.[29]

A similar analysis was put forth by Blair to explain the historical change he detected in the style of language, through which exaggeration and hyperbole gave way to calmness, precision, and simplicity. This modification he attributed to a basic intellectual development, the taming of the imagination and the concomitant rise of the understanding, which itself grew out of social change. Reigning supreme in the "infancy" of society, the imagination came to have less influence over men "in proportion as Society advanced" to a more "cultivated" state. Here again the causal chain was conceived as having three links: first society would advance, then thought, and finally language. As the *Encyclopaedia Britannica* stated, when any savage people finally emerged from their "barbarism, . . . it is obvious that the improvement and copiousness of their language would keep pace with their own progress in knowledge and in the arts of civil life."[30]

But if the advance of society and thought created linguistic progress, language itself brought about social and intellectual ameliora-

29. Stackhouse, *Reflections*, 45–46; Johnson, "Preface," in *Works* (1825 ed.), 5:47; Astle, *Origin and Progress of Writing*, 16.

30. Blair, *Lectures on Rhetoric*, 1:113–16; idem, *A Critical Dissertation on the Poems of Ossian, the Son of Fingal*, 2d ed. (London, 1765), 2–4, 30, 33; *Encyclopaedia Britannica*, 9:533:2–534:1.

tion, in several ways. For example, language played the role of the improver for society as a whole. Mandeville claimed that the invention of writing constituted the "last Step to Society," because no people could live peaceably without government, no government could subsist without laws, and no laws could be effectual for long without being written down. Wilson similarly contended that laws had less ambiguity in a nation possessing a good language. His list of the valuable advantages conferred on any people by such a language also included such items as fewer misunderstandings in contracts and conversation, greater clarity in the doctrines of faith and the conceptions of the learned, superior religious practices, and better poetry and prose. Looking specifically at the ancient Greeks, he noted that "it was their Language, and [the] Learning that was inseparably joined to it, that opened the Way both to their Laws, Trade, and Riches, and [to] the great Conquests that they made." Sheridan agreed that the Greeks, as well as the Romans, owed their splendor to the care they took in the cultivation of language. He believed that language, particularly as refined through the study of elocution, contributed enormously both to the benefit of individuals and to the wealth and adornment "of the state in general." Consequently, while the neglect of their speech provides a certain means of keeping a people in barbarism, the "refinement of language is a necessary step towards introducing politeness."[31]

Language was also universally treated as a powerful instrument of intellectual improvement. Such a view Johnson made explicit when, in a famous passage, he called the lexicographer the "slave of science" and "pioneer of literature," whose task it was "to remove rubbish and clear obstructions from the paths, through which Learning and Genius press forward to conquest and glory." But if the progress of language was a kind of bulldozer preparing a roadbed for intellectual advance, it was at the same time an engine pulling behind it sparkling new cargoes of thought. The "Advancement of the Arts and Sciences," wrote Hartley, "is chiefly carried on by the new Significations given to Words" in writing and reading. Stackhouse agreed, asking rhetorically how the sciences could make any progress "if learned Men are not allowed to form Terms and Fashions of Speech proper to illustrate new Discoveries?" In his view, however, the con-

---

31. Mandeville, *Fable*, 2:269; Wilson, *Many Advantages*, 4, 81; Sheridan, *British Education*, 132, 162; idem, *A Discourse*, 53–54; idem, *A Dissertation on the Causes of the Difficulties, Which occur, in learning the English Tongue* (London, 1761), 2.

tribution of language to the improvement of thought was much more profound. He believed that for any people to advance their stock of knowledge very far, they had to accustom themselves to speak with purity, elegance, energy, and even sublimity and magnificence. "And all this is nothing else but perfecting their own *Tongue*, and making it more Polite and Eloquent."[32]

At bottom, that language could have a progressive effect on thought followed from the fact, as Johnson wrote, that it "is only the instrument of science, and words are but the signs of our ideas." For Hartley, thinking of the individual, this fact implied the "great Use and Necessity of Words for the Improvement of our Knowlege [*sic*], and Inlargement of our Affections." He explained that words served to collect and unite ideas "from various Quarters," and to "transfer them both upon foreign Objects." As a result, the "Use of Words adds much to the Number and Complexity of our Ideas, and is the principal Means by which we make intellectual and moral Improvements." Sheridan went beyond the individual to look at the connection of ideas and words from a broader perspective. He observed that language was actually a transcript of ideas: the more perfect the transcript, the more precisely and forcefully was the intellect displayed; but however deficient the language, to that extent was knowledge afflicted. Consequently, he argued, only when language was in a state of excellence could any "sure progress" in the sciences be made or communicated.[33]

Beyond all these considerations, language was believed to contribute to intellectual *and* social progress in one more way: it provided a vessel to transport that improvement safely over the seas of time and space. Turgot certainly recognized the centrality of language to the temporal transmission of knowledge, by which each generation could build on the work of its predecessors. But perhaps even more than he did his British contemporaries perceive and emphasize the importance of the permeative as well as transmissive function of language. With regard to the linguistic shrinkage of space, Astle, for example, noted that through writing "distance is as it were annihilated, and the merchant, the statesman, and the scholar becomes present to every purpose of utility, in regions the most remote." And

32. Johnson, "Preface," in *Works* (1825 ed.), 5:23; Hartley, *Observations*, 1:269; Stackhouse, *Reflections*, 89, 51.

33. Johnson, "Preface," in *Works* (1825 ed.), 5:23; Hartley, *Observations*, 1:234, 287; Sheridan, *British Education*, 81, 142, 171–73.

Beattie remarked that printing, in particular, was useful not only for "promoting the improvement of arts and sciences" but also for "diffusing knowledge through all the classes of mankind."[34]

Conqueror of geographical and social distance, language could also vanquish time. Sheridan contended that it was the "only sublunary thing from which men may expect perpetuity to their labours," giving them a type of "immortality even in this world." He believed that language, in its highest state, preserved a perfect record of the works of the great geniuses of a people, which could even "be the means of perpetuating the British constitution either here or in some other country to the end of time." Writing, especially, was seen as linking the present with the future and the past. According to Astle, because writing enabled men to record and perpetuate their thoughts, by its means philosophy, science, and the arts had "derived all their successive improvements: succeeding generations have been enabled to add to the stock they received from the past, and to prepare the way for future acquisitions." When he proclaimed language the "invention which hath contributed more than all others to the improvement of mankind," he made clear how crucial the vessel of language was considered to be for that cumulative process of progress described long before by Bacon.[35]

As vessel and as instrument, then, language was believed to contribute to intellectual and social advance. The *Encyclopaedia Britannica* epitomized the views of contemporaries on this subject. Through the use of language, it asserted,

> man is raised above the brute creation; . . . by this means he improves every faculty of his mind, and, to the observations which he may himself have made, has the additional advantage of the experience of those with whom he may converse, as

---

34. Astle, *Origin and Progress of Writing*, i; Beattie, *Dissertations*, 318. For the views of Turgot and the image of language as a vessel, see "Tableau philosophique des progrès successifs de l'esprit humain. Discours prononcé en latin dans les écoles de Sorbonne, pour la clôture des Sorboniques" (Dec. 11, 1750), in *Oeuvres de Turgot et documents le concernant*, ed. Gustave Schelle, 4 vols. (Paris, 1913–23), 1:215; Frank E. Manuel, *The Prophets of Paris: Turgot, Condorcet, Saint-Simon, Fourier, and Comte* (Cambridge, Mass., 1962), 21, 29.

35. Sheridan, *British Education*, 193–94, 137–39; Astle, *Origin and Progress of Writing*, i, 10. Citing Turgot, Michel Foucault emphasizes how important the perception of language as the bringer of temporal continuity was to "progress, as defined in the eighteenth century": *The Order of Things: An Archaeology of the Human Sciences* (New York, 1970), 113.

well as the knowledge which the human race have acquired by the accumulated experience of all preceding ages; . . . it is by the enlivening glow of conversation that kindred souls catch fire from one another, that thought produces thought, and each improves upon the other, till they soar beyond the bounds which human reason, if left alone, could ever have aspired to.

Blair adduced a similarly comprehensive list of benefits deriving from language. Taking the historical point of view, he declared that, beginning in rudeness, language had finally become "a vehicle" by which the most delicate and refined sentiments and the most abstract conceptions could be intelligibly communicated; by which all the ideas that science discovered or the imagination created could be correctly named and understood; and by which an easy and speedy intercourse was carried on in society to provide the necessities of life. At present writing permitted thoughts to be propagated throughout the world, and it also provided the means of perpetuating the instructive memory of the past and transmitting ideas to the future. In brief, it was through speech and writing, the "two great arts" of language, that "men's thoughts are communicated, and the foundation laid for all knowledge and improvement."[36]

Clearly, eighteenth-century British students of language did not think of the connection between verbal communication, on the one side, and thought and society, on the other, as unidirectional. They believed that progress, like an alternating electrical current, flowed between the two elements of this circuit in both directions. With regard to thought and society, language was the improver as well as the improved.

THE SCHOOL OF LANGUAGES

In some of the most memorable pages of *Gulliver's Travels*, Jonathan Swift satirically disparaged such scientific institutions as the Royal Society, by means of an account of the Grand Academy of Lagado. Along with a number of crack-brained "projectors" of ludicrous technological, intellectual, and political schemes, the Academy included "the School of Languages, where three Professors sat in Consultation upon improving that of their own Country." One of the

36. *Encyclopaedia Britannica*, 9:542:1; Blair, *Lectures on Rhetoric*, 1:98–99, 135–36.

projects evolved by the linguists called for the complete abolition of words and the use of things alone in communication, "since Words are only Names for *Things*." The implementation of this project was designed both to lessen corrosion of the lungs and to create a "universal Language to be understood in all civilized Nations, whose Goods and Utensils are generally of the same Kind, or nearly."[37]

Like all great satire, this fictional flower of Swift's genius was planted firmly in fact. English Baconians and *virtuosi* of the middle and late seventeenth century had exhibited an intense distrust of existing language. They desired linguistic renovation in the direction of a one-to-one relation of words and things, in order to facilitate science by bringing language into closer harmony with nature. Some of them (including Samuel Hartlib, John Webster, Seth Ward, Cave Beck, George Dalgorno, Robert Boyle, John Wilkins, and Isaac Newton)—even formulated or at least heartily approved of schemes for a universal language.[38] It was undoubtedly ideas such as all of these that Swift was satirizing in *Gulliver*. But what has too often been forgotten, and what many contemporary readers of his book must have known, is that he, too, had once made proposals for reforming language.[39] In fact, Swift was merely one of many eighteenth-century Britons who had a substantial interest in bringing about linguistic improvement. As a group they constituted a real, and less absurd, version of the Lagado school of languages. The views they held and the projects they formulated represent nothing less than a conception of future progress in and through language.

Most of these projects concerned English and aimed at improving and then stabilizing and preserving that language. Swift set a half-century-long trend in motion when he advocated in 1712 that "some Method should be thought on for *Ascertaining* and *Fixing* our Language for ever, after such Alterations are made in it as shall be

37. Jonathan Swift, *Gulliver's Travels* (1726), in *Prose Works*, 11:185–86.

38. On seventeenth-century views of linguistic reform and the schemes proposed during that period for a universal language, see [Johann David] Michaelis, *A Dissertation on the Influence of Opinions on Language and of Language on Opinions* (London, 1769), iv–vi (translator's preface); Richard Foster Jones, "Science and Language in England of the Mid-Seventeenth Century," *Journal of English and Germanic Philology* 31 (1932): 315–31, reprinted with corrections in *The Seventeenth Century: Studies in the History of English Thought and Literature from Bacon to Pope* (Stanford, 1951), 143–60; James Knowlson, *Universal Language Schemes in England and France 1600–1800* (Toronto, 1975). (In spite of the title of his book, Knowlson does not discuss eighteenth-century British ideas about a universal language.)

39. For the full title of Swift's contribution see above, n. 13.

thought requisite." The general outlines and sometimes even the very words of this proposal were reiterated by later writers like Wilson, Stackhouse, George Harris, and Sheridan. Neither they nor Swift had any desire to make English completely changeless. "I do not mean," wrote Stackhouse, "that it should never be enlarg'd"; he recognized that commerce, war, and—especially—the increase of knowledge constantly made for additions to any language. The intention was simply, as Sheridan explained, first to "lay the foundation for regulating and refining our speech, till it is brought to the degree of perfection whereof in its nature it is capable; and afterwards of fixing it in that state to perpetuity, by a sure and settled standard." The erecting of such a standard would not mean the total elimination of linguistic change, since "in a living tongue changes are not to be prevented," but rather the conformity of all further alterations "to those rules, in order to render our language more regular and complete."[40] In essence, the inherent tendency of the language to change had to be brought under control, once sufficient improvements had been made in it.

A number of institutional mechanisms were suggested for achieving this dual goal, some of which emphasized the role of the state. Bishop Wilson, for instance, argued in favor of the production of better grammars and dictionaries. Through encouragement by the government and with use in the schools and universities, these linguistic handbooks would, "like Anchors, . . . most certainly keep [English] stedfast, if it was but once brought to a just Standard." Swift and Stackhouse had a more elaborate plan. They revived the late seventeenth-century proposals of Sprat, Evelyn, Dryden, and Defoe for a national society (similar to the Académie Française) to supervise the language. It would correct linguistic abuses such as abbreviation, establish definitive grammatical rules, and prescribe the lexicon. George Harris went even farther. He called for legislation to improve and preserve English, particularly by creating uniformity in spelling![41]

Others who had the same general goal did not rely on governmen-

40. Swift, A Proposal, in Prose Works, 4:14–15, 9; Stackhouse, Reflections, 189, 191–92; Sheridan, A Dissertation, 33; idem, British Education, 176. See also Wilson, Many Advantages, 5; George Harris, Observations upon English, 6, 13.

41. Wilson, Many Advantages, 80–81, 23–24, 40; Swift, A Proposal, in Prose Works, 4:13–14; Stackhouse, Reflections, 189–92; George Harris, Observations upon English, 13–14.

tal action for its accomplishment. The idea of an academy for linguistic regulation was specifically rejected by Johnson and Sheridan, on grounds of excessive interference with the liberty of the citizen. The alternative offered by Johnson was, of course, his *Dictionary of the English Language* (1755), through which, he hoped, the vernacular "may be fixed, and its attainment facilitated; by which its purity may be preserved, its use ascertained." He wanted the *Dictionary* to serve as a kind of linguistic periodical table, resolving English into its "minutest subdivisions" and "elemental principles." Thereby the "fundamental atoms of our speech might obtain the firmness and immutability of the primogenial and constituent particles of matter, . . . might retain their substance while they alter their appearance" in the course of use. Recognizing that change in language could never be entirely overcome, Johnson knew that his book would not achieve these ends. But he thought that although his incursion into English, like Caesar's invasion of Britain, could not be a complete conquest, it might at least "make it easy for some other adventurer to proceed further."[42]

Such a man Sheridan clearly felt himself to be, and he embarked on two related projects "*to correct, ascertain, and fix the English language.*" Although greatly admiring Johnson's work, in 1780 he produced his own grammar and "pronouncing dictionary." And because he believed that the real regulators of language were not academies but the people themselves, he set out to make the people better speakers of English. To attain this end, he ardently promoted the study of eloquence or rhetoric as an integral part of education. His scheme met with an enthusiastic reception in Edinburgh, where in 1761 he lectured successfully on elocution and English to more than three hundred Scottish gentlemen and professional men, including Hume and Boswell. Eager to lose what many of them considered to be the barbarousness of their native speech, and thereby to become more "polite," these Scots established the Select Society for Promoting the Reading and Speaking of the English Language in Scotland, under the auspices of the Select Society of Edinburgh. With Sheridan's help, this new organization planned to establish voluntary schools for the teaching of English to children and adults.[43]

42. Johnson, "Preface" and *Plan*, in *Works* (1825 ed.), 5:48–49, 20–21, 12; Sheridan, *British Education*, 271–72.
43. Sheridan, *British Education*, v, 273–77. On Sheridan's activities in Edinburgh and on the short-lived Select Society for Promoting English, see Davis D. McElroy,

Underlying all these various projects was a widespread expectation: English could be improved, with beneficial consequences. Comparing English to a healthy but untended plant, the *Encyclopaedia Britannica* declared that should its

> soil be cultivated with care, and a strong fence be placed around it, to prevent the idle or wicked from breaking or distorting its branches;—who can tell with what additional vigour it would flourish, or what amazing magnitude and perfection it might at last attain!

For Sheridan, the means of arriving at such perfection lay as much in the power of modern Britons as in that of classical Greeks and Romans. Indeed, although he did not consider contemporary English to be superior to Greek and Latin, he did agree with Wilson that, with proper care, it could eventually surpass the languages of the ancients, "as far as our Navigators have gone beyond their Seamen in discovering new Lands and Seas." English would then become what Sheridan called "a third classical language, of far more importance than the other two." The ramifications of such future linguistic progress seemed immense. Swift could think of nothing that "would be of greater Use towards the Improvement of Knowledge and Politeness." Sheridan asked rhetorically, if English in its "corrupt state" had carried a writer like Dryden so far, "what might we not hope for from it were it polished and refined?" But beyond the advantages to be conferred on literature alone, "nothing could be more desirable, nothing could more effectually contribute to the benefit and glory of this country," than to bring English to "as great a degree of perfection, stability, and general use" as Greek and Latin had once attained.[44]

Hence, the English language was commonly believed to be capable, through a variety of institutional methods, of advancing in the future and of bringing about nonlinguistic progress. Once achieved, the improved state of English would remain relatively permanent. Such stability, it was thought, would itself confer a significant benefit: the preservation of the language's function as the vessel of progress. As Beattie declared, everything "deserves praise, which is done

Scotland's Age of Improvement: A Survey of Eighteenth-Century Literary Clubs and Societies ([Pullman, Wash.], 1969), 56–59.

44. *Encyclopaedia Britannica*, 9:550:1; Sheridan, *British Education*, 176–77, 271, 254; idem, *A Discourse*, 8–11; Wilson, *Many Advantages*, 25–26, 28–29; Swift, *A Proposal*, in *Prose Works*, 4:5.

with a view to make language durable; for on the permanency of any tongue depends that of the literature conveyed in it." Language therefore required stability, as Wilson put it, in order that "Posterity may not lose the Wisdom of their Ancestors." This outlook explains why Stackhouse proposed that an academy of language bring English to "a competent Standard of Purity," so that "no Words, to which this Society shall give a sanction (whatever *new* ones they may think proper to receive) shall ever after be *antiquated* and exploded." Understanding the cumulative method of progress, he wanted to make certain that the writers of the past would continue eternally to be understood.[45]

The same intention motivated Johnson to produce his dictionary. As a proponent of the cyclical theory of the history of language, he did not believe it possible to keep English forever from decay. But he refused to acquiesce meekly in the prospect of inevitable decline, because what could not be prevented could at least be retarded. "Life may be lengthened by care," he wrote, "though death cannot be ultimately defeated: tongues, like governments, have a natural tendency to degeneration; we have long preserved our constitution, let us make some struggles for our language." And so he devoted years of lexicographical labor to the "hope of giving longevity to that which its own nature forbids to be immortal." Why linguistic endurance was so important he made explicit in assessing the value of the *Dictionary*:

> I shall not think my employment useless or ignoble, if, by my assistance, foreign nations, and distant ages, gain access to the propagators of knowledge, and understand the teachers of truth; if my labours afford light to the repositories of science, and add celebrity to Bacon, to Hooker, to Milton, and to Boyle.
>
> When I am animated by this wish, I look with pleasure on my book, however defective, and deliver it to the world with the spirit of a man that has endeavoured well.

Like Condorcet's proposed fireproof vault containing an encyclopedic compendium of all valuable knowledge, Johnson's *Dictionary* and the other programs for stabilizing English aimed at building an indestructible vessel for progress.[46]

---

45. Beattie, *Dissertations*, 262, 429n; Wilson, *Many Advantages*, 50; Stackhouse, *Reflections*, 192.

46. Johnson, "Preface," in *Works* (1825 ed.), 5:45–46, 49–50. On Condorcet's vault, see Keith Michael Baker, *Condorcet: From Natural Philosophy to Social Mathematics* (Chicago, 1975), 367.

Of course, the encyclopedia that Condorcet envisioned was to be written not in English but in a universal language. And, like him, some British writers looked forward to linguistic improvement beyond the vernacular alone, and particularly to the coming of a worldwide language. Ever since the appearance of the Port-Royal Grammar, there had been a widespread conviction that all languages possessed certain elements in common. James Harris and Beattie described in detail what they thought these elements to be. Others believed that the supposed existence of a universal grammatical structure, and even of universal morphemes, implied the possibility of ultimately creating a catholic tongue. For example, Rowland Jones and the philologist L. D. Nelme (fl. 1772–87) contended that the original, primitive language of mankind could be restored and made the basis of international verbal communication. Jones felt certain that his investigation of comparative philology had actually unearthed the "universal philosophical language," for which he compiled an extensive grammar and lexicon. Because of its basis in human history, he argued, such a system "must be far preferable, as well as more practicable, than the arbitrary real characters of Dr. Wilkins and others." Its adoption would consequently yield what both Jones and Nelme considered important results: the uniformity and spread of true religion around the world, the "advancement of learning in general," the reconciliation and reuniting of mankind, and the infusion of men with a spirit of "good-will and benevolence to all."[47]

Bishop Wilson's expectations were not so grandiose. But he did think that it was possible for the people of all European countries to learn a single grammar, which he called the key that could unlock their various languages "with great Ease, and take out any Treasures of Philosophy, Physick, or any other useful Knowledge that may be hidden in them." Similarly, Hartley anticipated the transformation in future ages of linguistic diversity into unity, a change that would be productive of greater human happiness. On the basis of his associationist psychology, he believed that just as life was presently a mixture of happiness and misery, "so all our Languages must, from the Difference of our Associations, convey Falsehood as well as Truth." Nevertheless, he projected,

47. James Harris, *Hermes*, in *Works*, 1:221, 282, 373–74; Beattie, *Dissertations*, 306–07, 322, 501–02; Jones, *Origin of Language*, sig. A2ʳ ("Preface"); idem, *Philosophy of Words*, 6, 11, 41; Nelme, *Origin and Elements*, x–xii, 15, 132–34.

since our imperfect Languages improve, purify, and correct themselves perpetually by themselves, and other Means, so that we may hope at last to obtain a Language, which shall be an adequate Representation of Ideas, and a pure Chanel [sic] of Conveyance for Truth alone, Analogy seems to suggest, that the Mixture of Pleasures and Pains, which we now experience, will gradually tend to a Collection of pure Pleasures only, and that Association may be the Means of effecting this.

So in Hartley's view, the emergence of a universal language was closely linked to the development of more accurate associations and, therefore, of greater pleasure among men. And like Condillac and Condorcet, he wanted and expected this language to be mathematical in nature. It appeared likely to him that "future Generations should put all Kinds of Evidences and Inquiries into mathematical Forms; . . . so as to make Mathematics and Logic, Natural History, and Civil History, Natural Philosophy, and Philosophy of all other Kinds, coincide *omni ex parte*." If the various branches of knowledge were not yet entirely ready for such methods, "they seem to tend to this more and more perpetually."[48]

Bentham, who learned much from Hartley, ultimately made a mathematical language his ideal. In writing his *Pannomial Fragments* during the early nineteenth century, he sought to create a verbal equivalent of mathematics, a moral geometry. But long before that time he had been preoccupied with the improvement of language, and thus he may appropriately serve as an epitome of the eighteenth-century British "school of languages." No less than Johnson was Bentham a lexicographer, for nearly all of his works were, at least in part, dictionaries. Indeed, he thought and wrote from the perspective of a supreme legislator of definitions. In this role he attempted simultaneously to correct linguistic abuses where he found them (especially in the law), to foster neologisms when necessary, and to stabilize language so that men could know what they did by understanding what they said. He recognized that this task was in some sense contradictory, and certainly fraught with difficulties. "Change the import of the old names," he admitted in his *Principles of Morals and Legislation* (written 1780), "and you are in perpetual

48. Wilson, *Many Advantages*, 30; Hartley, *Observations*, 1:316–17, 320–21, 351, 358. On Condillac and Condorcet, see Knight, *Geometric Spirit*, 171–75; Baker, *Condorcet*, 126–28.

danger of being misunderstood: introduce an entire new set of names, and you are sure not to be understood at all." Yet he could not give up the effort to improve and fix language. For he realized that science in general and moral science in particular depended on classification; in turn, the "distribution of things must in a great measure be dependent on their names: arrangement, the work of mature reflection, must be ruled by nomenclature, the work of popular caprice." To eliminate that caprice meant to bring about scientific progress, and so Bentham undertook and continued his lexicographical labors. Perhaps better than his eighteenth-century predecessors, he knew that "Complete success . . . is, as yet at least, unattainable." But like them he believed that the attempt to advance and stabilize language was inherently valuable:

> at the worst, it may accelerate the arrival of that perfect system, the possession of which will be the happiness of some maturer age. Gross ignorance descries no difficulties; imperfect knowledge finds them out, and struggles with them: it must be perfect knowledge that overcomes them.[49]

And how should that knowledge be gained and those difficulties defeated if not through improved language?

Language and progress, then, were intimately connected in the thought of the period. Linguistic history appeared to contemporaries to be progressive, on the whole. They believed that advances in verbal communication could continue, toward which end they proposed a number of institutionally oriented plans—sometimes carrying them out. And eighteenth-century British students of language considered these past and future improvements to be enormously important to human life. For although thought and society gave birth to linguistic advance, language itself provided not only an index of but an instrument and a vessel for intellectual and social progress.

49. Bentham, *Principles of Morals and Legislation*, 205n, 207n. For Bentham as lexicographer and mathematician of language, see Mary P. Mack, *Jeremy Bentham: An Odyssey of Ideas, 1748–1792* (London, 1962), 151–54; idem, *A Bentham Reader* (New York, 1969), xxxix, 44, 76, 240–41.

P*art Three*
Culminating Forms

Between 1777 and 1783 James Barry completed six enormous canvases commissioned by the London Society of Arts to decorate its Great Room. He intended these paintings, which have been called the "most considerable achievement" in the "grand style" by any British artist of the eighteenth century, "to illustrate one great maxim of moral truth, viz. that the obtaining of happiness, as well individual as public, depends upon cultivating the human faculties." In order to make the illustration clear, he proceeded historically, beginning with man in the "savage state, full of inconvenience, imperfection and misery" (the famous "state of nature," which actually fell "far short of the golden age and happiness some have unwisely imagined"), and following him through the "several gradations of culture and happiness."[1] The theme of this visually related story, as expressed in Barry's collective title for the paintings, was The Progress of Human Culture.

The notion that there had been or could be improvement in human affairs generally—in culture or civilization or even happiness— was rarely expressed by British writers in more than an implicit, cursory way before about 1760. Prior to the reign of George III, the idea of progress was almost always cast into less comprehensive forms, and particularly into those that concerned the arts and sciences, religion and religious knowledge, the pliability of man, and language. But during the three decades leading up to the outbreak of

1. James Barry, *An Account of a Series of Pictures, in the Great Room of the Society of Arts, Manufactures, and Commerce, at the Adelphi* (1783), in *The Works of James Barry, Esq.,* 2 vols. (London, 1809), 2:323, 325. The critical opinion referred to concerning Barry's series is found in Ellis Waterhouse, *Painting in Britain 1530 to 1790,* 4th ed. (Harmondsworth, Eng., 1978), 273:2. On Barry and one of the paintings mentioned, see above, chap. 2.

the French Revolution, a significant number of doctrines of general progress were put forth. Among these there were two basic types. One, expressed primarily by Scots, depicted history, in the march from rudeness to refinement, as broadly progressive within certain temporal and cultural limits. The other, of principally English provenance, ignored these limits and conceived of progress as indefinite in scope and duration. A large area of common ground underlay this difference in outlook and emphasis, but the diversity is important and should not be overlooked.[2] In any case, these doctrines of general progress represent the culminating forms of the idea during the eighteenth century, in the sense that they appeared latest in time, were more inclusive than those forms that had emerged earlier, and combined and extended the others.

In addition to taking on broader shapes, the idea of progress, whatever kind of expression it was given, appeared far more frequently in British writings after mid-century. Although this development is obviously difficult to quantify with any precision, we can find evidence of the idea on practically all sides from the later 1750s on, which was much less the case during the previous thirty years. Taken together, these two developments indicate that the historical outlook of the eighteenth century, rather than remaining constant, actually grew increasingly optimistic as the decades advanced. In short, the idea of progress was becoming more popular, and more influential. But how exactly did this change occur?

2. See below, chap. 8.

6 The Progress of Human Culture: England

Throughout the eighteenth century, British historical pessimism, while not negligible in quantity, was usually tempered with or limited by a concomitant optimism.[1] The clearest and most notable instance of this phenomenon was the controversy in England surrounding John Brown's *Estimate of the Manners and Principles of the Times* (1757–58). This debate generated a full-scale public consideration of the national destiny and the issue of luxury. At the same time, it marked the last great gasp of pessimism in the high eighteenth century, an outburst that was immediately succeeded by a wave of expressions of belief in general progress.

THE BROWN CONTROVERSY

Horace Walpole's description of himself in 1745 as "one of the *ultimi Romanorum*," alive at the fag end of his country's greatness, epitomized the gloom present among virtually all social groups in Britain toward the end of the War of the Austrian Succession and at the time of the second Jacobite Rebellion. For six or seven years after that war, this mood gave way to one of mixed concern and self-satisfaction. The military conflict had finally ended, but the Treaty of Aix-la-Chapelle brought the nation no tangible benefits for the decade of fighting and an expenditure of eighty million pounds. The economy entered a boom period, yet the people were disconcerted by a rising crime rate, the "gin mania" (which, however, began to subside as a result of legislation passed in 1751), and the terrifying concurrence in 1750 of earthquakes under and unusual storms and the Aurora Borealis over London. In these circumstances it is not surpris-

1. See above, chap. 1.

ing that an anonymous writer of 1754 could produce a pamphlet in which he consciously sought to depict human life in tones that were neither too cheerful nor too despairing. Then, beginning with the next year, came food shortages and economic deceleration (which probably meant higher unemployment, and certainly did bring a rise in consumer and producer prices and a decline in wages and the important re-export trade), tragic news of the catastrophe at Lisbon, and the start of the Seven Years' War. That this war went very badly at first for Britain and her allies, while the Newcastle administration seemed paralyzed by indecision in the face of its problems, served only to deepen the growing national despondency. As the inveterate political timeserver George Bubb Dodington recorded in his diary on May 27, 1755, the country "was sinking by degrees, and there was a general indisposition." By early 1757, with the awareness of a seemingly imminent French invasion, alarm intensified and depression became pronounced. As Bishop Warburton unhappily noted, "Never did public affairs wear a more melancholy aspect." The years 1756 and 1757 were, in Lecky's words, "among the most humiliating" in British history.[2]

It was in this climate of intense national pessimism that Brown published his book. "Estimate" Brown, who ultimately committed suicide in 1766 at the age of fifty, was an Anglican clergyman and a member of Warburton's circle. He established himself as a writer of note in 1751 with a volume of essays critical of Shaftesbury's moral philosophy. As his nickname testifies, however, he attained renown not for the theological utilitarianism of this earlier work but for the *Estimate* itself, the most famous and popular of the many jeremiads that appeared at the time. His announced task in writing the book was to search out the "peculiar Causes of our calamitous Situation,"

2. Walpole to Horace Mann, July 26, 1745 (o.s.), *Horace Walpole's Correspondence with Sir Horace Mann*, ed. W. S. Lewis et al., in *The Yale Edition of Horace Walpole's Correspondence*, ed. W. S. Lewis, in progress (New Haven, 1937–), 19:78; Anon., *A New Estimate of Human Life. Inscribed to The Reverend Dr. Young* (London, 1754), 5–7; *The Diary of the Late George Bubb Dodington, Baron of Melcombe Regis*, ed. Henry Penruddocke Wyndham, 4th ed. (London, 1823), 289; Warburton to Richard Hurd, Feb. 7, 1757, *Letters from a Late Eminent Prelate, to One of his Friends* (Kidderminster, [1809]), 174; William Edward Hartpole Lecky, *A History of England in the Eighteenth Century*, 8 vols. (New York, 1878–91), 2:492. For the economic situation see T. S. Ashton, *An Economic History of England: The 18th Century* (New York, [1955]), 54, 225; B. R. Mitchell with Phyllis Deane, *Abstract of British Historical Statistics* (Cambridge, 1962), 280, 347, 469.

to discover the "Source of all our public Miscarriages" at a "*Crisis* so important and alarming." He traced these desperate problems back to the practices and outlook of the upper strata of British society. Their manners he characterized as a "*vain, luxurious,* and *selfish* EFFEMINACY," which manifested itself both in the decline of education, music, and painting and in the omnipresence of personal vanity, dandyism, gluttony, gambling, avarice, and a tendency toward the reversal of the traditional behavior patterns of the sexes. With regard to the principles of the elite, he asserted that religion, patriotism, and the quest for fame through honor had largely disappeared. In brief, "SHOW and PLEASURE are the main Objects of Pursuit: . . . the general Habit of *refined Indulgence* is *strong,* and the Habit of *induring* is *lost:* . . . the general Spirit of *Religion, Honour,* and *public Love,* are weakened or vanished."[3]

Behind these trends in manners and principles, thought Brown, lay a crucial fact about the history of trade. In its first stages, commerce provided for necessities, extended knowledge, eradicated prejudices, and spread humanity in society. During its "middle and more advanced Period," it permitted conveniences, gave birth to art and science, created equitable laws, and diffused general plenty and happiness. All of these were purely beneficial results. But in its "third and highest Stage" commerce produced "dangerous and fatal" effects. "It brings in Superfluity and vast Wealth; begets Avarice, gross Luxury, or effeminate Refinement among the higher Ranks, together with general Loss of Principle." According to Brown, Britain had entered this final stage: "our present exorbitant Degree of Trade and Wealth . . . naturally tends to produce luxurious and effeminate Manners . . . together with a general Defect of *Principle.*"[4]

These economic facts and their direct consequences held immense importance for the author of the *Estimate* because he accepted Montesquieu's conception of the centrality of general causes in shaping the condition of every state. And, in Brown's view, among such causes—more significant even than the spirit of the laws of a country—were its manners and principles, upon which the "internal

3. [John Brown], *An Estimate of the Manners and Principles of the Times,* 1st ed., 2 vols. (London, 1757–58), 1:14, 11, sig. a2ʳ, 29–41, 45–48, 51, 55–56, 58, 61–64, 66; 2:68–70, 79–82, 100.
4. Ibid., 1:152–53, 181, 183, 161.

Strength of a Nation will always depend chiefly." In Britain's case, the effeminate manners and lack of principle among the ruling orders

> have produced a general Incapacity, have weakened the national Spirit of Defence, have heightened the national Disunion: And this national Disunion, besides it's [sic] proper and immediate Effects, being founded in Avarice for the Ends of Dissipation, hath again weakened the small Remainder of publick Capacity and Defence; and thus seems to have fitted us for a Prey to the Insults and Invasions of our most powerful Enemy.

Consequently, "by a gradual and unperceived Decline, we seem to be gliding down to Ruin" just like "degenerate and declining *Rome.*"[5]

Brown's analysis of Britain's apparently precarious situation proved popular, and the *Estimate* went through at least four editions by 1760. The periodical press published a considerable number of letters favorable to his assessment of the times, while pamphleteers echoed his views. A writer calling himself "Britannicus" claimed that his country, "once the boast and confidence of her friends, the envy and dread of her enemies, the nurse of heroes, the glory and admiration of mankind, is now, alas! a reproach among the nations, the school of licentiousness and unmanly luxury, lost to public spirit, and to every great and generous principle." The people suffered from a prevalence of profaneness, vanity, luxury, disregard for religion, and gross sensuality, which together "are a disgrace to, and tend to the utter ruin of, all civil societies." Not surprisingly, therefore, the author contended that Britain had been "brought to the brink of ruin by the degeneracy of her sons" and was "ripening every day for a state of slavery and dependence" at the hands of France. Even a decade later, after the French menace had disappeared, it was still possible for an anonymous writer to declaim against the "present very great profligacy," the "great and crying sins of the age," and the "monstrous degeneracy" and "very great depravity and corruption" that had "infected the whole nation." He discerned the source of the "present troubles and discontents" in an almost total "neglect (I might say contempt) of religion; an almost universal corruption of morals, and an idle luxury, which at once enervates, and renders us venal." Another anonymous pamphleteer, writing in 1769 under the obvious

5. Ibid., 1:12–13, 104, 152, 172, 181–82, 144, 120; 2:20–23. On the comparison of contemporary Britain with ancient Rome, see ibid., 1:108–13, 127; 2:198–200.

influence of Brown, lamented the "melancholy prospect" of the times. Attempting to prove that "England was never so immoral as at present," he examined in succession the degeneracy of the nobility, members of the traditional professions, physicians, merchants and craftsmen, women, and the lower orders. He concluded that society was "almost *universally* unhappy," largely because the "nation totters to the power of Gold."[6]

Of course, the *Estimate* had its critics, too, some of whom substantially misinterpreted it. For example, Sir Charles Hanbury Williams (1708–59), a diplomat and satirical writer, condemned Brown for indiscriminately attributing the faults of "the Great" to everyone, whereas the "common people of *Britain* are a respectable and powerful Body." (Brown actually confined his catalogue of vices to the ruling classes, believing that "the *People* are in general much more irreproachable than their *Superiors*.") Of more importance, Brown was charged by an anonymous critic with professing "to demonstrate that this is the worst of all Ages." This claim is directly related to Williams's assertion that the author of the *Estimate* favored the Greeks and Romans over the men of the eighteenth century, and to the statement made by a reviewer in the *Annual Register* (edited by Robert Dodsley and Edmund Burke) that the "disadvantageous picture given of modern times in this work, revived . . . the dispute concerning the preference of antient and modern times."[7]

In fact, however, Brown had no intention of entirely damning his own age or of doing battle against it on behalf of classical antiquity, but quite the reverse. He contended in a reply to his critics that his book contained "a Catalogue of Virtues, which adorn our Times and Country" as well as a litany of vices, and so indeed it did. It praised the spirit of liberty, the humanitarianism, and the sense of equity in the administration of justice that prevailed in Britain, which together

6. Britannicus, *Friendly Admonitions to the Inhabitants of Great-Britain, in general; and to the Clergy of the Church of England in particular* (London, 1758), 10, 17, 54, 2, 9; Anon., *An Address to the People of England, on the Manners of the Times* (London, 1767), sig. B^r, 2, 20, 7; Anon., *Another Estimate of the Manners and Principles of the Present Times* (London, 1769), 108, sig. B^r-2, 96, 106. For even later comments of the same type, see Petruchio, "On Luxury," *Sentimental Magazine* 1 (April 1773): 67:1–2; [John Wesley], *An Estimate of the Manners of the Present Times* (London, 1782), sig. a2^r, 5, 10–11, 20. On those who agreed with Brown in the late 1750s, see Simeon M. Wade, Jr., "The Idea of Luxury in Eighteenth-Century England," Ph.D. diss., Harvard Univ. (May 1968), 276, 301, 323–24.

7. [Sir Charles Hanbury Williams], *The Real Character of the Age* (London, 1757), 6–8, 10–11; Brown, *Estimate*, 1:23–26, 131; Anon. [Sam Barratt?], *Some Doubts Occa-*

meant that the "Manners of the Times are in many Instances amiable and alluring" and as yet far from *"abandoned Wickedness and Profligacy."* As for unfavorable comparisons with the past, Brown recognized that "there are Corruptions in *all* Times." Moreover, he argued that his country possessed a "political Constitution, superior to all that History hath recorded, or present Times can boast. . . . A Volume might be written in Proof and Display of this Superiority." For these reasons he asserted that in some respects "there is no Time nor Country delivered down to us in Story, in which a wise Man would so much wish to have lived in [*sic*], as our own."[8]

If, then, Brown did not wish to rail against the times in general, to characterize his age as the darkest ever, or even to uphold the ancients over the moderns, why did he paint so gloomy a picture of contemporary Britain? The answer lies in his assertion that the *"Permanency* or *Duration* of the State, is the main Object" of the *Estimate.* He envisioned this book as part of a larger work entitled "A History and Analysis of Manners and Principles in their Several Periods," which would begin with an examination of *"savage Life"* and proceed "through the several intermediate Periods of *rude, simple, civilized, polished, effeminate, corrupt, profligate,* to that of final DECLENSION and RUIN." Shifting from description to analysis, his history would also seek to discover how these various eras were generated, the advantages and disadvantages of each, and the best means of advancing rude periods toward polished life and of returning effeminate and corrupt ones to that "same *salutary Medium."* Much like Machiavelli and Bolingbroke, therefore, although Brown assumed that societies tended to follow a cyclical pattern, he nonetheless believed that the cycle could be broken. He knew that many writers had compared the life of a state to that of man, in that it moved from infancy to maturity to death. Yet he found this comparison "as groundless as it is common." For the "human Body is *naturally* mortal; the political, only so by *Accident."* Unlike man, whose very composition included the "Seeds of certain Dissolution," the state contained nothing in its internal construction that inevita-

sioned by the Second Volume of An Estimate of the Manners and Principles of the Times (London, 1758), 37; Anon., review of Brown's *Estimate, Annual Register* 1 (1759): 445:1.

    8. Brown, *Estimate,* 1:17–23, 28, 15, and 2.30, 23–26; [idem], *An Explanatory Defence of the Estimate of the Manners and Principles of the Times. Being An Appendix to that Work* (London, 1758), 35–36, 28.

bly made for death. And this observation seemed "confirmed by History: Where you see States, which, after being sunk in Corruption and Debility, have been brought back to the Vigour of their first Principles." To accomplish this difficult but "not altogether chimerical" revival, what was needed was "moral or political Physic," "Remedies . . . suited to the Disease." Such medicine Brown thought he offered in the *Estimate*, where Britons "were to be awakened and alarmed" regarding their present condition, in order to control the effects—but not to discourage the growth—of commerce and wealth. Should this nostrum be accepted, a positive change in manners and principles could rightly be expected, since the "most effectual Way to render Kingdoms *happy*, *great*, and *durable*, is to make them *virtuous*, *just*, and *good*." Having faith that his country might yet be saved, Brown argued that his book led to hope, not despair.[9]

This core of ultimate optimism, lying beneath and actually supporting a surface of pessimism, also broke through the gloom of some of Brown's supporters. At present in a "weak and languishing condition, and bowed down almost to the ground," the nation, felt Britannicus, "may still raise her head, recover her former health and vigour, and resume her native station of dignity and honour." He wrote to alert the people to the existence of a crisis of life and death, brought on by an "unmanly luxury" and a "selfish effeminacy," and to offer them speedy remedies. If he could kindle in their breasts the ardor for liberty, virtue, and religion, and animate them to check their vices while reviving the regard for principle, he believed that then "we may emerge from those depths of infamy into which we are sunk, and be once more a virtuous, and, of consequence, a happy and flourishing people." Likewise, the anonymous pamphleteer of 1769 claimed that when, as at present, "matters are at the worst they must mend," and he predicted a purging of the "Augean stable of the times" as individuals ridded themselves of immorality, after which there would come a utopia of peace and harmony.[10]

9. Brown, *Estimate*, 2:105, and 1:213–21; idem, *Defence of the Estimate*, 4–6, 37, 70, 55. In a way, Brown had arrived at what Pocock calls a "Machiavellian moment," that moment in conceptualized time when the state "was seen as confronting its own temporal finitude, as attempting to remain morally and politically stable in a stream of irrational events conceived as essentially destructive of all systems of secular stability": J. G. A. Pocock, *The Machiavellian Moment: Florentine Political Thought and the Atlantic Republican Tradition* (Princeton, 1975), vii. But Brown obviously rejected the view that any polity, and especially Britain, was inherently mortal.

10. Britannicus, *Friendly Admonition*, 17, 26, 2–3; Anon., *Another Estimate*, 110, 101–03, 112–14.

In these various ways, Brown and those influenced by his jeremiad combined pessimism and fear with optimism and hope. At the same time, however, the darker side of their views served to provoke replies with a far more sanguine and progressive tone, even before the tides of the Seven Years' War had begun to turn favorable. One of Brown's anonymous critics, for instance, confessed that the nation was "by no means so religious and virtuous, as it might and ought to be." But he found the general tenor of affairs to be positive, especially with regard to morality, learning, and religion. Of most significance, he objected to Brown's antimodern outlook on change. "Perhaps this ingenious Author has a Language of his own," he sarcastically remarked, "and may chuse to call those things by the name of *Corruptions*, or by some word synonymous to that, which the rest of the world agree in stiling [*sic*] Conveniences and Improvements." Williams, too, found Brown's charges unjustified, whether they were meant to apply to the whole people or only to the great. He protested that effeminacy was not the characteristic of the nation, and that the present existence of a spirit of humanity and charity (which Brown admitted) militated against the presumption of widespread irreligion. He also argued that the incidence of luxury had actually diminished since the previous century, and that in any case "our Trade will never be our Ruin." Addressing himself directly to the author of the *Estimate*, he proclaimed the age neither "so idle nor so ignorant as you supposed" and looked forward to a time when "you and I may yet see this distinguished Island rival *Greece* and *Rome*."[11]

In a quite different way, another critic retaliated by advancing an ironical and quasi-Mandevillian thesis. This anonymous writer argued that because the nation simultaneously had become, in Brown's terms, effeminate and had "arrived at a degree of prosperity none ever knew before," "therefore the prosperity of Britain is owing to the degeneracy of the people; quod erat demonstrandum." He declared that "we were little better than savages" in the age of Elizabeth, when the kingdom was "guided by wisdom and supported by integrity." Since that time, under the impact of "effeminacy," Britain had exchanged rude disquiet and brutal roughness for ease and polished manners. Abroad, its people now enjoyed respect for their politeness, whereas they had previously engendered fear because of their bravery; and would any man "prefer the fear of others to their respect?"

11. Barratt, *Some Doubts*, 72, 16; Williams, *Real Character*, 39, 2, 36, 46, 24, 16, 5.

Meanwhile, great advances had also been made in the sciences and the polite arts. In brief, "the advantage is all on the modern side. We are a more polite, a more learned, and a more respected people than we were in the time of Elizabeth." Nor would this progress give way to decline. The Romans could not derive such benefits from "effeminacy" because they adopted it when their empire had already begun to decline. But "we have assumed it in our full strength, and we must be immortal," with prosperity long continuing.[12]

With their positive assessment of the present when compared to the past and their hopes for the future, Brown's critics were really enunciating doctrines of general progress. Such an outlook on British history found additional proponents in 1759 and 1760, and they stated it with even more force and comprehensiveness.[13] Given their more sophisticated argumentation, however, these slightly later expressions of general progress represent much more than a reaction against Brownian negativism. Furthermore, they were written in a new national climate, created by the string of victories achieved by Britain and its allies in battles against the French from 1758 on. Citing these military advances and comparing England to France as eagle to pigeon, one "Swithin Swing" aggressively attacked Brown and his book and pointed out to him the "present condition of your country; as prosperous as it is honourable." Under the changed circumstances, Brown himself felt compelled to revise his views. In the process of defending his book, he conceded that the defective ruling manners and principles of the era had received some "sudden and courageous" reforms (on the basis of the urgings contained in the *Estimate*, of course), and that the "GENIUS of BRITAIN seems rising as from the *Grave*." The change was not complete, the evils not extirpated. Yet although the "perfect *Cure*" would "require the *Attention* and *Labour* of an *Age*," it was of at least some value "to have *check'd* the *Disease* at its *Crisis*." After 1759, the *annus mirabilis* of military triumphs in India and the Americas, even these minor worries largely disappeared from Britain for the time being. There dawned a new sense of national self-assurance and hope, symbolized by the themes of victory and confidence in the future depicted on the side panels of the golden royal coach constructed for the new king, George III. Britain's prospects soared amid renewed economic acceleration and the

12. Anon., *The Prosperity of Britain, proved from the Degeneracy of its People* (London, 1757), 4–7, 25, 18, 10–12, 17.
13. See below, in the section on "Indefinite Progress".

constant ringing of celebrational bells. Its greatness seemed certain, its possibilities limitless. Once again Horace Walpole captured the mood of the times when, in 1762, he wrote that "I shall burn all my Greek and Latin books; they are the histories of little people!"[14]

To be sure, gloom did not entirely vanish after 1758. It reappeared from time to time during the next three decades, especially with the disasters of the American Revolution (which led Walpole, ever sensitive to the national temper, to comment that calling Britain "Great" was a bad joke).[15] But it never regained even such limited force as it had previously possessed, until the era of the wars with revolutionary and Napoleonic France and the troubles associated with the birth of modern industrial society. For in the interim the idea of progress in its most general eighteenth-century form came to assume a strong grip on the British historical vision: as doctrines of general progress grew to be widespread and customary in English and Scottish thought, it was no longer possible for most educated Britons to succumb more than momentarily to pessimism. And part of the reason why these doctrines developed and became traditional lies in the mood of the late 1750s and early 1760s. On the one hand, the dramatic shift in the fortunes of the Seven Years' War raised national expectations to new heights, as illustrated by Brown's own conversion to a belief in the rejuvenation of Britain. On the other hand, even before this change occurred, the negativism of "estimators" like Brown called forth its antithesis. To some extent this response constituted rhetorical posturing or a defensive reaction aimed at strengthening the resolve of the country in a time of real crisis, yet overall its intensity endowed it with the ring of conviction. As the Brown controversy makes clear, then, in eighteenth-century Britain pessimism and fear not only were usually tempered with but also stimulated and were succeeded by optimism and hope, leading contemporaries to take their stand on the side of progress.

14. Swithin Swing [pseud.], *Letters to the Estimator of the Manners and Principles of the Times* (London, 1758), 37–42; Brown, *Defence of the Estimate*, 80–81, 83–84. Walpole's remark is quoted in R. K. Webb, *Modern England: From the Eighteenth Century to the Present* (New York, 1968), 73. Photographs and a description of the golden royal coach were included in a program in the television series "Royal Heritage" on P.B.S., narrated by Huw Weldon with J. H. Plumb as historical consultant: "The First Three Georges" (broadcast in the U.S. on Feb. 24, 1978). See also J. H. Plumb, *Royal Heritage: The Story of Britain's Royal Builders and Collectors* (London, 1977), 179–80.

15. Webb, *Modern England*, 73.

INDEFINITE PROGRESS

In anonymous prefatory comments of 1763 to an English version of Rousseau's *Émile*, the translator argued that the questioning of received opinions had produced "all the improvements in matters of science, politics, and religion, that have been made since those days of ignorance and barbarism," the dark ages. In light of these beneficial changes, he asked rhetorically,

> Is the human species arrived to its utmost degree of perfection? Hath society reached the summit of political happiness? Are there no farther improvements to be made in the science of government? No rank weeds to be still rooted up from the once overgrown and luxuriant soil of artificial religion?[16]

In essence, these remarks by a writer obviously under the influence of the Enlightenment amount to a brief statement that general progress had occurred in the past, plus a projection of that progress into the future. They thereby typify the English tendency during the eighteenth century, and especially after about 1760, not to place limits on the advancement of human life, but rather to imagine general progress as a temporally indefinite phenomenon.

The same approach also appears in the famous thirty-eighth chapter of Edward Gibbon's *Decline and Fall of the Roman Empire*, written in 1774 and published in 1781. There Gibbon inquired whether the calamities that destroyed Rome could recur in modern Europe. He foresaw no real possibility of the irruption of a new barbarian threat, and even if one did emerge the great moat of the Atlantic Ocean would permit European civilization to "revive and flourish in the American world." But should these considerations prove ill-founded, "there still remains a more humble source of comfort and hope," the fact of historical progress. Beginning as an abject savage, man had "gradually arisen to command the animals, to fertilise the earth, to traverse the ocean, and to measure the heavens." Admittedly, the course of improvement had been "irregular and various," with "vicissitudes of light and darkness" and moments of rapid downfall after ages of laborious ascent. Yet, overall, the "experience of four thousand years should enlarge our hopes, and diminish our apprehensions." Fear might be cast off because men could never lose

16. Anon., "Preface, by the Translator," in J. J. Rousseau, *Emilius and Sophia: Or, a New System of Education*, 4 vols. (London, 1763), 1:vii–viii.

the useful and necessary arts, so that "no people, unless the face of nature is changed, will relapse into their original barbarism." Hopes might continue to be held since mankind could "acquiesce in the pleasing conclusion that every age of the world has increased, and still increases, the real wealth, the happiness, the knowledge, and perhaps the virtue, of the human race." Consequently, when Gibbon asserted that "we cannot determine to what height the human species may aspire in their advances towards perfection," he meant not only that man was ignorant of the future but also that progress had no foreseeable limits. And its indefinite nature depended not a little on the historical fact of its acceleration: "infinitely slow in the beginning, and increasing by degrees with redoubled velocity."[17]

That such a man as Gibbon, caught up in the glories of antiquity and devoted to the study of historical decline, should take this position suggests how powerful the idea of progress had become by the 1780s. Moreover, for Gibbon and the translator of *Émile* the general progress of the past was an assumed fact, not an arguable theory. The same was true of others who had a more positive view of traditional Christianity than they. Thomas Astle, for instance, reflected unquestioningly and with pleasure in 1784 on the "improvements which have been made in most branches of science in the last three centuries." These had "humanized the mind" and decreased prejudices, and through the diffusion of knowledge among the people "many individuals are qualified to promote, in their respective stations, the arts, as well as the interests, of each community." On the basis of this general achievement, and with a fond desire for the increasing observation of the golden rule of behavior "laid down by our great Master," Astle found it reasonable to "indulge a hope, that every succeeding age will increase the knowledge, the virtue, and the happiness of mankind."[18]

Apart from the religious reference, this last statement bears a striking resemblance to Gibbon's remarks. In a different way, so does

17. Edward Gibbon, *The History of the Decline and Fall of the Roman Empire*, ed. J. B. Bury, 9th ed., 7 vols. (London, 1925), 4:176–81. It should be noted that Gibbon had not always believed in general progress. In his youthful *Essai sur l'étude de la littérature* (1761), he argued that erudition and belles lettres (for him, the knowledge of ancient literature) had been declining since the later seventeenth century: *The Miscellaneous Works of Edward Gibbon, Esq.*, ed. John, Lord Sheffield, 2d ed., 5 vols. (London, 1814), 4:19.

18. Thomas Astle, *The Origin and Progress of Writing* (1st ed., 1784; London, 1876), xxi.

a sermon preached before the annual meeting of the s.p.g. in 1773 by Jonathan Shipley (1714–88), bishop of St. Asaph, member of Lord Shelburne's circle, and William Shipley's brother. Shipley, too, well knew "what rapid improvements, what important discoveries" had relatively recently been made in knowledge "by a few countries, with our own at their head." Looking to the future, he suggested, much like Gibbon, that the center of civilization might possibly shift from Europe to America. There the descendants of the present colonists, possessed of the stock of learning accumulated by the old world and influenced by the "common progress of the human mind, should very considerably enlarge the boundaries of science." Partly as a result of the "gracious dispensation of Providence," the inhabitants of America appeared to Shipley already to show evidence of "strong tendencies towards a general improvement." He found it "difficult even to imagine to what heighth [*sic*] of improvement their discoveries may extend," and he believed that "they may make as considerable advances in the arts of civil government and the conduct of life" as in knowledge itself. What he called "the progressive improvement of human affairs" seemed to him to extend indefinitely into the ages to come.[19]

Whatever the nature of their religious orientation, each of these proponents of the idea of progress in its general form assumed improvement to be a fact for the past and expected it to continue indefinitely in the future. Presupposing the existence of historical progress, they felt no compulsion to examine its circumstances in detail. But five other men—William Worthington, Edmund Law, John Gordon, Richard Price, and Joseph Priestley—did feel the need to argue the case for past advance at length. And in the process they set forth the most comprehensive, extensive, and illuminating expression of the idea in eighteenth-century England.

Although they came from two different generations, the five had much in common. All of them were clergymen by profession. Worthington (1703–78) began his career in 1729 as a vicar in Shropshire before returning across the border to his native Wales, where from 1745 he simultaneously held the sinecure rectorate of Darowen in Montgomeryshire and the vicarage of Llanrhaiadr in Denbighshire. Born in Lancashire the same year as Worthington, Law spent most of

19. Jonathan [Shipley], *A Sermon Preached before the Incorporated Society for the Propagation of the Gospel in Foreign Parts; . . . February 19, 1773* (London, 1773), x–xi, xviii, xiii, xxii.

his long life in Cumberland. There he held the living of Greystoke from 1737 to 1743, when he became archdeacon of the diocese of Carlisle and rector of Great Salkeld, and for nineteen years before his death in 1787 he was bishop of Carlisle. A well-preferred pluralist, Gordon (1725–93) was rector of Henstead in Suffolk after 1758 and held several cathedral offices at Lincoln from the mid-1760s. As Dissenters, Price (1723–91) and Priestley (1733–1804) had neither such regular nor such lucrative ecclesiastical employment. The former served as minister at a number of Presbyterian churches in and around London, where he had grown up and been educated after moving from Wales. The latter, of a Yorkshire family, tended congregations at Needham Market in Suffolk (1755–58), at Nantwich in Cheshire (1758–61), at Leeds (1767–72), and finally at the New Meeting House in Birmingham (1780–91). Price and Priestley were on the radical fringe of eighteenth-century Christianity. But their Unitarianism (Price's being of the Arian variety) would not have been incomprehensible to Law, who was himself an extreme Latitudinarian. Worthington and Gordon, on the other hand, were much more conservative in their theology.

Philosophically, all except Price adhered closely to Lockean sensationalism. Price argued that some simple ideas (especially those of right and wrong) were immediately intuited by the understanding. Politically, each subscribed to some variety of Whiggism, ranging from Gordon's preference for the status quo to Priestley's and, especially, Price's ardent quest for reform. Whatever they conceived its true nature to be, Christianity provided a focus for their philosophical and political opinions, and indeed for their whole outlook. Priestley spoke for all of them when he made it clear to his readers that theology was his "original and proper province," for which he had a "justifiable predilection" because of the "superior dignity and importance of theological studies to any other whatever."[20] Yet in spite of—and sometimes because of—the primarily religious orientation of their lives, they also pursued a wide array of more secular activities. Gordon published sermons and devoted himself to his duties at Lincoln Cathedral, but in addition he wrote on the classics and education, engaged in local political frays, and undertook antiquarian research.

20. Joseph Priestley, *Experiments and Observations on Different Kinds of Air* (1774–86), 2d ed., 3 vols. (Birmingham, 1790), vol. 1, "Preface," in *The Theological and Miscellaneous Works of Joseph Priestley*, ed. John Towill Rutt, 25 vols. in 26 ([London, 1817–32]), 25:379.

Worthington was interested in education, and Law spent a dozen years as Master of Peterhouse and four as Knightbridge Professor of Moral Philosophy at Cambridge. Along with working for political reform during and after his intimate association with the Shelburne circle, Price devoted much time to writing on demographic and financial subjects. He achieved respect, as well as membership in the Royal Society, for his work in mathematics and political arithmetic. The others, too, had scientific concerns. Worthington wrote about geology, Gordon was an amateur archaeologist and botanist, and Law contributed to the popularization of the associationist psychology. Priestley, of course, undertook pioneering chemical research and, as a member of the Lunar Society in the 1780s, helped to harness science to technology during the early years of the Industrial Revolution. But he accomplished much in other fields as well. Historian, linguist, teacher (at the famous Dissenting academy in Warrington), confidant to Shelburne, writer on a myriad of subjects: he was the true universal man of eighteenth-century England.

Beyond their interest in science and secular affairs and their dominant religious preoccupation, the five were also bound by a complex chain of familiarity and intellectual ties. Price and Priestley had a close friendship that continued after the latter left Shelburne's coterie in 1780, and they shared many opinions even though disagreeing sharply about the immateriality of the soul and the freedom of the will. Priestley and Gordon praised Law's writings, and he approvingly cited theirs as well as Worthington's. In return, Worthington referred in print to Law.[21] To be sure, these sometimes purely literary connections neither establish a definite line of influence nor signify the existence of an intellectual "school." It is doubtful, in fact, whether

---

21. For references to each other, see William Worthington, *An Essay on the Scheme and Conduct, Procedure and Extent of Man's Redemption. Wherein is shewn, from the Holy Scriptures, that this great Work is to be accomplished by a gradual Restoration of Man and Nature to their primitive State* (1743), 2d ed. (London, 1748), 82n, 87n, 107n, 122n, 124n; Edmund Law, *Considerations on the Theory of Religion,* ed. George Henry Law, new ed. (London, 1820), 228n–229n, 232n, 252n, 254n–255n, 261n–263n, 268n, 279n, 294n, 297n (all citations are to this edition unless otherwise noted); [John Gordon], *A New Estimate of Manners and Principles: Being a Comparison between Ancient and Modern Times, In the three Great Articles of Knowledge, Happiness, and Virtue; Both with Respect To Mankind at Large and to This Kingdom in Particular,* 2 vols. (Cambridge, 1760–61), 1:vi, vin ("An Explanation of the Design of this Estimate"); Joseph Priestley, *Lectures on History and General Policy* (1788), American ed. (Philadelphia, 1803), Lecture LXVII, in *Works,* 25:428–29. Each of these citations has some bearing on the idea of progress.

any one of the five had a personal acquaintance with all of the others. Nevertheless, they certainly were mutually aware of each other, either directly or at secondhand. And this awareness centered upon an intersection of interests among them, in the common ground of the idea of progress. Occasionally drawing upon the work of one another, they formed a family of firm believers in the past and future progress of human culture on virtually all fronts.

Their views on the history and prospects of Britain illustrate this belief in broad improvement. Antedating by seven years Turgot's two famous Sorbonne *discours* on progress delivered in 1750, Worthington's *Essay on the Scheme and Conduct, Procedure and Extent of Man's Redemption* was probably the first piece of published writing in Britain to enunciate fully a doctrine of general progress. In this book of 1743 (reprinted with slight emendations in 1748), Worthington argued that his country had been advancing for centuries. "What vast Improvements," he declared, "must have been made in this country, since the time it was first conquer'd and civilized by the *Romans*, to bring it to its present state." Contemporary Britain abounded with "all the necessaries, conveniences, and superfluities of Life," flowed with wealth, and was "furnish'd with the most valuable commodities of all the known parts of the world, and polish'd with every Art that improves, or adorns Life!" The course of time had also brought governmental and social benefits as well as these material ones. The "Constitution was not brought to its present degree of perfection all at once," but rather through the "work of ages." Finally "established on its present happy Basis," it provided harmony to the whole nation, welfare to every individual, and security to the peasant as much as the prince. "And," Worthington wished, "may it long continue still advancing in perfection!" Writing two years later in his *Considerations on the Theory of Religion* (which went through seven continually revised and expanded editions between 1745 and 1784, several of which contained expanded annotations), Law echoed these observations on the constitution. He noted that Britons currently enjoyed "the blessing of *liberty* in that perfection which has been unknown to former ages," and which "includes every thing valuable in life, and has the greatest tendency to accelerate the progress" of the nation.[22]

Although he did not specifically mention Brown, Price was clearly

22. Worthington, *Essay*, 145, 153–54; Law, *Considerations*, 297–98.

Edmund Law

replying to the *Estimate* when in the great year 1759 he delivered a thanksgiving sermon entitled *Britain's Happiness*. Beginning with the "additions . . . made to our glory" by recent military triumphs, he adduced a long list of reasons why he and his countrymen ought to be thankful that "we now appear among the nations great, rich, prosperous and formidable." He believed that the national wealth "increases continually," and that the operation of British liberty had produced a more extensive enjoyment of personal security than ever before, the "greatest improvements . . . in all the sciences," and the elimination from Christianity of "a great deal of that shocking rubbish . . . thrown upon it by Popery." Certainly, Price admitted, the constitution had its flaws, and vice and irreligion did continue to exist. On the basis of their current "peculiar happiness," however, Britons should do their "utmost to push things to that point of perfection, which we have brought so nearly within our reach." In calling upon his fellow citizens to aim higher, Price differed from Brown only in assessing the present condition of the country more optimistically. For him, the future progress of Britain meant *further* advance, because so much had already occurred. The same was true of Gordon, who sought to refute the author of the *Estimate* by publishing a *New Estimate of Manners and Principles* in 1760 and 1761. His book built a case favoring modern over ancient times—with respect both to his own country and to mankind in general—in knowledge, happiness, and virtue. And it proclaimed that the progressive change in national manners and principles for which Brown wished "has in fact already happened."[23]

Priestley, too, saw wide-ranging advancement in his own nation. He promised the students taking his course in English history at Warrington "great pleasure . . . in tracing the security, the commerce, the power, and all the great advantages of our country, from their first rude beginnings . . . to the present age," which he characterized as an "advanced and highly improved state of society." How little could the Greeks and Romans have imagined that Britain would stand so high and even "go so infinitely beyond whatever they had attained to in respect to science, commerce, riches, power, and, I may add, happiness." The British had "particularly distinguished them-

23. Richard Price, *Britain's Happiness, and the proper Improvement of it, represented in a Sermon, Preach'd at Newington-Green, Middlesex, On Nov. 29. 1759* (London, 1759), 12, 6–7, 9–10, 17–18; Gordon, *New Estimate,* 1:ix ("An Apology to the Author of a former Estimate").

selves by their improvements in natural knowledge." Their constitution, which (until the 1790s) Priestley thought the best ever devised,
he hoped to see improved still further.[24]

Beyond Britain, he and the others agreed, there also had been and
would continue to be progress in the world as a whole. Law, for
instance, wrote of the "continual Improvement of the World in general," a phrase expressing his contention that "As the present world has
generally improved hitherto, we may expect that it shall continue to
do so." Likewise, Gordon thought that there had been "a continual
Tendency to the better in all human affairs." This meant that the
"world is, and has been from the earliest notice we have of it, in a
state of general improvement," with regard to everything that "can
be thought to raise or dignify our nature; and . . . consequently, it is
now in all respects of that sort, better than it ever was before." Yet,
Gordon suggested, if contemporaries had a right to self-congratulation
"on the high degree of perfection, to which the world has been advanced in our days," they might also "envy those, whom with our
fortunes and our honors we shall leave to be heirs also of greater
happiness." The entire process that he depicted was referred to by
Price in the 1780s as "the progressive course of human improvement." The world, he believed, "has hitherto been gradually improving," and such "are the natures of things that this progress must
continue," in spite of intervals that might interrupt but could not
destroy it. According to Worthington, history demonstrated that
"one generation has refined upon another, and every age has generally
added something to the foregoing," so as to render life more and more
"comfortable, easy, and happy." With the continuation of this advance, "Mankind, before the end of the world, shall recover from all
the ill consequences of the Fall, and be restored to their original
Perfection." Priestley had a similar outlook. The "state of the world
at present," he told his students in the 1760s and repeated in print in
1788, "and particularly the state of Europe, is vastly preferable to

24. Joseph Priestley, "Account of a Course of Lectures on the History of England,
and a Plan of the Course" (1765), in *Works*, 24:443; idem, "Account of a Course of
Lectures on the Constitution and Laws of England, and a Syllabus of the Course"
(1765), in *Works*, 24:446; idem, *Lectures on History*, Lectures XXXVII and I, in *Works*,
25:219, 33–34n; idem, *The History of the Present State of Discoveries relating to
Vision, Light, and Colours*, 2 vols. (London, 1772), vol. 1, "Dedication," in *Works*,
25:361; idem, *An Essay on the First Principles of Government; and on the Nature of
Political, Civil, and Religious Liberty* (1768), 2d ed., corr. and enl. (London, 1771), in
Works, 22:118.

what it was in any former period." Indeed, all things "valuable in society"—and especially whatever depended upon science—"have of late years been in a quicker progress towards perfection than ever," and there was the "greatest certainty" that posterity "will be *wiser*, and therefore the fairest presumption that they will be *better* than we are." "Thus," he concluded in a famous phrase, "whatever was the beginning of this world, the end will be glorious and *paradisiacal*, beyond what our imaginations can now conceive."[25]

Such statements should not suggest that these Englishmen were incurable optimists, looking at the world through a rosy haze and oblivious to potential obstacles or actual problems. On the contrary, they had what Priestley called "a deep conviction of the instability of all things" and were aware of the "misfortunes and hardships to which the most distinguished personages [in history] have been reduced." They thought that progress often took place hesitantly; that its path, in Worthington's words, "is steep and arduous, and Man ascends it with difficulty"; and that it often occurred intermittently in time and space, visiting various parts of the globe much like the ebb and flow of the tides. On rare occasions they even expressed fears that the great things they expected of the future might prove transient. "There is a danger that a state of society so happy will not be of long duration," wrote Price, and he referred darkly to what he thought had previously been the "progress of evil in human affairs." At least twice in his writings, Priestley described history as a cycle. "The progress of human life," he stated in terms reminiscent of Brown, "in general is from poverty to riches, and from riches to luxury and ruin."[26]

And yet, normally, they all believed with Worthington that in spite of its problems, the present age was "a *golden* one" when com-

25. Law, *Considerations*, sig. Q^r [225], 266; Gordon, *New Estimate*, 1:ii ("Explanation"), sig. D^r [49], 6, and 2:125; Richard Price, *The Evidence for a Future Period of Improvement in the State of Mankind, with the Means of Promoting It, Represented in a Discourse, delivered on . . . the 25th of April, 1787* (London, 1787), 20; idem, *Observations on the Importance of the American Revolution, and The Means of making it a Benefit to the World* (London, 1785), 3; Worthington, *Essay*, 143, 48; Priestley, *Lectures on History*, Lectures LXVI and XXXVIII, in *Works*, 24:425, 225; idem, *Essay on Government*, in *Works*, 22:122, 119, 9.

26. Priestley, *Lectures on History*, Lecture III, in *Works*, 24:49; idem, *A Course of Lectures on the Theory of Language, and Universal Grammar* (1762), Lecture XII, in *Works*, 23:193; Worthington, *Essay*, 127, 145–46; Price, *Observations*, 70. For a "tidal theory" of progress akin to that of Thomas Babington Macaulay (described below, chap. 9), see Gordon, *New Estimate*, 1:34, 41–43.

pared to former times. Furthermore, they not only expected advances in the future but saw improvement emerging out of the very evil of the past. Noting the opinion of men like Pierre Bayle and Voltaire that "history contains nothing but a view of the vices and the misery of mankind," Priestley commented that to him and many others this subject appeared "in a very different light." He argued, for example, that "wars, revolutions of empire, and the necessary consequences of them, have been, upon the whole, extremely favourable to the progress of knowledge, virtue, and happiness." These seeming catastrophes had brought with them the invention of many of the most useful arts of civil life and had done remarkable service to the cause of learning. Even so monstrous a crime as the notorious death of Jean Calas served to promote the "abhorrence of bigotry." Consequently, "those things with which the happiness of mankind, either in a private or social capacity, are most closely connected . . . have been chiefly promoted by events which, at first sight, appeared the most disastrous." With this historical vision in mind, Priestley went on to tell his students and readers that they ought to consider "what a foundation for future and general happiness" temporary evils like war might be laying.[27]

When these five men spoke of the progress of the world, they meant progress in all areas affecting human life. One such area was the physical environment, which appeared to them to be slowly improving. Priestley thought that the European climate had become more moderate over the ages, and Law agreed, adding that the "*natural advantages* of life"—the constitution of mankind and the earth— "have been at all times in themselves pretty equal, and rather improving, as they receive assistance, which they do very greatly, from the *acquired* ones." According to Worthington, the improvement of nature since the Flood was attested to by increases in the fertility of the soil, the health and longevity of the people, and the size of the human and animal population, as well as by the moderation of the

27. Worthington, *Essay*, 152; Priestley, *Lectures on History*, Lectures LXVII and LXVIII, in *Works*, 24:429–31, 433, 436; idem, *A Description of a New Chart of History, containing a View of the Principal Revolutions of Empire that have taken place in the World* (1769), 15th ed. (1816), in *Works*, 24:483. On bringing good out of evil, see also Gordon, *New Estimate*, 1:xviii ("Explanation"), 42–43. This notion is similar to Worthington's concept of the "Fortunate Fall": *Essay*, 51, 53; idem, *The Scripture-Theory of the Earth, throughout all its Revolutions, and all the Periods of its Existence, from the Creation, to the Final Renovation of all Things* (London, 1773), 422–27, 469–70.

earth's climate and topography. In short, he found all aspects of nature to be "in an improving and ameliorating state," and in proportion to the "progress, which, age after age, is made in improvements of this kind . . . the curse of the ground is removed and overcome."[28]

These opinions represent a partial modification of the prevailing eighteenth-century uniformitarian perspective on nature and human nature. Priestley and the others did in general "equally believe in *the uniformity of the laws of nature*, and that *man*, whose constitution is a part of the system of nature, was the same kind of being two thousand years ago that he is now." But this did not prevent them from conceiving of change itself, in its beneficial form, as one of the constant features of the operation of the world. As Worthington declared, "all parts of Nature are endued with a principle not only to preserve their state, but to advance it, and . . . every thing has a tendency to its own perfection. This is a general law impress'd upon Nature." Given this developmental theory, it is not surprising to find Worthington, more than half a century before Lamarck, adopting the transformist point of view in biology. Noting the observation of naturalists that carnivores possessed stomachs formed for animal food, he commented that "this might not have been any original constitution of nature, but at first contracted by habit, and derived down through their successive generations; and therefore may be worn off again by degrees" as nature continued to progress. Along similar lines, Gordon speculated that the earth might have provided a "place of abode for other animals, before it was fitted up for our reception," and that "some species of beings, even of mankind, may become extinct." He based the latter suggestion on the evidence that extinctions had in fact already occurred or were in process, in the cases of the giants mentioned in the Bible and pagan mythology and of certain wild beasts "scarce existing now, but in pictures and relations."[29]

If nature as a whole was progressive, so was learning or knowledge. Indeed, Worthington linked the two together, writing that "both seem to keep peace [sic] with each other, in their respective improvements." By knowledge he meant not mere erudition but

28. Priestley, *Lectures on History*, Lecture LXV, in *Works*, 24:416; Law, *Considerations*, 228nn, 231–33, 231n–33n; Worthington, *Scripture-Theory*, 404–15, 499, 426.

29. Priestley, *Experiments and Observations on Air*, "Preface," in *Works*, 25:382; Worthington, *Essay*, 190–91, 334; Gordon, *New Estimate*, 1:41n, 110n. For other statements of uniformitarianism, see Law, *Considerations*, 231; Gordon, *New Estimate*, 1:54, 102.

"natural and experimental Philosophy, Astronomy, and mathematical Learning," as well as "all other parts of useful Learning" (including theology). In these fields, he thought, such discoveries and improvements had been made as to "render the present age enlighten'd beyond the hopes and imaginations of former times." With these opinions all of the others wholeheartedly agreed. Gordon, for example, devoted one of the three sections of his book to proving the thesis that there had been "almost a continual improvement in human knowledge" over the centuries, and that "we ourselves, whatever high attainments we may boast, shall be far outdone by those, who come after." If the advance had only been "almost" continual, the reason lay partly in what he thought was the tendency of all disciplines to go through a middle period of development characterized by excessive rationalism and concern with ornament; and partly in what he and the others considered the "cloud of darkness . . . so fatal to letters" during the Middle Ages, which had made for "a most dreadful void" in learning. Since the Renaissance and Reformation, however, knowledge had revived and its improvement had accelerated. Progress seemed particularly conspicuous in natural philosophy during the relatively recent past, as Price pointed out. Priestley attempted to document this view in his histories of science, where he referred to the "astonishing improvements that have been made . . . in all the branches of real knowledge, in little more than two centuries." By means of projection, he formed a "most glorious" vision of the future, when the "progress of real knowledge may be expected to go on, not merely in an uniform manner, but to be constantly accelerated."[30]

Beyond knowledge alone, the arts and sciences as a whole—including both learning and useful or ornamental activities—also appeared to be advancing. Law wrote of "their continual *progress*," contending that "they always are, and have been, in the main, *progressive*," because improvements in the various sciences "derive some perfection on each sister art." Gordon made precisely the same claims, and he pointed to the importance of the institutional encour-

30. Worthington, *Scripture-Theory*, 422, 169–74, 263–64, iv; Gordon, *New Estimate*, 1:115, 73; idem, *Occasional Thoughts on the Study and Character of Classical Authors, on the Course of Literature, and the present Plan of a Learned Education* (London, 1762), 31–51; Price, *Evidence*, 14–16, 20; Priestley, *Discoveries relating to Vision*, "Preface," in *Works*, 25:367n; idem, *The History and Present State of Electricity, with Original Experiments* (1767; 3d ed., 1775), ed. Robert E. Schofield, 2 vols. (New York, 1966), 1:vi. See also Law, *Considerations*, 263, 263n, 268.

agement of progress in this area by praising the London Society of Arts and dedicating a portion of one of his books to that six-year-old organization. Priestley, too, believed that the sciences contributed to the advancement of the useful and "finer" arts, noting with regard to the latter that their great practitioners had tended to be alive in epochs abounding with eminent philosophers. As was customary in the eighteenth century, he identified the "remarkable periods in the history of the *arts and sciences*" as Greece at about the time of Alexander, Rome from the end of the Commonwealth to just after Augustus, the Italian Renaissance, and the seventeenth century in France and England. Of the present he said only that the "generous emulation by which we are actuated can only produce good effects." Looking ahead, he anticipated that "mankind, some centuries hence, will be as much superior to us in knowledge and improvements in the [useful] arts of life, as we are now to the Hottentots, though we cannot have any conception [of] what that knowledge or what those improvements will be."[31]

As for the future of the fine arts, Priestley was not quite so sanguine. He twice commented that they, unlike the sciences, had generally followed a cyclical course, declining into a taste for "superfluous decoration" after having attained a state of "real propriety and magnificence." In any case, such arts as "music, painting, and poetry, have perceivable limits, beyond which it is almost impossible to advance." This situation he attributed (as did others) to the inhibiting effects of past achievements, the general esteem for which constricted opportunities for emulation. And yet, he thought, the expansion of the range of human endeavor offered a partial remedy. "So wide a field is now open to the genius of man, that let some excel ever so much in one province, there will still be room for others to shine in others." In addition, because very few people could become completely acquainted with each of the growing number of great works of any one art, the triumphs of the past would not prove an insuperable obstacle to every artist. Consequently, to Priestley further progress in the fine arts seemed at least possible, even if not certain as in the case of science. Likewise, Gordon contended that in their middle period of development the fine arts, under the excessive influence of the imag-

31. Law, *Considerations*, 233, 250, 254; Gordon, *New Estimate*, 1:50–51, 53, [47]; idem, *Occasional Thoughts*, 37–38; Priestley, *Lectures on History*, Lectures L and XXXVI, in *Works*, 24:311, 214–17; idem, *Experiments and Observations on Air*, "Preface," in *Works*, 25:378.

ination, became subject to "false ornament and frippery refinement." But reason could lead them out of this "fairy land" and "back to the true source and test of art, that propriety, which is founded in nature."[32]

Priestley felt he could not conclude his remarks on the arts and sciences without calling the attention of his students to the great practical advantages derived from improvements in these areas. He was particularly concerned to point out how far humankind had advanced in such things as food, housing, and machinery, all of which he grouped under the heading of "conveniences" bringing more "comfort" to life. These and similar terms were employed by the others to emphasize what they saw as the progressive easing of living conditions. Beneficial changes in the useful arts, Law asserted, necessarily brought "a proportionable improvement of other natural advantages; such as health, strength, plenty, urbanity." These in turn enabled human beings to reap the benefits of nature "in ways more easy and compendious, with less time, labour, and expense," so that "every thing in life becomes more comfortable." Worthington placed special emphasis on improvements over the ages in agriculture and its implements, which had "undoubtedly render'd the toil and work of Men's hands, less and less burthensome to them." In recent times, he thought, discoveries in natural philosophy had helped to multiply the fruits of the earth. Meanwhile the "happy investigation of the *laws of motion*, and a dextrous application of the *mechanical powers*" had produced a situation in which "one Man can now perform with ease, what hath otherwise surmounted the united force of many." As a result, "a great part of the labour of life, hath been thrown back upon inanimate matter," and nature, being "brought in to this assistance of Man," had come to be commanded "in a great measure to do her own work."[33]

The implied correlation in these comments between increasing convenience and the progress of human power was made explicit by Price. He proclaimed that by means of relatively recent inventions

32. Priestley, *Lectures on Language*, Lecture XII, in *Works*, 23:193; idem, *Lectures on History*, Lecture XLIX, in *Works*, 24:312–13; Gordon, *Occasional Thoughts*, 21–22, 30.

33. Priestley, *Lectures on History*, Lecture XLIX, in *Works*, 24:313–14; Law, *Considerations*, 250; Worthington, *Essay*, 74–75, 143, 335. For other remarks by Priestley on the link between progress in the arts and sciences and the progress of knowledge, see *History of Electricity*, 1:xxi; *Discoveries relating to Vision*, "Dedication," in *Works*, 25:361.

(such as optical instruments, printing, and gunpowder) and discoveries (in navigation, mathematics, and natural philosophy), man had gained "new dignity" and great additions had been made to his powers. To this fairly traditional formulation he added a note that illuminates the impact of the visibility of scientific and technological advance on the eighteenth-century mind. Who, he asked,

> even at the beginning of this century, would have thought, that, in a few years, mankind would acquire the power of subjecting to their wills the dreadful force of lightning, and of flying in aerostatic machines? . . . Many similar discoveries may remain to be made, which will give new directions of the greatest consequence to human affairs; and it may not be too extravagant to expect that (should civil governments throw no obstacles in the way) the progress of improvement will not cease till it has excluded from the earth most of its worst evils, and restored that Paradisaical [*sic*] state which, according to the Mosaic History, preceded the present state.

Balloon flight and the harnessing of electricity: these contemporary symbols of enlarged human power seemed to Price almost the keys to a paradise of comfort. The same was true for Priestley, who even more than his friend knew the situation of English science from the inside. Writing about advances in chemistry, he argued that science provided the sole foundation for the useful arts, "which distinguish *civilized* nations from those which we term barbarous." For it was only by augmenting the knowledge of nature that "we acquire the great art of commanding it, of availing ourselves of its powers, and applying them to our own purposes." And because civilized human beings were finally comprehending the Baconian motto that knowledge is power, "human powers will, in fact, be enlarged; nature, including both its materials and its laws, will be more at our command; men will make their situation in this world abundantly more easy and comfortable"—even "*paradisiacal.*"[34]

Running parallel to and stimulating this continuing increase in the ease and convenience of life, thought Priestley and the others, was the progress of society itself. When they looked back on the past,

---

34. Price, *Observations*, 5, 5n; Priestley, *Experiments and Observations on Air*, "Dedication," in *Works*, 25:368; idem, *Essay on Government*, in *Works*, 22:9. See also Price, *Evidence*, 12.

they all saw advances in government and an enlargement of its blessings. According to Worthington, the enactment of better laws and the recognition and remedying of constitutional defects had produced improvements "from time to time . . . in civil Government" and "refinements . . . one age after another . . . in the art of Politicks." These changes meant greater security for the lives, liberty, and property of men, "so that now *every Man sits under his own vine and figtree,* and all orders and degrees of Men enjoy their rights and privileges in greater safety than was formerly known." Law and Gordon found convincing evidence of this more complete enjoyment of personal security in the modern European nations, when compared to those of antiquity.[35]

Likewise, Priestley held that the "science of civil government," although still in its infancy, was "gradually improving," so that it was now "certainly much more perfect" than it had been among the ancients. And he contended that it must continue to improve: if the best-formed state in the world were to be fixed in its present condition, it would at length undoubtedly become the worst. In the later editions of his *Considerations,* Law cited this observation with approval. As a political radical, Price quite naturally asserted that many improvements remained to be made "in the state of civil government." But he also believed, writing between 1785 and 1787, that the "liberality of the times" had already inaugurated such progress. The foundation in America of a new state based on liberty, the tendency in some Continental nations (especially France) toward a more equal system of political representation, and the European-wide "alleviation of the horrors of war" led him to expect a shaking of the remaining bastions of tyranny and the coming of universal peace. Though in practical politics his position lay far to the right of that of Price, Gordon also had high hopes for the future of civil government, which he thought would become "more and more perfect and complete." He found it plausible that "the wiser men grow, the better governments they will have," and he looked forward to a time when statesmen "would be better enabled to frame their different systems in such a manner, as should most effectually answer the end of all government, the general happiness of those who live under it." Ultimately, he asked, since the "progress of government" could be traced in its ex-

35. Worthington, *Essay,* 146–47, 152; Law, *Considerations,* 252, 252n; Gordon, *New Estimate,* 2:82–85, 56, 60–67.

tension from a single family to a city to a kingdom, "who can say, that it may not end at last in a much more comprehensive form?" Under a universal monarchy or federative community of states, the sentiments of nationalism would end and those of international brotherhood begin.[36]

To Gordon, these actual and potential changes in government constituted only part of the progress of society. Social advance, in his view, included the entire range of cooperative human activity, whose "natural progress . . . might perhaps be justly exhibited to our view by a scale, marked at proper intervals, with the following gradations— Necessity—Convenience—Ornament—Elegance—Propriety." Currently, his own culture was "somewhere upon the borders of the last division" of this sequence, having in many respects "made large advances of late towards some degree of *Propriety*." In formulating this analysis of the history of society, Gordon insisted that primitivist adoration of the state of nature (which he wrongly attributed to Rousseau), or even of the beginning of society, was ill-founded. For he believed that the state of nature did not provide adequately for subsistence and that human life required at least some "dignity and ornament," beyond considerations of mere "necessity or use alone," if it were to become truly happy. Such an antiprimitivist perspective led him to assert the superiority of "civilized Europeans" to noble savages, even with regard to courage and physical strength. Because he was, in part, replying to Brown's *Estimate*, it is not surprising to find him also singing the praises of commercial life. Should commerce become more extensive, he contended, it would "tend to better our condition; to improve our accommodations; and to raise the dignity and value of human life."[37]

36. Priestley, *Essay on Government*, in *Works*, 22:119, 121; Law, *Considerations*, 294n; Price, *Evidence*, 29–33, 24–25; idem, *Observations*, 1–2, 15, 20–21; idem, *Four Dissertations* (1767), 3d ed. (London, 1772), 138n; Gordon, *New Estimate*, 1:xiii ("Explanation"), and 2:56, 3, 86–87. Gordon was the only one of the five to discuss the Machiavellian question of the natural mortality of the state. Using the traditional analogy of the state to a ship, he conceded that, being built of perishable materials, it was "liable in time to decay." Therefore, it would require frequent repairs and sometimes almost complete rebuilding, "with only a few of the original principles preserved." When factions arose on board or dangerous waters and sudden tempests threatened, the only thing that could be safely concluded "is, that the more skil[l]fully this vessel is constructed, and the better the mariners on board, the greater the chance she has, as the phrase is, to weather it out." See *New Estimate*, 2:53–54, 54n–55n.

37. Gordon, *New Estimate*, 2:45, 53, 53n, 19–21, 19n–21n, 39, 42, 57–58, 109n, 4.

Priestley held a similar but more sophisticated conception of the history of society. He had read some of the writings of his Scottish contemporaries (especially Lord Kames, Adam Smith, and John Millar), and like a number of them he arranged the main outlines of social history on the basis of the development of economic organization: at first only a hunter, social man became a practitioner successively of pastoral life, agriculture, and commerce. This transition appeared to Priestley to bring human beings continually closer together in society, thereby increasing their interdependence and necessitating an ever-greater elaboration of the system of governance and justice. He approvingly characterized the entire process as "the *progress of refinement*," a gradual and interconnected shift from rudeness to improvement, barbarism to civilization, danger to security, and simplicity to complexity. After government and law, he assigned pride of place among the important elements in the refining of society to agriculture, "the only stable foundation of most of the improvements in social life." The encouragement of agriculture, however, depended upon its becoming "subservient to commerce," in order to produce the opportunity for the exchange of food for other commodities. And commerce offered still other advantages, in Priestley's view. It encouraged a cosmopolitan outlook and, therefore, peace; inculcated the principles of "strict justice and honour"; and, most important, excited industry and increased labor, "by the fruits of which a nation may procure themselves the conveniences they want; and thus human life be rendered much happier."[38]

These were the essential principles of Priestley's historical sociology. He thought that society was a "complex machine," and that people would "in time understand it better than those who now write about it." And yet, even if they recognized how little they knew about the nature of the social world, he and the others felt certain that society had moved over time in the right direction. "It has introduced some evils into life, which otherwise would have had no existence," wrote Gordon, "but then it has also been the happy means of many great advantages and comforts, of which without it we had been

38. Priestley, *Lectures on History*, Lectures XXXIX, IX, XLVII, XLIV, IV, XLIX, LI, in *Works*, 24:228–29, 83, 285–86, 271, 54, 300, 316–17. On the benefits of commerce, see also Gordon, *New Estimate*, 1:58; Worthington, *Essay*, 146, 169; Law, *Considerations*, 273n–274n.

Joseph Priestley

entirely destitute. And even for those ills, which necessarily attend it, it has provided, in most cases, correspondent remedies." Scoffing at claims of the past existence of a golden age, they rejected primitivism.[39]

But more than this, as their common approbation of increasing convenience and human power demonstrates, they had no real regrets about the passing of a simpler way of life. Therefore they could not share in Brown's attack on the new society of commerce and wealth around them. To be sure, in 1785 Price counseled the new American states to remain "bodies of plain and honest farmers" rather than to become "opulent and splendid merchants," corrupted by "Effeminacy, servility and venality." Indeed, he once observed that the "happiest state of man is the middle state between the *savage* and the *refined*, or between the wild and the luxurious." Nevertheless, in 1759 he replied to Brown by praising God for the unequalled "plenty and opulence we enjoy," and he never suggested that his age had fallen victim to injurious luxury. More positively, Gordon thought that commerce and luxury could encourage the progress of the arts, and Priestley launched a full-fledged defense of the villain of the *Estimate*. Since, in his opinion,

> a rich and flourishing state of society is the object of all wise policy, it were absurd to suppose that the proper use of riches was necessarily, and upon the whole, hurtful to the members of it. The more conveniences men are able to procure to themselves, the more they have it in their power to enjoy life, and make themselves and others happy. . . . The gratification of their taste for mere *ornament* in dress, equipage, &c., can do no real harm. Wants of this kind, more than all our other wants, promote industry, and are a most effectual means of circulating wealth. . . .
>
> Besides, in a country where there are more riches, there may generally be expected more improvements of all kinds, and consequently more *knowledge*.

He even believed that the "arts of luxury are, to a certain degree, favourable to liberty," because they enabled men to accumulate prop-

---

39. Priestley, *Lectures on History*, Lecture XLIX, in *Works*, 24:304; Gordon, *New Estimate*, 2:36. For negative comments on the possibility of a golden age, see Gordon, *New Estimate*, 2:119–20; Priestley, *Lectures on History*, Lecture XLIV, in *Works*, 24:269.

erty, which in turn stimulated the enactment of "equal laws to secure that property."[40]

In defending riches and luxury, Priestley found it necessary to argue against the Brownian thesis that they tended to make men effeminate and cowardly. A comparison of the common people of England with those of France, he claimed, proved that the former both lived more luxuriously *and* possessed "more strength of body, and more true courage." He conceded that excessively high living, with an immoderate indulgence of appetites, enfeebled the body and was the source of many other evils. But a life of material ease seemed to him far preferable to its usual alternative, a state of idleness and barbarity. Moreover, among a "people of the greatest wealth and luxury there is never found that treachery and cruelty which characterize almost all uncivilized and barbarous states; but commonly a higher and juster sense of honour, and a greater humanity of temper." It was even possible, he thought, for wealth to combine with virtue and religion, bringing the "greatest honour to human nature, and the greatest blessing to human societies."[41]

The thrust of these arguments is to suggest that the advance of civilization toward its commercial, eighteenth-century form, far from having injured human morality, had actually amended it. And, while recognizing that their world was hardly a paradise of virtue, Priestley and the others did confidently believe in moral progress. Law, for example, not only contended that the present times were "not worse than all before them, as to *morals*," but also supposed that they were "better in some respects, and that we have certain virtues of the first magnitude now in greater perfection." Along the same lines, Worthington and Gordon granted the moderns superiority over the ancients in virtue, and Price saw in his own age the "beginnings of a moral government" that was as yet "by no means carried to that degree of perfection, to which we have reason to expect it will be." The others equally anticipated further strides toward a condition in

40. Price, *Observations*, 77, 69; idem, *Britain's Happiness*, 5; Gordon, *New Estimate*, 1:65; Priestley, *Lectures on History*, Lectures LIV and L, in *Works*, 24:338–39, 310. Priestley noted that commerce "does not perfectly suit the true spirit" of a republic, and that excessive riches were a special danger there: *Lectures on History*, Lecture XLI, in *Works*, 24:239–40. But this opinion does not contradict his more detailed consideration of commerce and luxury in general, which in any case significantly outweighs the remarks on republics.

41. Priestley, *Lectures on History*, Lecture LIV, in *Works*, 24:338–39, 342.

which, as Gordon wrote, men "would comprehend more fully the duties, which they owed both to themselves and others," while becoming "better members of the community, and more friendly neighbours to each other." Part of the responsibility for this continuing moral progress was found in the beneficial effects of Christianity, and part in the ongoing improvement (parallel to the advancement of knowledge) in the understanding of the principles of morality.[42]

Past and future progress, then, was the rule in all major areas of human life. And in consequence of this general progress, happiness itself appeared to be increasing. Gordon set out to prove in his book that the moderns possessed more happiness, along with more knowledge and virtue, than the ancients, and he asserted that "this happiness is growing daily greater" and "will continue for ever to do so." Principally as a result of the continual progress of knowledge, he believed, each successive stage in his scale of the history of society was happier than the last. Taking a more cosmic view, Law envisioned the whole creation as rising along a "temporalized" Great Chain of Being by "a regular progress, in a growing happiness, through all eternity." Worthington saw in history the "gradual accomplishment" of a divine promise to bring about "a most glorious state" on earth, which would "make both rich and poor happy." When he took a comprehensive view of life, Price similarly thought that happiness was "the end, and the only end conceivable by us, of the divine providence and government." In a more restricted way, he also found that contemporary Britain had come to enjoy a "peculiar happiness," and he suggested with obvious pleasure that a recognition of the "happy state of the nation, may lead our thoughts to that time when the whole world shall enjoy the like happiness." This tendency to consider in both secular and religious terms the progress of the *bonheur* on which the eighteenth-century French so often focused was also apparent in Priestley. Having discussed the advance of human power and convenience, he noted that the men of the future would "grow daily more happy, each in himself, and more able (and, I believe, more disposed) to communicate happiness to others." The "summit of perfection and happiness," however, could only be at-

42. Law, *Considerations*, 279–82, 279n–82n, 290n; Worthington, *Essay*, 137–43, 326, 197 [misnumbered as 167]; Gordon, *New Estimate*, 2:2n, 4; Richard Price, *A Review of the Principal Questions and Difficulties in Morals* (London, 1758), 449–50, 392–93.

tained when the wills and wishes of human beings coincided with those of God.[43]

Before the achievement of this union of man with deity, true perfection was not to be expected on earth. "Nothing that is human," wrote Priestley, "can ever be absolutely perfect." Still, he felt certain that the "human species itself is capable of . . . unbounded improvement," so that "there is no situation man ever yet arrived at, or probably ever will arrive at, in which he can entirely acquiesce, so as to look out for no farther improvement." Though unable in this world to attain final *perfection*, man was *perfectible*. The plot of his course through time extended upward indefinitely. "We have," claimed Price, "the utmost scope for improvement, an everlasting progress before us, and infinite advances to make." Foreseeing no limits beyond which the advance could not be carried, he assigned to the human race a *"natural improveableness,"* a capacity for *"endless future progress in knowledge and happiness."*[44]

Price and Priestley had read Condorcet's biography of Turgot, which made available to them similar French opinions on perfectibility. But they did not need any assistance from across the Channel to look with pleasure upon the seemingly endless vista of human progressiveness. In any event, the English had already discovered perfectibility before Turgot gave it a vogue in France. Worthington,

43. Gordon, *New Estimate*, 1:xvii ("Explanation"), and 2:1, 4–5, 8–10, 12, 18–19, 53–55; Law, *Considerations*, 266; William King, *An Essay on the Origin of Evil* (1702), ed. and trans. Edmund Law, 4th ed., corr. (Cambridge, 1758), 109n [the notes in this volume were written by Law]; William Worthington, *A Sermon Preached in the Parish-Church of Christ-Church, London, . . . April the 21st, 1768* (London, 1768), 22; Price, *Principal Questions*, 441; idem, *Britain's Happiness*, 13, 16, 18, 22; Priestley, *Essay on Government*, in *Works*, 22:9; idem, *The Doctrine of Philosophical Necessity Illustrated* (London, 1777), "Dedication," in *Works*, 3:451. The question of how to define happiness was, of course, an important one in eighteenth-century thought, and it received a large variety of answers: see R. M. Wiles, "*Felix qui* . . . : Standards of Happiness in Eighteenth-Century England," *Studies on Voltaire and the Eighteenth Century* 58 (1967): 1857–60. In the context of this paragraph, "happiness" means what it meant for John Gay, "the sum total of pleasure": *Preliminary Dissertation Concerning the Fundamental Principle of Virtue or Morality* (1731), in L. A. Selby-Bigge, ed., *British Moralists: Being Selections from Writers Principally of the Eighteenth Century*, 2 vols. (Oxford, 1897), 2:277. Gordon was the only one of the five writers under consideration to define the term explicitly. His definition resembles Gay's and foreshadows Bentham's, emphasizing as it does the notion of a remainder of pleasure after the subtraction of pain: *New Estimate*, 2:104.

44. Priestley, *Lectures on History*, Lectures XLIII [added in American ed.] and LI, in *Works*, 24:256, 316; idem, *Essay on Government*, in *Works*, 22:8; Price, *Principal Questions*, 396; idem, *Evidence*, 12, 51n; idem, *Four Dissertations*, 151n–52n.

for instance, contended in the 1740s that "human nature is in a growing, progressive state, and is to advance to its perfection by a gradual increase." He believed that in the long process of recovery from the Fall the "Way to Perfection" was precipitous and full of hazards, and that human beings had as yet ascended only "a little way up the hill." Yet the history of past improvement made it clear to him how far they "were able to go towards perfection." In the same vein Law argued that regardless of the impediments lying most directly in the route to perfection, "we have encouragement enough left to proceed with cheerfulness and vigour in this same progress," because the state of "perfection in the world, has hitherto been [perpetually] *increasing*." To Gordon, this process of ongoing advancement was the only one that God could have instituted if human beings were to enjoy the greatest possible happiness. So man was "made and designed for continual improvement," endowed with "perfectionability."[45]

In light of this characteristic, mankind seemed to bear a striking resemblance to the individual human being. As Gordon observed, what is true of each man, "that his life will be happier, as he advances in years and grows more rational, is true also of the world at large." He did not consider the analogy to be perfectly exact, however, since mankind "can never feel the inconveniences of old age, but is perpetually renewed in strength and vigor." For Priestley, if the human species were, like the individual, ever to see its development cease, that terminus had to lie at a virtually infinite distance. He claimed that mankind was in any case still far from "any thing like what may be called their *mature* state. . . . And, allowing a period of *manhood*, in proportion to this long infancy . . . , three hundred and sixty thousand years will not be deemed a disproportionate age of the world [at the time of its demise]."[46]

This comment confirms what many of their remarks have already indicated, that all of these Englishmen treated the working out of progress and the perfectibility of man as long, gradual processes. How very slowly had mankind "advanced in political, and all kinds of improvements," wrote Priestley; "how gradual has been the progress

45. Worthington, *Essay*, 257, 127, 197; Law, *Considerations*, 172, 307–08; Gordon, *New Estimate*, 1:xvii ("Explanation"), 110n, and 2:46. The fourth edition of Law's book (London, 1759), 143, includes "perpetually."

46. Gordon, *New Estimate*, 2:124; Joseph Priestley, *Institutes of Natural and Revealed Religion* (1772–74), in *Works*, 2:367. See also Gordon, *Occasional Thoughts*, 36; Worthington, *Essay*, 7; Price, *Observations*, 3; idem, *Evidence*, 12.

of all discoveries in science, and of excellence in the arts." And though gradual, progress had not been uniform or steady. On the contrary, Worthington admitted, when man "has advanced a little way he makes a false step, and is borne down again, and it costs him much pains and labour to regain the ground he had lost." Using a different metaphor, Gordon noted that human affairs have "sometimes gone back a little; but then like those, who would overleap some opposing difficulty, they seem only to have made a voluntary retreat, in order to advance again with the greater spring." The notion of acceleration suggested here was emphasized by Priestley, who contrasted the sluggish advance of early man with the rapid rate of increase in improvement conspicuous during recent times. Price offered an explanation for the change. Although to date progress had been "irregular and various," the path of real improvement, "when it has once begun, is (like the motion of a descending body) an accelerated course. One improvement produces other improvements, and these others." Even the smallest advance might, through the operation of this multiplier effect, ultimately create an immense amount of progress.[47]

Hence, the improvement of man and the world, while dilatory and uneven at first, was picking up speed. But what was the source of all this progress? What could have transformed mankind into beings of ever-greater knowledge, power, happiness, and virtue? For all these believers in the general advancement of the world, the answer was, fundamentally, God: progress appeared to them to be a divine program. Worthington found it inescapable to conclude that, at the creation of the world, the "great Author and Moderator of it must have laid down some certain plan . . . which he constantly and invariably pursues in the conduct of the whole, and every part, . . . to the final consummation of all things." And what plan, he asked, could possibly be worthier of infinite wisdom and goodness "than that of melioration; and improvement of [the world], in all its parts; and in every capacity?" Though man did not possess enough insight to comprehend the totality of the program, thought Priestley, the deity was

47. Priestley, *Institutes*, in *Works*, 2:367; idem, *Lectures on History*, Lectures I and VI, in *Works*, 24:31, 72; idem, *History of Electricity*, 1:vi–vii; idem, *Essay on Government*, 1st ed. (London, 1768), 3; idem, *Miscellaneous Observations Relating to Education* (1778), in *Works*, 25:11; Worthington, *Essay*, 127, 86–92; Gordon, *New Estimate*, 2:52, 53n; Price, *Evidence*, 13, 35. Law was the only one of the five who considered progress to be essentially uniform: *Considerations*, 241.

in fact "ever bringing good out of evil, and gradually conducting things to a more perfect and glorious state."[48]

This theology of history had two characteristics of special note. To begin with, it treated the divine governance of earthly affairs as providential. According to Price, not only did the hand of God give shape to the broad course of history, but also "All events are subject to his superintendency," particularly those "where the fate of nations is concern'd." Providence seemed to him, therefore, to have intervened (with opposite results for Britain) in both the Seven Years' War and the American Revolution. For Priestley, similarly, history was "an exhibition of the conduct of Divine Providence," so that "all things past, present, and to come, are precisely what the Author of nature really intended them to be, and has made provision for." Because His finger was "really in every thing that happens," His operation in directing human affairs provided the "noblest object of attention to an historian." The other prominent feature of this theocentric philosophy of history was the emphasis it placed on the slow, measured pace of divine dispensations. "The government of the Deity," declared Price,

> proceeds gradually. . . . As he does not bring the *individuals* of the human race on the stage of mature life, before they have been duly prepared for it, by passing through the instruction and discipline of infancy and childhood, so neither does he bring the species to that finished state of dignity and happiness for which it is intended, without a similar introduction and education.

The "education of the human race," to use Lessing's famous phrase, was conceived of as proceeding in tandem with the increasing capacity of mankind to accept divine tutelage. As Worthington observed, God "disposes the several ages of the world, as it were, into so many seasons of the year; adapting his dispensations in each, to what is most becoming, for the improvement of the creation in general."[49]

48. Worthington, *Scripture-Theory*, 390–91; Priestley, *Lectures on History*, Lectures III and LXVIII, in *Works*, 24:47, 438; idem, *History of Electricity*, 1:iii. See also Gordon, *New Estimate*, 1:ii, xvi–xvii, and 2:107.

49. Price, *Britain's Happiness*, 14–16; idem, *Observations*, 3; idem, *Evidence*, 18; Priestley, *Lectures on History*, Lectures I–III, LXVI–LXVII, in *Works*, 24:28, 45, 421–22, 428–29; idem, *Philosophical Necessity*, in *Works*, 3:462; Worthington, *Scripture-Theory*, 444. See also Law, *Considerations*, 268, 172.

Although progress took place according to a program arranged by God, it did not appear to depend completely upon divine superintendance or intervention. Sometimes it was considered to be a self-perpetuating phenomenon. "Every present advance prepares the way for farther advances," Price commented, adding that progress resembled a "spark on a train that springs a mine." More often, however, improvement seemed to come through the instrumentality of man himself. Fully intending men to advance in all ways, thought Gordon, God gave them the ability to make progress. Therefore, the immediate source of human happiness was not nature but men themselves, because "she only supplies us with the materials and means, which it is the business of [human] Art to use and apply: and the degree of perfection in this case must depend on the degree of skill in those who make use of these means." In Worthington's terms, the divine scheme for the reformation of the world after the Fall could be realized only with the concurrence of mankind, the glorious future only with the individual and collective work of human beings. This fact, he held, both obliged and greatly encouraged them to "be ever pressing forward towards the mark, and going on unto perfection." For Price, the most powerful impetus for men to cooperate with God as willing instruments of progress arose from the improvement already achieved and the reasonable expectation of more to come. "And were all to contribute all they can . . . much would be done; and the world would make swift advances to a better state."[50]

Because Priestley was a necessitarian as well as a providentialist, he would not be expected to accord men a significant independent role in the working out of progress. Indeed, he contended that all conditions favorable to liberty, virtue, and happiness had to be ascribed not to human policies or desires but to the "good providence of God, wisely overruling the passions and powers of men to his own benevolent purposes." Yet if he could call human beings the "passive and blind instruments of their own felicity," he could also insist on the centrality to progress of their "endless craving" for improvement, and on the fact that God intended them to "be, as far as possible, *self-taught*." Moreover, he wished to animate mankind to achieve ever

50. Price, *Observations*, 3–4; idem, *Britain's Happiness*, 18; idem, *Evidence*, 5–6, 35–36, 51–52, 28–29; Gordon, *New Estimate*, 2:26–28, 44; Worthington, *Essay*, 192, 380–81, 40; idem, *Scripture-Theory*, 426–27, 502. See also Edmund [Law], *A Sermon Preached before the Incorporated Society for the Propagation of the Gospel in Foreign Parts . . . February 18, 1774* (London, 1774), ix; idem, *Considerations*, 30–32.

more in the future by enhancing their awareness of the accomplishments of the past. The apparent contradiction of these two views is resolved by the fact that Priestley ultimately argued for human cooperation with and not direction of the course of history: "let us learn," he declared, "to be content with the natural though slow progress we are in to a more perfect state. But let us always endeavour to keep things in this progress. Let us, however, beware, lest, by attempting to accelerate, we in fact retard our progress in happiness."[51]

For Priestley, then, just as much as for the others, men and women had a part to play in the process of general amelioration, albeit not an entirely autonomous one. This role, of course, was performed within the context of society, which Priestley called the "great instrument in the hand of Divine Providence, of this progress of the species towards perfection." Among these five Englishmen he alone claimed— like a number of the Scottish thinkers of his day—that progress in society depended heavily upon the division of labor (a term, but not a concept, that he derived from Adam Smith). Yet along with the others he also insisted upon the crucial nature of the progress of knowledge, about which Worthington stated flatly that "of all human means, none hath contributed so much to the improvement and advancement of human nature." Similarly, Gordon attacked Rousseau for denying that "knowledge seems to be the grand principle, on which all other improvements depend." He believed with Priestley that

> greater *command* of the powers of nature . . . can only be obtained by a more extensive and more accurate knowledge of them, . . . which can alone enable us to avail ourselves of the numerous advantages with which we are surrounded, and contribute to make our common situation more secure and happy.[52]

In the mansion of progress, therefore, while God was the superintending master and man the cooperative servant, learning was the key unlocking all the chambers.

51. Priestley, *Lectures on History*, Lectures III, XXXIII, and LI, in *Works*, 24:46, 206–07, 316; idem, *An Essay on a Course of Liberal Education for Civil and Active Life* (1764), in *Works*, 24:8; idem, *Essay on Government*, in *Works*, 22:124–25; idem, *History of Electricity*, 1:vi.

52. Priestley, *Essay on Government*, in *Works*, 22:8; idem, *Lectures on History*, Lecture XLIX, in *Works*, 24:305–06; idem, *Experiments on Air*, "Preface," in *Works*, 25:374; Worthington, *Essay*, 154; Gordon, *New Estimate*, 1:50, and 2:8–10, 12–13, 110.

Indefinite improvement, carried out gradually in society by an increasingly knowledgeable humankind and according to a divine program: such was the most comprehensive and sophisticated form of the idea of progress in English thought of the eighteenth century. From 1743 through the 1780s, the five men examined here gave detailed expression to this form of the idea in their published writings. That they were not unique in holding some variety of belief in unlimited progress is clear from the views of Gibbon and the translator of *Émile*, of Shipley and Astle. Furthermore, three of the five exercised a considerable influence on the English intellectual world. Price and Priestley were the most prominent Dissenters of the time and occupied a position of substantial respect in Nonconformist circles. The former (and, to a lesser degree, the latter also) helped to shape the opinions of the "Chathamites," that group of reformers centering on Shelburne. Priestley's audience included not only his readers (like Bentham) and a generation of students at one of the most advanced educational institutions in England, but also such members of the Lunar Society as Matthew Boulton, Erasmus Darwin, and Josiah Wedgwood. Law, too, molded the minds of students, becoming the mentor at Cambridge of a number of young men, most notably William Paley. What all of this means, quite simply, is that doctrines of general progress were clearly gaining wide currency in England during the second half of the century, and that the development of the idea of progress had reached its eighteenth-century zenith.

The same was true in Scotland. There, however, the belief in the progress of human culture assumed a different, more limited form.

7 The Progress of Human Culture: Scotland

There is no question that a considerable number of eighteenth-century Scottish thinkers undertook to analyze the long-term development of society, and that they depicted it as a historical transition from rudeness to refinement or from barbarism to civilization. Indeed, this vision of history has rightly been called "one of the leading principles" of the Scottish Enlightenment.[1] Nor is there any doubt that a whole constellation of factors prompted growing interest in the historical development of society. These influences included contemporary recognition of the marked contrast between seventeenth- and eighteenth-century Scotland, and between the modern Lowlands and more backward Highlands; the suddenly necessary quest after 1707 for new sources of Scottish national identity, and new national goals; the inevitable competition with and emulation of an England whose achievements and development were themselves fascinating to the junior partner in the Union; the emergence of vigorousness in the country's economy by about 1750; and the general preoccupation of Scottish intellectuals with the study of society. It is admittedly difficult to assess the relative importance of these and other factors in fostering the Scots' concern with social evolution. More crucial for our purposes is the issue of whether for

---

1. Duncan Forbes, "Introduction," in David Hume, *The History of Great Britain: The Reigns of James I and Charles I*, Pelican Classics ed. (Harmondsworth, Eng., 1970), 38 (hereafter cited as Forbes, "Introduction to Hume"). For the importance in the Scottish Enlightenment of the analysis of social development from rudeness to refinement, see also Hugh Trevor-Roper, "The Scottish Enlightenment," *Studies on Voltaire and the Eighteenth Century* 58 (1967): 1658; Andrew Skinner, "Natural History in the Age of Adam Smith," *Political Studies* 15 (Feb. 1967): 40–42; William C. Lehmann, *John Millar of Glasgow, 1735–1801: His Life and Thought and His Contributions to Sociological Analysis* (Cambridge, 1960), 99–100.

them the concept of social development from barbarism to civilization was equivalent to a belief in progress.

Obviously, perceiving development in history does not necessarily mean seeing improvement. On the basis of this distinction, it has been argued that the Scottish *literati* of the eighteenth century did not really believe in progress because—somewhat like Rousseau—they discovered in the past a course of social evolution that brought mankind many evils as well as blessings, and that paradoxically corrupted man as it was empowering him to reach new heights. Evidence for such an interpretation of contemporary Scottish thought is not entirely lacking. Gilbert Stuart (1742–86), for example, a historian of law and a book reviewer for London and Edinburgh magazines, in 1778 published a book that generally took a dim view of the shift from medieval rudeness to early modern refinement. And, though less pessimistic than he, other writers among his countrymen demonstrated a lively awareness of the costs of the civilizing process. Nevertheless, on the whole the Scots *did* consider the pattern of development that they discerned in history to be broadly progressive.[2]

Although the views of the *literati* on the progress of human culture are hardly monolithic, the similarities in them far outweigh the differences.[3] Unlike their English counterparts, the Scots relatively rarely thought in terms of an indefinite temporal range for improvement. And they were oriented more toward the past than toward the future: that is, they engaged more in recollection than in foresight.

2. Gilbert Stuart, *A View of Society in Europe in its Progress from Rudeness to Refinement: Or, Inquiries concerning the History of Law, Government, and Manners,* 2d ed. (Edinburgh, 1792), passim and esp. 2, 109, 128–35. The argument that the Scots' notion of historical development did not represent a belief in progress is contained in Forbes, "Introduction to Hume," 38; idem, "Introduction," in Adam Ferguson, *An Essay on the History of Civil Society* (1767), ed. Duncan Forbes (Edinburgh, 1966), xiv (the preliminary material in this volume is hereafter cited as Forbes, "Introduction to Ferguson"). For a contrary view, see Gladys Bryson, *Man and Society: The Scottish Inquiry of the Eighteenth Century* (Princeton, 1945), 14–15, 243. In spite of taking much the same position as Forbes on this issue, J. G. A. Pocock admits (in *The Machiavellian Moment: Florentine Political Thought and the Atlantic Republican Tradition* [Princeton, 1975], 503–04) that "it would clearly be possible to write a study of the Scottish school in which nearly all the emphasis lay on those aspects of their thought which were progressive." I am contending that this is not only possible but necessary—and historically correct.

3. The existence of differences has been recognized, but they still have not been satisfactorily specified: see Duncan Forbes, *Hume's Philosophical Politics* (Cambridge, 1975), xi; idem, "Introduction to Ferguson," xxii–xxiii.

Nor did they suggest that advances occurred equally or at all times in each department of life. In short, for them the general progress of culture had at least some limits.

FROM RUDENESS TO REFINEMENT

Those who adopted the historical perspective of advance from rudeness to refinement included the key figures of the eighteenth-century Scottish intellectual scene. Near the center was Henry Home, Lord Kames (1696–1782). Born in Berwickshire, he was educated at home until going to Edinburgh to receive legal training. He was admitted to the Faculty of Advocates in 1723, became a lord ordinary of the Court of Session in 1752, and was appointed commissioner of justiciary in 1763; in a society that assigned enormous power and prestige to its judiciary, few individuals had as much importance as he. In the city and on his nearby estates, he entertained the leading Scottish luminaries and participated wholeheartedly in the republic of letters of his day. Besides his judicial career, his activities encompassed not only the writing of many books (on topics ranging from legal history to literary criticism to agriculture), but also membership in several improving societies and encouragement of the careers of his younger friends. He self-consciously attempted to gather around himself a group of *élèves* and succeeded for a time in becoming a kind of father-figure to David Hume, Adam Smith, and James Boswell. At the age of thirty-four Hume called Kames, his distant relative, "the best Friend, in every respect, I ever possess," a claim supported later in his life by the fact that Kames always demonstrated great solicitude for the philosopher's career and served as his host during the writing of the *History of England*. John Millar, too, lived with the Kames family for a time and obtained his academic appointment at Glasgow in part on the recommendation of the judge, who also fostered the reputations of Smith and Hugh Blair by enabling them to deliver public lectures on rhetoric and belles lettres in Edinburgh. The works of William Robertson, and undoubtedly of Adam Ferguson as well, owed something to Kames's conversation and writings. Smith spoke for all the *literati* when he commented, "We must every one of us acknowledge Kames for our master."[4]

4. Hume to Kames, June 13, 1745, in *New Letters of David Hume*, ed. Raymond Klibansky and Ernest C. Mossner (Oxford, 1954), 17; Alexander Fraser Tytler, Lord Woodhouselee, *Memoirs of the Life and Writings of the Honourable Henry Home of*

Henry Home, Lord Kames

Over the long run, of course, the most influential Scots were Hume (1711–76) and Smith (1723–90) themselves. Hume's youth hardly seemed to mark him for greatness. The younger son of a gentry family of modest means whose estate lay near Edinburgh, he spent most of the decade after 1723 acquiring an education in the Scottish capital. After giving up his legal training and suffering an emotional breakdown, he traveled to France in 1734 and settled at La Flèche, where Descartes had received his Jesuit education. By the time Hume returned to Britain three years later, he had nearly completed the *Treatise of Human Nature* (published 1739–40). The signal contribution of this book to the development of modern philosophy has long been recognized, in spite of the fact that the *Treatise* failed to achieve for Hume the immediate renown he desperately craved. But even in his own time this youthful work—along with its later and more popularly written reincarnation, the two *Enquiries* of 1748 and 1751—stimulated and provoked his countrymen, as the replies of the common-sense school testify. He was much more than a writer of philosophy, however. The contemporary European-wide fame that he eventually came to enjoy derived less from the *Treatise* and *Enquiries* than from his volumes of essays on literary, economic, political, and religious subjects (published between 1741 and 1757), and from his *History of England* (1754–62). As a man of letters above all else, he played a crucial role in the intellectual circles and improving societies of Edinburgh, although his religious skepticism and the implications of his philosophy prevented him from gaining an academic position. The disappointment (in 1745) of his hopes for a university career, coupled with the limited financial resources of his family, forced him to find employment elsewhere: first as a private tutor, next in a series of civilian positions in the British military, then as keeper of the Advocates' Library in Edinburgh, and finally in the 1760s as secretary to the British ambassador in Paris and undersecretary of state for the Northern Department. While in Paris Hume made the acquaintance of most of the leading French philosophes. In 1769 he returned to Edinburgh and spent his last seven years among old friends.

One of these friends was Smith, son of a comptroller of customs in a small town on the north shore of the Firth of Forth. While a student

---

Kames, 2d ed., 3 vols. (Edinburgh, 1814), 1:218; Ian Simpson Ross, *Lord Kames and the Scotland of His Day* (Oxford, 1972), 75, 188, 94–95, 40, 191.

at the University of Glasgow from 1737 to 1740 Smith attended the lectures of Francis Hutcheson, thereafter becoming Snell Exhibitioner at Balliol College, Oxford. Neglected by the Oxford faculty (who he later said had "given up altogether even the pretence of teaching"), for the next six years he independently pursued the study of ancient and modern literature.[5] By the time he returned to Scotland in 1746, he had decided against a career in the church and began to attempt to obtain an academic position. Unsuccessful at first, he nonetheless improved his possibilities by having the opportunity to lecture publicly on rhetoric, belles lettres, and, finally, jurisprudence in Edinburgh from 1748 to 1751. In the latter year he was appointed professor of logic at Glasgow and moved soon thereafter to Hutcheson's old chair of moral philosophy, which he held until 1763. During his time at Glasgow, Smith lectured on literature as well as on law, government, and ethics, and in 1759 he published *The Theory of Moral Sentiments*, which emphasized the centrality of sympathy in the formation of moral judgments. The mid-1760s found him acting as traveling tutor to the young duke of Buccleuch, a situation that permitted him to spend much time among the philosophes and physiocrats on the Continent. This experience probably sharpened (but certainly did not fundamentally alter) his thinking on political economy, to which subject he devoted the ten years after his return to the Edinburgh area in 1766. The *Wealth of Nations*, begun in France, was finally published in 1776, and the next year Smith became commissioner of customs in the Scottish capital. He never again held a teaching position, although in 1787 he was elected Lord Rector of the University of Glasgow.

Although his posthumous reputation and influence lie far below those of Hume and Smith, William Robertson (1721–93) played at least as important a role as they or Kames did in the intellectual and cultural life of eighteenth century Scotland. Growing up in Midlothian, this son of a minister in the Church of Scotland attended Edinburgh University in the 1730s before obtaining the pastorate of Gladsmuir in East Lothian, which he held from 1743 to 1759. For three years thereafter he was minister of Greyfriars Kirk in Edinburgh. By the early 1750s, he had already become a leader of the emerging progressive "Moderate" party within the Scottish Church,

5. Adam Smith, *An Inquiry into the Nature and Causes of the Wealth of Nations*, ed. R. H. Campbell, A. S. Skinner, and W. B. Todd, 2 vols. continuously paginated (Oxford, 1976), 761.

a group that included such notable figures as Alexander "Jupiter" Carlyle, Adam Ferguson, and John Home. Soon the chief figure among the Moderates, he successfully strove to bring the Scottish kirk into touch with the changing intellectual, social, and economic climate of the age. His involvement in the controversy over Home's play *Douglas*, on the side of those clergymen who had attended its performance and of the minister-playwright himself, illustrated the temper of the progressives, as did his efforts to keep Hume and Kames from ecclesiastical persecution at the hands of the conservative "High-flyers" and his participation in local improving societies and in the first *Edinburgh Review*. Moreover, from 1762 to his death he was principal of the University of Edinburgh, enlarging its physical facilities and improving its faculty and medical school, and between 1766 and 1780 he served as moderator of the General Assembly of the Church of Scotland. Even with the pressure of all these duties, he found time to produce four major historical works: a *History of Scotland* (1759), *The History of the Reign of the Emperor Charles V* (1769), *The History of America* (1777), and a *Historical Disquisition concerning the Knowledge which the Ancients had of India* (1791). The first of these books won him both fame and appointment in 1763 as Historiographer Royal for Scotland, and his commitment to factual accuracy in research and objectivity in interpretation have continued to bring him praise as the "most impeccable of eighteenth century historians."[6]

Among the second rank of Scottish men of letters stand two professors, Adam Ferguson (1723–1816) and John Millar (1735–1801). As the youngest child of a Calvinist minister, Ferguson spent his early years in the respectable poverty of a Perthshire parish in the Highlands. Between 1738 and 1742 he studied mathematics, philosophy, and the classics at the University of St. Andrews, moving on to theological training at the University of Edinburgh (where his friends included Robertson, Kames, and Hugh Blair). He was ordained in 1745, the year of the second Jacobite rebellion, accepting the chaplaincy of the famous Black Watch Regiment. After serving nine years in the Highlands and abroad, he left both the military and the clergy in 1754 for reasons that remain unclear. But he continued to be an active communicant in the Scottish church, and, as a Moderate, he was for many years a lay member of the General Assembly. In 1757 he

6. J. B. Black, *The Art of History: A Study of Four Great Historians of the Eighteenth Century* (London, 1926), 122.

succeeded Hume as keeper of the Advocates' Library in Edinburgh and became tutor to the sons of Lord Bute. Two years later he was elected to the chair of natural philosophy at the University of Edinburgh, and in 1764 he became professor of pneumatics and moral philosophy there. His academic career spanned more than a quarter of a century, during which time he participated actively in the social and club life of the city. He also journeyed to the Continent (where he was in contact with the philosophes), served as secretary to a commission that negotiated with the American rebels in 1778, and published three books: *An Essay on the History of Civil Society* (1767), *Institutes of Moral Philosophy* (1768), and a *History of the Progress and Termination of the Roman Republic* (1783). After his retirement in 1785, Ferguson continued for many years to pursue intellectual work, publishing his Edinburgh lectures as *Principles of Moral and Political Science* (1792) and drafting a number of essays.

Compared with Ferguson, Millar led a sedentary life, never leaving Britain and rarely Glasgow and its environs. He, too, was the son of a minister (though his family was definitely gentry), and at the age of eleven in 1746 he became a student at his father's alma mater, the University of Glasgow, with the original intention of entering the clergy. There he spent at least six years, eventually attending the lectures and coming under the influence of the new professor of logic and moral philosophy, Adam Smith. Millar's activities during most of the 1750s are unknown, but between 1758 and 1760 he served as tutor to Kames's son. Admitted to the bar in the latter year, he practiced only briefly before his election in 1761 to the chair of civil law at Glasgow. He held that professorship for forty years, lecturing on Justinian, general jurisprudence, the principles of government, and the law of Scotland and England. All the while he was building a reputation for Glasgow as the chief Scottish center of legal studies. As a teacher he exercised an influence unmatched by that of any other Scot of the eighteenth century: his students included future attorneys, judges, and legal scholars of note; prominent ambassadors, members of Parliament, and royal councillors; and even a prime minister, William Lamb, second viscount Melbourne. Millar's most important published works were *The Origin of the Distinction of Ranks* (1771, revised and enlarged in 1779) and *An Historical View of the English Government* (1787–1803), both based on his lectures. Among those who read these books with interest were J. G. Herder, James Madison, Francis Jeffrey and other early contributors to the *Edin-*

burgh Review, Sir James Mackintosh, David Ricardo, and both Mills, the younger of whom once called Millar "perhaps the greatest of philosophical inquirers into the civilization of past ages."[7]

Kames, Hume, Smith, Robertson, Ferguson, and Millar were central figures not only in the intellectual life of the times but also on the broader stage of Scottish life generally. They unquestionably belonged to and were accepted as members of the country's elite. The official positions of Kames and Robertson located them behind only the principal Scottish politicians in overall importance. With the emphasis that the town fathers of Edinburgh and Glasgow placed on their universities, the professors in our group—Ferguson, Millar, and Smith—enjoyed a prestige and an influence virtually unknown in contemporary Oxford and Cambridge. In spite of his notoriety Hume, too, was an insider, as his official appointments and memberships in key societies testify. Elsewhere in the Enlightenment of western Europe, one can identify a few individuals, preeminently Turgot and Gibbon, who can properly be said to have had strong establishment ties. But only in Scotland, where the elite cherished and encouraged ideas and intellectual activity, did the Enlightenment come to be an integral part of the establishment.

Quite naturally, therefore, the views of these men on the evolution of society had the potential for a kind of influence that the ideas of Englishmen like Gordon and Worthington or even Priestley and Law could not match. But it was not just the famous and influential among eighteenth-century Scots whose writing depicted history as a progressive development from rudeness to refinement. James Dunbar (d. 1798) may be taken as an example of the lesser lights who adopted this same perspective. Although little is known about him, it is clear that he grew up in Moray and entered King's College, Aberdeen, in 1757, when Thomas Reid was lecturing there. He became an assistant regent at that institution in 1765 and a regent the next year, teaching Greek and moral philosophy in that capacity until 1794. These were illustrious years in the history of Aberdeen intellectual life, marked by the presence of the common-sense philosopher James Beattie, the aesthetician Alexander Gerard, and the theologian and rhetorician George Campbell. Reid, one of the founders of the

---

7. John Stuart Mill, "Modern French Historical Works" (1826), in *Collected Works of John Stuart Mill*, 29 vols. (Toronto, 1963–), vol. 20 (*Essays on French History and Historians*, ed. John M. Robson [1985]), 46. For Millar's influence, see Lehmann, *John Millar*, 145–63.

Aberdeen Philosophical Society, left for Glasgow in 1764, but the society continued its activities. Dunbar became a member in 1765 and presented papers on "The Equality of Mankind" and "The Influence of Place and Climate upon Human Affairs." This "acute frosty-faced little man of much erudition and great good nature"[8] was deeply interested in bringing about a full union of King's with Marischal College, but his efforts to rationalize teaching responsibilities and reform the curriculum met with resistance. In 1779 he published a tract on the American Revolution, and the next year saw the appearance of the work for which he is remembered (if at all), *Essays on the History of Mankind in Rude and Cultivated Ages*.

With the likely exception of Dunbar, these Scots were socially and intellectually well acquainted with one another, and they drew upon each other's work and ideas. Nonetheless, in terms of the basic elements of their thought they hardly formed a homogeneous group. It is true that they all rejected the rigid Calvinism of the traditional Scottish faith, but there uniformity ended. Hume of course established for himself a deserved reputation as the arch-skeptic of Britain, and although Smith never reached quite such an extreme position he did move increasingly farther away from orthodox Christianity toward an optimistic deism that emphasized Christian virtues and Stoicism. Robertson alone was by profession and inclination a true man of religion, like the English believers in general progress. His liberal religious views, however, were much the same as those of the laymen Kames, Millar, and Ferguson, all of whom attended worship services regularly and observed the customary rites of the Church of Scotland. The ecclesiastical opponents of the Moderates had harsh words for everyone in this group, even though they saved their most severe criticisms for Hume and Kames.

Politically, all were by the 1750s at least nominally Whigs, but, again, similarity extended no farther than that. Initially a Jacobite, Kames became by the 1730s a conservative Whig. His patriotism and fervent approval of the political and social status quo was matched by Robertson, who enjoyed the patronage of Bute and other key Scottish politicians, and by Ferguson, who supported official government policy because he believed that order and authority were necessary for the maintenance of civilized society. Hume and Smith, though by no

8. John Malcolm Bulloch, *A History of the University of Aberdeen, 1495–1895* (London, 1895), 163.

means "patriots," were also firmly committed to the Hanoverian regime. Although Hume appeared to some contemporaries to be a Tory (because of his relatively sympathetic treatment of the early Stuarts in the *History of England*) and Smith a member of Lord Rockingham's connection, both were in fact the most sceptical of Whigs: their "scientific" outlook on history did not permit them to accept at face value the dogmatic platitudes of orthodox Whiggism. On the other hand, neither of them was a political reformer like Millar, the ardent Whig, supporter of Charles James Fox, and typical "Commonwealthman" of the reign of George III.[9]

Eighteenth-century Scottish philosophy grew primarily out of the empirical tradition of Locke and Newton and the ethical theories of Shaftesbury and Hutcheson.[10] Hume carried Locke's epistemological insights to their skeptical and subjectivist limits, restricting the boundaries of knowledge to perceptions of objects (not the objects themselves), insisting upon the limitations of reason (the "slave of the passions"), and denying the possibility of proof for causation and of demonstration for matters of fact. It was in opposition to the working-out by Hume and Berkeley of this kind of conclusion implicit in Locke that there emerged at Aberdeen a "common-sense" school of philosophy, headed by Reid and associated also with Campbell, Beattie, and James Oswald. These philosophers claimed that experience *did* provide knowledge of the real external world, and they came close to reasserting the existence of innate ideas or self-evident principles implanted by God and recognized intuitively. Such principles Reid called "the common sense of mankind," though he also used that term to mean common experience and generally accepted opinions. In any event, common sense was usually thought to include belief in the existence of the material world, the uniformity of nature, the power of men over their wills and actions, and the

9. David Kettler, *The Social and Political Thought of Adam Ferguson* ([Columbus, Ohio], 1965), 84–96; Duncan Forbes, "'Scientific' Whiggism: Adam Smith and John Millar," *Cambridge Journal* 7 (Aug. 1954): 660–61; Elie Halévy, *The Growth of Philosophic Radicalism*, trans. Mary Morris (Boston, 1955), 140–42; Caroline Robbins, *The Eighteenth-Century Commonwealthman: Studies in the Transmission, Development and Circumstance of English Liberal Thought from the Restoration of Charles II until the War with the Thirteen Colonies*, Atheneum ed. (New York, 1968), 215.

10. This, of course, is not intended to deny the indirect influence of other traditions, such as the natural law tradition imported from the Continent by Gershom Carmichael and other lawyers.

difference between right and wrong. According to Reid and the other members of this school, the raw material from which knowledge was formed included not only sensations but also judgments based on the common sense and antecedent to the sensations themselves: the mind was beginning to seem far less passive than Locke and Hume had portrayed it.

The main lines of Reid's philosophy, accepted by Ferguson, were anticipated and, to at least some degree, influenced by Kames's *Essays on the Principles of Morality and Natural Religion*.[11] Both Kames and Ferguson were concerned to avoid the skeptical trap in which, as they thought, Hume had become ensnared. But they shared Hume's primary interest in moral philosophy, and with him and Reid they opposed both ethical rationalism and ethical egoism. In place of these theories, they adopted a moral philosophy that owed much to the ideas of Hutcheson and Shaftesbury. Hutcheson had argued that moral judgments and actions flowed from the feelings rather than from reason and were disinterestedly benevolent, not selfish (as Mandeville had previously contended). He, like Shaftesbury, had supposed the existence of an inborn, internal "moral sense" capable of approving and driving men toward virtue, which he had tended to identify with a benevolence whose most extensive form brought the greatest happiness to the greatest number. Hume accepted much of this analysis, and he, too, found disinterested benevolence to be a motive to virtuous (and, therefore, utilitarian) action. But for him motivation was more complicated than Hutcheson had considered it to be, and he attributed it to an observer's sympathetic sharing in the action-produced pleasure or pain experienced by someone else. Sympathy became the central feature of Smith's moral theory, largely replacing both the moral sense and utility. In his view, however, sympathy meant an observer's fellow-feeling for any passion experienced in either the actor or the person affected by the action, with regard to motives as well as effects. Kames, on the other hand, defined sympathy in essentially Humean terms, but he considered it merely one motive among several, including benevolence and self-interest, all governed by the moral sense. According to Ferguson, none of the other Scottish moralists had been able to arrive at a complete ethical theory because, in spite of the useful insight of the existence of a

11. Reid later contributed "A Brief Account of Aristotle's Logic" to Kames's *Sketches of the History of Man*.

moral sense, they had forgotten to ask what man ought to be rather than what he is.

Given these differences of outlook on religion, politics, and philosophy, it is obviously not possible to describe the seven Scots under consideration here as a "school." Nevertheless, they did form an intellectual community based upon a significant shared interest: the study of man in society, along scientific lines. This concern led them to insist that what Hume called "Moral philosophy, or the science of human nature" should have for its "only solid foundation" a Newtonian emphasis on experience and observation, through the "application of experimental philosophy to moral subjects." In their view, Locke and Hutcheson had already begun to fashion a true "science of man," itself the "only solid foundation for the other sciences." Their own task, they believed, was not only to improve this science but also to extend its range into the whole realm of social phenomena. As a result, they undertook the study of law and government, political economy and social structure, language and the history of civilization in general. From being moral philosophers, they self-consciously sought to become scientists both of man and of society. And in the process they grew from students of Locke, Newton, and Hutcheson into students of Montesquieu as well.[12]

12. David Hume, *An Enquiry concerning Human Understanding* (1748), sect. 1, in *Enquiries Concerning Human Understanding and Concerning the Principles of Morals, by David Hume*, ed. L. A. Selby-Bigge, 3d ed., rev. Peter H. Nidditch (Oxford, 1975), 5; idem, *A Treatise of Human Nature*, ed. L. A. Selby-Bigge, 2d ed., rev. Peter H. Nidditch (Oxford, 1978), xvi. See also Peter Gay, *The Enlightenment: An Interpretation*, 2 vols. (New York, 1966–69), 2:332–33; Bryson, *Man and Society*, 1, 52; Trevor-Roper, "Scottish Enlightenment," 1639–40.

In recent scholarship an increasing emphasis has been placed on the centrality to eighteenth-century Scottish thought of the "civic humanist" and "civil jurisprudential" traditions. It has become clear that these traditions were important enough in the Scottish Enlightenment to deserve recognition and careful study. But it is time to underscore once again the primacy of the heritage of Locke, Newton, and their successors among the major intellectual influences that shaped contemporary thought. Certainly, if the effect of concentrating on the perspectives of the civic humanist and jurisprudential traditions is, as J. G. A. Pocock contends, to make the emerging discipline of political economy seem "to have had far more to do with morality than with science," then we have lost sight of a crucial feature of Enlightenment ideas and dreams—the quest to duplicate outside the realm of physics the method and achievements of Newton. For Pocock's remark, see "Cambridge Paradigms and Scotch Philosophers: A Study of the Relations between the Civic Humanist and the Civil Jurisprudential Interpretation of Eighteenth-Century Social Thought," in Istvan Hont and Michael Ignatieff, eds., *Wealth and Virtue: The Shaping of Political Economy in the Scottish Enlightenment* (Cambridge, 1983), 251.

In all likelihood Montesquieu was their main source of inspiration for and principal teacher in the study of society.[13] Millar called him "the Lord Bacon in this branch of philosophy," and nowhere was his *De l'esprit des lois* (1748) read more avidly than among the Scottish *literati*. The Scots learned much from him and took up as their own his attempt to identify the causes of the customary practices and institutions of peoples, though for the most part they emphasized the social role of climate and geography less strongly than he. Looking back on nearly half a century of scholarship, Dugald Stewart, the last significant member of the Scottish Enlightenment, put Montesquieu's contribution in the proper context when he wrote that the Frenchman

> considered laws as originating chiefly from the circumstances of society, and attempted to account, from the changes in the condition of mankind, which take place in the different stages of their progress [i.e., development], for the corresponding alterations which their institutions undergo. It is thus, that in his occasional elucidations of the Roman jurisprudence, . . . we frequently find him borrowing his lights from the most remote and unconnected quarters of the globe, and combining the casual observations of illiterate travellers and navigators, into a philosophical commentary on the history of law and manners.
>
> The advances made in this line of inquiry since Montesquieu's time have been great.

Indeed they had, for Montesquieu, usually confining himself to a comparative and static method, only pointed the way to historical sociology.[14] He may have been the Bacon but the Scots were conjointly the Newton of this field.

13. But it is interesting that *De l'esprit des lois* received no review in the *Scots Magazine*, the principal journal of cultural and intellectual affairs at the time. Voltaire's works were being reviewed by this point. On the other hand, an English translation of Montesquieu's book was quickly arranged in Edinburgh, and it *was* noticed in the *Scots Magazine* 12 (1750): 352. (I owe this reference to my student Naomi Siegel.)

14. John Millar, *An Historical View of the English Government, from the Settlement of the Saxons in Britain, to the Revolution in 1688*, 4th ed., 4 vols. (London, 1818), 2:429n–30n; Dugald Stewart, "Account of the Life and Writings of Adam Smith, LL.D." (delivered 1793), in *The Collected Works of Dugald Stewart*, ed. Sir William Hamilton, 11 vols. (Edinburgh, 1854–60), 10:35. According to Forbes, the passage quoted in this paragraph reveals Stewart's contention that "Montesquieu himself used the progress of society as the organizing principle of his researches": "'Scientific'

Stewart attributed the advances of which he spoke to the Scots' practice of a "species of philosophical investigation" that he called "*Theoretical* or *Conjectural History*, an expression which coincides pretty nearly in its meaning with that of *Natural History*, as employed by Mr. Hume." The method of natural history represented the eighteenth-century response to a basic historiographical and anthropological problem pointed out by Stewart: with regard to the origins of language, arts and sciences, and government, "very little information is to be expected from history, for long before that stage of society when men begin to think of recording their transactions, many of the most important steps of their progress have been made." In light of this fact, how could the history of civilization be fully reconstructed? Part of the answer had been worked out as early as the seventeenth century, when travel literature and reports by missionaries were used by Continental writers to compare the customs of contemporary primitive societies with those already known from the existing record of the ancient Mediterranean peoples. The Scots continued to employ the technique of learning about the distant past from the "savage" present, going so far as to treat the nearby and still-backward Highlands as a kind of sociological museum or laboratory. We can note the clear similarity between this approach to the history of civilization and the "comparative method" of more recent anthropology in Ferguson's statement that it is in the present condition of Arab clans and American tribes "that we are to behold, as in a mirrour, the features of our own progenitors; and from thence we are to draw our conclusions with respect to the influence of situations, in which, we have reason to believe, our fathers were placed." The primitives, in other words, served as an aid to historical recollection, providing a "representation of past manners, that cannot, in any other way, be recalled."[15]

Whiggism," *Cambridge Journal* 7 (Aug. 1954): 646. Stewart certainly made no such claim, and it would be inaccurate to do so now. For Montesquieu neither truly believed in progress (see Gilbert Chinard, "Montesquieu's Historical Pessimism," in *Studies in the History of Culture: The Disciplines of the Humanities* [Menasha, Wis., 1942], 161–72), nor regularly adopted the perspective of historical social *development*. That such a perspective can sometimes be found in *De l'esprit des lois* (especially in Bk. XVIII), however, and that it represents an important first step in the transformation of political into social science, is argued in Thomas L. Pangle, *Montesquieu's Philosophy of Liberalism: A Commentary on "The Spirit of the Laws"* (Chicago, 1973), 177–93.

15. Stewart, "Account of Smith," in *Collected Works*, 10:36, 33; Ferguson, *Civil Society*, 80–81. For discussions of this aspect of natural history, see J. W. Burrow, *Evolution and Society: A Study in Victorian Social Theory* (Cambridge, 1966), 11–14;

Of course, this method could have been applied only on the assumption that human nature never varied in its fundamentals, and it is therefore not surprising that the uniformitarian hypothesis found acceptance as much among Scottish as English believers in general progress. "Mankind," declared Kames, "through all ages have been the same," in the sense that although the characters of men vary, their minds "are uniform with respect to their passions and principles." This meant, as Ferguson explained, that there was "not any sufficient reason to believe that men, of remote ages and nations, differ from one another otherwise than by habits acquired in a different manner of life." Or to invert the relationship as Robertson did, the human mind, whenever placed in the same situation, "will, in ages the most distant, and in countries the most remote, assume the same form, and be distinguished by the same manners." For a "human being, as he comes from the hand of nature, is every where the same."[16]

Hume discussed the uniformity of human nature more deeply and cautiously than did his Scottish contemporaries. "Would you know," he asked in a famous passage,

> the sentiments, inclinations, and course of life of the Greeks and Romans? Study well the temper and actions of the French and English: You cannot be much mistaken in transferring to

Frank E. Manuel, *The Eighteenth Century Confronts the Gods* (Cambridge, Mass., 1959), 15–19; Frederick J. Teggart, *Theory and Processes of History* (Berkeley, 1960), 93–96. On the Highlands as a museum, see Duncan Forbes, "The Rationalism of Sir Walter Scott," *Cambridge Journal* 7 (Oct. 1953): 32; idem, "Introduction to Ferguson," xxxviii–xl; Skinner, "Natural History in the Age of Adam Smith," 37–38.

16. [Henry Home, Lord Kames], *Introduction to the Art of Thinking* (1761), 2d ed. (Edinburgh, 1764), [1]; idem, *Sketches of the History of Man* (1774), new ed., 3 vols. (Edinburgh, 1813), 3:444 (Bk. III, Sk. iii, Ch. 3); Adam Ferguson, *Principles of Moral and Political Science; being chiefly a Retrospect of Lectures delivered in the College of Edinburgh*, 2 vols. (Edinburgh, 1792), 1:221; William Robertson, "A View of the Progress of Society in Europe, from the Subversion of the Roman Empire to the Beginning of the Sixteenth Century" [preliminary dissertation to *The History of the Reign of the Emperor Charles V*], Note VI, in *The Works of Wm. Robertson, D.D.*, 8 vols. (Oxford, 1825), 5:195; idem, *The History of America*, Bk. IV, in *Works*, 6:371. See also Adam Smith, "The Principles which lead and direct Philosophical Enquiries; illustrated by the History of the Ancient Logics and Metaphysics" (date of composition unknown), *Essays on Philosophical Subjects*, ed. W. P. D. Wightman and J. C. Bryce (Oxford, 1980), 121. Of the seven Scots discussed here, Dunbar was the only one who considered seriously the possibility of the transformation of nonhuman species, arguing that "perhaps of man alone it can be said in the strictest sense, Genus immortale manet": James Dunbar, *Essays on the History of Mankind in Rude and Cultivated Ages* (London, 1780), 305–06, 330, 404.

the former *most* of the observations which you have made with regard to the latter. Mankind are so much the same, in all times and places, that history informs us of nothing new or strange in this particular. Its chief use is only to discover the constant and universal principles of human nature.

The importance of the frequently overlooked qualifiers "much" and "*most*" is underscored by Hume's slightly later statement that "As far . . . as observation reaches, there is no universal difference discernible in the human species." He did not intend to suggest that there were no "characters peculiar to different nations and particular persons, as well as common to mankind." Rather, he meant both that these differences (and those among the various social strata) arose "necessarily, because uniformly, from the necessary and uniform principles of human nature," and that observation revealed a uniformity in the operation of the actions flowing from such differences.[17] Though they did not express themselves so meticulously or with equal circumspection, the rest of our group of Scots undoubtedly thought of human uniformity in this dual way.

Another technique used by the natural historians, which also rested on the assumption of uniformitarianism, explains why Stewart spoke of "theoretical" or "conjectural" history. For when neither the direct evidence of the existing historical record nor the indirect evidence of contemporary primitives was adequate, the Scots often resorted to what Kames called "supplying the want of positive facts by rational conjecture." If the historian were to use "all the light that is afforded, and if the conjectural facts correspond with the few facts that are distinctly vouchsafed, and join all in one regular chain, nothing further can be expected from human endeavours." As Stewart pointed out, such a procedure amounted to a demonstration of how historical events "*may have been* produced by natural causes," with reference to the "known principles of human nature." This explains Kames's statement that his historical sketches were a "natural history of man," Millar's comment that his *Origin of the Distinction of Ranks* was "intended to illustrate the natural history of mankind,"

17. Hume, *Human Understanding*, Sect. VIII, Part i, in *Enquiries*, 83; idem, "Of the Populousness of Ancient Nations" (1752), *Essays Moral, Political, and Literary*, ed. T. H. Green and T. H. Grose, new impression, 2 vols. (London, 1898), 1:382; idem, *Treatise*, 402–03. For an analysis of the sophistication of Hume's treatment of uniformitarianism, see S. K. Wertz, "Hume, History, and Human Nature," *Journal of the History of Ideas* 36 (July–Sept. 1975): 481–96.

and Hume's use of the title *The Natural History of Religion*. In this context, "natural" meant "normal," the opposite of "unusual," "exceptional," or "accidental."[18]

The Scots would have only partly accepted Stewart's claim that in most cases in the reconstruction of history

> it is of more importance to ascertain the progress that is most simple, than the progress that is most agreeable to fact; for, paradoxical as the proposition may appear, it is certainly true, that the real progress is not always the most natural. It may have been determined by particular accidents, which are not likely again to occur.

Ferguson made it clear that on the whole the "natural historian thinks himself obliged to collect facts, not to offer conjectures," and Smith and the other *literati* were equally committed to empiricism of the Voltairean *"Aux faits!"* variety, employing speculation as sparingly as possible. Nonetheless, they all aspired to much more than a mere recitation of the facts. They recognized with Stewart that "human affairs never exhibit, in any two instances, a perfect uniformity," because of the role of accident. And therefore, instead of confining themselves to what their pupil Francis Jeffrey called a "stupid amazement" with the "singular and diversified appearances of human manners and institutions," they sought to lay bare the underlying *normal* process by which civilization seemed to them to develop everywhere. Facts held much importance for them, but (except in the case of Robertson) only as the landmarks necessary—along with occasional conjecture—to the unearthing of "those steps by which men advance from a barbarous to a civilized state of society."[19]

18. [Henry Home, Lord Kames], *Historical Law-Tracts* (1758), 2d ed. (Edinburgh, 1761), 254, 22–23; idem, *Sketches*, 2:41 (Bk. II, Sk. i); Stewart, "Account of Smith," in *Collected Works*, 10:33–34; John Millar, *The Origin of the Distinction of Ranks*, 3d ed. (London, 1779), repr. in Lehmann, *John Millar*, 180 (this reprint is hereafter cited as Millar, *Ranks*). For the use of the term "natural," see Hume, *Treatise*, 474; idem, *An Enquiry concerning the Principles of Morals* (1751), Appendix III, in *Enquiries*, 307 and 307n; T. D. Campbell, *Adam Smith's Science of Morals* (London, 1971), 56; Teggart, *Theory and Processes of History*, 89–90; Arthur O. Lovejoy, "'Nature' as Aesthetic Norm," *Essays in the History of Ideas* (Baltimore, 1948), 71. Robertson stated his opposition to theoretical history in *The History of Scotland during the Reigns of Queen Mary and King James VI*, Bk. I, in *Works*, 1:3. But even he slipped into conjecture from time to time, as will appear below.

19. Stewart, "Account of Smith," in *Collected Works*, 10:37, 34; Ferguson, *Civil*

The natural history of mankind, then, was thought to consist of a series of fairly orderly and almost spontaneous stages through which virtually all peoples eventually passed as they moved from rudeness to refinement. It has been suggested that the Scots organized these stages along primarily economic lines, differentiating somewhat like Marx between an economic foundation and a social, political, and cultural superstructure.[20] Robertson took this view when he stated that in every examination of the "operations of men when united together in society, the first object of attention should be their mode of subsistence. Accordingly as that varies, their laws and policy must be different." Smith quite clearly accepted such a perspective in telling his students at Glasgow in 1762–63 that the "four stages of society are hunting, pasturage, farming, and commerce": for him, the status of a society's development was to be identified on the basis of the central element in its economic structure. Kames agreed and described an identical series of historical states of society, noting like Smith that the single exception to the order of the four-stage model was to be found among the American Indians, some of whom engaged in simple farming without having previously kept livestock herds.[21]

Both Hume and Ferguson outlined similar sets of economic steps, but neither they nor Dunbar envisioned the development of civilization in fundamentally economic terms. Ferguson subsumed historical changes in the mode of production under the heading of a broader shift from savagery through barbarism to polished life, a shift that

Society, 2–3, 75; [Francis Jeffrey], untitled review of Millar's *Historical View*, *Edinburgh Review* 3 (Oct. 1803): 157, 162; Tytler, *Memoirs of Kames*, 2:149–52. On Smith's use of "theoretical" history, see Campbell, *Smith's Science of Morals*, 79–80.

20. Skinner, "Natural History in the Age of Adam Smith," *Political Studies* 15 (Feb. 1977): 38, 40; idem, "Introduction," in Adam Smith, *The Wealth of Nations: Books I–III*, Pelican Classics ed. (Harmondsworth, Eng., 1970), 30–31. The first of these articles insightfully treats the whole subject of natural history among the Scots.

21. Robertson, *History of America*, Bk. IV, in *Works*, 6:298; Adam Smith, *Lectures on Jurisprudence*, ed. R. L. Meek, D. D. Raphael, and P. G. Stein (Oxford, 1978), 459, 14–16; Kames, *Law-Tracts*, 50n–51n, 60, 81, 90–91, 95, 207–08; idem, *Sketches*, 1:71–74 (Bk. I, Sk. i), and 2:368 (Bk. II, Sk. xii); idem, *Essays on the Principles of Morality and Natural Religion*, 2d ed. (1758), Pt. I, Essay vii, Ch. 7, in L. A. Selby-Bigge, *British Moralists: Being Selections from Writers Principally of the Eighteenth Century*, 2 vols. (Oxford, 1897), 2:320. Millar also emphasized the economic interpretation of the history of civilization, and this was undoubtedly the "one simple principle" to which (according to Jeffrey) he taught his students to refer the varied forms of human life: Millar, *Ranks*, 176, 203, 208, 284; Jeffrey, review of *Historical View*, *Edinburgh Review* 3 (Oct. 1803): 157.

depended on developments in social subordination and intellectual outlook as much as in the economy. He had no intention of arguing that the "pursuits of external accommodation . . . had a priority in the order of time, to those of political or mental attainment." This comment expresses the spirit of another of Robertson's generalizations, which deserves to be paired with the one previously noted: "the operations of man are so complex, that we must not attribute the form which they assume to the force of a single principle or cause."[22]

In any event, regardless of the principle or principles according to which they periodized history, all of the Scots agreed with Millar that there was in the course of civilization a series of complicated, interrelated changes encompassing every aspect of life and amounting to a transition from rudeness to refinement. A primitive people could devote its attention to only a very small number of objects associated with subsistence, and accordingly its ideas and feelings were "narrow and contracted." But just as its economy eventually became capable of providing much more than the bare necessities of existence, so "the most important alterations [were] produced in the state and condition" of the people. The population increased and the "connections of society" were extended. Property assumed more sophisticated forms, laws grew more numerous and governmental systems more complex. At the same time, these changes were "productive of suitable variations" in taste, sentiments, and the general system of behavior or manners, and ignorance gave way to knowledge. Millar called this process "a natural progress," by which he meant that the similarity of man's desires and faculties had "everywhere produced a remarkable uniformity in the several steps of his progression." He and the others knew that the uniformity was not complete and that the pace of change was far from identical among all peoples. Yet they believed, as Robertson put it, that in "every part of the earth, the progress of man hath been nearly the same, and we can trace him in

22. David Hume, "Of Commerce" (1752), *Essays*, 1:289; Adam Ferguson, *Institutes of Moral Philosophy. For the use of Students in the College of Edinburgh* (1768), 2d ed. (Edinburgh, 1773), 28–32; idem, *Civil Society*, 81–98, 184, 194, 205; idem, *Principles*, 1:240, 252; Robertson, *History of America*, Bk. IV, in *Works*, 6:320. Dunbar's division of history into three epochs emphasized increasing community integration: Dunbar, *History of Mankind*, 2–3. In the *History of England* far more than in the earlier essays, Hume tended to portray economic changes as dominant in the process of social and cultural development: Constant Noble Stockton, "Economics and the Mechanism of Historical Progress in Hume's *History*," in Donald W. Livingston and James T. King, eds., *Hume: A Re-evaluation* (New York, 1976), 313–14.

his career from the rude simplicity of savage life, until he attains the industry, the arts, and the elegance of polished society."[23]

The Scots' frequent discussion of the emergence of polished or refined conditions from rude or barbarous origins laid part of the groundwork for the continuing study by nineteenth-century social scientists of the development of civilization. In the hands of Millar, Robertson, and the others, however, the process of refinement was treated not only as development but also as *improvement*. For example, although their use of phrases like "the progress of refinement" without further qualification might easily seem value-free (given the range of eighteenth-century meanings for the term "progress"), it certainly was not. Rather, they intended such phrases to be synonyms for what Dunbar called "the progress of general improvement," and Kames "the natural progress of human improvement." Their alternative descriptions of the refining process make this clear. Thus, Hume wrote of the "improvement of human society, from rude beginnings to a state of greater perfection" and Robertson of how the medieval ancestors of modern Europeans "advanced from barbarism to refinement" until they reached "that degree of improvement in policy and in manners" associated with the early sixteenth century. For Smith, as a society advanced in civilization it partook of "the progress of improvement"; for Kames and Ferguson, the advance of the individual from infancy toward manhood provided an illuminating metaphor for the "similar progress of every nation, from its savage state to its maturity."[24]

To be sure, it was possible to extend this analogy in the direction of historical pessimism, as Robertson once did when he declared that the philosophical historian must trace man's evolution through the various "stages of society, as he gradually advances from the infant state of civil life toward its maturity and decline." And, indeed, the Scots were interested in and sometimes discussed the cyclical theory of history. Both Dunbar and Millar, for example, mentioned that it was often difficult to determine whether a particular people was ris-

23. Millar, *Ranks*, 176–77; idem, *Historical View*, 4:284–86; Robertson, *History of America*, Bk. IV, in *Works*, 6:246. See also Kames, *Sketches*, 2:48 (Bk. II, Sk. i).

24. Dunbar, *History of Mankind*, 297; Kames, *Law-Tracts*, 364, 368, sig. A3^r; idem, *Sketches*, 3:376 (Bk. III, Sk. iii, Ch. 3); David Hume, *The Natural History of Religion* (1757), Sect. I, in *Essays*, 2:310; Robertson, "Progress of Society in Europe," Sect. I, Introduction, in *Works*, 3:10; Smith, *Wealth of Nations*, 707; Ferguson, *Civil Society*, 1. See also Millar, *Ranks*, 176, 224.

ing or declining, because of the similarity between "corresponding points" in the "returns of the civil period." Casting his eyes on the "general revolutions of society," Hume noted that "there is an ultimate point of depression, as well as of exaltation, from which human affairs naturally return in a contrary direction, and beyond which they seldom pass either in their advancement or decline."[25] But infrequent remarks of this sort should not be construed as evidence that the Scots customarily considered the normal course of history to be cyclical rather than progressive.

On the contrary, such comments represent an almost ritualistic obeisance to a traditional yet time-worn and debatable historical theory. Ferguson knew that the most remarkable races of men, after becoming polished, "have in some cases returned to rudeness again." He was aware that this fact had lent credence to the apprehension that the advance of societies to greatness "is not more natural, than their return to weakness and obscurity is necessary and unavoidable," that "images of youth and old age, are applied to nations . . . supposed to have a period of life, and a length of thread . . . to be cut, when the destined aera is come." Still, he thought,

> it must be obvious, that the case of nations, and that of individuals, are very different. The human frame has a general course; it has, in every individual, a frail contexture, and a limited duration; it is worn by exercise, and exhausted by a repetition of its functions: But in a society, whose constituent members are renewed in every generation, where the race seems to enjoy a perpetuated youth, and accumulating advantages, we cannot, by any parity of reason, expect to find imbecilities connected with mere age and length of days.

25. Robertson, *History of America*, Bk. IV, in *Works*, 6:259; Dunbar, *History of Mankind*, 186–87; Millar, *Ranks*, 282–83; David Hume, *The History of England, from the Invasion of Julius Caesar to the Revolution of 1688*, new ed., 8 vols. (London, 1789), 3:297–98 (Ch. XXIII). It is worth noting that Robertson cited this remark of Hume's in his prolegomena to the era of Charles V: "Progress of Society in Europe," in *Works*, 3:18–19, 18n–19n. Other expositions of the cyclical theory can, of course, be found elsewhere in Hume's writings (especially in "Of the Rise and Progress of the Arts and Sciences" and *The Natural History of Religion*), and these are discussed below. Too much emphasis can be placed on this aspect of Hume's historical thought, however. For, as John B. Stewart rightly says, although Hume had conflicting ideas about the "pattern of time," his "study of the past had led him to presuppose that a unique, vast change in men's morals and science had taken place, and . . . this belief, not the weak logical thought of inclusive cycles, was the foundation of his historical writing": *The Moral and Political Philosophy of David Hume* (New York, 1963), 297.

So the decline of refined institutions was never inevitable, their duration "not fixed to any limited period."[26]

Nevertheless, as Kames observed, if nations were not *fated* to die
of old age, they could still become subject to deterioration from certain "diseases" associated with economic prosperity. That the Scots
identified and carefully investigated these maladies—especially luxury and the division of labor—is clear. But they did not believe, as has
sometimes been claimed, that corruption was built into the process
of refinement, that the commercial stage of social development inherently produced incurable social and psychological degeneration
along with (and because of) economic prosperity.[27] The Scots' pathology of historical diseases was not nearly as pessimistic, or as simple-
minded and reductionist, as this. Nor did it establish anything like a
necessary connection in their minds between the process of refinement, on the one hand, and decay, on the other.

Their analysis of the effects of commerce, chronologically the last
of the four modes of production, makes this clear. Historically, they
were certain, commerce and its attendant wealth had brought a
whole range of signal benefits to Europe. Robertson filled the long
preliminary dissertation to his account of the reign of Charles V with
examples of how, in the later medieval period and the Renaissance,
the "progress of commerce had considerable influence in polishing
the manners of the European nations, and in establishing among
them order, equal laws, and humanity." He especially emphasized
the role of commercial activity in fostering the growth of political
liberty and the arts and sciences at this time, as did Millar. Looking at
the same period, Smith asserted that the rising commerce and man-

26. Ferguson, *Civil Society*, 109, 208–09, 279–80; idem, *Institutes*, 293. Dunbar
also argued that the "progress of nations and of men" were "not exactly parallel,"
though they did correspond with regard to the "interval from infancy to manhood":
History of Mankind, 16.

27. Kames, *Sketches*, 3:204 (Bk. III, Sk. ii, Pt. 2). For the views cited, see J. G. A.
Pocock, *Politics, Language and Time: Essays on Political Thought and History* (New
York, 1971), 102–03; idem, *Machiavellian Moment*, 493–503; Albert O. Hirschman,
The Passions and the Interests: Political Arguments for Capitalism before Its Triumph
(Princeton, 1977), 104–07. A somewhat similar argument is made by Forbes, although
he recognizes that Ferguson, at least, did not believe in the *inevitability* of decadence
through civilization: Forbes, "Introduction to Ferguson," xiii–xiv, xxxviii. It is not
clear whether Professor Pocock's addition of a new "paradigm" to his interpretation of
eighteenth-century thought has altered his opinions about the connection between
refinement and decline: "Cambridge Paradigms and Scotch Philosophers," in Hont
and Ignatieff, *Wealth and Virtue*, 235–52.

ufacturing of the cities were the "cause and occasion" of the cultivation and further improvement of the countryside and also "gradually introduced order and good government, and with them, the liberty and security of individuals." The latter change he called "by far the most important of all their effects." Like Robertson and Hume, he moved beyond the confines of European history to argue a more general case for the beneficial consequences of commerce, writing of "that mutual communication of knowledge and of all sorts of improvements" which extensive international trade "naturally, or rather necessarily, carries along with it." Similarly, Ferguson believed that the commercial arts, although not absolutely essential to civilization, enabled mankind to subsist in increasing numbers, to make better use of their resources, and to wield their strength with superior ease and success.[28]

In celebrating its benefits, the Scots certainly did not claim that commerce never produced deleterious effects. They considered it to be potentially, in Ferguson's words, "a blessing or a curse, according to the direction [the human] mind has received." For although commerce brought prosperity, prosperity itself—whatever its source— could make men happy only when used properly. It was in this context that the Scots discussed the issue of luxury. Dunbar spoke for all of them when he observed that

> Luxury, according to its species and direction, may be pronounced to be either salutary or destructive. By its connexion with industry and active exertion, it is productive of the noblest effects. It is the parent of ingenious arts, and conducts a people to honour and distinction. Yet objects which are not only innocent, but beneficial in the pursuit, may prove dangerous in the possession.

Dunbar's differentiation between the good and bad aspects of luxury and the tentativeness of his phrase "may prove dangerous" provide

28. Robertson, "Progress of Society in Europe," Sect. I, Pts. x, i–ii, and Note XXX, in *Works*, 3:69, 73–74, 24–27, 29–32, and 5:314; Millar, *Ranks*, 217; idem, *Historical View*, 2:367–70, 375; Smith, *Wealth of Nations*, 411–12, 422, 627; idem, *Lectures on Rhetoric and Belles Lettres* (delivered 1762–63), ed. J. C. Bryce (Oxford, 1983), 137; Hume, "Of Commerce," "Of Refinement in the Arts" (1752), and "Of Interest" (1752), *Essays*, 1:288–89, 291–93, 303, 305–07, 325–26; Ferguson, *Principles*, 1:252–53. See also Dunbar, *History of Mankind*, 293.

the keynotes of the Scots' outlook on this great eighteenth-century issue.[29]

Hume thought that the positive side of luxury, which he named "innocent luxury, or a refinement in the arts and conveniences of life," was "advantageous to the public" in a variety of ways. It encouraged all the arts and sciences and, by stimulating demand for goods and services beyond mere necessities, enhanced the productiveness, employment opportunities, and incomes of the peasants as well as the middle class. These effects, in turn, increased the power of the state and enlarged the "basis of public liberty." Even sociability was promoted and the standard of morality improved by innocent luxury. In short, "*industry, knowledge,* and *humanity* . . . are found, from experience as well as reason, to be peculiar to the more polished and, what are commonly denominated, the more luxurious ages." Smith took this argument as the starting point for his analysis of the breakup of feudal society. He also told his Glasgow students that the Romans enjoyed greater tranquillity and security than ever before at just the time (in the reign of Trajan) that "Luxury, and the Refinement of manners . . . were as far advanced as they could be in any state."[30]

The "vicious" or "blameable" side of luxury, in Hume's terminology, was an excessive and all-engrossing gratification of the senses. All of the Scots criticized it as basically harmful both to the individual and to the state, but Kames was its most vociferous opponent. Among those afflicted by it, he contended, selfishness and lethargy increased, the growth of population was constricted, and manners, patriotism, and bravery all decayed. Ferguson added that it also wreaked political havoc by attracting respect and honor to men of mere wealth, rather than to those possessing the personal qualities and family background requisite to service in good government. In fact, thought Kames, vicious luxury had been "the ruin of every state where it prevailed," and along with Ferguson and Millar he argued that it was "above all, pernicious in a commercial state." But this did not mean that vicious luxury was either a disease peculiarly asso-

29. Ferguson, *Civil Society,* 112; idem, *Principles,* 1:255; Dunbar, *History of Mankind,* 351.

30. Hume, "Of Refinement in the Arts" and "Of Commerce," *Essays,* 1:299–307, 288–94; Smith, *Lectures on Jurisprudence,* 410–11, 420, 227, 661; idem, *Wealth of Nations,* 412–22; idem, *Lectures on Rhetoric,* 112. Hume's essay on refinement was originally entitled "Of Luxury."

ciated with commerce, or one inevitably fatal. Both Ferguson and Kames believed that it could appear long before the maturation of the commercial stage, a point vividly made in Hume's comment that the "TARTARS are oftener guilty of beastly gluttony, when they feast on their dead horses, than EUROPEAN courtiers with all their refinements of cookery." And Kames thought that it was possible for a country that had advanced economically until "depressed by luxury and self-ishness" to be restored to its progressive state through civic activity. "By such means a nation may be put in motion with the same advantages it had originally; and its second progress may prove as successful as the first."[31]

Thus, vicious luxury was to be avoided because of the threat it posed to any society, whether rude or refined, but even when it had insinuated itself among a people it could still be overcome. And, in fact, the Scots believed that it actually possessed at least some partially redeeming qualities. According to Millar, the luxurious enjoyment of great wealth required an exacting observation of the rules of justice, which in turn facilitated the "general intercourse of society." Hume argued that excessive luxury was "in general preferable to sloth and idleness, which would commonly succeed in its place, and are more hurtful both to private persons and to the public." Kames would not have accepted this contention but even he suggested (albeit somewhat inconsistently) that the public could actually gain from vicious luxury, which, like its innocent counterpart, encouraged commerce, manufacturing, and all the arts.[32]

Undoubtedly referring to Mandeville and himself, Hume remarked in 1751 that those who represented luxury as wholly or partially laudable rather than entirely pernicious could be said to "regulate anew our *moral* as well as *political* sentiments." Whether marking an intellectual revolution or not, such an opinion of luxury—in both its innocent and vicious varieties—was the norm among the Scots. For them, the bogy of the *Estimate* was far from being the malignant disease of commercial society so luridly de-

---

31. Hume, "Of Refinement in the Arts," *Essays*, 1:307–08, 302; Kames, *Sketches*, 1:89, 324–25, 473, 494, 509–12, 522–24 (Bk. I, Sks. i, v–vii), and 2:103–04, 150 (Bk. II, Sks. v–vii); idem, *Loose Hints upon Education, Chiefly Concerning the Culture of the Heart* (1781), 2d ed., enl. (Edinburgh, 1782), 38, 334; Ferguson, *Civil Society*, 248–49, 254–55; Millar, *Ranks*, 225, 228, 285; idem, *Historical View*, 4:230–31, 233, 251–55.

32. Millar, *Historical View*, 4:253–55; Hume, "Of Refinement in the Arts," *Essays*, 1:309; idem, *History of England*, 3:400 (Ch. XXVI); Kames, *Sketches*, 1:523 (Bk. I, Sk. vii), and 2:103–04 (Bk. II, Sk. v).

scribed by Brown. They approached this subject with a completely different spirit than he: like the English believers in general progress and unlike him, they did not reject the new eighteenth-century world of commerce and convenience. It was probably Brown whom Ferguson had in mind when writing that a moral censor accustomed to sleep on straw in a cottage would not propose that men return to caves and the woods for shelter, since "he admits the reasonableness and utility of what is already familiar; and apprehends an excess and corruption, only in the newest refinement of the rising generation." Considering the familiar to be the sole standard of behavior, the casuist who in one age condemned the use of coaches (as Brown did) "in another . . . would have no less censured the wearing of shoes." The Scots were not conservatives of this sort. To be sure, the excesses of vicious luxury did on the whole seem to them to constitute a real danger, and Kames, at least, occasionally worried that Britain was slowly falling into its toils.[33] But this peril, they believed, did not of necessity vitiate commerce or the development of society from rudeness to refinement, and in some respects it actually seemed to stimulate progress.

The Scots took much the same view of the division of labor. They had no doubt that, as a uniquely human phenomenon, it played a crucial role in the augmentation of human power and, indeed, in the whole process of refinement. For instance, Ferguson contended that "a people can make no great progress in cultivating the arts of life, until they have separated, and committed to different persons, the several tasks, which require a peculiar skill and attention." The reason, as both he and Hume pointed out, was that the savage or barbarian, "being employed in supplying all his different necessities, . . . never attains a perfection in any particular art." But through the "partition of employments, our ability encreases." This was especially true of the mechanical or useful arts, which advanced by having their different operations distributed among the greatest number of people. Such an arrangement, wrote Kames, saved time and promoted expertise. Smith agreed and added that it also encouraged technical innovation and the use of machines, since the man whose business in life was the performance of a small number of discrete tasks would tend to discover the cleverest way of going about them. In short, he

---

33. Hume, *Principles of Morals*, Sect. II, Pt. ii, in *Enquiries*, 181; Ferguson, *Civil Society*, 245; Kames, *Sketches*, 1:516, 518 (Bk. I, Sk. vii), and 2:104 (Bk. II, Sk. v).

believed, the division of employments was responsible for the "greatest improvement in the productive powers of labour," a contention that he supported with the famous illustration of the steps involved in pin-making.[34]

Because of the enhanced productivity that it occasioned, the division of labor, according to Smith, was "the great cause of the increase of public opulence" in any country. It enlarged the exchange of commodities and lowered their real price, so that "a general plenty diffuses itself through all the different ranks of society." In savage nations, men worked entirely for themselves and therefore could possess only the meager fruits of their own labor. But among cultivated peoples, who divided employments, necessities were far more liberally provided to all. And it was for this reason that "a common day labourer in Brittain [sic] has more luxury in his way of living than an [American] Indian sovereign" or than "an African king, the absolute master of the lives and liberties of ten thousand naked savages."[35]

The Scots thought that the division of labor produced more than purely economic benefits, however, arguing that it was essential for the advancement and success of almost every art, and the sciences, too. Smith was especially emphatic about its crucial function in the accumulation of knowledge. In "the progress of society," he asserted, philosophy or speculation became, like every other employment, the special and sole occupation of a single group of citizens and ultimately was subdivided into different branches. In the realm of the intellect no less than in other areas, this apportionment saved time and promoted the acquisition of expertise, with the result that "more work is done upon the whole, and the quantity of science is considerably increased." Thus, wrote Millar, "There can be no doubt that this division in the labours, both of art and of science, is calculated for promoting their improvement." By its means, Ferguson declared, polished nations attained "that air of superior ingenuity, under which

34. Ferguson, *Civil Society*, 180; Hume, *Treatise*, 485; Kames, *Sketches*, 1:151 (Bk. I, Sk. iv, Sect. 1); Smith, *Lectures on Jurisprudence*, 490–92, 341–47; idem, *Wealth of Nations*, 13–21. Agriculture was thought to be less susceptible of improvement through the division of labor: see Smith, *Wealth of Nations*, 16; Millar, *Historical View*, 4:153–54.

35. Smith, *Lectures on Jurisprudence*, 494, 489–91, 355, 338–47; idem, *Wealth of Nations*, 22, 24, 37. See also Ferguson, *Civil Society*, 181.

they appear to have gained the ends that were pursued by the savage in his forest, [namely] knowledge, order, and wealth."[36]

But were these benefits not almost or even completely nullified by simultaneous costs? Were they not necessarily compensated for and, in a kind of vicious circle, accompanied by losses of an enormous magnitude? Rousseau and, during the next century, Marx certainly answered such questions in the affirmative. It has sometimes been argued that the Scots did likewise: according to this theory, they held that in spite of—or, rather, because of—the material progress made possible by the division of labor, social health deteriorated and dehumanization arose in refined cultures.[37]

It is undoubtedly true that the Scottish *literati* expressed two related reservations about the effects of the division of labor. To begin with, they believed that it could easily force the lower classes of society into an existence with severely limited horizons. The constant application of a workman to one mechanical task, Kames observed, "confines the mind to a single object . . . : in such a train of life, the operator becomes dull and stupid, like a beast of burden." Laborers of this type would be incapable not only of real thought and inventiveness but also, as Millar put it, of drawing more than a little "improvement from the society of companions, bred to similar employments, with whom, if they have much intercourse, they are most likely to seek amusement in drinking and dissipation." Even where there was a political system designed to ensure equal rights, the result would be a two-tiered society, composed of what Ferguson referred to as "the few" and "the many." And in such circumstances, wrote Smith, "all the nobler parts of the human character may be, in a great measure, obliterated and extinguished in the great body of the people."[38]

36. Smith, *Wealth of Nations*, 21–22, 697; idem, *Lectures on Jurisprudence*, 492–93, 521, 347–49; Millar, *Historical View*, 4:141–44; Ferguson, *Civil Society*, 183–84, 189; idem, *Institutes*, 31. See also Kames, *Law-Tracts*, 52n; Robertson, "Progress of Society in Europe," Sect. I, Pt. vii, in *Works*, 3:61.

37. Forbes, "Introduction to Ferguson," xxxi–xxxvi; Pocock, *Machiavellian Moment*, 498–503; Robert R. Heilbroner, "The Paradox of Progress: Decline and Decay in *The Wealth of Nations*," in Andrew S. Skinner and Thomas Wilson, eds., *Essays on Adam Smith* (Oxford, 1975), 530–32.

38. Kames, *Sketches*, 1:152 (Bk. I, Sk. iv, Sect. 1); Millar, *Historical View*, 4:144–46, 151; Ferguson, *Civil Society*, 186–87; idem, *Principles*, 1:251; Smith, *Wealth of Nations*, 781–84; idem, *Lectures on Jurisprudence*, 539–40. See also Dunbar, *History of Mankind*, 424.

In addition, the Scots contended that the division of labor could prove harmful to the practice of citizenship. The ignorance and tunnel vision of the lower classes, Smith commented, prevented them from forming just judgments of either the real interest of their country or the ordinary duties of their private lives. They were equally incapable of defending their nation in war. Concentration on a narrow range of manual activities corrupted the courage of the typical workingman's mind and extinguished his martial spirit, making him regard the irregular, uncertain, and adventurous military life with abhorrence. It also corrupted his body, rendering him unable to exert his strength in any employment other than the one that perpetually occupied him. All of these considerations led Smith to conclude that the expertise of a laborer in a single, specialized function seemed to be "acquired at the expence of his intellectual, social, and martial virtues." Ferguson made a different point to the same effect. He argued that the full elaboration of the division of labor meant the creation of distinct groups engaged in military activities, statesmanship, and public administration, each of them separate from the other and from the great body of the people. Such a system, he claimed, gravely weakened a nation. It sapped the patriotism and destroyed the military character of common men by disqualifying them from the use of arms. Through its fragmentation and disjunction of employments, it left no one who could act in all the different roles, in the state and in the field, for which a national leader had to be qualified. In short, the separation of those "arts which form the citizen and the statesman, the arts of policy and war, is an attempt to dismember the human character, and to destroy those very arts we mean to improve," by depriving a people of what is necessary to their security and freedom.[39]

These are serious criticisms of the effects of the division of labor, relatively sophisticated forerunners of the ones later made by Marx. Unlike Marx, however, the Scots did not treat what Smith called the "disadvantages of a commercial spirit" as inevitably fatal to the refined stage of society in which they occurred. "To remedy these defects," said Smith in his Glasgow lectures on jurisprudence, "would be an object worthy of serious attention." If this remark indicates

39. Smith, *Wealth of Nations*, 781–82; idem, *Lectures on Jurisprudence*, 540–41; Ferguson, *Civil Society*, 181–82, 225–27, 230–32; idem, *Reflections Previous to the Establishment of a Militia* (London, 1756), 11–12. See also Kettler, *Social and Political Thought of Ferguson*, 100–01; Millar, *Ranks*, 285.

that the Scots were not without hope that the problems associated with the division of labor could be overcome, later comments in the *Wealth of Nations* point to a solution: government action to encourage public education and military training. Citing the example of the parish schools in Scotland and the relatively new charity schools in England, Smith argued that for a very small expense the state could establish a nationwide system of elementary instruction, which would facilitate the acquisition of the "most essential parts of education" by the "whole body of the people." Likewise, Millar thought that it was shortsighted, absurd, and even "revolting" to maintain that society could benefit from the ignorance of the laboring people. On the contrary, he claimed, the "great aim of the public" should be to counteract the natural tendency of mechanical employments by setting up schools designed to provide the "most useful, but humble class of citizens, that knowledge which their way of life has, in some degree, prevented them from acquiring." Ferguson, too, believed that general education was essential if the harmful effects of "mere wealth" on society were to be avoided. But he particularly insisted on the need for institutionally reuniting the "talents for the council and the field" in individual members of the elite, and for requiring military training and service in all citizens. Such state-imposed remedies, he and Smith contended, could prevent decay from draining the intellectual and physical strength of a commercial people.[40]

Thus, Dunbar once again spoke for his contemporaries when he said that the "subdivision of arts, which is so conducive to their perfection, degrades the character of the common artizan," causing him to fall into a torpor that "implies the absence or annihilation of every manly virtue"—"if the tendency of his occupation is not counteracted by some expedient of government."[41] The reservation is crucial. The Scots were surely concerned about the costs of the division of labor, yet they had no desire to forsake its enormous benefits. As one of the motor forces behind the progress of society from rudeness to refinement, it had to be allowed to operate, while its inherent dangers could and should be minimized through state intervention.

40. Smith, *Lectures on Jurisprudence*, 541; idem, *Wealth of Nations*, 781–87; Millar, *Historical View*, 4:158–61; Ferguson, *Principles*, 1:254; idem, *Civil Society*, 30–31, 227–32. The views of Ferguson and Smith did differ significantly on some issues related to proposals for a citizens' militia: see John Robertson, *The Scottish Enlightenment and the Militia Issue* (Edinburgh, 1985), esp. Chaps. 3, 7, 8.

41. Dunbar, *History of Mankind*, 402, 404.

No more than luxury was it considered to be a terminal historical disease.

The Scots' analysis of the two great problems that they associated with basic economic and social change, though hardly producing pessimism about the course of history, did tend to circumscribe their enthusiasm for the process of refinement. It led them to conceive of the progress of civilization in a more limited way than their English counterparts did. For they were suggesting, ultimately, that the over-all improvement of any nation became a conditional affair once the commercial stage of development had been reached. Thereafter, the continuing progress of society as a whole depended upon overcoming the potential obstacles introduced by luxury and the partition of employments. Such contingency, the Scots believed, was an integral feature of the natural history of mankind.

NATURAL HISTORY AND THE HISTORICAL RECORD

The Scots' awareness of the conditional or limited nature of progress, apparent in their assessment of luxury and the division of labor, also frequently manifested itself in their opinions about the historical development of the most important noneconomic fields of human activity. As their comments on the positive effects of the division of labor have already indicated, they thought that the arts and sciences were generally progressive: man, stated Ferguson, was a being who, originally ignorant and rude, was "advancing in knowledge and art." According to standard Scottish natural history, the practical arts came first, taking their rise from sheer necessity. With increased agricultural productivity, human beings gained the wherewithal and leisure to improve useful techniques and to invent the fine arts. Only then did knowledge become sufficiently systematic for the sciences to begin. Hume wrote more extensively and analytically on the totality of the arts and sciences than did the rest of his countrymen. But they certainly agreed with him that, after ancient glories and Gothic darkness, a revival of thought and culture had been initiated in Europe at the end of the Middle Ages. By the early seventeenth century, the "minds of men . . . seem to have undergone a general, but insensible revolution": the cultivation of letters spread, mechanical and liberal arts "were every day receiving great improvements," and as a consequence of this "universal fermentation" the ideas of men "enlarged themselves on all sides." At present, said Kames,

"European nations are daily improving in every art and in every science." What causes were responsible for such progress as this in the
arts and sciences as a whole? Hume's answer—personal liberty and
security, the mutual influence and rivalry of neighboring states, the
opportunity for true emulation, plus an active economy—was not
particularly controversial among the *literati*. But Kames would have
added to this list the arousal of a nation "out of a torpid state by some
fortunate change of circumstances," and the engagement of a people
in "some important action of doubtful event" (like a struggle for
liberty or resistance to foreign invasion).[42]

Of course, the Scots' impression of conditions in the Dark Ages
convinced them that the arts and sciences, as a unit, were not imper-
vious to decay. Kames tried to account for such decline by referring to
the problem of great predecessors, whose achievements could restrict
or destroy emulation. But only Hume ever claimed, like Bolingbroke,
that degeneration was in some respect built into the historical process. In his *History of England*, he once depicted the "rise, progress,
perfection, and decline of art and science" as a theme recurrent over
time. Elsewhere, he argued that when the arts and sciences arrive at
perfection in any country, "from that moment they naturally, or
rather necessarily decline, and seldom or never revive in that nation,
where they formerly flourished," because their soil has been exhausted. These rather somber observations, however, were not
Hume's definitive word on the subject, since he held that the existence of fresh soil made transplantation possible. "The arts and sciences," he wrote,

> indeed, have flourished in one period, and have decayed in
> another: But we may observe, that, at the time when they rose
> to greatest perfection among one people, they were perhaps
> totally unknown to all the neighboring nations; and though

42. Ferguson, *Principles*, 1:198; Hume, *History of England*, 3:297–98, 406 (Chs.
XXIII, XXVI), and 6:21 (Ch. XLV); idem, "Of the Rise and Progress of the Arts and
Sciences" (1742) and "Of Refinement in the Arts," *Essays*, 1:176–86, 195, 300–02;
Kames, *Sketches*, 1:322, 146–50, 128, 172, 280, 401 (Bk. I, Sks. iv–v). On progress in the
arts and sciences, see also Robertson, *History of America*, Bk. IV, in *Works*, 6:248;
Smith, "The Principles which lead and direct Philosophical Enquiries; illustrated by
the History of Astronomy" (written before 1758), *Essays on Philosophical Subjects*,
50; Ferguson, *Civil Society*, 167–68, 171–72, 175, 189; Dunbar, *History of Mankind*,
230–31; Millar, *Ranks*, 284, 217; idem, *Historical View*, 4:138, 143, 163–67. For some
reservations about the necessity of *political* (as opposed to *personal*) liberty for progress
in the arts and sciences, see Hume, "Of Civil Liberty" (1741), *Essays*, 1:157–59.

they universally decayed in one age, yet in a succeeding generation they again revived, and diffused themselves over the
world.

Given the fact that this remark was set in the context of a comparison
of ancient with modern times, it is likely that the revival Hume had
in mind was the Renaissance. If so, he found no evidence that the
ensuing diffusion would culminate in a new round of retrogression
within the foreseeable future. On the contrary, he specifically contended that the "general revolution . . . in human affairs" inaugurated during the fifteenth century had not suffered any setbacks to
date.[43] No more than his fellow *literati* did he present a clearly formulated cyclical theory of the development of art and science, even
though they all believed that significant reverses were always possible, and had actually occurred, in this broad field.

A similar noncyclical mixture of advancement and retrogression
was discerned by the Scots in the fine arts, in particular. Ferguson
thought that what he referred to as the "elegant and literary arts"
were based upon materials "which cannot be exhausted, . . . proceed
from desires which cannot be satiated," and therefore probably "will
ever make a part of the unrestrained progress of human nature." That
these arts were presently advancing and could potentially be
"cultivated to a high degree of refinement" in the future was maintained by Kames; that they had already made much "conspicuous"
progress seemed clear to Millar. Improvement of this sort, according
to Hume, often originated by accident or through "secret and unknown causes," and it tended to become marked in the necessarily
polite environment of monarchies (as opposed to republics). For Ferguson, the fine arts first grew up as a result of the leisure made available by the division of labor. Thereafter, the "monuments of art produced in one age remain with the ages that follow; and serve as a kind
of ladder," so that there has been a "mounting upon steps which ages
successively place."[44] Hearkening back to the traditional Baconian

43. Kames, *Sketches*, 1:150–51, 244–46 (Bk. I, Sk. iv); Hume, *History of England*,
3:297, 406–07 (Chs. XXIII, XXVI); idem, "Of the Rise and Progress of the Arts and
Sciences" and "Of the Populousness of Ancient Nations," *Essays*, 1:195, 197, 382. On
the decay of the arts and sciences in the Dark Ages, see Robertson, "Progress of Society
in Europe," Sect. I, Introduction, in *Works*, 3:16–17.
44. Ferguson, *Civil Society*, 217; idem, *Principles*, 1:293, 296–99; Kames,
Sketches, 2:420 (Bk. II, Sk. i, Sect. 2); idem, *Elements of Criticism* (1762), 6th ed., 2 vols.
(Edinburgh, 1785), 1:7 (Introduction), and 2:501–04 (Ch. XXV); Millar, *Historical*

principle of cumulative progress in learning, this metaphor suggested that the fine arts were likely to advance continuously.

Nevertheless, the Scots sometimes portrayed these arts as being quite vulnerable to deterioration. Kames, for example, held that there were several reasons why taste—on which, he said, the fine arts entirely depended—could assume a "retrograde motion" after having reached maturity. Chief among these were the debilitating effects of despotism, vicious luxury, and the quest for innovation (spawned by the desire to excel through originality). Ferguson and Hume especially emphasized the psychologically restricting influence of great models from the past, which the latter said "naturally extinguish" emulation and the ardor for creativity. Comparing the magnificent works of his predecessors with his own youthful efforts, and seeing the great disparity between them, the young artist "is discouraged from any farther attempts, and never aims at a rivalship with those authors, whom he so much admires." Neither Hume nor any of the other Scots ever suggested, as did Priestley, that there might be a way out of this difficulty, although Millar did claim that poetry could be "easily" transferred from a country where it had decayed to another nation.[45]

In contrast, the *practical* arts were not found to exhibit a substantial tendency toward decay. To be sure, Hume thought that the collapse of the Roman Empire proved destructive to them, although Kames was not convinced even of this. Both of them agreed with Robertson, however, that a necessary art of life would seldom go into decline and almost never be lost, because it remained in constant use. Indeed, as Ferguson wrote, such arts appeared from the natural history of mankind to "admit of perpetual refinements." The savage faced so much hardship in procuring the bare necessities of life, argued Millar, that he had no leisure or incentive to do more than merely subsist. Then, slowly and gradually, he made "those improvements which tend to multiply and accumulate the necessaries." As he developed further, noted Kames, he was "not long contented with simple necessaries: an unwearied appetite to be more and more comforta-

View, 4:313–14; Hume, "Of Eloquence" (1742) and "Of the Rise and Progress of the Arts and Sciences," *Essays*, 1:170, 176, 184–86.

45. Kames, *Sketches*, 1:171, 220–21, 248 (Bk. I, Sk. iv, Sect. 2); idem, *Elements of Criticism*, 2:500–01 (Ch. XXV); Ferguson, *Civil Society*, 217; Hume, "Of the Rise and Progress of the Arts and Sciences," *Essays*, 1:195–96; Millar, *Historical View*, 4:323–28.

bly provided, [led him] from necessaries to conveniences, and from these to every sort of luxury." Consequently, Ferguson explained, the practical arts were "continued, multiplied, and extended to supply a continued or increasing consumption, and to gratify multiplied and accumulating wants." Man "suits his means to the ends he has in view; and, by multiplying contrivances, proceeds, by degrees, to the perfection of his arts." The invention of new devices, especially, depended on the ability of individuals to pursue their own goals, and on the inheritance by one age of the techniques acquired during its predecessors.[46]

Progress in the practical arts, the Scots believed, increased human comfort, rendering the environment "more wholesome, and friendly to life," as Robertson put it. His reference to the invention and use of the compass, which "opened to man the dominion of the sea, and . . . put him in full possession of the earth," illustrates what the Scots thought was another effect of the improvement of these arts: greater power of humankind over nature. The theme of increased power over the external world was adopted by Dunbar, who urged his readers to "wage war with the elements" so as to assume command of them. Their rebellious nature could be broken, he asserted, because soil and climate were "susceptible of improvement, and variable, in a high degree, with the progress of civil arts." Along with the provision of comfort and the enlargement of power, certain social benefits seemed to accrue from advances in the practical arts. "The tendency of improvement in all the arts of life," Millar stated flatly, "has been uniformly the same; to enable mankind more easily to gain a livelihood by the exercise of their talents, without being subject to the caprice, or caring for the displeasure of others; that is, to render the lower classes of the people less dependent upon their superiors." If, as Ferguson argued, the onrush of technical change was stimulated by the freedom of individuals to seek their own ends, wealth and personal independence were promoted by that very change.[47]

Ferguson and the others devoted more attention to the fate of

46. Hume, *History of England*, 3:298 (Ch. XXIII); idem, "Of the Rise and Progress of the Arts and Sciences," *Essays*, 1:185; Kames, *Sketches*, 2:246 (Bk. II, Sk. ix), and 1:150, 220, 323 (Bk. I, Sks. iv–v); Robertson, *History of America*, Bk. IV, in *Works*, 6:248; Ferguson, *Civil Society*, 216–17, 168–70; idem, *Principles*, 1:242; Millar, *Ranks*, 183; idem, *Historical View*, 4:204.

47. Robertson, *History of America*, Bks. IV and I, in *Works*, 6:235, 237, 34; Dunbar, *History of Mankind*, 338, 342–43; Millar, *Historical View*, 4:128; idem, *Ranks*, 292, 295, 316; Ferguson, *Principles*, 1:242–44.

knowledge or learning than to any other facet of improvement in the arts and sciences, believing that in no respect was human progress "less questionable, than . . . in the attainment of knowledge." "Less questionable," of course, did not mean "absolutely certain and uniform," and not only because of the Dark Ages. For instance, Millar indicated that the science of psychology could be extended only within rather narrow limits. Smith dryly spoke of "that summit of perfection to which [philosophy] is at present supposed to have arrived, and to which, indeed, it has equally been supposed to have arrived in almost all former times." And even Ferguson contended that knowledge could give way to ignorance in a nation and was subject to diminution when men sought only to learn what their illustrious predecessors had taught.[48]

Such opinions did not prevent the Scots from claiming that there was, to use Hume's term, a "natural progress of human thought." That is, they affirmed with Robertson that the ideas of man "extend not beyond that state of society to which he is habituated," and that the "faculties of the human mind hold nearly the same course in their progress" everywhere. Robertson sketched the broad outlines of this course of natural intellectual progress with an analogy. "As the individual advances from the ignorance and imbecility of the infant state to vigour and maturity of understanding," he wrote, "something similar to this may be observed in the progress of the species." In the rude state of society, man's mental powers were "feeble and defective"; only among polished nations did his reason come to be exercised. Ferguson presented the transition in a different way: "the natural progress of knowledge . . . is, from particular specimens, to the general combination and system of the whole," from a concern with the facts themselves to the formulation of general laws whose application explains phenomena. In his posthumously published *Essays on Philosophical Subjects* (1795), Smith sought to reconstruct the history of thought in somewhat greater detail. A predecessor in this regard of Auguste Comte, he posited two great stages of mental development. In the first of these, entitled "superstition," savages showed little curiosity to discover the "hidden chains of events" that connect the "seemingly disjointed appearances of nature." Therefore, they ascribed every event whose operations did not seem perfectly regular

48. Ferguson, *Principles*, 1:271, 282; idem, *Civil Society*, 217; Millar, *Historical View*, 4:171; Smith, "History of Astronomy," *Essays on Philosophical Subjects*, 46.

(such as storms and comets) to the direction of "invisible and designing" powers—the gods, demons, witches, genies, and fairies of polytheism. But when the establishment of law brought order and security to society, and when subsistence ceased to be precarious, then the curiosity of human beings increased while their fears diminished. Leisure gave them more opportunity for and interest in a systematic explanation of unusual natural phenomena. It was mere wonder, then, and not any expectation of advantage from discovery that actuated humankind to move from superstition to "philosophy," the earliest branch of which, as Ferguson agreed, was natural philosophy or physics. Later, the same systematizing spirit gave birth to moral philosophy or ethics. "Logick, or the science of the general principles of good and bad reasoning," arose last, as proponents of each system of physics and ethics tried to expose weaknesses in the others.[49]

Over the long run, Smith suggested, the tendency of philosophical systems was toward simplification. Inventors equipped the earliest machines with a multitude of moving parts, he wrote, but succeeding mechanics discovered that the same effects could be more easily produced with fewer wheels having fewer principles of motion. Just so with systems of thought: their first formulators found it necessary to unite every pair of seemingly unrelated appearances with a separate causal chain, while later thinkers arrived at a single great connecting principle to explain "all the discordant phaenomena that occur in a whole species of things." Smith also concluded that whatever branch of thought had made the greatest advances at any moment would be the most fashionable and prestigious one of the time. In classical antiquity, he claimed, the queens of the sciences were rhetoric and logic, overshadowing natural philosophy (which had decayed after its early glory). The intellectual fire of Greece was passed on to Rome, but, as Hume declared, the barbarian invasions "overwhelmed all human knowledge . . . ; and men sunk [sic] every age deeper into ignorance, stupidity, and superstition; till the light of ancient science and history had very nearly suffered a total extinc-

49. Hume, *Natural History of Religion*, Sect. I, in *Essays*, 2:311; Robertson, *History of America*, Bk. IV, in *Works*, 6:354–55, 380, 283–84; Ferguson, *Principles*, 1:273, 279, 307; Smith, "History of Astronomy," *Essays on Philosophical Subjects*, 48–51; idem, *Wealth of Nations*, 767–70. Although he did not specifically cite Robertson or Hume in this context, Smith undoubtedly benefited from the *History of America* (in *Works*, 6:353) and the *Natural History of Religion* (Sects. I–V), both of which present a speculative account of superstition and polytheism similar to his.

tion." Very nearly yet not completely, since three repositories of learning remained. Robertson and Hume gave due credit, respectively, to the Muslims and Byzantine Greeks and to some Catholic clergymen for retaining a superior knowledge and preserving the precious literature of antiquity. From these sources there came by the twelfth century a new queen of the sciences, scholastic theology. Wrong-headed and elitist though Robertson considered it to be, it was recognized by him as the first sign of a human mind reawakening after centuries of lethargy, the "first production of the spirit of inquiry after it began to resume some degree of activity and vigour in Europe."[50]

Kames described the Renaissance as a time in which men "restored reason to her privileges," having begun to think for themselves rather than continuing slavishly to follow Aristotle. For Robertson, the fifteenth and sixteenth centuries were the pivotal period when the "human mind felt its own strength, broke the fetters of authority, . . . and, venturing to move in a larger sphere, pushed its inquiries into every subject, with great boldness and surprising success." From this point on, the Scots were sure, tremendous intellectual progress had been made. The advance started with physics, Millar noted, but he and the others also found it conspicuous in most disciplines and in method. Thus, Robertson could refer to the "universal progress of science, during the last two centuries," while Kames could write that "human understanding is in a progress toward maturity, however slow." Smith especially insisted on the role played in all this recent enlightenment by Newton, who, with his discoveries and scientific method, produced "the most happy, and, we may now say, the greatest and most admirable improvement that was ever made in philosophy."[51]

Reason, said Dunbar, "stands in need of culture, and arrives gradually at different stages of perfection." His contemporaries were well aware of this gradualness. Kames, for instance, thought it "lament-

50. Smith, "History of Astronomy," *Essays on Philosophical Subjects*, 66–69; idem, *Lectures on Rhetoric*, 181–82; Hume, *History of England*, 3:297–98, 454 (Ch. XXIII and Note L); Robertson, "Progress of Society in Europe," Sect. I, Pt. ix, and Notes X and XXVIII, in *Works*, 3:66–68, and 5:215, 299–300.

51. Kames, *Sketches*, 2:420–21 (Bk. III, Sk. i, Sect. 2), and 3:257 (Bk. III, Sk. iii, Ch. 1); Robertson, *History of Scotland*, Bk. II, in *Works*, 1:114; idem, *Charles V*, Preface, in *Works*, 3:[vii]; idem, "Progress of Society in Europe," Note XXVIII, in *Works*, 5:300; Millar, *Historical View*, 4:163–64, 275, 277, 280; Smith, *Lectures on Rhetoric*, 145–46; idem, "History of Astronomy," *Essays on Philosophical Subjects*, 103–05, 98.

able to observe the slow progress of human understanding and the faculty of reason." But he was also reflecting the outlook of his fellow Scots when he contended that the intellect "is in a progress toward maturity, however slow," and that "enlightened reason has un-masked [ancient] fables, and left them in their nakedness." Kames took comfort in these facts. Likewise, his cousin Hume looked at the "still imperfect State of our Knowlege [sic]" and wondered whether men could "ever reach a much more perfect State; while the rich have so many more alluring Appetites to gratify than that for Knowlege, and the poor are occupyed [sic] in daily Labour." Yet he told Turgot that he earnestly wished these doubts to be allayed, since the "con-trary Opinion is much more consolatory, and is an Incitement to every Virtue and laudable Pursuit." Such consolation and incitement he obviously felt when writing the *Treatise*. In that book, he deplored the "present imperfect condition of the sciences," while arguing that it was "impossible to tell what changes and improvements" could be wrought in all the sciences by a thorough acquaintance with human nature. Once the capital science of man was conquered, wrote the arch-skeptic in a military image, "we may every where else hope for an easy victory" in the struggle for intellectual progress.[52]

Hume's contemporaries would not have disagreed with his con-clusion that learning grew most vigorously in republics, where free-dom of thought prevailed. Except for Ferguson, however, the *literati* placed more importance than he on the role played by leisure and the security and tranquillity of life in the advancement of knowledge.[53] In any case all of them believed that knowledge was naturally pro-gressive and, historically, had progressed within certain limits, what-ever the causes.

Manners and morals, in their view, presented a similar picture. Along with Ferguson, Hume thought that there had been "a consider-able advancement" in moral philosophy, but he doubted whether it had as yet exerted any influence on practice. Nonetheless, the Scots were certain that morality improved with the passage of time. The

52. Dunbar, *History of Mankind*, 44; Kames, *Sketches*, 2:472–73 (Bk. III, Sk. i, Sect. 2); Hume to Turgot, June 16, 1768, in *The Letters of David Hume*, ed. J. Y. T. Grieg, 2 vols. (Oxford, 1932), 2:181; Hume, *Treatise*, xiii–xvi.

53. Hume, "Of the Rise and Progress of the Arts and Sciences," *Essays*, 1:184–87; Ferguson, *Civil Society*, 178; Smith, "History of Astronomy," *Essays on Philosophical Subjects*, 50, 67; Robertson, *History of America*, Bk. IV, in *Works*, 6:284; idem, "Prog-ress of Society in Europe," Sect. I, Introduction, in *Works*, 3:16.

"disposition and manners of men," wrote Robertson, "are formed by their situation, and arise from the state of society in which they live. . . . In proportion as it advances in improvement, their manners refine." Ferguson claimed that history revealed the "progress of moral apprehension and manners," and that the "tendency of this progress is to make the real welfare and peace of society, founded in justice, the rule of propriety and estimation in all the external actions of men." Likewise, Kames believed that the principles of morality, though originally rooted in human nature, grew up gradually and "advance[d] toward maturity." This process, though very slow, was nevertheless definitely recognizable and formed an integral part of the transition from rudeness to refinement.[54]

During the infancy of mankind, according to Kames, the desire for self-preservation reigned supreme, there were no established rules of conduct, and, given the prevailing intellectual limitations, the tyranny of appetites and passions prohibited the formation of general moral principles. As a direct consequence, at that early stage the innate moral sense was feeble in its operation, and "barbarity, roughness, and cruelty" were the norm. Smith argued slightly differently that the savage, finding himself in continual personal distress and danger, felt passions "all mounted to the highest pitch of fury" while paying little or no attention to the plight of his fellows. Not expecting sympathy from others, he offered them none and was "obliged to smother and conceal the appearance of every passion," thereby acquiring the habit of dissimulation and falsehood. Yet the vengeance of the savage, when he gave way to it, was "always sanguinary and dreadful," and he indulged in such great barbarities as the murder of infants whom he could not support. This whole situation changed, Smith agreed with Millar, when increasing security and affluence gave men more leisure "to exert the social affections, and to cultivate those arts which tend to soften and humanize the temper." Under the influence of these new circumstances, said Kames, a nation (like an individual) matured and eventually acquired "a refined taste in morals." Internal senses such as order, propriety, dignity, and grace, which had no value

54. Hume, *Treatise*, 469, 621; Ferguson, *Principles*, 1:300–02, 310, and 2:2; idem, *Civil Society*, 94, 246; Robertson, *History of America*, Bk. IV, in *Works*, 6:246; Kames, *Sketches*, 3:378, 102, 201 (Bk. III, Sk. iii, Ch. 3, Sect. 2; Sk. ii, Introduction, and Pt. 2); idem, *Essays on the Principles of Morality and Natural Religion*, 1st ed. (Edinburgh, 1751), 137, 143 (Pt. I, Essay ii, Ch. 9).

for the savage, came into use. The "selfish passions" were tamed and subdued, the "malevolent" or "stormy" passions extinguished themselves, and the "social affections" gained the ascendancy.[55]

Therefore, the Scots believed, a decisive difference existed between barbarous and polished people in morals and manners. Hume stated quite simply that "vice is much less frequent in the cultivated ages." Smith would not go so far. But he was convinced that the virtues founded upon humanity and sensibility to others were far more prominent among the members of civilized nations, whose passions were seldom so furious, desperate, or hurtful as those of early men. That there was what Millar called "a natural progress . . . from rude, to civilized manners," and that, as Kames insisted, the moral sense became increasingly acute through discipline and education in civilized society, seemed to Robertson to be borne out by European history since the Dark Ages. He observed that the spirit of chivalry inculcated more liberal and generous sentiments among the nobility and exerted a strong influence in "refining the manners of European nations." Later, the advance of science, literature, and commerce added further polish to manners, led to the exercise of greater humanity, and introduced "that civility and refinement by which [the countries of Europe] are now distinguished." Kames agreed with Robertson about the effect of the revival of letters on behavior, although the manners of the eighteenth century gave him pause. As for the future, Ferguson considered his own period merely "a transition to a better, in which malice, in the progress of information, will be corrected; and every other evil disposition or habit, resulting from [human] ignorance or false apprehensions will be suppressed."[56] This exceedingly cheerful prognostication, while unique among the *liter-*

55. Kames, *Principles of Morality and Natural Religion*, 1st ed., 136–46 (Pt. I, Essay ii, Ch. 9); idem, *Sketches*, 3:116, 202–04 (Bk. III, Sk. ii, Pt. 1, Sect. 2; Sk. ii, Pt. 2), and 2:83 (Bk. II, Sk. iii); idem, *Law-Tracts*, 59; Adam Smith, *The Theory of Moral Sentiments*, ed. D. D. Raphael and A. L. Macfie (Oxford, 1976), 205–10 (Pt. V, Ch. ii); Millar, *Ranks*, 238; idem, *Historical View*, 4:186–87. It should be recalled that the concept of an innate moral sense held by Kames was rejected by Smith, and that it constituted only a part of Hume's ethical theory.

56. Hume, "Of Refinement in the Arts," *Essays*, 1:309n; idem, *History of England*, 1:222 (Appendix I); Smith, *Theory of Moral Sentiments*, 204–05, 208–09, 341 (Pt. V, Ch. ii; Pt. VII, Sect. iv); Millar, *Ranks*, 176; [Henry Home, Lord Kames], *Principles of Equity* (Edinburgh, 1760), v; idem, *Principles of Morality and Natural Religion*, 1st ed., 142–48 (Pt. I, Essay ii, Ch. 9); idem, *Sketches*, 1:293, 306, 334 (Bk. I, Sk. v); Robertson, "Progress of Society in Europe," Sect. I, Pts. viii–x, in *Works*, 3:62–63, 65, 69; Ferguson, *Principles*, 1:182.

ati, is at least indicative of their optimism about the general historical trend of behavior patterns.

It is true, of course, that the Scots did not consider that trend to be uniformly positive, because they could never forget the actual or potential problems linked to luxury and the division of labor. Millar made this clear. He claimed that the transition from rudeness to refinement was inimical to courage and fortitude, because it accustomed human beings to a life of ease and tranquillity. Likewise, licentiousness appeared to him to be the "inseparable attendant of great opulence," although, in Europe, Christianity had significantly contributed to the retardation of that vice. The enrichment flowing from trade was "unfavourable to generosity, and to the higher exertions of benevolence," he thought, since individuals in a commercial society usually could not sacrifice their own pecuniary interest to the good of others. These are weighty charges. But Millar was no Rousseau (whose polemics against civilization he found "paradoxical"), and the other side of his moral balance sheet of the ages was more than offsetting. If the inhabitants of civilized societies showed less courage and fortitude than did their predecessors, still they had a "lively sensibility and exquisite fellow-feeling" that was previously absent. Their "manners . . . are softened, their social dispositions are awakened, and they feel more and more an attraction which leads them to conform their behaviour to the general standard." If they often exhibited excessive sexual passions, they also were comparatively abstemious in drinking. If they were incapable of great generosity and benevolence, yet "a limited and regulated charity" could be expected from them. And the "advancement of arts, manufactures, and commerce has a tendency to improve the virtue of justice in all its branches," a fact of supreme importance. For mere generosity without a precise observance of the rules of justice "is of less consequence to the prosperity and good order of society, than the latter, though without any considerable share of the former." In sum,

> it may be concluded, that the manners of an opulent and luxurious age are, upon the whole, favourable to the general intercourse of society. . . . [Under these circumstances, men] are likely to communicate to each other, and to enjoy, all that security, ease, and tranquillity, all that comfort and satisfaction which can reasonably be desired.[57]

57. Millar, *Historical View,* 4:175, 184–88, 212–13, 236, 245, 253–55.

In the shift from savage to civilized manners and morals, the benefits exceeded the costs.

The Scots believed that this transition was closely connected to the progress of government and law. For example, Hume and Millar contended that the slow expansion in the range of human affections, the "gradual advancement of a people in civilized manners," had a "natural tendency" to increase the small regard given to justice by savages. Or as Ferguson remarked, while men of real virtue "are destined to live, the states they compose are likewise doomed by the fates to survive, and to prosper."[58]

But for how long? The terminology used by Ferguson—"destined," "doomed," "fates"—bears a strong resemblance to that of Machiavelli in *The Prince* and the *Discourses*. In fact, the Scots were well acquainted with and sometimes seemed to approve of the Italian's related opinions that all things human were mortal and that the political affairs of all states followed a two-stage cycle (order-disorder, good-bad). Thus, Kames observed that "states are seldom stationary; but, like the sun, are either advancing to their meridian, or falling down gradually till they sink into obscurity." Smith spoke to his students of the "fated dissolution that awaits every state and constitution whatever." And Hume saw in history the "rise, progress, declension, and final extinction of the most flourishing empires," thinking as he did "that every government must come to a period, and that death is unavoidable to the political as well as to the animal body." Yet such views did not by any means lead to gloom. The operation of an inexorable political cycle and the "supposed fatality in human affairs" were rejected by Ferguson because he thought that no state ever suffered internal decay except from preventable failures: errors in its policy and vice and weakness of manners among its citizens. Similarly, without pretending that it could have immortality, Hume claimed that his proposed perfect commonwealth "would flourish for many ages," and he felt that this prediction was "a sufficient incitement to human endeavors."[59] If there

58. Hume, *Treatise*, 488–89; idem, *Principles of Morals*, Sect. III, Pt. i, in *Enquiries*, 192; Millar, *Ranks*, 238, 301; Ferguson, *Civil Society*, 280.

59. Kames, *Sketches*, 2:92 (Bk. II, Sk. iv); Smith, *Lectures on Jurisprudence*, 414; Hume, "Of the Study of History" (1741), "Whether the British Government inclines more to Absolute Monarchy, or to a Republic" (1741), and "Idea of a perfect Commonwealth" (1752), *Essays*, 2:389, and 1:126, 493 (cf. idem, *History of England*, 7:347 [Ch. LXII]); Ferguson, *Civil Society*, 279–80, 232–33.

was a Machiavellian "cycle of commonwealths" at all, its downturn could long be delayed.

That Hume and the others took this position was due in large measure to their assessment of the natural history of government and law from rudeness to refinement. According to Millar, the precautions instituted by a rude people for preventing injustice and maintaining order and peace were simple. Over time, however, experience, the gradual expansion of the understanding, the division of labor, and the accumulation of wealth all suggested new regulations for removing particular breaches of justice and for the security and enjoyment of material acquisitions. Therefore, in the "gradual progress of government" there was a recognizable movement toward more comprehensive and civilized "systems of policy." Like property, government exhibited a "natural growth," as Kames put it. "From that weak and infantine state in which both are found originally," he wrote, "both of them, by equal degrees of improvement, have arrived at that stability and perfection which they enjoy at present." He added that the evolution of law, in which he had a special scholarly interest, ran parallel to that of government and property: "In the social state under regular discipline, law ripens gradually with the human faculties," as many previously neglected duties are discovered to be binding on the conscience and can no longer be ignored by tribunals of justice. It was for this reason that civil and criminal jurisdiction "came gradually to be improved to its present state," one of "perfection," the "last and most shining period" of law.[60]

Neither Ferguson nor any of his countrymen had any primitivist regrets about all of these governmental and legal changes. He thought it unnecessary to refute the arguments of those who, "in judging of political establishments, recur to the first suggestions of nature, as the model of what mankind are forever bound to retain." For the institutions that "arise . . . from the instincts of nature, although they may serve for ages the purpose of political establishment, are however no more than a rude material on which the ingenuity of man is to be exercised" by removing their inconveniences and later drawing out their advantages. Kames made this point plain in his two reconstructions of the history of political forms. In one, every nation

60. Millar, *Historical View*, 3:2–3; idem, *Ranks*, 304; Kames, *Law-Tracts*, 35–36, 94, 19–20, 41, 46, 46n; idem, *Principles of Equity*, iv. See also Smith, *Theory of Moral Sentiments*, 341 (Pt. VII, Sect. iv).

was said to begin as a pure democracy ("the very worst form of government, if we make not an exception of despotism") and then, under the pressure of increasing population, to come to be led by a senate. "From this form of government, the transition is easy to a limited monarchy," which represented progress because mixed governments—whether republican or monarchical, depending on the size of the state—promoted human activity but seldom dangerous excesses. In Kames's alternative model, the mild government provided by a democracy proved inadequate for the repression of "dissocial passions" triggered by increasing opulence, and it was replaced by an absolute monarchy "contradictory to the liberty that all men should enjoy." This form, in turn, eventually lost its harshness as men became by degrees "regular and orderly under a steady administration." Government then returned at last to "its original temper of mildness and humanity," but without reinstating the turbulence of democracy.[61] Here the long-term trend was quite clearly toward a mixture of order and liberty, and, as in his other reconstruction, Kames presented the form of government coming latest in time as the best.

Once more, the course of affairs in Europe seemed to the Scots to confirm what natural history indicated. Millar agreed with Smith and Robertson that progress in commerce and the arts promoted freedom (even freedom for the masses in opulent and polished nations), and that this was exactly what had happened when a "spirit of liberty . . . was gradually infused into the great body of the people" even before the Reformation. Hume explored this development at greater length in his *History of England*, where he used the later Middle Ages and early modern period to illustrate the general thesis—first set forth by him in 1752—that progress in the arts was favorable to liberty. An important consequence of the revival of the arts after 1100, he argued, "was the introduction and progress of freedom; and this consequence

61. Ferguson, *Principles*, 1:257–58, 260–61; Kames, *Sketches*, 2:57–64 (Bk. II, Sks. ii–iii). As reported by a student, Smith's Glasgow lectures discuss the succession of political and legal forms at much greater length than do Kames's *Sketches*, and they mix natural with European history. According to Millar, however, the intent of the lectures was similar to that of the judge's remarks: "to trace the gradual progress of jurisprudence, both public and private, from the rudest to the most refined ages, and to point out the effects of those arts which contribute to subsistence, and to the accumulation of property, in producing corresponding improvements or alterations in law and government." See Smith, *Lectures on Jurisprudence*, 401–37, 200–330; Stewart, "Account of Smith," in *Collected Works*, 10:12.

affected men both in their *personal* and *civil* capacities." Personal liberty increased because, as agriculture improved and the use of money spread, manorial lords thought it advantageous to transform serfs into rent-paying freemen. In the end, "*personal* freedom became almost general in Europe," a circumstance that "paved the way for the increase of *political* or *civil* liberty," or at least for "the most considerable advantages of it." For with the subsequent enlargement of commerce and navigation came a further increase of industry and the arts, which led the nobles to dissipate their fortunes in the pursuit of expensive pleasures. Their financial embarrassment allowed the middle classes (who were creating a new, mercantile type of wealth) to acquire a share of the landed property. In some nations, the "privileges of the commons increased by this increase of property." But even in other countries, where powerful kings arose as the nobles declined, the "condition of the people . . . received great improvement," since they were released from the control of the "petty tyrants by whom they had formerly been oppressed rather than governed." As Smith recognized, Hume was the first of the Scots to point out how socio-economic changes contributed to the rise of liberty and effective government in Europe.[62]

Indeed, Hume believed that such improvements, once begun, had continued up to his own time. Free and absolute governments alike, he observed,

> seem to have undergone, in modern times, a great change for the better, with regard both to foreign and domestic management. The *balance of power* is a secret in politics, fully known only to the present age; and I must add, that the internal POLICE of states has also received great improvements within the last century. . . .
>
> But though all governments be improved in modern times, yet monarchical government seems to have made the greatest

---

62. Millar, *Ranks*, 284, 316; idem, *Historical View*, 2:431–35, and 3:1–2; Hume, "Of Refinement in the Arts," *Essays*, 1:306; idem, *History of England*, 3:302–04, 400, 404–05 (Chs. XXIII, XXVI); Smith, *Wealth of Nations*, 412. Ferguson said that the "commercial and political arts have advanced together" and that they "have been in modern Europe so interwoven, that we cannot determine which were prior in the order of time, or derived most advantage from the mutual influences with which they act and re-act upon the other": *Civil Society*, 261. This argument is found to be implicit in Hume, if the essay cited here is read in conjunction with "Of the Rise and Progress of the Arts and Sciences."

advances towards perfection. It may now be affirmed of civilized monarchies, what was formerly said in praise of republics
alone, *that they are a government of Laws, not of Men.* They
are found susceptible of order, method, and constancy, to a
surprising degree. Property is there secure; industry encouraged; the arts flourish; and the prince lives secure among his
subjects, like a father among his children. . . . It must, however, be confessed, that, though monarchical governments
have approached nearer to popular ones, in gentleness and stability; they are still inferior.

The progress of the rule of law (over will) and of personal—and, to
some extent, political—liberty was for Hume a central feature of
European history since the feudal age. The other Scots held essentially the same view, even though they thought with Kames and
Millar that the science of politics was advancing only slowly and had
far to go. Although none of them offered any predictions about the
political future, Ferguson and Dunbar did suggest that some sort of
international union was at least conceivable.[63]

In government and law, then, just as in the arts and sciences and
morals and manners, progress within certain limits and tempered by
certain conditions appeared to all these Scotsmen to be the keynote of
human development from rudeness to refinement. They took much
the same view when, subsuming all the facets of life under one head,
they generalized about the history of man. The thread running
through the longest book that Kames wrote was an attempt to depict
the "history of the [human] species in its progress from the savage
state to its highest civilization and improvement." But this did not
prevent him from arguing that vicious luxury, if left unchecked,
could ruin any nation. Millar thought that the "wonderful powers
and faculties" of man, "in a gradual progression from such rude beginnings, have led to the noblest discoveries in art or science, and to the
most exalted refinement of taste and manners." Therefore, he concluded, "how poor and wretched soever the aspect of human nature in
[its] early state, it contains the seeds of improvement, which, by long
care and culture, are capable of being brought to maturity." Yet he
also feared that, without efforts on the part of government to alleviate

63. Hume, "Of Civil Liberty" (1741), *Essays,* 1:161–62; Kames, *Sketches,* 2:200,
(Bk. II, Sk. viii, Sect. 7); Millar, *Historical View,* 4:295–96; Ferguson, *Civil Society,* 21–
22; Dunbar, *History of Mankind,* 272.

the deleterious effects of the division of labor, the mass of the people would never reap the benefits of a mature civilization. Men "tend to a perfection in the application of their faculties," wrote Ferguson, "to which the aid of long experience is required, and to which many generations must have combined their endeavours." Accordingly, "in the human kind"—alone among all the creatures of the earth— "the species has a progress as well as the individual; they build in every subsequent age on foundations formerly laid." Dunbar, too, believed that Homo sapiens was uniquely progressive. Like Ferguson, however, he added that "Degeneracy, as well as improvement, is incident to man."[64] The expression of such qualifications was typical of the Scots, and, though hardly a sign of pessimism, it distinguishes them from the English believers in indefinite progress.

Only occasionally did they sound very much like Worthington, Law, Gordon, Priestley, and Price. For example, in rare instances they advanced the theory that the course of history brought increased happiness to man. Hume contended that human happiness consisted of action, pleasure, and indolence. Providing for each of these three ingredients, the industry, knowledge, and humanity that were peculiar to the more refined societies not only rendered government great and flourishing but also made individuals "happy and prosperous." That being so, it seemed to him that "the ages of refinement are both the happiest and most virtuous." Turning his eyes to the future, Hume asked rhetorically whether there was a stronger foundation for any obligation "than to observe, that human society, or even human nature, could not subsist without the establishment of [justice]; and will still arrive at greater degrees of happiness and perfection, the more inviolable the regard is, which is paid to that duty?" For Ferguson, it was not increased attention to justice but the Baconian cumulative effect that would—or at least could—lead to increased happiness. Man, he remarked, "profiting by the experience of ages to come, may exhibit in some future time, a felicity of which these infant generations of men are not yet susceptible."[65] Except for their lack of a sense of absolute certainty, these comments about the future could easily have been made by Priestley.

64. Kames, *Sketches*, 1:sig. A^r, 65 (introductory paragraph and "Preliminary Discourse concerning the Origin of Man and of Languages"); Millar, *Ranks*, 198; Ferguson, *Civil Society*, 4–5; idem, *Principles*, 1:194–95; Dunbar, *History of Mankind*, 66, 3.
65. Hume, "Of Refinement in the Arts," *Essays*, 1:300–02; idem, *Principles of Morals*, Sect. III, Pt. ii, in *Enquiries*, 201; Ferguson, *Principles*, 1:335.

Even so, compared to the English the Scots rarely offered observations concerning the future, and those few tended to be rather tentative. Thus, Kames the judge hoped to see lawyers "soaring above their predecessors" and "purifying and improving" the law (but only if legal studies became a rational science). Taking a broader view, Dunbar wrote that "perhaps there are talents inherent in the species which at no time have been called forth into action, and which may yet appear conspicuous in some succeeding period." He also suggested that the soul of man "may open and expand itself in *energy* through the successive periods of [time's] duration." Millar once went so far as to mention the theory, advanced by "benevolent philosophers," that "human nature, by culture and education, is led to endless degrees of perfection," and he called it a "flattering, perhaps generally well-founded hypothesis." Much more in tune with the Scots' standard outlook, however, were the more modest statements by him and Kames, respectively, that man possessed a "wonderful capacity for improvement" and was "susceptible of high improvements in a well regulated society."[66]

Only in Ferguson's lectures on moral and political philosophy did limitless progress and human perfectibility become common themes. Man, he asserted, was "susceptible of indefinite advancement, engaged in a road of experience and discipline, which points him forward to his end." Because nothing human was perfect, this road continually approached more closely to but never reached "the infinite perfection of what is eternal," just like a hyperbola approaching ever nearer to an asymptote without touching it. "In a progress begun with this indefinite prospect," said Ferguson, "successive periods, even those of the greatest advancement, may be marked with their respective defects and imperfections." But this was to be expected, since there could only be progress where there was prior deficiency, and in any case experience tended "to exhaust the sum of possible errors, and to limit the choice at last to what is best." It was

---

66. Henry Home, Lord Kames, *Elucidations respecting the Common and Statute Law of Scotland* (1777), new ed. (Edinburgh, 1800), xiii (Preface); idem, *Law-Tracts*, 57; Dunbar, *History of Mankind*, 4; Millar, *Historical View*, 4:232–33; idem, *Ranks*, 218. In light of the first of Millar's remarks to be quoted here, the claim (in Jeffrey, review of *Historical View*, 158) that he "laughed at the dreams of perfectibility" does not appear to be tenable. See also John Craig, "Account of the Life and Writings of John Millar, Esq.," in Millar, *The Origin of the Distinction of Ranks*, 4th ed., corr. (Edinburgh, 1806), xlvii–xlix.

Adam Ferguson

impossible to specify "any rate of actual attainment" for man: even though he had all the necessary faculties and materials to make improvement, he could fail to use them, so that progress was "not always equable, nor exempt from interruptions." Yet there was "a principle of progression on which mankind advance in civilization, good order, and justice," and against which no bounds had been set.[67] Ferguson's "principle of progression" and Gordon's "perfectionability" were essentially identical.

Ferguson was certainly an exception: the Scots normally did not believe at all in the indefinite progress of the human species, or, at least, they did not believe in it with the kind of enthusiasm characteristic of their English contemporaries.[68] The difference between their views on general progress and those of the English is also visible in their assessment of the course of British history. Most of the time the Scots claimed that Britain had for centuries been slowly improving on all fronts. Thus, to illustrate his famous thesis that there was a "natural Progress of Opulence" in the shift from rudeness to refinement, Smith portrayed the annual produce of English land and labor as perpetually increasing from age to age, going all the way back to the first century B.C. (when the inhabitants of the country "were nearly in the same state with the savages of North America"). The enlargement of wealth and revenue seemed to him to have accelerated since the sixteenth century, and to have become particularly notable in the period beginning with the Restoration. Millar agreed that during the last century agriculture, commerce, and industry had improved to "a wonderful degree," and he, like Smith, traced this economic advance to the security and liberty provided by the British constitution.[69]

In the same period, Millar believed, philosophy had been "con-

67. Ferguson, *Principles*, 1:183–85, 181, 298, 313–14, 304, 310, 194, 54; 2:403–04.

68. It has been argued (in Forbes, "'Scientific' Whiggism," 649) that Smith did not believe in perfectibility, and this is undoubtedly true. As for Hume, it is incorrect to suggest (as Ernest Campbell Mossner does in *The Life of David Hume* [Austin, Tex., 1954], 543) that "what he found alien and untenable [in Ferguson's *Civil Society*] was surely the insistence upon the inevitability of progress, upon the principle of perfection." For Ferguson—in *Civil Society*—did not make progress seem inevitable, and it was only later that he wrote about a human principle of progression (not of perfection): see Kettler, *Social and Political Thought of Ferguson*, 52, 57–60. Still, the temperate Hume would undoubtedly not have accepted the belief in indefinite progress and perfectibility present in Ferguson's *Principles*.

69. Smith, *Wealth of Nations*, 376, 194–95, 106, 344–46, 424, 540; Millar, *Historical View*, 3:5–6, and 4:103–05, 132, 370. See also Hume, *History of England*, 5:482–83 (App. III); idem, "Of the Jealousy of Trade" (1752), *Essays*, 1:345–46.

stantly advancing in all the departments of science," as both natural phenomena and human artifices had been reduced to their principles. Hume was not as sanguine about the intellectual attainments of his own age, writing early in his career that "the utmost we have to boast of, are a few essays toward a more just philosophy; which, indeed, promise well, but have not, as yet, reached any degree of perfection." Still, improvement there had been. Every science had as yet been in its infancy in the reign of James I, whereas after the Restoration men like Boyle and Newton opened up the "only road which leads to true philosophy." The subsequent "progress of learning," along with the increase of liberty brought about by the Revolution, created "a sudden and sensible change in the opinions of men within these last fifty years," a change associated particularly with the decline of "superstitious reverence to names and authority." Several times in the *History of England* Hume expressed a rather low opinion of English achievements in the fine arts, although he did think that these had relatively recently entered a period of improvement. Kames found the beginning of this trend in the later fifteenth century, claiming that at present the "fine arts are gaining ground daily" and might eventually have London—or even Edinburgh—for their capital instead of Rome.[70]

As for the political side of life, the Scots were in agreement with Ferguson's comments that Britain "has carried the authority and government of law to a point of perfection, which they never before attained in the history of mankind," and that among his fellow citizens "the liberty of the subject is more secure perhaps than it ever has been under any other human establishment." Buttressing this perspective and setting it apart from the seventeenth-century belief in a perfect ancient constitution was a notable assumption: "the government which we enjoy at present has not been formed at once, but has grown to maturity in a course of ages." So said Millar, who divided the maturation process into three phases ("feudal aristocracy," "feudal monarchy," and "commercial government"). He contended that even before the last of these began, with the first Stuart, the constitution had become "a system of liberty." Since then it had received

---

70. Millar, *Historical View*, 4:304–05; Hume, "Of Civil Liberty," "Whether the British Government inclines more to Absolute Monarchy, or to a Republic," and "Of Refinement in the Arts," *Essays*, 1:159, 125, 306; idem, *History of England*, 6:197 ("Appendix to the Reign of James I"), and 8:332–37 (Ch. LXXI); Kames, *Sketches*, 1:495–96, 49, 173–74, 243–44 (Bk. I, Sk. vii; Prelim. Discourse; Bk. I, Sk. iv, Sect. 2).

"many improvements," particularly in the wake of the "memorable Revolution in 1688, which completed, and reduced into practice, a government of a more popular nature, and better fitted to secure the natural rights of mankind, than had ever taken place in a great nation." For with the Revolution came the "full establishment of a regular and free constitution" and, therefore, "political liberty, and the secure possession and enjoyment of property." Hume took essentially the same position as Millar, writing that "the privileges of the people have, during near two centuries, been continually upon the encrease," so that since the Revolution the British had happily enjoyed, if not the best system of government, at least "the most perfect and most accurate system of liberty that was ever found compatible with government."[71]

In his *History of England*, Hume vigorously argued that the tendency toward increased liberty and political improvement had manifested itself long before the accession of the Stuarts. The rude, violent Anglo-Saxons, he thought, were incapable of submitting to government and sought shelter in personal servitude, their lives and property not being protected by law. But affairs "took early a turn which was more favourable to justice and to liberty." With Magna Carta, men acquired more security for their property and liberties, and "government approached a little nearer to that end for which it was originally instituted, the distribution of justice, and the equal protection of the citizens." By the time of Henry VI, "considerable progress" had been made in the science of government, "which prognosticated a still greater." Such views led Hume—often accused of being a Tory historian—to the conclusion that those who

> from a pretended respect to antiquity, appeal at every turn to an original plan of the constitution, only cover their turbulent spirit and their private ambition under the appearance of venerable forms; and whatever period they pitch on for their model, they may still be carried back to a more ancient period, where they will find the measure of [political] power entirely different, and where every circumstance, by reason of the

71. Ferguson, *Civil Society*, 166; idem, *Principles*, 2:473; Millar, *Historical View*, 1:1–8, and 2:389–90, and 4:102–03; Hume, "Of the Protestant Succession" (1752) and "Of the Coalition of Parties" (1752), *Essays*, 1:472, 465; idem, *History of England*, 3:306 (Ch. XXIII), and 8:320 (Ch. LXXI). See also Smith, *Lectures on Jurisprudence*, 420–22, 264–74.

greater barbarity of the times, will appear still less worthy of imitation.[72]

A firmer denial of the doctrine of the ancient constitution can scarcely be imagined. For Hume as for the other Scots, the key to the political history of their nation was progressive change.

Englishmen like Price made similar pronouncements on politics and other aspects of British history, but they also projected past national progress into the future. This the Scots almost never did, and, in fact, they sometimes expressed rather serious reservations about what was to come. In spite of his assessment of the economic improvement that England had undergone, Smith, for example, noted ominously that two hundred years had elapsed since the beginning of the reign of Elizabeth, "a period as long as the course of human prosperity usually endures." Likewise, Hume worried whether Britain's trade would "not at last come to a *ne plus ultra*" and cease to expand, and he bemoaned the national debt, commenting that public credit, "the seeds of ruin," would destroy the nation if not destroyed itself. He also feared that the "levity and rebellious disposition" of the British might ultimately make them fit only for "absolute slavery and subjection," a concern that the Wilkite disturbances (when he was undersecretary of state) did nothing to lessen. On the other hand, it was the very possibility of silencing the "noise of dissension," of squelching the "refractory and turbulent zeal of this fortunate people," that made Ferguson apprehensive about a future turn to despotism in Britain. His interest in Roman history grew out of a sense of the parallelism in social conditions (if not yet in historical fate) existing between republican Rome, with its eventual corruption and decline, and his own nation. Kames several times asserted that the decay attendant upon vicious luxury had already begun to afflict Britain, and Dunbar found the state of public manners to be alarmingly low.[73]

---

72. Hume, *History of England*, 3:301–02, 305–06 (Ch. XXIII); 2:141–42 (App. II). Of course, Hume did not claim that the expansion of liberty was a continuous process. It was interrupted under the Tudors, who "assumed an authority almost absolute" before the introduction of "a new plan of liberty, founded on the privileges of the commons," in the seventeenth century: ibid., 5:489 (App. III).

73. Smith, *Wealth of Nations*, 425; Hume to Kames, March 4, 1758, and to Turgot, June 16, 1768, in *Letters of David Hume*, 1:271–72, and 2:180; Hume, "Of Public Credit" (1752) and "Of the Protestant Succession," *Essays*, 1:367–74, 479; Ferguson, *Civil Society*, 256, 167; Kettler, *Social and Political Thought of Ferguson*, 201–11;

Yet although the Scots were not nearly as optimistic as the English about the future of Britain, they did—like the English—discern *general* improvement in their nation's past, and especially in its recent history. Since the Revolution, wrote Robertson, the Scottish people had "refined their manners, made improvements in the elegancies of life, and cultivated the arts and sciences," while their commerce had "advanced in its progress, and government attained nearer to perfection." At the beginning of the Seven Years' War Ferguson may have castigated Britain for its lack of military preparedness and its excessive concentration on the pursuit of wealth, but he also saw many "Circumstances of which a Nation may be allowed to boast": "The happy Form of our Government; the sacred Authority with which our Laws execute themselves; the Perfection to which Arts are arrived; the Extent of our Commerce, and Increase of our People; the Degrees of Taste and Literature which we possess; the Probity and Humanity which prevail in our Manners." "Such is the height," he declared, "to which every improving Nation aspires, and at which but a few have arrived." Writing in 1752, the usually staid Hume became almost ebullient in his discussion of the past sixty years:

> Public liberty, with internal peace and order, has flourished almost without interruption: Trade and manufactures, and agriculture, have encreased: The arts, and sciences, and philosophy, have been cultivated. Even religious parties have been necessitated to lay aside their mutual rancour: And the glory of the nation has spread itself all over EUROPE; derived equally from our progress in the arts of peace, and from valour and success in war. So long and so glorious a period no nation almost can boast of: Nor is there another instance in the whole history of mankind, that so many millions of people have, during such a space of time, been held together, in a manner so free, so rational, and so suitable to the dignity of human nature.

With the eighteenth century, surely, the "dawn of civility and science"—which Hume thought had after 1485 broken through the

---

Kames, *Sketches*, 2:103–04, 145 (Bk. II, Sks. v, vii), and 3:234n–235n (Bk. III, Sk. ii, Pt. 2); Dunbar, *History of Mankind*, 51.

gloom of "a series of many barbarous ages"[74]—had itself given way to the full light of civilized day. British history, like the natural history of mankind, exhibited a progress from rudeness to refinement.

Explicitly recognizing the complexity of the whole problem of historical causation, the Scots did not arrive at a simple, general formula to explain this kind of progress.[75] It is possible, nevertheless, to divide the causes of progress about which they talked into two basic categories: factors external to nature and society, and those internal. In the case of the former, the Scots placed much less importance on the role of God in the shaping of history than did their English counterparts. With one exception, they had no theology of history comparable to that of Worthington or Priestley. On the basis of a sermon that Robertson delivered in 1755, it is reasonable to conclude that the leader of the Moderates saw an overarching "plan of God's providence" in the "government of the world," and that careful observers of civil as well as sacred history might "form probable conjectures" about this plan while discovering "a skil[l]ful hand, directing the revolutions of human affairs." This was an overall scheme for history, one which certainly conjoined civil and sacred history to promote the establishment of Christianity. But Robertson offered no other details about the divine plan, except to note (in his other remaining sermon, probably of 1788) that the divine plan included a prominent part for Britain to play. His historical writings belittled the concept of divine intervention in human affairs, and even the sermon of 1755 made clear that God's scheme for human history was almost invariably worked out through secondary causes. "The Almighty," he wrote, "seldom effects, by supernatural means, any thing, which could have been accomplished by such as are natural." To the extent that the other Scots believed in the divine ordering of human affairs, that belief was typified by Dunbar: "we observe the determinations of heaven to coincide with a regular and established order of second causes." Smith elaborated the point with a standard analogy. Just as the "wheels of the watch are all admirably adjusted to

---

74. Robertson, *History of Scotland*, Bk. VIII, in *Works*, 2:240; Ferguson, *Reflections Previous to the Establishment of a Militia*, 11. Hume, "Of the Protestant Succession," *Essays*, 1:475–76; idem, *History of England*, 3:296 (Ch. XXIII). See also Kettler, *Social and Political Thought of Ferguson*, 100–01.

75. On attitudes toward causation, see, for example, Robertson, *History of America*, Bk. IV, in *Works*, 6:320, 386.

the end for which it was made" by the watchmaker, so in the universe means are "adjusted with the nicest artifice to the ends which they are intended to produce," by "the wisdom of God." And the "system of human nature seems to be more simple and agreeable when all its different operations are in this manner deduced from a single principle." This principle was Smith's "invisible hand," really a conception of general providence virtually devoid of traditional Christian connotations (though not of metaphysical optimism) and leaving no room for divine intervention or miracles. As Kames asked, "Is it not obvious, that the great God of heaven and earth governs the world by inflexible laws, from which he can never swerve in any case, because they are the best possible in every case?" Even Ferguson, who had stronger traditional religious sensibilities than any of the others except Robertson, could write that while the "Author of Nature, has projected a scene of discipline and progression" for man and has given him all the tools for progress, that "effect is optional to him."[76]

Closely related to the role of the "invisible hand" was the part played in progress by the unforeseen or apparently accidental, sometimes referred to in sociological terminology as "the heterogeneity of ends" or "unintended social outcomes."[77] Hume believed that a people who examined the ancient periods of their government would see the "remote and commonly faint and disfigured originals of the most finished and most noble institutions," and would learn of the "great mixture of accident which commonly concurs with a small ingredient of wisdom and foresight in erecting the complicated fabric of the most perfect government." Even when intended aims were attained, their realization could occur in the most ironic fashion. Hence, the English owed the "whole freedom of their constitution" to the "absurdities" of the "frivolous" and "ridiculous" Puritans. In a

76. William Robertson, *The Situation of the World at the Time of Christ's Appearance, and its Connexion with the Success of his Religion, considered. A Sermon Preached before The Society in Scotland for propagating Christian Knowledge . . . On Monday, January 6. 1755* (Edinburgh, 1755), 3–6, 13; Dunbar, *History of Mankind,* 251; Smith, *Theory of Moral Sentiments,* 87, 184–85 (Pt. II, Sect. ii, Ch. 3; Pt. IV, Ch. i); Kames, *Sketches,* 3:293 (Bk. III, Sk. iii, Chap. 2); Ferguson, *Principles,* 1:314. For an example of Robertson's rejection of the concept of divine intervention, see "Progress of Society in Europe," Sect. V, Pt. ii, in *Works,* 3:45–46. On his unpublished sermon of 1788, see Jeffrey Smitten "Impartiality in Robertson's *History of America,*" *Eighteenth-Century Studies,* 19 (Fall 1985): 71–72.

77. For these terms, see Forbes, "'Scientific' Whiggism," 651; Louis Schneider, ed., *The Scottish Moralists on Human Nature and Society* (Chicago, 1967), xxix–xxx, xxxn.

similar vein, Smith described the rise of commerce and liberty during the later Middle Ages as a "revolution of the greatest importance to the publick happiness, . . . brought about by two different orders of people, which had not the least intention to serve the publick." Neither the feudal nobles, who hedonistically craved luxury goods, nor the merchants, who self-interestedly provided them, had "knowledge or foresight of that great revolution which the folly of the one, and the industry of the other, was gradually bringing about." Generalizing along the same lines, Ferguson contended that although nations did not consciously attempt to improve in wisdom or virtue, their peoples nevertheless received "instruction and habits of civilization, in the midst of labours bestowed in procuring their subsistence, accommodation, or safety." Striving to remove inconveniences or to gain immediate advantages, men "arrive at ends which even their imagination could not anticipate." If Oliver Cromwell was right to say that an individual never achieves more than when he does not know where he is headed, "it may with more reason be affirmed of communities, that they admit of the greatest revolutions where no change is intended." So every step taken by the multitude, even in "enlightened ages," is "made with equal blindness to the future; and nations stumble upon establishments, which are indeed the result of human action, but not the execution of any human design."[78]

A final external factor, the physical conditions of life, also seemed to the Scots to have a large impact on the process of human progress. "Necessity," Robertson stated, "is the great prompter and guide of mankind in their inventions." Ferguson agreed and, with Kames and Smith, noted that this principle was especially influential during the earliest phases of society. It was but a short step from such observations to an emphasis on the effect of climate upon progress. The generally accepted theory—similar to Arnold Toynbee's view of "challenge and response"—was stated by Dunbar: extremes of climatic "munificence and rigour, by withholding the motives to industry, or by rendering the ends desperate, often produce similar effects. A middle situation between those extremes is perhaps the most eligible in a moral light, as well as the most auspicious for civil progress." Except in the case of Ferguson, however, there was no attempt to treat

78. Hume, *History of England*, 3:306 (Ch. XXIII), and 5:183 (Ch. XL), 469 (App. III), and 7:20 (Ch. LVII); Smith, *Wealth of Nations*, 422; Ferguson, *Principles*, 1:241; idem, *Civil Society*, 122–23, 182.

climate as more than a generally conditioning factor in human affairs. Robertson, for instance, considered the "law of climate" to be subject to many exceptions, and Hume and Millar specifically rejected its use (as in *De l'esprit des lois*) to account for specific national characters or mental habits.[79]

As their treatment of climate implies, the Scots did not consider the role of man in the making of progress to be that of an inanimate cog driven solely by the outside forces of a larger machine. This does not mean that they universally subscribed to some version of the doctrine of free will (Hume and Kames, at least, were firmly in the necessitarian camp), but rather that they saw *within* the human being a natural tendency or instinct of enormous importance for the refining process. Kames wrote of the innate human "taste for variety" and "unwearied appetite to be more and more comfortably provided." Millar cited the "disposition"—as well as the capacity—of man "for improving his condition, by the exertion of which, he is carried on from one degree of advancement to another," adding that man is "Never satisfied with any particular attainment" and therefore pursues those "arts which render his situation more easy and agreeable." Or as Ferguson told his students, "Men are disposed to better themselves. They distinguish perfections from defects: they admire and contemn," and they refuse to acquiesce "in any precise measure of attainment already made." He variously called this instinct the "desire for perfection," the "principle of ambition," and the "*law of estimation, or of progression,*" and he claimed that it was "one of the strongest propensities in human nature." Although he once said that it was "an ultimate fact in the nature of man, and not to be explained by any thing that is previously or better known," he undoubtedly considered it to be intimately related to the desire for that ornament and wealth which, in his opinion, made men objects of consideration and symbolized social rank and condition.[80]

79. Robertson, *History of America*, Bk. IV, in *Works*, 6:440, 383, 385–86; Ferguson, *Principles*, 1:205, 242, 256; idem, *Civil Society*, 31, 108, 110–19; Kames, *Law-Tracts*, 90–91; idem, *Sketches*, 1:73, 77 (Bk. I, Sk. i); Smith, *Lectures on Jurisprudence*, 488–89, 336–39; Dunbar, *History of Mankind*, 207–09, 221–23, 231–32, 280–81 (cf. 228); Hume, *Treatise*, 316–17; idem, "Of Commerce," "Of Taxes" (1752), and "Of National Characters" (1748), *Essays*, 1:298–99, 356–57, 244–58; Millar, *Ranks*, 178–80. On climate, see Christopher J. Berry, "'Climate' in the Eighteenth Century: James Dunbar and the Scottish Case," *Texas Studies in Literature and Language*, 16 (Summer 1974): 281–92.

80. Kames, *Sketches*, 2:46 (Bk. II, Sk. i), and 2:323 (Bk. I, Sk. v); Millar, *Ranks*, 176,

Smith, too, spoke of the "natural effort which every man is continually making to better his own condition," of that desire for amelioration which "comes with us from the womb, and never leaves us till we go into the grave." This, he argued, was "a principle . . . capable of carrying on the society to wealth and prosperity," and one "frequently powerful enough to maintain the natural progress of things toward improvement" in spite of all the obstacles set up by government. The only notable difference between his analysis of the desire for betterment and that of Ferguson was that he specifically traced it back to an ultimate source, vanity:

> From whence, then, arises that emulation which runs through all the different ranks of men, and what are the advantages which we propose by that great purpose of human life which we call bettering our condition? To be observed, to be attended to, to be taken notice of with sympathy, complacency, and approbation, are all the advantages which we can propose to derive from it. It is vanity, not the ease, or the pleasure, which interests us. But vanity is always founded upon the belief of our being the object of attention and approbation.

Herein lies the connection between the ethical, sympathetic, approbation-seeking man of the *Theory of Moral Sentiments* and the economic man of the *Wealth of Nations*. For it was, after all, economic man that Smith and the others were describing when they discussed the instinctual quest for improvement. And, given this outlook on human nature, there can be little wonder that not only he but also Kames, Hume, Ferguson, Dunbar, and Millar all emphatically endorsed the economic policy of laissez-faire. Nor is it surprising that they struck a balance between the effects of external factors and human instinct in assessing the causes of progress. "That order of things which necessity imposes in general, though not in every particular country," declared Smith, "is, in every particular country, promoted by the natural inclinations of man." In Ferguson's words, "progress itself is congenial to the nature of man," so that "to advance . . . is the state of nature relative to him."[81]

218; Ferguson, *Institutes*, 90, 143; idem, *Principles*, 1:207, 235–36, 238–39, 243; idem, *Civil Society*, 8, 12. See also Dunbar, *History of Mankind*, 151. In comparison to Hume and Kames, Ferguson and Dunbar were far less deterministic.

81. Smith, *Wealth of Nations*, 673–74, 340–43, 540, 377; idem, *Lectures on Jurisprudence*, 487, 334–35; idem, *Theory of Moral Sentiments*, 50 (Pt. I, Sect. iii, Ch. 2);

Fulfillment of the instinctual desire for improvement, of course, could occur only within society. Man was recognized by the Scots to be an inherently social creature, fitted for community life and existing in that setting from very early times if not from his origin.[82] He could "subsist only in society," wrote Smith. As Hume explained, it was there alone that he could supply his defects and compensate for his infirmities. Moreover, it was there that his abilities were increased, making him "in every respect more satisfied and happy" than he could possibly be in a solitary condition. But if society provided man with the "additional *force, ability,* and *security*" required for progress, it also necessitated his making that progress in order to solve social problems and deal with social complexity. Human activity, stated Ferguson, resulted not only from mere physical wants but also from the "exigencies of human society, or its need of establishments, to restrain disorders, and to procure the benefits of which it is susceptible." Thus, taking a total view, Dunbar called society the "theatre on which our genius expands" and the "prime mover of all our inventive powers," distinguishing man from other animals in that "he rises to improvements which flow from the union of his kind."[83] Social life seemed to him and the other *literati* to be both the setting of and a basic precondition for progress.

To three of the characteristic features of that life the Scots assigned particularly important parts in the drama of progress. One of these was the division of labor; among Englishmen, only Priestley insisted upon its profound consequences with equal vigor. A second was government and law. Ferguson placed political factors among the most important of those circumstances leading to the progress (or decline) of nations, and he considered the conditions of politics to be part of the human "school of intellectual and moral improvement."

Ferguson, *Principles*, 1:249, 199. For statements of the laissez-faire point of view, see Kames, *Sketches*, 2:324 (Bk. II, Sk. x); Hume, *History of England*, 3:402 (Ch. XXVI), and 4:30 (Ch. XXIX); Ferguson, *Civil Society*, 143–44; idem, *Principles*, 1:244; Smith, *Wealth of Nations*, 686–88; Dunbar, *History of Mankind*, 295, 297; Millar, *Historical View*, 4:109–10.

82. For explicit statements to this effect, see Kames, *Law-Tracts*, 40–41, 80; idem, *Sketches*, 2:3, 18–19, 56 (Bk. II, Sk. i); Hume, *Treatise*, 493; idem, "Of the Origin of Government" (first published 1777), *Essays*, 1:113; Smith, *Theory of Moral Sentiments*, 85, 88 (Pt. II, Sect. ii, Ch. 3); Ferguson, *Civil Society*, 4, 6, 16, 53. Two of the Scots did not think that man's career began in society: Robertson, *History of America*, Bk. IV, in *Works*, 6:265; Dunbar, *History of Mankind*, 2.

83. Smith, *Theory of Moral Sentiments*, 85 (Pt. II, Sect. ii, Ch. 3); Hume, *Treatise*, 485; Ferguson, *Principles*, 1:205–06; Dunbar, *History of Mankind*, 5, 14.

Hume thought that great legislators deserved special praise for their work, because the benefits arising from a wise system of laws and governmental institutions—peace, security, and virtue, which "are so requisite to happiness"—were more appreciable even than those conferred by the arts and sciences. The provision of public order and safety seemed to the Scots to be of special significance for overall improvement. "If men do not enjoy the protection of regular government, together with the expectation of personal security, which naturally flows from it," remarked Robertson, "they never attempt to make progress in science, nor aim at attaining refinement in taste, or in manners." But, as Smith wrote, "when they are secure of enjoying the fruits of their industry, they naturally exert it to better their condition and to acquire not only the necessaries, but the conveniencies and elegancies of life." The "attainment of a just political order otherwise so necessary to the welfare of mankind," Ferguson declared, "is to be considered also as an occasion on which the principal steps of man's progress are made, or in which a scene is opened that gives scope to his active disposition."[84] Like the partition of employments, Hume's "government of laws," his "personal liberty," was held to be essential to the improvement of man in society.

No less important to human progress was a third prominent feature of social existence, knowledge. Looking at European history, Robertson placed the "progress of science" among the great causes that changed rude manners for the better and introduced "civility and refinement." Millar offered one explanation of why this was true more generally: "the advancement of natural knowledge, in all its branches, is highly subservient to the improvement of the common arts of life, and consequently, by promoting opulence and independence in the great body of the people, must contribute to inspire them with sentiments of liberty." Somewhat differently, Ferguson argued that any extension of knowledge concerning man or nature was "an accession of power" and led to "the command of events." This was so because the most cloistered intellectual ultimately "works for his community," his discoveries being to some degree diffused into every corner of society, and "separate communities mutually work for one another, for ages to come, and for mankind." Attainments in science,

84. Ferguson, *Principles*, 1:313, 265; Hume, "Of Parties in General" (1741) and "That Politics may be reduced to a Science" (1741), *Essays*, 1:127, 105; Robertson, "Progress of Society in Europe," Sect. I, Introduction, in *Works*, 3:16; Smith, *Wealth of Nations*, 405.

therefore, should be considered crucial "steps in the progress of the human species itself."[85] On this issue, at least, Ferguson and the others concurred completely with their English contemporaries.

Lacking the comprehensive theology of history adopted by men like Worthington and Priestley, the Scots offered no single replacement for it. They were content to do without a unifying causal system, and to point out how various external and internal factors—physical necessity and climate, the accidental or unintended, human nature, the social context, the division of labor, government and law, and knowledge—*all* helped to produce progress. The modest and undogmatic character of this historiographical position is typical of them, and it is intimately bound to their customary description of progress. How could they have traced human improvement to one all-encompassing cause or to a small, neat set of causal elements when they usually viewed that improvement, real though it seemed to be, as subject to certain limitations and restrictions, when they speculated on the future so seldom?

From rudeness to refinement: this perspective on human progress was not confined to the seven Scots discussed here, although they were the first to elaborate it in writing. Their unique position as intellectuals who were also key members of the Scottish establishment helped to give this perspective a considerable vogue north of the Tweed. Thus, to cite only its written manifestations,[86] the economist Sir James Steuart (1712–80) found "the regular progress of mankind, from great simplicity to complicated refinement" to constitute an important ingredient in the "distinct method of analysing so extensive a subject" as the political economy. He went on to argue that economies historically passed through three stages, pastoral, agrarian, and exchange, and he traced the rise of modern liberty to this change. Robertson and others from among the group considered here arranged for John Logan (1748–88), a Moderate minister in the Church of Scotland, to deliver in Edinburgh a series of lectures on the

85. Robertson, "Progress of Society in Europe," Sect. I, Pt. ix, in *Works*, 3:65, 69; Millar, *Historical View*, 4:168–69; Ferguson, *Principles*, 1:2–3, 280–81, 284. Dunbar took a more Rousseau-like perspective on this subject, but even he conceded that the benefits of knowledge outweighed the costs: *History of Mankind*, 148–49.

86. For its connection to the ethos of improvement surrounding the planning and building of the "New Town" of Edinburgh, see below, chap. 9.

philosophy of history. Logan began these by enunciating some first principles, among which were the beliefs that progress was characteristic of mankind and the key to history, and that improvement in human affairs resulted from the interconnected movement of all facets of social life out of barbarous origins. William Russell (1714–93), a miscellaneous writer and sometime-editor originally from Selkirkshire, produced a popular textbook on European history whose theme was the progress of the continent from rudeness to refinement since the fall of Rome. Such views also penetrated English thought, influencing Priestley to at least some degree, and animating some lengthy (and rather bad) verses by the eventual poet laureate Henry James Pye (1745–1813), down to his presentation of a "natural history" of early men and his worries about luxury.[87]

The case of James Burnett, Lord Monboddo (1714–99), illustrates the strength of the Scottish outlook on progress. Like Kames a Scottish law lord in the Court of Session, Monboddo remains best known for his writings on the development of language, his notorious inclusion of the orangutan within the human species, and his general eccentricity. That he was in many ways unique—"an original," in eighteenth-century parlance—is beyond question. For example, in an age that treated Newton and Locke as heroes, he rejected most of their physics and philosophy in favor of Aristotelianism and Platonism. His singularity extended to his opinions on progress. From one point of view, he does not appear to have been a believer in progress at all, but rather a chronological and cultural primitivist. Over and over again, he discoursed on the constant decline of civilized man, a decline that began very early in recorded history and became pronounced after the time of Augustus. At present, he thought, human beings were "very much degenerated both in mind and in body," and even in the arts and sciences "we confess how much we are fallen off." Monboddo assigned a great deal of the responsibility for this sorry state of affairs to the pursuit of ease and pleasure, in general, and

87. Sir James Steuart, An Inquiry into the Principles of Political Oeconomy, ed. Andrew S. Skinner, 2 vols. (Edinburgh, 1966), 1:28, 208–09; John Logan, Elements of the Philosophy of History, Part First (Edinburgh, 1781), 14–16, quoted in Thomas Preston Peardon, The Transition in English Historical Writing, 1760–1830 (New York, 1933), 52–53 (and, for comments on Russell, 65); William Russell, The History of Modern Europe from the Fall of the Roman Empire to 1763 (1779–84), new ed., 5 vols. (London, 1801), esp. 1:1–3, 189–203 (Letters I, XXI); Henry James Pye, The Progress of Refinement. A Poem. In Three Parts (Oxford, 1783), 4–6, 65, 91–98, and passim.

to modern commercial society, in particular, whose commerce and luxury had helped to make Europeans the most miserable animals on earth.[88]

If the other Scots would have opposed such historical pessimism, they would also have rejected the way in which, from another point of view, Monboddo *did* believe in progress. Civil society might make men unhappy and even miserable; it might, in fact, cause them to degenerate. But these effects, he claimed, merely supported the old saying that the corruption of the best things is the worst. For civilized life, with all its problems, was absolutely necessary for the advance of humankind toward perfection. Because of the Fall, man lost the true intelligence in which his perfection consisted. To regain it required the "cultivation of his intellect by arts and sciences," which as God foresaw could not exist "except in a state of civil society." Although these arts and sciences had decayed over the centuries, a deep reservoir of them had been filled by the ancient Egyptians and Greeks. Drinking from it, "we must improve our intellectual faculty, and consequently correct those vices and follies which are produced in civil life." Such improvement was sure to come, and soon, since the deity had planned a radically new environment where men would rid themselves of their corporeal frames and desires. Becoming pure intelligences not needing to pursue bodily pleasure, they would then be free to follow the wisdom of ancient metaphysics.[89]

This vision has a close affinity to English doctrines of general progress, in that it presents human improvement as perfectibility and as a divinely ordained program of indefinite duration. Such an outlook was alien to most of the Scots, but embedded within it was a focus that they would have understood: Monboddo made civil so-

88. [James Burnett, Lord Monboddo], *Of the Origin and Progress of Language*, 6 vols. (Edinburgh, 1773–92), vol. 1 (2d ed., 1774), ii–iii, 551n–552n [only vols. 1–3 had 2d eds.]; idem, *Antient Metaphysics*, 6 vols. (Edinburgh, 1779–99), 4:397–98, and 3:lxxviii, 103, 196, 271–72. For the condemnation of commercial society, see ibid., 3:193–95, and 5:70–80, 83.

89. Ibid., 3:282, 103–04; 4:64, 387, 387n; 5:88, 225, 235–40, 317–21; 6:141–46, 220–21, 254–55. Arthur O. Lovejoy was consequently right when, in his "Monboddo and Rousseau" (first published 1933), he linked the two men as primitivists—in some sense—who tended to destroy primitivism with perfectibility: *Essays in the History of Ideas* (Baltimore, 1948), 38–61. Monboddo was influenced or, at least, confirmed in his opinions by Rousseau, but his notion of perfectibility had strong underpinnings in theology and *Anticomanie* not clearly present in the Frenchman (and not discussed by Lovejoy, who did not refer to *Antient Metaphysics*, where those underpinnings are patent).

ciety the necessary context of progress (even, curiously, for the life to come). Indeed, the picture of the development of society that he drew was quite similar in both outline and detail to the one contained in the other Scots' account of the natural history of man. All nations, he wrote, "even the most polished and civilized, of which we read in history, were originally barbarians," and man at that time (that is, immediately after the Fall) was "a wild savage animal." "From such beginnings, however, men . . . advance to arts and sciences, and so on to refinement and politeness." This change had several components. In terms of social organization, the savage and solitary state gave way to life in small "herds" or groups, then to the "family" or clan stage, and finally to civil society. Economically, gathering was replaced successively by hunting, agriculture, and that money- and pleasure-oriented economic stage, trade and manufacturing. As for government, at first there was none at all. Then came "occasional government" to meet the needs of defense; the "state," with public deliberations among elders but without any system of law; a "more regular" state, based upon enforceable laws aimed only at public behavior; and the "most perfect form of polity" (like that of Sparta), in which the state added to its functions the provision of education and the regulation of private life. In the most important sphere of human activity, the arts and sciences, there was likewise a recognizable temporal order. The needs of subsistence and self-defense produced the "arts of life" (beginning with language), then leisure and the desire for ease and amusement led to the "pleasurable arts," and eventually curiosity and the quest for knowledge gave rise to the sciences.[90]

Monboddo's account of the refining process, therefore, bears a striking resemblance to that of the other Scottish *literati*. He may have had no use for their philosophical and religious "heresies" (as he frequently called their ideas), he may have seen only degeneration in the contemporary commercial society that they found largely congenial and progressive, he may have looked expectantly to the future of perfectible man while they normally concentrated on the past improvement of the species. But both he and they discovered in human history—or, at least, in some portion of it—a transition from rudeness to refinement.

90. Monboddo, *Origin and Progress of Language*, vol. 1 (2d ed.), 144–45, 394–95, 364–65; idem, *Antient Metaphysics*, 5:88, 323, 70–71, 63, 51–52, and 6:145, and 4:61, 40, 55. Monboddo probably comes closest to propounding the "civic humanist" ideal that Professor Pocock finds at the heart of eighteenth-century thought.

Likewise, his gloomy assessment of the post-Augustan world and his cherishing of classical antiquity would have seemed strange to Law and Gordon. With them, however, he firmly believed that God had a plan for the indefinite improvement of mankind. In his time Monboddo was unusual in combining the Scottish and English versions of the progress of human culture. Nonetheless, given his primitivistic and pessimistic side, he provides evidence of how compelling *some* form of the belief in general progress must have been during the second half of the eighteenth century. It took root all across Britain, even in the most unexpected places.

8 The Sources of Belief

Time and again, historians and other scholars have attempted to account in a general way for the rise of the idea of progress to a prominent position in European thought. Great importance has been attached by them to a number of disparate intellectual factors: the influence of traditional Christian historical conceptions; the triumph of the secular, scientific outlook and spirit over providentialism; the temporalization of the Great Chain of Being; and the spread of a new anthropology that emphasized the dignity, uniformity, and "malleability" of man. Attention has also been paid to the role of more purely social developments, including discontent over the state of society, the consequent desire for institutional reform and struggle for freedom, and the underlying "recovery of nerve" that made change thinkable and even welcome.[1]

The problem with the causal explanations based upon these various factors is not that they are clearly wrong, but that for the most part they have not yet been demonstrated to be right. They are generalizations too vast to rest comfortably on the usually slender supporting evidence on which they rest, too broad to allow for potential national or even local differences. Before it is possible to say that Europeans came to believe in progress for definite reasons, it is necessary to examine with care the opinions and circumstances first of individuals and then of groups.

1. For a summary of theories about the sources of the belief in progress, see W. Warren Wagar, "Modern Views of the Origins of the Idea of Progress," *Journal of the History of Ideas* 28 (Jan.–March 1967): 59–69. Some of the factors cited in this paragraph have been assigned importance in works not mentioned by Wagar: Arthur O. Lovejoy, *The Great Chain of Being: A Study of the History of an Idea* (Cambridge, Mass., 1936), 244–46; Franklin L. Baumer, *Religion and the Rise of Scepticism* (New York, 1960), 121–27, 67–77; Peter Gay, *The Enlightenment: An Interpretation*, 2 vols. (New York, 1966–69), 2:1–12, 56–57.

In the case of eighteenth-century Britain, specific causes—some social, some intellectual—have already been assigned for the popularity of each of the narrower doctrines of progress discussed in this book. But why did the most general doctrines gain so many adherents? What were the sources of the belief in the progress of human culture? Equally important, how can the existence of differences between English and Scottish versions of this belief be explained?

SOCIAL CONTEXT AND INTELLECTUAL TRADITION

J. B. Bury claimed that "passionate desire for reform was the animating force which propagated the idea of Progress in France." Having already undergone its revolution, and enjoying relatively "large political liberties," the British nation tended "to regard change with suspicion," so that during the eighteenth century the belief in progress did not "have the same kind of success, or exert the same kind of effect" north of the Channel as south.[2] This theory errs in several respects. The idea of progress was undoubtedly *less* popular in France, where the tendency toward historical pessimism remained quite pronounced, than in England and Scotland. The desire for political reform may have diminished under the first two Georges, but it never disappeared (as the propaganda of Walpole's opponents testifies) and actually became very strong in the 1760s and 1770s. From Bolingbroke to Wilkes and Wyvill to Millar, many members of the political nation countenanced the possibility of change in the system of government or even worked for that end.

Certainly, reformers were in the minority. Yet relative political stability and satisfaction with the constitution really encouraged rather than restricted the growth of the idea of progress. The *Anglomanie* of Montesquieu, Voltaire, and other philosophes had its British reflection: most Britons took great pride in their supposedly mixed and balanced constitution, as evidenced by the frequent reprintings of Jean Louis de Lolme's celebratory *The Constitution of England* (translated 1775) and by the popularity of Blackstone's equally approving *Commentaries* (1765–69). This pride and the confidence it engendered would have had little to do with *historical* optimism if it had derived solely from a comparison of domestic and

2. J. B. Bury, *The Idea of Progress: An Inquiry into Its Origin and Growth* (London, 1920), 217–18.

contemporary foreign systems of law and government. But it also had roots in a comparison of present with past conditions. Blackstone, for instance, concluded his massive work with a chapter that sketched the "history of our laws and liberties; from their first rise, and gradual progress, among our British and Saxon ancestors, till their total eclipse at the Norman conquest; from which they have gradually emerged, and risen to the perfection they now enjoy." Supporters of the status quo, like the apologist for the Rockingham administration who wrote *An Essay on the Constitution*, might proceed from the assumption that the "freedom of the subject in England is now arrived at the highest degree of perfection consistent with the nature of civil government" to the conclusion that "it is the duty of every good Englishman to cry, . . . ESTO PERPETVA, without adding any contradiction to this pious wish, by wishing for any innovation or pretence of improving it." Others, like Price and even Blackstone, might hope or expect just such improvement. In both cases, however, the superiority of the present constitution to its predecessors—as the government apologist stated, the "progress of English liberty, from its lowest ebb to that glorious height to which it has arrived"—was taken to be a fact.[3]

That the sense of living in an excellent or perhaps the best political system, one which had historically changed for the better, fostered the belief in general progress is illustrated by the dozen Englishmen and Scots considered at length in the previous two chapters. In their comments on Britain, nearly all of them specifically discussed or at least mentioned the greatness of the present constitution and the long-term improvement that had produced it. This fact is significant for two related reasons. First, these thinkers and many of their contemporaries recognized that favorable political conditions were crucial to the existence of a thriving society. "Wherever the true Principles of Liberty are best established," wrote a London attorney, "there Arts and Sciences, Trade and Commerce, refined Morality, pure Religion, wise and just Policy, all the Social Virtues, and all that tends to make Length of Days desirable, or to give a prospect of a

3. William Blackstone, *Commentaries on the Laws of England* (1765–69), ed. Edward Christian, 15th ed., 4 vols. (London, 1809), 4:442 (Bk. IV, Ch. xxxiii); Anon., *An Essay on the Constitution of England*, 2d ed. (London, 1766), vii, v. For Blackstone's views on the future advance of English law, see Daniel J. Boorstin, *The Mysterious Science of the Law: An Essay on Blackstone's "Commentaries"* (Cambridge, Mass., 1941), 74–81.

happy Futurity, are most likely to flourish and abound."[4] Because such principles appeared to be in effect, it was much easier than otherwise to think that their extra-political benefits were being enjoyed.

Second, a positive opinion of the constitution represented one—but only one—result of the visibility of progress in the high eighteenth century. The *fact* of many-sided change, of increasing power, speed, and productivity, unavoidably confronted the educated and culturally aware Briton. Anyone who read newspapers and magazines, traveled across the land, or participated in an improving society or club would have been cognizant of the scope of technological innovation. Mechanical inventions, more rapid and convenient methods of transportation, recently discovered industrial processes, and new agricultural implements and techniques all presented themselves to the observant eye. Equally striking were economic changes. In Scotland's leading industry, the production of linen cloth, output tripled in volume between 1736–40 and 1768–71. England and Wales, for which longer statistical series are available, also showed impressive gains in manufacturing and commerce. From the 1730s to the 1770s, the amount of coal shipped coastally from the northeastern fields more than doubled; iron and steel exports increased by between 75 and 80 percent. At the heart of the new textile industry, raw cotton imports rose by a factor of five between the 1750s and the 1780s.[5] Meanwhile, throughout much of Britain, new and deeper mines and more and sometimes much larger manufacturing facilities were being established during the half-century before the French Revolution.

The technological and economic changes so central to the onset of the Industrial Revolution could not have been overlooked by those Englishmen and Scots who wrote extensively about general progress.

4. Anon. ["a Gentleman of the Middle Temple"], *A Critical Review of the Liberties of British Subjects* (London, 1750), 4.

5. The figures cited are taken or calculated from data presented in T. C. Smout, *A History of the Scottish People, 1560–1830* (New York, 1969), 244–45; Peter Mathias, *The First Industrial Nation: An Economic History of Britain, 1700–1914* (New York, 1969), 465–66, 479, 482, 486. On technological change and the awareness of it, see above, chap. 2. Between 1750 and 1780 there was a proportionately smaller but still quite significant growth in the number of families with incomes above £50 per annum, who increased demand for consumer goods: Neil McKendrick, "The Consumer Revolution of Eighteenth-Century England," in McKendrick, John Brewer, and J. H. Plumb, *The Birth of a Consumer Society: The Commercialization of Eighteenth-Century England* (Bloomington, Ind., 1985), 24.

With the exception of Worthington, each of them spent a significant portion of his life in a city or town that was a commercial or even a manufacturing center. Some of them had a more intimate knowledge of the state of economic activity: Smith and Price by virtue of their familiarity with the available trade statistics, Millar through maintaining a private legal practice and serving as a case arbiter in the Glasgow mercantile community, Priestley because of his close ties to industrialists like Wedgwood and Boulton from Birmingham and its general vicinity. In addition, only Worthington and Law are not known to have participated in one or more improving societies. Even if these organizations did not keep them supplied with information on the latest techniques in the practical arts or on the contemporary marvels of power, speed, and efficiency, then direct experience did. Millar, for example, who owned a small farm, was one of the many Scottish agricultural "improvers," as was Kames. The latter even wrote books entitled *Progress of Flax-Husbandry in Scotland* (1766) and *The Gentleman Farmer. Being An Attempt to improve Agriculture, By subjecting it to the Test of Rational Principles* (1776). He also made a tour of a colliery (for which he designed a coal-hauling cart), a tile-making facility, and undoubtedly, the great new Carron Ironworks located near one of his estates. Price served as a relay for the transmission between experimenters like Benjamin Franklin and Priestley of the most current news on the theory and uses of electricity and balloons. Priestley himself, of course, was deeply involved in a number of technical projects undertaken by members of the Lunar Society, including the improvement of Watt's steam engine.[6]

To those who looked closely, economic and technological changes and the benefits they brought were visible during the *entire* eighteenth century. Writing in the year of his death, Alexander ("Jupiter") Carlyle (1722–1805), the Moderate minister in the Scottish Church who was on intimate terms with the leading members of the republic of letters in Edinburgh and Glasgow, could reflect that over the course of his long lifetime (and, in fact, since 1688) Scotland "has been prosperous, with an increase of agriculture, trade, and man-

---

6. John Craig, "Account of the Life and Writings of John Millar, Esq.," in John Millar, *The Origin of the Distinction of Ranks*, 4th ed. (Edinburgh, 1806), lxxxvii–lxxxviii, lxviii–lxix; Ian Simpson Ross, *Lord Kames and the Scotland of His Day* (Oxford, 1972), 227, 315, 320, 328–29, 331, 338, 356, 362; Robert E. Schofield, *The Lunar Society of Birmingham: A Social History of Provincial Science and Industry in Eighteenth-Century England* (Oxford, 1963), 195, 250, 201–03.

ufactures, as well as all the ornamental arts of life, to a degree unexampled in any age or country." As Smith understood, "In England the improvements of agriculture, manufactures and commerce began much earlier than in Scotland," and having thus entered the Union as the decidedly junior, more backward partner the Scots had come even farther than the English during the eighteenth century. But throughout Britain, even before the 1750s, innovation confronted the keen observer on all sides. As Daniel Defoe wrote in 1726, "the improvements that encrease, the new buildings erected, the old buildings taken down: New discoveries in metals, mines, minerals; new undertakings in trade; inventions, engines, manufactures, in a nation, pushing and improving as we are: These things open new scenes every day." Nineteen years later a popular handbook on Britain claimed that of all nations

> None has more improved the *Mechanic Arts*. . . . Here are made the best *Clocks, Watches, Barometers, Thermometers, Air Pumps,* and all Sorts of *Mathematical Instruments*. . . . They have found out the Way to polish the Insides of great Iron Guns, and to weigh up Ships that are sunk to the Bottom of the Sea. They have invented the Use of Cane Chairs and several Engines for printing Stuffs and Linen, &c. Glass, Tin, Copper, Brass, Earthen and Horn Ware, they have improved to Admiration. . . . For Merchandize and Navigation, except the *Hollanders,* none come near them; and their surprizing wealth arising from Trade, is a plain Demonstration of it.

And, the handbook added, that commercial wealth and the power of the state had "advanced exceedingly" since 1688, arable lands were "increased as well as improved," and there had been a "vast increase of Navigation and Commerce."[7] For at least some observers of the earlier eighteenth-century scene, it was possible to discover signs of ongoing progress in the material life of the nation.

But for many others this was not yet the case. As late as the 1740s,

---

7. Alexander Carlyle, *Autobiography* (Boston, 1861), 407; Adam Smith, *An Inquiry into the Nature and Causes of the Wealth of Nations,* ed. R. H. Campbell, A. S. Skinner, and W. B. Todd, 2 vols. continuously paginated (Oxford, 1976), 94; Daniel Defoe, *A Tour through the Whole Island of Great Britain* (1724–26), Everyman's Library rev. ed., 2 vols. in 1 (London, 1974), 2:133 ("The Author's Preface to the Third Volume"); Guy Miege, *The Present State of Great Britain, and Ireland,* rev. [Samuel] Bolton, 10th ed. (London, 1745), 136, 17 (Chs. X, V).

for instance, economic pamphleteers found only fluctuation and not real growth in national productivity over the previous fifty years, and it was commonly believed that total population had remained stagnant in the same period.[8] There was good reason for the popularity of such opinions: recent estimates indicate that before 1745 real national output grew at a rate of only 0.3 percent per annum, while population expanded even less rapidly or not at all. In the second half of the eighteenth century, however, the rates of growth increased sharply. Population expanded by between 0.4 and 0.9 percent per annum over that period, and perhaps as early as the later 1740s. The annual rate of growth in national output probably accelerated to about 0.9 percent after 1745, and to about 1.8 percent after 1780. If the "take-off into sustained growth" did not occur until 1783–1802, the way was being cleared for it during the preceding thirty or forty years. This is apparent from other considerations, as well. Although it had been going on slowly for centuries, the enclosures of farm land—the hinge on which other agricultural innovations turned—proceeded at an enormously increased pace (by private Acts of Parliament) during the first half of the reign of George III, as a direct result of the rising demand for and price of food. The number of patents granted was more than four times higher in the four decades after 1750 than in the three decades before. Less measurable but no less real was the building of great numbers of turnpikes and canals from mid-century on. In short, if one looks for the start of

> rapid, cumulative, structural [economic] change, with the onset of rates of growth of up to 2 per cent per annum, with all the implications this involved, the industrial revolution can be located in time and place. Britain saw the beginning of such a process between the 1740's and the 1780's. Here came a break with a tradition of economic life, and a pace of change, which had lasted for centuries.

The "new surge of energy" moved forward in the economy "with all the greater force, it would seem, for the long period of waiting that preceded it."[9]

8. Phyllis Deane, *The First Industrial Revolution* (Cambridge, 1965), 11, 18.
9. Mathias, *First Industrial Nation*, 3; J. D. Chambers, *The Vale of Trent, 1670–1800: A Regional Study of Economic Change*, in *Economic History Review Supplements*, no. 3 (London, [1955]), 15. The general picture of economic and demographic developments presented in this paragraph is drawn from John B. Owen, *The Eighteenth*

In light of this profound alteration of the demographic and economic situation, it is not surprising that from mid-century minor
poets like John Dyer (in *The Fleece* [1757]) glowingly described the
advance of agriculture, commerce, and manufacturing, while other
writers began to challenge the notion of a static or declining population; that the economist and Anglican cleric Josiah Tucker in 1757
listed many "curious" examples of English "Contrivance of the mechanic Powers" and went on to claim that "at *Birmingham*,
Wolverhampton, *Sheffield*, and other manufacturing Places, almost
every Master Manufacturer hath a new Invention of his own, and is
daily improving on those of others"; or that a minister from eastern
Perthshire, writing in 1790, could describe the developments beginning forty-five years before as follows:

> In a few years improvements were diffused through the whole
> country. The tenants, as if awaked out of a profound sleep,
> looked around, beheld his [sic] fields clothed with the richest
> harvests, his herds fattening in luxuriant pastures, his family
> decked in gay attire, his table loaded with solid fare, and won-
> dered at his former ignorance and stupidity. The landlord re-
> joiced in the success of his schemes [for agricultural improve-
> ment], and shared in the honours and profits of this new
> erection. The manufacturer, mechanic, and tradesman, re-
> doubled their efforts to supply the increasing demand for the
> conveniencies and elegancies of life.

In 1774 Arthur Young asked his readers to "consider the progress of
every thing in *Britain* during the last twenty years." The "great improvements we have seen in this period," he continued,

---

Century, 1714–1815 (New York, 1976), 123–39, 295–316; Deane, *First Industrial
Revolution*, 18–50, 69–83, 115–33; Mathias, *First Industrial Nation*, 1–19, 73, 186–
95. Its details are largely taken from more specialized works: on population, Michael
Drake, ed., *Population in Industrialization* (London, 1969), 1, and M. W. Flinn, *British
Population Growth, 1700–1850* (London, 1970), 16–24; on rates of output and on the
onset of the Industrial Revolution, Phyllis Deane and W. A. Cole, *British Economic
Growth 1688–1959: Trends and Structure*, 2d ed. (Cambridge, 1967), 80, 280, 285, and
M. W. Flinn, *Origins of the Industrial Revolution* (London, 1966), 1–18; on enclosures,
J. D. Chambers and G. E. Mingay, *The Agricultural Revolution, 1750–1850* (New York,
1966), 77–82, and J. H. Plumb, *England in the Eighteenth Century* (Harmondsworth,
Eng., 1963), 82; on patents, B. R. Mitchell with Phyllis Deane, *Abstract of British
Historical Statistics* (Cambridge, 1962), 268.

superior to those of any other, are not owing to the constitution, to moderate taxation, or to other circumstances of equal efficacy, ever since the Revolution, as the existence of these circumstances did not before produce equal effects. —The superiority has been owing to the quantity of wealth in the nation, which has, in a prodigious degree, facilitated the execution of all great works of improvement.

There is no coincidence in the fact that precisely in the years to which Young and the Perthshire minister referred, the years in which the Industrial Revolution began to get underway, economic writers like Hume, Tucker, and Smith began to work out theories of economic growth, culminating in Smith's views on the "natural progress of opulence."[10] Nor is it accidental that only two published statements of the belief in general progress—those of Worthington and Law— appeared before this time. Without question, the increase in the visibility of material progress from about mid-century on contributed much to the spread and popularity of that belief.

The same can be said of the favorable turn in the tides of the Seven Years' War after 1758, when a new sense of national confidence suddenly replaced Brownian pessimism.[11] But even taken together, the start of the Industrial Revolution and the welcomed string of great military victories do not completely explain the *emergence* of doctrines of general progress: after all, Worthington's *Essay* and Law's *Considerations* were written before the 1750s by men living at the time in quiet backwaters. Moreover, these two developments strongly affected both England and Scotland, and the overall constitutional situation was essentially the same (and was perceived in much the same way) in each country during the high eighteenth century. Yet the Scots' view of general progress was notably different from that of

10. A. R. Humphreys, *The Augustan World: Society, Thought, and Letters in Eighteenth-Century England* (New York, 1963), 64, 66–70, 79; D. V. Glass, "The Population Controversy in Eighteenth-Century England. Part I. The Background," *Population Studies* 6 (July 1952): 69–91; [Josiah Tucker], *Instructions for Travellers* (privately printed; [London], 1757), 20–21; Sir John Sinclair, ed., *The Statistical Account of Scotland*, 21 vols. (Edinburgh, 1791–99), 1:514; Arthur Young, *Political Arithmetic. Containing Observations on the Present State of Great Britain* (London, 1774), 49–50; J. M. Low, "An Eighteenth Century Controversy in the Theory of Economic Progress," *Manchester School of Economic and Social Studies* 20 (Sept. 1952): 311–30.
11. See above, chap. 6.

the English. How, then, can this distinction be accounted for on the basis of social considerations?

From one point of view, changes in government and material conditions certainly began later and, in relative terms, advanced more quickly north of the Tweed, where most of the seventeenth century had been a virtual dark age. According to the Perthshire minister, as late as 1745 "the state of this country was rude beyond conception. The most fertile tracts were waste, or indifferently cultivated, and the bulk of the inhabitants were uncivilized." Given Scotland's late but rapid change, it could be argued that our group of Scots conceived of the progress of human culture in more limited terms than the English because they had a much briefer experience of actual improvement—too short to trust in its continuation. But looking at the facts from a second angle, the reverse argument is equally possible. Exposed to the swift transformation of an almost medieval way of life (even if the turning point may have been closer to 1660 than to 1707), seeing the patent contrast between the modernity of Edinburgh and the archaisms of the Highlands, the Scots had a more dramatic awareness of beneficial change in society and thus a more powerful reason for rising expectations than did the English. This line of reasoning receives support from the views expressed by a parish minister from southwest Scotland. Comparing the circumstances of his parish sixty or seventy years earlier with

> its present state of improvement, in agriculture, the manners, dress, and mode of living among its inhabitants, and their present sentiments in religion, the great improvement they have made in agriculture and civilization will appear in the most striking point [of] view; and as they are still in a gradual train of improvement at present, it gives the most flattering prospects of their future progress in the course of time.

Further support for the second perspective comes from the many projects for improvement, culminating in the quest for the building of a new Edinburgh, that were so typical of Scotland during the second half of the century. From either set of facts it would be appropriate to come to the conclusion that our group of Scots should have had at least as strong a future orientation as their neighbors to the south did. But in fact they did not. These two perspectives, though not quite mutually contradictory, illustrate the great difficulty in relying on the social context alone for arriving at a convincing explanation of why the Scots and the English differed on the subject of the progress of human culture, let alone why at base both groups believed in such progress at all.[12]

Nor does such an explanation lie wholly in intellectual factors. No questions, Hume declared,

> are more difficult, than when a number of causes present themselves for the same phaenomenon, to determine which is the principal or predominant. There seldom is any very precise argument to fix our choice, and men must be contented to be guided by a kind of taste or fancy, arising from analogy, and a comparison of similar instances.[13]

In the present case, the most useful analogy is between botanical growth and the growth of doctrines of general progress. To develop, a plant typically needs both suitable soil and accommodating atmospheric conditions, which work intimately together. It cannot live at all without being established below the surface, and it cannot flourish unless circumstances above are optimal. Similarly, in Britain the belief in progress on all fronts developed because of a favorable intellectual grounding and a congenial social climate. It attained vigor only when that climate became most propitious, in the 1750s and later, but even then its sine qua non was a rootage in intellectual tradition.

This tradition centered on the four narrower doctrines of progress that had such substantial popularity both before and after 1750. The most general forms given to the idea of progress in the eighteenth century were in fact combinations and extensions of these. Each of the dozen Englishmen and Scots whom we have seen formulating notions about the broad improvement of human culture also subscribed to at least three of the narrower doctrines. Furthermore, they

12. Sinclair, *Statistical Account of Scotland*, 1:513; 9:329. On the contrast between seventeenth- and eighteenth-century Scotland, the classic statement has been Hugh Trevor-Roper, "The Scottish Enlightenment," *Studies on Voltaire and the Eighteenth Century* 53 (1967): 1635–58. (Trevor-Roper advances a version of the second argument discussed in this paragraph.) But his view of the later seventeenth century has recently been challenged as too bleak. See, for example, R. H. Campbell and Andrew S. Skinner, eds., *The Origins and Nature of the Scottish Enlightenment* (Edinburgh, 1982), 4, and several essays included in that book. On the "startling" scale of improvement in Scotland during the eighteenth century, see John Butt, *The Mid-Eighteenth Century*, ed. and completed by Geoffrey Carnall (Oxford, 1979), 200.

13. David Hume, *A Treatise of Human Nature*, ed. L. A. Selby-Bigge, 2d ed., rev. Peter H. Nidditch (Oxford, 1978), 504n.

often tended to arrive at the former through the conceptual "displacement" of the latter. That is, they extended beyond customary patterns of use modes of thinking about progress that had become traditional, thereby making them into something new and more inclusive than before: doctrines of general progress.

The process of displacement plays an important part in the development of all new concepts and theories in science, technology, philosophy, and most other fields and disciplines. We have already seen it at work on several occasions, most notably among those clerics whose belief in the improvement of Christianity and religious knowledge received support from the idea of the pilgrim's progress and from Baconian conceptions about the advancement of learning.[14] There and elsewhere, the use of a standard metaphor or mode of discourse—like the paradox of the ancients and the comparison of ancients with moderns, respectively—in a new setting or in a somewhat different but still recognizable form is perhaps the best indication that displacement has occurred. Nearly as good a sign is the explicit application of conclusions reached on one issue to another. And displacement can at least be inferred where intimately related topics are addressed in juxtaposition and treated, one after the other, in parallel fashion. Following Hume's suggestion, "a comparison of similar instances"—in the writings of Law, Smith, and the others—will reveal displacement functioning in these various ways and, therefore, will show how much the belief in general progress owed to the narrower doctrines of progress so common at the time.

But it will also demonstrate that such doctrines, considered individually, did not always exert an equal force on each of the two groups of men who arrived at that belief. This fact, more than any other, explains why the typically English and Scottish descriptions of the improvement of human culture were at once alike and different. Variety, wrote Kames, "however great, is never without some degree of uniformity; nor the greatest uniformity without some degree of variety."[15] Whether his aphorism applies, as he thought, to all phe-

14. On the theory of conceptual displacement and its wide applicability, see Donald A. Schon, *Displacement of Concepts* (London, 1963), esp. ix–34; as Schon makes clear, the argument of his book has a close connection to Ernst Cassirer's view of metaphor. For displacement and the Christian vision of history, see above, chap. 3.
15. [Henry Home, Lord Kames], *Elements of Criticism*, 6th ed. (Edinburgh, 1785), 1:331 (Ch. IX, Appendix).

nomena, it certainly fits the case of the most comprehensive forms of the idea of progress, and their sources, in eighteenth-century Britain.

UNIFORMITY: TRIUMPHANT MODERNITY AND PLIABLE MAN

As has already become clear, both the English and the Scots believed that the arts and sciences—as a whole and, with the partial exception of the fine arts, individually—were progressive. In the writings of each group, this opinion customarily appeared with another, that modernity had triumphed over antiquity in art and science, and comparison of the ancients and moderns often led to broader conclusions about the advance of human culture.

Hume knew, as did the others, that there had been a "celebrated controversy" concerning the ancients and moderns, and they were all familiar with at least some of the literature and basic issues involved in it. Wotton, for example, was cited by Worthington, Law, and Gordon, and the polemical writings of Hakewill, Perrault, and Swift were also quoted by them and Kames. As with other participants in the eighteenth-century version of the "war," they themselves rarely launched vituperative attacks upon antiquity. Millar apparently adopted an irreverent attitude toward classical literature, Gordon said that Plato looked at "the fleeting shadows of his own mind; [Aristotle] at a bead-roll of categories," and Price called the Peripatetic philosophy "barbarous," but more typical was the recognition that the ancients were hardly without merit. Gordon found it "impossible to survey them without perceiving many circumstances, which strike the mind with awful admiration," Dunbar asked who could possibly arraign their genius, and Ferguson admitted that "We are certainly indebted to them" in the "strain of our literature, together with that of our manners and policy." In fact, the Greeks and Romans actually seemed superior in a few areas. Hume, Smith, and—with reluctance—Gordon gave them the palm in eloquence or oratory, Millar in epic poetry, and Kames in melody and the practical side of music.[16]

16. David Hume, "Of the Standard of Taste" (1757) and "Of Eloquence" (1742), *Essays Moral, Political, and Literary*, ed. T. H. Green and T. H. Grose, new impression, 2 vols. (London, 1898), 1:282, 164, 170–73; William Worthington, *An Essay on the Scheme and Conduct, Procedure and Extent of Man's Redemption*, 2d ed. (London,

Even so, no one attempted to build a more inclusive case for antique supremacy. The common acceptance of uniformitarianism, of course, made the seventeenth-century theory of continual degeneration completely untenable. Worthington quoted Tertullian, Arnobius, and Pierre Bayle against it, while Gordon claimed that if the theory were true "there must have been an end of the world, and it's [*sic*] wickedness too, before this time." Thinking that physique, life span, courage, and genius "seem hitherto to have been naturally, in all ages, pretty much the same," Hume concluded that it was impossible to "presuppose any decay in human nature" and that the thesis about a previously youthful and vigorous world was "imaginary." An assertion of the essential sameness of man and the world over time, however, did little or nothing to counteract what he along with Law, Gordon, Kames, and Millar considered "a propensity almost inherent in human nature": the "humour of blaming the present, and admiring the past," the tendency to "declaim against present times, and magnify the virtue of remote ancestors."[17] The refusal of Hume and the others to subscribe to such historical pessimism followed in part from the results of their comparison of the ancients to the moderns.

They had no doubt at all that the knowledge or learning of the latter towered above that of the former. In "science and philosophy, the moderns have not only equalled, but surpassed the antients," wrote Dunbar. As Worthington put it, "by far the greatest and most useful part" of extant knowledge the "Moderns may properly call

1748), 171, 151 (unless otherwise noted, all references are to the second edition); Edmund Law, *Considerations on the Theory of Religion*, ed. George Henry Law, new ed. (London, 1820), 247n–248n, 227n; [John Gordon], *A New Estimate of Manners and Principles*, 2 vols. (Cambridge, 1760–61), 2:xxxii, and 1:vii ("An Explanation of the Design of this Estimate"), 75, 83–85; idem, *Occasional Thoughts on the Study and Character of Classical Authors* (London, 1762), 3–6, 31; Kames, *Elements of Criticism*, 1:422 (Ch. XIV), and 2:464 (Ch. XXIV); idem, *Sketches of the History of Man*, new ed., 3 vols. (Edinburgh, 1813), 1:223–24, 235–37 (Bk. I, Sk. iv, Sect. 2); [Francis Jeffrey], untitled review of Millar's *Historical View*, *Edinburgh Review* 3 (Oct. 1803): 156; Richard Price, *The Evidence for a Future Period of Improvement in the State of Mankind* (London, 1787), 14; James Dunbar, *Essay on the History of Mankind in Rude and Cultivated Ages* (London, 1780), 175; Adam Ferguson, *An Essay on the History of Civil Society*, ed. Duncan Forbes (Edinburgh, 1966), 170; Adam Smith, *Lectures on Rhetoric and Belles Lettres*, ed. J. C. Bryce (Oxford, 1983), 196.

17. Worthington, *Essay*, 3, 150–52; Gordon, *New Estimate*, 1:31–33, 3, 17; Hume, "Of the Populousness of Ancient Nations" and "Of Refinement in the Arts," *Essays*, 1:382, 443, 307; Law, *Considerations*, 225–27, 231, 283; [Henry Home, Lord Kames], *Introduction to the Art of Thinking*, 2d ed. (Edinburgh, 1764), 45; John Millar, *An Historical View of the English Government*, 4th ed., 4 vols. (London, 1818), 4:174–75.

their own." He had in mind "natural and experimental Philosophy, Astronomy, and mathematical Learning in all its branches." In these and "all other parts of useful Learning, such discoveries and improvements have of late years been made, es[p]ecially by our great luminary Sir *Isaac Newton*, as render the present age enlighten'd beyond the hopes and imaginations of former times." Such statements were not intended to suggest that modernity owed no intellectual debts to the past. On the contrary, the Baconian principle of the continual accumulation of knowledge was accepted on all sides. Gordon and Priestley enunciated it directly, as did Ferguson in his comment that when nations succeed one another "in the career of discoveries and inquiries, the last is always the most knowing. . . . The Romans were more knowing than the Greeks; and every scholar of modern Europe is, in this sense, more learned than the most accomplished person that ever bore either of those celebrated names." The same principle sometimes appeared in standard literary garb, as when Worthington cited the paradox of the ancients, and when Gordon used a version of the giant-and-dwarf metaphor by writing that "We can easily make all, that men formerly knew, our own; . . . we can calmly look down from our eminence, and see where they, who went before us, were misled and lost their way; can correct their mistakes, avoid their errors, and mark out, and pursue . . . the direct road, which leads to truth."[18]

Nonetheless, the obligation to classical predecessors was not thought to be exceedingly large. "That is the least part of our knowledge, which is derived from the fountains of Antiquity," stated Worthington, and Dunbar and Gordon specifically rejected the opinion of men like Louis Dutens that the intellectual achievements of recent centuries represented mere borrowings from antiquity. For ancient and modern knowledge appeared to differ not only quantitatively, through the cumulative effect, but also qualitatively, because of methodological considerations. Smith spoke of the great superiority of the Cartesian—and even more of the Newtonian—

18. Dunbar, *History of Mankind*, 174–75; Worthington, *Essay*, 171–73; Gordon, *New Estimate*, 1:54, 74, 50; Joseph Priestley, *An Essay on the First Principles of Government*, 2d ed., corr. and enl., in *The Theological and Miscellaneous Works of Joseph Priestley*, ed. John Towill Rutt, 25 vols. in 26 ([London, 1817–32]), 22:125–26, 141; idem, *A Course of Lectures on the Theory of Language, and Universal Grammar* (Warrington, 1762), in *Works*, 23:228; Ferguson, *Civil Society*, 29. See also Law, *Considerations*, 241; Hume, "Of Eloquence," *Essays*, 1:164.

method to that pursued by Aristotle and his followers. Gordon made the same point, contending that the ancients (including Plato and the classical grammarians, rhetoricians, and poets, as well as Aristotle)

> knew scarce anything as we do. They never searched into the hidden sources of science. . . . Their knowledge, in short, was drawn rather from their own brain, than from nature. They trusted more to fancy, than to facts: and, like those ingenious architects, who begin their building from the roof, they framed curious hypotheses, which had no foundation to support them. Whereas we, leaving the airy flights of imagination, have taken the surer, though more humble path of sober reason and chastized reflexion; and ground our deductions on correct experiments, and accurate observation.

The distinction seemed immensely important to Gordon because "whatever depends upon experiment and observation, (which all the nobler and more useful parts of knowledge do) is capable of continual improvement." It was especially because of the recognition of advances in method that Price and the others could "look down with pity on the ignorance of the most enlightened times among the antients."[19]

In practical arts and techniques, too, the moderns were presumed to have advanced far beyond their antique forerunners. Hume, for example, referred to the superiority of modernity in mechanical skills and navigation, which had contributed to the easier subsistence of men. Priestley and Price cited the use of glass, paper, mills, time-pieces, and that traditional triad, optical instruments, printing, and gunpowder, as conveniences of comparatively recent invention that the "ancients were obliged to do without" and that had added greatly to human dignity and power.[20]

The case of the fine arts seemed somewhat less clear-cut. But even there, it was believed, the moderns had done much to recommend them over antiquity. If Hume and others applauded the eloquence of

19. Worthington, *Essay*, 172 [misnumbered as 176]; Dunbar, *History of Mankind*, 199; Gordon, *New Estimate*, 1:103, 69–70, 73–82, 101; Smith, *Lectures on Rhetoric*, 145–46; Richard Price, *Observations on the Importance of the American Revolution* (London, 1785), 5.

20. Hume, "Of the Populousness of Ancient Nations," *Essays*, 1:412–13; Joseph Priestley, *Lectures on History and General Policy*, American ed., Lecture LI, in *Works*, 24:314; Price, *Observations*, 5.

the Greeks, he ranked them below the French in drama, while Gordon and Kames went further and preferred the modern theater as a whole, because the ancients did not possess so perfect an understanding of true virtue and indulged in "numberless improprieties" in the construction of their plays. As for poetry in general, Millar assigned Shakespeare pride of place, and Kames asserted that even the leading figure among the ancients, Homer, lacked "such ripeness of judgment and correctness of execution, as in modern writers are the fruits of long experience and progressive improvements, during the course of many centuries." He lodged similar charges against Pindar and Vergil. Hume thought that modern authors had an important advantage in that their characters displayed more humanity and decency than those of Homer, the Greek tragedians, and other ancient poets. Instances of modern precedence in didactic, dramatic, and elegiac poetry were put forth by Gordon, who also claimed that recent refinements had pushed literary criticism "much beyond" its classical "clumsiness." He conceded supremacy to antiquity in architecture and sculpture, but Kames did not, thinking that architecture and gardening had only lately become fine as well as useful arts. Modern music, he hoped, would eventually be able to rival that of the Greeks; indeed, it was already superior to theirs in harmony and theory.[21]

Throughout the arts and sciences, then, both English and Scottish believers in general progress found evidence of an impressive—though not in every area a complete—victory for modernity over antiquity. They were no different in this respect than the majority of contemporary British writers on the subject. In their case, however,

21. Hume, "Of Civil Liberty" and "Of the Standard of Taste," *Essays*, 1:159, 282–83; Gordon, *New Estimate*, 1:21–22, 86–99, 75–76; Kames, *Sketches*, 1:215, 217, 220, 223–25, 237 (Bk. I, Sk. iv, Sect. 2); idem, *Elements of Criticism*, 2:423, 430–31 (Chs. XXIII–XXIV), and 1:27–28 (Ch. I); Millar, *Historical View*, 4:341. Robertson said that the moderns "must be content to equal, without pretending to surpass the antients" in the "elegant and polite arts": William Robertson, *The Situation of the World at the Time of Christ's Appearance, and its Connexion with the Success of his Religion, considered* (Edinburgh, 1755), 39.

There is evidence of some degree of adherence to literary primitiveness among the Scots. See, for instance, Ferguson's early account of the development of poetry and prose: *Civil Society*, 171–75. In addition, he, Robertson, and to some extent Kames joined Hugh Blair in promoting and defending Macpherson's *Ossian* in the early 1760s: see Richard Sher, *Church and University in the Scottish Enlightenment: The Moderate Literati of Edinburgh* (Princeton, 1985), 242–61. But Ferguson's later opinions about the arts were rather different (see above, chap. 7), and the *Ossian* affair probably had more to do with Scottish nationalism than with any deeply felt primitivism, literary or otherwise.

comparison of the ancients with the moderns was not confined to the past and present state of art and science alone. They often extended the comparison to other considerations and thereby displaced the idea of progress so that it encompassed more than ever before. This process can be seen at work in the most limited way in Price. He wrote that "Standing on [Newton's] shoulders and assisted by his discoveries we see farther than he did" and then asked rhetorically, "who should say, that our successors will not see farther than we do?"[22] Here a metaphor traditionally associated with the war was extended in its temporal range, making progress seem an integral part of the future no less than of the past.

Another sort of extension occurred much more frequently: a broadening of the field of the war, so that it included new topics and enlarged the bounds of what was thought to be progressing. Thus, in the midst of his discussion of Western history between the Dark Ages and the sixteenth century, Robertson examined the question of whether the population of certain European countries was higher in the ancient or the modern era, decided in favor of the latter, and linked this conclusion to improvement in the arts and increased economic activity. Priestley also contended that "all the western parts of Europe had few inhabitants in ancient times in comparison of what they have at present." Likewise, both Hume and Gordon claimed that the moderns exhibited better manners and more humanity than the ancients and, therefore, lived in less violent political circumstances. Ferguson felt that the Greeks and Romans were more active and vigorous in performing their civic duties than the peoples of his own day, but he nevertheless held that "we shall be found to have greatly excelled any of the celebrated nations of antiquity" in politeness, gallantry, the upholding of honor, and the adherence to a civilized code of behavior in war.[23]

Frequently this type of extension of the war led to a depiction of human culture as generally progressive. Worthington attempted to prove an increase in the longevity of man over the centuries in part by

22. Price, *Evidence*, 21.

23. William Robertson, "A View of the Progress of Society in Europe," in *The Works of Wm. Robertson, D.D.*, 8 vols. (Oxford, 1825), 3:4; Priestley, *Lectures on History*, Lecture LX, in *Works*, 24:379; Hume, "Of Civil Liberty," *Essays*, 1:162; idem, *An Enquiry concerning the Principles of Morals*, Sect. II, Pt. ii, in *Enquiries Concerning Human Understanding and Concerning the Principles of Morals, by David Hume*, ed. L. A. Selby-Bigge, 3d ed., rev. Peter H. Nidditch (Oxford, 1975), 180–81; Gordon, *New Estimate*, 1:24, 104, and 2:xxii, 105–06; Ferguson, *Civil Society*, 29–30, 194, 203.

asserting that "these latter generations in general have the advantage of the ancients, and . . . may be said to outlive them," insofar as they mature faster. The moderns, he continued, "are more knowing in every art and profession of life, and more capable of business," than their ancestors were at twice a given age. Law cited these remarks to support his opinions on the continual improvement of the arts and conveniences, and immediately afterward he approvingly quoted Ferguson's statement that the human species had a progress just as did the individual. In the course of claiming that antiquity was greatly inferior to more recent eras in commerce, Dunbar stated that the "spirit of commerce, which actuates modern ages, has opened a new path of ambition," and that the "civil and moral order of the world is certainly advanced by this great revolution." Along the same lines, Millar wrote that the "modern European nations have carried the advantages of liberty to a height which was never known in any other age or country," specifically including the "ancient states, so celebrated upon account of their free government." For him, "In the history of mankind, there is no revolution of greater importance to the happiness of society than this." The separation of juridical from administrative and military affairs, said Smith in his early lectures on rhetoric, "is the great advantage which modern times have over antient," and he went on to call it the "foundation of that greater Security which we now enjoy both with regard to Liberty, property and Life" and to link it to the "increase of Refinement." Later, in the *Wealth of Nations*, he noted that the "superiority of modern artillery . . . over that of the antients, is very great" and then proceeded to draw an important conclusion from this obvious fact:

> In antient times the opulent and civilized found it difficult to defend themselves against the poor and barbarous nations. In modern times the poor and barbarous find it difficult to defend themselves against the opulent and civilized. The invention of fire-arms, an invention which at first sight appears to be so pernicious, is certainly favourable to the permanency and to the extension of civilization.[24]

24. Worthington, *Essay*, 1st ed. (London, 1743), 422–23, and 2d ed., 343–50; Law, *Considerations*, 250n–251n; Dunbar, *History of Mankind*, 293–94; John Millar, *The Origin of the Distinction of Ranks*, 3d ed., reprinted in William C. Lehmann, *John Millar of Glasgow, 1735–1801: His Life and Thought and His Contributions to Sociological Analysis* (Cambridge, 1960), 315 (this reprint is hereafter cited as Millar, *Ranks*); Smith, *Lectures on Rhetoric*, 176; idem, *Wealth of Nations*, 708. Hume had

A broad comparison of the antique past with modernity served Priestley as evidence of general progress in history. Attend, he said, "to every advantage which the present age enjoys above ancient times, and see whether [you] cannot perceive marks of things being in a progress towards a state of greater perfection." He claimed in this regard that a "thousand circumstances shew how inferior the ancients were to the moderns" in religious knowledge, government, laws, arts, commerce, conveniences, manners, "and, in consequence of all these, in *happiness.*" Hume devoted the longest of his essays to the subject of ancient versus modern population, the "most curious & important of all Questions of Erudition," which he explored in much greater depth than did Robertson or Priestley. Montesquieu and others had held that antiquity must have been more populous than the modern world because it was assumed to be the greater age. Hume's research prompted him to "favour the opposite opinion to that which commonly prevails," and in his exposition he rejected Montesquieu's assumption as well. The issue of the "comparative populousness of ages or kingdoms," he wrote, "implies important consequences, and commonly determines concerning the preference of their whole police, their manners, and the constitution of their government." He spelled out the implication as his essay proceeded: "human nature, in general, really enjoys more liberty at present, in the most arbitrary government of EUROPE, than it ever did during the most flourishing period of ancient times"; in domestic life and manners, "in the main, we seem rather superior"; as to political "justice, lenity, and stability," no modern European republic is not "equal to, or even beyond . . . the most celebrated in antiquity"; and "Trade, manufactures, industry, were no where, in former ages, so flourishing as they are at present."[25] In brief, Hume thought that the greater populousness of modern over classical Europe went hand in hand with broad-ranging progress.

The most extensive example of how the ancients-and-moderns controversy could be expanded into a doctrine of general progress is

previously made a similar point about artillery: David Hume, *The History of England, from the Invasion of Julius Caesar to the Revolution of 1688*, new ed., 8 vols. (London, 1789), 2:432 (Ch. XV).

25. Priestley, *Lectures on History*, Lecture LXVII, in *Works*, 24:424–25; Hume to Robert Wallace, Sept. 22, 1751, in *New Letters of David Hume*, ed. Raymond Klibansky and Ernest C. Mossner (Oxford, 1954), 29; Hume, "Of the Populousness of Ancient Nations," *Essays*, 1:412–13, 383–85, 397, 402, 409–10.

Gordon's *New Estimate*. As its very subtitle indicates, the form of this book is a *Comparison between Ancient and Modern Times, In the three Great Articles of Knowledge, Happiness, and Virtue*, by means of which the author sought to demonstrate that there had been a "continual *Tendency to the better* in all human affairs."[26] Not even Priestley or Hume treated the war at such length or made it so clearly the fundamental ground of their belief in progress. But they and the others were at one with Gordon in asserting the triumph of modernity, and in conceptually displacing the comparison of classical with recent times beyond its traditional boundaries.

A second topic on which the English and Scots agreed was the pliability of man and the implications of that characteristic for general progress. This is true in spite of claims that the Scots found pliability to be of only limited force in the face of inherent human propensities, and that their belief in progress belonged to "a different family-tree" than that of Priestley, for example, because it did not have the same underpinnings in psychological theory.[27] To be sure, the common-sense philosophy of the later eighteenth century demonstrated a considerable tendency to return to innatism, and Kames and Ferguson (and presumably Dunbar) were influenced by the common-sense point of view. Yet neither that influence nor the widely accepted notion of some type of inborn moral sense prevented the Scots from insisting, with the English, on the great importance of nurture to human thought and action and, therefore, to progress.[28]

On some occasions, this insistence appeared in the plainest possible terms in comments on the mental, emotional, and moral constitution of humankind. Kames and Hume several times asserted that children had "tender" or "ductile" minds, so that during childhood "every object strikes the mind with the force of novelty; and the mind, soft like wax, yields to every impression, good or bad." Hume believed that although the passions were "of a very stubborn and

---

26. Gordon, *New Estimate*, 1:ii ("An Explanation of the Design of this Estimate"). See also *Occasional Thoughts*, where the question of ancients versus moderns is the groundwork for Gordon's consideration of many matters, including the traditional curriculum focusing on the classics.

27. J. A. Passmore, "The Malleability of Man in Eighteenth-Century Thought," in Earl R. Wasserman, ed., *Aspects of the Eighteenth Century* (Baltimore, 1965), 35–36; Duncan Forbes, "'Scientific' Whiggism: Adam Smith and John Millar," *Cambridge Journal* 7 (Aug. 1954): 649.

28. On common-sense philosophy and the moral sense, see above, chap. 7. Only Worthington and Robertson did not discuss the pliability of man in published works.

intractable nature" compared to the sentiments and understanding, which were "easily varied by education and example," it would be incorrect to think that human conduct was also unalterable. For moralists, politicians, and parents could provide "a new direction to those natural passions," such as when they contributed to "the giving us a sense of honour and duty in the strict regulation of our actions with regard to the properties of others." Likewise, Smith argued that although moral sentiments (unlike the sense of beauty) were only partly alterable by habit and fashion, still they varied according to the "different situations of different ages and countries."[29]

Two of the Scots pointed to the powerful influences of the will and environmental conditioning. The "genius of man," wrote Dunbar, "is so flexible, so open to impressions from without, so susceptible of early culture, that between heredity, innate, and acquired propensities, it is hard to draw the line of distinction." He went on to claim that "all the capital distinctions in individuals, families or tribes, flow from causes subsequent to birth; from education, example, forms of government; . . . but above all, from the free determinations of the will." Ferguson asked whether anything was so fixed in the nature of man as to be unchangeable by habit or custom. In his answer, he observed that while the "qualities of the mind, and the distribution of enjoyment and suffering" were governed by unalterable laws, habit *could* substitute one affection or temper of mind for another, it being "an object of supreme concern that they should be made for the better." The capacity to make such changes he called

> probably the most interesting fact that occurs in the history of man. By this law of his nature, he is intrusted to himself, as the clay is intrusted to the *hands of the potter*; and he may be formed by himself in the course of that life he adopts, as the vessel is formed by the other, for purposes of *honour* or *dishonour*.
>
> It is not in vain, therefore that man is endowed with a power of discerning what is amiss or defective in the actual state of his own inclinations or faculties. It is not in vain that

29. [Henry Home, Lord Kames], *Loose Hints upon Education, Chiefly Concerning the Culture of the Heart*, 2d ed., enl. (Edinburgh, 1782), iii, 297, 300–02, 311, 26; idem, *Sketches*, 1:476n (Bk. I, Sk. vi), 154 (Bk. I, Sk. iv, Sect. 2); idem, *Art of Thinking*, 34; Hume, "Of Eloquence," *Essays*, 1:164; idem, *Treatise*, 486, 572, 517, 521, 533–34; Adam Smith, *The Theory of Moral Sentiments*, ed. D. D. Raphael and A. L. Macfie (Oxford, 1976), 200, 204 (Pt. V, Ch. ii).

he is qualified to apprehend a perfection far beyond his actual attainments. . . . The smallest efforts which they lead him to make, lay the foundations of habit, and point to the end of a progress in which he is destined, however slowly, to advance.

In light of his ability to choose his habits, concluded Ferguson, man possessed "in his nature, a principle of ductility or pliancy" and was to a large extent "the artificer of his own nature, as well as of his own fortune."[30]

Given this perspective on man, it is not surprising that Ferguson emphasized the great force exerted on human existence by habit, custom, and education (in the broad sense). The other Scots did the same, even though some of them would never have followed him in attributing so extensive a role to volition. Thus, the necessitarian Kames wrote that "Custom is a second nature," and Hume said that "the far greatest part of our reasonings, with all our actions and passions, can be deriv'd from nothing but custom and habit."[31] But if a qualified environmentalism was a central principle of the Scots' "science of man," they came closest to being Newtons of the moral world when they elaborated that principle along associationist lines.

It has been argued that except for Hume they rejected the psychology of association, and that they did not derive their belief in progress from it, even in part.[32] In fact, however, they were no less convinced than their English counterparts of its importance in mental operations. Hume, of course, gave association a prominent place in his *Treatise*, and in the first *Enquiry* he continued to describe it as a "universal principle" that had an "equal influence on all mankind." Smith's youthful lectures on rhetoric called "associations of our Ideas," along with the origin and development of the passions, "matters . . . of importance," while one of his posthumous essays discussed the basic way in which association functioned. His *Theory of*

30. Dunbar, *History of Mankind*, 425, 433; Adam Ferguson, *Principles of Moral and Political Science*, 2 vols. (Edinburgh, 1792), 1:223–27, 232, 201–02; idem, *Civil Society*, 11.

31. Ferguson, *Principles*, 1:207–12, 219; Kames, *Elements of Criticism*, 1:403n, 400–01, 418 (Ch. XIV); idem, *Historical Law-Tracts*, 2d ed. (Edinburgh, 1761), 249; idem, *Art of Thinking*, 8–9; Hume, *Treatise*, 116–18; idem, *An Enquiry concerning Human Understanding*, Sect. VIII, Pt. i, in *Enquiries*, 85–86. See also Smith, *Wealth of Nations*, 28–29; idem, *Theory of Moral Sentiments*, 194, 200 (Pt. V, Chs. i–ii); Millar, *Historical View*, 4:174, 290.

32. Gladys Bryson, *Man and Society: The Scottish Inquiry of the Eighteenth Century* (Princeton, 1945), 144–45; Forbes, "'Scientific' Whiggism," 649.

Moral Sentiments treated association as the source of custom. According to Dunbar, "associations of thoughts" took place by means of an analogical faculty, which had "vast power . . . in all the mental arrangements." Kames devoted a section of one of his books to "association of ideas," a subject that he thought was "a plentiful source of speculation" deserving careful investigation, and elsewhere he named it "the law of [mental] succession." This law—"which must be natural, because it governs all human beings"—seemed to him, as to Hume, to be of "great importance" in the "science of human nature." But unlike Hume he refused to confine its modes of operation to resemblance, contiguity, and cause and effect. Ferguson also considered the process of association to be "a general law of our nature," believing that through habit it not only linked ideas but also produced moral judgments (and the actions following from them), religious opinions, and the affections and passions.[33]

In ascribing so much significance to association, the Scots were in accord with the two members of the English group who explored this aspect of psychology. Law interested himself in associationism as early as 1731, when he published and may have had a hand in writing John Gay's *Preliminary Dissertation.* After profitably studying Hartley, he referred in an essay of 1758 to the principle of association as a "universal *Law of our Nature*" that had no less "extent and influence in the intellectual World, than that of Gravity . . . in the Natural." In support of its centrality, he claimed that association accounted for the formation of the moral sense, the "whole tribe of *affections*," the so-called "natural" passions, and indeed all the "predominant qualities" of the mind. Even more strongly than Law was Priestley influenced by *Observations on Man*: he called Hartley an

---

33. Hume, *Human Understanding,* Sect. III, in *Enquiries,* 23–24; Smith, *Lectures on Rhetoric,* 93; idem, "The Principles which Lead and Direct Philosophical Enquiries; Illustrated by the History of Astronomy," *Essays on Philosophical Subjects,* ed. W. P. D. Wightman and J. C. Bryce (Oxford, 1980), 40–41; idem, *Theory of Moral Sentiments,* 194 (Pt. V, Ch. i); Dunbar, *History of Mankind,* 77–78; Kames, *Loose Hints upon Education,* 327, 331; idem, *Elements of Criticism,* 1:17–19, 22, 66–67 (Ch. I and Ch. II, Pt. i, Sect. 5); Ferguson, *Principles,* 1:139, 222, 136–37, 75, 126–27, 141–42, 147, 151. For Hume's view of association as expressed in the *Treatise* and *Abstract,* see above, chap. 4.

Among the common-sense philosophers, Reid, at least, was not as hostile to Hartley as is usually claimed: see his MS. "Miscellaneous Reflections on Priestley's account of Hartley's Theory of the Human Mind," as summarized in James McCosh, *The Scottish Philosophy: Biographical, Expository, Critical, from Hutcheson to Hamilton* (1875), repr. ed. (Hildesheim, 1966), 473–74.

"extraordinary man" and his "revered master." Thinking himself to be "more indebted to this one treatise, than to all the books I ever read beside, the Scriptures excepted," he defended it in print against criticisms by the common-sense school and twice published an abridgment of it. This version excluded Hartley's chapters on morals and religion and the details of his analysis of vibrations, on the grounds that they made the theory of association itself too inaccessible. Priestley actually had no substantive reservations about the omitted materials and intended eventually to publish them (a goal he never fulfilled). But of the whole "new and extensive *science*" contained in the *Observations*, it was association that seemed absolutely crucial to him. This principle, he believed, "comprehends all the other affections of our ideas, and thereby accounts for all the phenomena of the human mind," including moral judgments and the operation of mental faculties, as well as accounting for human actions. In brief, it was "a principle of immensely extensive application, both theoretical and practical."[34]

To have pushed the science of the human mind to the point where the significance of association was recognized seemed, in itself, to constitute progress. "Knowledge of this kind," wrote Priestley, "tends, in a very eminent degree, to enlarge the comprehension of the mind, to give a man a kind of superiority to the world and to himself,

---

34. Edmund Law, "The Nature and Obligations of Man, As a sensible and rational Being," in William King, *An Essay on the Origin of Evil*, trans. and ed. Law, 4th ed., corr. (Cambridge, 1758), lvi–lix; idem, *Considerations*, 11n–12n; Joseph Priestley, *An Examination of Dr. Reid's Inquiry into the Human Mind on the Principle of Common Sense; Dr. Beattie's Essay on the Nature and Immutability of Truth; and Dr. Oswald's Appeal to Common Sense on Behalf of Religion* (1774; 2d ed., 1775), "Preface" and "Introductory Observations," in *Works*, 3:6, 10, 15–24; idem, *The Doctrine of Philosophical Necessity Illustrated* (1777; 2d ed., 1782), "Dedication," in *Works*, 3:451; idem, *Hartley's Theory of the Human Mind, on the Principle of the Association of Ideas; with Essays relating to the Subject of It* (London, 1775), [iii]–v, xviii, xxiv, xlii–xlvi ("Preface" and "Introductory Essays"); idem, *Miscellaneous Observations Relating to Education; More Especially as It Respects the Conduct of the Mind* (1778), "Preface," in *Works*, 25:[5].

It should be noted that although Price debated a number of philosophical issues with Priestley, especially the question of free will, he never challenged the principle of association. Nor did he attack Hartley, but only the materialist deductions that Priestley made from Hartley's theory. In fact, Priestley wrote that "ideas are only vibrations in the brain, which corresponds to what Dr. Price might call modifications of the mind; so that on this subject our opinions are not materially, if at all different": see *A Free Discussion of the Doctrines of Materialism and Philosophical Necessity, in a Correspondence between Dr. Price and Dr. Priestley* (1778), Part II, Third Communication, in Priestley, *Works*, 4:64.

. . . to lay a foundation for equable and permanent happiness." As Law stated, "the more we are acquainted with the faculties of our own *soul*, the better qualified we must be to regulate and improve them." For him, because man possessed "a degree of liberty, or active power," the chief application of psychological science concerned the formation of new and better associations and the proper regulation of the moral sense, which would "promote the highest degree of happiness in social life." Ferguson, too, thought that psychological knowledge brought power to man, "in applying the laws of his nature to the command of himself." Believing in the freedom of the will to choose between alternatives (the "foundation . . . upon which we may safely erect the fabric of moral science"), he argued that a person could improve his conduct by reviewing his habits and associations, weeding out those that were bad and cultivating better ones. This process seemed to him to be of the greatest moment, showing as it did that the "virtue of goodness . . . is surely improveable [*sic*]." Kames cited the decline of patriotism in Britain as an instance of how an "association of repugnant opinions" could "mislead people from a just way of thinking." He went on to contend, however, that such associations were capable of being overcome, because "though we cannot add to the train [of our ideas] an unconnected idea, yet in a measure we can attend to some ideas, and dismiss others." Put another way, "a choice is afforded; we can insist upon one, rejecting others. . . . So far doth our power extend; and that power is sufficient for all useful purposes."[35]

The progressive implications of the principle of association were pursued by Smith in an entirely different direction. He theorized that the causal connection between natural objects or occurrences was understood by means of an "association of their ideas," in which there was "no break, no stop, no gap, no interval" and which soothed the imagination. When phenomena presented themselves in a new way or order, the chain of explanatory ideas in the mind was incomplete, so that the imagination could not immediately comprehend the phenomena. "Wonder" then disturbed mental tranquillity. The only way in which the imagination could "fill up this interval" in its train of ideas was to postulate "a chain of intermedi-

35. Priestley, *Hartley's Theory*, 370–71 ("Conclusion"); Law, *Considerations*, 264, 13n–14n, 288; idem, "Nature and Obligations of Man," in King, *Origin of Evil*, lviii–lix; Ferguson, *Principles*, 1:3, 151–55, 233 (also 130–31, 208, 217), and 2:404; Kames, *Loose Hints upon Education*, 334–35; idem, *Elements of Criticism*, 1:19 (Ch. I).

ate, though invisible, events, which succeed each other in a train similar to that in which the imagination has been accustomed to move, and which link together those two disjointed appearances." According to Smith, it was in this fashion that "philosophical" systems had been formed, and he judged such systems on the basis of "how far each . . . was fitted to sooth [sic] the imagination, and to render the theatre of nature a more coherent, and therefore a more magnificent spectacle, than otherwise it would have appeared to be." In his view, the advance of science culminating (to date) in Newton amounted to a lengthening of the total chain of associated ideas that the mind used to understand the external world.[36]

Psychology in general and association in particular appeared to have application in one other sphere: education, in the narrower sense of the term. And it was when discussing this subject that thinkers like Kames and Priestley most firmly connected the pliability of man to general progress. Eight of the twelve Scots and Englishmen were members of the teaching profession during at least part of their lives, and most of this group, along with Kames, wrote books or essays on education. These works make it clear that their authors were in the mainstream of eighteenth-century British pedagogical thought. For example, they agreed with other writers of the time on the failures of prevailing educational practice. Kames, Ferguson, Gordon, and Priestley disparaged the customary emphasis on classical languages and literature, an emphasis, they felt, that had once but no longer served a good purpose. The limited amount of instruction available to the lower classes evoked harsh words from Millar and Ferguson, while Priestley's background in the progressive dissenting academies encouraged him to call the education offered by the English public schools and universities "remote . . . from the business of *civil life*." Smith had experience with the English universities and the Grand Tour, and he condemned both.[37]

The point of such criticism was to call attention to the need for reforms in education, of which the most significant appeared to be the establishment of a new goal for the instruction of youth. Surely,

36. Smith, "History of Astronomy," *Essays on Philosophical Subjects*, 40–42, 46–47, 104–05.

37. Kames, *Sketches*, 2:393 (Bk. III, Preface); idem, *Art of Thinking*, sig. a3ʳ [v]; Ferguson, *Civil Society*, 77–78, 186; Gordon, *New Estimate*, 2:xxiv–xxvi; idem, *Occasional Thoughts*, passim; Joseph Priestley, *An Essay on a Course of Liberal Education for Civil and Active Life*, in *Works*, 24:15–19, 8–10; Millar, *Historical View*, 4:160; Smith, *Wealth of Nations*, 761–62, 764, 772–73, 781. See also Price, *Evidence*, 42–44.

stated Kames, "the educating of a young man to behave properly in society, is of still greater importance than the making him even a Solomon for knowledge." The teaching of grammar and syntax meant far less to him and the others than the formation of good men and virtuous, benevolent citizens.[38]

It was with that end in mind that the English and Scottish believers in general progress described education as a method for improving the condition of pliable man. On some occasions they set this description in the context of the individual. Hume thought that education had "a mighty influence in turning the mind" toward pursuits that promoted private happiness. Or as Kames declared, "How important then is the art of education, when upon it in a great measure depend, not only our behaviour and conduct; but even our judgment and understanding, by which we are elevated above the brute creation!" Most of the time, however, the context was much broader. Thus, Priestley argued that society could "never arrive at perfection till those vices to which men are most prone be either eradicated or disguised," and that there was no method of doing so "but by early and deeply inculcating the principles of integrity, honour, and religion, on the minds of youth, in a severe and virtuous education." Such tuition seemed to Price to be "the only means of gaining free scope for the progress of truth; and of exterminating the pitiful prejudices we indulge against one another; and of establishing *peace on earth and goodwill amongst men.*" Because they opposed the imposition of a uniform, public system of instruction for children, these two Dissenters would only with reservations have accepted Kames's statement that "Education may well be deemed one of the capital articles of government. It is intitled to the nursing care of the legislature." But they would certainly have agreed with his observation that "no state has ever long flourished, where education was neglected." And although they were not so worried about luxury as he, they would not have objected when he found the care taken by parents in the education of their offspring to be the principal means "to stem the tide of corruption in an opulent and luxurious nation."[39] For both he

38. Kames, *Loose Hints upon Education*, 15, 82; idem, *Sketches*, 2:393, sig. Bb[4r] [391] (Bk. III, Preface). For some other comments on this subject, see Priestley, *Lectures on History*, Preface, in *Works*, 24:5; idem, *Miscellaneous Observations Relating to Education*, Preface, in *Works*, 25:6, 8; idem, *Essay on Government*, in *Works*, 22:44; Gordon, *New Estimate*, 2:xxiv–xxvi; Price, *Evidence*, 41, 47.

39. Hume, "Of Refinement in the Arts," *Essays*, 1:300; Kames, *Loose Hints Upon Education*, 296, 22, 198–99; idem, *Art of Thinking*, x; Priestley, *Lectures on History*,

and they saw in child-rearing and schooling a cure for moral and social diseases.

The analogy between education and "medicine of the mind" became patent in Smith, who (along with Millar and Ferguson) proposed to remedy the harmful effects of the division of labor on the working classes. After recommending universal military training as a method of overcoming the aversion of the common people to the soldier's life and duties, Smith remarked that

> happiness and misery, which reside altogether in the mind, must necessarily depend more upon the healthful or unhealthful, the mutilated or entire state of the mind, than upon that of the body. Even though the martial spirit of the people were of no use towards the defence of the society, yet to prevent that sort of mental mutilation, deformity and wretchedness, which cowardice necessarily involves in it, from spreading themselves through the great body of the people, would still deserve the most serious attention of government; in the same manner as it would deserve its most serious attention to prevent a leprosy or any other loathsome and offensive disease, though neither mortal nor dangerous, from spreading itself among them.

Smith thought that much the same thing could be said of his proposed national system of basic instruction, aimed at curing the "gross ignorance and stupidity which, in a civilized society, seem so frequently to benumb the understandings of all the inferior ranks of people." For the man who cannot properly use his intellectual faculties "seems to be mutilated and deformed in a still more essential part of the character of human nature" than does the coward. The state "derives no inconsiderable advantage" from the instruction of such people, since the "more they are instructed, the less liable they are to the delusions of enthusiasm and superstition" that lead to social insubordination and disorder.[40] If Bentham did not actually derive his conception of the legislator-as-moral-physician from Smith, he certainly could have done so.

Lectures LV–LVI, in *Works*, 24:342–43; Price, *Evidence*, 42. For Priestley's opposition to standardized state education, see *Essay on Government* and *Lectures on History*, Lecture XXXVIII, in *Works*, 22:40–54, and 24:223.

40. Smith, *Wealth of Nations*, 787–88. For some related comments by Millar and Ferguson as well as by Smith, see above, chap. 7.

In a more comprehensive way, Hume, too, considered education to be a connection between pliable man and the development of a good society. Human beings, he wrote, "are generally contented to acquiesce implicitly in those [social] establishments, however new, into which their early education has thrown them." Therefore, "general virtue and good morals in a state, which are so requisite to happiness, . . . must proceed entirely from the virtuous education of youth, the effect of wise laws and institutions." Even the "sense of justice and injustice is not deriv'd from nature, but arises artificially, tho' necessarily from education, and human conventions." And just as "publick praise and blame encrease our esteem for justice; so private education and instruction contribute to the same effect." Recognizing this to be true, parents are

> induc'd to inculcate on their children, from the earliest infancy, the principles of probity, and teach them to regard the observance of those rules, by which society is maintain'd, as worthy and honourable, and their violation as base and infamous. By this means the sentiments of honour may take root in their tender minds, and acquire such firmness and solidity, that they may fall little short of those principles, which are the most essential to our natures, and the most deeply radicated in our internal constitution.

Beyond early education in morals, Hume also recommended the study of history, because it not only amuses the fancy but also "improves the understanding, and . . . strengthens virtue." Without it, he claimed, "we should be for ever children"; with it, a man may be said "to have lived from the beginning of the world, and to have been making continual additions to his stock of knowledge." For a historical experience of past ages could "contribute as much to our improvement in wisdom, as if they had actually lain under our observation."[41]

---

41. Hume, *History of England*, 4:127 (Ch. XXXI); idem, "Of Parties in General" and "Of the Study of History," *Essays*, 1:127, and 2:389–90; idem, *Treatise*, 483, 500–01. On the value of historical study, see also Priestley, *Course of Liberal Education*, in *Works*, 24:12–15, 22–23.

Passmore overstates his case when he argues that, on the whole, education "comes off rather badly" in Hume, especially by comparison with its treatment in Locke: "Malleability of Man," 35–36. Hume was certainly not a complete environmentalist (but neither were most of his contemporaries or, for that matter, Locke: see above, chap. 4). He contended that "As a stream necessarily follows the several inclinations of

Hume did not himself focus on the role of association in education, but others did. According to Kames, "It is of importance in the education of youth, that this succession [of related thoughts or ideas] be preserved entire, free from ill-sorted ideas that have originally no relation." Because "our erroneous conceptions are the result of misguided education, or of wrong impressions made during childhood," he thought it "a chief concern of the tutor to prevent in his pupil an association between truth and error." Smith held that the "great secret of education is to direct vanity to proper objects," vanity being, in his view, the motor force impelling individuals to seek improvement. Pursuing his claim that the main application of Hartley's theory of the mind was in the instruction of youth, Priestley wrote some general observations on education in which he "made great use of the doctrine of Association." There he asserted that as "a necessary consequence of the principles of association, . . . the mind grows more callous to new impressions continually; it being already occupied with ideas and sensations which render it indisposed to receive others." By implication, the happiness or misery experienced over the entire course of life "depends, in a great measure, on the manner in which we begin our progress through it." Therefore, "too much attention cannot be given to education, and the conduct of early life. Supposing the present laws of our minds to continue, . . . our happiness to endless ages must depend on it."[42] For Priestley, the establishment of correct associations through education provided the key to human felicity and progress.

Whether they emphasized the association of ideas, nearly all of

---

the ground, on which it runs, so are the ignorant and thoughtless part of mankind actuated by their natural propensities. Such are effectually excluded from all pretensions to philosophy, and the *medicine of the mind,* so much boasted. But even upon the wise and thoughtful, nature has a prodigious influence." Yet three paragraphs later he could write that the "prodigious effects of education may convince us, that the mind is not altogether stubborn and inflexible, but will admit of many alterations from its original make and structure." He then went on to discuss how "Habit is another powerful means of reforming the mind, and implanting in it good dispositions and inclinations": "The Sceptic" (1742), *Essays,* 1:221–23. This is really the same thing that the majority of eighteenth-century British educationalists and Locke himself were saying.

42. Kames, *Loose Hints upon Education,* 328, 331; Smith, *Theory of Moral Sentiments,* 259 (Pt. V, Sect. iii); Priestley to Rev. John Bretland, Jr., Dec. 28, 1777, in John Towill Rutt, *Life and Correspondence of Joseph Priestley,* 2 vols. (London, 1831–32), 1:304; Priestley, *Miscellaneous Observations Relating to Education,* Sect. XII, in *Works,* 25:50–51. For Priestley's comment on the main use of Hartley's theory, see above, chap. 4.

Richard Price

the English and Scottish believers in general progress had a lively awareness of the latent power of education. For that power to achieve its full positive effect, they thought, pedagogy had to be reformed. As Price suggested, if only the true goal of education had been pursued in the past, "mankind would now have been farther advanced"; once reformed, education "will quicken the progress of *improvement*." Consequently, he found it almost impossible to insist strongly enough on the importance of education. But neither he nor anyone else would have made such insistence without a prior recognition of human pliability. "So much is left by the author of nature," he wrote,

> to depend on the turn given to the mind in early life, and the impressions then made, that I have often thought there may be a *secret* remaining to be discovered in education, which will cause future generations to grow up virtuous and happy, and accelerate human improvement to a greater degree than can at present be imagined.

Or as he said elsewhere,

> On the bent given to our minds as they open and expand, depends their subsequent fate; and on the general manage- ment of education depend the honour and dignity of our spe- cies. . . . I often think there may remain a secret in it to be discovered which will contribute more than any thing to the amendment of mankind. . . .
> . . . Improvement, in [education], must be in the highest degree useful. It has a particular tendency to perpetuate itself. . . . One generation thus improved communicates improve- ment to the next, and that to the next, till at last a progress in improvement may take place rapid and irresistable, which may issue in the happiest state of things that can exist on this earth.[43]

Kames, Smith, and Priestley felt that the formation of good asso- ciations was the secret to which Price referred. Even without the associationist perspective, however, Price's statements offer the clearest possible example of how, so frequently, the doctrine of pliability was extended in its field of reference from the individual to the multitude, was applied to education, and ultimately was dis-

43. Price, *Observations*, 56, 50; idem, *Evidence*, 34–36.

placed into a belief in general progress. Pliable man: in the hands of both the English and Scottish groups, this common notion—like that of triumphant modernity—grew into doctrines of progress in human culture.

VARIETY: LANGUAGE, RELIGION, AND PROGRESS

Much as they agreed about the question of ancients versus moderns and the import of education and human psychology, the English and the Scots nonetheless tended to have recognizably distinct ways of treating the relationship of language to progress. As a group the Scots showed much the greater interest in this subject, and they emphasized different aspects of it than did their counterparts to the south.

Nearly all the members of the Scottish group wrote on language,[44] and none with more influence than Smith. One of the major preoccupations of their language study is illustrated by his "Considerations concerning the First Formation of Languages" (originally published 1767), in which he attempted to reconstruct the outlines of early linguistic development. Stewart thought this essay to be "a very beautiful specimen of theoretical history," and it certainly does represent the application of "natural" historiography to yet another sphere of human life. Smith began by postulating the existence of two savages who had grown up apart from any society, had never been taught to speak, and therefore obviously stand for early human beings. His object was to deduce the manner in which they would have acquired language. He concluded that impersonal verbs and proper nouns would have arisen first, followed relatively soon by common nouns (through generalization), adjectives, and the use of inflection. The whole process, he believed, would have demonstrated an increasing capacity for abstraction and would have led to a more and more complex system of speech. In this hypothetical and naturalistic account, he made no effort to discuss directly the ultimate source of language. Some of his fellow-countrymen did, but with much equivocation, as reflected in Dunbar's statement that "language may be accounted in part *natural*, in part *artificial*: in one view

---

44. The exception is Millar, but even he was said by a student to have made "many profound and original observations" on language in his lectures: [Francis Jeffrey], untitled review of Millar's *Historical View, Edinburgh Review* 3 (Oct. 1803): 158.

it is the work of providence, in another it is the work of man." These Scots did not reject outright the theory of a divine origin, and—unlike other British students of language—they occasionally described speech as instinctive or innate. Yet, on the whole, they and Smith seem to have preferred to think of language in the same way that Monboddo did, as an art of strictly human provenance.[45]

In any event, origins mattered less to them than development. For they thought that, once invented, languages began a long career of constant, gradual change. And that change was usually considered to have been for the better: "In its progress toward perfection," wrote Kames somewhat redundantly, "a language is continually improving, and therefore continually changing." Smith specified how this could be so. When men first started to use speech, he argued, they tried to express the whole meaning of each event in a single word. Confronted by a growing number of different events, they were eventually forced to abandon this early arrangement in favor of one in which there was a word for each of the "metaphysical elements" that together constitute occurrences. "The [verbal] expression of every particular event, became in this manner more intricate and complex, but the whole system of the language became more coherent, more connected, more easily retained and comprehended."[46]

Having advanced so far, observed Smith, language did not then

45. Dugald Stewart, "Account of the Life and Writings of Adam Smith, LL.D.," *The Collected Works of Dugald Stewart*, ed. Sir William Hamilton, 11 vols. (Edinburgh, 1854–60), 10:37; Adam Smith, "Considerations concerning the First Formation of Languages, and the Different Genius of original and compounded Languages," in *Lectures on Rhetoric*, 203–18; Dunbar, *History of Mankind*, 61, 67–68. For Smith's influence, see Christopher J. Berry, "Adam Smith's *Considerations* on Language," *Journal of the History of Ideas* 35 (Jan.–March 1974): 130–31, 135, 138. On the question of whether language had a divine or human origin or was instinctive, see Kames, *Sketches*, 1:59–61 ("Preliminary Discourse, concerning the Origin of Men and Languages"); Ferguson, *Civil Society*, 3, 6; idem, *Principles*, 1:39–43, 287; idem, *Institutes of Moral Philosophy*, 2d ed., rev. and corr. (Edinburgh, 1773), 43–44. And see also [James Burnett, Lord Monboddo], *Of the Origin and Progress of Language*, 6 vols. (Edinburgh, 1773–92), vol. 1 (2d ed., 1774), viii–ix, 12, 39–41, 201, 207–09, 214, 378, 380, 488, 579.

In the first volume of his *Origin and Progress of Language*, Monboddo addressed such questions as the rise of articulate speech and presented a general conjectural account of the early development of linguistic structures: see, for example, ibid., 1:187–88, 256–57, 269, 297, 461–68, 475–82, 495–97, 518–31, 537–39, 569–73. The second volume deals with the history of the parts of speech at greater length.

46. Kames, *Sketches*, 1:250 (Bk. I, Sk. iv, Sect. 2); Smith, "Considerations," in *Lectures on Rhetoric*, 217–18. On the constant change of language, see also Ferguson, *Principles*, 1:44–45; Monboddo, *Origin and Progress of Language*, 1:666.

cease to develop but instead began to change in the direction of simplification, as the use of personal pronouns, auxiliary verbs, and prepositions replaced the previously intricate system of conjugation and declension. He contended that although a reduction in the number of moving parts produced better machines, the analogous simplification of language resulted in growing imperfection and decline, and on that basis he preferred the highly inflected classical Greek and Latin to modern European tongues. Ferguson considered linguistic decay to be at least possible, and Dunbar presented it as an inevitability once a language reached its highest state. But this view (explicitly rejected by Kames) did not prevent either of them from asserting that human psychological structure permitted or even forced language "to advance towards its perfection." Indeed, with the exception of Smith, the Scots normally thought of the overall natural history of language as a process of gradual yet astonishing improvement. The speculative mind, wrote Ferguson, "is apt to look back with amazement from the height [language] has gained," just as one who, "rising insensibly on the slope of a hill, should come to look from a precipice of an almost unfathomable depth, to the summit of which he could scarcely believe himself to have ascended." And what was true of language in general was true of the modern European tongues in particular, including English, all of which Robertson believed to have been slowly refined after the Renaissance.[47]

The Scots had as little to say about the future of language as about what was still to happen in other areas of human life. For example, they did not develop or promote any scheme for a universal system of speech or writing, cherished no Hartleyan dream of mathematically precise verbal communication, expressed no Bentham-like desire to legislate lexicographically a new world of words. Nor did they hope to see the government establish institutions that would regulate English, although Hume regretted that "Even to this day, no society has been instituted for the polishing and fixing of our language." The goal of linguistic permanence, however, seemed important to some of

47. Smith, "Considerations," in *Lectures on Rhetoric*, 218–26; Ferguson, *Principles*, 1:43–45; Dunbar, *History of Mankind*, 124, 138–39, 90; Kames, *Sketches*, 1:249–51 (Bk. I, Sk. iv, Sect. 2); Robertson, *The History of Scotland*, Bk. VIII, in *Works*, 2:242–46. Throughout the six volumes of his *Origin and Progress of Language*, Monboddo expressed a clear preference for the classical languages (especially Greek), while arguing that the decline of inflection made the modern European tongues inferior; he took up Smith's question of simplicity versus complexity in 1:568–69.

them, like Kames, which in part explains why he encouraged Scottish gentlemen to set up their own "school of languages" with Thomas Sheridan as its headmaster. Sheridan's lectures on correct English elocution led the Edinburgh Select Society—of which Kames, Hume, Robertson, and Ferguson were members—to create a subsidiary Select Society for Promoting the Reading and Speaking of the English Language. But even in the case of this organization, the future progress or even the permanence of language was not a passionate concern of the Scots: after all, to them promoting English meant ending a source of personal embarrassment (the use of "Scotticisms") and gaining in politesse more than it meant improving a medium of communication.[48]

As the principal form of human communication, language was assumed by them to exist in an intimate, reciprocal relationship with thought and society. "Language is the instrument of society," said Ferguson, "and . . . man is indebted to society for every exercise of his faculties, of which language is formed to express the attainment or the use."[49] Similarly, Smith's "Considerations" rested on the rationale that linguistic systems had developed in step with intellectual and social evolution. For the Scots as for most other contemporary students of language, this historical connection worked two ways: language was the improved as well as the improver.

The improvement of language, they believed, fundamentally depended on intellectual advance. "In proportion as minds are knowing, comprehensive, and ingenious," Ferguson declared, "language is copious and regular," because it represents "the emanation of idea in the mind of man." Therefore, asserted Dunbar, it "increases with the experience and discernment of mankind" and, "by the enlargement of the fund [of ideas], . . . is constantly enriched." In brief, as Kames wrote, it "is gradually improved to express whatever passes in the mind." Social change, and especially the refinement of manners, appeared to make some contribution to linguistic progress, but not

48. Hume, *History of England*, 6:167 ("Appendix to the Reign of James I"); Kames, *Sketches*, 1:250–51 (Bk. I, Sk. iv, Sect. 2). On Sheridan's lectures in Edinburgh during 1761 and their institutional result, see above, chap. 5.

49. Ferguson, *Principles*, 1:269. On the general relationship of language to society and thought, see also Hume, *Treatise*, 490; idem, *Principles of Morals*, App. III, in *Enquiries*, 306; idem, *History of England*, 5:483 (App. III); Kames, *Elements of Criticism*, 2:24 (Ch. XVIII, Sect. ii); Dunbar, *History of Mankind*, 91. The developmental linkage of language, thought, and society is assumed throughout Monboddo, *Origin and Progress of Language*, vol. 1.

nearly as much as that made by the development and accumulation of knowledge.[50]

When the Scots turned their attention to the role of language as the improver, they concentrated on the way in which linguistic communication seemed to constitute a vessel for progress. Notwithstanding the diversity of tongues, Ferguson contended, mankind's talent for language served to unite their efforts in

> one common purpose of advancement in the progress of intelligence. The lights of science are communicated, from the parts in which they sprang up, to the remotest corners of the habitable world. The works of singular genius are a common benefit to mankind; and the whole species, on every quarter, in every nation, and in every age, co-operates together for one common end of information, invention, science and art.

The use of writing, he added, was the primary means by which the human species could transmit the benefits of knowledge across space and time. Without it, said Kames, no branch of science could make progress; with the coming of its printed form, social attitudes had been changed for the better through the spread of rational principles and "a great revolution in learning."[51]

Because language acted as a secure, preserving vessel, Ferguson concluded, the "present age is perfecting what a former age began; or is now beginning what a future age is to perfect." By locating in verbal communication the source of the all-important Baconian cumulative effect, this statement offers one example of how the Scots' study of language sometimes grew into—or, at least, encouraged their acceptance of—a doctrine of general progress. Robertson and Kames provide further instances of the same process of displacement. In Robertson's published writings, the notion of a *general* trend toward

50. Ferguson, *Principles*, 1:287–88; Dunbar, *History of Mankind*, 93–94, 66, 109; Kames, *Elements of Criticism*, 2:270 (Ch. XX, Sect. v). See also Hume, "Of National Characters," *Essays*, 1:253. Climate and the "intermixture of different nations" were also mentioned as influences on the growth of language: Dunbar, *History of Mankind*, 112; Smith, "Considerations," in *Lectures on Rhetoric*, 220–21. For the general influence of the rise of the social arts and thought on language, see Monboddo, *Origin and Progress of Language*, 1:215–16, 236, 359, 577.

51. Ferguson, *Principles*, 1:36, 45, 296; Kames, *Sketches*, 2:384 (Bk. II, Sk. xii), and 1:136 (Bk. I, Sk. iv, Sect. 1); idem, *Loose Hints upon Education*, 311–12. On language as the improver, see Monboddo, *Origin and Progress of Language*, 1:385. Monboddo specifically described the state of language as an intellectual index: ibid., 1:154, 569, 574.

refinement in European history appeared earliest in a discussion of the refinement of *language*. There Robertson suggested that the rise of modern languages out of barbarism had much to do with "improvements in taste, in the arts, and in the sciences," and that these were in turn characteristic of the "polished nations of Europe." Such improvements were not to be found in backward Scotland, however, whose native tongue had never been able to advance. Likewise, it was a linguistic topic, the origin of diverse languages at Babel, that marked the starting point for Kames's *Sketches of the History of Man*. Conceiving that the confusion of tongues created a state of degeneracy, deprived men of society, and therefore "rendered them savages," he undertook in his book to "trace out [their] progress towards maturity in different nations" over the course of history.[52]

Thus, the Scots had a substantial interest in language and especially in its development and connection with thought and society, an interest that was intimately bound up with their conception of progress from rudeness to refinement. Among their English counterparts, however, deep concern with the whole subject of language was the exception rather than the rule. Linguistic history, in particular, received no attention at all in the published works of Law and Price, and very little more in those of Worthington and Gordon.[53] Priestley alone demonstrated the kind of curiosity about the development of language that was typical of the Scots.

In one set of his Warrington lectures, he insisted that no truly philosophical person could read history without observing "whatever occurs with respect to the *languages* of different ages and nations. Every thing relating to their rise, progress, and revolutions, will demand his attention." This program was put into practice in a book based on another course he offered at Warrington, *Lectures on the Theory of Language, and Universal Grammar* (privately printed, 1762). There Priestley argued that languages changed constantly, and that each of them underwent "a kind of regular growth, improve-

52. Ferguson, *Principles*, 1:47; Robertson, *History of Scotland*, Bk. VIII, in *Works*, 2:242–44; Kames, *Sketches*, 1:65 (Prelim. Discourse). The study of language was the organizing principle around which Monboddo built his theory of human history.

53. Worthington discussed the divine origin of language and, along with Priestley, the question of Babel: Worthington, *Essay*, 20, 96–97; Priestley, *Lectures on Language*, Lecture XIX, in *Works*, 23:242–44. Gordon's only comment on the history of language was—as might be expected—that English and French were in important respects the equals of or even superior to classical Greek and Latin: *New Estimate*, 1:85 (cf. 2:xiv–xv).

ment, and declension." Although he briefly examined the nature and causes of linguistic decay, he focused his attention primarily on the improving stage of the cycle. As depicted by him, the advance of language consisted of two fundamental elements. One of these was an increase in the size of vocabulary, proportional to the increasing experience and knowledge of man. The other was changes in grammatical structure, and in this context Priestley described the development of the parts of speech much as Smith did five years later. But unlike Smith, he did not find the overall tendency of the history of grammar to be in the direction of simplicity. Rather, it was toward coherence and connectedness in speech, whether through a more and more sophisticated system of inflection or through the employment of auxiliaries.[54]

Priestley's analysis of the regular process of linguistic development constituted an exercise in the kind of "natural" historiography so commonly practiced by the Scots. And as with them it led him to discover a transition from "barbarous language to a state of perfection," a "progress from [extreme] simplicity to refinement" in speech. There is more than coincidence in the fact that the topic on which he sounded most like his Scottish contemporaries was also the one to which he did not consistently apply the conception of indefinite progress. "There are certain limits beyond which the growth of a language cannot extend," he wrote. Indeed, "all the pains that we bestow upon a language, when it is sufficiently perfect for all the uses of it, serve only to disfigure it, to lessen its real value, and encumber it with useless rules and refinements."[55]

Not being entirely consonant with his standard view of history, this finding must have troubled Priestley. He certainly went to considerable lengths to soften its impact, especially with respect to his native tongue. Although in one place he could assert that English "seems to be as near to its meridian as possible," having become uniform and "arrived to its maturity and perfection" at about the time of Queen Anne, elsewhere he looked for it to "come in for some

54. Priestley, *Lectures on History*, Lecture LXVI, in *Works*, 24:421; idem, *Lectures on Language*, Lectures XI–XIV, XVII, in *Works*, 23:185–211, 227 (the quotation is on 191). Priestley's lectures on language, probably written in 1761 or 1762, appeared in print five years before Smith's "Considerations," which in turn constituted a part of his lectures on rhetoric delivered in 1762–63 and possibly as early as 1748–51. Under the circumstances, it seems unlikely that either man could have influenced the other.
55. Priestley, *Lectures on Language*, Lectures XII–XIV, in *Works*, 23:209, 200, 194–95.

share of [the] improvement" that the recent past led him to expect of all the sciences in the next age. For this hope to be fulfilled, of course, the study of language had to become a science itself. And so Priestley urged upon his students and readers the need to make exact observations of the actual use of words, observations leading to the recognition of linguistic "rules and laws." He had no use for the arbitrary regulation of a language by an academy, which he considered unnatural. But he wholeheartedly approved of the quest for "a *philosophical* and *universal language,* which shall be . . . much better adapted than any language now in use, to answer all the purposes of human life and science." He considered Bishop Wilkins's plan to have the greatest potential in this regard, and the adoption and use of some such scheme in a future age appeared to him to be less improbable than "many of the present actual discoveries in *philosophy* must have seemed to all men, but a century ago."[56]

The possibility of a catholic tongue intrigued Worthington and Gordon, too. According to the latter, the world-wide employment of a single language "would answer many valuable purposes," especially by shortening the road to true knowledge. In so doing, Priestley contended, a universal language would be "one of the last and greatest achievements of human genius." These comments show an interest in the future of language absent among the Scots, and they also illustrate how verbal communication and general progress were sometimes closely bound together in the thought of the five Englishmen. The connection became clearest when they discussed writing, which Law believed was "necessary to advance the progress of science." As writing improved, he asserted, it "drew along with it all the other arts; helping at once to spread and to perpetuate them." Worthington made a similar point, going so far as to declare the invention of writing to be the most beneficial and wonderful of all human discoveries, since it "makes us Masters of other Men's labours and studies, as well as of our own." In its printed form, writing seemed to Law to have "contributed infinitely to the perfection and progress of the sciences" in recent centuries. At the same time, in Price's view, it facilitated the "diffusion of [the] knowledge created."[57]

56. Ibid., Lectures XVIII, XII, XIX, and Introduction, in *Works,* 23:241, 195–97, 124, 248–50; idem, *The Rudiments of English Grammar* (1761), Preface, in *Works,* 23:8, 10.
57. Worthington, *Essay,* 258, 258n, 155–56; Gordon, *New Estimate,* 2:xvi; Priestley, *Lectures on Language,* Introduction, in *Works,* 23:124; Law, *Considerations,* 259, 259n, 249n; Price, *Evidence,* 25.

Priestley agreed with these observations on the effects of printing, and he saw in writing—considered generally—a vessel for intellectual progress: connecting as it did "the living, the dead, and the unborn," it could "convey wisdom and instruction to the latest posterity." Moreover, he held that language as a whole was "that art which is the means of preserving and bringing to perfection all other arts." Alone among the English believers in general progress, he also examined the other side of the connection between language and social and intellectual life. Historically, he was certain, the increasing sophistication of human society and understanding had impelled the invention of new words and better ways of using them. Even when a language had reached its greatest perfection, that attainment "ought rather to be considered as an argument for the improvement of the nation that uses it, than an encomium upon the language itself; the latter being only a consequence of the former." For "copiousness and refinement in language always keep pace with improvements in the arts and conveniences of life, and with the progress of science in a country." And whatever its condition, whether high or low, any form of verbal communication "takes a tincture from the civil policy, the manners, customs, employment, and taste, of the nation that uses it." Therefore, language could serve the historian as an index of progress, as a "measure of our intellectual powers" and a "great guide . . . in discovering the state of many other important circumstances."[58] Other British writers in the mainstream of eighteenth-century language study would have found this description entirely satisfactory.

In his wide-ranging treatment of language, then, Priestley stood between the Scots and the four other Englishmen. As was the case with the Scots, language lay near the center of his historical consciousness. In fact, his two earliest published works dealt with linguistics, and it was in those books that his belief in general progress first began to emerge. Furthermore, along with the Scots he had a profound awareness of how language benefited from as well as contributed to the advance of thought and society. To the limited extent that they wrote about verbal communication, Worthington, Law, Gordon, and Price emphasized only the second half of this dual relationship. Nor were they preoccupied, like their counterparts to the north, with the question of linguistic history. But some of them—and

58. Priestley, *Lectures on History*, Lectures XXXVI and VIII, in *Works*, 24:216, 78–80; idem, *Lectures on Language*, Lectures II–III, XI–XII, XVII–XVIII, and Introduction, in *Works*, 23:138, 131, 125, 185–86, 191–92, 194–95, 239, 227.

Priestley, as well—had an interest in the future of language, a topic that the Scots never explored. These four Englishmen considered language mainly as a tool for building progress, in the past and in generations to come. For the Scottish *literati*, it offered instead a revealing reflection of and window on the *pattern* of that progress: the transition from rudeness to refinement, characteristic of man virtually everywhere.

Priestley alone brought together these different attitudes to language. If his conception of linguistic history as a refining process did not in the end provide him with a model of human progress generally, it was because that conception was modified and even overridden by his typically English concern with the future.

That concern and the whole doctrine of indefinite progress that encompassed it went hand in hand with the eschatological outlook and the notion of improvement in religion. Indeed, the five Englishmen who formulated this distinctive doctrine would never have done so without having been immersed in the Christian vision of history. The Scots, of course, were far from ignoring theological issues, and some of them even showed substantial interest in the religious development of man. Taken as a group, however, they did not ground their belief in progress on traditional Christian historical conceptions. Such a grounding is unmistakable in the case of the Englishmen.

To them, progress in religion meant first and foremost the ongoing advance of religious understanding. Like so many other eighteenth-century British clerics, all five of them held that God had provided for mankind's spiritual education by means of a series of "dispensations." As Worthington declared, the divine scheme of redemption

> was opened and unfolded by degrees: The first discoveries of it were made by obscure hints, and general intimations given to particular persons: Then it was shadowed out by the types and figures of the mosaic Law; which was succeeded by the clearer predictions of the Prophets; which still were but *like a light shining in a dark place, till at length the day dawned, and daystar arose* when this mystery was fully revealed in the last and most perfect dispensation of the Gospel.

These dispensations, said Law, gradually enlarged the substance of religion, and every subsequent one marked "an improvement on all those that went before." Each was introduced "as soon as it was wanted, and in such a way as was most necessary," based upon the "respective circumstances and capacities" of the people living at each successive period. No other manner of proceeding could have been so appropriate. For there was a time, Price explained, when mankind was "too much in its infancy" to be capable of comprehending more than "dark preparatory dispensations"; the full divulgence of true religion had to be deferred "till the world was more improved, and therefore more capable of properly understanding it."[59]

The principle of a gradual, progressive revelation had intellectual appeal, in part, because it could be used polemically to explain Christianity's want of universality. Law utilized it for precisely that purpose, writing as he did before the complete quieting of the English deists.[60] But the principle's appeal derived also from the doctrine of progress in secular knowledge, in two ways. To begin with, since God had keyed his dispensations to the changing mental capacities of man, and since those capacities had unarguably been increasing over time, it seemed obvious that religious knowledge must, in Law's words, "have held pace in general with all other knowledge, from the beginning." "It would be strange, indeed," wrote Price, "if men were not likely to understand religion best, when they understood best all other subjects," especially given the commonly accepted axiom that the study of the divine works and word went together. In addition, the cumulative effect so visible in the other sciences appeared to apply equally to theology. The "same preparation of ages which is required to bring about advances in philosophical knowledge," Price noted, "is required also in religious knowledge." Because the Englishmen perceived this two-fold connection between secular and religious learning, they could claim with Gordon that the Gospel dispensation "is better understood now, than it was since inspiration ceased; now, when men's understandings are more refined, and their researches into truth more enlarged, than ever they were before!" Anticipating the continuation of past trends, they looked for more progress of this sort in the future. "We have grounds to expect a great increase of christian knowledge," declared Worthington. As Priestley put it, the darkness that for many centuries obscured the true religion "is past;

59. Worthington, *Essay*, 86, 95, 81–82; Law, *Considerations*, 92, 53, 164, 171–72; Price, *Evidence*, 16–18. See also Priestley, *Lectures on History*, Lecture LXVIII, in *Works*, 24:428–29; Gordon, *New Estimate*, 1:108–09.

60. Law, *Considerations*, 213–14 (and see also [3]-6). On the appeal of doctrines of religious progress in general, see above, chap. 3.

the *morning* is opening upon us; and we cannot doubt that the light will increase, and extend itself more and more into *the perfect day*."[61]

Related to this belief in the continuing improvement of religious knowledge was the notion of the progressive spread of true religion, which as we have seen also had substantial popularity in contemporary ecclesiastical circles. "True Religion," Worthington wrote, "which at first was confined to one Family, and afterwards to one Nation and corner of the World, has since by degrees so enlarged its Empire, as to be possess'd of vast Kingdoms and Territories." And its permeation of the earth would not cease until complete: "this we know assuredly," claimed Law, "that every people, nation, and language shall at length know and embrace the true religion; and all kingdoms of the world become the kingdom of Christ." He and Worthington pointed to the s.p.g. and the "standing ministry" as sources of the future spread of Christianity, whereas Gordon focused on the spiritual impact of European imperialism. But whatever its human causes, the eventual triumph and universality of the Gospel seemed inevitable and divinely ordained.[62]

To at least some of the Englishmen, Christianity appeared not only to be spreading and becoming better understood, but also to be improving in general. For instance, in the conclusion to his historical study of the corruptions of the faith, corruptions both doctrinal and institutional, Priestley contended that since the Middle Ages "we see the abuses gradually corrected, and Christianity recovering its primitive beauty and glory." Likewise, one of the main goals of Worthington's essay on the scheme of human redemption was to show that the true religion was "in its nature *progressive* towards a state of greater Perfection, with regard both to Knowledge and Practice." With that end in mind, he claimed that Catholicism had finally

61. Law, *Considerations*, 256, 31–32, 204–10; Price, *Evidence*, 18–19, 21, 27; idem, *Britain's Happiness and the proper Improvement of it* (London, 1759), 9–10; Gordon, *New Estimate*, 1:111–13; William Worthington, *A Sermon Preached in the Parish-Church of Christ-Church, London, . . . April the 21st, 1768* (London, 1768), 21–22; idem, *Essay*, 132–34, 374, iii; Joseph Priestley, *An History of the Corruptions of Christianity* (1782), Dedication, in *Works*, 5:4; idem, *Essay on Government*, in *Works*, 22:125, 131, 133.

62. Worthington, *Essay*, 124, 256; Law, *Considerations*, 200–04, 212–13; idem, *A Sermon Preached before the Incorporated Society for the Propagation of the Gospel in Foreign Parts . . . February 18, 1774* (London, 1774), iv–v, ix, xii–xvi, xxi–xxiii; Gordon, *New Estimate*, 1:110n. See also Price, *Evidence*, 4 [misnumbered as 3].

grown ashamed of its most egregious errors (especially its penchant for persecution), and that its clergy had become less scandalous in their lives and more learned in their theology. Meanwhile, Protestantism had also improved, by turning to toleration, moderation, and charity, thereby "promoting . . . the knowledge and practice of Virtue and Religion among us." To be sure, the "bold advances" of modern atheism, infidelity, and profane living might threaten to destroy morality and religion. Yet in spite of such problems, he was convinced, "the time will come when [Christianity] will yet have its due influence, and finally triumph over the obstinate prejudices and unruly lusts of Men, and every thing else that exalts itself against it."[63]

As expressed in these three basic forms, the belief in religious progress was no less typical of the five Englishmen than of most other British clergymen in the eighteenth century. In the case of Worthington, Price, and Priestley, the same can be said with respect to eschatology.[64] All three were keenly interested in the last things, and what they wrote on the subject placed them well within the confines of the prevailing eschatological tradition.

Like most contemporary commentators on the last things, they argued from the past fulfillment of some prophecies to the eventual realization of others, situated the millennium in the future, frequently cited the prediction in Daniel 12:4 about the increase of knowledge, and gave due attention to Antichrist (whom they identified with the papacy). Further, they tended to describe the course and timing of eschatological events in such a way as to bring them into the realm of the here and now. After studying the prophecies closely, Priestley and Worthington reached differing conclusions on whether the Parousia would precede or follow the millennium. But they agreed that Christ would not be physically present during this thousand-year period. Similarly, both of them minimized the catastrophic element in millennial changes. Priestley argued that the occurrence of an actual conflagration would be "exceedingly improbable," since most of the earth was incombustible. Therefore, it seemed evident to him that prophecies about the dissolution of the present environment and the appearance of a new one "must be figurative; denoting only great changes in the state of things, especially of

63. Priestley, *History of the Corruption*, in *Works*, 5:481; Worthington, *Essay*, ii, 135–37, 380. See also Price, *Evidence*, 21–22, 21n–22n, 27.

64. Gordon did not write about eschatological issues. Law's published references to them were extremely brief: see above, chap. 3.

kingdoms and empires, antecedent to the second coming of Christ, and the renovation of all things under him." Worthington expected a literal conflagration and discussed its causes and effects in detail. Yet he rejected Burnet's theory that it would take place prior to the millennium, claiming instead that it would merely complete the substantial renewal of nature to occur during that happy period.[65] Such interpretations reflected the tendency, prominent since the time of Whitby, to give prophecies about the last things an increased commensurability to human experience.

In much the same way, prophecies concerning the fall of Antichrist, which was to inaugurate the millennium, were endowed with a strong sense of immediacy. Price did not offer exact dates, but he thought that the "season fixed by prophecy for the destruction of the *man of sin* cannot be far distant," and to him the signs of the times showed "antichrist falling, and the *Millennium* hastening." Looking at the diminished power of the papacy, Priestley, too, believed that the downfall of Antichrist was "visibly hastening." Because he could perceive this "grand catastrophe growing nearer and nearer, perpetually," he predicted that it would "not be long before this world assumes another and more agreeable aspect." According to Worthington, the decline of the beast would continue until the mid-twentieth century, with the millennium dawning in 2001.[66]

65. William Worthington, *The Scripture-Theory of the Earth* (London, 1773), 396, 469, 475; idem, *Essay*, 263–64, 125, 276–77, 281–84, 293–94, 298–302; Joseph Priestley, *Institutes of Natural and Revealed Religion* (1772–74; 2d ed., 1782), in *Works*, 2:190, 365–67; idem, "Difficulties in the Interpretation of Some Prophecies not yet Fulfilled, and Queries relating to Them" (1788), in *Works*, 7:448–449; idem, *Discourses on the Evidence of Revealed Religion* (1794; enl. ed., 1796), in *Works*, 16:310–11 (the quotation is at 310n); Price, *Evidence*, 4, 8, 10–11, 19; idem, *Britain's Happiness*, 22–23. Clarke Garrett has argued that in the essay "Difficulties," Priestley adopted a new position favoring the personal presence of Christ in the millennium: *Respectable Folly: Millenarians and the French Revolution in France and England* (Baltimore, 1975), 131–32. I do not find this interpretation convincing. Priestley did eventually change his mind on the topic, but only at the very end of his life: see *Notes on All the Books of Scripture, for the Use of the Pulpit and Private Families* (1804), in *Works*, 14:502.

It should be noted that none of the three men under consideration here restricted the causation of the last things to the operation of natural laws. As mentioned previously (see above, chap. 6), they were all providentialists. Worthington specifically asserted that during the latter days, "without the use of any second causes at all, the sovereign Arbiter and Disposer of the universe may, by the power of his will alone, bring his great purposes to pass": *Scripture-Theory*, 464 (cf. 436).

66. Price, *Britain's Happiness*, 23; idem, *Evidence*, 25; Priestley, *Discourses on Revealed Religion*, in *Works*, 16:414–18; idem, *Lectures on History*, Lecture LXVII, in

What would be the nature of the coming new era? All three Englishmen described it in both spiritual and utopian terms, as did other eschatologists of the time. Price and Priestley saw it as, above all else, an age of worldwide righteousness and Gospel purity, since it was to be the kingdom of Christ realized on earth. Peace and love would prevail among all people, and war between nations would be unknown. But Price also mentioned liberty as one of the chief characteristics of the millennium, and Priestley foresaw the replacement of existing forms of government with "something very different from them, and greatly superior to them." Moreover, though they did not offer details, they thought of the millennium as a "prosperous state of things," in which "more ample and more effectual provision will be made for all the great interests of humanity." Finally, and encompassing all of its other aspects, both spiritual and secular, it would provide "happiness greater than can be now conceived," "happiness . . . placed upon the most solid foundation." Worthington's characterization of millennial life went even further. He looked not only for universal holiness, peace, better government, outward prosperity, and happiness, but also for a delivery of man from the Fall and of nature from the Curse. Mankind would live once again in "an earthly Paradise" comparable to the world of their original progenitors, except that it would ultimately be "much improved, exalted, refined, and spiritualized" when compared even to Eden.[67] Worthington's eschatology, no less than that of Priestley and Price, was not a primitivist but a progressivist dream.

This eschatology worked in tandem with the belief in religious progress to exercise a fundamental shaping influence on the English doctrine of indefinite human amelioration. In the broadest way, the Christian vision of history did for the Englishmen what the study of language did for the Scots: it endowed them with a strong feeling for the overall *pattern* of progress. As they conceived of it, the course of spiritual affairs over time was one of past improvement leading to and seemingly guaranteeing still more advances in the future, the whole

---

Works, 24:423; idem, *A Description of a New Chart of History*, in *Works*, 24:484; Worthington, *Essay*, 285–88.

67. Price, *Britain's Happiness*, 22–23; idem, *Evidence*, 51, 56; Priestley, *Institutes of Religion*, in *Works*, 2:365–71; idem, *Discourses on Revealed Religion*, in *Works*, 16:418; idem, *New Chart of History*, in *Works*, 24:484; Worthington, *Essay*, 199–201, 205, 208, 214–17, 237, 240–57, 261, 265, 270–77, 282, 291, 294–96, 317, 320–24, 333–48; idem, *Scripture-Theory*, 485 (quotation).

being marked with the imprimatur of the God who had planned it. Because religion still pervaded their lives and thought, because their underlying philosophy of history was really a theology of history, they could readily extend this pattern so that it applied as well to what a later age would consider to be the purely secular.

Among particular instances of the process of extension, several stand out. Near the end of his lectures on history, Priestley took up the subject of the "conduct of Divine Providence in the direction of human affairs." After mentioning the approaching downfall of Antichrist as part of a "divine drama," he noted that "we see a course of events in the history of the world terminating in the . . . benevolent purposes" of a wise and good deity. "Let an historian," he continued, "therefore, attend to every instance of improvement, and a better state of things . . . in history, and let him ascribe those events to an *intention* in the Divine Being to bring about that better state." Having established this line of reasoning, Priestley immediately went on to make one of his most complete and eloquent statements of belief in progress on all fronts, including human happiness. On a somewhat larger scale, one of Price's sermons shows a similar kind of extension or displacement at work. His topic was the evidence for a future period of improvement in the world, and his text was "Thy kingdom come" (Matthew 6:10). He began with the assumption that "there is a kingdom of Christ still to come" and encapsulated his theme in the following sentence: "That such a state of christianity lies before us between this and the end of time; or, that there is a progressive improvement in human affairs which will terminate in greater degrees of light and virtue and happiness than have been yet known, appears to me highly probable." The easy transition from eschatology to general progress, which appears over and over in the sermon, was made possible by Price's conviction that the prophecies actually contained evidence of future improvement in the world.[68]

Law started with the doctrine of progress in religious knowledge rather than with eschatology, but the end result was the same. The fundamental goal of his book on the theory (or "speculative part") of religion was to demonstrate that Christianity could not be objected to on the grounds of its lack of universality. To substantiate his position, he developed at great length the argument that God was revealing his truth gradually and in proportion to man's circum-

68. Priestley, *Lectures on History*, Lecture LXVII, in *Works*, 24:421–25; Price, *Evidence*, [1], 4–10.

stances and intellectual abilities. This argument, in turn, led him to
claim that human knowledge had been increasing, and, ultimately,
that there was a "Continual Improvement of the World in General."
The structure of the whole book is epitomized by its author's statement

> that God has all along acted equally and impartially for the
> good of mankind, in matters of religion; though in very differ-
> ent manners, according to their different circumstances and
> capacities; —that his several dispensations have been gradu-
> ally opened, so as regularly to rise out of, and improve upon
> each other; —and lastly, that the state of knowledge, and per-
> fection in the world, has hitherto been increasing.[69]

From attempting to prove that religious understanding was slowly
growing more perfect, Law finally came to assert that the process of
perfection could be seen in human life as a whole.

Through such conceptual displacement, the Englishmen made
the Christian vision of history into something more than it customarily had been, yet without really altering or secularizing it. This
the Scots could not do, since that vision had so much less meaning for
them. Not one of them was a true providentialist; not one ever wrote
a word on eschatology. Some of them—especially Hume and
Smith—held religious opinions that quite clearly lay beyond the
pale. Others at least occasionally showed a willingness to adopt certain attitudes associated more with the opponents than with the
defenders of Christianity. While professing his great regard for that
one true faith, Kames espoused a religious relativism with which the
philosophes would have been in sympathy. Ferguson expected an
afterlife of some kind but asserted in the most worldly way that
"Happiness is to be valued more for the present, than for the future."
And Dunbar followed the Enlightenment line of criticizing religion
for too often breeding violence and other "astonishing effects,"
"which disgrace reason and humanity."[70] In all probability, the label
"orthodox" can be applied only to Robertson, and even he was not
notable for manifesting the kind of religious warmth and strong tran-
scendental sense that marked the Englishmen, nor would his oppo-

69. Law, *Considerations*, 180, 171–72.
70. Kames, *Loose Hints upon Education*, 203–05; Ferguson, *Principles*, 1:322, 329,
331–32, 334; Dunbar, *History of Mankind*, 224.

nents in the Church of Scotland have agreed to apply that term to one who had done so much on behalf of ecclesiastical liberalization.

Since the Scots were, to varying degrees, more detached than their English brethren from the traditional Christian outlook, they could examine religion through a more secular lens. That they did so is nowhere clearer than in their treatment of the history of religion, which they tended to view from the perspective of later sociologists and anthropologists rather than from that of devout believers. For example, those of them who discussed the origin of religion traced it not to an initial divine dispensation but to the human experience of the natural world. They maintained that, confronted by terrifying storms and eclipses seemingly outside the regular course of nature, the earliest people arrived at a satisfying explanation of these discordant phenomena by positing the existence of invisible, interfering beings possessed of superhuman powers. Thus began polytheism, which most of the Scots considered to be, everywhere, the "most ancient religion of mankind," as Hume called it.[71]

Kames subdivided polytheism into a number of discrete stages, each of which he presumed to have had a unique mode of ascribing malevolent and benevolent purposes to the gods. Furthermore, he held that this transition eventually—and inexorably—terminated in monotheism, the "true religion." Therefore, the entire evolution amounted to a "gradual progress toward truth and purity" in religion. For Ferguson, too, the overall development of religious belief appeared to display this trend. The primitive, universally present conception of "intelligent power" exercising control over nature, he wrote, "is, like other articles in the progressive and variable nature of man, a foundation on which he may build; . . . one of the rude materials on which he himself is to exert his talent for art and improvement." He attributed the advance of religious opinions to the "progress of reason and more discernment," and particularly to the progress of knowledge about the natural world. Superstition, he argued, "has yielded only to the light of true religion, or to the study of

71. David Hume, "The Natural History of Religion," Sects. I–III, in *Essays*, 2:310 (quotation), 312–19. See also Kames, *Sketches*, 3:269–71, 289 (Bk. III, Sk. iii, Ch. 2); Smith, *Wealth of Nations*, 767; idem, "History of Astronomy," *Essays on Philosophical Subjects*, 48–51; Ferguson, *Civil Society*, 90; idem, *Principles*, 1:164–65; and see above, chap. 7. Ferguson claimed that the "plurality of Gods" was really an aggregate, formed very early in history, of the even earlier belief of each individual and people in a single, different god: *Principles*, 1:168–69.

nature, by which we are led to substitute a wise providence operating by physical causes, in the place of phantoms that terrify or amuse the ignorant." Kames concurred, observing that the rise of the mental faculties and natural knowledge leads "by sure steps, though slow, to one God."[72]

What is missing from these statements, when compared to the history of religious understanding offered by Law and Worthington, is any reference to a series of dispensations from God. To Kames and Ferguson, the development of theology was not the result of a special divine plan carried out by the Jews and then the Christians. It was simply an integral part of the omnipresent refining process, of "natural history." As Kames said, there was a "wonderful uniformity in the progress of religion through all nations," from the "savage state" to their "maturity." And this tendency to subsume religious history within the larger process of refinement emerged at a less general level of analysis, as well. Although Millar never wrote about the history of religion as a whole, when he dealt with the Reformation he described it not as God's way of perfecting the Gospel dispensation, but as the result of "certain fixed causes" associated with the refinement of early modern Europe. These causes—the progress of commerce, the arts, and knowledge—"contributed, on the one hand, to dispel the mist of superstition, and, on the other, to place the bulk of a people in situations which inspired them with sentiments of liberty."[73]

Besides Kames and Ferguson, Hume was the only Scot to write at length about the natural history of religion. Like them, he recognized a historical transition from polytheism or "idolatry" to the "doctrine of one supreme deity, the author of nature"; like them, he placed this transition within the context of the "improvement of human society, from rude beginnings to a state of greater perfection." Yet Hume denied that the masses of any nation were ever capable of adopting "theism" (as he called monotheism) on the basis of advances in reason and true philosophy. Rather, they were guided to it by "irrational and superstitious principles," such as when they raised up one god above the other members of the pantheon in order to "insinuate themselves into his favour." Because of its foundation in "adulation

72. Kames, *Sketches*, 3:270–72, 280–82, 286–90 (Bk. III, Sk. iii, Ch. 2); Ferguson, *Principles*, 1:167–68, 304–05; idem, *Civil Society*, 90–91.
73. Kames, *Sketches*, 3:297–98, 288–89, 376 (Bk. III, Sk. iii, Chs. 2–3); Millar, *Historical View*, 2:428–35.

and fears of the most vulgar superstition," the monotheism of the masses was "merely verbal," so that it could easily relapse into polytheism. In fact, "the principles of religion have a kind of flux and reflux in the human mind, and . . . men have a natural tendency to rise from idolatry to theism, and to sink again from theism into idolatry." And so, among the "greatest part of uninstructed mankind," polytheism was never for long replaced by belief, however unphilosophical, in a single deity.[74]

But what of the few, "the bystanders," who *were* able to investigate theological issues philosophically? In spite of his theory of fluctuations in popular religion and his conviction that monotheism was more inclined than polytheism to indulge in persecution,[75] Hume implied that there had been religious progress among just this limited group of sophisticated thinkers. For in his view they were the proponents of "true religion," to be distinguished from the "false religion"—whether polytheistic or monotheistic—blemished by superstition and enthusiasm. True religion, as he conceived of it, may well have been no more than the "simple, though somewhat ambiguous proposition, *that the cause or causes of order in the universe probably bear some remote analogy to human intelligence.*" If so, then on his own showing it could only have been the result of many centuries of intellectual preparation. "The farther we mount up into antiquity, the more do we find mankind plunged into polytheism. No marks, no symptoms of any more perfect religion." Even to have arrived at the theological system based on the questionable argument from design must have taken ages:

> We may as reasonably imagine, that men inhabited palaces before huts and cottages, or studied geometry before agriculture; as assert that the Deity appeared to them a pure spirit, omniscient, omnipotent, and omnipresent, before he was apprehended to be a powerful, though limited being with human passions and appetites, limbs and organs. The mind rises gradually, from inferior to superior: By abstracting from what is imperfect, it forms an idea of perfection: And slowly distin-

74. Hume, "Natural History of Religion," Sects. VI–VIII, I, III, in *Essays*, 2:328, 310, 330–31, 333–36, 318.
75. Ibid., Sect. IX, in *Essays*, 2:336–39. On "the bystanders" and the "few" who look at religion philosophically, see ibid., Sects. XII, VIII, in *Essays*, 2:344, 334.

guishing the nobler parts of its own frame from the grosser, it learns to transfer only the former, much elevated and refined, to its deity.[76]

How much longer must the process of intellectual refinement have required to reach the position where human intelligence, and nothing more, was transferred by analogy to the divine?

Whether Hume consciously considered the rise of true religion to be a matter of ongoing progress, he clearly was arguing that monotheism—in any form whatsoever—had not been the original, universal credo of mankind. This argument, like Law's theory of religious development, was intended to undermine an important polemical bastion of deism and other brands of "natural theology." Of course, Hume did not also share Law's interest in defending orthodoxy by adducing a series of ever-more perfect divine dispensations. Indeed, his essay "The Natural History of Religion" was really directed against all religions except one: not Christianity but Humean "true religion." And this exception was itself less theology than philosophy, into whose calm though obscure realms Hume escaped at the end of his book.[77] To the small degree that he left room for progress in religious history, that progress had essentially nothing to do with the Christian faith or the Christian God.

This was not true of Robertson, however. He was the sole member of the Scottish group ever to write about religious progress in the same way as the Englishmen. When still a young man, he delivered to the s.p.c.k. of Scotland a largely forgotten sermon that embodied a doctrine of improvement in religious knowledge strikingly similar to that of Law. "The light of revelation was not poured in upon mankind all at once, and with its full splendor," he declared. "The obscurity of

76. David Hume, *Dialogues Concerning Natural Religion* (first published 1779), ed. Norman Kemp Smith, 2d ed. (Indianapolis, 1947), 227; idem, "Natural History of Religion," Sect. I, in *Essays*, 2:310–11. For the distinction between "true" and "false" religion, see idem, "Of Superstition and Enthusiasm" (1741), *Essays*, 1:144–50. That Hume recognized a progress in true religion is also argued in Duncan Forbes, untitled review of Giuseppe Giarizzo's *David Hume politico e storico*, in *Historical Journal* 6 (1963): 289. See also Hume's comments on British religious progress in "Of National Characters," *Essays*, 1:251.

77. Hume, "Natural History of Religion," Sect. XV, in *Essays*, 2:363. Hume did not specifically mention the deists or other natural theologians. But he was clearly referring to them when he discussed and attempted to refute with "historical facts" certain "speculative opinions" on a primitive, universal theism: ibid., Sect. I, in *Essays*, 2:312–13.

the dawn went before the brightness of the noon-day." Elucidating this principle and urging its potency in opposing the "cavils" of "modern infidels," he asserted that the divine will

> was at first made known by revelations, useful indeed, but dark and mysterious. To these, succeeded others more clear and perfect. In proportion as the situation of the world made it necessary, the Almighty was pleased farther to open and unfold his scheme. And men came by degrees to understand this progressive plan of Providence, and to conceive how systems temporary and incompleat might serve to introduce that concluding and perfect revelation, which would *declare the whole council of God to man.*

At the same time, Robertson also claimed that Christianity had been "making its progress thro' the world." Given this fact, he expected a still-larger diffusion of the faith in the future: "after we have seen the light of the gospel penetrate into so many *dark places of the earth;* why doeth it seem incredible, that its splendor should, at last, fill the world, and scatter the remainder of the darkness which covereth the nations?" He was confident that this would happen, and foresaw what he called "the future and universal propagation of Christian knowledge," particularly because Europeans could utilize their science, other improvements, and commerce on the side of Christianity.[78]

What Priestley was among the Englishmen in the case of language study, Robertson was among the Scots on the subject of religious history: the exception who proved the rule. And, as with Priestley, he was only a partial exception at that. In his youthful sermon, he began to build his conception of religious improvement into a more general doctrine of progress, arguing briefly that the slow unfolding of divine truth was one example of how all the works of the deity—including "changes in the moral world"—"advance towards their finished and compleat state" in a "gradual and progressive" manner. He never fully elaborated this theory, and it certainly did not reappear in his later view of history as a strictly human transition from rudeness to refinement. In fact, when in later life he discussed religion from that vantage point, it had become no more than one of many kinds of grist for the mill of "natural history." The origin of religion was for him, by

78. Robertson, *Situation of the World,* 6–8, 37, 41–43.

William Robertson

then, the result not of a "dark and mysterious" dispensation from God but merely, as the other Scots believed, of the barbarous proclivity to ascribe the "extraordinary occurrences in nature to the influence of invisible beings." Instead of attributing the Reformation to the dawning of a more perfect divine revelation, he traced it to spreading secular knowledge, an increasingly bold "spirit of innovation," and a disgust with the haughty and hypocritical Catholic clergy.[79] Sacred history had given way before a concern with the secular process of human refinement.

Even for Robertson, therefore, ranking church official though he was, the Christian vision of history proved less influential in leading to a belief in general progress than it did for the five Englishmen. They extended religious history into a doctrine of indefinite human improvement. He and, more completely, the remaining Scots absorbed it within a concept of secular social development out of rudeness or barbarism.

RECOLLECTION AND FORESIGHT

Even before the 1750s, all four of the narrower doctrines of progress had become well-established intellectual traditions in Britain. By mid-century, they were pervasive enough that a majority of the literate, educated members of British society would have been familiar with and would have accepted most of them. The belief in progress on all fronts necessarily arose in close conjunction with rather than independent of these doctrines. But it was the result not so much of abstract generalization from them as of complicated interplay among them in the thought of Priestley, Kames, and the others. This interplay produced two basic patterns of recollection and foresight, which varied in proportion as the Englishmen and Scots treated the narrower doctrines of progress differently.

The comparison of ancient with modern achievements gave both groups a historical perspective from which they could see long-term improvement in the *past*. Whether this perspective was concentrated on the arts and sciences alone or expanded so as to take in other facets of life, it made visible an important trend in history: to date, there seemed to have been ongoing advances of a gradual, cumulative na-

79. Ibid., 7; idem, *History of America*, Bk. IV, in *Works*, 6:353; idem, *History of Scotland*, Bk. II, in *Works*, 1:108, 114–23.

ture, in spite of delays and even temporary setbacks (particularly during the Middle Ages). The cumulative effect, however, was only one of the mechanisms of progress. Another one, at least potentially, was located by the Scots as well as the English in the largely pliable nature of human beings. Psychologically, men and women seemed to be constructed for improvement. All that was needed to make them and human society better was to surround them from childhood with a better mental and moral environment, or, as Law and Ferguson believed, to show them their very real powers of self-command. In either case, reformed education and the establishment of appropriate habits seemed to provide a possible *future* cure for human ills.

To this extent, the two groups had essentially equal reasons for finding progress in previous centuries and expecting it of ages to come. Where their attitudes toward the past and future diverged was in their handling of language and religion. On neither subject did the Scots enter into a discussion of what was to happen, but only of what had happened. Their study of linguistic history, unmatched by any of the English except Priestley, produced a picture of historical progressiveness that frequently served them as a model of how man and his institutions had grown to refinement. And the notion of a refining process, supported by the evidence of improvement in the arts and sciences, became the context for the analysis of human evolution in its entirety, including religious developments. To nearly all the Scots, religious history was nothing more than an instance of the way in which civilized people had left barbarism and barbarous ideas behind. It did not provide them with an indication of the future course of events.

In contrast, this was precisely the most crucial thing it did for the English. The optimism that they continually expressed about the future, though reinforced by the psychological theory of pliable man, ultimately derived from the Christian vision of history. Their finding that many eschatological prophecies had already received fulfillment made them confident that the millennium was approaching; their opinion that religious understanding had been improving across the centuries, confirmed by what seemed to be the cumulative advance of secular knowledge, led them to expect ever more theological illumination in the ages ahead. And projection of this sort was facilitated by their certainty that the spiritual developments they anticipated actually comprised part—the best part—of God's plan for humankind. The strong future orientation of the English, which manifested itself even in their treatment of language, did not appear among their counterparts to the north, and for just the reason that its underpinnings lay in a theological view of the world and history that the Scots did not share.

This is not to say that the Scots were totally immune from looking forward in time. "No bias in human nature has greater influence, than curiosity about futurity," wrote Kames.[80] When from time to time they gave in to that curiosity, they tended to follow the English group in prognosticating a better state of affairs. That they nearly always did so with more hesitancy and caution than a man like Worthington was natural, for they saw no divine guarantee but only a human possibility that the problems attendant upon luxury and the division of labor would be overcome. That they did so at all was a function both of the hope raised in them by the theory of pliable man, and of their own historical and social experience. They and the English discovered in the past a course of broadly gauged improvement. For all of them, this reading of history was corroborated by the visibility of progress in Britain during the eighteenth century, and especially after about 1750. The personal, first-hand experience of progressive change could only have heightened their sense that advancement was a historical fact, could only have solidified their conviction that previous trends would endure.

"To man," said Ferguson,

> the proper subjects of knowledge are the present or the past:
> Yet, in some instances, the knowledge of these is a knowledge
> of the future also. Whoever knows an order of things that is
> established, or a description of a thing that is durable, knows
> the future respecting such matters, together with the present
> and the past.

This observation points to two significant facts about historical consciousness, both of which have relevance for the doctrines of general progress under consideration. First, the perception of the flow of time is a compound formed of two elements, recollection and foresight, though not always in the same measure. Hume was right when he remarked that man "looks backward to consider the first origin, at least, the history of [the] human race" and also "casts his eyes for-

---

80. Kames, *Sketches*, 3:310 (Bk. III, Sk. iii, Ch. 2). On the desire to know the future, see also Ferguson, *Civil Society*, 10; Joseph Priestley, *Experiments and Observations on Different Kinds of Air*, Preface, in *Works*, 25:383.

ward" to glimpse the situation of posterity.[81] He himself and most of the other Scots demonstrate, however, that the historical vision may sometimes be trained more in one direction than the other.

Second, foresight depends upon recollection, indeed upon its quality. As Hume insisted, "it is from past experience that we draw all inferences concerning the future." When that experience seems to display great uniformity, predictions can be made with confidence. But when the trend of the past and present appears less clear-cut, there is less willingness to project it onto the future. "Thus then we see, how necessary it is to form just conceptions of the past state of the world," wrote Law, "in order to judge in what condition it will probably be for the future. . . . If it has hitherto been really progressive, we find good reason to expect the same progress still farther." Being somewhat more fully certain than the Scots of past advances in every facet of life, and "especially with regard to that important point, *religion*," the English were more inclined than the *literati* of the north to have such an expectation.[82]

As these two groups prove, the idea of progress may—yet need not—wear both of Janus's faces. As they and their contemporaries illustrate, it can, like Proteus, assume many forms. But whether it was applied to art and science, spiritual affairs, language, the mind and morals, or human culture generally, it dominated historical thinking in high eighteenth-century Britain. Then and there, to engage in recollection or foresight or both meant, nearly always, to envision progress.

81. Ferguson, *Principles*, 1:319–20; David Hume, "Of the Dignity or Meanness of Human Nature" (1741), *Essays*, 1:152.

82. Hume, *Human Understanding*, Sect. VIII, Pt. 1, in *Enquiries*, 88; Law, *Considerations*, 290–94. For other examples of how recollection led the English to foresight, see also Joseph Priestley, *The History and Present State of Electricity*, ed. Robert E. Schofield, 2 vols. (New York, 1966), 2:ii (Preface); Price, *Evidence*, 14. Perhaps the earliest explicit statement by a British thinker that foresight depended upon recollection came in Thomas Hobbes, *Human Nature: or the Fundamental Elements of Policy* (1650), in *The English Works of Thomas Hobbes*, ed. Sir William Molesworth, 11 vols. (London, 1839–45), 4:16–17.

9 Conclusion

"No mind is much employed upon the present," wrote Samuel Johnson; "recollection and anticipation fill up almost all our moments."[1] This typically astute observation by the eighteenth century's great moralist reminds us why we have good cause, if we are interested in human nature, to be interested also in our own historical outlook and that of our predecessors. But at a time when the relevance and the methodological propriety of intellectual history and, especially, the history of ideas have been sharply challenged, it may perhaps be necessary in addition to emphasize that the socially oriented recollection and foresight of Johnson's own age had special historical significance. Simply put: the blossoming and spread of the idea of progress in England and Scotland during the eighteenth century is of central importance to the overall history of that idea itself, to British intellectual history, and even to the emergence of the modern world.

These are large claims, but the evidence for them is substantial. We can begin to understand how this is so by disposing of two long-standing myths. The first of these, that the British merely imported the belief in progress from France, is now quite clearly untenable. "The idea of Progress," wrote J. B. Bury, "could not help crossing the Channel," but it was "not indeed to be expected that the theory should have the same kind of success, or exert the same kind of effect in England." It would be fascinating to discover why this view ever

1. Samuel Johnson, *The History of Rasselas, Prince of Abyssinia*, in *The Yale Edition of the Works of Samuel Johnson*, ed. John E. Middendorf, 13 vols. to date (New Haven, 1958–), vol. 16 (*Rasselas and Other Tales*, ed. Gwin J. Kolb [1990]), Ch. XXX. See also idem, *The Rambler*, no. 41, in *Yale Edition*, vol. 3 (*The Rambler*, ed. W. J. Bate and Albrecht B. Strauss [1969]), 221–26; W. Jackson Bate, *Samuel Johnson* (New York, 1975), 299, 616n.

took hold among late nineteenth- and early twentieth-century historians of the idea. Responsibility may rest largely with the old notion of the eighteenth-century English having already had their revolution while the French still "needed" or at least anticipated one. But if so then the idea of progress comes to be concerned exclusively with the future—an orientation that contradicts Bury's own definition of the idea.[2] In any case, Bury and his predecessors and successors were thoroughly wrong: the idea grew up quite independently on the north side of the Channel, and many of the forms given to it there had a dramatically different appearance from the ones current in France during the Enlightenment. This is especially the case with regard to the views on religious progress so commonly held among the British clergy and so vitally important to English doctrines of general progress. Neither eschatology nor concepts of doctrinal development and progress in the spread of religion seem to have had any substantial impact on French Christian thought (or, of course, on the philosophes). Turgot's vision of indefinite human advance on virtually all fronts may have been the most comprehensive theory of progress in high eighteenth-century France, but its real connection to Christianity was slender. This is true in spite of his obviously deep-seated conviction that Christianity "enlightens the spirit, softens manners, and permits all the virtues and happiness to rule with her," as well as his remarks in the first Sorbonne lecture of 1750 on the positive historical effects of the true religion, especially during the Middle Ages.[3] In the area of speculation about religious progress, the only clear parallels with British thought are to be found in Germany, particularly with the writings of Lessing and Herder after 1780.

The relative independence of British from French thought on progress is evident in other ways as well. Those developments in psychology that culminated in the work of David Hartley all predated

---

2. J. B. Bury, *The Idea of Progress: An Inquiry into Its Origin and Growth* (London, 1920), 217–18, 2, 5.

3. Turgot, "Discours sur les avantages que l'établissement du christianisme a procurés au genre humain" (delivered July 3, 1750), in *Oeuvres de Turgot et documents le concernant*, ed. Gustave Schelle, 4 vols. (Paris, 1913–23), 1:198–203; Frank E. Manuel, *The Prophets of Paris: Turgot, Condorcet, Saint-Simon, Fourier, and Comte* (Cambridge, Mass., 1962), 40. There was some interest in eschatology among Jansenists, and especially the *convulsionnaires*, but "millenarianism in France never enjoyed the kind of informal acceptance it gained in protestant England": Clarke Garrett, *Respectable Folly: Millenarians and the French Revolution in France and England* (Baltimore, 1975), 19–26 (quotation on p. 21).

the relevant published work of Helvétius, La Mettrie, and Condillac, while relatively few of the commentators on education discussed in chapter 4 displayed familiarity with French educational writers other than Rousseau (whose influence was, in any event, overwhelmingly negative). Similarly, in the ongoing European warfare between ancients and moderns, the French, with the exception of Voltaire, appear to have been relatively little involved after 1719 (the year in which the Abbé Dubos published his *Critical Reflections on Poetry and Painting*).[4] Indeed, it was possible for Turgot to arrive at his broadly gauged vision of progress while supporting the claims of the ancients in poetry, painting, and music and denying the possibility of progress in the fine arts. The issues raised by the warfare between ancients and moderns simply did not have the same relevance for the ongoing development of the idea of progress in Enlightenment France as they did in Priestley's England and Hume's Scotland.[5]

The same cannot be said so unequivocally of language study, which seems to have attracted virtually every notable western European thinker of the later eighteenth century. Although it would hardly be appropriate to describe them as unoriginal borrowers, the British learned considerably more from their French contemporaries in this area than in any other. In addition, it is likely that at least some of the Englishmen and Scots who held doctrines of general progress eventually became familiar with the more important French work on the same subject. For instance, Antoine Yves de Goguet's *De l'Origine des loix, des arts, et des sciences; et de leurs progrès chez les anciens peuples* (1758), which adopted a four-stage theory of the economic development of civilization similar to that of Smith, was well enough known to have been translated and published in Edinburgh in 1761. Millar later cited the book in his own *Origin of the Distinction of Ranks*, as did Priestley in his *First Principles of Government* and Law in later editions of his *Considerations on the Theory of Religion*.[6] Yet there is no evidence that Goguet or any other French

4. A. Owen Aldridge, "Ancients and Moderns in the Eighteenth Century," in Philip R. Weiner, ed.-in-chief, *Dictionary of the History of Ideas: Studies of Selected Pivotal Ideas*, 4 vols. (New York, 1968–73), 1:80–86.

5. Turgot, "Tableau philosophique des progrès successifs de l'esprit humain. Discours prononcé en latin dans les écoles de Sorbonne, pour la clôture des Sorboniques" (Dec. 11, 1750), in *Oeuvres*, 1:227; Manuel, *Prophets of Paris*, 38–39.

6. On the debt of the British to the French in the area of language study, see above, chap. 5. For references to Goguet, see John Millar, *The Origin of the Distinction of Ranks*, 3d ed., repr. in William C. Lehmann, *John Millar of Glasgow, 1735–1801: His*

writer exercised more than minor influence on the emergence of the conception of general progress across the Channel.

This is certainly true of Turgot, for instance, whose views constitute the most sophisticated French analysis of general progress prior to the 1790s. His principal writings on progress, the two orations at the Sorbonne in 1750 and the fragmentary discourses on universal history written about 1751–52, were never published during his lifetime, and it is most unlikely that they became widely known in France let alone Britain (though Hume undoubtedly learned something of them after the beginning of his friendship with Turgot in the early 1760s). Even if his views had become popular, they could not have affected the relevant writings of Worthington and Law, first published in 1743 and 1745, respectively, nor could they have exerted a formative influence on Smith, who by the early 1750s—and possibly as soon as 1748—was already lecturing about the same four economic stages that Turgot described in his unpublished work. What is more, Turgot's theory of progress was in significant ways quite different from the English and the Scottish doctrines of general progress. He placed much more emphasis than either British version on the role of the genius in promoting improvement, and he conceived of progress in more cosmopolitan terms as being truly worldwide in its development, with the torch of advancement passing from one nation to another over many centuries.[7]

Thus, although eighteenth-century French cultural and intellectual trends were always quickly known across the Channel, there is every reason to conclude that the development of the idea of progress in Britain took place in a fundamentally independent way. If this is true with regard to a major idea of the age, it may well be that historians have for a very long time placed far too much emphasis on the degree to which contemporary French thought penetrated and led British. With the passing of Locke and Newton, British thought did not become derivative and dull, nor did the intellectual lights of Paris serve as hypnotizing beacons for every aspiring English or Scottish

Life and Thought and His Contributions to Sociological Analysis (Cambridge, 1960), 199n; Joseph Priestley, *An Essay on the First Principles of Government*, in *The Theological and Miscellaneous Works of Joseph Priestley*, ed. John Towill Rutt, 25 vols. in 26 ([London, 1817–32]), 22:119–121nn; Edmund Law, *Considerations on the Theory of Religion*, ed. George Henry Law, new ed. (London, 1820), 235n.

7. Ronald L. Meek, *Social Science and the Ignoble Savage* (Cambridge, 1976), 68–76, 99–115; Manuel, *Prophets of Paris*, 34–35.

thinker. Theirs was a vital, energetic, and relatively free intellectual climate in which ideas (and books) had a prominent place.

Moreover, the doubts that so frequently beset the French philosophes were both less common and less central among British thinkers and writers. We simply do not find the same kind of brooding pessimism in Smith, Gordon, Priestley, and even Hume that so often surfaced in Diderot, Montesquieu, and Voltaire. If we are to include many of the writers under study in this book as members of the Enlightenment (and how can we do otherwise?), then we must acknowledge that our definition of that great movement must be broad or general enough to accommodate a wide variety of views about the tendencies of history. And this suggests strongly that French ideas should not be taken as representative of the whole Enlightenment. France may have been the focal point of that part of the Enlightenment emphasizing criticism of the establishment, but Britain was, among other things, the center of historical optimism in the eighteenth century.

A second, and related, myth may also now be dispelled. Just as it has been standard practice to view the idea of progress as a French export, so there has been widespread agreement that the idea reached its high-water mark in Britain during the Victorian era. As Walter Houghton puts it, during the generation commencing about 1850 faith in progress "soared higher and [sang] more clearly than ever before, or since." Other historians, such as G. M. Young, have found an "almost universal faith in progress" in evidence as early as a decade or two before mid-century, and describe early Victorian thought as "regulated by the conception of progress." But whatever the precise chronology selected, it has for long been customary to refer glibly to "Victorian optimism," and to contend that "the central, the most characteristic belief of the Victorians, was the idea of progress"—a claim that has not been made for any other period.[8]

"Victorian optimism" was in fact a complicated and fragile mood. In an essay of 1857, significantly titled "Progress: Its Law and Cause," Herbert Spencer pointed to the complexity:

8. Walter E. Houghton, *The Victorian Frame of Mind, 1830–1870* (New Haven, 1957), 32–33; G. M. Young, *Victorian England: Portrait of An Age* (London, 1936), 1, 108; John Bowle, "Origins and Development of the Idea of Progress," in *Ideas and Beliefs of the Victorians: An Historic Revaluation of the Victorian Age* (New York, 1966), 33.

The current conception of Progress is somewhat shifting and indefinite. Sometimes it comprehends little more than simple growth—as of a nation in the number of its members and the extent of territory over which it has spread. Sometimes it has reference to quantity of material products—as when the advance of agriculture and manufactures is the topic. Sometimes the superior quality of these products is contemplated: and sometimes the new or improved appliances by which they are produced. When, again, we speak of moral or intellectual progress, we refer to the state of the individual or people exhibiting it; while, when the progress of Knowledge, of Science, of Art, is commented upon, we have in view certain abstract results of human thought and action.

According to the willing admission of one of its principal exponents, then, the optimism of the age seems rather clearly to have been neither singly focused nor uniformly expressed. As for its fragility, G. M. Trevelyan's comment more than forty years ago that "the famous Victorian belief in progress was a very conditional affair" points us in the right direction. The general improvement in material conditions gave great pleasure to nearly all observers. But because the Victorians "had no thought-out philosophic belief in progress as a universal law, true to all times and in all countries," because "few of them had a philosophic belief in a progress that would go on for ever, and some of them . . . thought the past had been better than the present," it was relatively easy for their pleasure at the sight of progress in manufacturing and in the conditions of life to be overwhelmed by social problems. Trevelyan was correct to note that "theories" of progress continued to remain relatively rare, coming from only a few thinkers like Spencer himself and Henry Thomas Buckle. Indeed, the optimism of the Victorian era hardly amounted to the uniform opinion that everything was destined to continue to get better everywhere, nor was it unchallenged by other, more pessimistic sentiments about the course of history. The more we learn of the Victorians the less enthusiastic about the possibility of ongoing progress they appear to have been.[9]

9. Herbert Spencer, "Progress: Its Law and Cause" (1857), *Essays on Education and Kindred Subjects* (London and New York: J. M. Dent and E. P. Dutton, n.d.), 153; G. M. Trevelyan, "Macaulay and the Sense of Optimism," in *Ideas and Beliefs of the Victorians*, 51.

When John Ruskin wrote that the "elements of progress and decline" were "strangely mingled in the modern mind," he expressed
an accurate understanding of the reality beneath the surface appearances of his century. For progress was just one of two "great polar
ideas" of the Victorians, the other being decadence, and contemporaries "surveyed their world, its past and its future, with alternate
hope and fear." Of course, notions of decadence and even cyclical
theories of history, all of which could be found in abundance during
the nineteenth century, were not new competitors for the idea of
progress. This time, however, the competition was much more severe than it had been in the high eighteenth century—severe enough
to permit us to conclude that in the Victorian era the idea of progress,
"whatever its effect upon those who embraced it, was much less
widely accepted than we have been led to believe."[10]

The fragile quality of the historical optimism of the age contrasts
starkly with what we now can say about the central years of the
previous century. As in the Victorian era, so in the period 1730–89 we
find many versions of the idea of progress; but we also uncover relatively little opposition to that idea. As we have seen, the cyclical
theory of history had few proponents then, and notions of decadence,
when they did appear, were quickly countered by the robustness of
the contemporary feeling that things were improving. The conclusion is heretical but inescapable: if we are to talk about an "optimistic" era, let us do so about mid-Georgian rather than mid-Victorian
times.

The eighteenth century was a particularly optimistic period in
Britain partly because the idea of progress was so thoroughly bound
up with every major field of thought at the time. In examining millennialism and the various doctrines of religious progress, we have seen
the close connections between the idea and contemporary theology
and religion. The continuing warfare between ancients and moderns,
along with all the doctrines of progress in the arts and sciences, illustrates how intimately the idea was related to the science or natural
philosophy of the age, and even to the organizational circumstances

10. John Ruskin, *Modern Painters*, Pt. IV, Ch. XVI, Sect. 17, in *The Works of John
Ruskin* ("Library Edition"), ed. E. T. Cook and Alexander Wedderburn, 39 vols. (Lon-
don, 1903–12), 5:327; Jerome Hamilton Buckley, *The Triumph of Time: A Study of the
Victorian Concepts of Time, History, Progress, and Decadence* (Cambridge, Mass.,
1966), 13, 33, 59, 61, 64; idem, *The Victorian Temper: A Study in Literary Culture*
(New York, 1961), 8.

of the study of the natural world. From the same context, the idea's tight links with then-current views on high culture, especially the writing of literature and the creation of works in the fine arts, are also revealed. Even clearer are the bonds between the idea of progress and contemporary thought about human nature, the human mind, and language. And as for many of the prominent social, economic, political, and historical theories of the eighteenth century, they are so closely tied to English and Scottish doctrines of general progress as to be inextricable. No other idea had such a multifarious existence in that age; no other idea gained so much from or contributed so much to activity in diverse fields of thought. The age of the Enlightenment saw the emergence of many elements of the modern mind, and, at least in Britain, the idea of progress had a crucial part to play in that development.

None of this is to say that the career of the idea reached its absolute apex in eighteenth-century Britain. There is no question that many, perhaps even a great majority of its most interesting forms were the products of later thinkers, and not just in Britain. No historian of the idea would deny that the nineteenth century was in many ways its heyday, that its credentials as one of the key features of the modern mind were fully solidified only then—in large measure because it was only then that its history began to be studied. But if we look at some of the principal British versions of the idea during the sixty or seventy years after 1789, we will immediately see how much they owed to the commentators on progress that are examined in this book. And this debt represents another crucial feature of the significance of the idea's development in the six or seven decades before the French Revolution.

"Influence" (like "causation") may have become a dirty word among many historians, but the concept remains crucial. Whether one can determine all or even most of the factors leading to an intellectual development or to the beliefs of an individual is irrelevant. Instead, it is useful to be alert to the ways in which ideas held by one person or group are picked up by others and thereafter elaborated in new ways, even if every detail about influence cannot be known.

Late eighteenth- and early nineteenth-century doctrines of progress provide a case in point. The radical intellectual and writer William Godwin, for instance, was an ardent believer in the view that "Man is perfectible, or in other words susceptible of perpetual improvement." His *Political Justice* (first published 1793) provoked as much controversy as any book written in England during the era of the French Revolution, and it did there what Condorcet's *Esquisse* did in France to popularize the concept of the perfectibility of man. There can be no doubt that Godwin's version of the idea of progress owed much to Joseph Priestley and Richard Price: he knew them and had read many of their writings with care. In fact, it is hardly too much to say that passages such as the following could have been written by Priestley or Price as easily as by Godwin:

> Is it possible for us to contemplate what [man] has already done, without being impressed with a strong presentiment of the improvement he has yet to accomplish? There is no science that is not capable of additions; there is no art that may not be carried to a still higher perfection. If this be true of all other sciences, why not of morals? If this be true of all other arts, why not of social institution?

Likewise, although Godwin rejected David Hartley's theory of vibrations, he not only adhered closely to the principal doctrine of association in *Observations on Man* but also adopted the Hartleyan emphasis on the pliability of man and the centrality of education. And his utopia, as described at the end of *Political Justice*, reads very much like a secularized version of the views of the millennium that Worthington and others had propounded earlier in the century.[11]

Similar connections can be uncovered for another early nineteenth-century radical who believed ardently in progress, Robert Owen. Owen's belief in the perfectibility of man and his attempt to develop a plan "for gradually ameliorating the condition of mankind" by establishing a new moral world, on both sides of the Atlantic, represent a doctrine of progress that had obvious eighteenth-century underpinnings. For example, millennialism played an important role in his ideas, and he has been described as "a typical eighteenth-century postmillennialist, believing that the millennium was simply a more perfect state of society." The following pronouncement from the introductory number of his journal *New Moral World* (1834) is typical

11. William Godwin, *Enquiry Concerning Political Justice and Its Influence on Morals and Happiness*, 3d ed., corr. (1797), ed. F. E. L. Priestley (Toronto, 1946), 1:86, 118–19, 398–421, 44–48, and 2:502–04; Peter H. Marshall, *William Godwin* (New Haven, 1984), 394–95.

of his attempt to portray each venture on which he embarked as constituting the start of the millennium:

> The rubicon between the Old Immoral and the New Moral World is finally passed: . . . . This . . . is the great Advent of the world, the second coming of Christ,—for Truth and Christ are one and the same. The first coming of Christ was a partial development of Truth to the few. . . . The second coming of Christ will make Truth known to the many. . . . The time is therefore arrived when the foretold millennium is about to commence.

This statement places Owen in line with the eighteenth-century scholarly eschatological tradition, and his comments on the development of truth also link him to the advancement of religious knowledge and the concept of a progressive revelation. Many of Owen's followers imitated their leader in adopting a strongly millennial outlook, and during the 1830s such Owenites as John Finch and James "Shepherd" Smith elaborated a vision of the millennium with a decidedly utopian and secular cast.[12]

Like Godwin, Owen was also a great believer in the power of education to mold character and reshape society for the better. He and his followers fully accepted the concept of the pliability of man, and although he did not himself subscribe to the psychology of association some of the Owenites did. In any event, Owen himself wrote that education (in the broad sense) "has not yet acquired that prominent rank in our estimation which it deserves; for, when duly investigated, it will be found to be, so far at least as it depends on our operations, the primary source of all good and evil, misery and happiness which exist in the world."[13] Hartley and the educationalists, Price and Smith, and the other believers in general progress would not have put the matter much differently.

It is not possible to specify with precision the sources of these views of Owen and his followers. Owen himself is known to have been a member of the Manchester Literary and Philosophical Society during the decade or so after 1787, so he would have become acquainted with the ideas of such other members as Thomas Barnes, the Arian who had much to say about education and progress in the

---

12. J. F. C. Harrison, *Quest for the New Moral World: Robert Owen and the Owenites in Britain and America* (New York, 1969), 91–135 (quotations 132–35).
13. Ibid., 140–47.

arts and sciences. Owen was later familiar with many professors in Glasgow and Edinburgh universities, and certainly many Owenite books and journals cited works by Ferguson, Hume, and Stewart. In addition, he spent much time with his new friend, Godwin, during the winter and spring of 1813, just when he was writing much of his fundamental statement on progress and social change, *A New View of Society*, and he continued to see Godwin frequently for the next five years.[14] But whatever the specific connections might have been, the point is that Owen and his followers were part of several strong intellectual traditions intimately connected to the development of the idea of progress in the eighteenth century. Those traditions *must* have played an important role in the development of the conception of progress held by Owen and his followers.

Similar kinds of connections with the eighteenth century are also apparent among the Romantics. M. H. Abrams has appropriately reminded students of literature that it is "an extreme historical injustice" to identify English Romanticism with "the cult of the noble savage and the cultural idea of a return to an early stage of simple and easeful 'nature.'" Far from being primitivists, as Crane Brinton put it long ago, the Lake Poets in their mature years "maintain the idea of progress, of growth; and faith in progress is intimately connected with their earlier faith in Nature." In Abrams's view, the "typical Romantic ideal . . . is an ideal of strenuous effort along the hard road of culture and civilization." This road is not a straight, inclined track but in fact an upward spiral, "a process of the self-formation, or self-education, of the mind and moral being of man from the dawn of consciousness to the stage of full maturity." The end result of the process is a reconciliation or reintegration of subject and object, of the spirit with its other, of man with nature, but at a new, higher level than at the beginning. For Coleridge, who epitomizes the English Romantic viewpoint in this regard, "all history, both of the race and of each human being, although it seems linear to short-sighted man, manifests itself to him who sees present, past, and future in one purview as a great circle from the One back to the One by way of the many."[15]

14. Ibid., 83–85; Marshall, *Godwin*, 310–11. On Barnes, see above, chap. 2 and chap. 4.

15. M. H. Abrams, *Natural Supernaturalism: Tradition and Revolution in Romantic Literature* (New York, 1971), 260, 183–88, 269–72; Crane Brinton, *The Political Ideas of the English Romanticists* (1926), repr. ed. (Ann Arbor, Mich., 1966), 227.

Such views as these unquestionably derived in part from German philosophy. But they also owed much to eighteenth-century English sources, particularly ones closely associated with the development of the idea of progress. Indeed, it is possible to identify a chain of influence stretching backward from Godwin himself. It has long been recognized that Wordsworth, Coleridge, and Southey were briefly "caught and held in the close web of logic" of *Political Justice*, even to the point of desiring to establish a Godwinian-based Pantisocratic community that would serve as a model of human perfectibility. When that web unraveled after the mid-1790s, as the first generation of Romantics turned toward a new philosophy and a new politics, important elements of Godwinism remained in their thought—especially the emphasis on perfectibility. But a significant part of the reason for this lasting impact lies in the fact that the Romantics shared with Godwin a common background in the British eschatological tradition.[16]

Abrams's analysis of the Lake Poets' relationship to millennialism offers a compelling instance of how "characteristic concepts and patterns of Romantic philosophy and literature are a displaced and reconstituted theology, or else a secularized form of devotional experience." Beginning with the eschatological climate that we have found in eighteenth-century Anglicanism and Dissent, the first generation of Romantics viewed the French Revolution as the introduction of a new world. Their expectations may have been shattered as the 1790s advanced, but the "millennial pattern of thinking . . . persisted, with this difference: the external means was replaced by an internal means for transforming the world." That is, traditional religious faith in the coming of the millennium had given way to a much more secular faith in a millennium brought on by political and social revolution, which itself was then replaced by faith in a millennium to be established through the human mind and imagination. As Abrams writes, "the mind of man confronts the old heaven and earth and possesses within itself the power . . . to transform them into a new heaven and new earth, by means of a total revolution of consciousness. This . . . is the high Romantic argument."[17]

Southey's *Colloquies* (1829) suggestively illustrates how old millennialism and new Romantic visions of progress were closely tied.

16. H. N. Brailsford, *Shelley, Godwin, and Their Circle* (1913), repr. ed. ([Hamden, Conn.,] 1969), 51–53; Marshall, *Godwin*, 123–33.

17. Abrams, *Natural Supernaturalism*, 64–65, 330–34.

The book's dialogue between the shade of Sir Thomas More and Montesinos centers on the tendencies of history, with More presenting an almost cheerless view of the present, especially the moral effects of the manufacturing system. In only one place is Montesinos able to avoid having More roundly negate his optimism. There he contends that a

> happier condition of society is possible than that in which any nation is existing at this time, or has at any time existed. The sum both of moral and physical evil may be greatly diminished by good laws, good institutions, and good governments. Moral evil cannot indeed be removed, unless the nature of man were changed; . . . physical evil must always, to a certain degree, be inseparable from mortality. But both are so much within the reach of human institutions that a state of society is conceivable almost as superior to that of England in these days, as that itself is superior to the condition of the tattoed Britons, or of the Northern Pirates from whom we are descended. Surely this belief rests upon a reasonable foundation, and is supported by that general improvement (always going on if it be regarded upon the grand scale) to which all history bears witness.

These hopes, Montesinos explicitly says, "are derived from the Prophets and the Evangelists." They rest upon his conviction that "the progress of knowledge and the diffusion of Christianity will bring about at last . . . something like that Utopian state of which the philosophers have loved to dream, . . . like that millennium in which Saints as well as enthusiasts have trusted." Thirty-five years after his flirtation with Pantisocracy, the poet laureate demonstrated that the millennialist perspective of men like Broughton, Hartley, Priestley, and Godwin himself had not disappeared.[18]

But it was not just eschatology that stimulated the Romantics to develop their views of progress. They also were influenced in this regard by the concept of the pliability of man, and the associationist psychology connected with it, which they shared with Godwin. For instance, Shelley was familiar with both Hartley and Helvétius, and

18. Robert Southey, *Sir Thomas More: or, Colloquies on the Progress and Prospects of Society*, 2 vols. (London, 1829), 1:27, 29–30, 32, 34. Abrams provides evidence from other Romantics (Wordsworth, Coleridge, and Shelley) of the altered millennialism that he calls "apocalypse by imagination": *Natural Supernaturalism*, 335–39, 342–44.

his fragmentary prose writings on metaphysics and on morals (both dating from about 1815) have a decidedly Hartleyan tone. He unquestionably learned much from his teacher Godwin, who convinced him of the perfectibility of man and may have introduced him to Hartley's ideas. But even when he had later turned away from materialistic psychology and Godwin's concept of progress through reason, and toward an imagination-inspired leap to a new level of perfection, his high hopes for mankind still rested on the belief that "Conversion is a psychological possibility." Similarly, Coleridge studied *Observations on Man* very closely in 1794, and the book remained important to him even after he had learned German philosophy. Indeed, as late as 1803 he was planning to write a comprehensive essay on its first volume, with new illustrations of the workings of association. Hartleyan psychology and moral philosophy proved so crucial to him because it offered a kind of "scientific confirmation" for his intuitive sense that "the religious experience of the annihilation of self and union with God could be supported by rational analysis."[19] The key Romantic emphasis on self-education, which both Shelley and Coleridge exemplify, required a firm underlying conviction that man was in fact educable. And it was precisely this conviction that lay at the heart of eighteenth-century British psychology and educational philosophy.

The pre-eminent Romantic from the north, Sir Walter Scott, also learned much from those of his predecessors who believed in general progress. For too long Scott's historical vision has been characterized as glorification of and nostalgia for the past, especially the medieval past. Certainly, there are elements of such an attitude in his novels, but for him, as Duncan Forbes and Hugh Trevor-Roper have reminded us, progress was "the organizing principle of history" and "the process of change was beneficent." He held that "his own age, and his own society, were preferable to the idleness, poverty and perpetual robbery of tribal life," and he believed in commercial, sci-

19. Carl Grabo, *The Magic Plant: The Growth of Shelley's Thought* (Chapel Hill, 1936), 145–52; Marshall, *Godwin*, 295–304; Brailsford, *Shelley, Godwin, and Their Circle*, 235–37; Richard Haven, "Coleridge, Hartley, and the Mystics," *Journal of the History of Ideas* 20 (Oct.–Dec. 1959): 478–81. A succinct statement of Shelley's mature vision of progress may be found in his preface to *The Revolt of Islam* (1818), in *The Complete Works of Percy Bysshe Shelley*, ed. Roger Ingpen and Walter E. Peck, 10 vols. (London, 1926–30), 1:239–42.

entific, and technological progress. As he observed in a letter urging his younger son to study history,

> Man only differs from birds and beasts because he has the means of availing himself of the knowlege [sic] which has been acquired by his predecessors. The swallow builds the same nest which its father and mother built and the sparrow does not improve by the experience of its parents. . . . It is not so with the human race. Our ancestors lodged in caves and wigwams where we construct palaces for the rich and comfortable dwellings for the poor. And why is this but because our eye is enabled to look back upon the past to improve on our ancestors['] improvements and to avoid their errors. This can only be done by studying history and comparing it with passing events.[20]

The fact that this comment might easily have been borrowed from the opening pages of Ferguson's *Essay on the History of Civil Society* suggests how much Scott's own outlook on history owed to the Scottish Enlightenment. He was in fact on intimate terms with Ferguson for many years, knew Robertson personally, and studied at the University of Edinburgh with their follower Dugald Stewart. Although it is not known whether he read them carefully, the major works of the members of the Scottish Enlightenment were all in his library. In any case, there can be no doubt that the intellectual atmosphere of his college years acquainted him with their principal ideas about history and society. At the very least their philosophical history "served as a catalyst for Scott, binding together and giving new significance to his large but fragmentary knowledge of history." For instance, as indicated by an early essay on the rise of feudalism written for Dugald Stewart, he looked beyond the particularities of a given situation to identify the "general origin" of that kind of development, and in doing so he hewed to the Scottish Enlightenment position that such

20. David Daiches, "Sir Walter Scott and History," *Études Anglaises* 24 (Oct.–Dec. 1971): 474, 464; P. D. Garside, "Scott, the Romantic Past and the Nineteenth Century," *Review of English Studies* 23 (May 1972): 147–61; Duncan Forbes, "The Rationalism of Sir Walter Scott," *Cambridge Journal* 7 (Oct. 1953): 28, 20, 26–27; Hugh Trevor-Roper, "Sir Walter Scott and History," *The Listener* 86 (Aug. 19, 1971): 228; Walter Scott to Charles Scott, Nov. 21, 1821, in *The Letters of Sir Walter Scott*, ed. H. J. C. Grierson, 12 vols. (London, 1932–37), 7:34.

matters proceed "upon principles common to all nations when placed in a certain situation." Writing to Southey nearly thirty years later, he praised the poet laureate's partially completed history of Brazil, contending that the "history of colonies has in it some points of peculiar interest as illustrating human nature. On such occasions the extremes of civilized and savage life are suddenly and strongly brought into contact with each other and the results are as interesting to the moral observer as those which take place on the mixture of chemical substances are to the physical investigator." This comment illuminates the frequent juxtaposition in his novels of Lowlanders with Highlanders.[21]

If the concept of progress from rudeness to civilization was implicit in Scott's thought and fiction, so, too, were concerns about the problems that might accompany such progress. At the end of the "hungry twenties" he wrote compassionately about the condition of the Irish and the British poor, observing that he was "no great believer in the extreme degree of improvement to be derived from the advancement of science; for every pursuit of that nature tends, when pushed to a certain extent, to harden the heart." He added that the "state of high civilization" to which the British had arrived in his own time was perhaps not a true blessing, because "while the *few* are improved to the highest point, the *many* are in proportion brutalized and degraded, and the same nation displays at the same time the very highest and the very lowest state in which the human race can exist in point of intellect. . . . As our numbers increased, our wants multiplied; and here we are, contending with increasing difficulties by the force of repeated inventions."[22] Smith, Ferguson, and Millar would have stated the problem in much the same terms. Hence, both in his conception of the advance of civilization from rudeness to refinement and in his worries about civilized life, Scott was very much the heir of the Scottish Enlightenment.

Moving beyond the Romantics, a similar inheritance from eighteenth-century predecessors can be found in the thought of

21. Peter D. Garside, "Scott and the 'Philosophical' Historians," *Journal of the History of Ideas* 36 (July–Sept. 1975): 497–500, 504–05, 510; Walter Scott to Captain Robert Scott, Sept. 30, 1790, and to Robert Southey, March 28, 1818, in *Letters of Scott*, 1:17, and 5:115; Forbes, "Rationalism of Scott," 24–25, 31–33.

22. Forbes, "Rationalism of Scott," 28; Scott to Maria Edgeworth, Feb. 4, 1829, in *Letters of Scott*, 11:127–28. On Scott's evaluation of commerce, both positive and negative, see Lawrence Poston III, "The Commercial Motif of the Waverley Novels," *ELH* 42 (Spring 1975): 62–64.

Scott's contemporary James Mill, that leading figure among the early Utilitarians and Philosophic Radicals (and a man described by his son as "the last of the eighteenth century"). It has rightly been said that a "scientifically" based belief in the progress of society became an essential part of the militant faith of Utilitarianism, and that Mill "brought with him from Scotland a conception of progress which was lacking in Bentham's thought." The version of progress that Mill offered to Utilitarianism was, of course, in part what his Edinburgh education had given him: a notion of a universally applicable advance from the savage to the civilized life. This concept undergirded his *History of British India* (1817), a book that played a considerable role in shaping the attitudes of British administrators in India during the nineteenth century. Mill's confidence in being able to write such a work—which included long chapters on religion and manners—without having ever visited India must have flowed from his sense of certainty in the principles of Scottish philosophical history. Again and again he used the yardstick of a stage-by-stage development from primitiveness toward a high level of civilization (as determined by contemporary Europe) to measure conditions in India, with the invariable finding that the country was currently located fairly near the beginning of the developmental scale. Thus, India ranked among the "uncultivated nations" in its degrading treatment of women, was considered to "have but just emerged from barbarism" because its people showed an excessive measure of rigid formality and ceremonialism in their behavior and exceptional mildness in their manners, and could be classified as "rude and ignorant" by virtue of its "defective" system of legal classification. Mill's scathing description of Indian religion was prefaced with an analysis of the growth of religion that probably came directly from the work of Hume and Smith. Indeed, they and the other major figures of the Scottish Enlightenment were frequently cited by Mill in this work.[23]

But if the elder Mill was, as his son wrote to Comte, "the last survivor of that great school" of eighteenth-century Scottish think-

---

23. John Stuart Mill, *Autobiography*, in *Collected Works of John Stuart Mill*, 29 vols. to date (Toronto, 1963–), vol. 1 (*Autobiography and Literary Essays*, ed. John M. Robson and Jack Stillinger [1981]), 213; Duncan Forbes, "James Mill and India," *Cambridge Journal* 5 (Oct. 1951): 23–25, 31–32; James Mill, *The History of British India*, 3d ed., 6 vols. (London, 1826), 1:383–85, 399–401, 421, 192–95, 282–87. For examples of citations to Robertson, Kames, Ferguson, Millar, and Hume, see ibid., 1:408n, 293n, 198n, 400n, 383n, 157n, 237n, 347n, 136n.

ers, his contribution to the Utilitarian vision of progress amounted to more than the mere importation of Scottish intellectual wares. For he had, according to his son, a "firm confidence . . . in the power of reason, the general progress of improvement, and the good which individuals could do by judicious effort," and he was convinced of the "unlimited possibility" of improving the human race. His were the kinds of high hopes for the future that had been much more common among eighteenth-century English believers in general progress than among their Scottish contemporaries, and these hopes explain his diligent work and writing over many years on behalf of reform. A crucial source of his optimism lies in the fact that for him *Observations on Man* was "the really master-production in the philosophy of mind," which he did his best to support and elaborate in his own *Analysis of the Phenomena of the Human Mind* (1829). His son quite rightly labeled him a disciple of Hartley; once he had thrown over the Scottish common-sense position, he could not refrain from advocating the principle of association—not even in the *History of British India*. For this reason it is true to say that the version of the idea of progress on which the Utilitarians were brought up sprang from English as well as Scottish sources.[24]

During the decades between the outbreak of the French Revolution and the First Reform Act, then, the major streams of contemporary British thought contained doctrines of progress that had close affinities to those of the high eighteenth century. This was still the case at mid-century, even though other influences (especially French ones) had by then also begun to make their presence felt, and still others (pre-eminently evolutionary theory) were about to do so. Two prominent intellectuals from the so-called mid-Victorian period make clear just how closely connected to its eighteenth-century roots the idea of progress still was in their day.

In his *System of Logic,* John Stuart Mill stated decisively his belief

24. John Stuart Mill to Auguste Comte, Jan. 28, 1843, in *Collected Works*, vol. 13 (*The Earlier Letters of John Stuart Mill, 1812–1848*, ed. Francis E. Mineka [1963]), 566; idem, *Autobiography*, "Letter to the Editor of the Edinburgh Review on James Mill" (1844), and "A Few Observations on Mr. Mill" (1833), in *Collected Works*, 1:105, 111, 71, 538, 589–90; James Mill, *History of British India*, 1:xiv–xv. Of course, there were probably French influences acting on James Mill, too, especially Condorcet and Helvétius: see Elie Halévy, *The Growth of Philosophic Radicalism*, trans. Mary Morris (Boston, 1955), 274, 282. But the Scottish and Hartleyan influences were of paramount importance. See also G. S. Bower, *David Hartley and James Mill* (New York, 1881), and above, chap. 4.

that the general tendency of history "is, and will continue to be, saving occasional and temporary exceptions, one of improvement; a tendency towards a better and happier state." He also contended that although no generalization could be made about the speed with which this advance occurred, the order and manner of the progress of mankind "may to a certain extent have definite laws assigned to it," because there was "a sort of necessity established in this respect by the general laws of human nature; by the constitution of the human mind." To a notable degree these mature opinions must have been shaped by continental writers of the first half of the nineteenth century, such as the Saint-Simonians and Comte, and in his *Autobiography* Mill tells us as much. But prior British thought about progress also played a prominent, and indeed formative, part in his views, which French thinkers later reinforced and enhanced.[25]

The concept of there being an order to human progress was, of course, central to the Scots' vision of development from rudeness to refinement, as well as to the subsidiary four-stage theory that they propounded long before Comte's theory of tripartite intellectual development. The younger Mill became familiar with their views during his childhood and adolescence, when he studied not only Hume but also Robertson, Ferguson, and Millar under his father's tutelage. The impact of this initial experience is frequently apparent in his writings. For instance, he used the four-stage theory at the outset of his *Principles of Political Economy* (1847), to elucidate at some length the differences between ages and between nations in the quantity, kind, and distribution of wealth. This discussion related economic, social, political, and intellectual developments within the separate stages, just as with the Scots. Likewise, he made it clear that the main principle of *On Liberty*—interference with the liberty of an individual is warranted only to prevent harm to others—did not apply to "those backward states of society in which the race itself may be considered as in its nonage," so that despotism might constitute "a

---

25. John Stuart Mill, *A System of Logic, Racionative and Inductive: Being a Connected View of the Principles of Evidence and the Methods of Scientific Investigation,* in *Collected Works,* vol. 8 (*A System of Logic,* ed. J. M. Robson [1973]), 913–14, 938; *Autobiography,* in *Collected Works,* 1:169, 171. Mill's reminder to Comte that such eighteenth-century Scottish thinkers as Hume, Ferguson, Smith, and Millar "intellectually resemble the French" suggests how Continental ideas may have supported and to some extent modified but did not radically alter his basic thought: Mill to Comte, Oct. 5, 1844, in *Collected Works,* 13:638; J. W. Burrow, *Evolution and Society: A Study in Victorian Social Theory,* paperback ed. (Cambridge, 1974), 15n4.

legitimate mode of government in dealing with barbarians." More than this, however, Mill's life-long concern with the problem of liberty, order, permanence, and progress reflected one of the Scots' own major interests. His conviction that "the only unfailing and permanent source of progress is liberty" is one for which their writings provide more than a little evidence. And the whole point of his calling attention to the problem of the tyranny of the majority was the same as their emphasis on the potential difficulties of a commercial civilization: to issue a warning that would prevent his own already advanced society from losing its progressiveness and stagnating like China or slipping into retrograde motion.[26]

But whatever might happen in particular nations, Mill fully expected mankind as a whole to continue on its improving course, as he said in the *System of Logic*. In arriving at this expectation, he relied heavily on two notions that had been of crucial importance to the development of the idea of progress in eighteenth-century Britain: the pliability of man and related principle of association, and the advancement of knowledge. Naturally, Mill had early been led by his father to read Hartley, at the age of fifteen or sixteen. A few years later he and the other young Philosophic Radicals used *Observations on Man* as a textbook in their study of analytical psychology, and they adopted the elder Mill's fundamental doctrine of "the formation of all human character by circumstances, through the universal Principle of Association, and the consequent unlimited possibility of improving the moral and intellectual condition of mankind by education." The "educated intellect" was to be the chief instrument of human improvement, the Philosophic Radicals believed, because of "a quality of the human mind, the source of everything respectable in man either as an intellectual or as a moral being, namely, that his errors are corrigible." It was the corrigibility of error that made possible the advancement of knowledge, which in turn led to wider progress. "Every considerable advance in material civilization has been preceded by an advance in knowledge: and when any great social change

26. John Stuart Mill, *Principles of Political Economy, with Some of Their Applications to Social Philosophy*, in *Collected Works*, vol. 2 (*Principles of Political Economy*, ed. J. M. Robson [1965]), 10–21; idem, *On Liberty*, in *Collected Works*, vol. 18 (*Essays on Politics and Society*, ed. J. M. Robson [1977]), 224, 272–75. See also Meek, *Social Science and the Ignoble Savage*, 223. For Mill's youthful reading of the Scots, see *Autobiography*, in *Collected Works*, 1:11, 15, 31, 71, 554–55, 558, 569, 578–79. As noted above, chap. 7, Mill offered especially high praise to Millar.

has come to pass . . . it has had for its precursor a great change in the opinions and modes of thinking of society." This outlook, of course, helps to explain why Mill felt compelled to write *On Liberty*, and it indicates the lineage of his position in that book, extending back through Godwin to Priestley and Gordon to the proponents of the moderns in the eighteenth century and thence to the *querelle* and Bacon himself. In *On Liberty* Mill even mentioned the eighteenth-century preference for the moderns over the ancients, siding with the former while nonetheless congratulating Rousseau on "dislocating the compact mass of one-sided opinion" on this question, thereby "forcing its elements to recombine in a better form and with additional ingredients."[27] Here, with the most famous flower of his philosophy, we find a doctrine of progress deeply rooted in soil made fertile a hundred years before.

The same can be said of Thomas Babington Macaulay, in spite of the substantial intellectual differences and public disagreements that he had with Mill. Macaulay has for long provided the prototypical example for textbook generalizations about "mid-Victorian optimism." Yet until his later twenties he did not believe in progress at all: for instance, as late as 1824 he expressed "doubt whether the changes on which the admirers of modern institutions delight to dwell have improved our condition so much in reality as in appearance."[28] The sources of his transformation into an ardent proponent of the idea of progress offer us an instructive lesson in that idea's history.

To begin with, Macaulay shifted from being an admirer of the ancients to being a champion of the moderns. As his horizons expanded beyond his classical education, completed at Cambridge in 1823, the praise offered to all things Greek in his earliest published essays soon disappeared. It was replaced by the opinion that all classical Greek discoveries in the moral sciences of government, legislation, and political economy "are not to be compared with those which have been made in England every fifty years since the time of

27. Mill, *Autobiography, On Liberty*, and *System of Logic*, in *Collected Works*, 1:71, 578, 125–27, 109–13; 18:231, 243, 253; 8:927. Elsewhere Mill showed much less inclination to make intellectual change the cause, rather than the effect, of economic or technological changes: *Principles of Political Economy*, in *Collected Works*, 2:20.

28. Thomas Babington Macaulay, "On the Athenian Orators" (1824), in *The Miscellaneous Works of Lord Macaulay*, ed. Lady Hannah Trevelyan (New York, [1897]), 8:154.

Elizabeth." By the time he wrote the famous essay on Bacon in 1837, very little positive feeling for the ancients remained. Even though he continued always to enjoy reading them, he now disparaged their achievements in literature, found their philosophy to be a treadmill requiring much exertion and accomplishing nothing useful, and minimized their general intellectual legacy by contending that it had been "so carefully improved that the accumulated interest now exceeds the principal."[29] In short, he had entirely realigned himself in the contest between the ancients and moderns. He was now capable of sounding the trumpets of progress in all the arts and sciences, past, present, and future, for which he has perhaps been too much remembered.

Meanwhile, two other significant themes began to appear in his essays. One was associationist psychology, with which he seems not to have been acquainted until 1827, when it suddenly began to appear in his writings with surprising frequency, starting even before James Mill's work on the mind had been published. During the next three years, he discussed association on several occasions, especially amid his arguments against the Utilitarians. He eventually claimed that he understood Hartley far better than they did. In spite of this exaggeration, he certainly was familiar enough with Hartleyan concepts to assert correctly a basic tenet of the theory of the pliability of man, that through association anything may become an object of desire or aversion.[30] Macaulay never specifically stated that this characteristic of human nature made progress possible. But he undoubtedly had as much faith in the educability (and corrigibility) of mankind as did J. S. Mill.

His other new theme during the second half of the 1820s was in fact as old as the Scottish Enlightenment: the philosophical history of the advancement from rudeness to refinement. "Not only the individual advances from infancy to manhood," Ferguson had written in 1767, "but the species itself from rudeness to civilization." Macaulay's observation made sixty years later was in fundamental agreement: the "progress of a nation from barbarism to civilization," he asserted, paralleled the "progress of an individual from infancy to

29. Idem, "History" (1828) and "Lord Bacon" (1837), in *Miscellaneous Works*, 1:215–21, 226; 4:17–18, 108–11, 128–30.
30. Idem, "John Dryden" (1828), "Mill's Essay on Government" (1829), and "Utilitarian Theory of Government" (1829), in *Miscellaneous Works*, 1:124, 130, 365, 396; 2:65–67.

mature age." The concept of what he elsewhere called the "progress of nations towards refinement" lay at the center of his increasingly sophisticated vision of the history of creative literature, which he began to develop in "Milton" (1825) and continued in other *Edinburgh Review* essays of the next few years. While exploring the historical fate of poetry, for instance, he argued that in their intellectual growth nations "first perceive, and then abstract," that they "advance from particular images to general terms." This was precisely the position adopted by Ferguson and Smith, and Macaulay's sense that in intellectual terms the people of "a rude state of society . . . are children [but] with a greater variety of ideas" was consonant with the Scots' analysis of the "natural history of thought." More generally, his insistence that historians always adopt the comparative point of view had the same goal as the Scots did: "to distinguish what is local from what is universal; what is transitory from what is eternal; to discriminate between exceptions and rules; to trace the operation of disturbing causes; to separate those general principles which are always true and everywhere applicable from the accidental circumstances with which, in every community, they are blended." So, too, did he urge concentration on "noiseless revolutions" rather than high politics alone, on "the changes of manners and morals, the transition of communities from poverty to wealth, from knowledge to ignorance, from ferocity to humanity." In this his goal was to "illustrate the operation of laws, of religion, and of education, and to mark the progress of the human mind."[31]

With these sentiments Macaulay closely echoed the Scots and their quest for a scientific understanding of the interlocking development of all aspects of society. How carefully he had studied his eighteenth-century predecessors is not clear, though certainly he read Millar and Robertson at an early stage, as well as Hume. His new connection (through the *Edinburgh Review*) with Millar's pupil Francis Jeffrey must have given him considerable exposure to their views during precisely the years when this theme appeared in his writings.[32] In any event, many of the positions that the Scots had taken

31. Adam Ferguson, *Essay on the History of Civil Society*, ed. Duncan Forbes (Edinburgh, 1966), 1; Macaulay, "John Dryden," "Milton" (1825), and "History," in *Miscellaneous Works*, 1:133, 136, 7, 9, 223–24, 230, 233, 237. See also Joseph Hamburger, *Macaulay and the Whig Tradition* (Chicago, 1976), esp. 21–23, 127–33.

32. T. B. Macaulay to Selina Mills Macaulay, Feb. 12, 1813, and Sept. 9, 1816, and to Hannah More, Nov. 11, 1816, in *The Letters of Thomas Babington Macaulay*, ed.

relating to the idea of progress became his own as the decade of the 1820s approached its end.

By the time of his attack on Southey's *Colloquies* in 1830, Macaulay's views on progress were essentially complete. It is not the case, as has too often been suggested, that he adhered to the naive proposition that everything had been improving and would ceaselessly and uniformly continue to do so, everywhere.[33] Rather, his was a complicated and subtle notion of progress whose essence is captured by the following statement about the course of British history: "Now and then there has been a stoppage, now and then a short retrogression; but as to the general tendency there can be no doubt. A single breaker may recede; but the tide is evidently coming in." This image, to which Macaulay recurred several times, illustrates two key points about his faith in progress. First, it was ordinarily expressed about British history, or sometimes other individual societies or nations, and not about universal history or mankind as a whole. His own country provided his preferred focus, and his observations on progress were intended to apply to the course of a single society's development. Second, his faith in progress was tempered by the understanding that if a tide could come in it could also eventually go out. This explains why he repeatedly wrote about the London of a distant future, where "a few lean and half-naked fishermen wash their nets amidst the relics of her gigantic docks, and build their huts out of the capitals of her stately cathedrals," or where a traveler from the then-advanced society of New Zealand "shall, in the midst of a vast solitude, take his stand on a broken arch of London Bridge to sketch the ruins of St. Paul's." In his own form of the old concept of *translatio imperii*, Macaulay understood, without gloom or regret, that the "sceptre may pass away from us," to be wielded by another nation whose own advance Britain had inaugurated.[34]

If Macaulay's vision of progress was not naively optimistic or simple-minded, neither did it narrowly focus on material or "mechanical" progress—the making of larger, more powerful, or faster

Thomas Pinney, 6 vols. (Cambridge, 1974–81), 1:17, 81, 82; Hamburger, *Macaulay and the Whig Tradition*, 178–79.

33. For a temperate version of this widespread interpretation of Macaulay, see Buckley, *Triumph of Time*, 32, 34–36, 48, 63.

34. Macaulay, "Southey's Colloquies" (1830), "Mill's Essay on Government," and "Ranke's History of the Popes" (1840), in *Miscellaneous Works*, 2:140, and 1:391, and 4:367; speech delivered in the House of Commons, July 10, 1833, in *Miscellaneous Works*, 9:192–93.

objects and the provision of a more comfortable life.[35] In fact, he found improvement in virtually every aspect of British life (except religion), and celebrated them all, in some of his most famous essays as well as in his *History*. "The history of England," he declared,

> is emphatically the history of progress. . . . In the course of seven centuries, the wretched and degraded race have become the greatest and most highly civilized people that ever the world saw; have spread their dominion over every quarter of the globe; . . . have carried the science of healing, the means of locomotion and correspondence, every mechanical art, every manufacture, everything that promotes the convenience of life, to a perfection which our ancestors would have thought magical; have produced a literature which may boast of works not inferior to the noblest which Greece has bequeathed to us; have discovered the laws which regulate the motions of the heavenly bodies; have speculated with exquisite subtilty on the operation of the human mind; have been the acknowledged leaders of the human race in the career of political improvement. The history of England is the history of this great change in the moral, intellectual, and physical state of the inhabitants of our own island.[36]

This is a Macaulay who cannot easily be classified as a Philistine, and whose views obviously resemble those of the eighteenth-century believers in general progress.

Nevertheless, it is true that from about 1830 he gave special attention to material progress, and with all the fervor of a convert. He did so, in large measure, because of Southey and other critics of contemporary life, who found fault with industry, technology, and their effects. The famous essay on Bacon implies that such critics had "unduly depreciated" the arts that "increase the outward comforts of our species." With his hero Bacon he therefore found it "necessary to assert that, as [these arts] have a most serious effect on human happi-

35. For examples of how "Macaulayan progress" is taken to mean material progress, see Houghton, *Victorian Frame of Mind*, 39–40; Buckley, *Triumph of Time*, 36; Pieter Geyl, *Debates with Historians* (Groningen, 1955), 31.

36. Macaulay, "Sir James Mackintosh" (1835), in *Miscellaneous Works*, 3:358–59, 349–50. For the exception of religion and theology, see "Ranke's History," in *Miscellaneous Works*, 4:367–73. Further comments on general progress are contained in the famous third chapter of Macaulay's *History of England from the Accession of James II*, Everyman's Library ed., 4 vols. (London, 1906), 1:210, 279, 310–21.

ness, they are not unworthy of the attention of the highest human intellects." More than this, however, Macaulay admitted that the critics of the new nineteenth-century world provoked an exaggerated response. "Rose-bushes and poor-rates, rather than steam-engines and independence," he snorted. Southey had discovered a way of comparing the effects of agriculture and manufacturing. "And what is this way? To stand on a hill, to look at a cottage and a factory, and to see which is prettier." When the picturesque has been made the test of political good, of the condition of life, Macaulay asked, is it any wonder that an opposite criterion of cultural excellence should be set up in antagonistic over-reaction?[37]

Thus, when Macaulay comes to the subject of material progress in his writings we find him growing particularly autocratic in tone, with discussion and even argument giving way before declamation and celebration. This tendency appears most clearly in his citation of the long-term accomplishments of the Baconian philosophy.

> It has lengthened life; it has mitigated pain; it has extinguished diseases; it has increased the fertility of the soil; it has furnished new arms to the warrior; it has spanned great rivers and estuaries with bridges of form unknown to our fathers; it has guided the thunderbolt innocuously from heaven to earth; it has lighted up the night with the splendor of the day; it has extended the range of human vision; it has multiplied the power of the human muscles; it has accelerated motion; it has annihilated distance; it has facilitated intercourse, correspondence, all friendly offices, all despatch of business; it has enabled man to descend to the depths of the sea, to soar into the air, to penetrate securely into the noxious recesses of the earth, to traverse the land in cars which whirl along without horses, and the ocean in ships which run ten knots an hour against the wind. These are but a part of its fruits, and of its first fruits. For it is a philosophy which never rests, which has never attained, which is never perfect. Its law is progress. A point which yesterday was visible is its goal today, and will be its starting-post to-morrow.[38]

37. Idem, "Lord Bacon" and "Southey's Colloquies," in *Miscellaneous Works,* 4:134–36; 2:103–04. See also John Clive, *Macaulay: The Shaping of the Historian* (New York, 1973), 486.

38. Idem, "Lord Bacon," in *Miscellaneous Works,* 4:131–32.

Neither Wotton at the end of the seventeenth century nor Gordon in the middle of the eighteenth could have put the case for the advance of the arts and sciences any more forcefully than this.

With Macaulay and Mill we see how crucial the idea of progress had become to British thought by the middle years of the nineteenth century, and how even in that era its roots still lay firmly planted in eighteenth-century soil. In all of the major intellectual movements between the 1790s and the 1850s this idea occupied an important or even a determinative position, and always its expression grew at least in part out of influences from the age of Hartley, Priestley, and Smith.

The development of the idea of progress in eighteenth-century Britain has great historical significance yet another way, for which Macaulay's concentration on "material progress" may serve as a symbol. From one point of view, Macaulay was simply doing what we have seen so many of his predecessors do, what had become culturally habitual: examining his own world, marveling at its accomplishments, and proclaiming them to be evidence of large-scale improvement. In this respect he partook of a world-view that had become traditional, with its beginnings in the seventeenth century and its period of intensive development during the sixty years after about 1730. From another perspective, however, he was also putting his finger on the pulse of the changed world around him. For between the 1760s and 1770s, when doctrines of general progress came to the fore, and the 1820s and 1830s, when Macaulay began to proclaim his historical optimism, lay the heart of the Industrial Revolution in Britain. This "first industrial revolution" not only fundamentally altered the British economy (while introducing the steam engine, the steam boat, and the iron bridges to which Macaulay referred) but also changed forever the whole way of life of millions of people. We have already seen how the beginnings of this profound transformation had the intellectual consequence of helping to stimulate the development of the idea of progress. But, like every major historical event, the Industrial Revolution was effect as well as cause: it may have fostered the growth of historical optimism in Britain, but it also benefited from that growing optimism.

Arthur Young, perhaps the most famous chronicler of the early stages of the transformation, illustrates this dual linkage. In his account of his travels through northern England in 1768, he described the building at Harecastle of the tunnel portion of Bridgewater's canal, whose goal was to facilitate shipments between Hull and Liverpool. He then observed,

> By such noble undertakings is the present age peculiarly distinguished. When agriculture, manufactures, and commerce flourish, a nation grows rich and great, and riches cannot abound, without exciting that general industry, and spirit for improvement, which at last leads to performing works, which, in poorer times, would be thought wonders.[39]

In effect, Young offers an interpretation of eighteenth-century economic history; one in which prosperity in all the main sectors of the economy produces industriousness and a quest for advancement, which themselves lead on to even greater works of even greater economic consequence.

There is much to be said for the view that the emergence of a spirit of improvement, an expectation of continued positive innovation, a belief in the value of hard work, and in progress, contributed signally to many of the dramatic social and economic changes associated with the birth of the modern world in Britain. Already during the age of Newton a spirit of improvement "was in the air, and it was in the air of economic life as well as of science and social agitation." By the middle of the eighteenth century it was becoming palpable. It could be found, for example, in Renfrewshire. There a parish minister, looking back from the vantage point of 1791, could remember how the husbandry of his parish and the whole west of Scotland had been, "about the middle of the century, in a most unprosperous state. . . . The spirit of improvement, however, which, about that time, appeared in Scotland, reached Renfrewshire; and a very favourable change has now taken place." Meanwhile, far to the south, there developed a "disinterested 'spirit of improvement'" in London, which issued in road acts, lighting and paving acts, a major building act that sought to standardize construction at a high level of quality, and the erection and repair of bridges—all with a view to enhancing the beauty, safety, and convenience of life in the city. The architect and builder John Gwynn (d. 1786) offered specific plans for the me-

---

39. [Arthur Young], *A Six Months Tour through the North of England*, 4 vols. (London, 1768–70), 3:309–12. See also Francis D. Klingender, *Art and the Industrial Revolution*, ed. and rev. Arthur Elton (New York, 1968), 17.

tropolis in his *London and Westminster Improved* (1766), and many of these ultimately came to fruition. Its own monument to the age of improvement in the capital, Gwynn's book articulated the point of view, subscribed to by most educated residents of the city for the next sixty years, that they had a social and civic obligation to make London better. According to Gwynn, the "publick magnificence" connected with the improvement of London would, among its other effects, tend "to promote industry, to stimulate invention and to excite emulation in the polite and liberal arts." It would even enhance the "love of elegance among all ranks and degrees of people, and that refinement of taste, which in a nobleman produces true magnificence and elegance, will in a mechanic produce at least cleanliness and decorum."[40]

Nowhere was such civic responsibility felt more keenly than in Edinburgh. In 1752, almost simultaneous with the beginning of London's age of improvement, there appeared a pamphlet entitled *Proposals for carrying on certain Public Works in the City of Edinburgh*, probably written by Sir Gilbert Elliott of Minto at the urging of the city's famous lord provost, George Drummond. The author argued that a capital city of beauty, good location, and convenient arrangement would "naturally become the centre of trade and commerce, of learning and the arts, of politeness, and of refinement of every kind." Once in place, these advantages would soon "diffuse themselves through the nation, and universally promote the same spirit of industry and improvement." London provided the author with a concrete example of this effect, as well as with a model for the former Scottish capital to emulate. "To enlarge and improve this city, to adorn it with public buildings, which may be a national benefit, and thereby to remove, at least to some degree, the inconveniencies to which it has hitherto been liable," was his primary goal. "So necessary and so considerable an improvement of the capital cannot fail to have the greatest influence on the general prosperity of the nation," according to the author, and it was therefore not too much to say that the "increase of our people, the extension of our commerce, and the

---

40. G. N. Clark, *Science and Social Welfare in the Age of Newton*, 2d ed. (Oxford, 1949), 94–95; Sir John Sinclair, ed., *The Statistical Account of Scotland*, 21 vols. (Edinburgh, 1791–99), 7:84; John Gwynn, *London and Westminster Improved* (London, 1766), xiv–xv, 1–4; John Summerson, *Georgian London*, 3d ed. (Cambridge, Mass., 1978), 121–32.

honour of the nation, are all concerned in the success of this project."
More people would mean greater consumption, which in turn would
yield a more rapid circulation of money and other commodities. This
"great spring which gives motion to general industry and improvement" would in the end bring "wealth and prosperity," as a "certain
consequence." Thus, by proposing the improvement of the city of
Edinburgh, he was in fact aiming at nothing less than the economic
and social advancement of all Scotland.[41]

Much like Young in his assessment of the Bridgewater canal, the
author of the *Proposals* argued that this goal was attainable because
the current environment was already an "improving" one.

> At no period surely did there ever appear a more general, or a
> better directed zeal for the improvement and prosperity of this
> country [i.e., Scotland]. Had we therefore this general spirit of
> our countrymen for our sole encouragement, we might rest
> assured that our proposals would meet with no unfavourable
> reception. But when we consider the rapid progress which our
> trade and manufactures have actually made within these few
> years, and attentively compare the present state of this coun-
> try as to these particulars, with what it was in former times, we
> are persuaded that an attempt to enlarge and beautify this me-
> tropolis, will now at length be deemed necessary.

This turned out to be excellent prophecy. By 1759 the drainage of the
North Loch had begun, and between 1763 and 1772 a bridge was
constructed over it. In 1767 James Craig's plan for a new town to the
north of the drained area was selected by the magistrates, and by the
1780s much of the building in this area was completed, along with
important new buildings in the old part of the city. The construction
of a second new town commenced just after the turn of the century,
and the partial development of Calton Hill followed. By then Edinburgh had become widely known as the "Modern Athens," and it
could even be compared favorably to London. To the extent that
many of the goals of the *Proposals* had been realized, the spirit of
improvement cited in that pamphlet, the vision of a more splendid
city and an economically more vigorous Scotland, should receive

41. *Proposals for carrying on certain Public Works in the City of Edinburgh,* quoted
in A. J. Youngson, *The Making of Classical Edinburgh, 1750–1840* (Edinburgh, 1966),
4, 6–11.

much of the credit. From its agricultural and literary improving societies to the modernization of its capital, Scotland in the later eighteenth century was alive with this attitude.[42]

Civic projects, however substantial, are merely one instance of the effect of this broad spirit of improvement, openness to change, and excitement about innovation as Britain entered, indeed created, the modern world. The whole atmosphere surrounding the Industrial Revolution provides perhaps the most compelling evidence for the impact of the idea of progress on the activities of the age. For example, as we have seen Samuel Johnson asserted that such ingenious trifles as automatons were valuable because they could show what was within reach, and because their mechanisms might eventually be employed not just to inspire wonder but rather "to drain fens, or manufacture metals." A key invention in the cloth-making industry proves Johnson's point. Against acquaintances who said that it was not possible to create a weaving "mill" that would use thread from Arkwright's water frame, Edmund Cartwright argued in 1784 that an automaton chess-player he had seen in London was already more mechanically complex than weaving would be. With this automaton as inspiration he invented the power loom by 1787. Forty-five years later a commentator on automatons claimed that this kind of connection was common.[43] Whether it was, there can be little doubt that the eighteenth century's faith in the progress of the practical arts and technology, as expressed in part in its fascination with mechanical marvels, yielded not just the skills but equally important the confidence and sense of the possible to produce the machinery that Macaulay eventually celebrated.

Of course, machinery and inventions were only part of what we call the Industrial Revolution. At least as important were the attitudes and practices of the factory owners, landlords, managers, merchants, and consumers. On his first visit to Birmingham in 1741,

42. *Proposals*, in ibid., 7–8; David Daiches, *Edinburgh* (London, 1980), 116–26; [John Britton], *Modern Athens, Displayed in a Series of Views: or Edinburgh in the Nineteenth Century* (1831), repr. ed. (New York, 1969), Preface, iii-v. This is also true in the Highlands, where during the last three or four decades of the century there was "an atmosphere of expectation of beneficent change about to take place, a hopefulness without parallel in Highland experience": T. C. Smout, *A History of the Scottish People, 1560–1830* (New York, 1969), 346.

43. Richard D. Altick, *The Shows of London* (Cambridge, Mass., 1978), 76:1–2. On Johnson's views, see above, chap. 2.

William Hutton (1723–1815), later the author of a substantial account of the city, found an ethos that he had not known elsewhere:

> I was much surprised at the place, but more at the people. They were a species I had never seen; they possessed a vivacity I had never beheld; I had been among dreamers, but now I saw men awake: Their very step along the street shewed alacrity. . . . Every man seemed to know and prosecute his own affairs: The town was large, and full of inhabitants, and those inhabitants full of industry.

From this experience Hutton arrived at the pleasing conclusion that commerce tended to improve its practitioners (by expanding the mind, removing prejudices, and polishing manners). But what was it about its practitioners that tended to improve commerce? Was it, as Hutton wrote, that the "view of profit, like the view of corn to the hungry horse, excites to action"? Surely the mere quest for wealth played some role in the origins of the Industrial Revolution, but this is a universal characteristic that does not by itself explain why the transformation occurred first in Britain. Nor does the fact that the industrious behavior of the citizens of Birmingham must have owed something to religious and psychological considerations, pre-eminently Nonconformist theology and child-rearing practices, the response of Dissenters to "withdrawal of status respect," and their need for achievement. After all, there were plenty of Calvinists on the Continent, as well as minority groups with psychological needs of at least equal potential significance.[44]

The Industrial Revolution was certainly "over-determined," and the list of factors that must be taken into account in seeking its origins is long. Yet it will not do to overlook or underestimate the influence of the idea of progress in this regard. The eighteenth century, writes a distinguished historian of the period, saw tremendous changes bring into existence in Britain "the first society dedicated to ever-expanding consumption based on industrial production." To be

44. W.[illiam] Hutton, *An History of Birmingham*, 3d ed. (Birmingham, 1795), 88–91, 85. See also Klingender, *Art and the Industrial Revolution*, 14. On the religious and psychological factors, see M. W. Flinn, *Origins of the Industrial Revolution* (London, 1966), 82–90; David S. Landes, *The Unbound Prometheus: Technological Change and Industrial Development in Western Europe from 1750 to the Present* (Cambridge, 1969), 73–74; Harold Perkin, "The Social Causes of the Industrial Revolution," *The Structured Crowd* (Brighton, 1981), 30.

successful, this innovation "required men and women to believe in growth, in change, in modernity; to believe that the future was bright, far brighter than the past; to believe, also, that what was new was desirable, whether it was the cut of a dress, the ascent of a balloon, or a new variety of auricula." We are also told by one economic historian that eighteenth-century British merchants were unusually "energetic, pushful, and open to innovation," and that the landowners exhibited a similar "spirit of innovation." The society in which they lived is now described by another economic historian as "increasingly curious, increasingly questing, increasingly on the move, on the make, having a go, increasingly seeking to experiment, wanting to improve." The evidence cited for this view of British society includes the popularization of science and technology, the encyclopedias of the day, new institutions such as the London Society of Arts and the many local societies of a similar bent, and new educational movements. And a social historian informs us of "the profound change in human expectations of the improvement of life in this world," stemming from the Renaissance, the scientific revolution and its sequelae, the schools and academies of the eighteenth century, and the philosophical societies that "harnessed this spirit to the actual improvement of agricultural and industrial processes." In each case we are presented with some facet of the various doctrines of progress in the arts and sciences that we have seen expressed so widely and vigorously by such a broad spectrum of thinkers and writers. On the basis of available evidence it seems appropriate to conclude that because the Industrial Revolution is a truly major historical discontinuity, its origins "are more likely to lie in other, exogenous, possibly non-economic discontinuities." And if for that reason "the spurt in all forms of innovational activity must necessarily be explained in some other, possibly non-economic, discontinuity in eighteenth-century (or, conceivably, seventeenth-century) history," as there is good cause to think, then the dramatic development of the idea of progress that we have examined in this book must be borne in mind as a key factor in the making of the Industrial Revolution.[45] In light of the complex interrelationship between this

45. J. H. Plumb, "The Acceptance of Modernity," in Neil McKendrick, John Brewer, and Plumb, *The Birth of a Consumer Society: The Commercialization of Eighteenth-Century England* (Bloomington, Ind., 1985), 316; Landes, *Unbound Prometheus*, 52, 69; Peter Mathias, "Who Unbound Prometheus? Science and Technical Change, 1600–1800," *The Transformation of England: Essays in the Economic and*

idea and this revolution, there can be little wonder that Macaulay and many other admirers of the modern industrial world placed such great emphasis on the advance of science and technology, or that they thereby succeeded in establishing an identification between doctrines of progress in those areas and the belief in progress as a whole. This in turn explains how in the later twentieth century those people who, like Southey before them, have concerns about the effects of science and technology could want to "stop progress before it goes too far."[46] As we have seen, the idea of progress had begun its career in a Baconian guise, and the Industrial Revolution re-established that concentration on a permanent basis.

In 1931 Charles Beard declared that the world "is largely ruled by ideas, true and false." An idea, he said, "contains within itself a dynamic power to move individuals and nations, to drive them in the direction of effecting the ends and institutions implicit in it." And, he added, "the ideas of every epoch in history are related, usually with one dominant concept setting the key-tone for the others."[47] Not long after Beard wrote these words, the West learned to its horror how much some ideas should be distrusted. Since then historians have been persuaded further that ideas, even whole climates of thought, could have sources of a non-intellectual nature—and even that (to use a Marxian metaphor) the intellectual world could be superstructure resting on a social and economic foundation. They have also become suspicious of monolithic "climates of opinion," and simple conceptions of how a set of ideas hangs together. But none of this education in reality should lessen the natural desire to study ideas and their growth; to recognize that they may sometimes have their own internal pattern of filiation, perhaps connected with factors outside the world of thought but not necessarily determined by them; or to accept the fact that a social and economic foundation might turn out, on excavation, to have a partially intellectual sub-basement.

The idea that Beard had principally in mind was progress. Here is an idea that unquestionably has been a driving force in the world. It

---

Social History of England in the Eighteenth Century (New York, 1979), 66; Perkin, "Social Causes," *Structured Crowd*, 30; Flinn, *Origins of the Industrial Revolution*, 81.

46. See above, chap. 1.

47. Charles Beard, "Introduction" to the American edition of Bury, *Idea of Progress* (New York, 1932), ix–x.

helped to shape the views of prominent intellectuals during the nineteenth century, and therefore modern thought. It influenced significantly the transformation of life that we call the Industrial Revolution, and therefore the emergence of the modern world itself. Most important, however, it was at the very core of British thought during the eighteenth century—so much so that Beard's phrase "dominant concept" is an apt way of describing its position. It was itself given many shapes by the thinkers and writers of the time, and as it became increasingly multifaceted its connections with other aspects of contemporary thought diversified and expanded. Rarely has a single idea played so central a part in an intellectual world. To begin to understand that world requires that we recognize the significance of the idea of progress within it.

Appendix

Any attempt to rectify the weaknesses in existing historical scholarship on the idea of progress must take into consideration recent discussions of the historiography of thought in general. Since the 1960s, many practitioners of this field—which is also sometimes known as intellectual history, the history of ideas, or *Geistesgeschichte*—have reassessed its traditional goals, subject matter, and methods. From among the results of these efforts three strands of significant criticism can be identified.

One critique is "contextualist" in outlook and relates closely in its assumptions to the sociology of knowledge. It claims that too much attention has been paid by historians to the content or substance of ideas and too little to the extra-intellectual context in which they arise, exist, and have effect. This is a charge especially applicable, it is often said, to Arthur O. Lovejoy and, even more, his followers, some of whom have written about the belief in progress. They can rightly be considered a self-proclaimed school of the "history of ideas" that has intentionally treated ideas largely in a vacuum, with little or no reference to the surrounding social environment, in order to reconstruct the "unconscious mental habits" of past ages. But the charge has far less appropriateness with regard to the American founders of "intellectual history" in the mid-twentieth century (including such historians as Crane Brinton, Franklin L. Baumer, and John C. Greene), who have always emphasized the need to understand the social causes and effects of ideas and assumptions. In any case, this criticism seeks to encourage a more *social* history of ideas than has existed before. It demands a recognition of the fact that because talking and thinking are at base two among many social activities, historical texts—in the words of John Dunn—"will only be fully understood if they are seen as complicated instances of these social activities." So the function and dynamics of ideas require exploration at least as much as their content. And their multitudinous reasons for existing must be exposed, reasons flowing not only from intellectual influences but also from stylistic traditions, the unconscious, and socio-economic and political pressures.[1]

1. John Dunn, "The Identity of the History of Ideas," *Philosophy* 43 (April 1968): 88; Peter Gay, "The Social History of Ideas: Ernst Cassirer and After," in Kurt H. Wolff

Another line of criticism is "popular" in perspective. It depicts the materials used by traditional intellectual historians—the works of famous and influential thinkers and writers—as inadequately representative of the thought of the past. It contends that such sources enable the historian to reconstruct only the mental world of an elite, not that of ordinary people. This critique frequently rests on the assumption that at any one time multiple climates of opinion exist, each of which is inherently valuable and corresponds to a particular social or educational stratum. These climates are never completely integrated into a homogeneous whole, and thus the historiographical desiderata become the recovery of the more popular as well as the more elite world-views, and the analysis of their mutual interaction.[2] In principle, these goals closely parallel those of traditional intellectual history, whose theorists have always recognized both the importance of using diverse

---

and Barrington Moore, Jr., eds., *The Critical Spirit: Essays in Honor of Herbert Marcuse* (Boston, 1967), 110–20; idem, *The Enlightenment: An Interpretation*, 2 vols. (New York, 1966–69), 1:427. For other examples of the "contextualist" critique, see Hajo Holborn, "The History of Ideas," *American Historical Review* 73 (Feb. 1968): 692; Felix Gilbert, "Intellectual History: Its Aims and Methods," *Daedalus* 100 (Winter 1971): 93–94; Leonard Krieger, "The Autonomy of Intellectual History," *Journal of the History of Ideas* 34 (Oct.–Dec. 1973): 510–12. Francis Oakley mounts a strong defense of Lovejoy's approach, and in the process offers an insightful discussion of virtually every aspect of recent debates over intellectual history and the history of ideas, in *Omnipotence, Covenant, & Order: An Excursion in the History of Ideas from Abelard to Leibniz* (Ithaca, 1984).

On the concern of traditional intellectual historians with the social context of ideas, see Franklin L. Baumer, "Intellectual History and Its Problems," *Journal of Modern History* 21 (Sept. 1949): 197–201; Crane Brinton, *Ideas and Men: The Story of Western Thought* (Englewood Cliffs, N.J., 1950), 7–8, 15–17; John Higham, "Intellectual History and Its Neighbors," *Journal of the History of Ideas* 15 (June 1954): 341, 347.

2. For the "popular" critique, see Gilbert, "Intellectual History: Its Aims and Methods," 87–88, 91, 94; Robert Darnton, "In Search of the Enlightenment: Recent Attempts to Create a Social History of Ideas," *Journal of Modern History* 43 (March 1971): 122–24, 132; Krieger, "Autonomy of Intellectual History," 509–10. Along with such French scholars as Robert Mandrou and Jean Ehrard, Darnton is one of the chief recent practitioners of a historiography of thought that probes beneath the elites. Although it is distinct from such an approach, his work has clear affinities to the *mentalités* school, which is left out of account here, as is the related "popular culture" approach associated with followers of Clifford Geertz. It is true, in a sense, that both of these movements represent critiques of older approaches to the history of thought. But in their insistence that ideas "must somehow be connected to mundane realities" because "consciousness is not a separate realm but a way of being in the world" (see Bruce Kuklick's contribution to "What Is Intellectual History?," *History Today* 35 [Oct. 1985]: 53:2–3), and in their concentration on rituals and non-written artifacts, they are separated from traditional intellectual history by what seems to me to be an unbridgeable gulf. Social history and intellectual history increasingly go their own ways.

materials and also the simultaneous existence of multiple mental climates.[3] In practice, however, until recently most attention has been paid to the dominant elites and the works of the great thinkers, a fact nowhere more apparent than in the study of the history of the idea of progress.

Proponents of these criticisms by no means advocate abandoning the historical study of ideas. As Peter Gay writes, "surely the pursuit of an idea into its past or its future, the search for roots or fruits, is a historical enterprise as legitimate as it is important."[4] But a third type of criticism, associated especially with Quentin Skinner, is less sanguine and appears on the surface to be devastating to the writing of intellectual history in general, and the history of individual ideas in particular. Skinner agrees that pure "textualism"—that is, concentration on written works without reference to the environment in which they were composed and read—is an insufficient method. It leads, he believes, to certain historiographical mistakes or "mythologies": discovering in a given text something that is not really present, such as a contribution to the history of an idea, a case of intellectual influence of one author on another, or supposed coherence instead of actual inconsistency; and missing the real meaning of a work by conflating its content with its significance. He argues that the use of "contextualism"—that is, reference to religious, political, and economic factors in the environment in which a writer lived—can aid in avoiding these mythologies, but only to some extent. For although the context serves as a tool to clarify the "meaning" of statements in a "text," by itself it does not permit an "understanding" of those statements, which in addition requires a grasp of their "intended illocutionary force" (that is, "*how* what was said was meant").[5]

3. Baumer, "Intellectual History and Its Problems," 192; idem, *Main Currents of Western Thought: Readings in Western European Intellectual History from the Middle Ages to the Present*, 1st ed. (New York, 1952), 5–6; Brinton, *Ideas and Men*, 8–10; Higham, "Intellectual History and Its Neighbors," 340–41; John C. Greene, "Objectives and Methods in Intellectual History," *Mississippi Valley Historical Review* 44 (June 1957): 63.

4. Gay, "Social History of Ideas," 111.

5. Quentin Skinner, "Meaning and Understanding in the History of Ideas," *History and Theory* 8 (1969): 3–53 (and especially 45–48). Along with several other relevant essays, Skinner's many writings on methodology are cited in Lotte Mulligan, Judith Richards, and John Graham, "Intentions and Conventions: A Critique of Quentin Skinner's Method for the Study of the History of Ideas," *Political Studies* 27 (March 1979): 84n. His general approach to the historical study of political ideas is shared by J. G. A. Pocock: see *Politics, Language and Time: Essays on Political Thought and History* (New York, 1971), 3–41; *Virtue, Commerce, and History: Essays on Political Thought and History, Chiefly in the Eighteenth Century* (Cambridge, 1985), 1–34. Elsewhere, Pocock says that he is "not engaged in doing" either intellectual history or the history of ideas, but rather is a historian of what "used to be and sometimes still is called 'the history of political thought,'" which he would prefer to call political "discourse": see his contribution to "What Is Intellectual History?," 52:1–3.

With these considerations in mind, Skinner offers an alternative methodology that centers on the recovery of an author's "intentions": specifically, on what a text was intended to mean and how this meaning was intended to be taken by readers. He seeks to focus interest especially on "the deep truth that concepts must not be viewed simply as propositions with meanings attached to them; they must also be thought of as weapons (Heidegger's suggestion) or as tools (Wittgenstein's term)." The assumption underlying this approach is clearly that all statements in texts are embodiments of particular intentions, on particular occasions, addressed to particular publics. In Skinner's view, the only historiographical method satisfactory for recovering such intentions involves a complex linguistic analysis of the entire range of communications that could have been performed at the moment of a writer's "utterances," plus a determination of the relation of these utterances to the field of relevant contemporary language conventions. In short, "we need to focus not on texts or unit ideas, but rather on the entire social and political vocabularies of given historical periods."[6]

According to Skinner, however, even if this method were employed it would "be a mistake even to try . . . to write" the history of an idea, "tracing the morphology of a given concept over time." Such an endeavor is "necessarily misconceived," and "even if we restrict the study of an 'idea' to a given historical period . . . there is still an underlying conceptual confusion in any attempt to focus on a[n] idea itself as an appropriate unit of historical investigation." Skinner contends that this approach suffers greatly from its natural tendency to hypostatize the idea in question, "whether it is the doctrine of equality, progress, Machiavellism, the social contract, the great chain of being, the separation of powers, and so on." In a passage worth quoting at length, he explains further that as

> the historian duly sets out in quest of the idea he has characterized, he is very readily led to speak as if the fully developed form of the doctrine was always in some sense immanent in history, even if various thinkers failed to "hit upon" it, even if it "dropped from sight" at various times, even if an entire era failed (note the implication that they *tried*) to "rise to a consciousness" of it. Similarly, the story of the development of such a doctrine very readily takes on the kind of language appropriate to the description of a growing organism. The fact that ideas presuppose agents is very readily discounted, as the ideas get up and do battle on their own behalf.

Consequently, Skinner insists that such historical accounts "can never go right," for the "notion that any fixed 'idea' has persisted is spurious." This

---

6. Skinner, "Meaning and Understanding," 48–49; idem, contribution to "What Is Intellectual History?," 51:3.

means, he concludes, that "there *is* no history of the idea to be written, but only a history necessarily focused on the various agents who used the idea, and on their varying situations and intentions in using it." Such an account would not really retain the form of the history of an idea at all. Rather, it could only be a history of all the intention-laden "statements made with the given expression" that constitutes the idea. And this "would of course be an almost absurdly ambitious enterprise. But it would at least be conceptually proper."[7]

The logical inconsistency of this conclusion is patent. If there is no persistent fixed idea, how can "agents" have "used" it? How can they have made statements with the "given expression" that constitutes it? Skinner has brought in by the back door what he sought to throw out by the front. Indeed, to do so is only a natural necessity if he wishes to talk about the history of ideas at all. Except for Platonists, few philosophers or historians would today disagree that ideas do not have a *nature* but only a *history*, and that the "history of ideas is not a chronology of things, but the story of the development of consciousness."[8] Of course ideas are not disembodied entities, floating through the cosmos and occasionally penetrating the minds of individuals who then proceed to make a contribution to their history. Nor are atoms really miniature solar systems; but for conceptual purposes it is often useful to treat them as such. Just so with ideas: they have no life apart from the men and women who think with and about them. Yet to understand this thinking and its history in more than the most fragmentary fashion requires treating ideas *as if* they were things, objects suitable for human use. And such reification need extend no further than the mere act of generalized definition. An idea defined in this general way is analogous to a specified quantity of water. That water will take on the shape of whatever container into which human hands may pour it, though its molecular configuration and volume remain constant. Similarly, an idea—like utopia or the great chain of being or progress—will be molded by human minds and writings into many forms, while never losing its essential characteristics. It is the task of the historian of that idea to search out these forms and to understand them in their unity and diversity, and in their humanness. Such an undertaking may well be ambitious, but it is as conceptually legitimate as pragmatic.

With respect to Skinner's strictures on intentionality, the historian may observe their spirit if not their every letter. Naturally, care must be taken to avoid misunderstanding a book or passage by failing to interpret properly its author's motives for writing. In fact, however, the intentions underlying some works can never be recovered in their entirety. Little or—in the case of

7. Idem, "Meaning and Understanding," 48, 35–36, 10–11, 38–39.
8. Louis O. Mink, "Change and Causality in the History of Ideas," *Eighteenth-Century Studies* 2 (Fall 1968): 13, 25.

an anonymous pamphlet, for example—nothing at all may be known about a writer, leaving his or her aims shrouded in darkness. Furthermore, intentionality in intellectual creation is actually a far more complex subject than suggested by Skinner's comparison of it to that in simple actions. As regards intentions versus performance, it is sometimes true of writers as it is of artists that what a creator ultimately says in his work "can sometimes be quite different from what he wanted to say and thought he succeeded in saying."[9] Then, too, a Hobbes does not sit down to write a *Leviathan* because he has the definite intention of performing a single action to bring about a specific result, and does not shape each of his propositions as Heideggerian "weapons." Such a work and the ideas it contains emerge out of an intricate web of concerns, some of them unconscious and therefore at least partially unrecoverable. But in instances where the intentionality of texts *is* discoverable, the historian of an idea need not feel overwhelmed by the burden of virtually infinite labors that the Skinnerian methodology seems to impose on him. For he can make use of the work of other scholars, particularly those who have studied the aims and language of relevant individual authors or groups of authors in particular periods.[10] Francis Bacon long ago knew what Skinner seems to have lost sight of, that learning is a cooperative, cumulative enterprise.

As for the problem of defining linguistic conventions operating when a given text was composed and read, commentators on Skinner have rightly noted that language changes continually, bringing gradual, subtle transformations to the meaning of terms. Hence, it is never possible to formulate a comprehensive vocabulary for any historical period. In addition, truly creative thinkers (like Bentham, for instance) have frequently fought against contemporary linguistic constraints, enlarging the boundaries of language with neologisms not immediately understood.[11] In spite of these complicat-

9. John Canaday, "Let's Not Try to Explain June Leaf," *New York Times*, Nov. 18, 1973, Sect. 2, 25:5–8. Nonetheless, the concept of the "disappearance of the author" and, indeed, post-structuralist criticism generally seem to me to be of quite limited value in intellectual history, in spite of the claims to the contrary made in recent years by a few historians. See, for example, essays by Dominick La Capra and E. M. Henning in La Capra and Steven L. Kaplan, eds., *Modern European Intellectual History: Reappraisals and New Perspectives* (Ithaca, 1982).

10. Bhikhu Parekh and R. N. Berki, "The History of Political Ideas: A Critique of Q. Skinner's Methodology," *Journal of the History of Ideas* 34 (April–June 1973): 169, 183. Mulligan, Richards, and Graham, "Intentions and Conventions: A Critique of Quentin Skinner's Method," offers an especially insightful review of Skinner's theory and practice regarding intentions.

11. Parekh and Berki, "History of Political Ideas," 167–68. Skinner has replied to various criticisms of his own analysis of the history of ideas, but without blunting their forcefulness: "Some Problems in the Analysis of Political Thought and Action," *Political Theory* 2 (Aug. 1974): 277–301. Pocock offers some interesting observations about innovation in language: *Virtue, Commerce, and History*, 12–17.

ing considerations, it still is useful and necessary for the historian of an idea to avoid anachronistic misreadings of texts by immersing himself in the parlance of the age he examines. Reference to contemporary dictionaries and encyclopedias can also prove helpful in this process. At base, although Skinner seems not to realize it, such philological research constitutes merely one more facet of the effort to establish a social context. Political and economic factors and language *all* shape the environment in which writing and reading take place.

Clearly, to write anything approaching a *complete* history of an idea in any era demands that this environment be taken into account. Only in the light of the social context is it possible to comprehend fully the dynamics of an idea, the human sources of its birth and development and the human consequences of its existence.[12] And yet, as J. G. A. Pocock has persuasively argued, before setting forth on the difficult exercise of establishing the historical relation of ideas to social realities, another type of inquiry can—and should—be undertaken:

> and that is to ascertain, by normal critical interpretation, what the ideas were that were in use at a particular time, what in fact they said and implied, and on what commonly accepted assumptions and methods they were based. To embark on a sociology of ideas without an accurate and extensive knowledge of the ideas' primary meaning and secondary implications is a dangerous venture, even if we believe that only the sociological approach will bring us to their true significance; and assuredly a systematic survey of the ideas used for certain purposes in a certain period can be peculiarly destructive of the clichés of intellectual history. There is a Namierism of the history of ideas as there is of the history of Parliament, and it consists of identifying the concepts, assumptions, and languages actually involved in given periods and areas of human life.[13]

12. I cannot agree with Stefan Collini's broad statement that "in general, the 'social context' of intellectual activity turns out to have a limited explanatory role in practice," although I am quite sympathetic to his further contention that "this is particularly true the more one grapples with the details of any particular episode in the intellectual life of the past": see his contribution to "What Is Intellectual History?," 47:3. It seems to me that social context generally *does* exercise considerable influence in determining the questions that are under examination in a given era, in shaping the broad debates and answers that these questions provoke, and in setting the general direction that thinkers from specific social backgrounds are following. Narrower controversies, subsidiary problems, and twists and turns during a thinker's career are often decided on purely intellectual grounds.

13. J. G. A. Pocock, "Machiavelli, Harrington and English Political Ideologies in the Eighteenth Century," reprinted in *Politics, Language and Time*, 105–06. See also Pocock's *The Ancient Constitution and the Feudal Law: A Study of English Historical Thought in the Seventeenth Century*, 2d ed. (New York, 1967), 130.

This preliminary, more limited sort of enterprise is especially appropriate wherever the historical investigation of certain ideas either has barely begun or, as in the case of the idea of progress in the eighteenth century, has yielded contradictory results.

If the writing of a comprehensive account of the history of an idea would require a thorough study of the social context, it would also call for an analysis of the views held by all groups of people in a society, not just those of an intellectual elite. Such a project, however, is almost doomed to failure for periods before the nineteenth century at earliest, when the limitations of literacy restricted the leaving of *written* records of mental outlook to a small fraction of the total population.[14] Moreover, although the exploration of the mental world of the non-elite is desirable, as it enables us to understand more of the past, surely there can be nothing inherently or even politically illegitimate about concentrating on great thinkers and their readers, opponents, and popularizers.[15] The further a historian can proceed in discovering the extent to which an idea or climate of opinion permeated all levels of society, the better. But to advance only part way is ever the necessary precondition to reaching any final destination.

Thus, the "popular" and "contextualist" critiques rightly set ultimate goals for the history of thought that some of its practitioners have too often forgotten. Yet the historian of special ideas or of climates of opinion may—indeed, often must—begin to fulfill these aims by setting his or her sights somewhat lower. Again, Skinner correctly points out certain methodological pitfalls lying along the path to the ends in question. But the existence of such snares does not compromise the conceptual propriety of the historical study of an idea, nor does avoiding them need to become an impossibly difficult, enervating task in linguistic analysis. To write the history of an idea, even in less than a full-fledged way, *is* a historiographically feasible and legitimate endeavor.

14. This is not, of course, to deny that a *mentalité* can be reconstructed from other than written records, by employing, for example, some of the methods of the anthropologist. But the result would not be in the field of what I consider to be intellectual history.

15. Some intellectual historians are sensitive on this matter, however, as Bruce Kuklick points out: "What Is Intellectual History?," 53:2–3. But see the defense of a concentration on the elite in Pocock, *Virtue, Commerce, and History*, 18.

Bibliographical Essay

The following discussion is meant only to point out the second-ary works that I have found particularly helpful in preparing this book, or that are especially relevant to one or more of the preceding chapters. It is not intended as a comprehensive statement of books and articles cited in foot-notes or consulted during research for this study. Nor does it deal with primary source materials, since the footnotes contain full references to them. I should say, however, that where standard editions of eighteenth-century works exist, I have done my utmost to use them; in other cases I have referred to editions that I believe to be the best and most widely available. This procedure has sometimes led me to cite from more than one collected edition of the works of a given author (such as Samuel Johnson), or from both a collected edition and those individual works never included in it (as with Joseph Priestley).

For works mentioned more than once in this bibliography, the second and later references use only the author's last name and a short title. The *Journal of the History of Ideas* is abbreviated as *JHI, Studies on Voltaire and the Eighteenth Century* as *SVEC*, and *Eighteenth-Century Studies* as *ECS*.

CHAPTER 1: INTRODUCTION

There are several general, philosophically oriented treatments of the idea of progress. Of these, only Charles Van Doren's *The Idea of Progress* (New York, 1967) aims at comprehensiveness, but the chief virtue of this work is to make clear that the idea may take various forms (such as the belief in intellectual progress, progress in the fine arts, economic progress, and so forth). More tendentious but also more useful are Morris Ginsberg, *The Idea of Progress: A Revaluation* (London, 1953), and Joseph Needham, *Integrative Levels: A Revaluation of the Idea of Progress* (Oxford, 1937). Like Van Doren, Arthur O. Lovejoy and George Boas attempt in their *Primitivism and Related Ideas in Antiquity* (Baltimore, 1937) to distinguish among various broad visions of history. Nathan Rotenstreich takes a sometimes helpful look at "The Idea of

Historical Progress and Its Assumptions" in *History and Theory* 10 (1971): 197–221.

On the *history* of the idea, W. Warren Wagar, "Modern Views of the Origins of the Idea of Progress," *JHI* 28 (Jan.–March 1967): 55–70, provides a thoroughly informed introduction to late nineteenth- and twentieth-century approaches to the whole subject. I learned much from Wagar's account. Still the best general history is that of J. B. Bury: *The Idea of Progress: An Inquiry into Its Origin and Growth* (London, 1920), published in an American edition in 1932 with an illuminating introduction by Charles A. Beard. As I have argued in the text, Bury's book suffers from a number of deficiencies. The most serious of these are an excessively narrow definition of the idea, an almost exclusive concentration on renowned thinkers, and a tendency to locate the "real" history of the idea in France. Overall, however, *The Idea of Progress* remains the single most outstanding work on the subject.

For comprehensiveness of scope and judiciousness of interpretation, it is not rivaled by Jules Delvaille, *Essai sur l'histoire de l'idée de progrès jusqu'à la fin du XVIIIᵉ siècle* (Paris, 1910), which nevertheless does examine a wider range of thinkers. Sidney Pollard, *The Idea of Progress: History and Society* (London, 1968), and Robert Nisbet, *History of the Idea of Progress* (New York, 1980), offer little that is not in Bury; the latter is principally based on secondary literature and contains no scholarly apparatus. More useful in much shorter compass are Carl Becker, "Progress," in *Encyclopedia of the Social Sciences*, 15 vols. (New York, 1930–35), 12:495:1–499:2; Georg G. Iggers, "The Idea of Progress: A Critical Reassessment," *American Historical Review* 71 (Oct. 1965): 1–17; and George H. Hildebrand, "Introduction," in Frederick J. Teggart, ed., *The Idea of Progress: A Collection of Readings*, rev. ed. (Berkeley, 1949), 3–30. Another collection of readings with a very good (if brief) introduction is W. Warren Wagar, ed., *The Idea of Progress Since the Renaissance* (New York, 1969). Wagar has also written a stimulating, finely documented study of the fate of the idea since the mid-nineteenth century, which includes two valuable introductory chapters on the idea's definition and origins: *Good Tidings: The Belief in Progress from Darwin to Marcuse* (Bloomington, Ind., 1972). A short but good recent account of the history of the idea since about 1700 is Georg G. Iggers, "The Idea of Progress in Historiography and Social Thought Since the Enlightenment," in Gabriel A. Almond, Marvin Chodorow, and Roy Harvey Pearce, eds., *Progress and Its Discontents* (Berkeley, 1982), 41–66. All the literature on the history of the idea of progress per se ought to be read in conjunction with John Passmore's excellent *The Perfectibility of Man* (New York, 1970), which deals with a somewhat different but related theme.

The importance of the idea in eighteenth-century thought is an unresolved issue, to which this book addresses itself in the context of one country only. For a wider perspective on this issue, see Peter Gay, *The Party of Hu-*

manity: Essays in the French Enlightenment (New York, 1964), 270–73, and idem, *The Enlightenment: An Interpretation*, 2 vols. (New York, 1966–69), 2:98–125, which argue that the men of the Enlightenment were not consistently optimistic about the course of history and rarely constructed any all-encompassing "theory" of progress. Support for this position can be drawn from Peter Burke, "Tradition and Experience: The Idea of Decline from Bruni to Gibbon," in G. W. Bowersock, John Clive, and Stephen R. Graubard, eds., *Edward Gibbon and the Decline and Fall of the Roman Empire* (Cambridge, Mass., 1977), 97–119 (a book which also appeared as *Daedalus* 105 [Summer 1976]); H. R. Trevor-Roper, "The Idea of the Decline and Fall of the Roman Empire," in W. H. Barber et al., *The Age of Enlightenment: Studies Presented to Theodore Besterman* (Edinburgh, 1967), 413–30; and Stow Persons, "The Cyclical Theory of History in Eighteenth Century America," *American Quarterly* 6 (Summer 1954): 147–63. Further confirmation appears in work done on the French philosophes: Lester Gilbert Krakeur [Crocker], "Diderot and the Idea of Progress," *Romanic Review* 29 (April 1938): 151–59; Gilbert Chinard, "Montesquieu's Historical Pessimism," in *Studies in the History of Culture: The Disciplines of the Humanities* (Menasha, Wis., 1942), 161–72; and especially Henry Vyverberg, *Historical Pessimism in the French Enlightenment* (Cambridge, Mass., 1958), an excellent and wide-ranging book.

That the idea of progress was, nevertheless, quite popular in eighteenth-century Europe, or at least more popular then than ever before, is the view presented in a considerable number of books. R. V. Sampson's *Progress in the Age of Reason: The Seventeenth Century to the Present Day* (Cambridge, Mass., 1956), stands pre-eminent among these. On eighteenth-century France in particular, there is the late Charles Frankel's *The Faith of Reason: The Idea of Progress in the French Enlightenment* (New York, 1948), which I consider to be the most outstanding work ever written on any portion of the history of the idea. The optimistic outlook of the Encyclopedists has also been studied: Nelly Noémie Schargo, *History in the Encyclopédie* (New York, 1947), 183–95. For individual philosophes who believed in progress, see especially the first two chapters of Frank E. Manuel's superb *The Prophets of Paris: Turgot, Condorcet, Saint-Simon, Fourier, and Comte* (Cambridge, Mass., 1962); and F. C. Green, *Rousseau and the Idea of Progress* (Oxford, 1950). Bruce Mazlish takes an interesting and provocative approach to Voltaire and Condorcet as well as to Vico, in his *The Riddle of History: The Great Speculators from Vico to Freud* (New York, 1966). Most but not all of the discussion of the eighteenth century is on France in Nannerl O. Keohane's "The Enlightenment Idea of Progress Revisited," in *Progress and Its Discontents*, 21–40.

By comparison with France, eighteenth-century Britain has received very little attention from students of the history of the idea. R. S. Crane's groundbreaking article "Anglican Apologetics and the Idea of Progress,

1699–1745," first published in 1934 and now available in his *The Idea of the Humanities and Other Essays Critical and Historical*, 2 vols. (Chicago, 1967), 1:214–87, was a revelation to me. It illustrates convincingly how the idea could have deep roots in the Christian tradition, and it first suggested to me that the belief in progress might well have been widespread in Georgian Britain, even though Crane himself concentrates on only a small number of Anglican clergymen. Lois Whitney, in *Primitivism and the Idea of Progress in English Popular Literature of the Eighteenth Century* (Baltimore, 1934), is more concerned with the first item in her title than with the second. A member of the Lovejoy school of the history of ideas at Johns Hopkins, she does not locate her subject at all in the social context. Several of her major generalizations cannot be supported by the evidence she presents, particularly the claim that the notion of continual degeneration remained popular after 1700. But she does probe beneath the level of the intellectual elite, and I have found her source references useful in doing my own research. To the extent that Ernest Lee Tuveson deals with the eighteenth century, rather than with the sixteenth and seventeenth, in *Millennium and Utopia: A Study in the Background of the Idea of Progress* (1949), Harper Torchbook ed. (New York, 1964), he reconfirms Crane's view that the idea of progress owed much to Christian historical conceptions at the time. As with Crane, however, he limits himself to an examination of a small number of eighteenth-century men. My disagreement with his interpretation of the secularization of eschatology is elaborated in chapter 3, above. His book is an excellent one, however, which has proved deservedly influential and from which I have learned a great deal.

Of course, the idea of progress was not the only pattern of recollection and foresight in Britain. On alternatives to it, see (besides Whitney's *Primitivism*) Simeon M. Wade, Jr., "The Idea of Luxury in Eighteenth-Century England," Ph.D. diss. (Harvard Univ., May 1968); and James William Johnson, "Swift's Historical Outlook," *Journal of British Studies* 4, no. 2 (May 1965): 52–77. As I have contended in the text, however, historical pessimism became increasingly less popular during the eighteenth century and was often limited by an accompanying optimism.

My general view of eighteenth-century European thought and of the Enlightenment owes a great deal to Gay, *The Enlightenment*, which has become a true classic. Its stature has made it a lightning rod for challenge— particularly challenge to its French emphasis, as historians seek to understand the diverse forms that the Enlightenment took in Europe and America. A preliminary report in this area is represented by the articles on individual countries in Roy Porter and Mikuláš Teich, eds., *The Enlightenment in National Context* (Cambridge, 1981). Much less comprehensive than Gay's book but still highly informative (especially regarding contemporary conceptions of time) is Norman Hampson, *The Enlightenment* (Baltimore, 1968).

Franklin L. Baumer's *Modern European Thought: Continuity and Change in Ideas, 1600–1950* (New York, 1977) not only gives an illuminating depiction of the eighteenth-century mind but also relates the world-view of that period to those that came before and after. To this group of basic works I would add Robert R. Palmer's *Catholics and Unbelievers in Eighteenth Century France* (Princeton, 1947), a superb reminder that the age of the Enlightenment was more than the philosophes alone, and that we can often best understand an intellectual movement by examining the ideas and polemics of its enemies.

For eighteenth-century philosophy, I have constantly referred to John Herman Randall, Jr., *The Career of Philosophy*, 2 vols. (New York, 1962–65); Frederick Copleston, *A History of Philosophy*, new rev. ed., 9 vols. to date (Westminster, Md., 1963–), vols. 5 and 6; and Ernst Cassirer, *The Philosophy of the Enlightenment*, trans. Fritz C. A. Koelln and James P. Pettegrove (Princeton, 1951), a splendid work of many merits. For religious ideas, I have relied heavily on Gerald R. Cragg, *The Church and the Age of Reason, 1648–1789*, rev. ed. (Harmondsworth, Eng., 1970); Frank E. Manuel, *The Eighteenth Century Confronts the Gods* (Cambridge, Mass., 1959); and Franklin L. Baumer, *Religion and the Rise of Scepticism* (New York, 1960). On science there is now a worthy introduction: Thomas L. Hankins, *Science and the Enlightenment* (Cambridge, 1985). Charles Coulston Gillispie's *The Edge of Objectivity: An Essay in the History of Scientific Ideas* (Princeton, 1960) remains essential.

Indirectly, this book has been influenced by several general accounts of the eighteenth-century philosophy of history. In addition to works by Gay and Mazlish already mentioned, these include R. N. Stromberg, "History in the Eighteenth Century," *JHI* 12 (April 1951): 295–304; Hugh Trevor-Roper, "The Historical Philosophy of the Enlightenment," *SVEC* 27 (1963): 1667–87; and Friedrich Meinecke, *Historism: The Rise of a New Historical Outlook*, trans. J. E. Anderson (London, 1972). Each of the three suggests that the idea of progress was a central part of contemporary historical conceptions.

With regard to British intellectual history, the primary work of reference for the period remains Sir Leslie Stephen's *History of English Thought in the Eighteenth Century* (3d ed., 1902), repr. ed., 2 vols. (New York, 1962), which can profitably be read in tandem with his *English Literature and Society in the Eighteenth Century* (London, 1904). Both books are highly opinionated, and the former is colored by its author's agnosticism. Though less comprehensive than Stephen, two more recent works offer superior interpretive introductions to the subject: Basil Willey, *The Eighteenth Century Background: Studies on the Idea of Nature in the Thought of the Period* (London, 1940); and Gerald R. Cragg, *Reason and Authority in the Eighteenth Century* (Cambridge, 1964). I have used each with profit. A. R. Humphreys, *The Augustan World: Society, Thought, and Letters in Eighteenth-Century England* (New York, 1963), pursues intellectual, cultural, and social history in continuously interesting fashion; it has been too much neglected. Also largely forgotten is Bernard M. Schilling, *Conservative England and the Case against Voltaire* (New York, 1950), the first half of which contains a wealth of material on many subjects not suggested by its title. More recent accounts of the situation of eighteenth-century British thought include John Redwood, *Reason, Ridicule and Religion: The Age of Enlightenment in England, 1660–1750* (Cambridge, Mass., 1976), which is primarily concerned with theology and natural philosophy and offers a rather curious chronological definition for the Enlightenment in England; Margaret C. Jacob, *The Newtonians and the English Revolution, 1689–1720* (Ithaca, 1976), which emphasizes the role of political and social issues in the emergence of Newtonianism; and Roy Porter, "The Enlightenment in England," in *The Enlightenment in National Context*, 1–18, an interesting but not entirely convincing beginning on a subject that demands attention. James Sambrook, *The Eighteenth Century: The Intellectual and Cultural Context of English Literature, 1700–1789* (London, 1986), is a very useful survey from the literary point of view.

One important but under-studied aspect of British thought and culture is authorship, publishing, and readership. Older works that have not yet been altogether superseded include R. W. Chapman, "Authors and Booksellers," in A. S. Turberville, ed., *Johnson's England: An Account of the Life & Manners of His Age*, 2 vols. (Oxford, 1933), 2:310–30; and A. S. Collins, *Authorship in the Days of Johnson: Being a Study of the Relation between Author, Patron, Publisher and Public, 1726–1780* (London, 1927), and its companion volume *The Profession of Letters: A Study of the Relation of Author to Patron, Publisher and Public, 1780–1832* (London, 1928). More recent are J. W. Saunders, *The Profession of English Letters* (London, 1964), and the relevant sections of Marjorie Plant, *The English Book Trade: An Economic History of the Making and Sale of Books*, 2d ed. (London, 1965). All of these matters have lately begun to receive more study, and deservedly so. Four recent publications are especially noteworthy: Roy McKeen Wiles, "The Relish for Reading in Provincial England Two Centuries Ago," in Paul J. Korshin, ed., *The Widening Circle: Essays on the Circulation of Literature in Eighteenth-Century Europe* ([Philadelphia], 1976); Terry Belanger, "Publishers and Writers in Eighteenth-Century England," in Isabel Rivers, ed., *Books and their Readers in Eighteenth-Century England* (New York, 1982), 5–25; Graham Pollard, "The English Market for Printed Books," *Publishing History* 4 (1978): 7–48; and Alvin Kernan, *Printing Technology, Letters & Samuel Johnson* (Princeton, 1987), a wide-ranging account.

On British political and social thought, one book stands out, Caroline Robbins's *The Eighteenth-Century Commonwealthman: Studies in the Transmission, Development and Circumstance of English Liberal Thought from the Restoration of Charles II until the War with the Thirteen Colonies*, Atheneum ed. (New York, 1968). Its full references have given me a number of valuable leads. It can be supplemented with J. G. A. Pocock, "Machiavelli, Harrington and English Political Ideologies in the Eighteenth Century" and "Civic Humanism and its Role in Anglo-American Thought," reprinted in *Politics, Language and Time: Essays on Political Thought and History* (New York, 1971), which set the stage for his ongoing work on the "civic humanist paradigm" in English political "discourse." This line of scholarship is well represented by the interesting if sometimes arcanely written essays brought together in his *Virtue, Commerce, and History: Essays on Political Thought and History, Chiefly in the Eighteenth Century* (Cambridge, 1985), and the last major section of *The Machiavellian Moment: Florentine Political Thought and the Atlantic Republican Tradition* (Princeton, 1975). The latter book overreaches itself on the subject of the Scots, but it, too, is already a classic and has stimulated a number of useful studies on Scottish thought, noted below. Along with John Dunn (especially in his "The Politics of Locke in England and America in the Eighteenth Century," in John W. Yolton, ed., *John Locke: Problems and Perspectives* [Cambridge, 1969], 45–80), Pocock has sought to minimize the influence of Locke on eighteenth-century political thought. A strong and effective reply has been mounted by Isaac Kramnick, "Republican Revisionism Revisited," *American Historical Review* 87 (June 1982): 629–64, which properly distinguishes between the era of Bolingbroke and the later part of the century. Meanwhile, H. T. Dickinson offers a useful introduction to the whole field of political thought in his *Liberty and Property: Political Ideology in Eighteenth-Century Britain* (London, 1977), which seeks to link political ideas and political action and is especially concerned with the role and influence of Locke's ideas. In spite of its density, Elie Halévy's *The Growth of Philosophic Radicalism*, trans. Mary Morris (Boston, 1955), has much to recommend it, especially its opening capsule summary of main currents of thought between Locke and Bentham. On the latter, Mary P. Mack, *Jeremy Bentham: An Odyssey of Ideas, 1748–1792* (London, 1962), has shaped my interpretation of that late English philosophe as a point of transmission to the nineteenth century.

Roland M. Stromberg, *Religious Liberalism in Eighteenth-Century England* (Oxford, 1954), provides a path through the thicket of Georgian religious opinions, including deism, not least by helping to distinguish the major theological positions from each other. Cragg's *Reason and Authority* and the later portions of Redwood's *Reason, Ridicule and Religion* are also valuable in this area. There is also some interesting material in Alan D. Gilbert, *The Making of Post-Christian Britain: A History of the Secularization of Modern Society* (London, 1980). As for Methodism, the book by Bernard Semmel, *The Methodist Revolution* (New York, 1973), is an excellent introduction to the ideas of John Wesley and his followers. Gordon Rupp's *Religion and England, 1688–1791* (Oxford, 1986) appeared too late for use in this book.

From among the multitude of good works on literary history, I mention only a few that have been of special value to me: Bonamy Dobrée, *English Literature in the Early Eighteenth Century, 1700–1740* (Oxford, 1959), useful to me not only as a reference tool but also as a source of my belief that the "Augustan Age" had ended by the 1730s; its worthy successor in the Oxford History of English Literature series, John Butt, *The Mid-Eighteenth Century*, ed. and completed Geoffrey Carnall (Oxford, 1979); Ian Watt, *The Rise of the Novel: Studies in Defoe, Richardson and Fielding* (Berkeley, 1960), and Pat Rogers, *The Augustan Vision* (London, 1974), both of which are studies in cultural and social as much as literary history; James William Johnson, *The Formation of English Neo-Classical Thought* (Princeton, 1967), valuable notwithstanding its over-insistence on the centrality of classical elements in eighteenth-century thought (culminating in Gibbon); the subtle, penetrating, brilliant study by Paul Fussell, *The Rhetorical World of Augustan Humanism: Ethics and Imagery from Swift to Burke* (Oxford, 1965); and Walter Jackson Bate, *From Classic to Romantic: Premises of Taste in Eighteenth-Century England* (Cambridge, Mass., 1946), especially good on the philosophical world of literature. This is also the place to recognize Bate's magnificent biography, *Samuel Johnson* (New York, 1975), which I have consulted frequently.

As for historiography, the shift away from antiquarianism and toward more modern historical pursuits is reflected in David C. Douglas, *English Scholars, 1660–1730*, 2d ed., rev. (London, 1951); and Thomas Preston Peardon, *The Transition in English Historical Writing, 1760–1830* (New York, 1933). I would argue that this change in interest derived, in part, from the opening of new historical vistas associated with the belief in progress. This point is also made, briefly, in Dorothy A. Koch, "English Theories Concerning the Nature and Uses of History," Ph.D. diss. (Yale Univ., May 1946), xxxiii. Of interest for the sake of contrast is Herbert Davis, "The Augustan Conception of History," in J. A. Mazzeo, ed., *Reason and the Imagination: Studies in the History of Ideas, 1600–1800* (New York, 1962), 213–29.

On Scottish thought, the relevant chapters of Henry Thomas Buckle's *History of Civilization in England* (1857–61) are still a good place to start; they have been conveniently reprinted, with a good introduction, as *On Scotland and the Scotch Intellect*, ed. H. J. Hanham (Chicago, 1970). My own introduction to Scottish thought was considerably influenced by two still vital articles, John Clive's and Bernard Bailyn's "England's Cultural Provinces: Scotland and America," *William & Mary Quarterly*, 3d ser., 11 (April 1954): 201–13, and Hugh Trevor-Roper's "The Scottish Enlightenment," *SVEC* 58 (1967): 1635–58; and by Gladys Bryson, *Man and Society: The Scottish Inquiry of the Eighteenth Century* (Princeton, 1945). Trevor-Roper's account does much in brief compass, and it provoked the Scots among the audience that first heard it as a paper in Edinburgh; to some extent that response has continued, in scholarly form. Bryson's account is old-fashioned in the sense that it takes almost no account of the social context, but it nevertheless remains the best book on the Scots' *ideas*.

Since about 1970, however, a great deal of innovative work has been done on Scottish thought in the age of the Enlightenment, and we now know much more about the context as well as the origins and development of the Scottish Enlightenment. A sound introduction, innovative but for its chapter on Scottish social thought, is Anand C. Chitnis, *The Scottish Enlightenment: A Social History* (London, 1976). Jane Rendall, *The Origins of the Scottish Enlightenment* (London, 1978) is an excellent anthology, with much informative and sensible interpretive material; it has superseded Louis Schneider, ed., *The Scottish Moralists on Human Nature and Society* (Chicago, 1967). The insightful work of Nicholas Phillipson, which is not yet brought together in book-length form, is accessible through his "The Scottish Enlightenment," in *The Enlightenment in National Context*, 19–40; "Towards a Definition of the Scottish Enlightenment," in Paul Fritz and David Williams, eds., *City & Society in the 18th Century* (Toronto, 1973), 125–47; and especially "Culture and Society in the 18th Century Province: The Case of Edinburgh and the Scottish Enlightenment," in Lawrence Stone, ed., *The University in Society*, 2 vols. (Princeton, 1974), 2:407–48. See also the book that Phillipson co-edited with Rosalind Mitchison, *Scotland in the Age of Improvement: Essays in Scottish History in the Eighteenth Century* (Edinburgh, 1970), which contains a number of first-rate essays on intellectual, social, and political history. Phillipson is one of the contributors to Istvan Hont and Michael Ignatieff, eds., *Wealth and Virtue: The Shaping of Political Economy in the Scottish Enlightenment* (Cambridge, 1983), much of which circles around the "civic humanist" and "civil jurisprudential" paradigms described in Pocock's contribution. These approaches are analyzed critically in Anand C. Chitnis's forceful "Agricultural Improvement, Political Management and Civic Virtue in Enlightened Scotland: An Historiographical Critique," *SVEC* 245 (1986): 475–88. A somewhat different set of approaches is contained in R. H. Campbell and Andrew S. Skinner, eds., *The Origins and Nature of the Scottish Enlightenment* (Edinburgh, 1982); the authors of its essays cover education, medicine, science, legal studies, and—*pace* Trevor-Roper—the late seventeenth-century emergence of a new Scotland. This volume and *Wealth and Virtue* together define the current state and direction of scholarship, with one quite notable exception: Richard Sher's seminal *Church and University in the Scottish Enlightenment: The Moderate Literati of Edinburgh* (Princeton, 1985). Sher offers a fascinating perspective on the intellectual world of eighteenth-century Edinburgh, including two of its key institutions. Of course, the book is not a history of the Scottish Enlightenment per se, inasmuch as it concentrates on the Edinburgh Moderates (and really on their institutional and political activities more than their ideas) and says relatively little about the legal profession or Edinburgh science. But its point of view is a welcome one, and the book will prove to be a challenge to the next generation of Scottish Enlightenment scholarship.

The interpretation of British history—considered as a whole—that I offer in chapter 1 is drawn in part from general works. Of these, I have particularly benefited from J. H. Plumb's older but still useful *England in the Eighteenth Century* (Harmondsworth, Eng., 1963); John B. Owen's fine introduction to the entire period, *The Eighteenth Century, 1714–1815* (New York, 1976); Asa Briggs, *The Age of Improvement, 1783–1867*, corr. ed. (London, 1960), packed with helpful detail; and Daniel A. Baugh, ed., *Aristocratic Government and Society in Eighteenth-Century England* (New York, 1975), a collection of important articles. English historians await an up-to-date synthesis on the eighteenth-century in the forthcoming New Oxford History of England series.

Of more specialized books, Plumb's *The Growth of Political Stability in England, 1675–1725* (Harmondsworth, Eng., 1969), demonstrates that relative political quiescence did not arrive until the high eighteenth century. Isaac Kramnick shows how Walpole and his supporters worked to establish this stability in the face of considerable opposition: *Bolingbroke and His Circle: The Politics of Nostalgia in the Age of Walpole* (Cambridge, Mass., 1968). Even with the many challenges to them, the writings of the Namier school—of which Sir Lewis's *The Structure of Politics at the Accession of George III*, 2d ed. (London, 1968), was the prototype—rightly point to the track on which stability ran between Walpole and the third Hanoverian king. That the desire for political reform during the high eighteenth century was always present, rarely controllable, and never truly effective is shown by John Cannon, *Parliamentary Reform, 1640–1832* (Cambridge, 1973). That it eventually intensified, but only in the second half of the period, and without wrecking the establishment, can be seen from George Rudé, *Wilkes and Liberty: A Social Study of 1763 to 1774* (Oxford, 1962); and John Brewer, *Party Ideology and Popular Politics at the Accession of George III* (Cambridge, 1976), which led me to several useful sources. Among recent works on parties, see Linda Colley's *In Defiance of Oligarchy: The Tory Party 1714–60* (Cambridge, 1982), which contains a chapter on "The Content of Toryism," and Reed Browning's *Political and Constitutional Ideas of the Court Whigs* (Baton Rouge, 1982), with its contrasting chapter entitled "The Structure of Court Whig Thought." Brewer, Colley, and Browning all help to tie ideas and politics together.

Scottish politics are the subject of several good recent works. These include John M. Simpson, "Who Steered the Gravy Train, 1707–66?," in Phillipson and Mitchison, *Scotland in the Age of Improvement*, 47–72; Alexander Murdoch, *"The People Above": Politics and Administration in Mid-*

Eighteenth-Century Scotland (Edinburgh, 1980); and John Stuart Shaw, *The Management of Scottish Society, 1707–1764: Power, Nobles, Lawyers, Edinburgh Agents and English Influences* (Edinburgh, 1983).

As for social history, Scotland has for some time been well served by one book in particular: T. C. Smout's superb *A History of the Scottish People, 1560–1830* (London, 1969), stylishly written and impeccably researched. To this has now been added the good brief introduction by Bruce Lenman, *Integration, Enlightenment, and Industrialization: Scotland 1746–1832* (Toronto, 1981). Until recently there was nothing comparable for England in the period 1730–89, although one could turn to a number of more narrowly or differently focused accounts that were produced primarily in the 1960s and 1970s. Impressionistic sketches of eighteenth-century English social history by notable scholars are contained in James L. Clifford, ed., *Man versus Society in Eighteenth-Century Britain: Six Points of View* (New York, 1972). Harold Perkin presents a fairly compelling analysis of the "old society" in *The Origins of Modern English Society, 1780–1880* (London, 1969), chap. 2, from which it is possible to discern the "dynamic equilibrium" mentioned in my text. For the aristocracy, this view of British social life receives support from H. J. Habakkuk, "England," in Albert Goodwin, ed., *The European Nobility in the Eighteenth Century: Studies of the Nobilities of the Major European States in the Pre-Reform Era* (New York, 1963), 1–21; and from G. E. Mingay, *English Landed Society in the Eighteenth Century* (London, 1963). For the lower classes, it is confirmed in M. Dorothy George, *England in Transition: Life and Work in the Eighteenth Century* (Harmondsworth, Eng., 1953), and in G. D. H. Cole and Raymond Postgate, *The British People, 1746–1946* (London, 1961). These two works show evidence of unrest, discontent, and mobility, but not of class consciousness, high levels of social antagonism, and rapid changes in the social status of individuals. But from the 1780s on, the "old society" was being transformed: see the famous, much-debated book by E. P. Thompson, *The Making of the English Working Class* (New York, 1963).

Suddenly, however, the social history of the eighteenth century has begun to attract more attention. The most broadly ranging recent survey is Roy Porter, *English Society in the Eighteenth Century* (Harmondsworth, Eng., 1982), written with Porter's usual energetic style. From one side of the political spectrum comes Maxine Berg's *The Age of Manufactures: Industry, Innovation and Work in Britain, 1700–1820* (London, 1985). From the other come a pair of extraordinary books by J. C. D. Clark, who is not at all reluctant to confront what in the past two decades has become historiographical orthodoxy about the seventeenth, eighteenth, and early nineteenth centuries: *English Society, 1688–1832: Ideology, Social Structure and Political Practice during the Ancien Regime* (Cambridge, 1985), and *Revolution and Rebellion:*

State and Society in England in the Seventeenth and Eighteenth Centuries (Cambridge, 1986). Clark's volumes are at least as much political history as social, and they offer a very full review of relatively recent work in both areas.

Works on economic history are discussed below, in the context of chapter 8.

CHAPTER 2: ANCIENTS AND MODERNS, ARTS AND SCIENCES

The origins of the belief in the progress of the arts and sciences has been traced in Edgar Zilsel, "The Genesis of the Concept of Scientific Progress," *JHI* 6 (July 1945): 325–49; A. C. Keller, "Zilsel, the Artisans, and the Idea of Progress in the Renaissance," *JHI* 11 (April 1950): 235–40; and now A. C. Crombie, "Some Attitudes to Scientific Progress: Ancient, Medieval and Early Modern," *History of Science* 13 (1975): 213–30. Hans Baron has done the same for the Battle of Ancients and Moderns: "The *Querelle* of the Ancients and the Moderns as a Problem for Renaissance Scholarship," *JHI* 20 (Jan. 1959): 3–22. The whole history of this battle (or war, as I prefer to call it) is surveyed in A. Owen Aldridge, "Ancients and Moderns in the Eighteenth Century," in *Dictionary of the History of Ideas: Studies of Selected Pivotal Ideas*, 4 vols. (New York 1968–73), 1:76:1–87:2; and Gilbert Highet, *The Classical Tradition: Greek and Roman Influences on Western Thought* (Oxford, 1949), 261–88. Its best known metaphor has happily received the attention of Robert K. Merton, whose *On the Shoulders of Giants: A Shandean Postscript* (New York, 1965) is a great pleasure to read. My treatment of the seventeenth-century stages of the war depends heavily on Hippolyte Rigault, *Histoire de la querelle des anciens et des modernes* (1856), in *Oeuvres complètes de H. Rigault*, 4 vols. (Paris, 1859), vol. 1; and on Baumer, *Modern European Thought*, 117–37. For France in particular, there is Hubert Gillot, *La Querelle des anciens et des modernes en France* (Paris, 1914); and Paul H. Meyer, "Recent German Studies of the Quarrel between the Ancients and the Moderns in France," *ECS* 18 (Spring 1985): 383–90. For seventeenth-century England, Richard Foster Jones, *Ancients and Moderns: A Study of the Rise of the Scientific Movement in Seventeenth-Century England*, 2d ed. (Berkeley, 1965), is unmatched; I have been especially influenced by Jones's interpretation of Bacon and his delineation of the war's stages. Several essays by him on related topics appear in *The Seventeenth Century: Studies in the History of English Thought and Literature from Bacon to Pope* (Stanford, 1951). On the very end of the century, there are two articles of interest by Joseph M. Levine: "Ancients, Moderns, and History: The Continuity of English Historical Writing in the Later Seventeenth-Century," in Paul J. Korshin, ed., *Studies in Change and Revolution: Aspects of English Intellectual History, 1640–1800* (Menston, Yorkshire, 1972), 43–75; and "Ancients and Moderns Reconsidered," *ECS* 15 (Fall 1981): 72–89.

On the eighteenth-century phase of the war, I have mostly had to find my own way. Three older articles by Herbert Weisinger were of considerable help in identifying promising sources: "The Study of the Revival of Learning in England from Bacon to Hallam," *Philological Quarterly* 25 (July 1946): 221–47; "The Idea of the Renaissance and the Rise of Science," *Lychnos* [Annual of the Swedish History of Science Society] (1946–47), 11–35; and "English Treatment of the Relationship between the Rise of Science and the Renaissance, 1740–1840," *Annals of Science* 7 (Sept. 28, 1951): 248–74. Richard D. Altick's fascinating *The Shows of London* (Cambridge, Mass., 1978) helps to make contemporary attitudes toward technology comprehensible, and I reached several useful sources through it. Further clues came from Herbert M. Schueller, "The Quarrel of the Ancients and the Moderns," *Music and Letters* 41 (Oct. 1960): 313–30, which concerns eighteenth-century musicology; from René Wellek's *The Rise of English Literary History* (Chapel Hill, N.C., 1941) and his magisterial *A History of Modern Criticism*, 6 vols. to date (New Haven, 1955–), vol. 1; and from Francis D. Klingender, *Art and the Industrial Revolution*, ed. and rev. Arthur Elton (New York, 1968). John D. Scheffer, "The Decline in Literature and the Fine Arts in Eighteenth-Century England," *Modern Philology* 34 (Nov. 1936): 155–78, was useful in defining issues, even though its conclusions seem incorrect to me.

On the place of classical studies and classical scholarship in the eighteenth century, see especially Rudolf Pfeiffer, *History of Classical Scholarship from 1300 to 1850* (Oxford, 1976), 143–63; R. M. Ogilvie, *Latin and Greek: A History of the Influence of the Classics on English Life from 1600 to 1918* (London, 1964), esp. 34–73; and M. L. Clarke, *Classical Education in Britain 1500–1900* (Cambridge, 1959), 46–73. All of these works suggest in one way or another that the position of the ancient Greek and Latin classics was becoming less important during the eighteenth century.

There are now two fine books on eighteenth-century scientific societies: Roger Hahn, *The Anatomy of a Scientific Institution: The Paris Academy of Sciences, 1666–1803* (Berkeley, 1971), a prototype for in-depth studies; and, more broadly and less deeply, James E. McClellan III, *Science Reorganized: Scientific Societies in the Eighteenth Century* (New York, 1985). But much work needs to be done on contemporary "improving" societies. For Europe as a whole a good start was made with Hahn's "The Application of Science to Society: The Societies of Arts," *SVEC* 25 (1963): 829–36, but this has not been followed up. On English developments, in particular, valuable work has been done by Robert E. Schofield, especially his *The Lunar Society of Birmingham: A Social History of Provincial Science and Industry in Eighteenth-Century England* (Oxford, 1963), but also "The Society of Arts and the Lunar Society of Birmingham," *Journal of the Royal Society of Arts* 107, nos. 5035 (June 1959) and 5037 (August 1959): 512–14, 668–71. We now know much about the London Society of Arts, thanks to D. G. C. Allan: see his *William Shipley: Founder of the Royal Society of Arts* (1968; 2d. ed., London, 1979), which reprints some important documents; and "The Society of Arts and Government, 1754–1800: Public Encouragement of Arts, Manufactures, and Commerce in Eighteenth-Century England," *ECS* 7 (Summer 1974): 434–52. There is also John L. Abbott, "Dr. Johnson and the Society (ii)," *Journal of the Royal Society of Arts* 115, no. 5130 (May 1967): 486–91, which helps us to rethink Johnson's views on science and technology, as, more generally, does Richard B. Schwartz, *Samuel Johnson and the New Science* (Madison, Wis., 1971).

On Scotland, the standard work is Davis D. McElroy, *Scotland's Age of Improvement: A Survey of Eighteenth-Century Literary Clubs and Societies* ([Pullman, Wash.], 1969). It can now be supplemented with three important articles by Roger Emerson: "The Philosophical Society of Edinburgh, 1737–1747," and "The Philosophical Society of Edinburgh, 1768–1783," *British Journal for the History of Science* 12 (1979): 154–91, and 18 (1985): 255–303; and "The Social Composition of Enlightened Scotland: The Select Society of Edinburgh, 1754–1764," *SVEC* 114 (1973): 291–329.

Finally, I note two fairly recent studies that came to my attention at the end of my work on this chapter: I. F. Clarke, *The Pattern of Expectation, 1644–2001* (New York, 1979), which deals with ideas of the future, including science fiction, and led me to two useful eighteenth-century sources; and Murray Krieger's general assessment of "The Arts and the Idea of Progress," in *Progress and Its Discontents,* 449–69.

CHAPTER THREE: THE CHRISTIAN VISION OF HISTORY

The general problem of the connection between Christianity and the idea of progress is considered in several books from which I have learned much. These include John Baillie, *The Belief in Progress* (New York, 1951); Rudolf Bultmann, *History and Eschatology: The Presence of Eternity* (New York, 1957); Herbert Butterfield, *Christianity and History* (New York, 1950); Christopher Dawson, *Progress and Religion: An Historical Enquiry* (New York, 1929); and Karl Löwith, *Meaning in History* (Chicago, 1949). Becker, "Progress," summarizes much of what they have to say and, by example, illustrates their weaknesses. Theodore Olson, *Millennialism, Utopianism, and Progress* (Toronto, 1982), promises much but remains in familiar territory, with familiar sources and conclusions.

On doctrines of progress in religion, the classical and medieval groundwork is laid out in Crane, "Anglican Apologetics," and in a justly famous essay by Theodor E. Mommsen, "St. Augustine and the Christian Idea of Progress: The Background of the City of God," *JHI* 12 (June 1951): 346–74. Gerhart B. Ladner, *The Idea of Reform: Its Impact on Christian Thought and Action in the Age of the Fathers,* enl. ed. (New York, 1967), contains some material on the conception of doctrinal development. More is provided, for a later period, by Owen Chadwick, *From Bossuet to Newman: The Idea of Doctrinal Development* (Cambridge, 1957), which, however, is not very helpful on eighteenth-century Britain. My discussion of the appeal of doctrines of progress in religion depends, in part, on interpretations of the social history of the contemporary church in several works: Stromberg, *Religious Liberalism*; G. R. Cragg, "The Churchman," in Clifford, ed., *Man versus Society*, 54–69; and the still-serviceable but in many ways out-of-date book by John H. Overton and Frederic Relton, *The English Church from the Accession of George I to the End of the Eighteenth Century (1714–1800)* (London, 1906). Michael R. Watts's *The Dissenters: From the Reformation to the French Revolution* (Oxford, 1978) is the first major treatment of its subject in many years; it is packed with useful information. Although more recent, Andrew L. Drummond and James Bullock, *The Scottish Church, 1688–1843: The Age of the Moderates* (Edinburgh, 1973) is not much more useful than Overton and Relton is for England. Sher's *Church and University* has much more to offer in understanding the Church of Scotland and its issues, as has Ian D. L. Clark, "From Protest to Reaction: The Moderate Regime in the Church of Scotland, 1752–1805," in Phillipson and Mitchison, *Scotland in the Age of Improvement*, 200–24. William Ferguson, *Scotland 1689 to the Present* (New York, 1968), has a sensible and informative chapter on "Religious Life, 1689–1761."

Leroy Edwin Froom offers a general history of eschatology in his *The Prophetic Faith of Our Fathers: The Historical Development of Prophetic Interpretation*, 4 vols. (Washington, D.C., 1946–54). Though marred by a blatant fundamentalist premillennialism, this massive work rests on a veritable mountain of sources, which I have found usable to good advantage. Less helpful but more objective is Ernest Tuveson's "Millenarianism," in *Dictionary of the History of Ideas*, 3:223:1–225:2, which includes a short bibliography. For broad interpretation, there is Norman Cohn, "Réflexions sur le Millenarisme," *Archives de sociologie des religions* 3 (Jan.–June 1958): 103–07.

Cohn's challenging *The Pursuit of the Millennium: Revolutionary Messianism in Medieval and Reformation Europe and Its Bearing on Modern Totalitarian Movements*, 2d ed. (New York, 1961), has by now achieved the status of a standard account for the period between late antiquity and the early sixteenth century. For that century and the next, much the best recent work has been done on England, for which the latest survey is Katharine R. Firth, *The Apocalyptic Tradition in Reformation Britain 1530–1645* (Oxford, 1979). But what Keith Thomas has to say on the whole subject in his brilliant *Religion and the Decline of Magic* (New York, 1971) is also very much to be observed. A considerable literature has grown up on eschatology in the Puritan and Restoration eras. Some of it, appearing in *Past and Present* between

1969 and 1972, represents historiographical jousting. More temperate and informative are Charles Webster, *The Great Instauration: Science, Medicine and Reform 1626–1660* (London, 1975), probably the best book on seventeenth-century English thought, and the essays in Peter Toon, ed., *Puritans, the Millennium and the Future of Israel: Puritan Eschatology 1600 to 1660* (Cambridge, 1970). The earlier chapters of Tuveson's *Millennium and Utopia* are still worth reading on this period and the Restoration. Christopher Hill has written on *Antichrist in Seventeenth-Century England* (London, 1971); his book opens up previously unexplored territory but errs in its unsupported views on the eighteenth century.

For eighteenth-century British eschatology as a whole, there is relatively little to report. J. A. DeJong deals with this topic as part of his *As the Waters Cover the Sea: Millennial Expectations in the Rise of Anglo-American Missions, 1640–1810* (Kampen, 1970), and I have been led to some of my sources by him and by Froom, *Faith of our Fathers*, vol. 2. On the first decades of the century, see Frank E. Manuel, *Isaac Newton, Historian* (Cambridge, Mass., 1963), which suggests that concern with the last things was not limited to a few wild-eyed ecclesiastics; and Hillel Schwartz, "The French Prophets in England: A Social History of a Millenarian Group in the Early Eighteenth Century," Ph.D. diss. (Yale Univ., Dec. 1974), now published as *The French Prophets: The History of a Millenarian Group in Eighteenth-Century England* (Berkeley, 1980). Schwartz provides a useful example of popular eschatology. This topic is also discussed in Thompson, *Making of the English Working Class*, for the 1790s, and in J. F. C. Harrison, *The Second Coming: Popular Millenarianism 1780–1850* (New Brunswick, N.J., 1979), for the whole era of the Industrial Revolution. The scholarly eschatology of the era of the French Revolution is treated in Clarke Garrett, *Respectable Folly: Millenarians and the French Revolution in France and England* (Baltimore, 1975), which, like Harrison's book, contains some valuable hints about earlier eighteenth-century trends. I have also profited from sources used in Bernard Capp, *English Almanacs, 1500–1800: Astrology and the Popular Press* (Ithaca, 1979), and D. P. Walker, *The Decline of Hell: Seventeenth-Century Discussions of Eternal Torment* (Chicago, 1964). The association of apocalyptic fears with earthquakes emerges in T. D. Kendrick, *The Lisbon Earthquake* (Philadelphia, [1957]); and G. S. Rousseau, "The London Earthquake of 1750," *Cahiers d'histoire mondiale* 11 (1968): 436–51. On British eschatology during the entire century, there is nothing to match the book on America written by James West Davidson, *The Logic of Millennial Thought: Eighteenth-Century New England* (New Haven, 1977), a suggestive and impressive work.

My emphasis on the continuation of supernaturalism conflicts with the standard view of the eighteenth century, stated, among other places, in Tuveson's *Millennium and Utopia* and "Swift and the World-Makers," *JHI*

11 (Jan. 1950): 54–74; and in J. H. Plumb, "Reason and Unreason in the Eighteenth Century: The English Experience," part of his *In the Light of History* (New York, 1972), 3–24. For the earlier background to notions of divine intervention, see Francis Oakley's stimulating historical analysis of "the distinction between the absolute and ordained or ordinary powers of God," in *Omnipotence, Covenant, & Order: An Excursion in the History of Ideas from Abelard to Leibniz* (Ithaca, 1984). Supernaturalism and related issues are viewed in broader eighteenth-century context in my "Secularization in British Thought, 1730–1789: Some Landmarks," in W. Warren Wagar, ed., *The Secular Mind: Transformations of Faith in Modern Europe* (New York, 1982), 35–56. I was glad to discover that the importance of the concept of "providence" in the eighteenth century has lately received at least some attention: Georges Gusdorf, "Déclin de la providence?," *SVEC* 153 (1976): 951–99; Henry F. May, "The Decline of Providence?," *SVEC* 154 (1976): 1401–16. Further scholarship in this area is much to be desired.

CHAPTER 4: MEDICINE OF THE MIND

Eighteenth-century British "anthropology" and moral philosophy have been summarized in L. A. Selby-Bigge, ed., *British Moralists: Being Selections from Writers Principally of the Eighteenth Century*, 2 vols. (Oxford, 1897), 1:xi–lxx ("Introduction"). For the French side, the best and fullest guide is Lester Crocker, *An Age of Crisis: Man and World in Eighteenth Century French Thought* (Baltimore, 1959). Arthur O. Lovejoy gives these subjects his usual careful, revealing scrutiny in *Reflections on Human Nature* (Baltimore, 1961). There is much related material in Maurice Mandelbaum's penetrating *History, Man, & Reason: A Study in Nineteenth-Century Thought* (Baltimore, 1971), which contains chapters on the pre-1800 background. The widespread notion of "The Malleability of Man in Eighteenth-Century Thought" was first studied historically by John Passmore, in Earl R. Wasserman, ed., *Aspects of the Eighteenth Century* (Baltimore, 1965), 21–46, a groundbreaking article; see also his *Perfectibility of Man*, 149–70. I do not accept all of Passmore's interpretation and prefer the term "pliability." John O. Lyons, *The Invention of the Self: The Hinge of Consciousness in the Eighteenth Century* (Carbondale, Ill., 1978), probes a different but very important aspect of contemporary psychological ideas, leading to Romantic attitudes.

Apart from a relatively few pages (on the great thinkers) in Daniel N. Robinson's *An Intellectual History of Psychology*, 3d ed. (Madison, Wis., 1986), there is no reliable recent account of the history of eighteenth-century psychology. Its *historiography*, however, is treated in G. S. Rousseau, "Psychology," in Rousseau and Roy Porter, *The Ferment of Knowledge: Studies in the Historiography of Eighteenth-Century Science* (Cambridge, 1980), 143–

210. There are two general accounts of the history of associationism: Howard C. Warren, *A History of the Association Psychology* (New York, 1921), which shows its age; and David Rapaport, *The History of the Concept of Association of Ideas*, trans. L. Juhasz (New York, 1974), which deals with the great figures only, from Bacon to Kant. Somewhat more useful, though necessarily more circumscribed, is Robert M. Young, "Association of Ideas," in *Dictionary of the History of Ideas*, 1:111:1–118:1, in which it is suggested that the principle of association played a fundamental role in the development of the idea of progress. Another aspect of the importance of this brand of psychology in eighteenth-century thought appears from Martin Kallich's *The Association of Ideas and Critical Theory in Eighteenth-Century England: A History of a Psychological Method in English Criticism* (The Hague, 1970).

On the rise of associationism before Hartley, there is virtually no recent work. But see Stephen Ferg, "Two Early Works by David Hartley," *Journal of the History of Philosophy* 19 (April 1981): 173–89, on the anonymous publications of 1741 and 1747; I do not agree with Ferg about the authorship of these works. Turnbull receives some attention in David Fate Norton, *David Hume: Common Sense Moralist, Sceptical Metaphysician* (Princeton, 1982). Hartley himself has had his share of commentators, of whom the best are Robert Marsh, "The Second Part of Hartley's System," *JHI* 20 (April 1953): 264–73; Maria Heider, *Studien über David Hartley. (1705–1757)* (Bergische Gladbach, 1913); and Barbara Bowen Oberg, "David Hartley and the Association of Ideas," *JHI* 37 (July–Sept. 1976): 441–53. But see also Nancy Moore, "David Hartley: The Bicentenary of 'Observations on Man,' 1749," *Hibbert Journal* 48 (Oct. 1949): 73–79; and R. C. Oldfield and Lady Kathleen Oldfield, "Hartley's 'Observations on Man,'" *Annals of Science* 7 (Dec. 28, 1951): 371–81. These works help to locate Hartley's place in the history of thought. His influence in England and America appears from Richard Haven, "Coleridge, Hartley, and the Mystics," *JHI* 20 (Oct.–Dec. 1959): 477–94; Donald J. D'Elia, "Benjamin Rush, David Hartley, and the Revolutionary Uses of Psychology," *Proceedings of the American Philosophical Society* 114 (April 13, 1970): 109:1–118:2; and G. S. Bower, *David Hartley and James Mill* (New York, 1881), useful in spite of its age. As I have noted in the chapter 4, I reject the conclusions of Margaret Leslie in "Mysticism Misunderstood: David Hartley and the Idea of Progress," *JHI* 33 (Oct.–Dec. 1972): 625–32. A major study of Hartley remains a desideratum. More work could also be used on Tucker: Meyrick H. Carré's "Abraham Tucker and the Joint Stock Universe," *Cambridge Journal* 4 (Aug. 1951): 688–97, has unfortunately had no successors.

For the general history of education in eighteenth-century Britain, recourse must be had to W. H. G. Armytage, *Four Hundred Years of English Education*, 2d ed. (Cambridge, 1970), and to Nicholas Hans, *New Trends in Education in the Eighteenth Century* (London, 1951), until we have a more up-to-date general survey. Peter Thomas Conmy, *Studies in English Education during the Eighteenth Century* (Oakland, Calif., 1946), is unsatisfactorily short. Some light is shed on the period after 1760 in Brian Simon, *Studies in the History of Education 1780–1870* (London, 1964), which is, however, politically tendentious. There are some interesting essays in James A. Leith, ed., *Facets of Education in the Eighteenth Century*, SVEC 167 (1977), but no broad study of England; Leith's own "Introduction: Unity and Diversity in Education during the Eighteenth Century," 13–27, does contain some helpful observations on the English situation. The circumstances of Scottish education are well summarized in Smout, *History of the Scottish People*. Frank Musgrove briefly explores discontent with the later eighteenth-century educational system in "Middle Class Families and Schools: Interaction and Exchange of Function between Institutions," *Sociological Review*, n. s., 7 (Dec. 1959): 169–78. I am not convinced by his "Two Educational Controversies in Eighteenth-Century England. Nature and Nurture: Private and Public Education," *Paedagogica Historica* 2 (1962): 81–93. M. G. Jones, *The Charity School Movement: A Study of Eighteenth Century Puritanism in Action* (Cambridge, 1938), is still the best book on the subject. The Dissenting academies are covered in H[erbert] MacLachlan's *English Education under the Test Acts: Being the History of the Nonconformist Academies, 1662–1820* (Manchester, 1931). Lawrence Stone, "Literacy and Education in England 1640–1900," *Past and Present* 42 (Jan. 1968): 69–139, has importance beyond the history of education alone.

CHAPTER 5: LANGUAGE AND PROGRESS

The study of language in eighteenth-century Britain needs a good, general treatment like that of Pierre Juliard on France, *Philosophies of Language in Eighteenth-Century France* (The Hague, 1970), which includes a most useful chapter on the relationship between language and progress in contemporary French thought. A point of departure can be found in Donald A. Sears's bibliographical essay, "Eighteenth Century Work on Language," *Bulletin of Bibliography* 28 (Oct.–Dec. 1971): 120–23, which I have used extensively, although it is far from complete. Scott Elledge concentrates on the major figures—especially Johnson, Priestley, Smith, and Monboddo—in "The Naked Science of Language, 1746–1786," in Howard Anderson and John S. Shea, eds., *Studies in Criticism and Aesthetics, 1660–1800: Essays in Honor of Samuel Holt Monk* (Minneapolis, 1967), 266–95. Alex Page creates some interesting categories of linguistic attitudes in his "The Origin of Language and Eighteenth-Century English Criticism," *Journal of English and Germanic Philology* 71 (Jan. 1972): 12–21. A specialized work that, however, does cover the whole century is Sterling Andrus Leonard, *The Doctrine of Correctness in English Usage 1700–1800* (Madison, Wis., 1929). It contains a few serious errors but uses many sources, to which I have had recourse. Hans Aarsleff's *The Study of Language in England, 1780–1860* (Princeton, 1967) includes some material on the pre-1780 background, mainly of a philosophical nature, although it focuses primarily on John Horne Tooke's *Diversions of Purley* (1786–98) and his later influence. One figure whom I discuss in the text has been studied carefully: see Stephen K. Land, "James Beattie on Language," *Philological Quarterly* 51 (Oct. 1972): 887–904.

A European-wide context is supplied by Lia Formigari's provocative essay, "Language and Society in the Late Eighteenth Century," *JHI* 35 (April–June 1974): 275–92. The seventeenth-century English background is sketched in Richard Foster Jones, "Science and Language in England in the Mid-Seventeenth Century," now reprinted in *The Seventeenth Century*, 143–60. Notwithstanding its title, James Knowlson's *Universal Language Schemes in England and France 1600–1800* (Toronto, 1975) does not consider eighteenth-century Britain.

I have derived some of my ideas for this chapter from studies that examine the linguistic opinions of several philosophes: Manuel, *Prophets of Paris* (on Turgot); Isabel F. Knight, *The Geometric Spirit: The Abbé de Condillac and the French Enlightenment* (New Haven, 1968); and Keith Michael Baker, *Condorcet: From Natural Philosophy to Social Mathematics* (Chicago, 1975). Indeed, it was Keith Baker who first interested me in the relationship between language study and the idea of progress.

CHAPTER 6: THE PROGRESS OF HUMAN CULTURE: ENGLAND

The most important work on contemporary opinions of luxury, and the only one to deal extensively with the Brown controversy, is Wade, "The Idea of Luxury." Luxury also receives attention in Kramnick, *Bolingbroke and His Circle*, and its most influential French commentators in Ellen Ross, "Mandeville, Melon, and Voltaire: The Origins of the Luxury Controversy in France," *SVEC* 155 (1976): 1897–1912. Although there is still much to be said on this whole subject, we are fortunate to have now John Sekora, *Luxury: The Concept in Western Thought, Eden to Smollett* (Baltimore, 1977), of which two chapters are on the eighteenth century as a whole while most of the rest of the book focuses on Smollett. In addition, Pocock's work often points out worries over luxury.

In the context in which I consider Gibbon, David P. Jordan's *Gibbon and His Roman Empire* (Urbana, Ill., 1971) was helpful, as was Per Fugulum, *Edward Gibbon: His View of Life and Conception of History* (Oslo, 1953). Besides what is said about him, valuably but rather briefly, in Crane's "Anglican Apologetics," 239–51, and Tuveson's *Millennium and Utopia*, 141–46, Worthington has not been studied. On Law, the discussion by Crane (259–74) is quite revealing and influenced me considerably; his view of the Great

Chain of Being is analyzed in Arthur O. Lovejoy's celebrated *The Great Chain of Being: A Study of the History of an Idea* (Cambridge, Mass., 1936), a book that has influenced me in many ways. There is a short biographical sketch of Law by his pupil William Paley in the "new" edition of *Considerations on the Theory of Religion*, ed. George Henry Law (London, 1820). Both Worthington and Law have rather uninformative articles on them in the *Dictionary of National Biography*. Gordon does not; he is discussed in Crane, "Anglican Apologetics," 279–83, and further information about his political and ecclesiastical career is given in Sir Francis Hill, *Georgian Lincoln* (Cambridge, 1966), esp. 44–47.

Neither Price nor Priestley has been particularly well served by modern scholars. Both are treated in connection with the Nonconformist intellectual tradition in Anthony H. Lincoln's old but still valuable *Some Political and Social Ideas of English Dissent, 1763–1800* (Cambridge, 1938). By contrast, Peter Brown views them in the context of Lord Shelburne's political circle: *The Chathamites: A Study in the Relationship between Personalities and Ideas in the Second Half of the Eighteenth Century* (London, 1967). Jack Fruchtman, Jr., gives them a Pocockian anchoring in the civic humanist tradition in *The Apocalyptic Politics of Richard Price and Joseph Priestley: A Study in Late Eighteenth-Century English Republican Millennialism*, Transactions of the American Philosophical Society, 73 (Philadelphia, 1983), which has only recently come to my attention. Though much of Fruchtman's analysis is sound and interesting, particularly his distinctions between the two figures, the attempt to view them as thinkers who grafted millennialism onto the "republican tradition" ultimately does not succeed: they were more a part of a tradition of scholarly eschatology, and they did not think that citizens had a responsibility to create the conditions necessary for the coming of the millennium. Even so, Fruchtman's book and the emergence of two new journals, *The Price-Priestley Newsletter* and *Enlightenment and Dissent*, should stimulate scholarship regarding both men.

On Price alone, see Carl B. Cone, *Torchbearer of Freedom: The Influence of Richard Price on 18th Century Thought* (Lexington, Ky., 1952), the only thing even approaching a standard work; and William D. Hudson, *Reason and Right: A Critical Examination of Richard Price's Moral Philosophy* (London, 1970). The book that explores Price's view of history most perspicaciously is Henri Laboucheix, *Richard Price Théorician de la Révolution Américaine, la philosophe et le sociologue, le pamphlétaire et l'orateur* ([Paris], 1970), which has now appeared in English as *Richard Price as Moral Philosopher and Political Theorist* (*SVEC*, vol. 207), trans. Sylvia and David Raphael (Oxford, 1982).

Priestley has a good bibliography—Ronald E. Crook, *A Bibliography of Joseph Priestley 1733–1804* (London, 1966)—but not an adequate biography. Anne Holt's *A Life of Joseph Priestley* (London, 1931) is fairly superficial;

F. W. Gibbs, *Joseph Priestley: Revolutions of the Eighteenth Century* (Garden City, N.Y., 1967), concentrates on its subject's scientific work, which is nevertheless handled more interestingly in Schofield, *Lunar Society*. The "Editor's Introduction" to John A. Passmore, ed., *Priestley's Writings on Philosophy, Science, and Politics* (New York, 1965), is a useful survey of Priestley's thought. But until a full-length intellectual biography appears, Basil Willey's chapter, "Joseph Priestley and the Socinian Moonlight," in *Eighteenth Century Background*, will remain the best introduction. Fortunately, there are several recent specialized articles that are leading the way toward a more sophisticated interpretation of Priestley. See, especially, Robert E. Schofield's "Joseph Priestley, Natural Philosopher," *Ambix* 14 (Feb. 1967): 1–15, and "Joseph Priestley: Theology, Physics, and Metaphysic," *Enlightenment and Dissent*, no. 2 (1983): 69–81; John G. McEvoy's "Joseph Priestley, Natural Philosopher: Some Comments on Professor Schofield's Views," *Ambix* 15 (June 1968): 115–33, and "Enlightenment and Dissent in Science: Joseph Priestley and the Limits of Theoretical Reasoning," *Enlightenment and Dissent*, no. 2 (1983): 47–67, as well as his multipart "Joseph Priestley, 'Aerial Philosopher': Metaphysics and Methodology in Priestley's Chemical Thought, from 1772 to 1781," *Ambix* 25 (March 1978): 1–55, 25 (July 1978): 93–116, 25 (Nov. 1978): 153–75, and 26 (March 1979): 16–38, and his "Electricity, Knowledge, and the Nature of Progress in Priestley's Thought," *British Journal for the History of Science* 12 (1979): 1–30. In addition, there is the important piece that McEvoy co-authored with J. E. McGuire, "God and Nature: Priestley's Way of Rational Dissent," *Historical Studies in the Physical Sciences* 6 (1975): 325–404.

CHAPTER 7: THE PROGRESS OF HUMAN CULTURE: SCOTLAND

A good sense of the overall context of Scottish thought can be had from John Ramsay, *Scotland and Scotsmen in the Eighteenth Century*, 2 vols. (Edinburgh, 1888), vol. 1, and Henry Grey Graham, *Scottish Men of Letters in the Eighteenth Century* (London, 1901). Also important in this regard is Alexander Fraser Tytler of Woodhouselee, *Memoirs of the Life and Writings of the Honourable Henry Home of Kames*, 2d ed., 3 vols. (Edinburgh, 1814).

The three best treatments of Scottish "natural history" are Andrew Skinner, "Natural History in the Age of Adam Smith," *Political Studies* 15 (Feb. 1967): 32–48, from which I have learned much; H. M. Höpfl, "From Savage to Scotsman: Conjectural History in the Scottish Enlightenment," *Journal of British Studies* 17, no. 2 (Spring 1978): 19–40, with which I do not always agree; and the recent essay by Roger L. Emerson, "Conjectural History and Scottish Philosophers," *Historical Papers* [of the Canadian Historical Association] (1984), 63–90, a searching and innovative look at the background of conjectural history. In a related vein, Duncan Forbes's "'Scientific' Whiggism: Adam Smith and John Millar," *Cambridge Journal* 7 (Aug. 1954): 643–70, is a fundamental and stimulating article, although I am unable to accept some of Forbes's views on the Scottish attitude toward progress. Although it also concentrates on the French, Ronald L. Meek's *Social Science and the Ignoble Savage* (Cambridge, 1976) identifies the most important Scottish contributions to the four-stage theory, offering sensible, well-considered conclusions about them. Another monograph of broad importance is John Robertson, *The Scottish Enlightenment and the Militia Issue* (Edinburgh, 1985), which distinguishes between Hume and Smith, on the one hand, and the Moderates, on the other; it is very much in the mainstream of examinations of the civic humanist tradition. A modern example of the traditional tendency to see the Scots as precursors of modern social scientists is Alan Swingewood, "Origin of Sociology: The Case of the Scottish Enlightenment," *British Journal of Sociology* 21 (June 1970): 164–80.

In comparison with the Englishmen studied in chapter 6, the individual Scots under examination here have in recent years received very careful treatment. On Kames, the leading books are Ian Simpson Ross, *Lord Kames and the Scotland of His Day* (Oxford, 1972), and William C. Lehmann, *Henry Home, Lord Kames, and the Scottish Enlightenment: A Study in National Character and in the History of Ideas* (The Hague, 1971). Both are reliable, as is Arthur E. McGuinness, *Henry Home, Lord Kames* (New York, 1970), especially on Kames's *Elements of Criticism*. There is an excellent recent article on Kames as legal thinker: David Lieberman, "The Legal Needs of a Commercial Society: The Jurisprudence of Lord Kames," in *Wealth and Virtue*, 203–34.

Ernest Campbell Mossner's *The Life of David Hume*, 1st ed. (Austin, Tex., 1954), is full and reliable, on everything except Hume's ideas themselves. For these there are many worthy guides. On his philosophy, I have often referred to J. A. Passmore, *Hume's Intentions* (Cambridge, 1952), which is illuminating without being overly technical; and to John B. Stewart, *The Moral and Political Philosophy of David Hume* (New York, 1963), an underrated study with a sensible chapter on Hume's vision of history. Among the spate of recent studies, I find D. F. Norton's *David Hume* (referred to under chapter 4) the most stimulating and persuasive. On Hume's history-writing, there are two useful introductory essays in the volume that Norton edited with Richard H. Popkin, *David Hume: Philosophical Historian* (Indianapolis, 1965); another one by Duncan Forbes introducing his edition of Hume's *History of Great Britain* (Harmondsworth, Eng., 1970); and that of H. R. Trevor-Roper, "David Hume as Historian," in D. Pears, ed., *David Hume: A Symposium* (London, 1963), 89–100. See also the chapters on Hume in Meinecke's *Historism* and J. B. Black's aging *The Art of History: A Study of Four Great Historians of the Eighteenth Century* (London, 1926). In many respects, the best book on Hume's historical and political outlook is Duncan

Forbes, *Hume's Philosophical Politics* (Cambridge, 1975), which has supplied me with a number of good leads. For economics, Eugene Rotwein offers a complete introduction in his *David Hume: Writings on Economics* (Madison, Wis., 1970). Amid an enormous journal literature, for the purposes of this book there is one short essay of special significance: Constant Noble Stockton, "Economics and the Mechanism of Historical Progress in Hume's History," in Donald W. Livingston and James T. King, eds., *Hume: A Reevaluation* (New York, 1976), 296–320.

Smith has still not been given a modern, comprehensive biographical treatment to equal that accorded him by Dugald Stewart's "Account of the Life and Writings of Adam Smith, LL.D.," in *The Collected Works of Dugald Stewart*, ed. Sir William Hamilton, 11 vols. (Edinburgh, 1854–60), 10:3–98, although we are promised such a book to conclude the Glasgow Edition of the Works and Correspondence of Adam Smith. Meanwhile, we have R. H. Campbell and A. S. Skinner, *Adam Smith* (New York, 1982), a slim but impressively researched account. My interpretation of Smith's thought draws extensively on the work of Andrew Skinner, including the long introduction to his edition of *The Wealth of Nations* (Harmondsworth, Eng., 1974), 11–97; the pieces brought together in *A System of Social Science: Papers Relating to Adam Smith* (Oxford, 1979); and his "Adam Smith: An Economic Interpretation of History," in Skinner and Thomas Wilson, eds., *Essays on Adam Smith* (Oxford, 1975), 154–78. The latter book is a collection of essays by many hands which makes an outstanding contribution to Smith studies. Of special note here is Robert L. Heilbroner's "The Paradox of Progress: Decline and Decay in The Wealth of Nations," 524–39. Another invaluable recent work is T. D. Campbell, *Adam Smith's Science of Morals* (London, 1971), a careful, insightful analysis that ought to be read along with the editors' introduction to the definitive edition of *The Theory of Moral Sentiments*, ed. D. D. Raphael and A. L. Macfie (Oxford, 1976), 1–52. Gordon Bartley Strong, *Adam Smith and the Eighteenth Century Concept of Social Progress* (Chicago, 1932), in spite of its promising title, is unintelligible. Along with several relevant essays in *Wealth and Virtue*, current thinking about Smith and "civic humanism" is represented by Donald Winch, *Adam Smith's Politics: An Essay in Historiographic Revision* (Cambridge, 1978).

For Robertson there is no modern life at all. Again, Dugald Stewart can help bridge the gap: "Account of the Life and Writings of William Robertson, D.D." (delivered 1796), in *Collected Works of Stewart*, 10:99–242. But Sher's *Church and University* gives us our first in-depth look at the man himself, much of it through unpublished correspondence that illuminates Robertson's ecclesiastical and university dealings. A longer study of him, with more attention to his historical interests as well as his more public roles, is greatly to be desired, as Sher agrees. For interpretation of the historian, we are finally beginning to move beyond the fairly superficial accounts in Meinecke's *His-*

torism and Black's *Art of History*. Paths were broken some years ago by R. A. Humphreys, *William Robertson and His "History of America"* (London, 1954), and E. Adamson Hoebel, "William Robertson: An Eighteenth-Century Anthropologist Historian," *American Anthropologist* 61 (Aug. 1960): 648–55. Jeffrey Smitten offers much more penetrating analyses, and appropriately demands that we see Robertson as more than a contributor to the development of social science-oriented history, in "Robertson's *History of Scotland*: Narrative Structure and the Sense of Reality," *Clio* 11 (Fall 1981): 29–47; and "Impartiality in Robertson's *History of America*," *ECS* 19 (Fall 1985): 56–77. Now there is D. J. Womersley's more broadly gauged "The Historical Writings of William Robertson," *JHI* 47 (July–Sept. 1986): 497–506, which views the histories as gradually developing in the direction of what was to be the Romantic stance. All of these lead to skepticism about some points in the general interpretation offered in the editor's introduction to Robertson, *The Progress of Society in Europe: A Historical Outline from the Subversion of the Roman Empire to the Beginning of the Sixteenth Century*, ed. Felix Gilbert (Chicago, 1972). I am now convinced that Gilbert places too much emphasis on Robertson's providentialism.

By all odds the best book on Ferguson is David Kettler, *The Social and Political Thought of Adam Ferguson* ([Columbus, Ohio], 1965), from which I have had much help. W. C. Lehmann's *Adam Ferguson and the Beginnings of Modern Sociology* (New York, 1930) makes for difficult reading because of its style; it is typical of the earlier twentieth-century tendency to see the Scots as the first sociologists and anthropologists, and very little more. I have also benefited from the long and important editor's introduction to Adam Ferguson, *An Essay on the History of Civil Society*, ed. Duncan Forbes (Edinburgh, 1966), although I think it errs in several respects, as discussed in the text references. I find myself in general agreement with John Andrew Bernstein, "Adam Ferguson and the Idea of Progress," *Studies in Burke and His Time* 9 (Spring 1978): 99–118. For the civic-humanist point of view, see Gary L. McDowell, "Commerce, Virtue, and Politics: Adam Ferguson," *Review of Politics* 45 (1983): 536–52.

For Millar, the only biographical study of note is John Craig's "Account of the Life and Writings of John Millar, Esq.," in the 4th ed. of Millar's *The Origin of the Distinction of Ranks* (Edinburgh, 1806). This can be supplemented with material in William C. Lehmann, *John Millar of Glasgow, 1735–1801: His Life and Thought and His Contributions to Sociological Analysis* (Cambridge, 1960), which is more than an intellectual biography. It not only gives personal details not available elsewhere but also places its subject in the context of contemporary thought and culture. To a more limited extent, this is also true of two unsigned, untitled review articles by Francis Jeffrey, one of Millar's leading pupils: *Edinburgh Review* 3 (Oct. 1803): 154–81, and 9 (Oct. 1806): 83–92. On interpretation, one must turn to

Forbes's fine "'Scientific' Whiggism," and now to Michael Ignatieff, "John Millar and Individualism," in *Wealth and Virtue*, 317–43, which brings Millar into the civic humanist context.

There is a brief study of one important aspect of Dunbar's thought: Christopher J. Berry, "'Climate' in the Eighteenth Century: James Dunbar and the Scottish Case," *Texas Studies in Literature and Language* 16 (Summer 1974): 281–92. Bury refers briefly to him in the notes to *The Idea of Progress*. Unfortunately, neither tells us anything about the man. For the little that is known about him, see John Malcolm Bullock, *A History of the University of Aberdeen, 1495–1895* (London, 1895), 163. Monboddo was "discovered" by Arthur O. Lovejoy in his important "Monboddo and Rousseau," reprinted in *Essays in the History of Ideas* (Baltimore, 1948), 38–61, a book full of judicious shorter studies. There are also some insightful pages in Tuveson's *Millennium and Utopia*. In spite of these promising beginnings, a biography did not appear for some time, and it is not as comprehensive as could be wished: E. L. Cloyd, *James Burnett, Lord Monboddo* (Oxford, 1972). The old *Lord Monboddo and Some of His Contemporaries* (London, 1900), by William Knight, contains much correspondence and still serves to make the mental atmosphere of eighteenth-century Edinburgh come alive.

CHAPTER 8: THE SOURCES OF BELIEF

My analysis of the social milieu in which doctrines of general progress arose and became popular depends in large measure on a reading of main trends in economic history. For this there are a number of outstanding works on which to draw, many of them coming from the 1960s, a boom period in this field of scholarship. Many kinds of statistical information are supplied by B. R. Mitchell with Phyllis Deane, *Abstract of British Historical Statistics* (Cambridge, 1962). The place of the eighteenth century in the big picture of economic history can be discovered in Phyllis Deane and W. A. Cole, *British Economic Growth 1688–1959: Trends and Structure*, 2d ed. (Cambridge, 1967), and in Peter Mathias, *The First Industrial Nation: An Economic History of Britain, 1700–1914* (New York, 1969). The seventeenth and eighteenth centuries are superbly covered in Charles Wilson, *England's Apprenticeship, 1603–1763* (London, 1965), which is much more than economic history; the eighteenth century itself in T. S. Ashton's *An Economic History of England: The 18th Century* (New York, [1955]). The best summary of the Industrial Revolution remains Phyllis Deane's *The First Industrial Revolution* (Cambridge, 1965). A succinct causal analysis is offered in M. W. Flinn, *Origins of the Industrial Revolution* (London, 1966). The history of science and technology is interwoven with economic change in David S. Landes's classic, *The Unbound Prometheus: Technological Change and Industrial Developments in Western Europe from 1750 to the Present* (Cambridge,

1969), chap. 1; and in A. E. Musson and Eric Robinson, *Science and Technology in the Industrial Revolution* (Manchester, 1969). On this subject, Schofield's *Lunar Society* presents a fascinating case study. The single best book on rural developments is still J. D. Chambers and G. E. Mingay, *The Agricultural Revolution, 1750–1850* (New York, 1966). The broader effects of economic change are interestingly presented by John W. Osborne in his *The Silent Revolution: Industrial Revolution in England as a Source of Cultural Change* (New York, 1970), to my mind an unfairly neglected work. Peter Mathias covers much ground in up-to-date fashion in *The Transformation of England: Essays in the Economic and Social History of England in the Eighteenth Century* (New York, 1979). A promising beginning in a new but quite important field are the essays in Neil McKendrick, John Brewer, and J. H. Plumb, *The Birth of a Consumer Society: The Commercialization of Eighteenth-Century England* (Bloomington, Ind., 1985).

On Scotland in particular, the basic works are Henry Hamilton, *An Economic History of Scotland in the Eighteenth Century* (Oxford, 1963), and the relevant parts of R. H. Campbell's *Scotland since 1707: The Rise of an Industrial Society* (Oxford, 1965), as well as his "The Industrial Revolution: A Revision Article," *Scottish Historical Review* 46 (1967): 37–55. There are newer, more narrowly focused studies of interest: the essays relating to agricultural improvement in T. M. Devine, ed., *Lairds and Improvement in the Scotland of the Enlightenment* (Dundee, 1979); R. H. Campbell, "The Enlightenment and the Economy," and T. M. Devine, "The Scottish Merchant Community, 1680–1740," both in *Origins and Nature of the Scottish Enlightenment*, 8–25, 26–41, respectively. T. C. Smout brings us rather well up-to-date in his "Where Had the Scottish Economy Got to by the Third Quarter of the Eighteenth Century?," in *Wealth and Virtue*, 45–72.

I arrived at my interpretation of how the narrower doctrines of progress were extended before finding Donald A. Schon, *Displacement of Concepts* (London, 1963). But that work, which is eminently readable, confirmed me in my opinions by giving them a certain amount of theoretical support.

The only one of the dozen Englishmen and Scots whose view of the War of Ancients and Moderns has been studied in any detail is Hume: Ernest Campbell Mossner, "Hume and the Ancient-Modern Controversy, 1725–1752: A Study in Creative Scepticism," *University of Texas Studies in English* 28 (1949): 139–53. On eschatology, there is less detailed analysis of Priestley and Price than one might want in Fruchtman's *Apocalyptic Politics*, and less appreciation of the tradition of scholarly eschatology—but at least he does not limit his consideration to the period after the commencement of the French Revolution, which is the normal starting point for discussion. Frank Manuel's *The Eighteenth Century Confronts the Gods* is helpful on Hume's views regarding the development of religion, but most of the book is devoted to Continental writers.

Although Priestley's associationism receives attention in many studies, Ronald B. Hatch, "Joseph Priestley: An Addition to Hartley's *Observations*," *JHI* 36 (July–Sept. 1975): 548–50, is unique in examining his handling of *Observations on Man*. For Hume the best guide is Passmore, *Hume's Intentions*, 105–31. Ruth Watts, "Joseph Priestley and Education," *Enlightenment and Dissent*, no. 2 (1983): 83–100, says the essential. Smith's work on language has recently attracted attention: see Christopher J. Berry, "Adam Smith's *Considerations* on Language," *JHI* 35 (Jan.–March 1974): 130–38; and Stephen K. Land, "Adam Smith's 'Considerations Concerning the First Formation of Languages,'" *JHI* 38 (Oct.–Dec. 1977): 677–90.

CHAPTER 9: CONCLUSION

In thinking about the differences between Britain and France, I was helped by Robert R. Palmer's truly classic *Catholics and Unbelievers in Eighteenth Century France*, noted above. It will be clear from the text that I have reservations about applying to England and Scotland generalizations based on France, and this is especially true regarding the idea of progress. The views of Gay and Vyverberg on the French philosophes do not seem to hold across the Channel. On Turgot, the relevant chapter in Manuel's *Prophets of Paris* is seminal, but there is interesting information regarding the evolution of his four-stage theory in Meek's *Social Science and the Ignoble Savage*, as well as in the editorial matter of his reader *Turgot on Progress, Sociology and Economics* (Cambridge, 1973).

For the belief in progress of the nineteenth century as a whole, I have been strongly influenced by J. W. Burrow, *Evolution and Society: A Study in Victorian Social Theory* (Cambridge, 1966), a ground breaking essay, as well as by the less innovative but quite informative revisionist book by Jerome Hamilton Buckley, *The Triumph of Time: A Study of the Victorian Concepts of Time, History, Progress, and Decadence* (Cambridge, Mass., 1966). From the latter I was able to track down a number of important sources. On the more radical thinkers of the late eighteenth and early nineteenth centuries examined in this chapter, two books stand out: Peter H. Marshall, *William Godwin* (New Haven, 1984), and J. F. C. Harrison, *Quest for the New Moral World: Robert Owen and the Owenites in Britain and America* (New York, 1969)—both well-documented and judiciously interpreted accounts. My view of the Romantic attitudes toward progress is shaped by M. H. Abrams's splendid *Natural Supernaturalism: Tradition and Revolution in Romantic Literature* (New York, 1971), which is learned, stylish, and convincing. The pleasantly old-fashioned *The Political Ideas of the English Romanticists*, repr. ed. (Ann Arbor, Mich., 1966), by Crane Brinton, still has much to recommend it and covers a wide range of material. Richard Haven's "Coleridge, Hartley, and the Mystics," *JHI* 20 (Oct.–Dec. 1959): 477–94, makes clear how strong was Hartley's influence. H. N. Brailsford, *Shelley, Godwin, and Their Circle* (1913), repr. ed. ([Hamden, Conn.], 1969) has stood the test of time and offers much of interest on the subject of the belief in progress. For Scott there is substantial relevant work, first and foremost Duncan Forbes, "The Rationalism of Sir Walter Scott," *Cambridge Journal* 7 (Oct. 1953): 20–35. Forbes's illuminating investigation has now been followed up. See, for example, two articles by Peter D. Garside, "Scott, the Romantic Past and the Nineteenth Century," *Review of English Studies* 23 (May 1972): 147–61, and "Scott and the 'Philosophical' Historians," *JHI* 36 (July–Sept. 1975): 497–512; Hugh Trevor-Roper's "Sir Walter Scott and History," *The Listener* 86 (Aug. 19, 1971): 225–32; and David Daiches, "Sir Walter Scott and History," *Études Anglaises* 24 (Oct.–Dec. 1971): 458–77. I was led to several sources, especially in Scott's correspondence, by these articles.

On Scott's contemporary James Mill, there is yet another crucial article by Duncan Forbes: "James Mill and India," *Cambridge Journal* 5 (Oct. 1951): 19–33. To this can be added the introductory essay by William Thomas to his modern abridgment of *The History of British India* (Chicago, 1975). Still a first-rate study, relevant to both Mills, is Halévy's *Growth of Philosophic Radicalism*. On John Stuart, the best recent book is Bernard Semmel, *John Stuart Mill and the Pursuit of Virtue* (New Haven, 1984). But John M. Robson, *The Improvement of Mankind: The Social and Political Thought of John Stuart Mill* (Toronto, 1968), is also essential for the question of Mill's attitude toward progress. Macaulay comes to life in the account of the earlier part of his career called *Macaulay: The Shaping of the Historian* (New York, 1973), by John Clive. His views on progress receive insightful if usually indirect treatment in Joseph Hamburger, *Macaulay and the Whig Tradition* (Chicago, 1976), a book which should help to remove its subject from the niche to which he is typically consigned.

On urban planning and related conceptions, John Summerson, *Georgian London*, 3d ed. (Cambridge, Mass., 1978) is a standard work, as is David Daiches, *Edinburgh* (London, 1980). The latter seeks to relate the building of the New Town to Enlightenment ideas, a difficult proposition to establish, but at least some evidence for it is available in A. J. Youngson, *The Making of Classical Edinburgh, 1750–1840* (Edinburgh, 1966), which also contains large excerpts from the *Proposals* of 1752. Two other essays touch on this latter subject: Phillipson's "Culture and Society in the 18th Century Province," and Peter Reed, "Form and Context: A Study of Georgian Edinburgh," in Thomas A. Markus, ed., *Order in Space and Society: Architectural Form and Its Context in the Scottish Enlightenment* (Edinburgh, 1982), 115–53.

Works on economic history are mentioned earlier, under chapter 8.

Index

Abrams, M. H., 391, 392
Accident, role of, 310–11
Acton, Lord, 4
Adam, Robert, 72
Aikin, John, 40, 45, 48, 69
Akenside, Mark, 67
Alembert, Jean le Rond d', 10, 32n, 51, 65, 120
Alison, Archibald, 63–64
Ancient constitution, 305, 306–07
Ancients, paradox of the, 22, 27, 97, 332, 335
Ancients and Moderns, war of: 8, 12, 401; 17th-century, 22–26; 18th-century, 26–28, 34–47, 333–41; terms defined, 28–29; and learning, 47–52, 334–36; and practical skills and techniques, 53–62, 336; and fine arts, 62–76, 333, 336–37; and language, 191–92, 206; and Brown controversy, 217; and general progress, 333, 338–41, 377
Antichrist, 107, 108, 125, 367, 369; papacy and, 110, 119–21, 366; destruction of, 130–31
Anticlericalism, 99, 101
Antiquity, classical: loss of prestige, 21; 18th-century veneration for, 36–38. *See also* Greece and the Greeks; Rome and the Romans
Apocalypticism, 108, 109, 110, 115–16
Art and science, defined, 29–34 passim
Arts and sciences: differences in progress between, 25–26, 45; meaning of terms, 29–34; general views of development and progress of, 34–47, 84, 234–37, 284–86, 333; and society, 76–77; and improving institutions, 76–84; goal of uniting, 82; and division of labor, 279–81; order of development, 289, 319; recovery of, 318.

See also Belles lettres and polite literature; Fine arts; Learning; Practical skills and techniques
Associationism. *See* Psychology
Astle, Thomas, 188, 198, 200, 201, 224, 252
Augustine, 86–87, 93, 101, 104

Bacon, Francis, 21–22, 23, 24, 29, 76, 90, 109, 187, 201, 401, 405–06, 422
Bailey, Nathan (or Nathaniel), 30–31
Balloons, 60–62, 76
Barnes, Thomas, 43, 82, 83, 171–72, 390
Barrow, John, 31, 41, 42, 63, 69, 83
Barry, James, 53, 55, 69, 74, 211
Baumer, Franklin L., 417
Beard, Charles, 414
Beattie, James, 51, 67, 163, 177, 261, 263; on language, 183, 187, 188, 193, 197, 199, 201, 206–07, 208
Belles lettres and polite literature: decline in, 24, 25; definitions of, 33; progress in, 63–74 passim
Bentham, Jeremy, 10, 349, 397; on art and science, 32; on ancients and moderns, 40, 50; and psychology and education, 162, 177–78; on language, 179, 196, 209–10, 422
Benwell, William, 40–41, 45, 52, 53, 56, 63, 65
Berkeley, George, 10, 42
Blackstone, William, 322–23
Blair, Hugh, 255, 259, 337n; on ancients and moderns, 27, 29, 34–35, 37; on arts and sciences, 45, 47–48, 52, 63; on language, 181, 182, 188, 192, 193–94, 195, 198, 202
Bolingbroke, 14–15, 16, 41, 218, 285, 322
Boswell, James, 39, 40, 205, 255
Boyle, Robert, 51, 106, 110, 113, 203

455

Milton, John, 67, 73, 87
Miracles, 111–12, 113, 118
Mommsen, Theodor, 86, 104
Monboddo, Lord (James Burnett), 11,
181, 185, 194, 317–20, 355n, 356n,
357n, 358n, 359n
Monotheism, 371, 372, 373
Montesquieu, 215, 265, 266, 322, 340,
385
Moral sense, 139, 146, 147, 156, 264,
293, 294, 341, 344, 346
Morals and manners, 146–48, 159–62,
172, 175–76, 244–45, 292–96, 307,
338
More, Henry, 87, 106, 110, 111, 113, 128
Moss, Charles, 95, 103

Napleton, John, 91, 102
National debt, 307
Natural history, 267–71, 289–90, 354,
360, 371–74, 375–77
Nature, laws of: uniform, 106, 110,
309–10; divine intervention in opera-
tion of, 113–14, 122–24, 367n
Necessity. See Free will and necessity
Nelme, L. D., 208
Neoclassicism, 30, 73–74
New heavens and earth, 107–8, 128–29
Newcastle, Duke of, 75
Newton, Isaac: as inspiration or influ-
ence, 9, 10, 11, 30, 49, 51, 57, 76, 84,
135, 136, 151, 152, 153, 156, 166, 186,
291, 305, 317, 347; on divine inter-
vention, 113–14; as eschatologist,
116n; and universal language, 203
Newton, Thomas, 100, 120, 129, 131
Noble savage, 14, 391
North, Brownlow, 93, 103

Original sin, 85, 148
Osbaldeston, Richard, 93
Owen, Robert, 389–91
Owenism, 116, 116n, 390–91

Paine, Thomas, 10
Paley, William, 165, 166, 252
Papacy, 110, 119, 130
Parousia. See Second Coming
Parsons, James, 184, 189, 193
Patents, 60, 327
Perfectibility of man, 246–47, 302–04,
304n, 318, 319, 388–89, 392
Perrault, Charles, 23, 25, 333
Pessimism, historical: in Enlighten-
ment, 5; in French thought, 5, 13,

322; in British thought, 13–17, 213–
16, 222, 317–18; tempered with opti-
mism, 16, 99–101, 190, 218–222, 318;
and perfectibility, 318n. See also His-
tory, general theories of
Philosophes, 9–10, 105–06, 136, 257,
258, 260, 270; and language, 180, 185,
195
Physico-theology, 110–14
Pilgrim's progress, idea of, 101–02
Pliability of man, 12, 144–49, 162–77
passim, 341–54 passim, 378, 379, 389,
390, 393–94, 400–01, 402
Pocock, J. G. A., 254n, 419n, 423
Polite arts. See Fine arts
Polytheism, 371, 372, 373
Pope, Alexander, 36
Population, 38, 327, 328, 340
Power, progress of human, 237–38, 288,
406
Practical skills and techniques: and war
of ancients and moderns, 24, 27, 53–
62 passim; progress in, 53–62, 237–
38, 287–88, 326, 336, 404–07; and division of labor, 279–80; and liberty,
288
Price, Richard, 226–27, 325, 359, 361,
362, 389; on progress of Britain, 230;
aspects of belief in general progress,
231–47 passim; on commerce and
luxury, 243; on perfectibility of man,
245; on providence, 249; on sources of
progress, 249, 250; influence of, 252,
389; on ancients and moderns, 333,
336, 338; on association, 345n; on education, 348, 353; on religious progress, 364, 368, 369; on eschatology,
366, 367
Priestley, Joseph, 132, 226–27, 325, 341,
383, 385; and Hartley, 162, 168; on
language, 181, 359–61, 360n, 362,
363, 375, 378; on education, 168, 347,
348, 351; on progress of Britain, 230–
31; aspects of belief in general progress, 231–48 passim; on commerce and luxury, 241, 243–44;
familiarity with Scots, 241, 317; on
perfectibility of man, 246; on sources
of progress, 248–51 passim; on providence, 249, 250; necessitarianism of,
250–51; on division of labor, 251;
314; influence of, 252, 261, 389; on
ancients and moderns, 335, 336, 338,
340; on association, 344–45, 345n,
351, 353; on religious progress, 364–
65; on eschatology, 366–67, 368, 369

Date Due